Communications in Computer and Information Science   646

Commenced Publication in 2007
Founding and Former Series Editors:
Alfredo Cuzzocrea, Dominik Ślęzak, and Xiaokang Yang

More information about this series at http://www.springer.com/series/7899

Lin Zhang · Xiao Song
Yunjie Wu (Eds.)

Theory, Methodology, Tools and Applications for Modeling and Simulation of Complex Systems

16th Asia Simulation Conference
and SCS Autumn Simulation Multi-Conference
AsiaSim/SCS AutumnSim 2016
Beijing, China, October 8–11, 2016
Proceedings, Part IV

 Springer

Editors
Lin Zhang
Beihang University
Beijing
China

Yunjie Wu
Beihang University
Beijing
China

Xiao Song
Beihang University
Beijing
China

ISSN 1865-0929   ISSN 1865-0937 (electronic)
Communications in Computer and Information Science
ISBN 978-981-10-2671-3   ISBN 978-981-10-2672-0 (eBook)
DOI 10.1007/978-981-10-2672-0

Library of Congress Control Number: 2016946015

Printed on acid-free paper

This Springer imprint is published by Springer Nature
The registered company is Springer Science+Business Media Singapore Pte Ltd.

Preface

AsiaSim/SCS AutumnSim 2016 (the 2016 International Simulation Multi-Conference) was a joint conference of the 16th Asia Simulation Conference and the 2016 Autumn Simulation Multi-Conference. The Asia Simulation Conference (AsiaSim) is an annual international conference started in 1999. In 2011, the Federation of Asian Simulation Societies (ASIASIM) was set up and the AsiaSim became an annual conference of ASIASIM. The SCS Autumn Simulation Multi-Conference (SCS AutumnSim) is one of the premier conferences of the Society for Modeling and Simulation International (SCS), which provides a unique opportunity to learn about emerging M&S applications in many thriving fields. AsiaSim/SCS AutumnSim 2016 was the first conference jointly sponsored by ASIASIM and SCS and organized by the China Simulation Federation (CSF), Science and Technology on Special System Simulation Laboratory (STSSSL), and Beihang University (BUAA). It was also co-sponsored by the China Simulation Federation (CSF), the Japanese Society for Simulation Technology (JSST), the Korea Society for Simulation (KSS), the Society for Simulation and Gaming of Singapore (SSAGSG), the International Association for Mathematics and Computers in Simulation (IMACS), the Chinese Association for Artificial Intelligence (CAAI), China Computer Federation (CCF), the China Electrotechnical Society (CES), the China Graphics Society (CGS), and the China Ordnance Society (COS).

This conference is a big event that provides a unique opportunity to learn about emerging M&S research achievements and applications in many thriving fields, focusing on the theory, methodology, tools and applications for M&S of complex systems; it provides a forum for the latest R&D results in academia and industry.

The papers contained in these proceedings address challenging issues in M&S theory and methodology, model engineering for system of systems, high-performance computing and simulation, M&S for smart city, robot simulations, M&S for intelligent manufacturing, military simulation, as well as cloud technologies in simulation applications.

This year, AsiaSim/SCS AutumnSim received 639 submissions. Submissions came from around 15 countries and regions. After a thorough reviewing process, 267 papers were selected for presentation as full papers, with an acceptance rate of 41.8 %. These papers are published in the proceedings in the four volumes, 643–646. Volume 643 mainly addresses the issues of basics of M&S theory and methodology. Volume 644 discusses M&S for intelligent manufacturing and military simulation methods. In Vol. 645, cloud technologies in simulation applications, simulation and big data techniques are covered. And Vol. 646 presents M&S applications and simulation software.

The high-quality program would not have been possible without the authors who chose AsiaSim/SCS AutumnSim 2016 as a venue for their publications. Also, we would like to take this opportunity to thank the ASIASIM Federation for allowing us to host AsiaSim 2016 in Beijing.

We also thank the members of the Program Committee for their valuable effort in the review of the submitted papers. Finally, we would also like to thank our technical co-sponsors and sponsors. Your contributions and support have helped to make AsiaSim/SCS AutumnSim 2016 a memorable and successful event.

We hope that you enjoy reading and benefit from the proceedings of AsiaSim/SCS AutumnSim 2016.

October 2016   Lin Zhang
                                                                              Xiao Song
                                                                              Yunjie Wu

Organization

Sponsors

Federation of Asian Simulation Societies (ASIASIM)
The Society for Modeling & Simulation International (SCS)

Co-Sponsors

China Simulation Federation (CSF)
Japanese Society for Simulation Technology (JSST)
Korea Society for Simulation (KSS)
Society for Simulation and Gaming of Singapore (SSAGSG)
International Association for Mathematics and Computers in Simulation (IMACS)
Chinese Association for Artificial Intelligence (CAAI)
China Computer Federation (CCF)
China Electrotechnical Society (CES)
China Graphics Society (CGS)
China Ordnance Society (COS)

Organizers

China Simulation Federation (CSF)
Science and Technology on Special System Simulation Laboratory (STSSSL)
Beihang University (BUAA)

Honorary Chairs

Chuanyuan Wen, China
Robert M. Howe, USA
Yukio Kagawa, Japan
Sadao Takaba, Japan
Sung-Joo Park, Korea
Tianyuan Xiao(†), China

General Chairs

Bo Hu Li, China
Qinping Zhao, China

Deputy General Chair

Agostino Bruzzone, Italy

General Co-chairs

Satoshi Tanaka, Japan
Jonghyun Kim, Korea
Axel Lehmann, Germany
Zicai Wang, China
Xianxiang Huang, China

Program Committee Chair

Lin Zhang, China

Program Committee Co-chairs

Bernard Zeigler, USA
Tuncer Ören, Canada
Ralph C. Huntsinger, USA
Xiaofeng Hu, China
Soo-Hyun Park, Korea
H.J. Halin, Switzerland
Kaj Juslin, Finland
Roy E. Crosbie, USA

Ming Yang, China
Xiaogang Qiu, China
Satoshi Tanaka, Japan
Jin Liu, China
Min Zhao, China
Shiwei Ma, China
Francesco Longo, Italy
Agostino Bruzzone, Italy

Program Committee

Anxiang Huang, China
Yoonbae Kim, Korea
Yu Yao, China
Fei Xie, USA
Toshiharu Kagawa, Japan
Giuseppe Iazeolla, Italy
Mhamed Itmi, France
Haixiang Lin, Netherlands
Henri Pierreval, France
Hugh HT Liu, Canada
Wolfgang Borutzky, Germany
Jong Sik Lee, Korea
Xiaolin Hu, USA
Yifa Tang, China

Wenhui Fan, China
Bernard Zeigler, USA
Mingduan Tang, China
Long Wang, China
ChaoWang, China
Doo-Kwon Baik, Korea
Shinsuke Tamura, Japan
Pierre Borne, France
Ratan Guha, USA
Reinhold Meisinger, Germany
Richard Fujimoto, USA
Ge Li, China
Jinhai Sun, China
Xinping Xiong, China

Changjian Bi, China
Jianguo Cao, China
Yue Dai, China
Minrui Fei, China
Chen Guo, China
Fengju Kang, China
Guoxiong Li, China
Jin Liu, China
Shiwei Ma, China
Jipeng Wang, China
Zhongjie Wang, China
Hongjun Zhang, China
Qinping Zhao, China
Guomin Zhou, China
Gary S.H. Tan, Singapore
Francesco Longo, Italy
Hong Zhou, China
Shin'ichi Oishi, Japan
Zhenhao Zhou, China
Beike Zhang, China
Alain Cardon, France
Xukun Shen, China
Yangsheng Wang, China
Marzuki Khalid, Malaysia
Sergio Junco, Argentina
Tieqiao Wen, China
Xingsheng Gu, China
Zhijian Song, China
Yue Yang, China

Yongsheng Ding, China
Huimin Fan, China
Ming Chen, China
Javor, Andras, Hungary
Nabendu Chaki, India
Koji Koyamada, Japan
Osamu Ono, Japan
Yunjie Wu, China
Beiwei Guo, China
Ni Li, China
Shixuan Liu, China
Linxuan Zhang, China
Fei Tao, China
Lei Ren, China
Xiao Song, China
Xudong Chai, China
Zonghai Chen, China
Yuhao Cong, China
Guanghong Gong, China
Zhicheng Ji, China
Weidong Jin, China
Bo Hu Li, China
Ma Ping, China
Shaojie Mao, China
Zhong Su, China
Jianping Wu, China
Min Zhao, China
Huizhou Zheng, China

Organization Committee Chair

Yunjie Wu, China

Organization Committee Co-chairs

Shixuan Liu, China
Zaijun Shi, China
Linxuan Zhang, China
Ni Li, China
Fei Tao, China

Beiwei Guo, China
Xiao Song, China
Weijing Wang, China
Lei Ren, China

General Secretaries

Shixuan Liu, China
Xiao Song, China

Special Session Chairs

Ni Li, China
Linxuan Zhang, China

Publication Chairs

Shiwei Ma, China
Xiao Song, China

Publicity Chairs

Fei Tao, China
Baiwei Guo, China

Awards Committee Chairs

Lin Zhang, China
Axel Lehmann, Germany

Awards Committee Co-chair

Yifa Tang, China

Awards Committee Members

Sung-Yong Jang, Korea
Wenhui Fan, China
Xiao Song, China

Contents – Part IV

Simulation Software

Social Simulations

Verification, Validation and Accreditation (VV&A) of M&S

M&S Applications

A Basic Proxy System Design for Integrating Complicated Distributed Simulation Systems

Xiaodong Zhu[✉], Ge Li, Peng Wang, and Xibao Wang

School of Information System and Management,
National University of Defense Technology, Changsha, China
{zhuxiaodong,geli,wangpeng_nudt}@nudt.edu.cn,
xbwang1990@126.com

Abstract. A management and control infrastructure comprising a macro-control system and some proxy systems can be used to integrate heterogeneous and distributed simulation systems. This paper proposes a design of a basic proxy system based on DDS (Data Distribution Service). It discusses the function, architecture and operating process of a proxy system. The weaponry proxy system is used as an example to specify the details of the running principle and process of the function modules. At last, we use a case study to illustrate the feasibility and performance of the proxy system in integrating complicated distribution simulation systems.

Keywords: Management and control infrastructure · Macro-control · Proxy · DDS

1 Introduction

The weapon performance in actual combat relays not only on the weapon itself but also on the corresponding environment it deals with. To conduct multi-weaponry system joint simulation experiment under operational conditions will highly improve the reliability of simulation, shorten the development cycle, promote the standardized management of life-cycle simulation service and reduce the expenses considerably.

Currently, advanced distributed simulation technology is the main supporting method used in weaponry system joint simulation. It builds a time and space coupling joint simulation running environment using network for information exchanging to combine the existing and geographically distributed simulation systems [1]. However, it is hard to interoperate and integrate various simulation systems due to the incompatibility in time advance mechanism, underlying service, data format and other aspects.

A complicated distributed simulation system usually consists of independent subsystems. Each subsystem has its own management module. In the process of integration,

X. Zhu—This work is supported by the National Nature Science Foundation of China (Grant No. 61374185).

L. Zhang et al. (Eds.): AsiaSim 2016/SCS AutumnSim 2016, Part IV, CCIS 646, pp. 3–12, 2016.
DOI: 10.1007/978-981-10-2672-0_1

we use a hierarchical management and control method, building a macro-control system and some proxy systems, to ensure centralized management of the whole system and alleviate the complication of the system development and integration by taking advantage of the current resources instead of developing new subsystems [2]. The macro-control system is a system-level central management system which manages and controls all systems. The proxy system is a subsystem-level local management system which cooperates with the macro-control system to manage all the simulation resources which possessed by the particular subsystem [3].

A proxy is a simulation system that is connected to two different infrastructure solutions. It comprises the common elements—entities and events—that are shared between the two solutions and uses the interface provided by the infrastructure for simulation systems [4]. Two different subsystems communicate with each other through their own proxy system other than communicate directly so that each subsystem can be insulated from outer simulation environment.

This paper is structured as follows. In Sect. 2, we discuss the basic functions of a common proxy system. Section 3 describes the function modules of the proxy system and details of the design of particular modules. Section 4 presents the operating process of the proxy system. Section 5 uses a case study to test the performance of the proxy system. Finally, we draw conclusions.

2 Functions of the Proxy System

Complicated distributed simulation systems usually run on networks with different demands of time such as high real time and non-real time. For example, the simulation repository access, experimental preparation and post-mortem analysis require a non-real time environment while simulation management, data display and time synchronization make claims on real time. Therefore, we design the proxy system to be suitable for multi-layer networks including Ethernet and high-speed real time network such as reflective memory network. The proxy system will transmit data on different networks based on the urgency of the mission.

The proxy system operates on the computer which takes control of the subsystem. It interacts with the other programs on the computer by inter-process communication. Therefore the proxy system has a promising prospect for reusability. On one aspect, the function modules of the proxy system have low coupling because the difference among all the proxy systems is mainly in data transformation module while the other parts, such as time synchronization module, have little interaction with the data transformation module so that they can all be reused. On the other aspect, we shield the proxy system from the underlying network and remain the consistency of interface. In that way, we can modify and extend the communication function conveniently.

The proxy system should provide services as follows:

Basic Gateway. The proxy system handles the information exchange between the subsystem and its outer environment. It works as an intelligent convertor which ensures that the data formats are converted properly and both data sender and data receiver can recognize them [5].

Data Filtering. The proxy system possesses the function of data identification so that it can make sure the subsystem receive proper data and reject uninterested data.

Checking Network Connection. The proxy system deals with the common problems in the distributed environment such as network interruption. It checks the state of the subsystem and report to the macro-control system real-timely to make sure that the joint simulation runs in completely connected networks.

Executing Command from Macro-control System. The proxy system can respond to the command from the macro-control system during all simulation periods. For example, it helps the macro-control system manage the starting and ending of the simulation programs in subsystem and sends feedback to report the execution.

3 Detailed Design of Function Modules

Different proxy systems shares a similar architecture which means most parts of the proxy system can be reused and only a few specific requirement need to be customized. In the following sections, we explain the detailed design of the function modules using the proxy system built for the weaponry subsystem as an example.

The proxy system for weaponry subsystem comprises eight modules as it shows in Fig. 1. They are network middleware interface module (NMIM), simulation repository access interface module (SRAIM), shared memory communication module (SMCM), TCP communication interface module (TCPCM), UDP communication interface module (UDPCM), log recording module (LRM), time synchronization module (TSM) and data parsing and transformation module (DPTM).

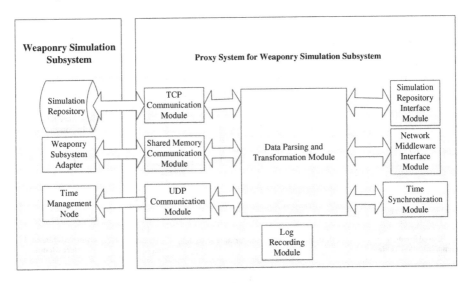

Fig. 1. Function structure of the proxy system

DPTM is the core function module of the proxy system which schedules and coordinates various modules. It is mainly responsible for parsing the data that the proxy system receives and transforming the format of the data that the proxy system transmits. The module parses protocol and transforms format of the data from the macro-control system and the other proxy systems through the network NMIM. And then it passes the transformed data to SMCM which transmits the data mainly to the subsystem adaptor software. Moreover, the module also parses and transforms the data that comes from SMCM including the state information and run time data information of the subsystem and then transmits it to NMIM. Furthermore, the module parses all requests from the macro-control system for information on the simulation repository of the weaponry subsystem. The requests and responding are transmitted by TCPCM. Beyond that, the module processes the UTC time synchronization information which comes from UDPCM and goes to TSM [6]. After that, the information is transmitted to the time synchronization node of the weaponry subsystem through UDPCM. In addition, the module passes information like the command from the macro-control system and state feedback from the subsystem to LRM so that they can be displayed and stored.

We describe the running process of DPTM in two parts. The first part transmits data through NMIM and SMCM based on DDS. The second part transmits data through UDPCM and TCPCM.

For the first part, DPTM mainly deals with simulation control command information and simulation report information as it shows in Fig. 2.

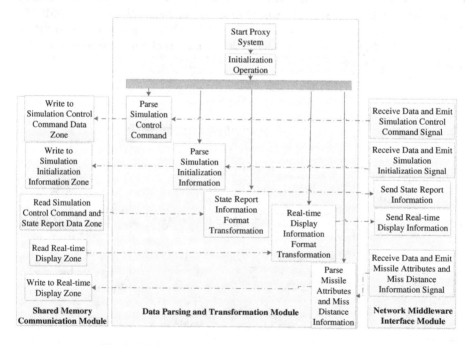

Fig. 2. Working flow of DPTM with NMIM and SMCM

As we can see, when the proxy system starts running, DPTM conducts initial process to get NMIM and SMCM ready for subsequent data transmission. When NMIM receives the data such as command like simulation start or initialization from the macro-control system, it passes the data to DPTM which will analyze and transform them afterwards. The processed data goes to SMCM to get read in. After that, SMCM sends the corresponding report information to DPTM which transforms the format of the information and send it to NMIM. The real time data of the subsystem, such as the entity attributes of the missile and the miss distance information [7, 8], will also be read by SMCM and sent to DPTM and NMIM.

For the second part, UDPCM mainly transmits the Universal Time Coordinate (UTC) timestamp information and time communication information in broadcast mode. TCPCM is designed particularly for giving the macro-control system access to the weaponry subsystem simulation repository. The request information on the repository from the macro-control is received by TCPCM over TCP and then transmitted to DPTM for parsing and transformation. After that, DPTM passes the processed data to the simulation repository of the weaponry subsystem through TCPCM. The corresponding information from the repository will return to TCPCM and then goes to the macro-control system after processed by DPTM. The specific running process of this part is present in Fig. 3.

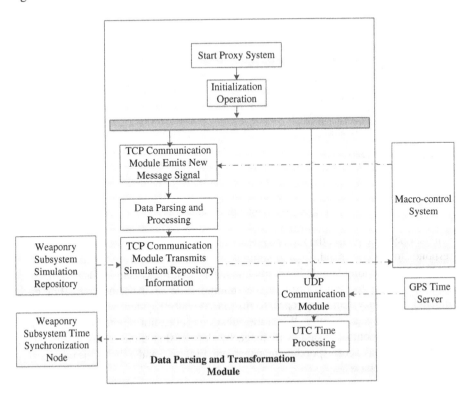

Fig. 3. Working flow of DPTM with TCPCM and UDPCM

4   Working Process of the Proxy System

The proxy system works in two phases, the initialization phase and the operation phase [9].

In the initialization phase, the proxy system is mainly responsible for transmitting the check command and initialization command and parsing the broadcast initialized scenario file from the macro-control system to the subsystem. In the meantime, the proxy system receives the report information from the subsystem to the macro-control system. Figure 4 shows the working process in the initialization phase.

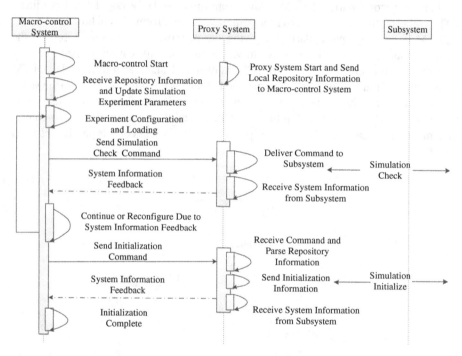

Fig. 4. Working flow of initialization

In the operation phase, the proxy system plays a role of two aspects. On one aspect, it responds to the command, such as simulation stop or pause, from the macro-control system. When the joint simulation starts, the macro-control system sends command to the proxy system to take control of the running state of the subsystem. For each command, the subsystem must report to the macro-control system whether it executes successfully or unsuccessfully. When the subsystem does not report over a period of time, the macro-control system will judge by default that there exists a subsystem breakdown and make corresponding management. Figures 5 and 6 shows the two aspects of the operation phase.

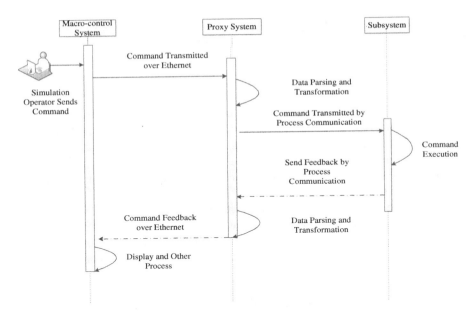

Fig. 5. Working flow of macro-control system when simulation runs

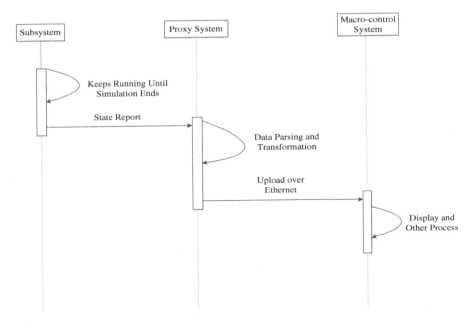

Fig. 6. Working flow of proxy system when simulation runs

To clarify, when we run a hardware-in-the-loop simulation, the macro-control system cannot send the simulation pause command. Besides, the proxy system will selectively accept the simulation command on the basis of the current mode in which the simulation runs. If a subsystem is not needed in one experiment, the proxy system for that subsystem will block all the simulation command.

5 Case Study

In this section, we present the test results of the simulation running with a full digital weaponry simulation subsystem and a guidance and control hardware-in-the-loop simulation system. The management and control infrastructure is used in the simulation. Each subsystem has its own proxy system to communicate with the macro-control system and the other subsystem. To describe the properties of the proxy system we designed, here we present two test results:

(1) After the missile is launch off, the guidance and control subsystem will track the missile and send its state information to the macro-control system, such as the speed, height, distance, pitch angle of the missile and so on. The macro-control system then displays of the track of how the state information of the missile changes on screen. The result is shown in Fig. 7.

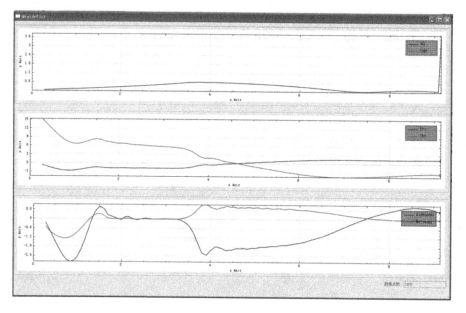

Fig. 7. State information of the missile received by macro-control system

The result indicates that the data is transmitted between the macro-control system and the guidance and control subsystems successfully through the proxy system. From the shape of each curve shown in the Fig. 7, we can say that the proxy system runs stably. The communication between subsystems and macro-control system is guaranteed by the proxy systems.

(2) After the missile is launch off, the guidance and control subsystem will send the state information of the missile to the weaponry subsystem to adjust the parameters of

the anti-missile missile which belongs to the weaponry subsystem. It is shown in Table 1 that the proxy system for the weaponry subsystem receives the state information at 2.789 s, 2.839 s and the other times.

Table 1. Messages transmitted between two proxy systems

Weaponry subsystem	Guidance and control subsystem
Missile Display updated! Missile time: 2.789	Real-time data updated! Time:78.4375
Missile Display updated! Missile time: 2.839	Real-time data updated! Time:78.5
Missile Display updated! Missile time: 2.939	Real-time data updated! Time:78.5625
Missile Display updated! Missile time: 2.989	Real-time data updated! Time:78.625
Missile Display updated! Missile time: 3.039	Real-time data updated! Time:78.6875

The result indicates that the data is transmitted between two different proxy systems successfully. Considering that the proxy system for the guidance and control subsystem received data from the subsystem, and the proxy system for the weaponry subsystem sent data to the subsystem, we can say that the communication between the two subsystems is guaranteed by the proxy system.

In general, the proxy system supports the communication successfully not only between subsystems and macro-control system, but also among different subsystems.

6   Conclusion

This paper first described the management and control infrastructure designed for complicated distributed simulation systems emphasizing the significance of the proxy system. We then presented basic functions of the proxy system and how they work in joint simulation. Our case study indicates that the design of our proxy system is successful and feasible. The proxy system has a promising prospect in joint simulation because it guarantees functional communication among different systems and insulates subsystems in the meantime so that we can put existing subsystems into joint simulation just by developing proxy systems for each of them. In that way, we can save much time, money and effort in joint simulation.

In fact, due to the similarity of the function and working process of all proxy systems, we can build a standard proxy system covering all the reusable parts. For instance, functions like data filtering, checking network connection and executing macro-control system command, which are needed by all proxy systems, can be integrated together to form a more powerful module. In future work, we will continue to study the versatility of proxy systems. We will study all the reusable parts of proxy system and design a general data model specifically for the management and control infrastructure in order to customize a specific proxy system for certain subsystem fast and conveniently.

References

1. Duan, W., Ge, Y.-Z., Qiu, X.-G.: Management and control techniques for distributed simulation system. In: 2010 Fifth International Conference on Frontier of Computer Science and Technology (FCST), pp. 9–16 (2010)
2. Xu, X., Li, G.: A management and control infrastructure for integrated real-time simulation environment. In: 17th IEEE/ACM International Symposium on Distributed Simulation and Real Time Applications (2013)
3. Wang, C., Hou, H.-T., Li, Q., et al.: A proxy-based composition method for distributed SMP2 models. Emerg. Mater. Mech. Appl., 171–194 (2012)
4. Tolk, A.: Engineering Principles of Combat Modeling and Distributed Simulation, USA, pp. 200–202 (2012)
5. Cai, Z.-W., Chen, Z.-B., Li, G.: The gateway research on interconnection in parallel and distributed simulation. Control Autom. 26(22), 127–129 (2010)
6. Wang, X., Wang, J.: Clock synchronization method for distributed real-time simulation based on multilayer network architecture. In: Xiao, T., Zhang, L., Fei, M. (eds.) AsiaSim 2012, Part III. CCIS, vol. 325, pp. 246–254. Springer, Heidelberg (2012)
7. Korkealaakso, P.M., Rouvinen, A.J., Moisio, S.M., et al.: Development of a real-time simulation environment. Multibody Sys. Dyn. 17(2/3), 177–194 (2007)
8. Boukerche, A., Zhang, M., Shadid, A., et al.: DEVS approach to real-time RTI design for large-scale distributed simulation systems. Simul.: J. Soc. Comput. Simul. 84(5), 231–238 (2008)
9. Liu, X.-M., Rao, H.: Modeling and analysis of mobile agent-based distributed simulation system. J. Syst. Simul. 18(z2), 350–353 (2006)

Dynamical Flocking of Multi-agent Systems with Multiple Leaders and Uncertain Parameters

Fusheng Wang and Hongyong Yang[(⊠)]

School of Information and Electrical Engineering,
Ludong University, Yantai 264025, China
hyyang@yeah.net

Abstract. Dynamical flocking of multi-agent systems with multiple leaders is studied. Supposing topologies are dynamically changed with jointly-connected, flocking algorithm of multi-agent systems with time-varying delays is proposed. Multi-agent systems with uncertain parameters and time-varying delays is investigated, and sufficient conditions are given for flocking control of multi-agent systems with dynamical topologies. Finally, simulations are provided to prove the effectiveness of the conclusion.

Keywords: Flocking control · Multi-agent systems · Uncertain parameters

1 Introduction

Distributed cooperative control of multi-agent systems has attracted great attention in the fields of control theory, mathematics, computer science, etc. Consensus is an important research problem of distributed cooperative control of multi-agent systems, which has been studies deeply [1–10].

Consensus of multi-agent systems means to reach agreement state with the evolution of time. Average consensus of continuous-time agents with delayed information and jointly-connected topologies is investigated, and a sufficient condition for average consensus of multi-agent system by employing Barbalat's Lemma in [1]. Multi-agent systems with time delays is studied in [2, 3], finite-time consensus algorithm for multi-agent with disturbance is researched in [4, 5]. Dynamical flocking is said as containment control with multiple leaders to drive followers moving into a target area (convex hull formed by the leaders). In [6], necessary and sufficient containment criteria with time delay are established for continuous-time and sampled-data sysems. In [7], containment control problem for second-order systems with time-varying delays is considered. In [8, 9], containment control of multi-agent systems with directed topology and communication time-delays and communication noises is investigated. In [10], containment control for multiple Lagrangian systems with multiple dynamic

H. Yang—Supported by the National Natural Science Foundation of China (No. 61273152, 61673200).

leaders in the presence of parametric uncertainties and external disturbances is studied. In [11], containment control of uncertain nonlinear multi-agent systems with multiple dynamic leaders under switching directed topologies is considered.

In this paper, dynamical flocking containment control of second-order multi-agent systems with multiple stationary leaders and time-varying delays is studied. The innovation of this paper is that distributed containment control algorithm for uncertain multi-agent systems with jointly-connected topologies is presented. By applying linear matrix inequality method, the convergence of the algorithm for the multi-agent systems with disconnected topologies is studied on Lyapunov-Krasovskii method.

2   Preliminaries

Let $G = \{V, E\}$ be an undirected graph of order n, where $V = \{v_1, v_2, \ldots, v_n\}$ is the set of nodes, $E = \{(v_i, v_j) : v_i, v_j \in V\}$ is the set of edges. If $(v_j, v_i) \in E$, then v_j is the neighbor of v_i. The set of the neighbors of node v_i is denoted by $N_i = \{v_j \in V | (v_i, v_j) \in E, j \neq i\}$. The union of a collection of graphs $G_1, G_2, \ldots, G_m$ with the same note set V, is defined as the graph G_{1-m} with the note set V and edge set equaling to the union of the edge sets of all of the graphs in the collection. Moreover, $G_1, G_2, \ldots, G_m$ is jointly-connected if its union graph G_{1-m} is connected [12].

The weighted adjacency matrix $A = [a_{ij}]$ of undirected graph G satisfying $a_{ij} > 0$ if $(i, j) \in E$, $a_{ij} = 0$, otherwise. The Laplacian corresponding to the undirected graph G is defined as $L = [l_{ij}]$, where l_{ij} is defined as follows:

$$l_{ij} = \begin{cases} -a_{ij}, & i \neq j \\ \sum_{j \in N_i} a_{ij}, & i = j \end{cases}$$

Consider an infinite sequence of nonempty, bounded and contiguous time-intervals $[t_r, t_{r+1})$, $r = 1, 2, \ldots$, with $t_1 = 0$ and for some constant $T_a > 0$. In each interval $[t_r, t_{r+1})$ there is a sequence of subintervals $[t_{r,j}, t_{r,j+1})$, $j = 1, 2, \ldots, m_r$ with $t_{r,1} = t_r$ and $t_{r,m_r+1} = t_{r+1}$ satisfying $t_{r,j+1} - t_{r,j} \geq T_b$, $J = 1, \ldots, m_r$ for some integer $m_r \geq 1$. Such that the communication topology switches at $t_{r,j}$ and it does not change during each subinterval $[t_{r,j}, t_{r,j+1})$. Let $\sigma(t) : [0, +\infty) \to \Gamma$, $\Gamma = \{1, 2, \ldots, N\}$ be a piecewise constant switching function, where N denotes the total number of all possible topologies. Suppose the multi-agent system consisting of n followers and m leaders in this paper. The communication topology of multi-agent systems at time is denoted by $G_{\sigma(t)}$ and the corresponding Laplacian matrix is denoted by $L_{\sigma(t)}$.

3   Flocking Control of Uncertain Multi-agent Systems

Consider second-order multi-agent systems of n followers and m leaders, and using $F = \{1, 2, \ldots, n\}$ and $L = \{n+1, n+2, \ldots, n+m\}$ to denote, respectively, the followers' set and the leaders' set. Suppose that the dynamics of agent i is described by the following equation

$$\dot{q}_i(t) = p_i(t - \tau(t)),$$
$$\dot{p}_i(t) = u_i(t - \tau(t)), \quad i = 1, \ldots, n, n+1, \ldots, n+m. \tag{1}$$

where $p_i(t) \in \mathbb{R}$ and $u_i(t) \in \mathbb{R}$ are the position vector, the velocity vector, and the control input vector, respectively. $\tau(t)$ is the time-varying communication delay.

Assumption 1. The time-varying communication delay $\tau(t)$ in the multi-agent system (1) is bounded, i.e., there exists $h > 0$ satisfying: $0 \leq \tau(t) < h$, $t \geq 0$.

Assumption 2. The communication topologies generated by n followers and m leaders, in each interval $[t_r, t_{r+1})$, $r = 1, 2, \ldots$, are jointly connected.

Assumption 3. There exists a connectivity subset for multi-agent systems in each non-overlapping time intervals $[t_{r,j}, t_{r,j+1}) \subset [t_r, t_{r+1})$, $j = 1, 2, \ldots, m_r$. For each follower, there exists at least one leader that has a path to the follower in the connectivity subset.

Considering the case of stationary leaders, and suppose the control protocol of second-order multi-agent systems is

$$u_i(t) = -k_1 p_i(t) - \sum_{j \in N_i} (a_{ij} + \Delta a_{ij}(t))(q_i(t) - q_j(t)), \quad i \in F; \tag{2}$$

$$p_i(t) = 0, \quad i \in L.$$

where $k_1 > 0$, and $\Delta a_{ij}(t)$ is the uncertain parameter with $\Delta a_{ii}(t) = 0$.

Definition 1. L is the Laplacian matrix of graph G, and $\Delta L(t) = [\Delta l_{ij}(t)]$ is the uncertain matrix of graph G defined by $\Delta l_{ij}(t) = \begin{cases} -\Delta a_{ij}(t), & i \neq j \\ \sum_{j \in N_i} \Delta a_{ij}(t), & i = j \end{cases}$, where

$$L = \begin{bmatrix} L_F & L_{FL} \\ 0_{m \times n} & 0_{m \times m} \end{bmatrix}, \quad \Delta L(t) = \begin{bmatrix} \Delta L_F(t) & \Delta L_{FL}(t) \\ 0_{m \times n} & 0_{m \times m} \end{bmatrix}, \quad L_F \in \mathbb{R}^{n \times n}, \quad \Delta L_F(t) \in \mathbb{R}^{n \times n},$$
$$L_{FL} \in \mathbb{R}^{n \times m}, \quad \Delta L_{FL}(t) \in \mathbb{R}^{n \times m}.$$

Definition 2. Norm bounded parameter uncertainty $\Delta L(t)$ and $\Delta L_F(t)$ satisfying

$$\Delta L^T(t) \Delta L(t) \leq \alpha^2 I_{n+m} \tag{3}$$

$$\Delta L_F^T(t) \Delta L_F(t) \leq \alpha^2 I_n \tag{4}$$

According to Definition 1, the system (1) and (2) can be written as

$$\dot{x}_F(t) = -H_1 x_F(t - \tau(t)) - H_2 x_L(t - \tau(t)) \tag{5}$$

$$\dot{x}_L(t) = H_3 x_L(t - \tau(t)) \tag{6}$$

where
$$H_1 = \begin{bmatrix} 0_{n \times n} & -I_n \\ E_F & k_1 I_n \end{bmatrix}, \qquad H_2 = \begin{bmatrix} 0_{n \times m} & 0_{n \times m} \\ E_{FL} & 0_{n \times m} \end{bmatrix}, \qquad H_3 = \begin{bmatrix} 0_{m \times m} & I_{m \times m} \\ 0_{m \times m} & 0_{m \times m} \end{bmatrix},$$

$E_F = L_F + \Delta L_F(t)$, $E_{FL} = L_{FL} + \Delta L_{FL}(t)$, $x_F(t) = [q_F^T(t), p_F^T(t)]^T$, $q_F(t)$ denotes the position vector of followers, $p_F(t)$ denotes the velocity vector of followers.

Let $\tilde{x}_F(t) = x_F(t) + H_1^{-1} H_2 x_L(t)$, Eq. (5) can be written as

$$\dot{\tilde{x}}_F(t) = -H_1 \tilde{x}_F(t - \tau(t)) \tag{7}$$

where $H_1^{-1} = \begin{bmatrix} k_1 E_F^{-1} & E_F^{-1} \\ -I_n & 0_{n \times n} \end{bmatrix}$.

Lemma 1 [13]. For any real differentiable vector function $x(t) \in \mathbb{R}^n$ and any $n \times n$ dimensional constant matrix $W = W^T > 0$, we have the following inequality

$$h^{-1}[x(t) - x(t - \tau(t))]^T W[x(t) - x(t - \tau(t))] \leq \int_{t-\tau(t)}^t \dot{x}^T(s) W \dot{x}(s) ds.$$

where $t \geq 0$, $0 \leq \tau(t) \leq h$.

Lemma 2 [14]. Let $\Xi = \Xi^T$, F_1, F_2, $H(t)$ be a matrices with appropriate dimensions, and matrix $H(t)$ satisfied $H^T(t)H(t) \leq I$, then

$$\Xi + F_1 H(t) F_2 + F_2^T H^T(t) F_1^T < 0,$$

satisfied if and only if there exists a positive constant $\varepsilon > 0$ satisfied

$$\Xi + \varepsilon^{-1} F_1 F_1^T + \varepsilon F_2^T F_2 < 0.$$

Lemma 3 [15]. For undirected graph G_F, if Assumption 3 holds, then E_F is positive definite, $-E_F^{-1} E_{FL}$ is a non-negative matrix and the sum of the entries in every row equals 1.

Lemma 4. Let $x_L = [x_{n+1}, \ldots, x_{n+m}]^T$, $x_F = [x_1, \ldots, x_n]^T$, if $x_F \to -H_1^{-1} H_2 x_L$, then the containment control of the multi-agent system can be achieved.

Proof. From Lemma 3, we can get the proof.

Theorem 1. Consider a second-order dynamic system (1) of n followers and m leaders with the switching topologies. When Assumptions 1, 2 and 3 hold, for each subinterval $[t_{r,j}, t_{r,j+1})$, if there exists a constant $\varepsilon > 0$, such that

$$\Pi_\sigma^i = \begin{bmatrix} \Pi_{11} & \Pi_{12} \\ * & \Pi_{22} \end{bmatrix} < 0, \quad i = 1, 2, \ldots, n_\sigma. \tag{8}$$

where $\Pi_{11} = -\frac{1}{h} I_{2 \times d_{\sigma F}^i} + \varepsilon I_{2 \times d_{\sigma F}^i}$, $\Pi_{22} = (\frac{1}{\varepsilon} - \frac{1}{h}) I_{2 \times d_{\sigma F}^i} + (h + \varepsilon h^2) \bar{H}_{\sigma 1}^i{}^{\mathrm{T}} \bar{H}_{\sigma 1}^i + h \alpha^2 J_\sigma^i$,

$\Pi_{12} = \frac{1}{h} I_{2 \times d_{\sigma F}^i} - \bar{H}_{\sigma 1}^i + \varepsilon h \bar{H}_{\sigma 1}^i$, $J_\sigma^i = \begin{bmatrix} 0_{d_{\sigma F}^i} & 0_{d_{\sigma F}^i} \\ I_{d_{\sigma F}^i} & 0_{d_{\sigma F}^i} \end{bmatrix}$. Then, the control protocol (2)

solves the containment control problem of second-order systems with time-varying delays and uncertain topologies.

Proof. Define a common Lyapunov-Krasovskii function for system (7) as follows

$$V(t) = \tilde{x}_F^{\mathrm{T}}(t) \tilde{x}_F(t) + \int_{t-h}^t (s - t + h) \dot{\tilde{x}}_F^{\mathrm{T}}(s) \dot{\tilde{x}}_F(s) ds \tag{9}$$

Taking the derivative of $V(t)$ along the trajectories of (9) yields

$$\dot{V}(t) = \sum_{i=1}^{n_\sigma} \left\{ \left[-H_{\sigma 1}^i \tilde{x}_{\sigma F}^i (t - \tau(t)) \right]^{\mathrm{T}} \tilde{x}_{\sigma F}^i(t) + \tilde{x}_{\sigma F}^i{}^{\mathrm{T}}(t) \left[-H_{\sigma 1}^i \tilde{x}_{\sigma F}^i (t - \tau(t)) \right] \right. \tag{10}$$
$$\left. + h \dot{\tilde{x}}_{\sigma F}^i{}^{\mathrm{T}}(t) \dot{\tilde{x}}_{\sigma F}^i(t) - \int_{t-h}^t \dot{\tilde{x}}_{\sigma F}^i{}^{\mathrm{T}}(s) \dot{\tilde{x}}_{\sigma F}^i(s) ds \right\}$$

From Assumption 1, since $\tau(t) < h$, $h > 0$, we get

$$-\int_{t-h}^t \dot{\tilde{x}}_{\sigma F}^i{}^{\mathrm{T}}(s) \dot{\tilde{x}}_{\sigma F}^i(s) ds \leq -\int_{t-\tau(t)}^t \dot{\tilde{x}}_{\sigma F}^i{}^{\mathrm{T}}(s) \dot{\tilde{x}}_{\sigma F}^i(s) ds \tag{11}$$

According to Lemma 1, we can get

$$-\int_{t-\tau(t)}^t \dot{\tilde{x}}_{\sigma F}^i{}^{\mathrm{T}}(s) \dot{\tilde{x}}_{\sigma F}^i(s) ds \leq -\frac{1}{h} [\tilde{x}_{\sigma F}^i(t) - \tilde{x}_{\sigma F}^i(t - \tau(t))]^{\mathrm{T}} [\tilde{x}_{\sigma F}^i(t) - \tilde{x}_{\sigma F}^i(t - \tau(t))] \tag{12}$$

we have

$$\dot{V}(t) \leq \sum_{i=1}^{n_\sigma} \left\{ -\tilde{x}_{\sigma F}^i{}^{\mathrm{T}}(t) H_{\sigma 1}^i \tilde{x}_{\sigma F}^i(t - \tau(t)) - \tilde{x}_{\sigma F}^i{}^{\mathrm{T}}(t - \tau(t)) H_{\sigma 1}^i{}^{\mathrm{T}} \tilde{x}_{\sigma F}^i(t) \right.$$
$$+ h \tilde{x}_{\sigma F}^i(t)^{\mathrm{T}} (t - \tau(t)) H_{\sigma 1}^i{}^{\mathrm{T}} H_{\sigma 1}^i \tilde{x}_{\sigma F}^i(t - \tau(t))$$
$$\left. - \frac{1}{h} \left[\tilde{x}_{\sigma F}^i(t) - \tilde{x}_{\sigma F}^i(t - \tau(t)) \right]^{\mathrm{T}} \left[\tilde{x}_{\sigma F}^i(t) - \tilde{x}_{\sigma F}^i(t - \tau(t)) \right] \right\}$$
$$= \sum_{i=1}^{n_\sigma} y_\sigma^i{}^{\mathrm{T}} \Omega_\sigma^i y_\sigma^i$$

where $y_\sigma^i = \left[\tilde{x}_{\sigma F}^i{}^{\mathrm{T}}(t), \tilde{x}_{\sigma F}^i{}^{\mathrm{T}}(t - \tau(t)) \right]^{\mathrm{T}}$, and

$$\Omega_\sigma^i = \begin{bmatrix} -\frac{1}{h} I_{2 \times d_{\sigma F}^i} & \frac{1}{h} I_{2 \times d_{\sigma F}^i} - H_{\sigma 1}^i \\ \frac{1}{h} I_{2 \times d_{\sigma F}^i} - H_{\sigma 1}^i{}^{\mathrm{T}} & -\frac{1}{h} I_{2 \times d_{\sigma F}^i} + h H_{\sigma 1}^i{}^{\mathrm{T}} H_{\sigma 1}^i \end{bmatrix}.$$

According to Lemma 2,

$$\Psi_\sigma^i = \begin{bmatrix} 0 \\ I_{2\times d_{\sigma F}^i} \end{bmatrix} B_\sigma^{i\,\mathrm{T}} \begin{bmatrix} I_{2\times d_{\sigma F}^i} & h\bar{H}_{\sigma 1}^i \end{bmatrix} + \begin{bmatrix} I_{2\times d_{\sigma F}^i} & h\bar{H}_{\sigma 1}^i \end{bmatrix}^{\mathrm{T}} B_\sigma^i \begin{bmatrix} 0 \\ I_{2\times d_{\sigma F}^i} \end{bmatrix}^{\mathrm{T}}, \quad \Omega_\sigma^i < 0$$

they equivalent to

$$\Phi_\sigma^i + \varepsilon^{-1} \begin{bmatrix} 0 \\ I_{2\times d_{\sigma F}^i} \end{bmatrix} \begin{bmatrix} 0 \\ I_{2\times d_{\sigma F}^i} \end{bmatrix}^{\mathrm{T}} + \varepsilon \begin{bmatrix} I_{2\times d_{\sigma F}^i} & h\bar{H}_{\sigma 1}^i \end{bmatrix}^{\mathrm{T}} \begin{bmatrix} I_{2\times d_{\sigma F}^i} & h\bar{H}_{\sigma 1}^i \end{bmatrix} = \Phi_\sigma^i + \Xi_\sigma^i < 0,$$

where $\quad \Xi_\sigma^i = \begin{bmatrix} \varepsilon I_{2\times d_{\sigma F}^i} & \varepsilon h\bar{H}_{\sigma 1}^i \\ \varepsilon h\bar{H}_{\sigma 1}^{i\,\mathrm{T}} & \varepsilon h^2 \bar{H}_{\sigma 1}^{i\,\mathrm{T}} \bar{H}_{\sigma 1}^i + \frac{1}{\varepsilon} I_{2\times d_{\sigma F}^i} \end{bmatrix}, \quad \varepsilon > 0.$ $\quad$ Definition $\quad$ 2,

$$\Delta L_{\sigma F}^{i\,\mathrm{T}}(t) \Delta L_{\sigma F}^i(t) \le \alpha^2 I_{d_{\sigma F}^i}, \qquad B_\sigma^{i\,\mathrm{T}} B_\sigma^i \le \begin{bmatrix} 0_{d_{\sigma F}^i \times d_{\sigma F}^i} & 0_{d_{\sigma F}^i \times d_{\sigma F}^i} \\ \alpha^2 I_{d_{\sigma F}^i} & 0_{d_{\sigma F}^i \times d_{\sigma F}^i} \end{bmatrix}, \qquad \text{then}$$

$$\Phi_\sigma^i \le \begin{bmatrix} -\frac{1}{h} I_{2\times d_{\sigma F}^i} & \frac{1}{h} I_{2\times d_{\sigma F}^i} - \bar{H}_{\sigma 1}^i \\ \frac{1}{h} I_{2\times d_{\sigma F}^i} - \bar{H}_{\sigma 1}^{i\,\mathrm{T}} & -\frac{1}{h} I_{2\times d_{\sigma F}^i} + h\bar{H}_{\sigma 1}^{i\,\mathrm{T}} \bar{H}_{\sigma 1}^i + h\alpha^2 J_\sigma^i \end{bmatrix}, \quad \text{where } J_\sigma^i = \begin{bmatrix} 0_{d_{\sigma F}^i} & 0_{d_{\sigma F}^i} \\ I_{d_{\sigma F}^i} & 0_{d_{\sigma F}^i} \end{bmatrix}.$$

Therefore, if Eq. (8) holds, then $\Omega_\sigma^i < 0$, i.e., $\dot{V}(t) < 0$. The system (7) is asymptotically stable. Since $V(t)$ is nonincreasing and bounded below by 0, then $V(t)$ must approach a limit as $t \to \infty$. Note that

$$0 \ge \int_0^t \sum_{i=1}^{n_\sigma} y_\sigma^i(s)^{\mathrm{T}} \Omega_\sigma^i y_\sigma^i(s) ds \ge \int_0^t \dot{V}(s) ds = V(t) - V(0)$$

and $\sum_{i=1}^{n_\sigma} y_\sigma^{i\,\mathrm{T}} \Omega_\sigma^i y_\sigma^i < 0$. It follows that $\int_0^{+\infty} (\sum_{i=1}^{n_\sigma} y_\sigma^i(s)^{\mathrm{T}} \Omega_\sigma^i y_\sigma^i(s)) ds$ exists and finite. We have $y_\sigma^i = 0$, i.e., $\tilde{x}_{\sigma F}^i(t) = \tilde{x}_{\sigma F}^i(t - \tau(t)) = 0$, $t \to +\infty$. Then by induction, it has $\lim_{t \to +\infty} x_F(t) = \lim_{t \to +\infty} x_F(t - \tau(t)) = -H_1^{-1} H_2 x_L(t)$, $\lim_{t \to +\infty} q_F(t) = -E_F^{-1} E_{FL} q_L(t)$.

Therefore, containment control of the second-order multi-agent systems with time-varying delays and uncertain topologies can be achieved.

4 Simulations

Considering the dynamic switching topology with 5 followers and 3 leaders shown in Fig. 1, and using $F = \{1, 2, 3, 4, 5\}$ and $L = \{6, 7, 8\}$ to denote, respectively, the followers' set and the leaders' set, where the connection weights of each edge is 1. Suppose the communication topology of the multi-agent system randomly switches in G1 to G3 at $t = kT$, $k = 0, 1, \ldots$, where $T = 0.5s$.

From the communication topology of the union of a collection of simple graphs $G1 \sim G3$, the system matrix $L_{\sigma F}$ can be obtained. Using the Matlab's LMI toolbox to solve (8) we get $k_1 > 4.3278$, $h < 0.4621$. Let $k_1 = 4.4$, and let $\tau(t) = 0.2 + 0.2 \sin t$ is the time-varying delays of multi-agent systems in the experiments. The initial position

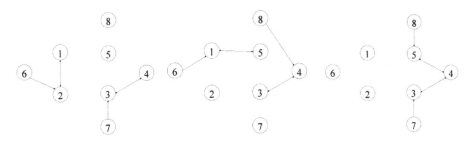

Fig. 1. Communication topology of the multi-agent systems

of followers and leaders are taken $q_1(0) = (1, 1)$, $q_2(0) = (1, 3)$, $q_3(0) = (3, 1)$, $q_5(0) = (5, 3)$, $q_6(0) = (7, 10)$, $q_7(0) = (10, 7)$, $q_8(0) = (10, 10)$, respectively. The initial velocity of followers and leaders are taken $p_1(0) = (1, 1)$, $p_3(0) = (1, 1)$, $p_4(0) = (2, 2)$, $p_5(0) = (3, 3)$, $p_6(0) = p_7(0) = p_8(0) = (0, 0)$, respectively.

For $\Delta L_{\sigma F} = \alpha \sin(t) * L_{\sigma F}$ with $\alpha = 0.1$, state trajectories of all agents are shown in Fig. 2, which shows that those followers can asymptotically convergence to the triangle formed by three leaders, i.e., the containment control of multi-agent systems can be achieved.

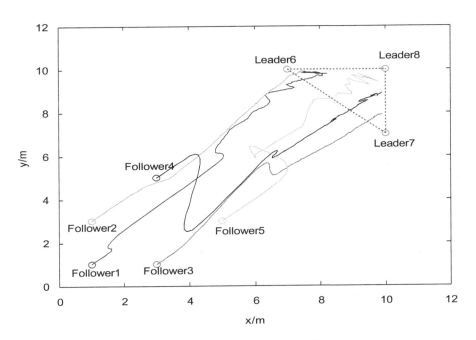

Fig. 2. Moving trajectories of multi-agent systems with uncertain topologies

5   Conclusion

In this paper, dynamical flocking containment control for second-order multi-agent systems with multiple leaders and jointly-connected topologies is studied. Flocking control algorithm of multi-agent systems with time-varying delays and uncertain parameters is proposed. The convergence of multi-agent systems is analyzed on Lyapunov-Krasovskii method, and some sufficient conditions in terms of linear matrix inequalities(LMIs) are obtained for flocking containment control of multi-agent systems.

References

1. Lin, P., Qin, K., Zhao, H., Sun, M.: A new approach to average consensus problems with multiple time-delays and jointly-connected topologies. J. Franklin Inst. **349**(1), 293–304 (2012)
2. Yang, H.Y., Zhang, Z.X., Zhang, S.Y.: Consensus of second-order multi-agent systems with exogenous disturbances. Int. J. Robust Nonlinear Contr. **21**(9), 945–956 (2011)
3. Yang, H.Y., Zhu, X., Cao, K.: Distributed coordination of fractional order multi-agent systems with communication delay. Fract. Calc. Appl. Anal. **17**(1), 23–37 (2014)
4. Li, S., Du, H., Lin, X.: Finite-time consensus algorithm for multi-agent with double-integrator dynamics. Automatica **47**(8), 1706–1712 (2011)
5. Yang, H., Guo, L., Zhang, Y., Yao, X.: Movement consensus of complex fractional-order multi-agent systems. Acta Automatica Sinica **40**(3), 489–496 (2014)
6. Yan, F., Xie, D.: Containment control of multi-agent systems with time delay. Trans. Inst. Meas. Contr. **36**(2), 196–205 (2014)
7. Liu, K., Xie, G., Wang, L.: Containment control for second-order multi-agent systems with time-varying delays. Syst. Contr. Lett. **67**(5), 24–31 (2014)
8. Qi, B., Lou, X., Cui, B.: Containment control of second-order multi-agent systems with directed topology and time-delays. Kybernetes **43**(8), 1248–1261 (2014)
9. Wang, Y., Cheng, L., Hou, Z., et al.: Containment control of multi-agent systems in a noisy communication environment. Automatica **50**(7), 1922–1928 (2014)
10. Yang, D., Ren, W., Liu, X.: Fully distributed adaptive sliding-mode controller design for containment control of multiple Lagrangian systems. Syst. Contr. Lett. **72**(10), 44–52 (2014)
11. Wang, W., Wang, D., Peng, Z.: Distributed containment control for uncertain nonlinear multi-agent systems in non-affine pure-feedback form under switching topologies. Neuro-computing **152**(3), 1–10 (2015)
12. Lin, P., Jia, Y.: Consensus of a class of second-order multi-agent systems with time-delay and jointly-connected topologies. IEEE Trans. Autom. Contr. **55**(3), 778–784 (2010)
13. Sun, Y.G., Wang, L., Xie, G.: Average consensus in networks of dynamic agents with switching topologies and multiple time-varying delays. Syst. Contr. Lett. **57**(2), 175–183 (2008)
14. Peterson, I.R., Hollot, C.V.: A Riccati equation approach to the stabilization of uncertain linear systems. Automatica **22**(4), 397–411 (1986)
15. Meng, Z., Ren, W., You, Z.: Distributed finite-time attitude containment control for multiple rigid bodies. Automatica **46**(12), 2092–2099 (2010)

A Novel Method of Pedestrian Detection Aided by Color Self-similarity Feature

Dong-yang Shen[1], Mei-hua Xu[1(✉)], and Ai-ying Guo[1,2]

[1] School of Mechatronic Engineering and Automation,
Shanghai University, Shanghai, China
mhxu@shu.edu.cn
[2] Department of Electrical Engineering,
Shanxi Light Industry Vocational and Technical College, Xianyang, China

Abstract. Pedestrian detection has been widely applied in intelligent surveillance and driver assistant systems. The histogram of the oriented gradient (HOG) is the most commonly used feature in pedestrian detection algorithms, which is computationally intensive and results in slow detection speed. This paper proposes a method of pedestrian detection, which is based on color self-similarity (CSS) feature and AdaBoost classifier. The color self-similarity (CSS) feature calculates the ratio of two rectangles to measure the self-similarity in HSV color space, and then the AdaBoost classifier is used to screen out the detection windows containing pedestrian. Tests show that this method has the same detection accuracy and faster detection speed compared with HOG detectors.

Keywords: CSS · AdaBoost · HSV · Pedestrian detection

1 Introduction

Pedestrian detection has been widely applied in intelligent surveillance and driver assistant systems [1], but the shape of the pedestrian, clothing, light and other factors increase the difficulty of pedestrian detection. So it is difficult to get a fast pedestrian detection method with high detection rate.

The classic work of real-time target detection is face detection proposed by Viola and Jones [2], whose fast speed is based on Haar-like features and AdaBoost classifier. Haar-like features are directly built on the image very fast and has scale invariance which can be applied to multi-scale detection. Cascade classifier selects some strong classifiers by AdaBoost algorithm and cascades the strong classifiers by coarse-to-fine, which can quickly rule out a large number of windows without targets. But Haar-like features have poor performance on pedestrian detection. Currently, the mainstream pedestrian feature is the histogram of oriented gradient (HOG) feature proposed by Dalal and Triggs [3], which is a multi-dimensional feature combined with the SVM classification algorithm to achieve good results, but it is slow. Overall, this feature calculates the gradient of image to characterize the outline of pedestrians which is slow and changes with scale, so it is also slow on multi-scale.

© Springer Science+Business Media Singapore 2016
L. Zhang et al. (Eds.): AsiaSim 2016/SCS AutumnSim 2016, Part IV, CCIS 646, pp. 21–29, 2016.
DOI: 10.1007/978-981-10-2672-0_3

The variable clothing of pedestrians increases the difficulty of pedestrian detection, but pedestrians have locally symmetric self-similarity. In the field of pedestrian detection, erect pedestrian is divided into three parts: the head, torso and lower limbs. Each part is symmetrically self-similar, such as the head, left arm right arm of torso, legs of lower limbs. Walk et al. [4] proposed a global self-similarity feature based on color self-similarity, which was combined with HOG feature to improve the detection rate, but it extracted high-dimensional symbiotic characteristics, which results high calculation complexity [5, 8, 9].

In this paper, the color self-similarity (CSS) feature is built in HSV color space to characterize the color self-similarity of pedestrians.

2 Color Self-similarity

Color feature is a common feature which is not widely applied in pedestrian detection [6], because most of the color features of pedestrian image are determined by the clothing and background. However, the human body has structural characteristics, and the color of the body also has structural self-similarity [7]. The color self-similarity (CSS) feature proposed by Walk et al. [4] did deep analysis on the local color of pedestrians in the image. The local similar structure of pedestrian is effective, such as the human torso and two arms. Figure 1(a) is the original pedestrian image. Face and arm skin color is similar (see Fig. 1(b)). The color of pedestrians' clothing is also self-similar (see Fig. 1(c, d)).

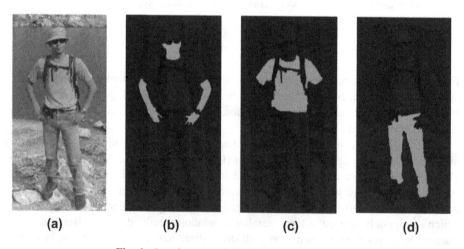

(a)   (b)   (c)   (d)

Fig. 1. Local structural similarity of pedestrians

CSS feature proposed by Walk et al. [4] divides the 128×64 images into 8×8 blocks and calculates the histogram information of every block in HSV color space, a total of $16 \times 8 = 128$ blocks. The histogram intersection is used to calculate the distances between the first block and the other 127 blocks, the second block and the subsequent 126 blocks are calculated as well. Finally the feature with $128 \times (128 - 1)/2 = 8128$ dimensions is got. The calculation steps are as follows:

(1) Converting an RGB image to HSV color space;
(2) Calculating the color histogram of each block:

128×64 image is divided into 8×8 blocks without overlap; the histogram of every block is calculated in H, S and V channels, which is set by three bins. The histogram is calculated with trilinear interpolation to minimize aliasing, according to formula (1).

$$chlh(x_1, y_1, c_1) \leftarrow chlh(x_1, y_1, c_1) + chlh(x, y)\left(1 - \frac{x - x_1}{dx}\right)\left(1 - \frac{y - y_1}{dy}\right)\left(\frac{chl(x, y) - c_2}{dc}\right)$$

$$chlh(x_1, y_1, c_2) \leftarrow chlh(x_1, y_1, c_2) + chlh(x, y)\left(1 - \frac{x - x_1}{dx}\right)\left(1 - \frac{y - y_1}{dy}\right)\left(\frac{chl(x, y) - c_1}{dc}\right)$$

$$chls(x_1, y_1, c_1) \leftarrow chls(x_1, y_1, c_1) + chls(x, y)\left(1 - \frac{x - x_1}{dx}\right)\left(1 - \frac{y - y_1}{dy}\right)\left(\frac{chl(x, y) - c_2}{dc}\right)$$

$$chls(x_1, y_1, c_2) \leftarrow chls(x_1, y_1, c_2) + chls(x, y)\left(1 - \frac{x - x_1}{dx}\right)\left(1 - \frac{y - y_1}{dy}\right)\left(\frac{chl(x, y) - c_1}{dc}\right) \quad (1)$$

$$chlv(x_1, y_1, c_1) \leftarrow chlv(x_1, y_1, c_1) + chlv(x, y)\left(1 - \frac{x - x_1}{dx}\right)\left(1 - \frac{y - y_1}{dy}\right)\left(\frac{chl(x, y) - c_2}{dc}\right)$$

$$chlv(x_1, y_1, c_2) \leftarrow chlv(x_1, y_1, c_2) + chlh(x, y)\left(1 - \frac{x - x_1}{dx}\right)\left(1 - \frac{y - y_1}{dy}\right)\left(\frac{chl(x, y) - c_1}{dc}\right)$$

Where (x_1, y_1) is the center coordinate of block; (x, y) is the coordinate of the statistical point; c_1, c_2 are the adjacent color intervals of coordinate point (x, y) in the color channel; dx, dy are respectively block width and height; dc is the interval of statistical histogram interval.

(3) Calculating block color histogram similarity: Histogram intersection is used to calculate the similarity of the color histogram of blocks in H, S and V color channels respectively, which are summed as the similarity of block. Similarity is calculated as Eq. (2) below:

$$Dist(M, N) = \sum_{HSV} \sum_{i=1}^{3} \min(M(i), N(i)) \quad (2)$$

(4) Feature normalization: L2-norm is used to normalize histogram distance calculated by last step as Eq. (3):

$$Dist(M, N)' = \frac{Dist(M, N)}{\sqrt{Dist(M, N)^2 + \varepsilon}} \quad (3)$$

Where M, N are block histograms, i is the bins of the histogram (i = 1, 2, 3).

Using trilinear interpolation can effectively minimize aliasing. But there is little interaction between the pixel color, according to the structure of the image sensor. And the calculation process of trilinear interpolation is relatively time-consuming. Meanwhile, it is very complex to calculate the color self-similarity of blocks using histogram intersection. Those parts are improved in the calculation steps:

(1) Converting an RGB image to HSV color space;
(2) Extracting rectangular block feature: R_1 is defined as 8×8 rectangular block, and the sum of the matrix blocks are calculated in H, S and V channels respectively:

$$Sum_{R_1 H} = \sum_{x,y \in R_1} S_H(x, y) \tag{4}$$

$$Sum_{R_1 S} = \sum_{x,y \in R_1} S_S(x, y) \tag{5}$$

$$Sum_{R_1 V} = \sum_{x,y \in R_1} S_V(x, y) \tag{6}$$

(3) Calculating the similarity of rectangular blocks: The ratio of rectangular block R_1 and R_2 is calculated in H, S and V channels, which is summed as the similarity of blocks. Similarity is calculated as Eq. (5) below:

$$F(R_1, R_2) = \frac{Sum_{R_1 H}}{Sum_{R_2 H}} + \frac{Sum_{R_1 S}}{Sum_{R_2 S}} + \frac{Sum_{R_1 V}}{Sum_{R_2 V}} \tag{7}$$

The improved feature extraction algorithm still calculate the similarity of different blocks as the order done by Walk et al. [4]. The 128×64 image is divided into 8×8 blocks without overlap getting $16 \times 8 = 128$ blocks in total. The $128 \times (128-1)/2 = 8128$ dimensions feature is calculating the similarity of each blocks.

3 AdaBoost Algorithm

AdaBoost is an iterative algorithm, whose core idea is training different weak classifiers form the same training set and then putting them together to form a strong classifier. This algorithm is achieved by changing the data distribution, which determines the weight of each sample by each time correctly classifying each sample in training set and the accuracy of the previous overall classification. The new data set with modified weights is sent to the lower classifier training. The classifiers got from each training are mixed together as the final decision classifier. AdaBoost classifier is used to rule out some unnecessary features of the training data and to focus on the key data.

$T = \{(x\_1, y\_1), (x\_2, y\_2) \ldots (x\_N, y\_N)\}$ is given as a training set, where $x \in X$, $X \subset R^n$ and y_i belongs to the mark set $\{0, +1\}$. The goal of AdaBoost is training different weak classifiers form the same training set and then putting them together to form a strong classifier. The algorithm process is as follow:

(1) Initializing the weight of training data: Each training sample is given the same weight at the beginning: 1/N

$$D_1 = (w_{11}, w_{12} \ldots w_{1i} \ldots w_{1N}), w_{1i} = \frac{1}{N}, i = 1, 2, \ldots N \tag{8}$$

Next, if a sample point has been accurately classified, it will has lower probability to be selected to construct the next training set; on the contrary, if a sample point has not been accurately classified, its weight is increased.

(2) For m = 1, 2,..., M:

(a) Using Training data set with weight distribution D_m to get the basic binary classifier:

$$G_m(x) : x \rightarrow \{-1, +1\} \tag{9}$$

(b) Computing the classification error rate of $G_m(x)$ on the training data set:

$$e_m = P(G_m(x) \neq y_i) = \sum_{i=1}^{N} w_{mi} I(G_m(x) \neq y_i) \tag{10}$$

(c) Computing the coefficient α_m of $G_m(x)$ which represents the weight of $G_m(x)$ in the final classification:

$$\alpha_m = \frac{1}{2} \log \frac{1 - e_m}{e_m} \tag{11}$$

Seen from the above formula, when $e_m \leq 1/2$, $\alpha_m \geq 0$, and α_m increases with e_m decreasing. It means that the basic classifier with smaller classification error rate plays the greater role in the final classification.

(d) Updating training dataset weight distribution:

$$D_{m+1} = (w_{m+1,1}, w_{m+1,2} \ldots w_{m+1,i} \ldots w_{m+1,N}),$$
$$w_{m+1,i} = \frac{w_{mi}}{Z_m} \exp(-\alpha_m y_i G_m(x_i)), i = 1, 2, \ldots, N \tag{12}$$

The weight of the positive samples by $G_m(x)$ classifier are increased, while the weight of correctly classified samples are decreased. In this way, AdaBoost method can focused on samples which is difficult to classify. Z_m is a normalizing factor so that D_{m+1} becomes a probability distribution:

$$Z_m = \sum_{i=1}^{N} w_{mi} \exp(-\alpha_m y_i G_m(x_i)) \tag{13}$$

(3) Constructing a linear combination of basic classifiers:

$$f(x) = \sum_{m=1}^{M} \alpha_m G_m(x) \tag{14}$$

The final classifier is as follows:

$$G(x) = sign(f(x)) = sign\left(\sum_{m}^{M} \alpha_m G_m(x)\right) \tag{15}$$

4 Fast Pedestrian Detection

The improved CSS feature is extracted faster and the AdaBoost classifier can quickly select the windows containing pedestrians, so that the speed of pedestrian detection has been effectively improved [10]. Further, CSS feature has scale invariance, which can be

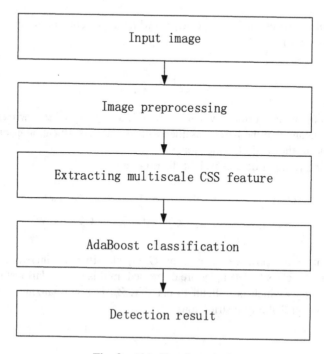

Fig. 2. Algorithm flow chart

used in multi-scale pedestrian detection by scaling feature to fit the scale of the current position and size. This avoids the multi-scale image pyramid construction, integral image pre-processing and calculation, which reduces the detection time. Correlation algorithm is shown in Fig. 2.

5   Results

In this paper, the experiments are carried out on the INRIA [11] pedestrian database. INRIA database is the most common database in Pedestrian Detection, which contains the original image and the corresponding annotation file and contains a wide range of scenarios used to train the model and detect. INRIA database has 614 positive samples (containing 2416 pedestrians) and 1218 negative samples; testing database has 288 positive samples (containing 1126 pedestrian) and 453 negative samples. In the image, most of the human is standing position with height greater than 100 pixels. In the experiment, training set consists of 2416 positive pedestrian samples and 4872 negative samples, which intercept four images from each of the 1218 negative sample images randomly. Test set consists of 1126 positive pedestrian samples and 2265 negative samples, which intercept five images from each of the 453 negative sample images randomly.

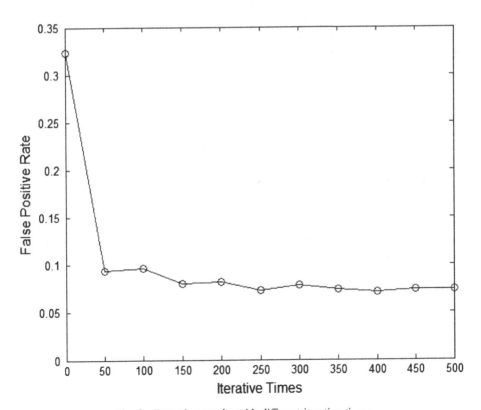

Fig. 3. Detection results with different iterative times

Table 1. The performance of HOG + SVM and CSS + AadaBoost

Method	Accuracy rate	Recall rate	Detection time
HOG + SVM	93.44 %	95.03 %	17.74 s
CSS + AadaBoost	92.67 %	94.50 %	2.51 s

Fig. 4. Detection results.

Computer configuration: Intel(R) Core(TM)i5 2.8 GHz, 12 GB RAM, 64-bit Windows7.

Simulation environment: Matlab R2013a

In this paper, AdaBoost classifier training algorithm is applied to train the classifier. Figure 3 shows results of the iteration times from 1–500 classification, which shows that classification results are stable at around 250 iteration times. So the classifier is trained with 250 iteration times, in this paper.

On the INRIA pedestrian database, the proposed method is compared with HOG + SVM. Recall rate (Eq. 16), accuracy rate (Eq. 17), detection time and other parameters are applied to evaluate the performance.

$$P(recall\ rate) = \frac{TruePositive}{Positive} \times 100\% \tag{16}$$

$$P(accuracy\ rate) = \frac{TruePositive}{TurePositive + FalsePositive} \times 100\% \tag{17}$$

According to Table 1, the accuracy rate and the recall rate of proposed method and HOG + SVM methods differ by no more than 0.8 %. For a 640×480 image, this method is 7 times speedup compared with HOG + SVM detector with training model, multi-scale spatial sliding window and testing windows integration. The actual test results are shown in Fig. 4.

6 Conclusion

Experimental results show that the method of pedestrian detection proposed in this paper has the same close detection performance with the traditional HOG + SVM pedestrian detection method, which is based on color self-similarity and AdaBoost classifier. But it is faster than the traditional method and achieves fast pedestrian detection. It fully verifies the effectiveness and rapidity of the method proposed in this paper.

Acknowledgments. This work is supported by the National Natural Science Foundation of China (Grant: 61376028).

References

1. Enzweiler, M., Gavril, D.M.: Monocular pedestrian detection: survey and experiments. IEEE Trans. Pattern Anal. Mach. Intell. **31**(12), 2179–2195 (2009)
2. Viola, P., Jones, M.J.: Robust real-time face detection. Int. J. Comput. Vis. **57**(2), 137–154 (2004)
3. Dalal, N., Triggs, B.: Histograms of oriented gradients for human detection. In: IEEE Computer Society Conference on Computer Vision and Pattern Recognition (CVPR), pp. 886–893 (2005)
4. Walk, S., Majer, N., Schindler, K., et al.: New features and insights for pedestrian detection. In: IEEE Computer Society Conference on Computer Vision and Pattern Recognition (CVPR), pp. 1030–1037 (2010)
5. Dollar, P., et al.: Pedestrian detection: an evaluation of the state of the art. IEEE Trans. Pattern Anal. Mach. Intell. **34**(4), 743–761 (2012)
6. Wang, Q., Pang, J., Qin, L.: Justifying the importance of color cues in object detection: a case study on pedestrian. In: Jin, J.S., Xu, C., Xu, M. (eds.) The Era of Interactive Media, pp. 387–397. Springer, New York (2013)
7. Goto, Y., Yamauchi, Y., Fujiyoshi, H.: CS-HoG: color similarity-based HoG. In: Frontiers of Computer Vision (FCV), pp. 266–271 (2013)
8. Guo, L., Zhao, Z., Nie, Q., et al.: Pedestrian detection with HOG in region of leg. Comput. Eng. Appl. **49**(1), 217–221 (2013)
9. Yao, X., Li, X., Zhou, J.: Pedestrian detection method based on edge symmetry and HOG. Comput. Eng. **38**(5), 179–182 (2012)
10. Sermanet, P., et al.: Pedestrian detection with unsupervised multi-stage feature learning. In: 2013 IEEE Conference on Computer Vision and Pattern Recognition (CVPR). IEEE (2013)
11. INRIA'S person dataset [EB/OL] (2005). http://pascal.inrialpes.fr/data/human/

An Ameliorated Two Segment Large-Scale Terrain Real-Time Rendering Technology

Jiang Zhang[(✉)], Lian-xing Jia, and Bo Liu

PLA Academy of National Defense Information, Wuhan, China
liongdancing@qq.com, {jialianxing,liubo_email}@163.com

Abstract. In this paper, the traditional terrain data preprocessing technology is improved. By using the Jiugongge hierarchical model, the non-redundant data storage method in block and the hierarchical index and ordinal index of the terrain block, a multi resolution hierarchical model of terrain is constructed. On this basis, it realizes the real-time rendering of large scale terrain with the sectional drawing method. The experimental results show that, compared with the traditional method based on four rendering tree, this method can effectively reduce the terrain data loading time, improve the fluency of the real-time rendering of large scale terrain.

Keywords: Large scale terrain · Real time rendering · Multi resolution level · Sectional drawing

1 Introduction

In the elements of the virtual environment, terrain model not only to generate near real terrain realistic visual effect, more important is to be able to simulate real terrain on the solid ground of various interference, in order to ensure the simulation credibility. The basic data of terrain visualization include the elevation data of the terrain, the image data of the characteristic of the landform and the vector data of the human character. In our country, we use digital elevation model (DEM), digital ortho image (DOM) and digital line model (DLG) to define the height, image and vector data. With these digital geo environmental data as support, using the visualization technology, we can build a realistic 3D terrain environment, and its contents are multi layer, dynamic, can be arbitrarily scaled, and not restricted by scale.

However, for large-scale terrain environment, its coverage area is wide, and the amount of data involved is large. And then triggered a lot of problems in real-time rendering of large-scale terrain, such as loading time is too long, the scene is not coherent, such as roaming. Therefore, how to reasonably deal with the massive terrain data has become the focus of the field of large-scale terrain real-time rendering.

This paper focuses on the large-scale terrain real-time rendering technology, terrain data the multi-resolution hierarchy structure, and the use of sub type of large-scale terrain real-time rendering method to solve massive data real-time terrain rendering provides effective solutions.

© Springer Science+Business Media Singapore 2016
L. Zhang et al. (Eds.): AsiaSim 2016/SCS AutumnSim 2016, Part IV, CCIS 646, pp. 30–37, 2016.
DOI: 10.1007/978-981-10-2672-0_4

2 The Multi-resolution Hierarchy Model

In order to meet the requirements of real-time rendering, the hierarchical model of the terrain block is usually used to meet the requirement of real-time rendering. The top layer is the lowest resolution level, the lowest level is the highest resolution level of the terrain block, so as to construct a multi-level and view independent multi resolution detail level.

2.1 Jiugongge Hierarchical Structure

Traditional terrain layering is based on two and four tree structure. But the two structures need lots of memory space, and in the implementation of more complex, based Jiugongge structure of terrain simplification method can well solve these problems.

Jiugongge is a multiple level model 3, is actually a nine binary tree, each of the 3×3 points for the synthesis of the one upper point. As shown in Fig. 1, the initial resolution of the terrain is r_0, then the l layer for r_1 resolution:

$$r_1 = r_0 \times 3^l \tag{1}$$

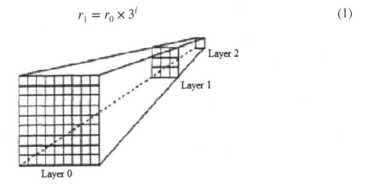

Fig. 1. The hierarchical structure of Jiugongge

In terrain rendering, from view from the region and from area near to viewpoint and the different resolution, as shown in Fig. 2(a) shows, dashed circle where the regional (i.e. the middle shelf of Jiugongg) need higher resolution, which in turn outward continue to reduce LOD.

Jiugongge terrain blocks as shown in Fig. 2(b) shown, due to the center point of view of block and squares in the middle of the grid coincide, so there is no need to the second block, multi resolution transform are concentrated in the eighth frame around. Assuming the number of LOD layers is l, and when l is equal to 3 the simplified rate of squares is about 0.9 %, while the traditional four fork tree simplification rate was 8.37 %. At the same time squares algorithm reduces a view segmentation, the total number of vertex processing is greatly reduced. Obviously the squares method can make the segmentation operation is greatly reduced, simplify the calculation, improve the efficiency of simplified.

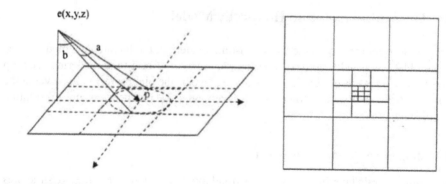

(a) LOD division of view region   (b) Terrain blocks

Fig. 2. Real time layered computation of LOD of Jiugongge

2.2 Non-redundant Data Storage Method in Block

In order to store the hierarchical multi-resolution terrain data, most of the traditional methods is the Pyramid model. The core of this model is to construct a Pyramid for each terrain block, in which the elevation point corresponding to the different resolution terrain blocks is stored. But this method will cause large data redundancy, that means large amounts of data are repeated in different level, and the redundancy is proportional to layer number.

Aiming at the defects of the Pyramid model, this paper uses a non redundant memory block model. The basic idea of the model is that only the new vertex is stored, which appears in the subdivision process of Jiugongge, so that only the unsaved data is saved. That means the saved data is no longer stored repeatedly for each layer. By this means

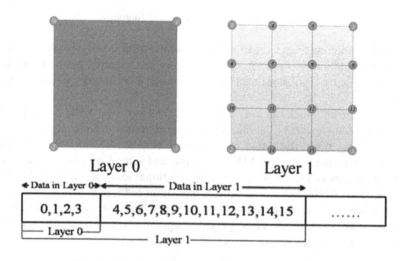

Fig. 3. The non-redundant data storage mode in block

the redundant data in a block is eliminated. Figure 3 shows the non redundant data storage in block.

As shown in Fig. 3, layer 0 comprising four vertices of the terrain blocks 0 to 3. The vertices' elevation values are stored with numbered in order from left to right, according to row first, and the storing location is beginning from the starting position of data field of terrain file. Then, Layer 1 is formed through the squares split of layer 0 which generates the new vertices 4 to 15 stored by the same method. The data redundancy is zero by this storage mode different from the Pyramid method, and there is only a small amount of redundancy in each block boundaries for the original terrain. So the memory overhead is reduced.

2.3 Index Strategy of Terrain Block

According to the characteristics of the Jiugongge block, the starting offset of hierarchical data and end offsets in the segment of the terrain data files can be expressed as

$$Offset(n)_{begin} = \begin{cases} 0, & n = 0 \\ (3^{n-1} + 1) \times (3^{n-1} + 1), & n \geq 1 \end{cases} \tag{2}$$

$$Offset(n)_{end} = (3^n + 1) \times (3^n + 1) - 1, n \geq 0 \tag{3}$$

The above formula can achieve data level positioning, and lay the foundation for the retrieval of memory based data.

When the data is loaded into memory, the storage mode is consistent with the order in the terrain file data field, which forms a linear sequence. In order to easily access the height of the linear sequence in the process of drawing, the index file is generated during the pretreatment process, and the index file is the table structure of the permanent memory. Because of the same data storage mode of each terrain block, it is necessary to construct a set of unified index files to meet the needs of all terrain blocks. We have established the level index and ordinal index two index files, record the level number of each vertex in the terrain block and its sequence number in the hierarchy.

During the preprocessing stage, starting from the layer 0, by dot interlaced scanning according to the resolution level of node length, the corresponding vertex hierarchy information and serial number information are written into the corresponding index file, and the elevation values are stored in the data field of terrain file. According to the above operation, the vertex elevation is composed of a sequence of low to high order, while the index file records the mapping relations between the 2D coordinates of each vertex and the hierarchy. When scheduling, based formulas (2) and (3) those files are loaded layer by layer. When drawing, due to memory the elevation data linear sequence sequential storage and memory terrain data files field order consistent directly offset is calculated on the basis of the hierarchical indexing and ordinal index can be obtained corresponding vertices of the elevation values.

In the following we take a 4 × 4 terrain block as an example to explain the mapping relationship between the 2D coordinates of the vertices, the index files and the vertex elevation values.

As shown in Fig. 4, for a label of 12 vertices, whose coordinates are (2, 2). Query to establish the hierarchy index and ordinal index shows that the height of the vertex information is located in the first layer of the data sequence, the number of 8. Therefore, when reading the vertex elevation data, first calculate the first layer of data starting offset is 4, and then calculate the height of the peak value of the data sequence in the offset of 4 + 8 = 12. So that the corresponding elevation value can be obtained directly.

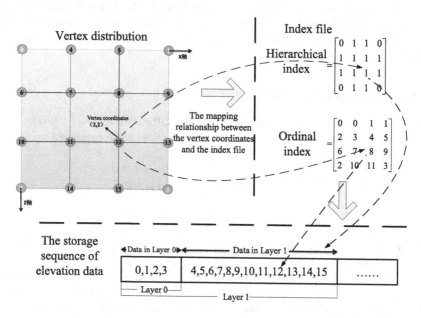

Fig. 4. The mapping relationship between the 2D coordinates of the vertices, the index files and the vertex elevation values

3   Sectional Terrain Rendering

Large scale terrain simulation needs to be performed in the range of hundreds of kilometers, or even thousands of kilometers. In order to realize the real-time visualization of massive terrain data, a sectional terrain rendering method is used. As shown in Fig. 5, it consists of a preprocessing stage and a real time rendering stage.

1. Pretreatment stage. First on the original elevation data of block processing, dividing it into the terrain blocks of the same size; then for each terrain block, establishing Jiugongge structure, in order to build a viewpoint has nothing to do with the multi-resolution hierarchy structure; used to block non redundant data storage method, effectively reduce the redundancy of the elevation data in low memory, and index files are generated, in order to draw quick access to the corresponding level vertex elevation data.

2. Real time rendering stage. Using multi thread mechanism enable data scheduling and drawing at the same time, main thread first using data pre strategy to determine

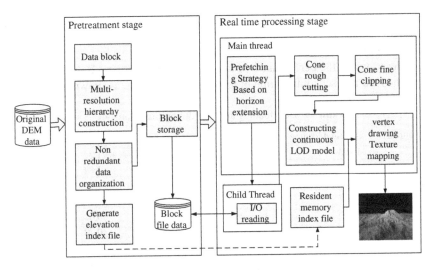

Fig. 5. The two steps of terrain real-time rendering

the need to dispatch the terrain block, and then the fine tailoring method to construct a continuous LOD model of terrain data needs to be drawn, by index file quick access to vertex elevation data; thread implementation based on external data scheduling and data unloading.

4   Experimental Results and Analysis

Experimental raw data from the Georgia Institute of Technology to provide large-scale terrain data Sound Puget. Sound Puget terrain data contains 16385×16385 elevation data points, the sampling interval is 10 m, the terrain coverage is about 163 km × 163 km, the original elevation data file size is 512 M, the original texture size is 768 M.

In the preprocessing stage, we stratified the terrain elevation data by Jiugongge model stratified, and saved block data by non-redundant data storage method. The terrain is divided to 1025×1025 blocks. Similar to the terrain elevation files, the original texture data is firstly divided into block, the number of treatment, for each texture image block, using Mipmap texture multi-resolution hierarchy construction, and the DXT1 format of texture compression. The information of the experimental data is shown in Table 1.

Table 1. List of experimental data

Terrain data	Terrain resolution	Terrain file size		Texture file size	
		Before treatment	After treatment	Before treatment	After treatment
Puget sound	16385×16385	512 M	533 M	768 M	170 M

From Table 1 we can see that elevation data memory overhead is not large, due to non-redundant data storage method. Compared with the literature [5], this research adopts the memory overhead is reduced by about 90 %.

In order to verify the performance of the method, we have carried out experimental tests on the load and scheduling time of terrain elevation data, as shown in Table 2.

Table 2. Data loading and scheduling time statistics

Frame number	Required loading data (M)	Real time loading data (M)	I/O operation time (ms)
1	1.193	1.193	21.2
162	1.578	0.376	3.88
388	1.297	0.094	1.18
4509	1.327	0.372	3.38
5330	1.446	0.024	0.67
7374	1.508	0.094	0.70
8208	1.384	0.366	3.31
10000	1.203	0.009	0.41

The experimental results show that because all data must be transferred from the external memory in first frames, so I/O operation time is relatively longer. Compared with the traditional method, the real-time load data of each frame is significantly reduced, the scheduling efficiency is significantly improved, and the real-time performance is not related to the I/O. It shows that the method is feasible and effective.

In addition, we also test the effect of this method in real time rendering. In the Sound Puget scene, we roamed 10000 frames according to the fixed path with 1024×768 window size, by using the way of geometric model and texture. With the same sequence of frames, when the error threshold is equal to 2, the system average frame rate is 67fps and memory consumption peak is 85 m, which fully meet the requirements of real-time rendering.

5   Concluding Remarks

The large-scale terrain rendering technology is the key problem of the research of 3D visual simulation. This paper improved the traditional terrain data of multi-resolution hierarchy, using segmented rendering method based on Pretreatment Technology scheduling adjacent frames required data, ensure the viewpoint in the rotating movement of terrain scene roaming coherence.

References

1. Liang, H.: Research of Battlefield Information Visualization Technology for Common Operational Picture. National University of Defense Technology (2007) (Ch)
2. Hou, S.: Research and Realization of 3D Battlefield Situation Information System. PLA Information Engineering University (2008) (Ch)

3. Chen, H.: Research on the Key Visual Technology in Large Scale Warfare Simulation Platform. Harbin Engineering University (2010) (Ch)
4. Qiu, H.: Research on some Key Technology of Modeling and Rendering of Complex Scenes in Virtual Battlefield. University of Electronic Science and Technology of China (2011) (Ch)
5. Lmdstrom, P., Yascucci, V.: Visualization of Large Terrams Made Easy, pp. 363–370 (2001)

A Handover Decision Algorithm
with an Adaptive Threshold Applied in HAPS
Communication System

Shu-yan Ni[✉], Shan Jin, and Hai-li Hong

Equipment Academy,
Huairou, Beijing 101416, China
daninini@163.com

Abstract. The platform disturbances of high altitude platform station (HAPS) communication systems increase the possibility of handover. Because the disturbance is not regular, the change rate of the received signal strength (RSS) varies in a large range. While different change rates call for different handover thresholds, which brings about a challenge to the handover decision algorithm. In order to solve this problem, this paper designs a prediction based handover decision algorithm with an adaptive threshold. This algorithm predict the values of RSS using time series analysis model and dynamically adjust the handover initiation time according to the prediction. The simulation results show that, while ensuring communication quality, the algorithm can reduce unnecessary handovers caused by platform disturbances and thus realize preferable handover performance with any attenuation rate of RSS.

Keywords: HAPS · Handover thresholds · Adaptive threshold · Time series

1 Introduction

High altitude platform station (HAPS) communication systems, characterized by extensive ranges, and preferable communication results, as well as strong damage resistance, mobility, and flexibility, have been widely applied in the field of military and civilian communication [1]. However, due to the instability of the HAPS, one of the important reasons, their application is limited. The changes of cell coverage caused by platform disturbances can lead to the instability of the quality of communication links of users, which increases the probability and frequency of handovers. This phenomenon puts forward a challenge for the design and application of handover algorithms [2].

In ground cellular networks, the handover algorithms mainly include the one based on the received signal strength (RSS) and that assisted by speed and position information (SPA). The advantage of RSS algorithm can be widely applied and easily implemented. While, it also presents a disadvantage that in the fixed threshold the handover performance is easily affected by different speeds of users and false decisions

© Springer Science+Business Media Singapore 2016
L. Zhang et al. (Eds.): AsiaSim 2016/SCS AutumnSim 2016, Part IV, CCIS 646, pp. 38–47, 2016.
DOI: 10.1007/978-981-10-2672-0_5

are likely to occur owing to some factors such as shadow fading [3]. The SPA algorithm is to set the dynamic thresholds of handover decision by using user information such as speed and position combining with the cell coverage. The advantage is that the adaptive adjustment of threshold of handover decision can be realized in the handover process for users using different network speeds. While the disadvantage is that the algorithm is very complex.

For HAPS communication systems, the platform disturbance is irregular, which means that it is difficult to establish a valid function relation between the speed and position information and the cell coverage area. Therefore, the handover decision algorithm assisted by speed and position information is not applicable. While conventional RSS-based and its improved algorithms (such as RSSTH algorithm employing a hysteresis margin and an absolute threshold) mainly use a fixed threshold. When the threshold is too low, frequent handovers are likely to happen; in contrast, if the threshold is too high, it is supposed to increase the non-handover probability. However, the selection of the optimal threshold is related to the change rate of signal strength. Due to the constant change of the signal strength, the algorithms with a fixed threshold is not suitable for HAPS systems. In view of this, the author proposes a prediction based handover decision algorithm with an adaptive threshold on the basis of the RSSTH algorithm.

2 Handover Decision Problems

In the practical handover process, due to the existence of shadow fading coherence, the RSS of users using different mobile speeds descends in various trends, thus calling for different threshold values of handovers. The optimal handover is supposed to make full use of the channel resources of current service cell on the premise of guaranteeing the communication quality. The author approximately explains the variation of signal strength in the process of signal handovers of mobile users in the target cell and then defines the following parameters:

T_h: The execution time of handovers;

$\bar{v}$: The average radial velocity of the handover execution getting away from the center of the cell;

d_h: The handover execution distance, which represents the radial distance between the positions corresponding to the moments t_s and t_{th}.

Let $\Delta t_h = t_s - t_{th} = d_h/\bar{v}$, there are three situations under different handover decision conditions;

(1) $\Delta t_h < T_h$: The threshold of handover decision is too high. In the condition, the handover initiation position is close to the coverage edge of the original cell and the signal quality of current communication links fails to maintain the correct transmission. Therefore, the communication access still is not completed in the target cell, which leads to the interruption of communication;

(2) $\Delta t_h > T_h$: The threshold of handover decision is too low. In the context, the handover initiation position is far away from the coverage edge of the original cell, which makes the mobile users prematurely access to the target cell. In this way, the resources of the current cell are not employed sufficiently, which is likely to result in users' frequent handover in the neighbor cells, that is, the Ping-pong effect.

(3) $\Delta t_h = T_h$: This is the optimum moment of handover decision. Under such circumstance, the resources of the current service cell are used fully with the utilization of the optimal threshold of handover decision on the premise of ensuring normal communication. Under such condition, $T_h = d_h/\bar{v}$.

In the handover decision algorithm, the value of d_h reflects that of the threshold. If the value of T_h is a constant, the setting of the optimal handover decision threshold is related to $\bar{v}$. The bigger the $\bar{v}$ is, the lower the handover threshold is supposed to be so that the handover can be triggered as soon as possible. The smaller the $\bar{v}$ is, the higher the handover threshold is supposed to be, so as to make the handover be triggered close to the edge of the cell and take full advantage of resources of the current cell. For the handover decision algorithm with a fixed threshold, it is obviously impossible to set the optimal handover threshold under different change conditions of signal strength.

3 Handover Decision Algorithm with an Adaptive Threshold

In order to realize handover under the optimal handover opportunity, the handover threshold needs to be dynamically adjusted according to the signal attenuation rate. Therefore, in this paper, the signal strength is predicted based on the improvement of traditional RSSTH algorithm combining with the autoregressive integrated moving average model (ARIMA) to achieve the purpose of adaptive handover. Specific design ideas are as follows:

In the detection process of handovers, detection signals need to be processed by layer 1 and layer 3. During each detection period T_a of handovers, the terminal samples the RSS in a T_a period to obtain the input sequence $Y_i = \{y(n), y(n-1), \ldots y(n - i+1)\}$ of layer 1 formed by i sampling values. Then M_k is output after the average processing of layer 1. Afterwards, M_k undergoes weighted filtering on layer 3 to be further filtered and therefore eliminate the influence of shadow fading. By doing so, the measurement value F_k in the measurement report is acquired. The expression of the weighted filtering is as follows:

$$F_k = (1 - \alpha)F_{k-1} + \alpha M_k \qquad (1)$$

Where, F_k represents the measurement result output after the filtering of layer 3. Suppose that the initial value is $F_0 = M_1$, and F_{k-1} denotes the result which is filtered at the previous moment. Besides, $\alpha = (1/2)^k$, where k is a filter coefficient and determined by the upper-layer network [4]. All F_k is recorded by the system to serve as the training sequence for prediction, and the sequence length l increases with the extension of the communication time. In the initial stage, when the sequence length is less than l, in view of the difficulties in establishing a precise prediction model, it is more appropriate to adopt the RSSTH algorithm with a fixed threshold. Here, if the handover decision meets the following requirements, then

$$\begin{cases} P_{r0} < P_0 \\ P_{r0} \le P_{r1} - H_0 \end{cases} \tag{2}$$

Where, P_0 and H_0 are the threshold values of the RSSTH algorithm with a fixed threshold. While P_{r0} and P_{r1} signify the signal strengths in the service cell and the target cell, respectively. When the sequence length is equal to l, the signal strength can be precisely predicted in a short time using the existing sequence of signal strengths. Under such condition, when the measurement values meet the following relations, the algorithm for predicting signal strength is executed.

$$\begin{cases} P_{r0} < P_1 \\ P_{r0} \le P_{r1} - H_1 \end{cases} \tag{3}$$

Where, P_1 and H_1 represent the predicted initiation threshold of the algorithm with an adaptive threshold. The application of a proper threshold value can decrease the times of executing unnecessary predictions and the resource consumption. When the detection results satisfy the requirements, P_{r0} is predicted in m steps, where the value of m is related to the detection period T_s and the execution time T_h of handovers. The longer the prediction steps m are, the lower the precision of the predicted values is. Therefore, m is set in the following ways:

$$m = \frac{T_h + \Delta T}{T_s} \tag{4}$$

Where, ΔT is the prediction margin. According to the setting of Sect. 3, $T_s = 0.5$ s and $T_h = 1$ s. Suppose that $\Delta T = 0$, then $m = 2$. In this paper, the simulation and analysis process is carried out based on $m = 2$.

Suppose that P_{pre} is obtained through prediction in m steps. If the relation between P_{pre} and the communication threshold P_{th} meets the following requirement $P_{pre} \le P_{th}$, Then the handover is conducted; otherwise, it needs to continue to monitor.

The procedure of the algorithm is shown in Fig. 1.

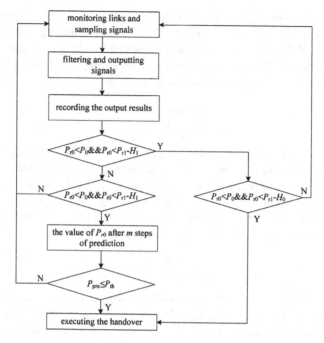

Fig. 1. The principle of the handover decision algorithm with an adaptive threshold

4   Simulation Analysis

4.1   Setting Simulation Conditions

The MATLAB software is used to carry out Monte Carlo simulation. Meanwhile, the simulation scene is established in the rectangular coordinate system. Suppose that the platform works at a high altitude of 22 km and the distance between the centers of adjacent beams is 6 km. In order to facilitate the simulation analysis, only the performance parameters of users' handover between the beam under the platform and its adjacent beams are analyzed. The coordinates of the initial position and motion trajectories of users are randomly generated in a rectangular frame of 4×4.

Suppose that the platform swings with the y axis as the center, and swing angle $\theta_h(°)$ obeys Gauss distribution whose mean value and standard deviation are 0 and σ_h [5]. σ_h is set to 0.5 in simulation. The relative displacement between the users and the platform is reflected by the fast random movement of users by taking the platform as a reference. Gauss-Markov model is used to generate the motion trajectory.

The handover decision is performed by using the mobile station to assist the control of handovers on the basis of signal strength of forward links. Meanwhile, the antennas with equal beamwidth are used in the platform and the directive gain G_t of each beam is set according to the literature [6].

4.2   Analysis and Processing of Prediction Effect

In the handover process, as containing obvious tend terms, the detection signal sequence belongs to the non-stationary time series. Therefore, the ARIMA model [7] is used. The target sequence can be converted to a stationary time series by means of the difference method. Suppose that $t = n$, the observed values of the stabilized detection signals are $Z_n, Z_{n-1}, Z_{n-2},\dots$. For the ARIMA model, the sequence length is supposed to affect the prediction effects. If the sequence length is too short, it is difficult to explore the correlation in the sequence, which leads to the low prediction precision. The longer the sequence length, the more precise the established model is, but the longer the operation period of the algorithm is also. Considering the prediction precision and operation time, in this paper, suppose that the sequence length l is equal to 30, and the prediction $\hat{Z}_n(m)$ of least mean square error of forward m steps can be expressed as:

$$\hat{Z}_n(m) = E(Z_{n+m}|Z_n, Z_{n-1}, \cdots Z_{n-29}) \tag{5}$$

The prediction error is:

$$e(m) = Z_{n+m} - \hat{Z}_n(m) = \sum_{j=0}^{m-1} \psi_j a_{n+m-j} \tag{6}$$

Obviously, the prediction error is affected by the value of σ_a. For the handover of detection signals, σ_a is mainly related to the variance of shadow fading. In the detection process of handovers, the influence of shadow fading on the sampling signals can be reduced through the filtering on layer 3, and the filtering effect is related to the filter coefficient. Under the simulation conditions, the sampling data of a group of signal strength are randomly generated. Meanwhile, three filter coefficients are set with the corresponding weighted values α being 0.1, 0.5 and 0.9, respectively. Based on the different weighted values, the results of three groups of output sequences of handover detection are shown in Fig. 2.

By comparing the output sequences of detection signals with different filter coefficients, it can be seen that improving the filter coefficient can obviously reduce the jitter of output signal strength in the measurement report of handovers. Meanwhile, it also can decrease the influence of shadow fading. However, the enlargement of the filter coefficient is expected to weaken the traceability for signals.

Every 30 continuous data points of each group are input to carry out the prediction of 2 steps using the ARIMA model. Then, the root-mean-square errors (RMSEs) of the predicted values of the three groups of data are separately solved, as shown in Table 1.

By comparing the RMSEs, it can be seen that when the ARIMA model is used to predict the signal strength, the greater the weighted value, the lower the randomness of the input sequence values is. Under such condition, a higher prediction precision can be obtained to improve the precision of the handover decision. However, the greater the weighted value is, the weaker the possibility of tracing signals. Therefore, $\alpha = 0.5$ is selected as the weighted value of the filter in the entire analysis process of this paper.

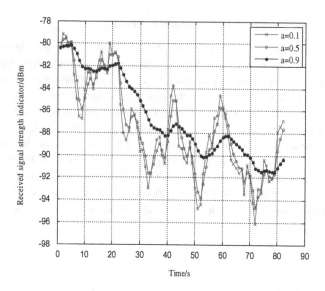

Fig. 2. The output result of layer 3 corresponding to different weighted values

Table 1. The RMSEs of the predicted values

The weighted value α	The root-mean-square errors (RMSEs)/dB
0.1	2.770595
0.5	1.943008
0.9	0.478330

Due to the existence of the shadow fading and the uncertainty of motion, the RSS changes randomly. For any handover decision algorithm, the instantaneous large-scale variation of the RSS is likely to cause interruption of communication or unnecessary handovers. The weaker the current RSS is, the larger the possibility of interruption caused by fading fluctuation, and therefore the higher the probability of handovers. Compared with the excessive handovers, the interruption of communication is more intolerable. In order to avoid the case that the handover is not triggered in time because the predicted values are higher than true values, the author adopts the confidence interval to compensate the predicted values. That is to say, the lower limit of the confidence interval of the predicted value is used as the prediction result to avoid the occurrence of the above case. For a normal process, the confidence interval with the confidence of $(1-\beta)100\ \%$ is:

$$\hat{Z}_n(m) \pm N_{\beta/2}\sqrt{\sum_{j=0}^{m}\psi_j^2}\,\sigma_a \qquad (7)$$

Where, $N_{\beta/2}$ is the quantile of a standard normal distribution that makes $P(N > N_{\beta/2}) = \beta/2$ valid. With different values of β, the relation between the confidence interval and the true value is presented in Fig. 3.

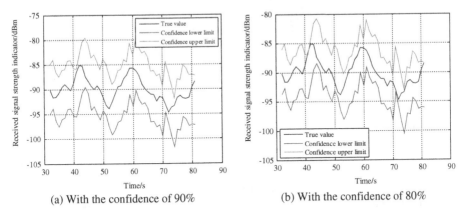

(a) With the confidence of 90%   (b) With the confidence of 80%

Fig. 3. The confidence intervals of the predicted values with different confidences

By comparing the differences of the true values with the upper and lower limits of the confidences in different confidence intervals, it can be found that the higher the confidence is, the larger the differences. Under such circumstance, a higher possibility that the true values are located within the confidence interval of predicted values can be acquired. The lower limit value of confidence interval is selected as the output result of prediction. Therefore, in the selection of confidence, it is supposed to select the confidence corresponding to the confidence interval whose lower limit value is slightly smaller than the true value. This paper employs the lower limit value of the confidence interval of predicted value with a confidence of 80 % as the output result of prediction, which is the basis of handover decision.

4.3   Performance Verification of the Proposed Algorithm

In order to compare the handover adaptation of the algorithm with an adaptive threshold proposed in this paper under different handover scenes, the handover performance of the algorithm is simulated. The simulation results of the algorithm with an adaptive threshold and the RSSTH algorithm are compared in Figs. 4 and 5:

It can be seen from the figure that, when Hys = 0.3 dB, the handover decision algorithm with an adaptive threshold shows less average handover times are less while similar average interruption times compared with the RSSTH algorithm. Although the average interruption times of the proposed algorithm are slightly higher than the statistical results when Hth = −88 dBm and Hys = 0.3 dB, the average handover times are obviously more preferable. When Hys = 0.5 dB and Hth = −88 dB, the average handover times of the proposed algorithm are close to that of the RSSTH algorithm,

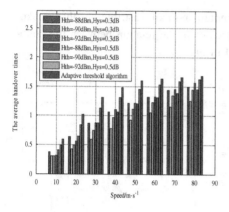

Fig. 4. The average handover times

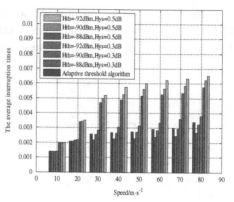

Fig. 5. The average interruption times

while the average interruption times are obviously lower. In addition to the less average handover times, the proposed algorithm has lower interruption times as well, which makes it more adaptive to the handover under conditions of different speeds.

5 Conclusions

In the HAPS communication system, when the handover decision algorithm with a fixed threshold is adopted, it is hard to set a reasonable threshold of handover decision to adapt to different attenuation rates of signals. In this paper, the algorithm with an adaptive threshold is proposed to predict the current signal strength by using the time series prediction model based on the known signal strengths. The purpose is to explore the time of triggering handover in advance and set a dynamic threshold of handover decision. Meanwhile, the author also puts forward a compensation method using the lower limit value of the confidence interval to avoid that the handovers are triggered too late due to the prediction errors. The simulation results show that under different speed conditions, the algorithm with an adaptive threshold can trigger less handovers while ensuring the lower average interruption times. Meanwhile, it also can satisfy the requirements for setting the handover threshold at different attenuation rates of signal strength. The results provide a certain reference for the handover decision in the HAPS communication systems.

References

1. Zheng, J.: Modeling and performance simulation for high altitude platform communication system based on OPNET. National University of Defense Technology, April 2010
2. Li, S.: Studies on call admission control and handover techniques for high altitude platform communications systems. National University of Defense Technology, October 2010

3. Jin, S., Ni, S., Hong, H.: Mobile communication handover algorithm research. J. Ordnance Equip. Eng. 1(37), 151–154 (2016)
4. Liu, J.: Research on handover and handover self-optimization method in LTE system. Xi'an Electronic Technology University, January 2009
5. Guan, M., Guo, Q., Gu, X.: Model and evaluation for performance effects by instability of HAP for HAPS communication. Acta Electron. Sin. 10(10), 1948–1953 (2012)
6. Thornton, J., Grace, D., Capstick, M.H., Tozer, T.C.: Optimizing an array of antennas cellular coverage from a high altitude platform. IEEE Trans. Wirel. Commun. 2(3), 484–492 (2003)
7. Zhang, W.: Study of method on non-stationary time series prediction. Lanzhou University of Technology, May 2007

An Overview of Simulation-Oriented Model Reuse

Ying Liu[1,2], Lin Zhang[1,2(✉)], Weicun Zhang[3], and Xiaolin Hu[4]

[1] School of Automation Science and Electrical Engineering, Beihang University,
Beijing, 100191, China
707051795@qq.com, zhanglin@buaa.edu.cn

[2] Engineering Research Center of Complex Product Advanced Manufacturing Systems,
Ministry of Education, Beijing, 100191, China

[3] School of Automation and Electrical Engineering,
University of Science and Technology Beijing, Beijing, 100083, China
weicunzhang@263.net

[4] Department of Computer Science, Georgia State University, Atlanta, GA 30314, USA
huxiaolin@gmail.com

Abstract. Simulation-oriented model reuse (SOMR) technology is an important way to improve the efficiency of modeling and simulation (M&S) and the credibility of simulation results. Recently, following the rapid development of the new technologies (cloud computing, service-oriented architecture (SOA), Web-based simulation, etc.), a mass of tools and architectures on SOMR technologies have been put in use, meanwhile a large number of related papers on SOMR have been published. This paper aims to describe the essence of SOMR briefly through investigating and summarizing the existing researches on SOMR. The contributions of this paper includes: (1) introducing the concepts and evolution process of SOMR; (2) analyzing the motivation and requirements of SOMR; (3) summarizing the general process and the categories of SOMR; and (4) providing a description and comparison of SOMR technologies.

Keywords: M&S · SOMR · Credibility · SOA

1 Introduction

M&S technology is more and more widely used on applications in various fields. With the development and utilization of a large number of simulation models, SOMR has become a major theoretical issue in the field of M&S.

In the process of simulation, the complete system modeling process should include two parts: mathematical modeling and simulation modeling. Simulation modeling process is the transformation of non formal model or mathematical model into a simulation model that a computer system can identify and run, which is also called "twice modeling". In this paper, SOMR process mainly refers to the process of "twice modeling".

As early as 1984, Zeigler and Oren et al. [1] provided some methods about the heterogeneous integration of models. Until 1986, Ron Huhn et al. [2] first explicitly proposed the issues of SOMR. It then began to be much accounted of by many

© Springer Science+Business Media Singapore 2016
L. Zhang et al. (Eds.): AsiaSim 2016/SCS AutumnSim 2016, Part IV, CCIS 646, pp. 48–56, 2016.
DOI: 10.1007/978-981-10-2672-0_6

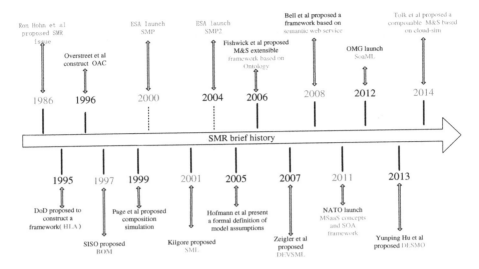

Fig. 1. SOMR development history

organizations and scholars, model reuse technology has made a great progress in the past decades, as shown in Fig. 1.

The following is a brief review of the development history and evolution process of SOMR technology from three aspects.

SOMR theories: In 1996, Anita et al. [3] considered the context of simulation, and constructed the model hypothesis description framework. In 2000, Dale et al. [4] explicitly pointed out the significance of the simulation concept model, and proposed to focus on conceptual model (CM) reuse. In 2007, Bell et al. [5] proposed architecture of SOMR based on semantic service web. In 2014, Tolk et al. [6] proposed a new paradigm using composable cloud-based M&S service, and so on.

SOMR methods and technologies: there are some classical methods and technologies, for example, Meta Model technology [7], Component technology, Basic Object Model (BOM [8]), MDA technology, SMP/SMP2 [9, 10] for model reuse standard modeling specification, Modeling language (SRML [11], Modelica [12], etc.) to support the reuse, open source simulation modeling language (SML), reuse-oriented modeling runtime environment (COTS [13], Simulink, etc.), Semantic Web Service technology, etc. Recently there are methods based on networked simulation environment, ontology language, SOA framework technology and so on. For instance, model language based on the SOA (SoaML [14]), model language based on DEVS (DEVSML [15]), modeling and simulation as a service framework (MSaaS [16]), Modeling and simulation framework based on ontology, model ontology schema based on DEVS (DEVSMO), implementing model reuse based on conceptual simulation model, etc.

Evolution process of SOMR: The simulation technology has experienced the evolution process from the distributed to the networked, from the networked to the ontological and multi-agent, and from the ontological and multi-agent to the servitization. The SOMR technology also experienced the similar evolution process, besides in this process it gone through several stages of the evolution of reuse level as shown in Fig. 2.

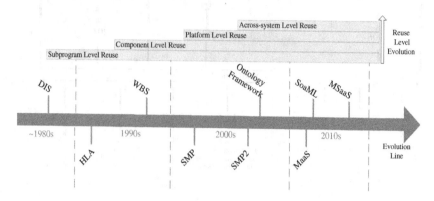

Fig. 2. SOMR evolution process

This paper comprehensively expounds the research of SOMR from the thinking aspects of Why, How and What. *Why*? Why do we research on the SOMR technology? *How*? How to design and use a simulation model in detail for reuse? *What*? What are the international standards, tools and applications for SOMR based on the primary methods and technologies? Finally, a conclusion and a research prospection on SOMR are presented.

2   Motivation and Requirements

2.1   Motivation

1. **Simulation Model redundancy.** The process of M&S produces a large number of repetitive, redundant description information of simulation model, simulation data and other related data, as a result, a large number of resources are wasted. Researchers and engineers generally want to make full use of the existing simulation system and simulation model resources to quickly build a simulation system to meet the needs of different applications.
2. **High complexity of the system.** The more complex the system is, the more complex the model is, and the problem of model reuse is more prominent. Generally, people have accumulated a large number of multi-domain subsystem models, which can compose a complex system. If these models can be correctly and efficiently reused, it will greatly reduce the cost of developing a model, and improve the efficiency of model evaluation.
3. **The heterogeneity of the model.** Complex simulation system usually consists of a large number of heterogeneous component models, and the heterogeneity is mainly reflected in the heterogeneous of modeling methods, modeling tools,

simulation environment and so on. Due to the multidimensional heterogeneous, it is very difficult to reuse and integrate.

4. **Model reusability decision.** In the process of M&S, there is a lack of necessary information that related to the decision of model reusability. In addition, most simulation models are established and described based on programming language or simulation language, and do lack of a unified description of the abstract model for supporting the SOMR. Model reusability decision is the premise and foundation of SOMR.

5. **Less research on SOMR.** At present, there is much and mature research about the reuse of simulation software and simulation application system. On the contrary, the research on SOMR is less, especially in the systematic theory and method.

2.2   Requirements

SOMR is a systemic and also a systematic engineering. It runs through the various stages of whole life cycle of simulation model, including the process of requirement analysis, design, construction, VV&A, application, maintenance and management, etc. Referring to the system engineering, modeling and simulation theory, project management and other multi-disciplinary knowledge system, we present a system requirement framework of the research on SOMR in Fig. 3.

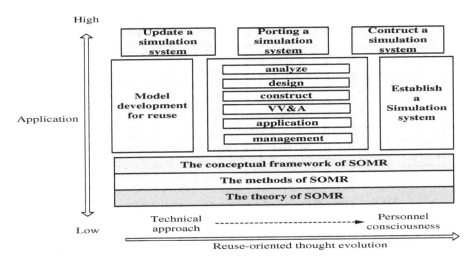

Fig. 3. A system requirement framework of SOMR research

From Fig. 3, we can analyze that the system requirements of SOMR actually include five parts: (1) the basis of SOMR; (2) the whole life cycle of SOMR; (3) the implement and management of SOMR; (4) the tools of SOMR; and (5) the relative standards of SOMR. With the mature technical approaches are established, people who involved in the process of M&S should have the consciousness of SOMR, then the SOMR technology can be really used in the real world.

3   The General Process, Category of SOMR

3.1   The General Process of SOMR

The process of SOMR is similar to the software reuse, but there are differences which can be reflected in two aspects. One side, in the modeling phase, we modify the existing model and then reuse. On the other side, in the simulation phase, we try to construct a simulation environment for supporting reuse, or establish a simulation system framework in order to use the reusable model priority. Also, the process of SOMR is more focused on the description of specific simulation contexts. This paper summarizes a general model reuse process, as shown in Figs. 4 and 5.

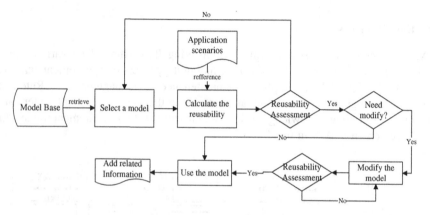

Fig. 4. A general process of modifying the existing model

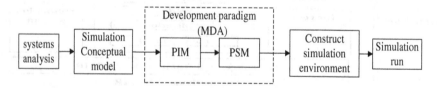

Fig. 5. A general process of constructing a simulation framework

The general process of modifying the existing model in modeling stage is illustrated in Fig. 4. In this process, according to different contexts and the actual development needs, we retrieve one or more similar simulation models ready to reuse from the model base of the simulation system; then, a new context is described as a reference constraint, and the reusability of the model can be determined. At last, one of the correct models will be chosen by the evaluation results. If it is necessary for us to modify the model to satisfy the demand, another credibility assessment should be made until the model is correct.

The general process of constructing a simulation environment or simulation framework for supporting reuse is illustrated in Fig. 5. In this process, the MDA architecture is used to develop models and build a simulation environment to meet the running conditions of the simulation based on the support of the reuse-oriented HLA simulation framework. Among them, the development pattern and simulation framework can be replaced by the other pattern and framework of SOMR according to the actual demands.

3.2   The Category of SOMR

Based on the category of software reuse proposed by Pidd Michael, and the definition of SOMR provided by Robinson and Nance, SOMR can be described into three aspects, each of which has different categories according to the reuse technologies as shown in Fig. 6.

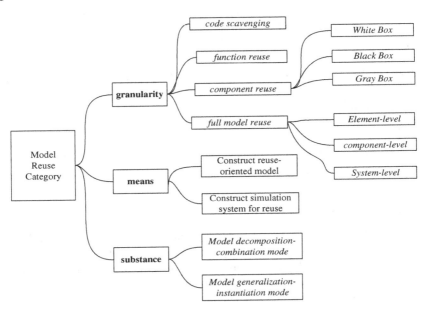

Fig. 6. The categories of SOMR

4   The Methods and Comparison of SOMR Technologies

4.1   The Methods and Technologies of SOMR

(1) The methods of standardized model specification and model base

The standardized model specification and model base is convenient for interoperation and integration of model, so it is more reusable for model. For instance, the EATI specification based on conceptual models of the mission space (CMMS), basic object model (BOM), simulation model portability standard (SMP/SMP2), system entity structure/model base (SES/MB).

(2) The methods of the simulation model representation

Establishing a model representation method which can satisfy the demand of the multi-form system, multi-domain concept, platform-independence is an efficient way to promote reusing. Examples of simulation languages representation methods are CSSL, GPSS, SLAM, etc. Examples of general modeling languages representation methods are UML, SMDL, XML, SRML, SML, model representation based on meta-model, etc.

(3) The methods of the generalized model

Generalized model reuse method is a kind of method that emphasis on the generalization through the way of inheritance, composition, and parameterization to reuse the basic model. For example, NASA/LaSRC's object-oriented simulation framework LaSRS++ [17] and NASA/KSC generic simulation model (GSM), etc.

(4) The methods of the M&S environment to support the reuse

Almost all the simulation development and running environments are designed to support model reuse to a certain extent. For example, COTS simulation development kit, Simulink, Sim2000, OneSAF, etc.

(5) The methods of the simulation model framework

Such as, the model reuse and composition technology described by the DEVS, the simulation composition technology, extensible modeling and simulation framework XMSF [18], etc.

(6) The methods of model engineering

Model Engineering (ME [19, 20]) that focuses on solving the issues of model heterogeneity and model reuse covers in the specific knowledge framework of the model. The key technology of ME includes the process of modeling in model life cycle, modeling language and model description, model base, model reuse and composition, engineering model supporting environment and tools.

4.2 The Comparison of the Methods and Technologies

Overall, in the terms of the simulation model representation, the model representation is unified, which reduces the complexity of the integration, but it does not care about the semantic issues, and the supporting on open simulation framework are congenitally deficient. Although general model is a good way, it is very hard to implement. Based on the model framework, the model reuse methods are usually used in the field of combinatorial simulation reuse, and there are limitations. The method based on the standard model specification and model base is a more eclectic approach. The method based on model engineering approach provides a more comprehensive way. No matter what method we use, standardization, abstraction, hierarchy is the premise and foundation of SOMR.

5 Conclusion and Future Work

SOMR mainly involves two problems: (1) how to use mature technologies and methods to develop a model for supporting reuse, and (2) how to build a simulation application system or environment to reuse a model. Before that, how to determine and assess the reusability of the simulation model is the basis and premise of SOMR.

MSaaS is a feasible and popular architecture for SOMR following the rapid development of the cloud computing, cloud simulation and other emerging technologies. ME is also a good way to achieve parts of functions of SOMR by providing systematic, quantitative project management and control theory, techniques, methods, standards and tools. They are both to improve the reusability and credibility of models.

It should be pointed out that the SOMR technologies, of which can support the personalization, the servitization, and the intelligence will be a popular development direction of M&S. However, there are many challenges and issues for SOMR to deal with including high reliability, controlled model management, reusable model composition and service composition, mature theory and method system, and so on.

Acknowledgment. Authors gratefully acknowledge the support of National Natural Science Foundation of China (Grant No. 61374199); National High-Tech Research and Development Plan of China (No. 2013AA041302). Natural Science Foundation of Beijing (No. 4142031).

References

1. Ören, T.I., Zeigler, B.P., Elzas, M.S.: Simulation and Model-Based Methodologies: An Integrative View. Springer, Heidelberg (1984)
2. Huhn, R., et al.: Issues in simulation model integration, reusability and adaptability. In: Winter Simulation Conference (1986)
3. Pos, A., Borst, P., et al.: Reusability of simulation models. Knowl. Based Syst. **9**, 119–125 (1996)
4. Pace, D.K.: Simulation Conceptual Model Development Issues and Implications for Reuse of Simulation Components (2000)
5. Bell, D., De Cesare, S., Lycett, M., et al.: Semantic web service architecture for simulation model reuse. In: IEEE International Symposium on Distributed Simulation and Real-Time Applications, pp. 129–136. IEEE Computer Society (2007)
6. Tolk, A., Mittal, S.: A necessary paradigm change to enable composable cloud-based M&S services. In: IEEE Simulation Conference, pp. 356-366 (2014)
7. Hawryszkiewycz, I.T.: A meta model for modeling collaborative systems. J. Comput. Inf. Syst. **45**(3), 63–72 (2016)
8. Peng, G., Mao, H., Wang, H., et al.: BOM-based design knowledge representation and reasoning for collaborative product development. J. Syst. Sci. Syst. Eng. **25**, 159–176 (2016)
9. Nemeth, S., Demarest, P.: Research and Development in Application of the Simulation Model Portability Standard (2010)
10. Lei, Y.L., Nian-Le, S.U., Jing-Jie, L.I., et al.: New simulation model representation specification SMP2 and its key application techniques. Syst. Eng. Theory Pract. **31**(4), 553–572 (2010)
11. Kalman, M., Havasi, F.: Enhanced XML validation using SRML. Comput. Sci. **4**(4) (2013)

12. Fritzson, P.A.: Principles of Object-Oriented Modeling and Simulation with Modelica 3.3. Wiley-IEEE Press (2014)

13. Rosa, W., Packard, T., Krupanand, A., et al.: COTS integration and estimation for ERP. J. Syst. Softw. **86**(2), 538–550 (2013)

14. Tounsi, I., Hrichi, Z., Kacem, M.H., et al.: Using SoaML models and event-b specifications for modeling SOA design patterns. In: 15th International Conference on Enterprise Information Systems, pp. 294–301 (2013)

15. Hu, J., Huang, L., Cao, B., et al.: Executable modeling approach to service oriented architecture using SoaML in conjunction with extended DEVSML. In: IEEE International Conference on Services Computing, pp. 243–250 (2014)

16. Wang, S., Wainer, G.: A mashup architecture with modeling and simulation as a service. In: Wang, J., Cellary, W., Wang, D., Chen, S., Li, T., Zhang, Y. (eds.) WISE 2015. LNCS, vol. 9418, pp. 247–261. Springer, Heidelberg (2015)

17. Glaab, P., Madden, M.: Benefits of a unified LaSRS++ simulation for NAS-wide and high-fidelity modeling. In: Digital Avionics Systems Conference. IEEE (2014)

18. Katherine, D., Morse, L., Tolk, D.A., et al.: XMSF as an Enabler for NATO M&S (2012)

19. Zhang, L., Zhang, X., Song, X., et al.: Model engineering for complex system simulation. J. Syst. Simul. **25**(11), 2515–2516 (2013)

20. Zeigler, B.P., Zhang L.: Service-oriented model engineering and simulation for system of systems engineering. In: Yilmaz, L. (ed.) Concepts and Methodologies for Modeling and Simulation, pp. 19–44. Springer International Publishing, Switzerland (2015)

Multi-model Switching Method Based on Sphere-Based SVM Classifier Selector and Its Application to Hydrogen Purity Multi-model Soft Sensor Modeling in Continuous Catalytic Reforming

Yi-Fan Shuang and Xing-Sheng Gu[(✉)]

Key Laboratory of Advanced Control and Optimization or Chemical Processes,
Ministry of Education, East China University of Science and Technology,
Shanghai, China
xsgu@ecust.edu.cn

Abstract. The process of continuous catalytic reforming is complex and changeable. Usually, a single model soft sensor is hardly to grantee the accuracy of the prediction result, so it is necessary to adopt the multi-model strategy to improve the model performance. The process of sub model combination of the multi-model soft senor could be considered as a multi-class classification issue. The main idea of the proposed method in this paper aims to solve this issue with Support Vector Machine (SVM). The proposed approach is to build a sphere structure to cover the same-class samples as much as possible, and these sphere-based structure can be considered as a selector of those SVM classifiers. Experimental results show that the proposed method is suitable for particular use in SVM multi-class classification, and the switched-based multi-model soft sensor for hydrogen purity in continuous catalytic reforming based on the proposed method has a higher prediction accuracy.

Keywords: Soft sensor · Multi-model · Multi-class classification · Support Vector Machine

1 Introduction

Chemical process contains a massive amount of immeasurable variables. Usually, these variables are very important in the reaction process. So, it is meaningful to find some way to measure these variables. Soft sensor techniques have been widely used to solve this problem, and have made some achievements [1, 2]. Data-driven soft sensor is based on measurable historical samples. However, chemical process has the properties of nonlinear and multi-modes (various working conditions). The properties of historical samples are changing with these working conditions. So a single model for the complex system may result in poor prediction performance and over-fitting problems.

To solve such problems, many researchers have presented the multi-model soft sensor for the complex problem [3]. Building a multi-model soft sensor has three main steps:

© Springer Science+Business Media Singapore 2016
L. Zhang et al. (Eds.): AsiaSim 2016/SCS AutumnSim 2016, Part IV, CCIS 646, pp. 57–72, 2016.
DOI: 10.1007/978-981-10-2672-0_7

(1) Historical samples identification.

The historical samples are changing with the different operating conditions, it is supposed to be clustered around those different working conditions. The clustering algorithms have been introduced by researchers to classify the historical samples. Zhi-Gang et al. [4] introduced fuzzy C-means (FCM) and Zhou and Zhang [5] introduced modified K-means algorithms to improve the model precision.

(2) Sub model building.

After clustering the historical samples, the data would be divided into several parts. The next step is to build every sub model by using those clustered historical samples. The most common data-driven soft sensor methods are based on machine learning methods such as Artificial Neural Networks (ANN) [6], Support Vector Machines (SVM) [7] and Gaussian Processes Regression (GPR) [8].

(3) Sub model combining.

The final step of building a multi-model soft sensor is combining the sub models. Usually, there are two ways: the switcher mode [9–11] and the weighted combination mode [12, 13].

However, in a practical application, the mentioned sub model combining methods have lots of deficiencies. First, using a weighted combination mode to combine the sub models is equivalent to admitting that the sub models are subject to a linear relationship, but this assumption is rarely valid [14]. Second, the switcher mode is mainly to build a classifier to recognize the relevant working conditions. Well, due to the complexity of the chemical process, the working conditions are changeable and complicated and it could be considered as a multi-class classification issue. SVM is supposed to be among the best classification tools available today. But it is originally designed for binary classification. How to extend it effectively for multi-class classification is still an on-going issue [15]. There are two kinds of multi-class solution: "One Versus One, OVO" [16] and "One Versus Rest, OVR" [17, 18]. However, the OVO strategy often needs a voting process to decide the final classification result, and it may sometimes cause the error accumulation problems. And the OVR strategy might increase the difficulty in building the SVM classifier because of the imbalanced datasets between different classes [19].

In this paper, a sphere-based SVM classifier selector for OVO issue is proposed. We have built several SVM classifiers for each binary classification. Then we introduces a novel sphere-based algorithm to identify the correct SVM classifier. Finally, this method has been used in the process of building a multi-model soft sensor for hydrogen purity prediction. The result shows that the proposed algorithm has improved both the accuracy of the multi-class classification issue and the predict value of the multi-model soft sensor.

This paper is organized as follows. First, we will give a brief overview of SVM classification and Gaussian Process soft sensor modeling method in Sects. 2 and 3. In Sect. 4, we will address the proposed sphere-based classifier selector algorithm, and the relevant experimental result will be described in Sect. 5. Finally, the conclusions and discussions will be drawn in Sect. 6.

2 Support Vector Machine

Support Vector Machine (SVM) is a useful classification tool widely used in various fields. It was proposed by Vapnik in the last century [7]. The main idea of SVM is to find the optimal separator between two classes to maximize the margin of separation in the training data. The kernel functions are introduced to solve the non-linear problems. Kernel function maps feature vectors to a high dimensional space and to compute a hyperplane to make the dataset separable.

For classification issue, assume there is a set of training data $Z = \{Z_i\}_{i=1}^{n} = \{(x_1, y_1), \ldots, (x_n, y_n)\}$, where $x_i \in X$ is the input vector and $y_i \in \{-1, +1\}$ is the output vector. Let $\phi : X \to F$ be a feature mapping with a dot product denoted by $<., .>$.

The classification function of SVM becomes an optimal problem as follows:

$$\min_{\omega \in F, b \in R} \frac{1}{2} \|\omega\|^2 + C \sum_i \xi_i \tag{1}$$

$$\text{s.t.} y_i(<x_i, \omega> + b) + \xi_i \geq 1, \ \xi_i \geq 0, z_i \in Z$$

Where term C is the regularization and term ξ_i are slack variables. The solution can be written as

$$\omega = \sum_i^n \alpha_i y_i x_i \tag{2}$$

Where α_i are Lagrange multiples for the dual problem of formula (1). Furthermore,

$$\sum_i^n \alpha_i y_i = 0 \tag{3}$$

$$0 \leq \alpha_i \leq C \tag{4}$$

$$\alpha_i(y_i(<x_i, \omega> + b) - 1 + \xi_i) = 0 \tag{5}$$

Vector x_i is called a support vector (SV), where $\alpha_i \neq 0$. Term b is calculated a posteriori.

So, the classifier function is:

$$f(x) = \left(\sum_i^n \alpha_i y_i x_i\right)^T x + b = \sum_i^n \alpha_i y_i <x_i, x> + b \tag{6}$$

With the kernel function, the function can be written as follows:

$$f(x) = \sum_i^n \alpha_i y_i < \phi(x_i), \phi(x) > + b \tag{7}$$

3 Gaussian Processes

Gaussian Processes [20] is a new machine learning method based on Bayesian learning theory [21] and Gaussian stochastic process. Its predict output is determined by the mean function and the covariance function, which is suitable for high dimension, strong nonlinear characteristics and other complex problems, and has been widely used in the application of nonlinear regression, classification and probability estimation.

For a training dataset $D = \{(x_i, y_i) | i = 1, 2, \ldots, n\}$, where $x_i \in R^d$ is a d-dimension input vector, y_i is the output vector, n is the number of this dataset. Gaussian Process Regression is to determine the distribution of the target output based on the given input samples.

Let f be a Gaussian Process, its characteristics can be determined by the mean function and covariance function that is:

$$f \sim GP(m, k) \tag{8}$$

Where m is the mean function, and k is the covariance function.

The main idea of Gaussian Process Regression is to find out the mapping relationships between the input samples and the output samples by using the training dataset D. Thus, the corresponding predictive output $\hat{y}_*$ can be obtained by the new test input x_* through the mapping relationships.

According to the principle of Gaussian Process, the training output y and the prediction output $\hat{y}_*$ are subject to the joint Gaussian distribution:

$$\begin{bmatrix} y \\ \hat{y}_* \end{bmatrix} \sim N \left\{ 0, \begin{bmatrix} K(X, X) & K_*(X, x_*) \\ K(X, X) & K_*(X, x_*) \end{bmatrix} \right\} \tag{9}$$

In formula (9), $K(X, X)$ is the Symmetric covariance matrix of training samples, $K_*(X, x_*)$ is the covariance matrix between training samples and test samples, and $k_*(x_*, x_*)$ is the test samples' own covariance. They can be described as follows:

$$K(X, X) = \begin{bmatrix} k(x_1, x_1) & k(x_1, x_2) & \cdots & k(x_1, x_n) \\ k(x_2, x_1) & k(x_2, x_2) & \cdots & k(x_2, x_n) \\ \vdots & \vdots & \ddots & \vdots \\ k(x_n, x_1) & k(x_n, x_2) & \cdots & k(x_n, x_n) \end{bmatrix} \tag{10}$$

$$K_*(x_*, X) = [k(x_*, x_1) \quad k(x_*, x_2) \quad \cdots \quad k(x_*, x_n)] \tag{11}$$

According to the Bayesian posterior probability formula, the predictive output $\hat{y}_*$ obeys the following Gaussian distribution:

$$p(\hat{y}_* \mid D, x_*) \sim N(\mu, \sigma^2) \tag{12}$$

In the real industry process, the history data often contain noise, and it can be considered as white Gaussian noise, which is obey the distribution $\varepsilon \sim N(0, \sigma_n^2)$, so the predictive output will change to be:

$$\hat{y}_* = \mu = K_* (K + \sigma_n^2 I)^{-1} y \tag{13}$$

$$\mathrm{var}(y_*) = \sigma^2 = k_* - K_* (K + \sigma_n^2 I)^{-1} K_*^T \tag{14}$$

In Gaussian Process, covariance function reflects the correlation between the input vectors. The squared exponential covariance function is one of the common covariance function, which can be described as follows:

$$k(x_i, x_j) = \sigma_f^2 \exp\left[\sum_{u=1}^{d} \frac{-(x_u^{(i)} - x_u^{(j)})^2}{2l_u^2}\right] \tag{15}$$

Considering the noise:

$$\mathrm{cov}(x_i, x_j) = k(x_i, x_j) + \sigma_n^2 \delta(x_i, x_j) \tag{16}$$

In order to facilitate the calculation, formula (16) can be modified as follows:

$$\mathrm{cov}(x_i, x_j) = v_1 \exp\left(-\frac{1}{2}\sum_{u=1}^{d} \omega_u (x_u^{(i)} - x_u^{(j)})^2\right) + v_2 \delta_{ij} \tag{17}$$

Where, d is the input vector dimension, v_1 represents the prior knowledge, $\omega_u (u = 1, 2, \ldots, d)$ is the weighting factor of the input, v_2 represents the noise covariance, and δ_{ij} is the Kronecker factor.

In (17), the parameter list $\theta = \{v_1, \omega_1, \omega_2, \ldots, \omega_d, v_2\}$ are hyper-parameters, which can be solved by the maximum likelihood method, and the negative log likelihood function can be written as follows:

$$L(\theta) = -\frac{1}{2} y^T (K + \sigma_n^2 I)^{-1} y - \frac{1}{2}\lg|K + \sigma_n^2 I| - \frac{n}{2}\lg 2\pi \tag{18}$$

Formula (18) could be solved by using the optimization algorithm, and finally the hyper-parameters will be obtained. With these determination list θ, we can obtain the corresponding predictive output through formulas (13) and (14).

4 Sphere-Based Classifier Selector

For One-Versus-One (OVO) issue in multi-class classification. The classifier is supposed to be divided into several parts. So that an N classes problem would be divided into $N(N - 1)/2$, that is, C_N^2 parts. In this situation, during the process of classification, the new input vector x absolutely needs to select the right classifier for itself. To solve this problem, the traditional solution is based on voting [22]. The main idea of this method is voting for the best result based on all the classifiers' output. This method is simple and feasible, but the computation and accuracy would be influenced by the increment of the number of classes and datasets.

The main idea presented in this paper is to select the right classifier for each input vector. This idea is inspired by the features of sphere. For a convex multi-class dataset, there could be a sphere structure to cover the same-class subset of this dataset. If we could shape those spheres and build relevant models, then it will be easier to select the correct classifier for the input vector.

4.1 Shaping the Sphere

Assume there is a set of same-class training data $D \in Z$, $D = \{D_i\}_{i=1}^m = \{(x_1, y), \ldots, (x_m, y)\}$ where $y = 1$ or $y = -1$. There could be a sphere $\Theta(o, R)$ covering all the training data, where term o is the center of the sphere, and term R is the radius of the sphere. Term o can be determined by the following formula:

$$o : x_i = \arg\min \sum_{j}^{m-1} dist(x_i, x_j), i = 1, \ldots, m, i \neq j \qquad (19)$$

Where function $dist(\cdot, \cdot)$ is the distance between different samples. Usually, this function can be considered as Euclidean distance, Manhattan distance, or cosine similarity. We choose Euclidean distance here, so formula (19) will transform to:

$$o : x_i = \arg\min \sum_{j}^{m-1} \|x_i - x_j\|, i = 1, \ldots, m, i \neq j \qquad (20)$$

Formula (20) means that o, the center of the sphere, is just the input vector x_i itself, which its summation of the Euclidean distance between the other input vectors is minimum.

Through this way, the center of the sphere will be established in the middle of the same-class subset as much as possible, and could effectively avoid the following phenomenon which is shown in Fig. 1(a).

Figure 1(b) illustrates this idea that through (20) we can find the center of the sphere or the training data easily.

The next step is to determine the radius of the sphere. In order to cover the same-class data samples as much as possible. We define the radius R as follows:

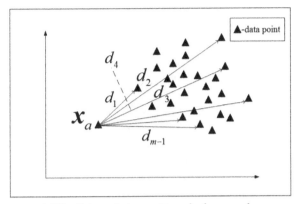

(a)The distance between x_a and other samples

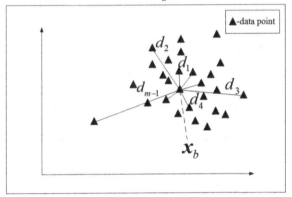

(b) The distance between x_b and other samples

Fig. 1. Example of the second situation

$$R = \max\ dist(x_o, x_j), j = 1, \ldots, m, o \neq j \qquad (21)$$

Where x_o is the center point which can be determined by (20). Replaced by Euclidean distance, the formula will be changed as follows:

$$R = \max \|x_o - x_j\|, j = 1, \ldots, m, o \neq j \qquad (22)$$

Through formulas (20) and (22), we can obtain both the center o and the radius R. With these, the sphere is then established. Figure 2 is a sample of this method.

Obviously, the noise in the dataset may have certain effects on the accuracy of this algorithm, so it is necessary to do some data cleaning works before it, so that the validity of this method can be guaranteed.

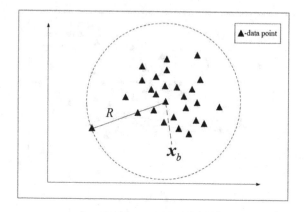

Fig. 2. The sphere structure of a same-class dataset.

4.2   The Selector of Multi-class Classifier

Suppose there is a k-classes multi-class dataset. We can build several spheres $\Theta_i(o_i, R_i)$, $(i = 1, \ldots, k)$ for each class of the dataset. Meanwhile, we could use the SVM classification algorithm to build corresponding classifiers for every two-classes samples. Let $SVM_{i,j}$ represent the SVM classifier of class i and class j, so there should be $k(k-1)/2$ classifiers. For the new input vector x, we can select the right classifier as the following method.

Let $L = \{d_i\} = \{d_1, d_2, \ldots, d_k\}(i = 1, 2, \ldots, k)$, where d_i is the distance between the input vector x and the center o_i of the sphere Θ_i. These distances indicate the vector x's deviate degree from o_i. It's obvious that we can reference these distances to select the right classifier. The intuitive idea is that we can choose the smallest two distances

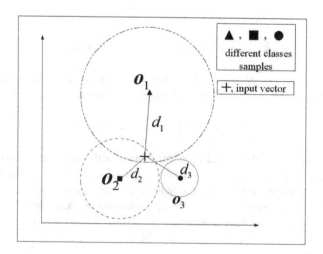

Fig. 3. Example of classifier selection

from L, for example d_2 and d_4, accordingly, we select classifier $SVM_{2,4}$. However, this simple idea needs to be improved, as it may be effected by the physical dimension, which will be illustrated in Fig. 3.

In Fig. 3, the smallest two distances is d_2 and d_3, but the correct classifier is supposed to be $SVM_{1,2}$. This error is caused by the physical dimension of each radius, in order to avoid this phenomenon, we make a change to calculate the list V:

$$V = \{v_i\} = \frac{L}{R_i} = \left\{ \frac{d_1}{R_1}, \frac{d_2}{R_2}, \ldots, \frac{d_k}{R_k} \right\} \tag{23}$$

We choose the smallest two elements from V, and their sequence number determine the corresponding classifier. So far, we have introduced this algorithm, and it will be summarized as Algorithm 1.

X_i-training data of class i, m_i-the dimension of X_i)

Initiate :List $O = \{\}$, $R = \{\}$, $V = \{\}$

$c_1, c_2 = 0$

      ▷ O stores the center of every sphere

      ▷ R stores the radius of every sphere

      ▷ V stores the distances

For $i = 1$ to k **do**

$$O(i) = \arg\min_{X_i(o)} \sum_j^{m_i 1} dist(X_i(o), X_i(j))$$

      ▷ $dist$ is a distance function

End for

For $i = 1$ to k **do**

For $j = 1$ to m_i **do**

$$R(i) = \max dist(O(i), X_i(j))$$

End for

End for

For $i = 1$ to k **do**

$$V(i) = \frac{dist(x, O(i))}{R(i)}$$

End for

$c_1 = $ smallest element's sequence number of V

$c_2 = $ the second smallest element's sequence number of V

Return c_1, c_2

---

5   Experimental and Result Discussion

5.1   The Re-contacting Process of the Continuous Catalytic Reforming.

Hydrogen is an important byproduct of the continuous catalytic reforming process, which is separated from the reforming reaction product. In order to enhance the purity of the hydrogen, a catch pot is designed in the continuous catalytic reforming process. Figure 4 is a simplified flow chart of this process.

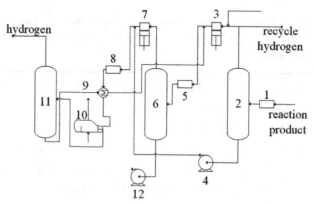

1—reaction product air cooler; 2—separator; 3,7—booster; 4,12—pump ; 5,8—air-cooler; 6—1#recontact reaction tank; 9—precooler; 10—refrigerator; 11—2# recontact reaction tank;

Fig. 4. The re-contacting process.

According to the re-contacting process, we choose the feed temperature of the reforming catch pot, the feed temperature of the 1#recontact reaction tank, the feed temperature of the 2#recontact reaction tank, the pressure of the reforming catch pot, the pressure of the 1#recontact reaction tank, the pressure of the 2#recontact reaction tank and the recycle hydrogen purity of the reforming process as the auxiliary variables for the soft sensor.

5.2   Datasets

One of the datasets used in this experimental is obtained from a real chemical plant. We plan to use this production data to build a multi-model soft sensor to predict the hydrogen purity of the catalytic reforming process. The production data has been filtered and clustered to be a 4-class multi-class dataset by the Clustering by Fast Search and Find of Density, CFSFD algorithm [21], and the clustering result is shown in Fig. 5.

In order to fully reflect the performance of the algorithm proposed in this paper, we have added another three multi-class datasets, which can be obtained from the UCI

Machine Learning Repository[1] database. For all the dataset, we divided into training and testing sets in a ratio as 80:20. Table 1 shows the basic information about these datasets.

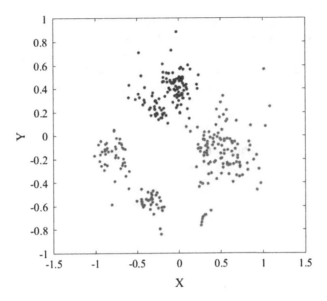

Fig. 5. Clustering result of the real chemical plant history data.

Table 1. Basic information of datasets

Data set	Classes	Attributes	Instances
Chemical plant data	4	7	313
Iris flower	3	4	150
Wine	3	13	178
Seeds	3	7	210

All the datasets have been normalized by a linear transformation of the feature values into the [0, 1] range.

5.3   Classifier Selection

For these multi-class datasets, we adopt the OVO strategy to build enough classifiers for each binary classification. We then use the algorithm (SCS) proposed in Sect. 3 in

---

[1] Available at: http://archive.ics.uci.edu/ml/index.html.

this paper to build corresponding selector for these classifiers. To evaluate this algorithm, we use formula (24) to calculate the selection accuracy F:

$$F = \frac{C}{T} \times 100\% \qquad (24)$$

Where T is the total number of the test data, and C is the correct number of the output of the SCS algorithm. We affirm that once the selected SVM classifier is relevant to the input data, then this output should be considered as a correct result. For example, there is an input test data, which belongs to class 2, if the output of the SCS is $SVM_{2,j}$, $(j = 1,2,..., k)$ we consider it as a correct prediction result. The result of the SCS is shown in Table 2.

Table 2. Result of classifier selection.

Data set	Accuracy
Chemical plant data	100%
Iris flower	100%
Wine	100%
Seeds	98.6%

Table 2 shows that the proposed algorithm has a good performance in the classifier selection.

5.4   Multi-class Classification

For these dataset, we have introduced "Voting", and the proposed SCS method to solve the multi-class problems with SVM in an "OVO" manner. We have built relevant SVM classifiers for each two-class samples. In order to reflect the performance of this algorithm or idea, we have introduced the "accuracy" as the performance indicator. The results of classification experiment are shown in Table 3.

Table 3. Result of classification.

Data set	Accuracy	
	SCS-SVM	Voting-SVM
Chemical plant data	86.7%	76.7%
Iris flower	98.7%	97.4%
Wine	96.5%	93.1%
Seeds	92.6%	85.2%

From Table 3, we can see that on average the proposed method in this paper achieves the best average results in accuracy, which demonstrate the effectiveness of the algorithm.

5.5   Multi-model Soft Sensor

In catalytic reforming process, the purity of the by-product hydrogen gas is an important unmeasurable process variable, which should be strictly monitored and controlled. However, a single model soft sensor is hard to guarantee the prediction accuracy. So, we apply the multi-model soft sensor as a solution, and its structure is shown in Fig. 6.

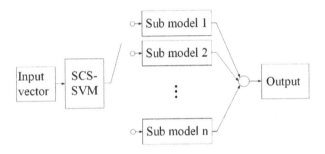

Fig. 6. The structure of multi-model soft sensor.

All the operation data is collected from the DCS in the plant and have been clustered and filter into a 4-class datasets. We introduced the Gaussian Process Regression to build each sub-model. We then applied the proposed method in this paper to combine all the sub-models. To evaluate the performance of this model, three quantitative evaluation is introduced, namely root mean square error (RMSE), absolutely percentage error (MAPE), and mean absolutely difference (MAD).

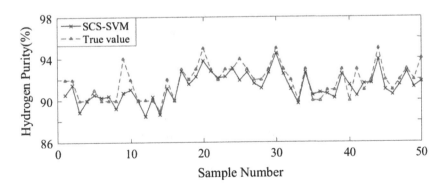

Fig. 7. Testing result of SCS-SVM multi-model

For a comparison, the voting and SVM based multi-model soft sensor (Voting-SVM), and the weighted combination based multi-model soft sensor (WCMM) have been developed. The experiment results are shown in the following.

Figures 7, 8, 9 and Table 4 illustrate that the proposed method has a better average performance than the Voting-SVM based multi-model soft sensor. Meanwhile, Fig. 5 also shows that the Voting-based multi-class classification may lead a poor result, for the last part of the testing samples are obviously wrongly classified.

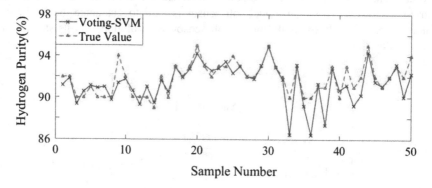

Fig. 8. Testing result of Voting-SVM multi-model

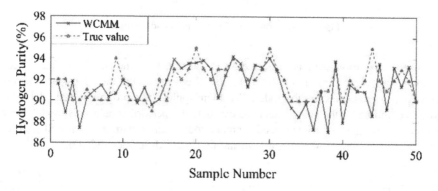

Fig. 9. Testing result of Voting-SVM multi-model

Table 4. Error result of multi-model soft sensor

Method	Testing results		
	RMSE	MAPE	MAD
SCS-SVM	0.9811	0.0080	0.7304
Voting-SVM	1.2100	0.0087	0.7846
WCMM	1.7253	0.0139	1.2802

6 Conclusion

The combination of sub models of the multi-model soft sensor can be considered as a multi-class classification problems. However, the tradition method is not suitable for this issue. In this paper, we proposed a sphere-based classifier selector for SVM classifier to solve this problem. The real chemical plant dataset and the public multi-class dataset have been used as an experiment in this paper. Relevant results reflect a good performance and have validated the proposed idea in this paper. Therefore, the method mentioned in this paper can act as an efficient solution for the building of the multi-model soft sensor.

Acknowledgements. This work is supported by the National Natural Science Foundation of China (Grant No. 61573144, 61174040), Shanghai Commission of Science and Technology (Grant no. 12JC1403400), and the Fundamental Research Funds for the Central Universities.

References

1. Kano, M., Nakagawa, Y.: Recent developments and industrial applications of data-based process monitoring and process control. Comput. Aided Chem. Eng. **21**(6), 57–62 (2006)
2. Kadlec, P., Gabrys, B., Strandt, S.: Data-driven soft sensors in the process industry. Comput. Chem. Eng. **33**(4), 795–814 (2009)
3. Lü, Y., Yang, H.-Z.: A Multi-model approach for soft sensor development based on feature extraction using weighted Kernel fisher criterion. Chin. J. Chem. Eng. **22**(22), 146–152 (2014)
4. Zhi-Gang, S., Wang, P.-H., Shen, J., Xiang-Jun, Yu., Lü, Z.-Z., Lu, L.: Multi-model strategy based evidential soft sensor model for predicting evaluation of variables with uncertainty. Appl. Soft Comput. **11**(2), 2595–2610 (2011)
5. Zhou, L.-F., Zhang, H.-N.: Research on multi-mode MPC based on clustering multi-modeling. J. Chem. Ind. Eng. **59**(10), 2546–2552 (2008)
6. Franklin, J.: The elements of statistical learning: data mining, inference and prediction. J. Roy. Stat. Soc. **173**(173), 693–694 (2010)
7. Vapnik, V.N.: Statistical Learning Theory. Encycl. Sci. Learn. **41**(4), 3185 (2010)
8. Williams, C.K.I., Rasmussen, C.E.: Gaussian processes for regression. Adv. Neural Inf. Process. Syst. **27**(6), 514–520 (1996)
9. Battistelli, G., Mosca, E., Tesi, P.: Adaptive memory in multi-model switching control of uncertain plants. Automatica **50**(3), 874–882 (2014)
10. Gao, F., Li, S.-B.E., Kum, D., Hui, Z.: Synthesis of multiple model switching controllers using [formula omitted] theory for systems with large uncertainties. Neurocomputing **157**, 118–124 (2015)
11. Kim, J., Kim, H.J.: Consistent model selection in segmented line regression. J. Stat. Plan. Infer. **170**, 106–116 (2016)
12. Ciupak, M., Ozgazielinski, B., Adamowski, J., et al.: The application of dynamic linear bayesian models in hydrological forecasting: varying coefficient regression and discount weighted regression. J. Hydrol. **530**, 762–784 (2015)
13. Leamer, E.E.: S-values and Bayesian Weighted All-Subsets Regressions. European Economic Review **81**, 15–31 (2015)

14. Lei, Y., Yang, H.-Z.: Combination model soft sensor based on Gaussian process and Bayesian committee machine. Ciesc Journal **64**(12), 4434–4438 (2013)
15. Hao, P.-Y., Lin, Y.-H.: A new multi-class support vector machine with multi-sphere in the feature space. In: Okuno, H.G., Ali, M. (eds.) IEA/AIE 2007. LNCS (LNAI), vol. 4570, pp. 756–765. Springer, Heidelberg (2007)
16. Sánchez-Maroño, N., Alonso-Betanzos, A., García-González, P., Bolón-Canedo, V.: Multiclass classifiers vs multiple binary classifiers using filters for feature selection. In: The 2010 International Joint Conference on Neural Networks (IJCNN), Barcelona, pp. 1–8 (2010)
17. Galar, M., Fernández, A., Barrenechea, E.: An overview of ensemble methods for binary classifiers in multi-class problems: experimental study on one-vs-one and one-vs-all schemes. Pattern Recogn. **44**(8), 1761–1776 (2011)
18. Hong, J.-H., Cho, S.-B.: A probabilistic multi-class strategy of one-vs.-rest support vector machines for cancer classification. Neurocomputing **71**(18), 3275–3281 (2008)
19. Gonzalez-Abril, L., Angulo, C., Velasco, F., et al.: A note on the bias in SVMs for multiclassification. IEEE Trans. Neural Netw. **19**(4), 723–725 (2008)
20. Williams, C.K.I., Rasmussen, C.E.: Gaussian processes for regression. In: Advances in Neural Information Processing Systems vol. 27, no. 6, pp. 514–520 (1996)
21. Emilio, S.O., Juan, G.S., Martín, J.D., et al.: BELM: Bayesian extreme learning machine. IEEE Trans. Neural Networks **22**(3), 505–509 (2011)
22. Saha, S., Ekbal, A.: Combining multiple classifiers using vote based classifier ensemble technique for named entity recognition. Data Knowl. Eng. **85**(8), 15–39 (2013)
23. Alex, R., Alessandro, L.: Clustering by fast search and find of density peaks. Science **344** (6191), 1492–1496 (2014)

Weighted Feature Correlation and Fusion Saliency

Yiwen Dou[1,2], Kuangrong Hao[1(✉)], and Yongsheng Ding[1]

[1] Engineering Research Center of Digitized Textile & Apparel Technology,
Ministry of Education, College of Information Science and Technology,
Donghua University, Shanghai, China
krhao@dhu.edu.cn
[2] College of Computer and Information,
Anhui Polytechnic University, Wuhu, China

Abstract. In this paper, we propose a novel feature correlation and fusion approach for multiple visual focuses content associational problem. Integrating various visual attention models to extract the visual focus of the image in the visual database, a weighted fusion of visual focuses will be obtained in good accuracy and the corresponding visual focus set will also be built subsequently. Then, the correlation matrix based on normalized mutual information and structural similarity index measurement will be computed within visual focus set. Through scanning correlation matrix in turn, the corresponding focus fusion process will be carried on and we use the weighted saliency model to compute visual focus of fusion focus. Compared with the state-of-the-art methods such as Itti, IS, GBVS, IF, NCS, MS and ISRW, higher robustness and accuracy rate are the main outstanding advantages of the presented approach. Experimental results on high noise interference confirm the validity of our approach.

Keywords: Visual focus · Saliency detection · Normalized mutual information (NMI) · Structural similarity index measurement (SSIM) · Weighted feature correlation and fusion saliency (WFCFS)

1 Introduction

Visual saliency detection has become an important part of image and video processing and the research of visual saliency is of great significance in image compression [1, 2], stereo matching [3, 10], video processing [4] and image retrieval [5] etc. The most famous visual saliency detection models is Itti's [6] model which is supported by feature integration theory. However, the visual attention of the image can not only be processed in the spatial domain. The image can be transformed by Fourier transforms and then the visual saliency image can be extracted in the frequency domain from the sign function of DCT coefficients. This is famous image signature (IS) saliency model which is proposed by Hou, Harel, and Koch [7]. A very important bottom-up saliency model is graph-based visual saliency (GBVS [8]) which is used graph and dissimilarly measure to find saliency area. A worth noting literature is [9] which is presented with non Itti's center-surrounding theory and its main theoretical basis is that the saliency

© Springer Science+Business Media Singapore 2016
L. Zhang et al. (Eds.): AsiaSim 2016/SCS AutumnSim 2016, Part IV, CCIS 646, pp. 73–81, 2016.
DOI: 10.1007/978-981-10-2672-0_8

area should be used surrounding patches to express the sparse reconstruction residual of the central patch by a non local sample. But, these models nearly have not advantages for the integrity of the visual focus. This phenomenon has changed in recent years. In [10], the authors propose an integrated visual detection model which is conducive to reduce the defects caused by single visual attention model, and bring the advantages of different visual attention model. Another saliency model needed to use prior knowledge is presented in [11] which has been given us a certain degree inspiration from this paper. Unfortunately, it may not get so much sampling in real application to ensure reliable prior knowledge. At last, we notice [12] which gives us an important inspiration. The authors combine mutual information [13] with saliency model and result in mutual saliency model which can be used to deal with the deformable registration problem in medical images. Inspired by this paper, we continue to develop and put forward the necessity of adding structural similarity index measurement (SSIM [14]). The weighted feature correlation and fusion saliency is proposed where the focus correlation process is added content-based correlation detection.

The main contributions of our paper can be summarized as followed.

- A novel visual focus correlation algorithm based on MI and SSIM is proposed.
- The fusion algorithm of associated visual focus is introduced with regard to save the energy distribution within original visual focus.
- In view of getting visual focus representation, we design a weighted fusion of many state-of-the-art visual focuses extraction algorithm which is embedded our above algorithms.

The rest of this paper is organized as follows. In Sect. 2, we review some important related works including visual saliency and normalized mutual information. In Sect. 3, a novel correlation detection algorithm is presented for visual saliency and the detailed fusion processing. In Sect. 4, the efficiency and effectiveness of our algorithm are tested by some experimental results. In Sect. 5, the whole paper is concluded and we give three further directions.

2 Related Works

2.1 Visual Attention Mechanism

According to many literatures [15–17] discussed about visual attention mechanism theory has been existed, we have no idea concerning about its theory. The key of this paper is how to apply the theory to obtain integrated target so as to serve for visual servo and detection.

In reality applications, visual scene reduction will bring much more advantages especially on robustness. According to the results as shown in Fig. 1, we can conclude that the acquired location of focus using visual saliency mechanism is quite stable and accurate under different level Gaussian noise. Therefore, it can assure the servo detection stability after utilizing visual saliency mechanism in a complex scene.

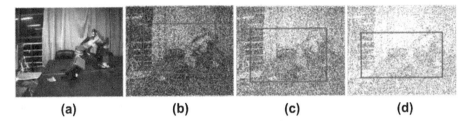

(a)   **(b)**   **(c)**   **(d)**

Fig. 1. Effects on visual focus with different level Gaussian noise. The real scene is captured by a 1/3 inch Sony Color CCD camera with 640×480 square pixels at 30 Hz frame rate. (a) Original image. (b) ~ (d) Adding man-made Gaussian noise in original image and respectively setting different parameters; (b) Mean equals zero and variance equals 0.5. (c) Mean and variance both equals 0.5. (d) Mean equals 1.0 and variance equals 0.5

2.2 Normalized Mutual Information

Mutual information [13], as a measure in the area of information theory, is often be used to test the similarity of two stochastic variances. In order to normalize the amount of mutual information to [0, 1], the normalized mutual information [18] is usually defined as follows:

$$NMI(\text{A}, \text{B}) = \sqrt{\frac{MI^2(\text{A}, \text{B})}{H(\text{A}) \times H(\text{B})}} \tag{1}$$

where, A and B are two gray images.

The basis of the principle of maximum mutual information is that the value of mutual information will reach the maximum when the spatial position of the two images is consistent.

2.3 Structural Similarity Index Measure

Structural similarity index measurement [14] is an important feature similarity index in many aspects of image analysis and processing. In real application, supposing there are two local window which is respectively named as A and B. Then, the local SSIM can be expressed as follows after simple setting parameters.

$$SSIM(A, B) = \frac{(2\mu_a \mu_b + C_1)(2\sigma_{ab} + C_2)}{(\mu_a^2 + \mu_b^2 + C_1)(\sigma_a^2 + \sigma_b^2 + C_2)} \tag{2}$$

where the estimation of brightness, contrast and structure similarity are means (μ_a and μ_b), standard deviation (σ_a and σ_b) and covariance (σ_{ab}) respectively. Constant C_1 and C_2 are attributed by avoiding meaningless phenomenon which $(\mu_a^2 + \mu_b^2)$ and $(\sigma_a^2 + \sigma_b^2)$ become zero simultaneously.

3 Weighted Feature Correlation and Fusion Saliency

Most of visual focus extraction algorithms are based on pixels' values. It will result in unassociated with the visual focus content itself because the real obtained visual focus only denotes a certain saliency features of color, originates and motion directions.

From the second rows of Fig. 2, it can be known that the content integrity of visual attention region is separated by the visual model. The main reason for this phenomenon is that those focuses are not able to achieve the correlation relations between those focuses.

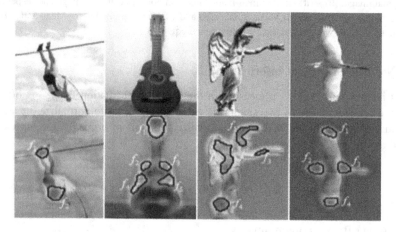

Fig. 2. Content integrity of saliency objects is destroyed by visual attention regions extracted by Itti. (All Images are coming from MSRA Salient Object Database and f_i (i = 1,2,...) is the i-th visual saliency region in each image of the second rows.)

In view of comprehensiveness and accuracy of extracting saliency area, we decide to integrate several state-of-the-art visual saliency models to extract saliency area. After saliency extraction, a focus set will be obtained from one image which is denoted as $F = \{f_1, f_2, ..., f_n\}$. Then, according to above equations, an integrated judgment matrix can be obtained as follows:

$$\begin{bmatrix} 0 & NMI_{f_1f_2} - \theta & \cdots & \cdots & NMI_{f_1f_n} - \theta \\ SSIM_{f_2f_1} - \eta & 0 & \cdots & \cdots & NMI_{f_2f_n} - \theta \\ \vdots & \vdots & \ddots & \vdots & \vdots \\ SSIM_{f_{n-1}f1} - \eta & SSIM_{f_{n-1}f_2} - \eta & \cdots & 0 & NMI_{f_{n-1}f_n} - \theta \\ SSIM_{f_nf_1} - \eta & SSIM_{f_nf_2} - \eta & \cdots & SSIM_{f_nf_{n-1}} - \eta & 0 \end{bmatrix}_{n \times n} \quad (3)$$

where θ is the threshold of NMI and η is the threshold of SSIM. Then, a combine matrix will be built according to the above matrix elements whose definition is presented by positive logic expression which is set zero when the element is less than threshold and set one when the element is greater than threshold.

Algorithm 1. Proposed weighted feature correlation and fusion saliency.

Inputs:

SMA - saliency map of image A (extracted by weighted saliency model).

Outputs:

RA - an uncorrelated feature map cellular array;

FA - the saliency index array of RA.

1: Label different focus areas of SMA and build a saliency index array FA.

2: Cut scale normalized rectangles from original color images according to FA and then build a saliency areas cellular array RA.

3: Use eq. (1) and (2) to calculate correlation matrix and use eq. (4) to justify possible fusion areas till combine matrix becomes zero.

4: Build a combine focus sets F_Combine and simplify it.

5: Call fusion_update algorithm till achieve all combination process in F_Combine.

6: Return 1 and recheck if all saliency areas do not need to be combined.

The correlation and fusion focus will be justified by following combine label matrix:

$$Combine\_lable = (a_{ij})_{nn}^{i<j} \wedge (a_{ji})_{nn}^{j<i} \tag{4}$$

where a_{ij} and a_{ji} are all the elements of combine matrix. Once the value calculated by Eq. (4) is one, it means that the i-th and j-th saliency areas need to be combined. Given a color image A, the pseudo-code of weighted feature correlation and fusion saliency model is described in **Algorithm 1**.

4   Experimental Result and Discussion

In our experiments, we provide a number of real natural scene images for comparison, and these images are coming from MSRA Salient Object Database where contains all kinds of images for visual saliency model testing and even gives three observers' subjective visual saliency maps.

From Fig. 3, it can be found that the integrity of saliency region extracted by our proposed WFCFS algorithm can be hold and the result is superior to the rest of seven different visual attention models.

From Table 1, we can find that in spite of the highest coverage rate of primary focus, ISRW also has highest coverage rate of non focus and the proportion of focus area.

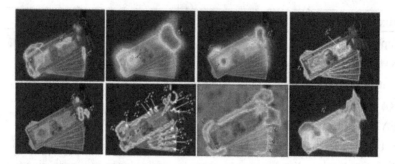

Fig. 3. Saliency extracting results of eight different visual saliency models. From left to right, the first row respectively shows the results of Itti, IS, GBVF and IF. And the results of NCS, MS, ISRW and WFCFS are shown in the second from left to right. and f_j^i ($j = 1,2,...,8. i = 1,2,...$) is denoted as the i-th visual saliency region in the j-th visual saliency models.

Table 1. Eight indexes of extracting result by different saliency models

Item	Primary focus coverage rate (%)	Non focus coverage rate (%)	Focus proportion (pixles)	Focus number (pic.)	Run time (ms)
Itti	0.0751	0.3431	16339	3	0.8892
IS	0.0124	0.3448	1491	2	0.9360
GBVS	0.0222	0.3403	3302	3	3.12
IF	0.0627	0.3518	14390	2	0.2964
NCS	0.0112	0.3490	1700	3	2.7924
MS	0.1932	0.3327	42346	19	0.1872
ISRW	0.3572	0.6395	119603	6	20.2489
WFCFS	0.1954	0.3236	43966	1	20.5609

After adding Gaussian noise with different noisy intensity, the saliency regions are extracted by different visual saliency models. From Fig. 4, the goose object is full included in the saliency area obtained by WFCFS before adding Gaussian noise and in spite of adding different strength Gaussian noise, it has nearly no change. This situation is completely opposite to IS. When the noise variance reaches to 0.9, its saliency area almost overlap the whole image. Others has little changing on visual integrity, saliency robust and Euler number which are shown in Fig. 5.

From visual integrity shown in Fig. 5a, whether the original image adds noise or not, the overlap ratio of the saliency area calculated by WFCFS and the subject saliency area is very high. But the visual integrity index of Image Signature is closed to WFCFS's where it also conforms to the results of the subjective comparisons in Fig. 4. At the same time, we also find that the visual integrity of other saliency models are not very good and even NCS, it only reaches to 0.6. In Fig. 5b, it shows that the saliency robustness of WFCFS is the

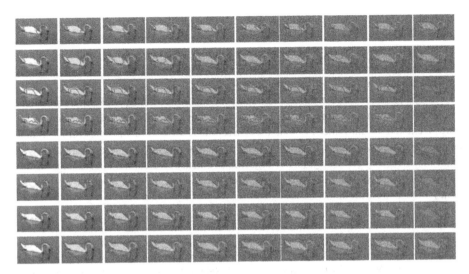

Fig. 4. The subjective observation results of saliency region extracted by different saliency models when adding different noise intensity to original image. It respectively shows the results of Itti, IS, GBVF, IF, NCS, MS, ISRW and WFCFS from the first to the eighth row. The first left column shows the visual saliency maps of original image. From the second to the tenth column, the original image is added with Gaussian noise which is zero mean and the variance from 0.1 to 0.9.

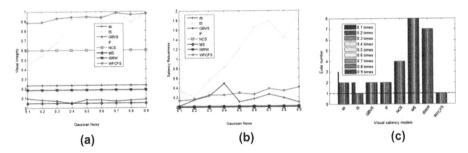

Fig. 5. Comparisons of the objective results under noise interrupting. (a) Visual integrity, (b) saliency robustness, (c) Euler number

best while GBVS's is the second rank and IS's is the worst. The saliency area of other saliency models shows very robust and nearly can not be seen any influence. In Fig. 5c, the visual integrity of WFCFS always holds one Euler number.

5   Conclusions and Future Work

In this paper, we have summarized several classical approach to visual saliency extraction based on visual saliency mechanism and an important feature correlation strategy is introduced for computing correlation level. We have subsequently proposed a weighted visual saliency model which is embedded with feature correlation and fusion. We design a weighted feature correlation and fusion saliency which can be used to integrate several visual focuses representation of visual saliency models. Many corresponding experiments shows WFCFS own good visual saliency description in high noise which means to fit the real application.

This research has not finished universal verification currently and three directions will be extended in the future. Firstly, our visual saliency algorithm will be tested by all images existed in all saliency databases. Secondly, there are only "several" visual saliency models who have been integrated in our algorithm at present and this will result in universal verification of our algorithm. Thirdly, we can take advantage of the feature descriptor correlation calculation which may be a method to improve the efficiency of our algorithm.

Acknowledgements. This work was supported in part by the National Nature Science Foundation of China (Nos. 61473077, 61473078, 61503075), the Key Project of the National Nature Science Foundation of China (No. 61134009), Cooperative research funds of Hong Kong and Macao scholars (No. 61428302) and the National Natural Science Funds Overseas, Shanghai Pujiang Program (15PJ1400100), Specialized Research Fund for Shanghai Leading Talents, Program for Changjiang Scholars from the Ministry of Education, Innovation Program of Shanghai Municipal Education Commission (No. 14ZZ067), and the Fundamental Research Funds for the Central Universities (Nos. 15D110423, 2232015D3-32), Project of the Shanghai Committee of Science and Technology (No. 13JC1407500), Provincial Natural Science Research Project of Anhui province higher education promotion plan (TSKJ2014B06) and Provincial Natural Science major project of Anhui Province (KJ2015ZD06).

References

1. Lee, S.-H., Choi, S.-B., Lee, M., et al.: Non-uniform image compression using a biologically motivated selective attention model. Neurocomputing **67**, 350–356 (2005)
2. Gupta, R., Khanna, M.T., Chaudhury, S.: Visual saliency guided video compression algorithm. Signal Process. Image Commun. **28**, 1006–1022 (2013)
3. Jiang, Q., Shao, F., Jiang, G., et al.: A depth perception and visual comfort guided computational model for stereoscopic 3D visual saliency. Signal Process. Image Commun. **38**, 57–69 (2015)
4. Ji, Q.-G., Fang, Z.-D., Xie, Z.-H., et al.: Video abstraction based on the visual attention model and online clustering. Signal Process. Image Commun. **28**, 241–253 (2013)
5. Wang, X.-Y., Yong-Jian, Yu., Yang, H.-Y.: An effective image retrieval scheme using color, texture and shape features. Comput. Stan. Interfaces **33**, 59–68 (2011)
6. Borji, A., Itti, L.: State-of-the-art in visual attention modeling. IEEE Trans. Pattern Anal. Mach. Intell. **35**, 185–207 (2013)
7. Hou, X., Harel, J., Koch, C.: Image signature: high lighting sparse salient regions. IEEE Trans. Pattern Anal. Mach. Intell. **34**, 194–201 (2012)
8. Harel, J., Koch, C., Perona, P.: Graph-based visual saliency. In: Advances in Neural Information Processing Systems, Proceedings of the 2006 Conference, vol. 19, pp. 545–552 (2007)

9. Xia, C., FeiQi, G.S., et al.: Nonlocal center–surround reconstruction-based bottom-up saliency estimation. Pattern Recognit. **48**, 1337–1348 (2015)

10. Jing, H., He, X., Han, Q., et al.: Saliency detection based on integrated features. Neurocomputing **129**, 114–121 (2014)

11. Li, J., Fang, S., Tian, Y., et al.: Image saliency estimation via random walk guided by informativeness and latent signal correlations. Signal Process. Image Commun. **38**, 3–14 (2015)

12. Yangming, O., Sotiras, A., Paragios, N., et al.: DRAMMS: deformable registration via attribute matching and mutual-saliency weighting. Med. Image Anal. **15**, 622–639 (2011)

13. Yaman, M., Kalkan, S.: An iterative adaptive multi-modal stereo-vision method using mutual information. J. Vis. Commun. Image Representation **26**, 115–131 (2015)

14. Wang, Z., Bovik, A.C., Sheikh, H.R., et al.: Image quality assessment: from error visibility to structural similarity. IEEE Trans. Image Process. **13**, 600–612 (2004)

15. Hou, W., Gao, X., Tao, D., et al.: Visual saliency detection using information divergence. Pattern Recognit. **46**, 2658–2669 (2013)

16. Sun, J., Jiangchuan Xie, J., Liu, J., et al.: Image adaptation and dynamic browsing based on two-layer saliency combination. IEEE Trans. Broadcast. **59**, 602–613 (2013)

17. Fellrath, J., Ptak, R.: The role of visual saliency for the allocation of attention: evidence from spatial neglect and hemianopia. Neuropsychologia **73**, 70–81 (2015)

18. Ren, J., Jiang, X., Yuan, J.: Learning LBP structure by maximizing the conditional mutual information. Pattern Recognit. **48**, 3180–3190 (2015)

A Two-Stage Simulation Optimization Method Based on Metamodel

Zhizhao Liu, Wei Li, and Ming Yang[(⊠)]

Control and Simulation Center, Harbin Institute of Technology, Harbin, China
{liuzhizhao2007,fleehit}@163.com, myang@hit.edu.cn

Abstract. For reducing the sample size of costly simulation system, we propose a novel method named a two-stage simulation optimization method based on metamodel. A small sample is taken to get some useful information for reducing the search space. Then, several optimal values are achieved based on some metamodels of reduced spaces. Finally, the optimal solutions are taken into the simulation system to get the best solution. Six typical test functions are demonstrated that two-stage simulation method can reduce the running times effectively and the results are normally better than the classical metamodel-based simulation optimization method.

Keywords: Simulation optimization · Metamodel · Support vector machine · Particle swarm optimization

1 Introduction

A metamodel is "a simplified mathematical description of a simulation model that represents the system's input–output relationship with a function" [1]. When the simulation system is large and costly, a metamodel may be very effective, which has been popular in the fields of simulation sensitivity analysis, simulation uncertainty analysis, simulation optimization and so on. Simulation optimization based on metamodel is discussed by Fu [2, 3], Barton [4, 5], Van Beers and Kleijnen [6] and the applications are also popular [7–10]. In general, more training points could achieve a better metamodel [11]. But the time consuming problem of simulation systems restricts the sample size of training data. Therefore, how to achieve the optimization solution by less sample points is an outstanding problem for simulation optimization based on metamodel.

In recent years, several researches tried to decrease running times during metmodeling. An important idea is to have a sequential method to construct metamodel. It begins with a small size sample and adds some new samples until the metamodel has a high precision, which generates sample points as few as possible. A general frame is proposed for the optimization of plastic injection molding process parameters [12]. Chen and Zhou [13] introduce sequential experimental designs for a special metamodel named stochastic Kriging. Chen et al. [1] and Shang et al. [14] also focus on the sequential experimental methods, respectively for interpolation-based metamodels and least square support vector machine. Therefore, the purpose of the researches above is

© Springer Science+Business Media Singapore 2016
L. Zhang et al. (Eds.): AsiaSim 2016/SCS AutumnSim 2016, Part IV, CCIS 646, pp. 82–91, 2016.
DOI: 10.1007/978-981-10-2672-0_9

to construct a highly precise metamodel for the whole search space by less training sample points.

In this paper, we discuss the optimization of multi-input single-output continuous system, which is so complex that we must use a large sample to get an approved metamodel. In this case, even by the sequential method it needs too many sample points. This paper tries to solve the problem on another track. As the optimal value is in a little range and the search space is not, there is no need to get a highly precise metamodel in the whole search space. Therefore, we try to get some useful information to focus some little search spaces in the first step and obtain the optimization with some metamodels of the little spaces in the second step, which is the two-stage simulation optimization method based on metamodel.

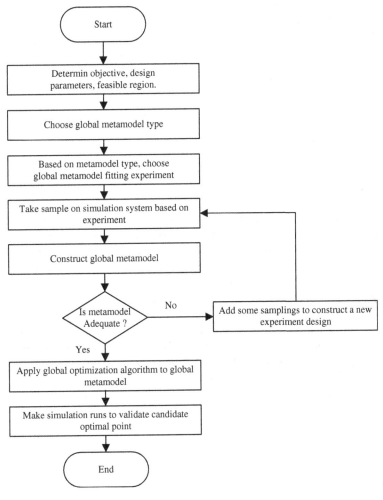

Fig. 1. Strategy of simulation optimization based on global metamodel [4]

Section 2 describes the theory of classical simulation optimization based on global metamodel. In Sect. 3, we give the frame of a two-stage simulation optimization method based on metamodel and introduce the procedure. In Sect. 4, six illustrative test functions are used to show the good character of the proposed method. Finally, Sect. 5 gives the conclusion and some thoughts for the future research.

2   A Review of Simulation Optimization Based on Global Metamodel

Metamodel is an alternate model, which is an expression of mathematical function that has a similar input-output relationship of simulation system. As the metamodel runs quickly by a computer, the time of simulation optimization is cut down compared with the optimization directly on simulation system.

The main strategy of global metamodel-based simulation optimization is shown in Fig. 1. The steps of simulation based on metamodel are divided into three parts. Firstly, the training set and predicting set are generated on the simulation system, which are used to construct metamodel. If the metamodel is adequate, the second step is to apply optimization algorithm on the metamodel. Finally, the optimization solution is taken into simulation system to validate.

3   Two-Stage Simulation Optimization Method Based on Metamodel

The classical metamodel-based simulation optimization method demands a highly precise metamodel. In this study, less training sample points are applied to construct a rough metamodel. Although the precision is not adequate, the rough metamodel can indicate the tendency of system's input–output relationship. Figure 2 gives a diagram of input–output relationship of a rough metamodel and a simulation system. From the figure, it is shown that there is a deviation of optimization solution and optimal value between metamodel and simulation system. Sometimes, the optimal point of metamodel might correspond a local optimal point of simulation system as shown in Fig. 2, especially for a lowly precise metamodel. In this figure, the optimal point of simulation system is near the local optimal points of metamodel. So in order to get the optimal point based on metamodel, we can find the local optimal points of metamodel and search the optimal one near these local ones on the simulation system. For solving this problem, we proposed a multimodal optimization method for simulation systems, which is the stage one in this paper [15].

The second stage is to get the optimal points near every local ones. The range of local space can be expressed in Eq. (1).

$$\Psi_{i,j} = \left[\alpha_{ij,\max}^k - (b_j - a_j)/v \cdot \eta, \alpha_{ij,\max}^k + (b_j - a_j)/v \cdot \eta \right] \tag{1}$$

where $A_{i,\max}^k = \left[\alpha_{i1,\max}^k, \alpha_{i2,\max}^k, \ldots, \alpha_{im,\max}^k \right], 1 \leq i \leq v$. $A_{i,\max}^k$ is the local optimal points of metamodel, v is the number of local optimal points, $1 \leq j \leq n$, n is the dimension of

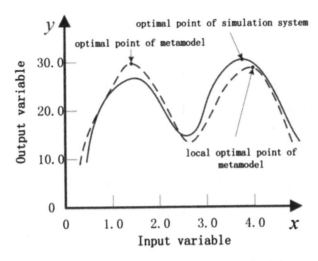

Fig. 2. Input–output relationship of metamodel and simulation system

input variables, η is a constant coefficient, $\eta \in [0\,1]$. As the input–output relationship near local optimal points is $A^k_{i,\text{max}}$ simple, we need little sample points to construct new precise metamodels for every local space. The strategy of a two-stage simulation optimization method based on metamodel is shown in Fig. 3.

Suppose that a simulation system has n input variables and one output, noted as $X = \{x_1, x_2, \ldots, x_n\}$ and Y. The simulation optimization is to find a solution X^* that the responding output Y^* is the optimal value. In this section, we search the maximum output as shown in Eq. (2). The other situation can be solved by transforming the output into its opposite number. The two-stage simulation optimization method based on metamodel is illustrated as bellows.

$$\max Y = f(X) \tag{2}$$

Stage I. Multimodal optimization based on a rough metamodel

(a) Sampling and Metamodeling.
 We choose Support Vector Machine (SVM) metamodel, which is fitting for small sampling. Select a proper experiment design method for sampling, and then build a SVM metamodel of simulation system. The SVM metamodel is as shown in Eq. (3).

$$f(x) = \sum_{i=1}^{l} (\alpha_i - \alpha_i^*) K(x, x_i) + b \tag{3}$$

(b) Multimodal optimization.
 We choose Particle Swarm Optimization (PSO) as the multimodal optimization

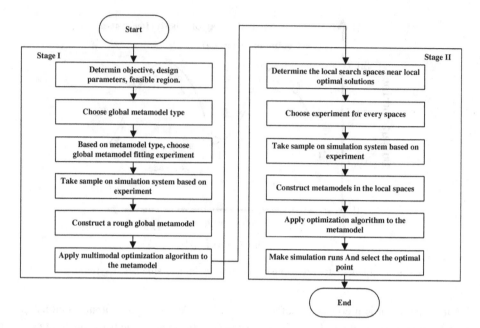

Fig. 3. Strategy of a two-stage simulation optimization method based on metamodel

method [11]. Suppose that the PSO individual $A_i^k = [\alpha_{i1}^k, \alpha_{i2}^k, \ldots, \alpha_{im}^k]$ and the predicted fitness from SVM metamodel $\hat{F}^k = [\hat{\beta}_1^k, \hat{\beta}_2^k, \ldots, \hat{\beta}_n^k]$, where $k = 1, 2, \ldots, n, m$, is the number of input variables and n is the size of PSO population. The parameters of PSO algorithm is modified properly, making individuals could not skip from local optimum. After repeated iteration as in Eq. (4), all population individuals are stable near several local optimal points.

$$v_{ij}(t+1) = \mathrm{w} \cdot v_{ij}(t) + C_1 r_{1j}(t)(P_{ij}(t) - x_{ij}(t)) + C_2 r_{2j}(t) \cdot (P_{gj}(t) - x_{ij}(t))$$
$$x_{ij}(t+1) = x_{ij}(t) + v_{ij}(t+1)$$

$$(4)$$

Some individuals at the last generation will be rejected if their fitness is too bad. The screening equation is shown in Eq. (5).

$$\hat{\beta}_i^\xi \geq C_{ps} \cdot \hat{\beta}_{max}^\xi \tag{5}$$

where $\hat{\beta}_i^\xi$ is the predicted fitness of individual A_i^ξ at the ξth generation. ξ is the number of last generation. $\hat{\beta}_{max}^\xi$ is the maximum value of individual fitness until the ξth generation. C_{ps} is a constant and its maximum value equals to 1.

(c) Getting local optimal solutions.

Confirm the number and values of local optimal points as follows:

(i) In consideration of magnitude difference, the population individuals of PSO algorithm at the last generation are standardized as shown in Eq. (6).

$$\tilde{\alpha}_{ij}^{\xi} = \left(\alpha_{ij}^{\xi} - b_j\right)\Big/(a_j - b_j) \tag{6}$$

where α_{ij}^{ξ} is the j th variable of individual $A_i^{\xi} \cdot a_j$ is the maximum value of the j th variable and b_j is the minimum one.

(ii) Every individual A_i^k can be seen as a cluster, so there are n clusters, denoted by $G_1, G_2, \ldots, G_n$. The distance s_{ij} can be given in Eq. (7) and the distance matrix $S = \{s_{ij}\}$.

$$s_{ij} = \sqrt{\sum_{k=1}^{m} (\alpha_{ik} - \alpha_{jk})^2} \tag{7}$$

(iii) Get the minimum value from the matrix S, denoted by s_{ij}. The cluster $G_j = \{A_{j,1}^{\xi}, A_{j,2}^{\xi}, \ldots, A_{j,t}^{\xi}\}$ is incorporated into the cluster $G_i = \{A_{i,1}^{\xi}, A_{i,2}^{\xi}, \ldots, A_{i,r}^{\xi}\}$. We get the new cluster $G_i = \{A_{i,1}^{\xi}, A_{i,2}^{\xi}, \ldots, A_{i,r}^{\xi}, A_{j,1}^{\xi}, A_{j,2}^{\xi}, \ldots, A_{j,t}^{\xi}\}$. Go to the step (2) until only one cluster exist.

(iv) Hierachical diagram can be drawn and the number of clusters can be determined from the linkage distance. The clusters are denoted by $G_1, G_2, \ldots, G_v$.

(v) From the cluster $G_k = \{A_{k,1}^{\xi}, A_{k,2}^{\xi}, \ldots, A_{k,t}^{\xi}\}$, we can get the corresponding fitness set $H_k = \{\hat{F}_{k,1}^{\xi}, \hat{F}_{k,2}^{\xi}, \ldots, \hat{F}_{k,t}^{\xi}\}$. The maximum value of set H_k is the local optimal value denoted by $\hat{F}_{k,\max}$. The corresponding input variable value is $A_{k,\max}^{\xi}$. Through the v kinds of clusters, we can get v local optimal values denoted by $\hat{F}_{1,\max}, \hat{F}_{2,\max}, \ldots, \hat{F}_{v,\max}$ and the corresponding input variable values denoted by $A_{1,\max}^{\xi}, A_{2,\max}^{\xi}, \ldots, A_{v,\max}^{\xi}$.

Stage II. Simulation optimization near the optimal solutions based on metamodel

(a) Determining the local search spaces.
Based on the local optimal points $A_{1,\max}^{\xi}, A_{2,\max}^{\xi}, \ldots, A_{v,\max}^{\xi}$, get the local spaces based on Eq. (1), noted as $\Phi_i = \{X | x_j \in \Psi_{i,j}\}, 1 \le i \le v$.

(b) Sampling and metamodeling
This step is the same as step (a) of stage one. The experiment design is Latin Hypercube Sampling (LHS), which is a small sampling method. Among the $\Phi_i = \{X | x_j \in \Psi_{i,j}\}, 1 \le i \le v$, some SVM metamodels are built.

(c) Simulation optimization based on metamodel
As Genetic Algorithm (GA) is robust for global optimization, GA is applied on the SVM metamodels and get the optimal solutions of every local spaces, noted as $A_1^*, A_2^*, \ldots, A_v^*$.

(d) Getting the optimal solution

Take $A_1^*, A_2^*, \ldots, A_v^*$ into the simulation system and get the output values $F_1^*, F_2^*, \ldots, F_v^*$. The maximum value $F_{max}^* = \max\{F_1^*, F_2^*, \ldots, F_v^*\}$ and the responding input is A_{max}^*. Therefore, A_{max}^* is the optimal solution and F_{max}^* is the optimal value.

4 Numerical Examples

In order to evaluate the performance of our proposed method, numerical analysis should be done. As test functions have exactly optimal value, we use six different mathematical problems, which are convenient to evaluate the optimization result. All the test functions need to be searched the minimum value. The details of six functions are as belows.

(1) Ackley function

$$f(x) = -20 \cdot e^{-0.2\sqrt{\frac{1}{2}(x_1^2 + x_2^2)}} - e^{\frac{1}{2}[\cos(2\pi x_1^2) + \cos(2\pi x_2^2)]} + 20 + e$$

where $-5 \le x_i \le 5$, $i = 1, 2$, $f_{min} = 0$.

(2) Beale function

$$f(x) = (1.5 - x_1 + x_1 x_2)^2 + (2.25 - x_1 + x_1 x_2^2)^2 + (2.625 - x_1 + x_1 x_2^3)^2$$

where $-4.5 \le x_i \le 4.5$, $i = 1, 2$, $f_{min} = 0$.

(3) Bird function

$$f(x) = \sin(x_1)e^{[(1-\cos(x_2))^2]} + \cos(x_2)e^{[(1-\sin(x_2))^2]} + (x_1 - x_2)^2$$

where $-5 \le x_i \le 5$, $i = 1, 2$, $f_{min} = -106.764537$.

(4) Booth function

$$f(x) = (x_1 + 2x_2 - 7)^2 + (2x_1 + x_2 - 5)^2$$

where $-10 \le x_i \le 10$, $i = 1, 2$, $f_{min} = 0$.

(5) Carrom table function

$$f(x) = -\left[\cos(x_1)\cos(x_2)e^{|1-(x_1^2 + x_2^2)^{0.5}/\pi|}\right]^2 \Big/ 30$$

where $-10 < x_i \le 10$, $i = 1, 2$, $f_{min} = 24.1568155$.

(6) Chichinadze function

$$f(x) = x_1^2 - 12x_1 + 11 + 10\cos(\pi x_1 / 2) + 8\sin(5\pi x_1) - (1/5)^{0.5}e^{-0.5(x_2 - 0.5)^2}$$

where $-30 \le x_i \le 30$, $i = 1, 2$, $f_{min} = -43.3159$.

Table 1. Results of metamodels by two methods

Function	Proposed method		Classical method	
	Total number of sampling data	Optimal value	Total number of sampling data	Optimal value
Ackley	171	0.00232	310	0.000148
Beale	92	1.06([a])	142	9.32
Booth	39	0.0634([a])	142	0.729
Carrom table	151	−24.05([a])	382	−23.31
Bird (1)	102	−105.36([a])	85	−91.47
Bird (2)	102	−105.36([a])	142	−102.5731
Chichinadze(1)	104	−31.57([a])	56	−11.13
Chichinadze(2)	104	−31.57([a])	142	−10.77
Chichinadze(3)	104	−31.57([a])	217	−18.64
Chichinadze(4)	104	−31.57([a])	246	−32.79

[a] Denote the proposed method has a better result than the classical method.

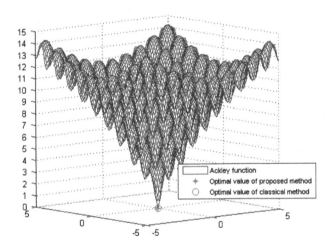

Fig. 4. Optimization results of two methods for Ackley function

The proposed method in this paper is used to get the optimal points of test functions. In the stage one, every input variable is divided into n_d equal parts and the values are the boundary values. The training sets are all the combinations of two variables. The sizes of training sets are 121, 36, 64, 9, 121, 36 (n_d = 10, 5, 7, 2, 10, 5). The predicting sets are designed by LHS of size 20. In the stage two, the training sets are designed by LHS and GA based on SVM is applied. The total number of sampling data is $N_{total} = N^1_{train} + N^1_{predict} + N^2_{train} + N^2_{validation}$, where N^1_{train} is the number of training data in stage one. $N^1_{predict}$ is the number of predicting data in stage one. N^2_{train} is the number of training data in stage two. $N^2_{validation}$ is the number of local optimal points.

In the classical method, Multiple Correlation Coefficient (R^2) is a common performance measures to evaluate metamodel as shown in Eq. (8).

$$R^2 = 1 - \sum_{i=1}^{n} (y_i - \hat{y}_i)^2 \bigg/ \sum_{i=1}^{n} (y_i - \bar{y})^2 \tag{8}$$

where y_i is the i th output value. $\hat{y}_i$ is the ith predictive value, $i = 1, 2, \cdots, n$. $\bar{y}$ is the mean of outputs. If R^2 of metamodel is more than 0.9, SVM metamodel is adequate. The training sets of SVM metamodels are designed by the same method of proposed method in stage one. For Ackley function, Beale function, Booth function and Carrom table function, the sizes of training sets are 289, 121, 121, 361. For Bird function and Chichinadze function, R^2 is satisfied in a small sample, but the optimization result is bad. So we analyses with different training sets. The sizes of predicting sets are 20 for all the test functions.

The results of these two methods are shown in Table 1. From the tables, we can see that in general the proposed method uses less training data and obtains more precise solutions than the classical method for the test functions except for Ackley function. For Ackley function, the optimal solutions of proposed method and classical method are respectively (−0.000748, 0.000324) and (−0.000005, −0.000052), which can be seen that the optimal solutions of the two methods both have a high precision as shown in Fig. 4. Although the optimal value of proposed method is a little more than the one of classical method, the number of sampling data by the proposed method is much less than that by classical method. The proposed method has a good character, which has two main reasons. One is to get some information from a rough metamodel, which needs much less training points than classical metamodel. Another is to have a highly precise metamodel in a local space, which can get a good optimal solution. So the proposed method effectively cut down the running times of simulation systems and achieved a better optimal solution.

5 Conclusion

In this study, a two-stage simulation optimization method based on metamodel is proposed, which is a novel track of simulation optimization based on metamodel. The first stage is to narrow down the search space, which only needs a rough metamodel. In the second stage, some new samples are generated and GA based on SVM is applied to get the local optimal solution. From numerical analysis, it is shown that the training data is less and the optimal solution is better than classical metamodel-based simulation optimization method in general.

In fact, this paper introduces a frame of two-stage simulation optimization method based on metamodel. The multimodal optimization method in stage one and the simulation method in stage two can be other methods. For example, kriging metamodel or artificial neural network (ANN) can replace SVM in stage one and polynomial metamodel can be the metamodel in stage two. If the local space is also large after stage one, we can repeat the stage one until the local space is little enough.

During stage one, the metamodel has no index to evaluate whether the metamodel is suitable for the proposed method. Even if $R^2 \geq 0.9$, the next work might lead bad results. So the further research is to give another index for metamodel in stage one. In addition, many real simulation systems are stochastic systems. In order to test the effect, the proposed method can be applied into this circumstance, which might give a new idea for the research on stochastic simulation systems.

Acknowledgements. This research is supported by the National Natural Science Foundation of China (Grant No. 61403097).

References

1. Chen, E.J., Li, M.: Design of experiments for interpolation-based metamodels. Simul. Model. Pract. Theory **44**, 14–25 (2014)
2. Fu, M.C.: Handbook of Simulation Optimization. Springer, New York (2014)
3. Chau, M., Fu, M.C., Qu, H.S., Ryzhov, I.O.: simulation optimization: a tutorial overview and recent developments in grandient-based methods. In: Proceedings of the 2014 Winter Simulation Conference, pp. 21–35. IEEE Press, Savanah (2014)
4. Barton, R.R.: Simulation optimization using metamodels. In: Proceedings of the 2009 Winter Simulation Conference, pp. 230–238. IEEE Press, Austin (2009)
5. Barton, R.R., Meckesheimer, M.: Metamodel-based simulation optimization. Handbooks Oper. Res. Manage. Sci. **13**, 535–574 (2006)
6. Van Beers, W.C.M., Kleijnen, J.P.C.: Kriging interpolation in simulation: a survey. In: Proceedings of the 2004 Winter Simulation Conference, pp. 113–121. IEEE Press, Washington, DC (2004)
7. Kaminski, B.: A method for the updating of stochastic kriging metamodels. Eur. J. Oper. Res. **247**(3), 859–866 (2015)
8. Kusiak, J., Sztangret, L., Pietrzyk, M.: Effective strategies of metamodelling of industrial metallurgical processes. Adv. Eng. Softw. **89**, 90–97 (2015)
9. Kuznik, F., Lopez, J.P.A., Baillis, D., Johannes, K.: Phase change material wall optimization for heating using metamodeling. Energy Build. **106**, 216–224 (2015)
10. Wang, G.G., Shan, S.: Review of metamodeling techniques in support of engineering design optimization. J. Mech. Des. **129**(4), 370–380 (2007)
11. Geleder, L.V., Das, P., Janssen, H., Roels, S.: Comparative study of metamodelling techniques in building energy simulation: guidelines for practitioners. Simul. Model. Pract. Theory **49**, 245–257 (2014)
12. Dang, X.P.: General frameworks for optimization of plastic injection molding process parameters. Simul. Model. Pract. Theory **41**, 15–27 (2014)
13. Chen, X., Zhou, Q.: Sequential experimental designs for stochastic kriging. In: Proceedings of the 2014 Winter Simulation Conference, pp. 3821–3832. IEEE Press, Savanah (2014)
14. Shang, W.F., Zhao, S.D., Shen, Y.J.: Application of LSSVM with AGA optimizing parameters to nonlinear modeling of SRM. In: 3rd IEEE Conference on Industrial Electronics and Applications, pp. 775–780. IEEE Press, Singapore (2008)
15. Liu, Z.Z., Li, W., Yang, M.: A multimodal optimization method for simulation systems. In: 26th European Modeling and Simulation Symposium, pp. 289–294. Dime University of Genoa Pess, Bergeggi (2014)

Internet Communication Engine (ICE) Based Simulation Framework (ISF)

Hang Ji[1,3], Xiao Song[1,3(✉)], Xuejun Zhang[1,3], Jing Bi[2], and Haitao Yuan[1,3]

[1] School of Automation Science and Electrical Engineering, Beihang University, Beijing, China
jihangchn@163.com, songxiao@buaa.edu.cn
[2] School of Software Engineering, Beijing Engineering Research Center for IoT Software and Systems, Beijing University of Technology, Beijing, 100124, China
[3] Engineering Research Center of Complex Product Advanced Manufacturing System, Ministry of Education, Beijing, China

Abstract. Most existing HLA based simulation frameworks do not support simulation on WAN. To tackle this problem, we propose an Internet Communication Engine (ICE) based framework (ISF) that is capable of running on WAN, generating simulation codes automatically, and managing simulation procedures efficiently. ICE as well as its several powerful services is adopted to build discrete event driven applications and provide network communications. A use case of antimissile system is implemented with this framework, which is validated to have useful functions and be stable with running simulations on both LAN and WAN.

Keywords: Automatic code generation · Simulation management · ICE

1 Introduction

Communication middleware is gaining popularity through their rich set of features helping the development of complex systems. In this paper we consider applying a novel communication middleware, Internet Communication Engine (ICE) [1], to simulation system and implementing the system's framework. The related works are introduced as two separate subsections as follows.

Most current simulation framework designs are still in the stage of model-code-run, which means that users have to create a model of the target system, program the simulation based on the model, and then run the simulation [2–4]. However, model-and-run simulation framework emerged for it can ease the burden of developing complicated codes [17]. G.D. Kapos [5] introduces DEVSys, an integrated framework for utilizing existing systems modeling language (SysML) models and automatically producing executable discrete event simulation code. However, DEVSys emphasizes more on profile diagrams design and model transformation, as a result whose simulator implementation and case study are not fully supported. W.T. Tsai [6] presents a service-oriented modeling and simulation framework for rapid development of distributed applications. An automatic code generation tool is developed to covert language specification into the executable codes. C. Yang [7] introduces a parallel simulation

© Springer Science+Business Media Singapore 2016
L. Zhang et al. (Eds.): AsiaSim 2016/SCS AutumnSim 2016, Part IV, CCIS 646, pp. 92–101, 2016.
DOI: 10.1007/978-981-10-2672-0_10

framework Ivy that has similar target and capacity with ISF. But both of above works did not elaborate communication schemes and test their performances on WAN.

The High Level Architecture is the IEEE standard for distributed simulation [8] and its actual implementation is provided by Run Time Infrastructure (RTI) [9, 14]. When building a simulation framework HLA-RTI could provide a professional and efficient guide. However, several problems remain unsolved in current HLA-RTIs. For example, though RTIs normally run well in LANs, when take them into WAN, firewalls on the entrance of inner networks to WAN will block RTIs' underlying communications. Nowadays papers [10, 11] indicate that service provisioning of HLA-RTI as Web services feasible, but until now only a few commercial products integrate Web-based technologies and functions. In addition, HLA-RTI interface specification's binding with programming languages cause some programming interoperability issues. The dependency of the interface description to the HLA-RTI from the specific simulation model is a critical disadvantage in extending applications.

In the sections follow, outline design of ISF are presented first. Following this detail designs and implementation are concluded and experience applying ISF to an anti-air use case is described. At last are future work and conclusion.

2   Overview of Framework Design

ICE is a powerful object-oriented communication middleware; it provides basic service modules such as slice, IceStorm and object-oriented communications. However, these modules are not enough for model-and-run applications. Therefore we propose a generic platform to provide conceptual and pragmatic support for DES-based simulation by developing model prototypes based code generation, event management, time management, entity management and WAN functions as Fig. 1 shows.

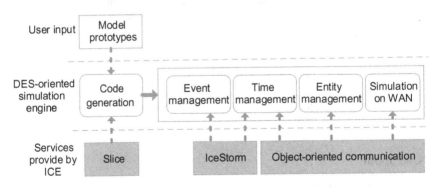

Fig. 1. ICE based framework. Modules with gray background provide by ICE, others developed by this paper.

At the bottom of ISF are the services provide by ICE:

- **Slice:** Ice offers slice language for declaring interfaces and types for building network. It is the fundamental abstraction mechanism for separating object interfaces from their implementations; it will be compiled for a particular implementation language by a compiler built in Ice.

- **IceStorm:** Different data protocols that a simulation entity uses to communicate with others are abstracted as topics. Topics are arranged by IceStorm's topic manager. When a new entity is created during the simulation, ISF dynamically generates the topic names it would subscribe or publish and registers above-mentioned names to IceStorm. When the entity sends an event, IcsStorm would locate the receiver through look up the variable *topic* inside the event.

- **Object-oriented communication:** As ICE is a powerful object-oriented communication middleware. It provides flexible communication methods to establish and manage communication connections on both LAN and WAN.

In the middle layer of ISF is the DES-oriented simulation engine:

- **Discrete Event Simulation (DES):** Discrete Event Simulation has been an active research topic since the beginnings of the computer industry [12, 16]. It is used for modeling physical systems as a collection of processes that consume and produce actions or events that take place at discrete timestamps. The physical system is viewed as comprising some number of physical processes that interact in some fashion [13]. Each physical process is modeled by a logical process while interactions between physical processes are modeled by exchanging events between the corresponding logic processes.

- **Code generation:** It automatically generates simulation code by adopting slice specification and parsing user input.

- **Simulation management:** Including event management, time management, entity management and simulation on WAN.

On the top of ISF is the user input. Users are required to provide related information about their simulation models in format of Extensible Markup Language (XML), which is a markup language that defines a bunch of rules for encoding documents in a format both human-readable and machine-readable.

3   Practical Implementations of ISF

In this section we present the practical realizations of ISF from user level to the bottom level by elaborating their implementations and analyzing their typical features.

3.1   User Input

The structure of user input could be specified as three layer form as Fig. 2-(a) shows. The attribute of first layer declares the models' names. During the following steps, each model would produce a C++ class, which can be instantiated repeatedly during the simulation to achieve dynamic generating worker entities. Giving the fact that the simulation is based on discrete events, the second layer describes the topic types that entity would receive. Eventually, the third layer contains the activities of entity receiving new event, including the declarations of new variables, the operations of states and variables, and the new events that triggered. This three layer architecture refines the necessary details of whole simulation running, based on which the frame would be constructed effectively and efficiently, so that users could just focus on establishing model logic rather than paying attention to network communication and process management.

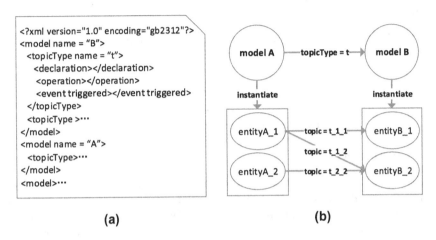

```
<?xml version="1.0" encoding="gb2312"?>
<model name = "B">
  <topicType name = "t">
    <declaration></declaration>
    <operation></operation>
    <event triggered></event triggered>
  </topicType>
  <topicType >···
</model>
<model name = "A">
  <topicType>···
</model>
<model>···
```

(a)   (b)

Fig. 2. Layout of user input and how *topicType* converts to topic during the simulation

There is a special issue to be concerned, as one model may be instantiated to many simulation entities during the simulation, these entities shall share the same kinds of topic types. In order to distinguish different entities, ISF introduces a nomenclature of topics, *topicType* add entity identifier add target identifier. As Fig. 2-(b) shows, there is a *topicType* t publishes by model A and subscribes by model B. A as well as B creates two entities. As consequence of this enactment, when an event, whose *topicType* is t, produces from A_1 to B_2, the topic of the event would set as t_1_2.

3.2   Code Generation

Three main steps included. First of all, ISF extracts network related information from XML document and arrange them into a new text document that meets Slice-language's syntax and semantic rules. At the same time ISF keeps on analyzing XML document and gets the model related information, based on which model classes would be generated (Fig. 3).

Second, ISF invokes compiling services provided by Ice to create network communication APIs, based on which each model could connect to other models and get access to their operations. Put it more bluntly, one entity send events via acquiring the other entity's function handle, which is provided by network communication APIs. The worker model projects encapsulate network APIs and models' business logic from model classes.

At last, users can place these projects, as well as the project of manager model, to different nodes to form distributed simulation environment. In the process of simulation, ISF generates new worker entities dynamically through instantiating their model projects.

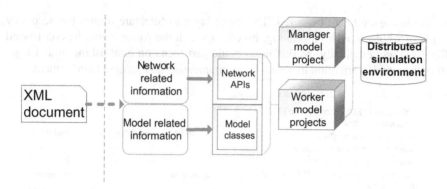

Fig. 3. Automatic code generation process

3.3 Event Management

To build a holonomic simulation framework and construct a sound DES-oriented simulation environment, the design for event's style is momentous significant. A discrete event should have two important attributes concerned with time, the send time represents the simulation time when the event was generated and the receive time describes the simulation time when the event is to take effect. In our case of designing the layout of event, we make it as Fig. 4-(a) shows. In addition, the *sendName* and the *receiveName* express identifies of two communication parties. The *content* is the messages that this event transferring, it can be designed by users on the basis of actual requirements.

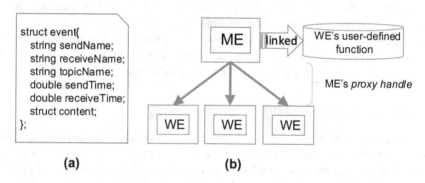

Fig. 4. Event management and entity management

3.4 Entity Management

Inside ISF we present two kinds of entities, manager entity (ME) and worker entity (WE). Figure 4-(b) displays their relationships.

ME is in charge of several affairs, including registering IceBox and IceStorm services which helps to execute event transferring, locating topic manager's endpoint, and creating its *proxy handle*. Before the simulation ME would distribute this handle to each WE. WEs could report their logical time to ME via this handle while simulation is running, in which case ME is able to manage all WEs' temporalities in case of some WEs are advanced or lagged in time. In addition, to increase the commonness of WEs and the efficiency of ISF, all WEs' user-defined functions are gathered to a function library, which is linked to ME. Whenever a WE is in demand of executing a specific function, the *proxy handle* that ME transmitted could help.

A standard WE includes three built-in functions. The first one is responsible for acquiring ME's proxy handle. The second function deals with the events WEs receive. When WEs receive an event, they would pick up the content, react upon the information, and trigger new events, which would be stored to future event list (FEL). The third function processes FELs. As every WE has a logic time and each event has a receive time, this function publishes corresponding events from future event list when its logic time arrives.

3.5 Time Management

As Fig. 5 shows, the time management algorithm is based on several essentials.

1. All of WEs have a same logic time, they can only move forward for one step if ME gives an advance signal to them.
2. The information of currently running WEs is recorded in ME. At every step, ME broadcasts an advance signal to each WE giving the permissions to advance and waits for theirs messages of executing successfully. When every WE calls back, next step starts.
3. As each ME acquires its advance signal, it would check its FEL to publish events that have same receive time with logic time.
4. Whenever a ME receives an event it subscribes, it would react upon the event and write new events to its FEL.

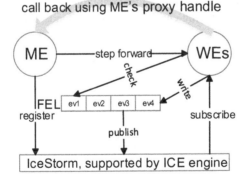

Fig. 5. Time management of ISF

3.6 Simulation on WAN

One of the ISF's most significant features is it supports simulation on Internet. ICE supports Internet Protocol versions 4 and 6 in all language mappings [1]. Users can employ either a host name that is resolved via the Domain Name System (DNS), an IPv4 address in dotted quad notation, or an IPv6 address in 128-bit hexadecimal format and enclosed in double quotes when they deploy the simulation nodes. The simulation process can be specified as Fig. 6. For example, Host1 visits RouterB's port 12337 to get access to Host3's services on port 13337.

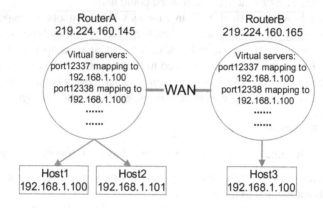

Fig. 6. Simulation on WAN with ISF

4   Case Study

To verify the performance of ISF, a simple anti-air case is implemented. The elementary procedure is shown in Fig. 7. Blue missile entities are launched to attack red target, simultaneously red missile entities are launched to block blue missile entities. The initial locations of red target, blue missile and red missile are (500, 500), (0, 0), and (300, 0) in 2-D plane. Three kinds of events included: red target sends events with topic type *t1* to inform blue missile producing entities every ten seconds; blue missile sends events

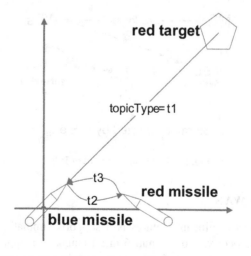

Fig. 7. Use case of antimissile (Color figure online)

with topic type *t2* every one second when its entities are on the way toward red target, position information is included in *t2* so that red missile could updates its entities' positions in time; red missile sends events with topic type *t3* when a red missile entity catches up with its tracking target, in which case these pair of entities perish.

Same scenarios are run under ISF and KD-RTI [9, 15], a software supports simulation using HLA-RTI. During the simulation every step represents one second. Every ten step red target notices blue missile to produce an entity, at the same time red missile launches an entity to trace the blue missile. During the tracing blue missile transmits its positions to red missile every one step. The speed of blue missile and red missile are 1.0 per step and 1.2 per step separately. The calculations of updating positions are relatively inferior so the experiments mostly test communication efficiency. The results depicts in Fig. 8. 8-(a) presents time consumptions of KD-RTI, ISF with LAN and ISF with WAN within 250 steps, it takes them 5.8 s, 3.1 s and 9.3 s separately. 8-(b) shows rates of producing 500 entities. All of simulations are super-real-time and ISF with LAN performs superior than HLA-RTI infrastructure. Several reasons can be put forward to explain this situation. Firstly ICE is a lightweight middleware and IceStorm provides powerful subscribe/publish service to enhance communication efficiency; Then every HLA-RTI entity are an object class and there lacks of an effective management of same kinds of entities, but ISF put all same kinds of entities under one model and communications are operating between models, furthermore ISF adopts topics to distinguish different entities inside a model; At last, time management of ISF is simple but still flexible. Nevertheless, ISF supports simulation in Internet which is not a widely used function in current HLA-RTI products.

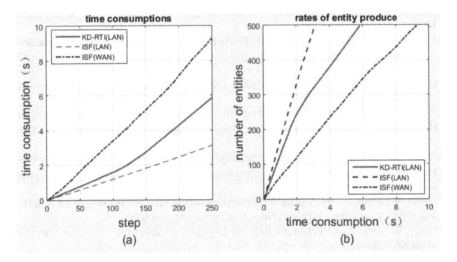

Fig. 8. Result of running the set use case

5 Conclusion and Future Works

In this paper we implemented a simulation framework that integrated automatic code generation, event management, time management and entity management. ISF adopts a powerful middleware ICE as communication toolkit and performs efficient in running discrete event driven systems. Future works include providing visual functions for ISF's inputs and outputs, developing more common-used simulation management methods to render options for operating more systems.

References

1. ZeroC Inc. Ice 3.5.1 Documentation, pp. 17–30 (2013)
2. Wang, W., Wang, W., Zhu, Y., Li, Q.: Service-oriented simulation framework: an overview and unifying methodology. Simulation: Trans. Soc. Model. Simul. Int. **83**(3), 221–252 (2011)
3. Wagner, G., Nicolae, O., Werner, J.: Extending discrete event simulation by adding an activity concept for business process modeling and simulation. In: IEEE Proceedings of the 2009 Winter Simulation Conference, pp. 2951–2962 (2009)
4. Ashtiani, M., Abdollahi Azgomi, M.: A distributed simulation framework for modeling cyber attacks and the evaluation of security measures. Simul. Trans. Soc. Model. Simul. Int. **90**(9), 1071–1102 (2014)
5. Kapos, G.-D., Dalakas, V., Nikolaidou, M., Anagnostopoulos, D.: An integrated framework for automated simulation of SysML models using DEVS. Simul. Trans. Soc. Model. Simul. Int. **9**(6), 717–744 (2014)
6. Tsai, W.T., Fan, C., Chen, Y., Paul, R.: A service-oriented modeling and simulation framework for rapid development of distributed application. Simul. Model. Pract. Theory **14**(6), 725–739 (2006). Elsevier
7. Yang, C., Chi, P., Song, X., Lin, T., Chai, X.: An efficient approach to collaborative simulation of variable structure systems on multi-core machines. Cluster Comput. **19**, 29–46 (2015). Springer
8. IEEE. Standard 1516 (HLA Rules), 1516.1 (Federate Interface Specification) and 1516.2 (Object Model Template) (2000)
9. Pan, K., Turner, S.J., Cai, W., Li, Z.: Multi-user gaming on the grid using a service oriented HLA RTI. In: 13th IEEE/ACM International Symposium on Distributed Simulation and Real Time Applications, pp. 48–56 (2009)
10. Zhang, H., Wang, H., Chen, D.: Integrating Web Services Technology to HLA-based Multidisciplinary Collaborative Simulation System for Complex Product Development, pp. 420–426. IEEE (2008)
11. Zhang, W., Feng, L., Hu, J., Zha, Y.: An approach to service provisioning of HLA RTI as web services. In: IEEE: Asia Simulation Conference, pp. 2–6 (2008)
12. Nance, R., Sargent, R.: Perspectives on the Evolution of Simulation. Syracuse University SURFACE (2002)
13. Miller, R.J.: Optimistic Parallel Discrete Event Simulation on a Beowulf Cluster of Multi-core Machines (2010)
14. Hao, J.: Research and Implementation of Interconnection Technology of Multi-federations in HLA. Nation University of Defense Technology (2003)
15. Zhao, X., Jing, H., Chang, W.: Research on the Flight Simulation System Based on HLA/KD-RTI. Journal of Air Force Engineering University (2005)

16. Song, X., Zhang, L., He, D.J., Ren, Z.Y.: A DEVS based modelling and methodology-COSIM. Appl. Math. Inf. Sci. **6**(2), 417–423 (2012)
17. Xiao, S., Xudong, C., Li, Z.: Modeling framework for product lifecycle information. Simul. Model. Pract. Theory **18**(8), 1080–1091 (2010)

A Survey of the BCI and Its Application Prospect

Xiashuang Wang, Guanghong Gong$^{(\boxtimes)}$, Ni Li, and Yaofei Ma

School of Automation Science and Electrical Engineering,
Beihang University (BUAA), Beijing 100191, China
ggh@buaa.edu.cn

Abstract. Over the past several decades, the Brain-computer interface (BCI) technology has attracted considerable attentions from researchers in the field of aerospace, military simulation, neural engineering, oceanic engineering and pattern recognition. In this paper, we explore the developing process, framework of a BCI system, feature extraction and classification models of machine learning and application on the basis of the latest research for BCI. Meanwhile, challenges of the BCI technology in aerospace systems and space explorations are analyzed. Finally, the application prospects in the modeling and simulation field to support combat training in complex situations are pointed out.

Keywords: BCI · Feature extraction · Machine learning · Aerospace application

1 Introduction

1.1 Emergence and Development of BCI

A BCI provides the central nervous system (CNS) with new outputs that are neither neuromuscular nor hormonal. A BCI is a system that measures CNS activities and convert them into artificial outputs that replace, restore, enhance, supplement, or improve natural CNS outputs and thereby change the ongoing interactions between the CNS and its external or inter environment [1]. Han Berger (1924), a professor of psychiatry at the University of Jena in Germany, discovered that electrical signals produced by human brains could be recorded from the scalp. After fourteen years of further research, Han Berger and Herbert Jasper (1938) envisaged that EEG could also be used for human communication [2].

Now, nearly a century after epochal discovery of Berger, possibility is becoming reality. Although the reality is new and tentative, its excitement and potential are driving the burgeoning field of BCI study. In the past 20 years, many scientists have conducted a variety of researches on BCI and application [3]. Events having significant influence on the development of BCI are shown in Fig. 1. Worldwide BCI technology research has been carried out for many years, the U.S. military expressed a high degree of concern, President Obama administration announced the "promote technological innovation and neurological brain research program", aims to explore the working mechanism of human brain, and eventually develop therapies for diseases of the brain

L. Zhang et al. (Eds.): AsiaSim 2016/SCS AutumnSim 2016, Part IV, CCIS 646, pp. 102–111, 2016.
DOI: 10.1007/978-981-10-2672-0_11

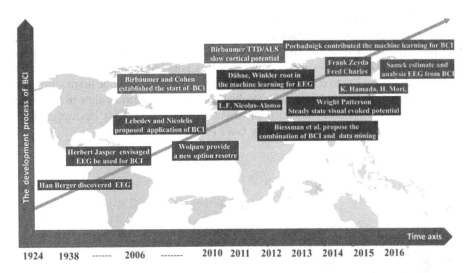

Fig. 1. The development process of BCI

in 2013. The U.S. DARPA announced that it will invest $300 million to support the plan of BCI in 2014 [4].

According to Wolpaw's survey, in the last decade, A BCI has turned from a field with six to eight research groups into aburgeoning career with more than 100 groups worldwide. The BCI research involves many fields widely, including cognitive brain science, military, communications engineering, signal detection and processing, pattern recognition, mathematics, psychology and other multidisciplinary. As an interdisciplinary technology, research and development of the BCI system need cooperation of all kinds of subjects, simultaneously, with the deepening of the BCI technology, also will push the fusion and development of these disciplines.

1.2 Framework of BCI System

There are two types of BCI: invasion and non-invasion. The invasive brain signals are recorded by brain implanted microelectrodes, and the noninvasive brain signals are recorded from cerebral cortex of humans. Owing to invasive methods have a surgical risk, we are interested in noninvasive BCI [5]. In Principle, a framework of BCI system mainly includes four components: signal acquisition, signal processing, feature and classification, external control and feedback devices [6]. As shown in the following Fig. 2.

Many studies of BCI in military are based on this framework. For instance, we provide evidence to control sensorimotor EEG while piloting a flight simulator and attending a double task simultaneously. The subjects are trained to learn how to manage a flight simulator, use the BCI system, and execute the tasks independently. Afterward, the EEG data are collected during a first flight where subjects are required to concurrently use the BCI, and a second flight where they are required to simultaneously use the BCI and execute the tasks. Results showed that the concurrent use of the BCI system during the flight simulation does not affect the flight performances. However, BCI performances decrease from the 83 to 63 % while attending additional alertness and vigilance tasks [7]. This work shows that it is possible to successfully control a BCI system during the execution of multiple tasks such as piloting a flight simulator with an extra cognitive load induced by tasks [6, 8]. Such framework aims to foster the knowledge on BCI systems embedded into flight simulator and robotic devices to allow the simultaneous execution of secondary tasks [9].

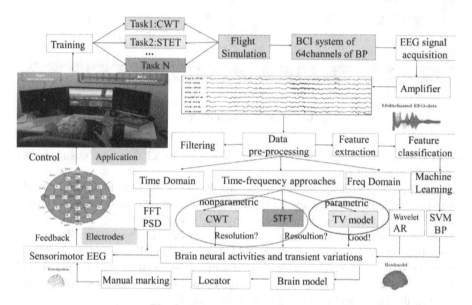

Fig. 2. Framework of BCI system

2 Sources of EEG Signals and Core Technology

2.1 Sources of EEG Signals

In specific experiments, EEG are recorded by a variety of different electrophysiological and metabolic approaches. This greatly simplified diagram shows the production of a normal motor action by the many CNS areas that collaborate to control spinal motoneurons and thereby activate muscles, as shown in the Fig. 2. The red color indicates that all the CNS areas adapt to optimize muscle control. This diagram B shows the BCI system mediated action by the same CNS areas, which now collaborate to optimize the control by the cortical area that produces the brain signals that the BCI translates into its output commands. The BCI assigns to the cortex the output role normally performed by spinal and thereby asks that the CNS areas adapt to optimize an entirely new kind of output. This change in the target of CNS adaptation is indicated in the illustration by the fact that the color of all these green areas no matches the BCI (Fig. 3).

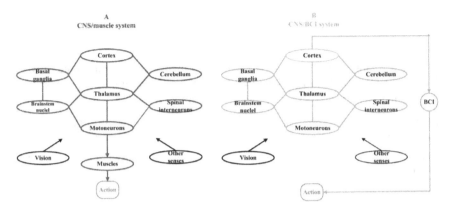

Fig. 3. CNS production of muscle-based action versus CNS production of BCI-based action (Color figure online)

2.2   Signal Processing and Feature Extraction Technology

Signal processing and analysis are the core part of the BCI system, and its essence is the signal feature extraction and pattern classification. It converts the recorded EEG to output signals controlling the external devices. Dietch published with FFT transform analysis of the article for the first time in 1932. With the further development of signal processing technology, the classical time domain analysis method has been developed [10]. There are many feature extraction technologies including time-spatial pattern analysis, statistical analysis, chaos analysis [6], spatial filtering method, AR model coefficient, fast FFT, single neuron separation and wavelet packet transform. The time domain method mainly analysis geometric properties of EEG, such as wave form analysis, such as amplitude, mean, variance, skew and so on. Meanwhile, frequency domain analysis method is mainly based on the frequency band power and coherence [11]. Through the BCI system, it will be converted into a series of external control commands, which is essentially a pattern recognition process of the signal [12–14]. Signal analysis generally consists of three steps:

In the first step, the recorded data is passed through a band-pass filter of 5–50 Hz to eliminate the lower and upper extra frequencies [14].

In the second step, in order to evaluate the proposed system in real-time applications, several temporal durations were considered. Each setting time data is divided into non-overlapping segments with the length equal to each sweep.

For feature extraction step two methods were employed to each observation, which is defined as follows:

1. FFT-Based Feature: This feature extraction method applies the Fast Fourier Transform on each segment, then divides the result by N, which is the all samples of Fourier transform of segment, then the amplitudes in the main frequencies construct the feature vector. The mathematical representation is as follows:

$$feature = \frac{|FFT\{x_n\}|_{f=MF}}{N} \tag{1}$$

Where, x_n is the segmented data in each sweep length, $|\cdot|$ is the absolute operator, FFT $\{\cdot\}$ is the Discrete Fourier Transform, MF is the main twinkling frequency and N is the total number of samples in frequency domain.

2. PSD-Based Feature: This feature extraction method calculates the Power Spectral Density (PSD) of each segment by calculating the Fourier transform of the auto-correlation of each segment. Where R_{xx}^n is the autocorrelation function of the n_{th} segment $x_n(t)$.

$$feature = \frac{|FFT\{R_{xx}^n\}|_{f=MF}}{N} \tag{2}$$

2.3   Feature Classification Technology and Evaluation

Signal classification is achieved through the classifier, including two types of linear and nonlinear. Linear classifier includes linear discriminant analysis (LDA) and fisher discriminant analysis. Nonlinear classifier includes support vector machine (SVM), Bayesian-Kalman Filter, artificial neural nets (ANN), genetic algorithm (GA), fuzzy algorithm (FA), deep learning [15, 16]. However, supervised learning (classification) is facing a new challenge is how to deal with the EEG data [17]. Currently, classification problem of big data is widespread, but traditional classification algorithms cannot process big data [18].

Decision tree model. As a classical classification algorithm, the decision tree uses a top-down recursive way and crushes one by one to construct. At each node of the tree, the information gain is used to measure the properties of the selected test. Rules can be extracted from the generated decision tree. However, there is the problem of excessive memory to BCI big data [19]. Franco-Arcega proposed a method to construct a decision tree from large-scale data to solve the some limited conditions of current algorithm. It can make use of all the data in the training set, but does not need to save all them in memory. The experimental results show that calculation speed of this method is faster than the other current decision tree algorithm in big data problems [20]. Yang presents a fast incremental optimization decision tree algorithm that can process BCI big data with noise. Compared with the traditional decision tree algorithm of mining data, the advantage of this algorithm is that it has the ability to dig data in real time. When the mobile data stream is unlimited, it can store complete data for training decision model. The advantage of this model can prevent explosive growth and prediction accuracy in the data stream containing noise. Simultaneously, it can also generate compact decision tree with higher prediction accuracy. Ben-Haim proposed a algorithm to build a decision tree classifier. It is running in a distributed environment, and is applicable to big data sets and data flow just like BCI data. The method can improve the efficiency compared with the serial decision tree in the premise of the accuracy error approximation.

Support vector machine model. As a machine learning method based on statistical learning theory. SVM can automatically find out the support vectors which have a better ability to classify. Therefore, the classifier can be constructed to maximize interval between classes, and have better adaptability and higher accuracy [21]. But this method has two bottlenecks for big data classification: First, computation-intense, that cannot be used for large data set. Second, the prediction of fitting model of robust and nonparametric confidence intervals is often unknown. In view, Lau proposed an on-line learning algorithm for SVM, and generalization ability is better and faster to use less support vector [11, 22]. Laskov proposed a fast, numerically stable and robust machine learning methods of incremental support vector.

For the problem of EEG data classification, on the basic of principal component analysis of incremental kernel and conjugate gradient of least squares SVM algorithm, Kim proposed for feature extraction and classification algorithms for big data. The algorithm requires less memory, without storing large matrix, can better solve the classification problem of big data. The linear hyper-planes generated by LDA and SVM classifiers were used to classify the whole dataset. For evaluating the performance of the proposed system, the mean accuracy of the all subjects was calculated. The accuracy for each classifier is defined as follows:

$$Accuracy = \frac{TP + TN}{TP + TN + FP + FN} \tag{3}$$

Where, True-Positive (TP) and False-Negative (FN) are the numbers of truly classified and misclassified observations with positive label, respectively. True-Negative (TN) and False-Positive (FP) are the same as TP and FN with negative label.

Next, for measuring the feasibility of the proposed system, the Information Transfer Rate (ITR) was calculated. This measuring index takes into account both the speed and the accuracy of the system to select the best sweep length with the appropriate feature extraction method. ITR is defined as follows:

$$V = \log_2 N + P \log_2 P + (1 - P) \log_2[(1 - P)(N - 1)] \tag{4}$$

Where, N is the number of the system classes, P is the classifier accuracy, and V indicates the information available in each of the trials in bits/trial unit. In the (4), the information, V can be measured in bits/min [23].

3 Five Categories of Applications of BCI

A BCI can records brain signals and extracts specific features from them, and translates these features into artificial outputs that act on the body itself or the outside word. The following Fig. 4 shows the five categories of applications of BCI. Each of the relevant examples are enumerated.

3.1 Replacement

A BCI output might replace natural output that has been lost as a result of injury or disease. It will play a role in the future war? For example, in military fighting, a pilot who can no longer manipulate battle-plane might use the BCI to control the flight and complete the operation of the aircraft. Just like the science fiction film "Avatar" in the scene, through the idea of control of another "body" to fight, the real formation of the Avatar arm. It can be predicted that BCI technology can not only provide the help for the body injured, but it will bring a profound change in the future war [24]. In these examples the BCI outputs replace lost natural output [4, 7].

3.2 Restoration

A BCI output might restore natural output. For example, a person with spinal cord injury whose arms and hands are paralyzed might use of a BCI to stimulate the paralyzed muscles via implanted electrodes so that the muscles move the limbs. Accordingly, the BCI can help the injured soldiers to restore the nervous function and behavior [25, 26].

3.3 Enhancement

A BCI output might enhance natural CNS output. For example, using BCI techniques in aerospace systems and space explorations, one can think that an astronaut operates a robot device by only imagining. This astronaut not only reduces the brain fatigue of pilots, but also enhances the reliability and fault tolerance of aerial vehicles.

3.4 Supplement

A BCI output might supple natural CNS output. For example, a person who is controlling the position of a computer cursor with a hand-operated joystick might use a BCI to select items that the cursor reaches. Or a person might use the BCI to control a third arm and hand of robot. In these cases, the BCI supplements natural neuromuscular output with an additional, artificial output.

3.5 Improvement

A BCI output might conceivably improve natural CNS output. In ocean engineering, for detection of mine-like objects (MLOs) inside scan sonar imagery have used BCI systems to improve computer vision and human vision capabilities alone [27]. Another example, for whose arm movements have been impaired by stroke. Sensorimotor cortex use a BCI that measures signals from the damages cortical areas and then stimulates muscles or controls an orthotic device so as to improve arm movements. The first two kinds of application of a BCI are the purposes of most current BCI research. Simultaneously, the other applications are also possible.

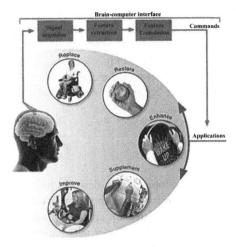

Fig. 4. The basic design and operation of a BCI system

4   Existing Problems and Prospect

Due to BCI technology is a relatively complex, involving the contents and related fields. Therefore, the BCI technology itself and its application are still in the exploratory stage. To allow the BCI technology out of the laboratory should be used in practice, there are many problems to be solved.

- Processing of BCI data

BCI data have the characteristics of sparse attributes, super high dimension, high noise and complex relationship, which leads to the difficulty in processing and analyzing the traditional machine learning algorithms.

- Stability and versatility of BCI performance

The ground soldier have been tested that using the BCI based controlled system is 9.18 % less than using the non-BCI based controlled system. However, there is no usable commercial BCI in our daily lives for the current state. Despite it has many advances, researchers and developers still struggle with the critical problem that stability and versatility of BCI performance.

- Development of application field

With the continuous development and improvement of BCI technology, we need to develop new application areas. Meanwhile, we also need research how to combine the various technologies and different application areas, and develop a practical, comprehensive BCI application system. For example, to apply BCI techniques to space system control, some special issues such as: human physiology in space, microgravity, and effects of radiation must be thoroughly studied within the context of BCI techniques because these issues may have profound influences on brain activities. In addition, there are other significant challenges that include low throughput, high error rate, autonomy, cognitive load for the development of BCI techniques. These challenges exist for both restoration and space mission applications, but more demanding in the latter application. It is hoped that the study of human cognition will offer some inspiration to find the relationship between human and their behavioral capacities. It will help us to establish the better behavior model of soldiers to support the combat training in the military simulation.

5   Conclusions

In this paper, we review the development, framework, processing models and application prospect of the BCI system based on the current research status of BCI. The study of BCI is becoming a new frontier hot spot with brain science, military, rehabilitation engineering, data mining and computer automatic control fields. Overall, the research of BCI is in the development stage, existing low speed in communication. For future studies, we suggest that the researchers spend longer time to test to the target, and increase the communication and integrative studies between the various related subjects. With the continuous development and integration of various disciplines, it is believed that it will promote its development to a higher level of science and technology, and will be applied in more fields, and benefit human ultimately.

References

1. Gao, S., Wang, Y., Gao, X., et al.: Visual and auditory brain–computer interfaces. IEEE Trans. Biomed. Eng. **61**(5), 1436–1447 (2014)
2. Wolpaw, J., Wolpaw, E.W.: Brain-computer interfaces: principles and practice. OUP USA (2012)
3. Tangermann, M., Müller, K.-R., Aertsen, A., et al.: Review of the BCI competition IV. Front Neurosci. **6**(55), 2 (2012)
4. George, K., Iniguez, A., Donze, H., et al.: Design, implementation and evaluation of a brain-computer interface controlled mechanical arm for rehabilitation. In: 2014 IEEE International Instrumentation and Measurement Technology Conference (I2MTC) Proceedings, pp. 1326–1328 (2014)
5. Nam, S., Kim, K.H., Kim, D-.S.: Motor trajectory decoding based on fMRI-based BCI—A simulation study. In: 2013 International Winter Workshop on Brain-Computer Interface (BCI), pp. 89–91 (2013)
6. Sato, T., Okuyama, Y., Sakai, M.: Simulation study of a P300 speller for single-lead hybrid BCI. In: 2013 Proceedings of SICE Annual Conference (SICE), pp. 2017–2023 (2013)
7. Vecchiato, G., Borghini, G., Aricò, P., et al.: Investigation of the effect of EEG-BCI on the simultaneous execution of flight simulation and attentional tasks. Medical & Biological Engineering & Computing, 1–11 (2015)
8. Looned, R., Webb, J., Xiao, Z.G., et al.: Assisting drinking with an affordable BCI-controlled wearable robot and electrical stimulation: a preliminary investigation. J. Neuroengineering Rehabil. **11**(1), 1 (2014)

9. Kasper, R.W., Cecotti, H., Touryan, J., et al.: Isolating the neural mechanisms of interference during continuous multisensory dual-task performance. J. Cogn. Neurosci. **26**(3), 476–489 (2014)

10. Chen, S-.C., Hsu, C-.H., Kuo, H-.C., et al.: The BCI control applied to the interactive autonomous robot with the function of meal assistance. In: Proceedings of the 3rd International Conference on Intelligent Technologies and Engineering Systems (ICITES 2014), pp. 475–483 (2016)

11. Baig, M.Z., Mehmood, Y., Ayaz, Y.: A BCI system classification technique using median filtering and wavelet transform. In: Dynamics in Logistics, pp. 355–364. Springer, Switzerland (2016)

12. Höller, Y., Bergmann, J., Thomschewski, A., et al.: Comparison of EEG-features and classification methods for motor imagery in patients with disorders of consciousness. PLoS ONE **8**(11), e80479 (2013)

13. Pfurtscheller, G., Allison, B.Z., Bauernfeind, G., et al.: The hybrid BCI. Front. Neurosci. **4**, 3 (2010)

14. Duan, L., Xu, Y., Cui, S., et al.: Feature extraction of motor imagery EEG based on extreme learning machine auto-encoder. In: Proceedings of ELM-2015, vol. 1, pp. 361–370. Springer (2016)

15. Aljshamee, M., Nadir, S., Malekpour, A., et al.: Discriminate the brain responses of multiple colors based on regular/irregular SSVEP paradigms. J. Med. Bioengineering **5**(2) (2016)

16. Hennrich, J., Herff, C., Heger, D., et al.: Investigating deep learning for fNIRS based BCI. In: 2015 37th Annual International Conference of the IEEE Engineering in Medicine and Biology Society (EMBC), pp. 2844–2847 (2015)

17. Lemm, S., Blankertz, B., Dickhaus, T., et al.: Introduction to machine learning for brain imaging. Neuroimage **56**(2), 387–399 (2011)

18. Fazli, S., Danóczy, M., Schelldorfer, J., et al.: ℓ 1-penalized Linear Mixed-Effects Models for high dimensional data with application to BCI. NeuroImage **56**(4), 2100–2108 (2011)

19. Lin, H., Yang, S., Midkiff, S.P.: RABID–a general distributed R processing framework targeting large data-set problems. In: 2013 IEEE International Congress on Big Data (BigData Congress), pp. 423–424 (2013)

20. Farid, D.M., Zhang, L., Rahman, C.M., et al.: Hybrid decision tree and naïve Bayes classifiers for classification tasks. Expert Syst. Appl. **41**(4), 1937–1946 (2014)

21. Kumar, A., Mohanty, M.N., Routray, A.: Design of support vector machines with time frequency kernels for classification of EEG signals. In: 2010 IEEE Students' Technology Symposium (TechSym), pp. 330–333 (2010)

22. Lau, H.-Y., Tong, K.-Y., Zhu, H.: Support vector machine for classification of walking conditions of persons after stroke with dropped foot. Hum. Mov. Sci. **28**(4), 504–514 (2009)

23. Resalat, S.N., Afdideh, F.: Real-time monitoring of military sentinel sleepiness using a novel SSVEP-based BCI system. In: 2012 IEEE EMBS Conference on Biomedical Engineering and Sciences (IECBES), pp. 740–745 (2012)

24. Leeb, R., Friedman, D., Müller-Putz, G.R., et al.: Self-paced (asynchronous) BCI control of a wheelchair in virtual environments: a case study with a tetraplegic. Comput. Intell. Neurosci. **2007** (2007)

25. Gomez-Pilar, J., Corralejo, R., Nicolas-Alonso, L.F., et al.: Neurofeedback training with a motor imagery-based BCI: neurocognitive improvements and EEG changes in the elderly. Med. Biol. Eng. Comput. 1–12 (2016)

26. Craelius, W.: The bionic man: restoring mobility. Science **295**(5557), 1018–1021 (2002)

27. Barngrover, C., Althoff, A., Deguzman, P., et al.: A Brain–Computer Interface (BCI) for the Detection of Mine-Like Objects in Sidescan Sonar Imagery (2016)

An Improved Jousselme Evidence Distance

Haiying Wang, Wei Li, Xiaochao Qian, and Ming Yang[✉]

Control and Simulation Center, Harbin Institute of Technology,
Harbin 150080, People's Republic of China
whydiana@163.com, {frank,myang}@hit.edu.cn,
everqxc@hotmail.com

Abstract. Evidence distance can be used in uncertainty simulation result validation, especially when the simulation model has epistemic uncertainty. Jousselme evidence distance (JED) and a modified Jousselme evidence distance (MJED) are introduced and analyzed first. Then the paper points out problems that they have when they measure the difference between two bodies of evidence: JED will measure two bodies of general evidence unreasonably; The distance value of MJED will be too large sometimes. An improved Jousselme evidence distance (IJED) is proposed to solve these problems. IJED can measure the dissimilarly between category evidence and general evidence as JED and MJED. And the distance value of IJED is within reasonable range when it measures two bodies of general evidence. Furthermore, IJED can measure the difference better when probability distribution parameters of the variable for the body of evidence change. Two numerical examples are illustrated to compare the three distances.

Keywords: Evidence distance · Jousselme distance · Simulation · Uncertainty

1 Introduction

Evidence theory is proposed by Dempster [1] and Shafer [2], because of which it is also known as Dempster–Shafer theory. Evidence theory provides a representation for uncertainty that permits the specification of more structure than possibility theory and less structure than probability theory [3]. The body of evidence represents the state of beliefs about the situation based on the given observations. One is able to compare algorithms for efficiency by quantifying distances between the bodies of evidence from these algorithms and a selected criteria body of evidence. The distance for two bodies of evidence has been applied in computing approximations of belief functions, belief functions clustering, evidential data classification and evidential sensor reliability assessment areas [4]. Evidence distance can be applied in simulation result validation. When a simulation model includes epistemic uncertainty, model outputs can be transformed into cumulative distribution functions which are the type of p-box. Evidence theory contains definitions of CPF and CBF [3] which are similar to the left-hand and right-hand boundary in a p-box. Therefore simulation outputs can be transformed into evidence theory to validate the simulation model through evidence distance.

Dissimilarity measures for bodies of evidence are found in some literature. Tessem [5] uses pignistic transform to turn a belief function into the least committed probability

L. Zhang et al. (Eds.): AsiaSim 2016/SCS AutumnSim 2016, Part IV, CCIS 646, pp. 112–120, 2016.
DOI: 10.1007/978-981-10-2672-0_12

distribution. The dissimilarity is thus calculated in a probability space. Bauer [6] introduced two other measures based on pignistic probabilities. Liu [7] used jointly Tessem's distance with Dempster's conflict to define a new conflict measure. Jousselme [8] gave a geometrical interpretation of evidence body and proposed the evidence distance which used the Jaccard coefficient as a similarity measure between focal elements. The Jousselme evidence distance satisfies all the requirements for a metric. Han [9] transformed the body of evidence into fuzzy set theory and then used the dissimilarity in fuzzy set theory to define the dissimilarities between bodies of evidence. Peng [10] proposed a modified distance of evidence by changing the denominator of Jousselme distance.

This paper studied and compared JED and MJED and then proposed an improved Jousselme evidence distance (IJED) to overcome existing problems of them. This paper is organized as follows. Section 1 recalls formulas of JED and MJED. And then Sect. 1 analyzes problems they have. Section 2 proposes IJED and represents advantages of the distance proposed. Section 3 constructs several different distributions of variables to illustrate advantages of IJED further.

2   Jousselme Evidence Distance and a Modified Distance

JED and MJED is defined as Definitions 1 and 2.

Definition 1. Let m_1 and m_2 be two BPAs on the same frame of discernment Θ, containing N mutually exclusive hypotheses. $\Theta = \{1, 2, \ldots N\}$. The power set of Θ, represented by $P(\Theta)$, is the set containing all possible subsets of Θ and consists of 2^N elements. $P(\Theta)$ is shown in Eq. (1).

$$P(\Theta) = \{\emptyset, 1, \ldots, N, (1,2), (1,3), \ldots, (N-1,N), (1,2,3), \ldots, \Theta\} \tag{1}$$

The JED between m_1 and m_2 is defined as:

$$d_{BPA}(m_1, m_2) = \sqrt{\frac{1}{2}(\|\vec{m}_1\|^2 + \|\vec{m}_2\|^2 - 2\langle \vec{m}_1, \vec{m}_2 \rangle)} \tag{2}$$

Where, $\vec{m}_1, \vec{m}_2$ is vectors of BPAs; $\|\vec{m}\|^2 = \langle \vec{m}, \vec{m} \rangle$; $\langle \vec{m}_1, \vec{m}_2 \rangle$ is defined as:

$$\langle \vec{m}_1, \vec{m}_2 \rangle = \sum_{i=1}^{2^N} \sum_{j=1}^{2^N} m_1(A_i) m_2(A_j) \frac{|A_i \cap A_j|}{|A_i \cup A_j|} A_i, A_j \in P(\Theta) \tag{3}$$

Definition 2. m_1 and m_2 is defined the same as in Definition 1. The MJED between m_1 and m_2 is defined as:

$$md_{BPA}(m_1, m_2) = \sqrt{\frac{\|\vec{m}_1\|^2 + \|\vec{m}_2\|^2 - 2\langle \vec{m}_1, \vec{m}_2 \rangle}{\|\vec{m}_1\|^2 + \|\vec{m}_2\|^2}} \tag{4}$$

Where $\|\vec{m}\|^2$ and $\langle \vec{m}_1, \vec{m}_2 \rangle$ is defined the same as Definition 1.

The range of JED and MJED values is [0,1]. And the larger dissimilarity between two bodies of evidence, the greater distance values will be. After research, the problems of the two methods are as follows.

Problem 1. For two disjoint bodies of evidence, the intersection of each focal from m_1 and each focal from m_2 is 0, i.e. $\langle \vec{m}_1, \vec{m}_2 \rangle = 0$. Therefore Eq. (2) is converted as follow.

$$d_{BPA}(m_1, m_2) = \sqrt{\frac{1}{2}(\|\vec{m}_1\|^2 + \|\vec{m}_2\|^2)} \tag{5}$$

If and only if m_1 and m_2 are both category evidence (The body of evidence only have one focal element), $\|\vec{m}_1\|^2 = 1$ and $\|\vec{m}_2\|^2 = 1$. At this time $d_{BPA}(m_1, m_2) = 1$. But in most cases, at least one of them is general evidence (The body of evidence have more than one focal element). Therefore $\|\vec{m}_1\|^2 + \|\vec{m}_2\|^2 < 2$, $d_{BPA}(m_1, m_2) < 1$. That is when there are intersection of two bodies of evidence, the value of JED is not 1 but less than 1, which is unreasonable.

Problem 2. The distance value of MJED can be seriously large sometimes. More detail is represented in Example 1.

Example 1. Two cumulative probability distribution curves in Fig. 1 is denoted as y-r and y-s. We get m_r and m_s by outer discrete method (ODM) [11], where the number of focal is 8. Then we use JED and MJED to measure the dissimilarity of m_r and m_s. The distance values are listed in Table 1.

The result of JED and MJED is 0.1584 and 0.4481 respectively. The difference of m_r and m_s is small from Fig. 1. Therefore the distance value of MJED is obviously too large. Bring $\|\vec{m}_r\|^2$ and $\|\vec{m}_s\|^2$ into Eqs. (2) and (4) and then we have:

$$d_{BPA}(m_r, m_{s1}) = \sqrt{\frac{0.25 - 2\langle \vec{m}_r, \vec{m}_s \rangle}{2}}$$

$$md_{BPA}(m_r, m_{s1}) = \sqrt{\frac{0.25 - 2\langle \vec{m}_r, \vec{m}_s \rangle}{0.25}}$$

The denominator under root sign of JED is 2. The denominator under root sign of MJED is 0.25. Because in most case $\|\vec{m}_1\|^2 + \|\vec{m}_2\|^2 < 2$, the distance value of MJED can be very large sometimes. The smaller $\|\vec{m}_1\|^2 + \|\vec{m}_2\|^2$ is, the larger value of MJED will be. We also use examples that JED and MJED have to illustrate that IJED can measure the dissimilarly between category evidence and general evidence as JED and MJED.

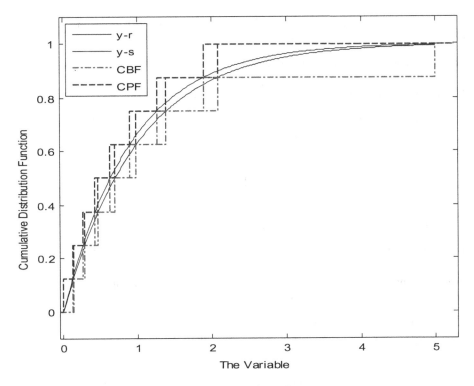

Fig. 1. Curves and transformation process

Table 1. Intermediate variables and values of JED and MJED

Intermediate variables			Distance values	
$\|\vec{m}_r\|^2$	$\|\vec{m}_s\|^2$	$\langle \vec{m}_r, \vec{m}_s \rangle$	JED	MJED
0.1250	0.1250	0.0999	0.1584	0.4481

3 Improved Jousselme Evidence Distance

To solve problems above, this paper proposes an improved distance based on Jousselme evidence distance. It is defined as below.

Definition 3. The IJED between m_1 and m_2 is defined as:

$$id_{BPA}(m_1, m_2) = 1 - \sqrt{\frac{2\langle \vec{m}_1, \vec{m}_2 \rangle}{\|\vec{m}_1\|^2 + \|\vec{m}_2\|^2}} \qquad (6)$$

Where, $\|\vec{m}\|^2$ and $\langle \vec{m}_1, \vec{m}_2 \rangle$ is defined the same as Definition 1. It has the following properties.

(1) Boundedness. $id_{BPA}(m_1, m_2) \in [0, 1]$;

Proof: From Jousselme distance [8], we know $d_{BPA}(m_1, m_2) \in [0, 1]$, thus $0 \le \sqrt{\frac{1}{2}(\|\vec{m}_1\|^2 + \|\vec{m}_2\|^2 - 2\langle \vec{m}_1, \vec{m}_2 \rangle)} \le 1$. Then we get $2\langle \vec{m}_1, \vec{m}_2 \rangle \le \|\vec{m}_1\|^2 + \|\vec{m}_2\|^2$. Since $\|\vec{m}_1\|^2 + \|\vec{m}_2\|^2 > 0, \langle \vec{m}_1, \vec{m}_2 \rangle \ge 0$, we have

$$0 \le \frac{2\langle \vec{m}_1, \vec{m}_2 \rangle}{\|\vec{m}_1\|^2 + \|\vec{m}_2\|^2} \le 1$$

Therefore we get $0 \le id_{BPA}(m_1, m_2) \le 1$.

(2) Reflexivity.

Proof: By property 1, we can see $id_{BPA}(m_1, m_2) \in [0, 1]$. And when $m_1 = m_2 = m$, $id_{BPA}(m_1, m_2)$ is always equal to 0, where $0 \in [0, 1]$.

(3) Symmetry. $id_{BPA}(m_1, m_2) = id_{BPA}(m_2, m_1)$.
(4) $id_{BPA}(m_1, m_2) = 1$, if and only if $\langle \vec{m}_1, \vec{m}_2 \rangle = 0$.

IJED has solved two problems which have been shown in Sect. 1.

To problem 1. For two disjoint bodies of evidence, i.e. $\langle \vec{m}_1, \vec{m}_2 \rangle = 0$, we have $id_{BPA}(m_1, m_2) = 1 - 0 = 1$. Therefore IJED can measure such two bodies of evidence correctly.

To problem 2. When IJED measure the difference of two bodies of evidence, the distance value won't be too large. We use Example 1 to illustrate that. The results of JED, MJED and IJED are listed in Table 2.

Table 2. Values of three distances in Example 1

Body of evidence	JED	MJED	IJED
m_r and m_{s1}	0.1584	0.4481	0.1060

From Table 2, we can see that the value of MJED is too large, while results of JED and IJED are within reasonable range.

4 Comparing Three Distances Under Several Probability Distributions

Not like probability theory that can represent the probability of each single element, evidence theory can only represent the probability of some sets due to insufficient information[12]. So evidence theory can be approximately understood as estimate of probability theory. This section designs two experiments (Examples 2 and 3) based on different probability distribution situations. We use ODM to transform into the body of evidence. Then three distances are used to measure these bodies of evidence. Example 2 fixes the standard deviation of the distribution and change the mean of the distribution. In contrast, Example 3 fixes the mean of the distribution and change the of the distribution standard deviation. Since evidence is an approximation of probability theory, the dissimilarity will be smaller when two probability distributions get closer.

Example 2. The abscissa of cumulative normal distribution, N(2.5,1), is 0 to 5. We gain the body of evidence m_{00} by ODM, where the number of focal is 8. In the same way we gain the body of evidence m_{01} by ODM from cumulative normal distribution N1(2.5 + mu,1). The variable mu varies from −6 to 6 and the step is 0.02. Figure 2 shows distance curves of JED, MJED and IJED.

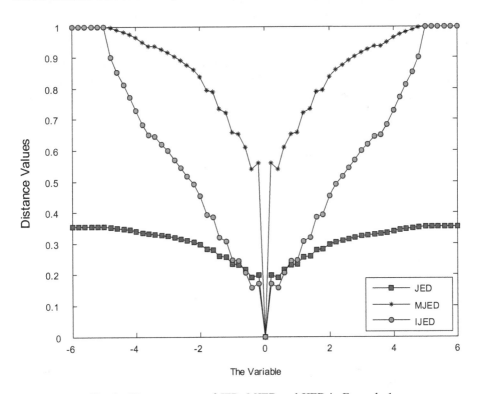

Fig. 2. Distance curves of JED, MJED and IJED in Example 1

When mu < 0, the distance between m_{00} and m_{01} gets smaller as mu increases; When mu > 0, the distance between m_{00} and m_{01} gets larger as mu increases; the distance gets smallest value when m_{00} and m_{01} are equal, i.e. mu = 0. As a whole, all the three curves are reflecting the real trend. Furthermore, we draw conclusions as below.

(1) m_{01} is close to m_{00} when mu = ±0.2, so the distance of them should be small. The value of JED and IJED is about 0.2, which is reasonable. However the value of MJED is about 0.55, which is obviously large. The reason for unreasonable value of MJED is due to its denominator.

(2) Since there is no intersection between m_{00} and m_{01}, their distance should be 1 when $|mu| > 5$. The value of MJED and IJED is 1. But the value of JED is 0.3536, which is not reasonable. When $2 \leq |mu| \leq 6$, values of JED vary from 0.2962 to 0.3536. As we can see, the varying interval is small.

(3) The distance of IJED varies more uniformly with the change of probability distribution parameters than other two distances. It is helpful for people to make decisions when the distance varies uniformly. For example, there are three bodies of evidence and the distance between them and a selected criteria body of evidence. When the distance varies uniformly, we can know the difference between m_1 and m_2 is about equal to the difference between m_2 and m_3.

Example 3. The body of evidence m_{02} is obtained from cumulative normal distribution N(2.5,1) and the number of focal is 8. The body of evidence m_{03} is obtained from cumulative normal distribution N2(2.5,sigm), where sigma varies from 0.5 to 1.5 with step 0.2. And the number of focal for m_{03} is 8 too. Figure 3 shows distance curves of JED, MJED and IJED.

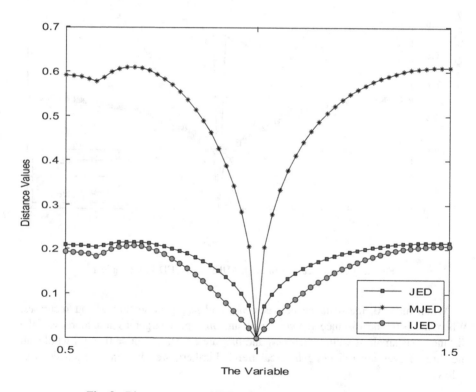

Fig. 3. Distance curves of JED, MJED and IJED in Example 2

The difference between m_{02} and m_{03} should decrease first and then increase when sigma increased from 0.5 to 1.5. When sigma = 1, the difference should be 0. From Fig. 3, all the three curves are reflecting the real trend. We can see that MJED still has the problem of large distance values. Values of JED and IJED change similarly. The later varies more uniformly.

5 Conclusions

In summary, this paper proposes a new distance between two bodies which is called IJED. IJED overcomes some problems that JED and MJED existed. And it has the following advantages: It can measure two bodies of evidence with no intersection; The value of IJED is within a reasonable range; The distance varies uniformly with the change of probability distribution parameters. As a result, IJED can measure difference between bodies of evidence better in simulation result validation and help people make decisions based on results. However IJED has not been proven to meet the triangle inequality, so it doesn't satisfy all the requirements of the distance. When the difference changes monotonously through theoretical analysis, the distance value of these three methods is not always absolutely monotonous. These problems need further research.

References

1. Dempster, A.P.: Upper and lower probabilities induced by a multivalued mapping. In: Yager, R.R., Liu, L., Szczuka, M.S., Düntsch, I., Yao, Y. (eds.) Classic Works of the Dempster-Shafer Theory of Belief Functions. STUDFUZZ (LNAI), vol. 219, pp. 57–72. Springer, Heidelberg (2005)
2. Shafer, G.: A Mathematical Theory of Evidence. Princeton University Press, Princeton (1976)
3. Helton, J.C., Johnson, J.D.: Quantification of margins and uncertainties: Alternative representations of epistemic uncertainty. Reliab. Eng. Syst. Safety **96**, 1034–1052 (2011)
4. Loudahi, M., Klein, J., Vannobel, J., Colot, O.: New distances between bodies of evidence based on Dempsterian specialization matrices and their consistency with the conjunctive combination rule. Int. J. Approximate Reasoning **55**, 1093–1112 (2014)
5. Tessem, B.: Approximations for efficient computation in the theory of evidence. Artif. Intell. **61**, 315–329 (1993)
6. Bauer, M.: Approximation algorithms and decision making in the Dempster-Shafer theory of evidence — An empirical study. Int. J. Approximate Reasoning **17**, 217–237 (1997)
7. Liu, W.: Analyzing the degree of conflict among belief functions. Artif. Intell. **170**, 909–924 (2006)
8. Jousselme, A., Grenier, D., Bossé, É.: A new distance between two bodies of evidence. Inf. Fusion **2**, 91–101 (2001)
9. Han, D., Onera, J.D., Han, C., Yang, Y.: New dissimilarity measures in evidence theory. In: 14th International Conference on Information Fusion, pp. 1–7 (2011)

10. Hu, P.Y., Zenghui, S.H.: A modified distance of evidence. J. Electron. Inf. Technol. **35**, 1624–1629 (2013)
11. Tonon, F.: Using random set theory to propagate epistemic uncertainty through a mechanical system. Reliab. Eng. Syst. Safety **85**, 169–181 (2004)
12. Bae, H., Grandhi, R.V., Canfield, R.A.: Uncertainty quantification of structural response using evidence theory. AIAA J. **41**, 2062–2068 (2003)

Finite-Time Stability Analysis of Fractional-Order High-Order Hopfield Neural Networks with Delays

Pan Wang[✉]

Applied Mathematics, Xuchang University, Xuchang 461000, China
wp521009@126.com

Abstract. In this paper, a class of fractional-order high-order Hopfield neural networks with delays are considered. By using the generalized Gronwall inequality, some new sufficient conditions are established to ensure the existence and uniqueness of the nontrivial solution. Moreover, finite-time stability of the fractional-order neural networks is proposed in fixed time intervals. Finally, an example is presented to illustrate the effectiveness of our results.

Keywords: High-order Hopfield neural networks · Fractional order · The generalized Gronwall inequality · Finite-time stability

1 Introduction

It is well known that the fractional calculus is a classical mathematical notion and a generalization of ordinary differentiation and integration to arbitrary (non-integer) order. However, the fractional calculus did not attract much attention for a long time due to the lack of application background and its complexity. Until only very recently, researchers pointed out that the fractional calculus plays an important role in modeling and many systems in interdisciplinary fields, such as viscoelastic systems, dielectric polarization, electromagnetic waves, heat conduction, robotics, biological systems, finance and so on [3,7,12]. Nowadays, studying on fractional-order calculus has become an active research field.

As we know, compared with the classical integer-order models, fractional-order derivatives provide an excellent instrument for the description of memory and hereditary properties of various materials and processes. Therefore, it may be more accurate to model by fractional-order derivatives than integer-order ones. Since fractional calculus has the memory, some researchers recently introduced it to neural networks to form fractional-order neural models. Also, it has been pointed out that fractional derivatives provide neurons with a fundamental and general computation ability that can contribute to efficient information processing, stimulus anticipation and frequency-independent phase shifts of oscillatory neuronal firing [11]. More recently, efforts have been made to investigate the complex dynamics of fractional-order neural (see [2,9]). Furthermore, note

© Springer Science+Business Media Singapore 2016
L. Zhang et al. (Eds.): AsiaSim 2016/SCS AutumnSim 2016, Part IV, CCIS 646, pp. 121–130, 2016.
DOI: 10.1007/978-981-10-2672-0_13

that fractional-order recurrent neural networks might be expected to play an important role in parameter estimation (see [4,8,16]). Therefore, the incorporation of fractional derivatives and integrals into the neural networks is a great improvement in modeling and it is worthwhile to study.

Nowadays much work has been done about the stability, such as Lyapunov stability, asymptotic stability, uniform stability and exponential stability, which are all concerned with the behavior of systems within an infinite time interval. However, in some practical applications the main concern is the behavior of systems over a finite time interval. Actually most real neural systems only operate over finite time intervals. In such cases, it is necessary to care more about the finite-time behavior of systems than the asymptotic behavior over an infinite time interval. The concept of finite-time stability was introduced by Kamenkov for the first time [10], which was system property concerning the quantitative behavior of the state variables over an assigned finite time interval. Given a bound on the initial condition, a system is said to be finite-time stable if its state norm does not exceed a certain threshold during the specified time interval [1]. It was demonstrated that finite-time stable systems might have not only faster convergence but also better robustness and disturbance rejection properties [5]. Thus, a considerable number of results on finite-time stability for autonomous or non-autonomous systems have been achieved, for example, see [13,14,18,19] and references therein.

Motivated by the above, we consider the following fractional-order high-order Hopfield neural networks with delays:

$$
{}^{c}D_t^{\alpha}x_i(t) = -a_i x_i(t) + \sum_{j=1}^{n} b_{ij} f_j(t, x_j(t - \gamma_{ij})) + \sum_{j=1}^{n}\sum_{l=1}^{n} c_{ijl} g_j(t, x_j(t - \tau_{ijl}))
$$
$$
\times g_l(t, x_l(t - \sigma_{ijl})) + L_i, \ t \in [0, T], \ i = 1, 2, \ldots, n. \tag{1}
$$

where ${}^{c}D^{\alpha}$ is the Caputo's fractional derivative and $0 < \alpha < 1$, n corresponds to the number of units in a neural network, $x_i(t)$ corresponds to the state vector of the ith unit at the time t, a_i represents the rate with which the ith unit will reset its potential to the resting state in isolation when disconnected from the network and external inputs, b_{ij} and c_{ijl} are the first- and second-order connection weights of the neural network, $\gamma_{ij} \geq 0$, $\tau_{ijl} \geq 0$ and $\sigma_{ijl} \geq 0$ correspond to the transmission delays, L_i denote the external inputs, and f_j and g_j are the activation functions of signal transmission, $i, j, l = 1, 2, \ldots, n$.

Here, the initial conditions associated with system (1) are of the form $x_i(s) = \phi_i(s)$, $s \in [-\eta, 0]$, $i = 1, 2, \ldots, n$, where $\eta = \max\limits_{1 \leq i,j,l \leq n} \{\gamma_{ij}, \tau_{ijl}, \sigma_{ijl}\}$. If the initial value $\phi(t) = (\phi_1(t), \phi_2(t), \cdots, \phi_n(t))^T$, we denote the norm $\|\phi\| = \sup_{t \in [-\eta, 0]} \|\phi(t)\|$, $\|\phi(t)\| = \max\limits_{1 \leq i \leq n} \{|\phi_i(t)|\}$.

The paper is organized as follows. In Sect. 2, we introduce some notations and definitions and state some preliminary results which are needed in later sections. In Sect. 3, we establish the existence and uniqueness of the nontrivial solution. In Sect. 4, finite-time stability of the system (1) is proposed in fixed time intervals. In Sect. 5, we give an example to demonstrate the feasibility of our results.

2 Preliminaries

In this section we present some definitions, lemma and recall the well-known results about fractional differential equations.

Definition 1 ([15]). *The fractional integral (Riemann-Liouville integral) $I_{t_0,t}^\alpha$ with fractional order $\alpha \in \mathbb{R}^+$ of function $x(t)$ is defined as*

$$I_{t_0,t}^\alpha x(t) = \frac{1}{\Gamma(\alpha)} \int_{t_0}^t (t - \tau)^{\alpha-1} x(\tau) d\tau,$$

where $\Gamma(.)$ is the gamma function, $\Gamma(\alpha) = \int_0^{+\infty} t^{\alpha-1} e^{-t} dt$.

Definition 2 ([15]). *The Riemann-Liouville derivative of fractional order α of function $x(t)$ is given as*

$$D_{t_0,t}^\alpha x(t) = \frac{d^n}{dt^n} \frac{1}{\Gamma(n-\alpha)} \int_{t_0}^t (t - \tau)^{n-\alpha-1} x(\tau) d\tau,$$

where $n - 1 < \alpha < n \in \mathbb{Z}^+$.

Definition 3 ([15]). *The Caputo derivative of fractional order α of function $x(t)$ is defined as follows*

$$^c D_{t_0,t}^\alpha x(t) = \frac{1}{\Gamma(n-\alpha)} \int_{t_0}^t \frac{x^{(n)}(\tau)}{(t - \tau)^{\alpha-n+1}} d\tau,$$

where $n - 1 < \alpha < n \in \mathbb{Z}^+$.

Lemma 1 ([17]). *(Generalized Gronwall Inequality) Suppose $\alpha > 0$, $k(t)$ is a nonnegative function locally integrable on $0 \leq t < H$ (some $H \leq +\infty$), and $g(t)$ is a nonnegative, nondecreasing continuous function defined on $0 \leq t < H$, $g(t) \leq M = const$, and suppose $f(t)$ is nonnegative and locally integrable on $0 \leq t < H$ with $f(t) \leq k(t) + g(t) \int_0^t f(s) ds$, then*

$$f(t) \leq k(t) + \int_0^t \left\{ \sum_{m=1}^{+\infty} \frac{[g(t)\Gamma(\alpha)]^m}{\Gamma(m\alpha)} (t - s)^{m\alpha-1} k(s) \right\} ds, \ t \in [0, H).$$

Corollary 1 ([17]). *Under the hypothesis of Lemma 2, let $k(t)$ be a nondecreasing function on $0 \leq t < H$, then*

$$f(t) \leq k(t) E_\alpha [g(t)\Gamma(\alpha)t^\alpha], \ t \in [0, H),$$

where E_α is the Mittag-Leffler function in one parameter.

Lemma 2 ([6]). *(Gronwall-Bellman inequality) Assume that function $u(t)$ satisfies*

$$u(t) \le a(t) + \int_0^t f(s)u(s)\mathrm{d}s, \ t \in [0,T], \ T \le \infty,$$

where $u(t)$, $a(t)$, $f(t) \in C[0,T]$, and $f(t) \ge 0$, then

$$u(t) \le a(t) + \int_0^t f(s)a(s)\exp\left\{\int_s^t f(r)\mathrm{d}r\right\}\mathrm{d}s, \ t \in [0,T].$$

If, in addition, $a(t)$ is nondecreasing, then

$$u(t) \le a(t)\int_0^t f(s)\mathrm{d}s, \ t \in [0,T].$$

3   Existence and Uniqueness of Solution

In this section, we will consider the existence and uniqueness of solution to system (1) by using the fixed point theorem. To establish our main results, it is necessary to make the following assumption.

Lemma 3. *The continuous function $x_i : [-\eta, T] \to \mathbb{R}^n$ is said to be a solution of the system (1), if and only if*

$$x_i(t) = \begin{cases} \phi_i(0) + \displaystyle\int_0^t \frac{(t-s)^{\alpha-1}}{\Gamma(\alpha)}\Bigg[-a_i x_i(s) + \sum_{j=1}^n b_{ij}f_j(s, x_j(s-\gamma_{ij})) \\ \quad + \displaystyle\sum_{j=1}^n \sum_{l=1}^n c_{ijl}g_j(s, x_j(s-\tau_{ijl}))g_l(s, x_l(s-\sigma_{ijl})) + L_i\Bigg]\mathrm{d}s, \ t \in [0,T], \\ \phi_i(t), \ t \in [-\eta, 0], \ i=1,2,\ldots,n. \end{cases} \tag{2}$$

Proof. The steps of the proof are: (i) the sufficiency of the condition (2). when $t \in [-\eta, 0]$, $x_i(t) = \phi_i(t)$, $i=1,2,\ldots,n$ is obviously the solution to the system (1).

For $t \in [0,T]$, applying Riemann-Liouville fractional derivative D_t^α on both sides of the condition (2) and using properties of the fractional derivative, we have

$$D_t^\alpha x_i(t) = \phi_i(0)\frac{t^{-\alpha}}{\Gamma(1-\alpha)} - a_i x_i(t) + \sum_{j=1}^n b_{ij}f_j(t, x_j(t-\gamma_{ij}))$$

$$+ \sum_{j=1}^n \sum_{l=1}^n c_{ijl}g_j(t, x_j(t-\tau_{ijl}))g_l(t, x_l(t-\sigma_{ijl})) + L_i, \ i=1,2,\ldots,n.$$

Considering $0 < \alpha < 1$ and using the relationship between the Caputo fractional derivative and the Riemann-Liouville fractional derivative, one can easily obtain

$$D_t^\alpha x_i(t) = {}^cD_t^\alpha x_i(t) + \phi_i(0)\frac{t^{-\alpha}}{\Gamma(1-\alpha)}, \ i=1,2,\ldots,n.$$

Thus, we get

$$^c D_t^\alpha x_i(t) = -a_i x_i(t) + \sum_{j=1}^n b_{ij} f_j(t, x_j(t - \gamma_{ij}))$$

$$+ \sum_{j=1}^n \sum_{l=1}^n c_{ijl} g_j(t, x_j(t - \tau_{ijl})) g_l(t, x_l(t - \sigma_{ijl})) + L_i, \ i = 1, 2, \ldots, n.$$

(ii) the necessity of the condition (2).

From system (1), we can easily get its solution is $x_i(t) = \phi_i(t)$, $i = 1, 2, \ldots, n$, $t \in [-\tau, 0]$. If $t \in [0, T]$, applying the Riemann-Liouville fractional integral I_t^α on both sides of system (1), we get

$$I_t^\alpha [^c D_t^\alpha x_i(t)] = \int_0^t \frac{(t - s)^{\alpha - 1}}{\Gamma(\alpha)} \left[- a_i x_i(s) + \sum_{j=1}^n b_{ij} f_j(s, x_j(s - \gamma_{ij})) \right.$$

$$\left. + \sum_{j=1}^n \sum_{l=1}^n c_{ijl} g_j(s, x_j(s - \tau_{ijl})) g_l(s, x_l(s - \sigma_{ijl})) + L_i \right] ds.$$

In accordance with properties of the fractional derivative $0 < \alpha < 1$, we have

$$x_i(t) = \phi_i(0) + \int_0^t \frac{(t - s)^{\alpha - 1}}{\Gamma(\alpha)} \left[- a_i x_i(s) + \sum_{j=1}^n b_{ij} f_j(s, x_j(s - \gamma_{ij})) \right.$$

$$\left. + \sum_{j=1}^n \sum_{l=1}^n c_{ijl} g_j(s, x_j(s - \tau_{ijl})) g_l(s, x_l(s - \sigma_{ijl})) + L_i \right] ds, \ i = 1, 2, \ldots, n.$$

This completes the proof of the Lemma 3.

(H_1) The activation functions f_j, g_j satisfies the Lipschitz condition, i.e. there exist positive numbers H_{jf}, H_{jg} such that

$$|f_j(t, x) - f_j(t, y)| \le H_{jf} |x - y|, \ |g_j(t, x) - g_j(t, y)| \le H_{jg} |x - y|, \ j = 1, 2, \ldots, n.$$

(H_1) There exist positive constants M_j, N_j, $j = 1, 2, \ldots, n$ such that $|f_j(t, x)| \le M_j$, $|g_j(t, x)| \le N_j$ for $j = 1, 2, \ldots, n$, $x \in \mathbb{R}$.

Theorem 1. *Assume that (H_1) and (H_2) hold, then system (1) has a unique continuous solution on $[0, T]$.*

Proof. Let $x(t) = (x_1(t), x_2(t), \cdots, x_n(t))^T$ and $\tilde{x}(t) = (\tilde{x}_1(t), \tilde{x}_2(t), \cdots, \tilde{x}_n(t))^T$ be any two different solutions to system (1), then $x(t)$ and $\tilde{x}(t)$ both satisfy the condition (2).

Also, let $z(t) = x(t) - \tilde{x}(t)$, one can obtain $z(t) = 0$ for $t \in [-\eta, 0]$. That is to say, system (1) has a unique continuous solution for $t \in [-\eta, 0]$.

While for $t \in [0, T]$, we get

$$z_i(t) = \int_0^t \frac{(t-s)^{\alpha-1}}{\Gamma(\alpha)} \Big\{ -a_i z_i(s) + \sum_{j=1}^n b_{ij}[f_j(s, x_j(s - \gamma_{ij})) - f_j(s, \tilde{x}_j(s - \gamma_{ij}))]$$

$$+ \sum_{j=1}^n \sum_{l=1}^n c_{ijl}[g_j(s, x_j(s - \tau_{ijl}))g_l(s, x_l(s - \sigma_{ijl}))$$

$$- g_j(s, \tilde{x}_j(s - \tau_{ijl}))g_l(s, \tilde{x}_l(s - \sigma_{ijl}))] \Big\} ds, \quad i = 1, 2, \ldots, n,$$

then

$$\|z(t)\| \le \max_{1 \le i \le n} \Big\{ \int_0^t \frac{(t-s)^{\alpha-1}}{\Gamma(\alpha)} \Big\{ a_i |z_i(s)| + \sum_{j=1}^n b_{ij} H_{jf} |z_j(s - \gamma_{ij})|$$

$$+ \sum_{j=1}^n \sum_{l=1}^n c_{ijl}[M_j H_{lg} |z_l(s - \sigma_{ijl})| + M_l H_{jg} |z_j(s - \sigma_{ijl})|] \Big\} ds \Big\}.$$

Let $z^*(t) = \sup_{\theta \in [-\eta, 0]} \|z(t + \theta)\|$, then we have

$$z^*(t) \le \max_{1 \le i \le n} \Big\{ a_i + \sum_{j=1}^n b_{ij} H_{jf} + \sum_{j=1}^n \sum_{l=1}^n c_{ijl}(M_j H_{lg} + M_l H_{jg}) \Big\} \int_0^t \frac{(t-s)^{\alpha-1}}{\Gamma(\alpha)} z^*(s) ds.$$

Applying the generalized Gronwall inequality on the above equation, it follows that

$$\|z(t)\| \le z^*(t) \le 0 \cdot E_\alpha \Big\{ \max_{1 \le i \le n} \Big[a_i + \sum_{j=1}^n b_{ij} H_{jf} + \sum_{j=1}^n \sum_{l=1}^n c_{ijl}(M_j H_{lg} + M_l H_{jg}) \Big] t^\alpha \Big\}.$$

Hence we can obtain $x(t) = \tilde{x}(t)$ for $0 \le t \le T$. This completes the proof.

4 Finite Time Stability

In this section, sufficient conditions for finite time stability are derived for a class of fractional order neural networks (1) with order $0 < \alpha < 1$.

Assume that $x(t) = (x_1(t), x_2(t), \cdots, x_n(t))^T$ and $y(t) = (y_1(t), y_2(t), \cdots, y_n(t))^T$ are any two solutions of (1) with different initial functions $x_i(s) = \phi_i(s)$, $y_i(s) = \varphi_i(s)$, $s \in [-\eta, 0]$, $i = 1, 2, \ldots, n$. Let $y(t) - x(t) = e(t) = (e_1(t), e_2(t), \cdots, e_n(t))^T$, one has the error system

$$\begin{cases} {}^cD^\alpha e_i(t) = -a_i e_i(t) + \sum_{j=1}^n b_{ij}[f_j(t, x_j(t - \gamma_{ij})) - f_j(t, \tilde{x}_j(t - \gamma_{ij}))] \\ \qquad + \sum_{j=1}^n \sum_{l=1}^n c_{ijl}[g_j(t, x_j(t - \tau_{ijl}))g_l(t, x_l(t - \sigma_{ijl})) \\ \qquad - g_j(t, \tilde{x}_j(t - \tau_{ijl}))g_l(t, \tilde{x}_l(t - \sigma_{ijl}))], \\ e_i(t) = \phi_i(t) - \varphi_i(t) = \psi_i(t), \quad t \in [-\eta, 0], \quad i = 1, 2, \ldots, n, \end{cases} \qquad (3)$$

where $\psi(t) = (\psi_1(t), \psi_2(t), \cdots, \psi_n(t))^T$, is the initial function of system (3), define the norm $\|\psi\| = \sup\limits_{t\in[-\eta,0]} \|\psi(t)\| = \max\limits_{1\leq i\leq n}\{\sup\limits_{t\in[-\eta,0]} |\psi_i(t)|\}$.

Definition 4. *System (1) is said to be finite-time stable w.r.t. $[t_0, J, \delta, \varepsilon]$, if and only if $\|e_0\| \leq \delta$ implies $\|e(t)\| \leq \varepsilon$, $\forall t \in J = [t_0, t_0 + T]$, where $e(t_0) = e_0$, t_0 is the initial time of observation, δ, ε, T are real positive numbers and $\delta < \varepsilon$.*

Theorem 2. *Assume that (H_1), (H_2) hold and*

$$\sqrt{\frac{10 + (5\omega + \beta\omega + 2\beta)e^{(\omega+2)t}}{\omega + 2}} \leq \frac{\varepsilon}{\delta}, \ t \in [0, T], \tag{4}$$

where

$$\beta = \frac{5\Gamma(2\alpha - 1)(B^2 + 2C^2)(1 - e^{-2\eta})}{4^\alpha \Gamma^2(\alpha)},$$

$$\omega = \frac{10\Gamma(2\alpha - 1)(A^2 + B^2 e^{-2\gamma} + C^2 e^{-2\sigma} + C^2 e^{-2\tau})}{4^\alpha \Gamma^2(\alpha)}, \ A = \max\limits_{1\leq i\leq n}\{a_i\},$$

$$B = \max\limits_{1\leq i\leq n}\left\{\sum_{j=1}^{n} b_{ij} H_{jf}\right\}, \ C = \max\limits_{1\leq i\leq n}\left\{\sum_{j=1}^{n}\sum_{l=1}^{n} c_{ijl} H_{jg} N\right\}, \ N = \max\limits_{1\leq j\leq n}\{N_j\}.$$

Then system (1) is finite time stable with respect to $\{0, [0, T], \delta, \varepsilon\}$.

Proof. According to the property of the fractional order $0 < \alpha < 1$, one can obtain that system (3) is equivalent to the following fractional integral:

$$e_i(t) = \psi_i(0) + \int_0^t \frac{(t-s)^{\alpha-1}}{\Gamma(\alpha)}\bigg[-a_i e_i(s) + \sum_{j=1}^{n} b_{ij}[f_j(s, x_j(s - \gamma_{ij})) - f_j(s, \tilde{x}_j(s - \gamma_{ij}))]$$

$$+ \sum_{j=1}^{n}\sum_{l=1}^{n} c_{ijl}[g_j(s, x_j(s - \tau_{ijl}))g_l(s, x_l(s - \sigma_{ijl})) - g_j(s, \tilde{x}_j(s - \tau_{ijl}))g_l(s, \tilde{x}_l(s - \sigma_{ijl}))]\bigg]ds.$$

From assumptions of Theorem 2, and the properties of norm $\|\cdot\|$, obviously,

$$\|e(t)\| \leq \|\psi(0)\| + \int_0^t \frac{(t-s)^{\alpha-1}}{\Gamma(\alpha)}A\|e(s))\|ds + \int_0^t \frac{(t-s)^{\alpha-1}}{\Gamma(\alpha)}B\|e(s - \gamma)\|ds$$

$$+ \int_0^t \frac{(t-s)^{\alpha-1}}{\Gamma(\alpha)}C\|e(s - \sigma)\|ds + \int_0^t \frac{(t-s)^{\alpha-1}}{\Gamma(\alpha)}C\|e(s - \tau)\|ds,$$

one has

$$\|e(t)\| \leq \|\psi(0)\| + \int_0^t \frac{(t-s)^{\alpha-1}}{\Gamma(\alpha)}Ae^s e^{-s}\|e(s))\|ds + \int_0^t \frac{(t-s)^{\alpha-1}}{\Gamma(\alpha)}Be^s e^{-s}\|e(s - \gamma)\|ds$$

$$+ \int_0^t \frac{(t-s)^{\alpha-1}}{\Gamma(\alpha)}Ce^s e^{-s}\|e(s - \sigma)\|ds + \int_0^t \frac{(t-s)^{\alpha-1}}{\Gamma(\alpha)}Ce^s e^{-s}\|e(s - \tau)\|ds$$

$$\leq \|\psi(0)\| + \frac{1}{\Gamma(\alpha)}\left(\int_0^t (t-s)^{2\alpha-2}e^{2s}ds\right)^{1/2} \times \left[\left(\int_0^t A^2 e^{-2s}\|e(s)\|^2 ds\right)^{1/2}\right.$$

$$+\left(\int_0^t B^2 e^{-2s}\|e(s-\gamma)\|^2 ds\right)^{1/2} + \left(\int_0^t C^2 e^{-2s}\|e(s-\sigma)\|^2 ds\right)^{1/2}$$

$$\left.+\left(\int_0^t C^2 e^{-2s}\|e(s-\tau)\|^2 ds\right)^{1/2}\right]. \tag{5}$$

Note that $\int_0^t (t-s)^{2\alpha-2}e^{2s} < \frac{2e^{2t}}{4^\alpha}\Gamma(2\alpha-1)$, one obtains

$$\|e(t)\| \leq \|\psi(0)\| + \frac{1}{\Gamma(\alpha)}\left(\frac{2e^{2t}}{4^\alpha}\Gamma(2\alpha-1)\right)^{1/2} \times \left[\left(\int_0^t A^2 e^{-2s}\|e(s)\|^2 ds\right)^{1/2}\right.$$

$$+\left(\int_0^t B^2 e^{-2s}\|e(s-\gamma)\|^2 ds\right)^{1/2} + \left(\int_0^t C^2 e^{-2s}\|e(s-\sigma)\|^2 ds\right)^{1/2}$$

$$\left.+\left(\int_0^t C^2 e^{-2s}\|e(s-\tau)\|^2 ds\right)^{1/2}\right]. \tag{6}$$

It follows from (6) that

$$\|e(t)\|^2 \leq 5\|\psi(0)\|^2 + \frac{10e^{2t}\Gamma(2\alpha-1)}{4^\alpha \Gamma^2(\alpha)} \times \left[\int_0^t A^2 e^{-2s}\|e(s)\|^2 ds\right.$$

$$+\int_0^t B^2 e^{-2s}\|e(s-\gamma)\|^2 ds + \int_0^t C^2 e^{-2s}[\|e(s-\sigma)\|^2+\|e(s-\tau)\|^2]ds\bigg]$$

$$\leq 5\|\psi(0)\|^2 + \frac{10e^{2t}\Gamma(2\alpha-1)}{4^\alpha \Gamma^2(\alpha)} \times \left[\int_{-\gamma}^0 B^2 e^{-2s}e^{-2\gamma}\|e(s)\|^2 ds\right.$$

$$+\int_{-\sigma}^0 C^2 e^{-2s}e^{-2\sigma}\|e(s)\|^2 ds + \int_{-\tau}^0 C^2 e^{-2s}e^{-2\tau}\|e(s)\|^2 ds$$

$$+\int_0^t (A^2 + B^2 e^{-2\gamma} + C^2 e^{-2\sigma} + C^2 e^{-2\tau})e^{-2s}\|e(s)\|^2 ds\bigg].$$

Note that $e(t) = \psi(t)$, $t \in [-\eta, 0]$, and $\|\psi\| = \sup\limits_{s\in[-\eta,0]} \|\psi(s)\|$, one obtains

$$\|e(t)\|^2 \leq \left[5 + \frac{5e^{2t}\Gamma(2\alpha-1)(B^2+2C^2)(1-e^{-2\eta})}{4^\alpha \Gamma^2(\alpha)}\right]\|\psi\|^2 + \frac{10e^{2t}\Gamma(2\alpha-1)}{4^\alpha \Gamma^2(\alpha)}$$

$$\times (A^2 + B^2 e^{-2\gamma} + C^2 e^{-2\sigma} + C^2 e^{-2\tau})\int_0^t e^{-2s}\|e(s)\|^2 ds,$$

which is equivalent to

$$\|e(t)\|^2 e^{-2t} \leq \left[5e^{-2t} + \frac{5\Gamma(2\alpha-1)(B^2+2C^2)(1-e^{-2\eta})}{4^\alpha \Gamma^2(\alpha)}\right]\|\psi\|^2 + \frac{10\Gamma(2\alpha-1)}{4^\alpha \Gamma^2(\alpha)}$$

$$\times (A^2 + B^2 e^{-2\gamma} + C^2 e^{-2\sigma} + C^2 e^{-2\tau})\int_0^t e^{-2s}\|e(s)\|^2 ds,$$

then

$$\|e(t)\|^2 e^{-2t} \le (5e^{-2t} + \beta)\|\psi\|^2 + \omega \int_0^t e^{-2s}\|e(s)\|^2 ds.$$

By using the Gronwall-Bellman inequality, it yields

$$\|e(t)\|^2 e^{-2t} \le (5e^{-2t} + \beta)\|\psi\|^2 + \int_0^t \omega(5e^{-2t} + \beta)\|\psi\|^2 \exp\left(\int_s^t \omega du\right) ds$$

$$= \frac{10e^{-2t} + (5\omega + \beta\omega + 2\beta)e^{\omega t}}{\omega + 2}\|\psi\|^2.$$

Therefore

$$\|e(t)\| \le \sqrt{\frac{10 + (5\omega + \beta\omega + 2\beta)e^{(\omega+2)t}}{\omega + 2}}\|\psi\|,$$

it follows that when $\|\psi\| < \delta$, if (4) is satisfied, then $\|e(t)\| < \varepsilon$, from Definition 4, system (1) is finite-time stable. This completes the proof.

5   An Example

Consider the following fractional-order shunting inhibitory cellular neural network with delays:

$$^c D^\alpha x_i(t) = -a_i x_i(t) + \sum_{j=1}^2 b_{ij} f_j(t, x_j(t - \gamma_{ij}))$$

$$+ \sum_{j=1}^2 \sum_{l=1}^2 c_{ijl} g_j(t, x_j(t - \tau_{ijl})) g_l(t, x_l(t - \sigma_{ijl})) + L_i, \ i = 1, 2, \ (7)$$

where $t \in [0, 1]$ and $a_1 = 0.2$, $a_2 = 0.3$, $L_1 = 0.01$, $L_2 = 0.03$, $c_{111} = c_{222} = 0.01$, $c_{112} = c_{211} = 0.02$, $c_{121} = c_{212} = 0.03$, $c_{122} = c_{221} = 0.04$, $(b_{ij})_{2\times2} = \begin{pmatrix} 0.3 & 0.5 \\ 0.4 & 0.2 \end{pmatrix}$, $\gamma_{ij} = \tau_{ijl} = \sigma_{ijl} = 0.1$, $f_j(t, x) = g_j(t, x) = 0.5(|x + 1| - |x - 1|)$, $\phi_i(t) = 0.5 + t$, $t \in [-0.1, 0]$, $i, j, l = 1, 2$. Obviously, $M_j = N_j = H_{jf} = H_{jg} = 1$, $j = 1, 2$, $\eta = 0.1$.

Taking $\alpha = 0.6$, then all the conditions in Theorem 2 is satisfied. Therefore, we obtain the existence, uniqueness of the continuous solutions of system (7). Further, it needs to verify the finite-time stability w.r.t. $\{t_0 = 0, \delta = 0.1, \varepsilon = 1, \eta = 0.1\}$. when $\alpha = 0.6$, it could be verified that $\gamma = 0.5390$, $\omega = 5.6799$, from the inequality

$$\sqrt{\frac{10 + (5\omega + \beta\omega + 2\beta)e^{(\omega+2)t}}{\omega + 2}} \le \frac{\varepsilon}{\delta},$$

it could be obtained that the estimated time of finite-time stability is $T = 0.4099$.

References

1. Amato, F., De Tommasi, G., Pironti, A.: Necessary and sufficient conditions for finite-time stability of impulsive dynamical linear systems. Automatica **49**, 2546–2550 (2013)
2. Arena, P., Caponetto, R., Fortuna, L., Porto, D.: Bifurcation and chaos in noninteger order cellular neural networks. Int. J. Bifurc. Chaos **8**, 1527–1539 (1998)
3. Bastos, N.R.O., Ferreira, R.A.C., Torres, D.F.M.: Discrete-time fractional variational problems. Signal Process. **91**, 513–524 (2011)
4. Beer, R.D.: Parameter space structure of continuous-time recurrent neural networks. Neural Comput. **18**, 3009–3051 (2006)
5. Bhat, S.P., Bernstein, D.S.: Continuousfinite-time stabilization of the translational and rotational double integrators. IEEE Trans. Autom. Control **43**, 678–682 (1998)
6. Corduneanu, C.: Principles of Differential and Integral Equations. Allyn and Bacon, Boston (1971)
7. Hilfer, R.: Applications of Fractional Calculus in Physics. World Scientific York, Singapore (2000)
8. Huang, H., Huang, T.W., Chen, X.P.: A mode-dependent approach to state estimation of recurrent neural networks with Markovian jumping parameters and mixed delays. Neural Netw. **46**, 50–61 (2013)
9. Kaslik, E., Sivasundaram, S.: Nonlinear dynamics and chaos in fractional-order neural networks. Neural Netw. **32**, 245–256 (2012)
10. Kamenkov, G.: On stability of motion over afinite interval of time. J. Appl. Math. Mech. USSR **17**, 529–540 (1953)
11. Lundstrom, B.N., Higgs, M.H., Spain, W.J., Fairhall, A.L.: Fractional differentiation by neocortical pyramidal neurons. Nat. Neurosci. **11**, 1335–1342 (2008)
12. Magin, R.L.: Fractional Calculus in Bioengineering, Begell House, Connecticut, conn, USA (2006)
13. Moulay, E., Perruquetti, W.: Finite time stability conditions for non-autonomous continuous systems. Int. J. Control **81**, 797–803 (2008)
14. Moulay, E., Perruquetti, W.: Finite time stability and stabilization of a class of continuous systems. J. Math. Anal. Appl. **323**, 1430–1443 (2006)
15. Podlubny, I.: Fractional Differential Equations. Academic Press, San Diego (1999)
16. Raol, J.R.: Parameter estimation of state space models by recurrent neural networks. IET Control Theory A **142**, 114–118 (1995)
17. Wang, F.F., Chen, D.Y., Zhang, X.G., Wu, Y.: The existence and uniqueness theorem of the solution to a class of nonlinear fractional order system with time delay. Appl. Math. Lett. **53**, 45–51 (2016)
18. Yang, X.J., Song, Q.K., Liu, Y.R., Zhao, Z.J.: Finite-time stability analysis of fractional-order neural networks with delay. Neurocomputing **152**, 19–26 (2015)
19. Zha, W., Zhai, J., Fei, S., Wang, Y.: Finite-time stabilization for a class of stochastic nonlinear systems via output feedback. ISA Trans. **53**, 709–716 (2014)

Dynamic Data Analysis of High-Speed Train Based on MEMD and Compressive Sensing

Zhidan Wu$^{(\boxtimes)}$ and Weidong Jin

School of Electrical Engineering, Southwest Jiaotong University,
Chengdu 610031, China
281348144@qq.com, wdjin@home.swjtu.edu.cn

Abstract. Aiming at the characteristics of multi-channel vibration signal of high-speed train, this paper proposes a data analysis method based on Multivariate Empirical Mode Decomposition (MEMD) and compressive sensing. The method decomposes vibration signal using MEMD to obtain a series of Multivariate Intrinsic Mode Functions (MIMF), and extracts information entropy of these MIMF components, constituting the original high-dimensional feature set. Then compressive sensing algorithm is adopted to compress the high-dimensional feature to eliminate redundant and undesirable feature, obtaining the low-dimensional optimal feature. The experimental results of classification and identification of conditions via Support Vector Machine (SVM) show the good classification performance is 100 % of proposed method in each channel, verifying the effectiveness of the proposed method.

Keywords: High-speed train · Multivariate empirical mode decomposition · Compressive sensing · Multivariate intrinsic mode function · Information entropy

1 Introduction

To fully monitor the whole movement state of the key parts of the high-speed train, the measurement of 6 degrees of freedom of each rigid body (such as vehicle body, frame, etc.) is necessary, so there exists strong correlation among the arranged sensor channels. Mandic [1] extended the empirical mode decomposition method from single to multivariate. The proposed MEMD method decomposes multi-channel data into multi-scale data, meanwhile, the correlation information among channels get the greatest degree of retention. In the analysis of fault feature, the information entropy [2] is widely applied to describe the quantity of random components contained in signal or the complexity of waveform. As a new data processing method, compressive sensing [3] can achieve low-dimensional representation of high-dimensional data, where the low-dimensional feature is more effective and separable compared with redundant high-dimensional feature.

Aiming at the characteristics of many freedoms of motion and strong non-linearity of high-speed train, in this paper, the multi-channel data is jointly processed by MEMD, combined with the background of vehicle dynamics. Then, the information entropy feature extraction is carried out for MIMFs from decomposition, obtaining

© Springer Science+Business Media Singapore 2016
L. Zhang et al. (Eds.): AsiaSim 2016/SCS AutumnSim 2016, Part IV, CCIS 646, pp. 131–139, 2016.
DOI: 10.1007/978-981-10-2672-0_14

original high-dimensional feature. After that, reduce the dimension using compressive sensing, and obtain the low-dimensional feature with redundant and secondary feature removed. Finally, SVM is adopted to classify the low- dimensional feature after dimensional reduction. The classification results verify the effectiveness and the advantages of the algorithm proposed. Data analysis process based on MEMD and compressive sensing is shown in Fig. 1.

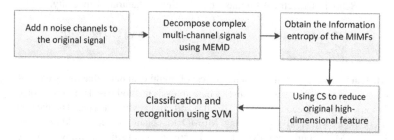

Fig. 1. Flow chart of the proposed method

2   Multivariate Empirical Mode Decomposition

The monitoring data of high-speed train is a multi-channel signal measured by a number of sensors, and there are important mutual information among each channel signal [4]. The analysis of multi-channel signal by traditional EMD often need to analyze each channel signal individually, or integrate the multi-channel signal into a single channel signal before analysis. These methods will result in different number of MIMFs of channels, which is not conducive to the comparison of the same frequency scale among different channels. And for high-speed train signal, the merger of multiple channels subjectively may lead to ignore the characteristics of the signal itself, causing interference to the follow-up feature analysis [5].

The original EMD algorithm is extended from one dimension to multi dimension, which is convenient for the cluster fusion of multidimensional data. Rehman et al. [1] proposed MEMD method, the method first projects multi-dimensional signal to directions of the vector, and then obtain the projection envelope of the signal in the direction respectively, and finally define the mean value of the multi-dimensional signal by calculating the mean of the envelope. The proposition of MEMD realizes the multi-channel conjoint analysis of multivariate signal synchronously, obtaining the common pattern of different channels and ensuring that MIMFs match on quantity and scale. Solve the problem of mode calibration of multi-channel signals.

The multivariate empirical mode decomposition algorithm is as follows [4]:

Defined observation signal $x = [x_1, x_2, \ldots, x_q]^T$ and the *lth* direction vector in the direction vector set D, $D^l = \left[d_1^l, d_2^l, \ldots, d_q^l \right]$. The basic steps of the MEMD are:

(1). Determination of direction vector set D;
(2). Calculate the *lth* projection $p^l(t)$ of x on D^l, for $l = 1, 2, \ldots, L$, and find the time instants t_m^l corresponding to the maxima of the set of projected signals $p^l(t)$;

(3). Interpolate $\left[t_m^l, x_m^l\right]$ to obtain the multivariate envelope curves $E^l(t)$;

(4). Calculate the mean of the L multi-dimensional envelopes: $M(t) = \frac{1}{L}\sum_{l=1}^{L} E^l(t)$

(5). Extract the "detail" $R(t) = V(t) - M(t)$, if $R(t)$ fulfills some stoppage criterion for a MIMF, apply the above procedure to $V(t) - R(t)$, else, repeat for $R(t)$.

Processing the multiple channels data of high-speed train signal synchronously by MEMD could realize the calibration of common scale characteristics among different channels, which is conducive to the research and comparison of the mutual information and self-information on different characteristic scales of each channel signal, and is convenient to analyze physical meaning and characteristics of signal itself.

3 Compressive Sensing

As a new technique of data acquisition, compressive sensing [6] has been a hot issue for researchers because it breaks through the restriction of Nyquist sampling rate. It is widely applied in fault diagnosis, feature extraction, data dimension reduction [7, 8] and so on. The original signal can be reconstructed accurately from these measurements by a series of reconstruction algorithms. From the point of view of signal processing, compressive sensing is to project the high dimensional signal to be processed into a low-dimensional space to realize the signal compression. The basic idea of the algorithm [6] is as follows:

Assume the original data X is sparse (can be compressed) in a transform domain, so there is a sparse measurement matrix $R(n \times m)$ that satisfies the condition RIP [3]. Projection dimension reduction of original high dimension data $X(n \times 1)$ obtaining the low-dimensional representation of $X(m \times 1)$, where $n \ll m$, and in the low-dimensional space, the main information of the original high dimensional data X can still be maintained well. Then the original signal X can be reconstructed from the low-dimensional space V by the optimization algorithm.

Achlioptas [9] prove that the random Gauss matrix R in

$$R_{ij} = \sqrt{S} \times \begin{cases} 1 \ with\ probability\ 1/2S \\ 0\ with\ probability\ 1-1/2S \\ -1\ with\ probability\ 1/2S \end{cases}$$ satisfies the condition RIP when S is 2 or 3.

$R = \{R_{ij}\}$ as a measurement matrix to reduce the dimension of original data;

The specific steps of compressive sensing algorithm are as follows:

(1) Sparse the original high dimensional data X according to the formula $X = \psi\theta$, where θ is a sparse representation of X in a certain transform domain, and ψ sparse matrix;

(2) The measurement matrix $R(n \times m, R = A\Psi)$ is used to observe the sparsity of the signal X, obtaining low-dimensional observation vector $V(m \times 1, V = A\Psi\theta)$;

(3) The original data X is accurately reconstructed from the low-dimensional space V via the optimization algorithm.

The main steps of compressive sensing include sparse representation of the original signal, selection of the observation matrix and reconstruction of the original signal. In the application of fault feature analysis of high-speed train, the reconstruction of original signal is omitted. The measurement matrix of compressive sensing is applied in dimension reduction of original high-dimensional feature set of various working conditions of high-speed train directly. Finally, the obtained low-dimensional observation result is carried for the fault analysis of the high speed train monitoring signal.

4 Experimental Data Processing and Analysis

4.1 Data Introduction

Test monitoring data is from a certain type of high-speed train. The simulation data collected by 58 sensors installed on different positions of high-speed train bogie. The sampling frequency is 243 Hz, and the total sampling time is 3.5 min. States include the normal working condition, the air spring shock conditions, the anti-hunting demolition condition and the lateral damper demolition condition, and 3 hybrid faults conditions mixed by 3 single faults two by two, i. e the air spring shock + the anti-hunting demolition condition, the air spring shock + the lateral damper demolition condition, the anti-hunting demolition + the lateral damper demolition condition. The data in this paper is collected by the running speed of 200 km/h, and the fusion data of the six channels is as the original data. By simulating the fault status of high-speed train, the vibration signal data monitored by sensors installed on different positions will reflect the different characteristics of vibration signal of normal state and fault state of the high-speed train suspension system.

4.2 Multivariate Empirical Mode Decomposition of Signal

To further reduce the aliasing phenomenon in MEMD method, this paper proposed noise assisted MEMD. Multi-channel signal data is added with n noise channels signal, whose length are equal to the original signal, as auxiliary signal channel. So it constitutes a composite channel signal. Decompose the composite channel signal by MEMD method, and obtain MIMFs of multi-channel independent with all the MIMFs in noise channel removed. Figure 2 is the MEMD decomposition result (only the first 8 MIMFs) of vehicle body acceleration (channel 1- channel 6) with the lateral damper demolition condition. Visibly, the MIMF layers of different channel are the same, and the waveform of the same frequency are alignment and exist differences.

4.3 Information Entropy Feature Extraction

In fault feature analysis, information entropy index is widely used to describe the number of random component contained in the signal or the complexity of waveform. In this paper, 3 information entropy (sample entropy, permutation entropy and multi variate multi-scale sample entropy) are used to analyze the fault monitoring signals of high-speed train bogie.

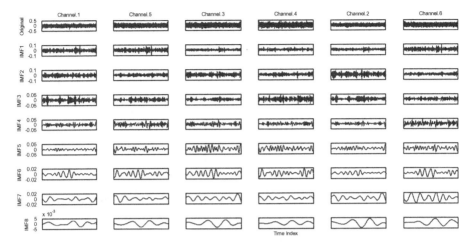

Fig. 2. Decomposition results of the signal of 6 channels with MEMD

Sample entropy is a new time series complexity measure method proposed by Richman [10]. Its calculation is independent of the length of data, so it is very convenient and practical. Permutation entropy can be used to analyze the complexity and Irregular degree of signal. It characterize complex system signal in a simple way quantitatively [11]. Multivariate multi-scale sample entropy is a new type of data analysis method proposed by Ahmed [12]. It can analyze multi-channel signal directly, and measure the possibility of generating new patterns in time series.

The experiment has intercepted operating data of 2 s (486 sample points) as a sample, and selected 102 samples of 7 working conditions respectively. Extract sample entropy, permutation entropy and multivariate multi-scale sample entropy of the first 17 MIMFs obtained from the MEMD decomposition of 7 working conditions. Figure 3(a), (b), (c) are sample entropy, permutation entropy and multivariate multi-scale sample entropy curve distribution individually of 6 acceleration channels fusion data of the vehicle body of 7 working conditions.

Shown as Fig. 3(a), the permutation entropy of the first and last several MIMFs are overlapped. The permutation entropy distribution curve of most of MIMFs of 7 working conditions is mutual independent, and there is a certain interval and distinction effectively. The sample entropy, multivariate multi-scale sample entropy curve distribution as shown in Fig. 3(b), (c) have similar conclusions. It illustrates that the extracted 3 entropy feature are effective in the classification of 7 working conditions. It also shows that the entropy feature to classify the fault type, some features are effective, but some are secondary and redundant, which has negative effect on the classification and recognition. Therefore, it is necessary to eliminate the redundant and undesired features, which can effectively reduce the feature dimension based on the full use of high dimensional feature, and improve the efficiency of algorithm.

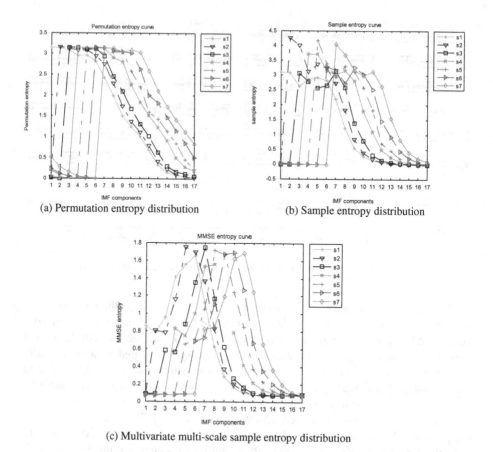

(a) Permutation entropy distribution   (b) Sample entropy distribution

(c) Multivariate multi-scale sample entropy distribution

Fig. 3. 3 information entropy distribution of MIMF components

4.4   Data Feature Analysis Based on Compressive Sensing

The extracted 17 dimensional sample entropy feature, permutation entropy feature and multivariate multi-scale sample entropy feature of the 7 working conditions above respectively, constitute 51 dimensional features, forming high dimensional feature matrix ($51 \times 102 \times 7$). Compressive sensing algorithm is used to reduce dimension of original feature, extracting the low-dimensional optimal feature that can reflect the inherent law of each condition. The optimal dimension is 3 (Determined by the maximum value point of the relationship curve between the embedding dimension and the Fisher ratio) in this paper.

Figure 4(a), (b) are low-dimensional feature spatial distribution after dimension reduction by compressive sensing of 7 working conditions of acceleration of the vehicle body (channel 1–channel 6) and acceleration of first frame (channel 7–channel 12) respectively.

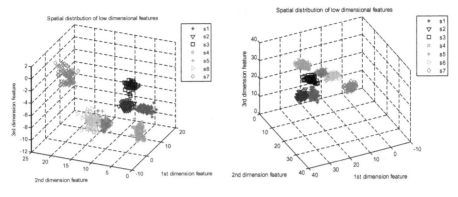

(a) Acceleration of the vehicle body   (b)   Acceleration of first frame

Fig. 4. The 3-dimensional feature spatial distribution of 7 working conditions

From Fig. 4, for the elimination of redundant features and undesirable features, the 3-dimensional feature value spatial distribution of low-dimensional feature can classify the 7 working conditions. Overall, samples of 7 working conditions show good intra class aggregation and inter class separability in 3-dimensional feature space.

4.5   Classification Result

The classification and identification of the fault condition need to be realized through the design of the classifier. Considering of the length of the experimental data is limited, SVM with the advantages of small sample classification is applied to achieve fault classification. To verify the validity of this method, the data test is compared with the other two methods, and the results are shown in Table 1.

Note: Method 1: Extract 3 information entropy of 12 IMF component after EEMD, and get a 36-dimensional feature, then select 10-dimensinal feature via Fisher ratio (recognition rate is the average rate of six channels); Method 2: Use Fisher ratio to select 17-dimensional feature form the 51 dimensional feature obtained above; Method 3: The method proposed in this paper.

Locations: 1–Acceleration of vehicle body; 2–Displacement of vehicle body; 3–Acceleration of the first frame of framework; 4–Displacement of the first frame of framework; 5–Acceleration of the second frame of framework;6–Displacement of the second frame of framework.

Analysis of Table 1, in the dynamic performance data analysis of high speed train, MEMD decomposition combined with compressive sensing method generally has better recognition effect than traditional method. The recognition rate of the 7conditions are basically up to 100 %, which proves that the dimension reduction by compressive sensing does have the effect of eliminating redundant features and undesirable features, so the low-dimensional feature after dimension reduction has better separability, and greatly improve the efficiency of computing synchronously.

Table 1. Recognition rate of classification of 3 methods (%)

Locations	Method 1	Method 2	Method 3
1	77.6732	94.3621	99.1758
2	79.3546	96.2338	100
3	83.2991	93.9560	100
4	74.5786	94.9527	99.1758
5	80.9178	93.7063	98.9011
6	82.7544	92.4937	100

5 Conclusions

The method based on MEMD and compressive sensing is proposed in this paper. Decomposes a composite multi-channel data signal added with a noise channel signal into a series of MIMFs with different frequency components adaptively by MEMD, each component containing different local characteristics of the signal. Extract 3 information entropy (sample entropy, permutation entropy, multivariate multi-scale sample entropy) of the first 17 MIMFs, forming the original high-dimensional set. Complete the fusion analysis of multi-channel data and simultaneous feature extraction. Analyzing the common modes of different channels is helpful to find the vibration mode of exact physical meaning. Compressive sensing is adopted to reduce dimension, with retention of useful information at utmost, eliminating redundant and undesirable features. It proves that the features after dimensional reduction contribute more to the classification and recognition of the 7 working conditions of high-speed train, and improves the operation efficiency. And the classification results using SVM also verify the effectiveness and advantages of the proposed algorithm for dynamic data analysis of high-speed trains.

References

1. Rehman, N., Mandic, D.P.: Multivariate empirical mode decomposition. Proc. Royal Soc. A **466**(2117), 1291–1302 (2010)
2. Shannon, C.E.: A mathematical theory of communication. ACM SIGMOBILE Mobile Comput. Commun. Rev. **5**(1), 3–55 (2001)
3. Shao, W.-Z., Wei, Z.-H.: The basic theory of compressed sensing: Retrospect and Prospect. J. Image Graph. **01**, 1–12 (2012)
4. Liu, Y.: Research on BCI signal processing based on multivariate EMD. Yanshan University (2013)
5. Fleureau, J., et al.: Multivariate empirical mode decomposition and application to multichannel filtering. Signal Process. **91**(12), 2783–2792 (2011)
6. Baraniuk, G.R.: Compressive sensing. IEEE Signal Process. Mag. **24**(4), 118–121 (2007)
7. Shen, Y.: Research on data detection and compression method of power system based on compressive sensing theory. Jiangsu University (2012)

8. Liu, B., Ping, F., Meng, S.-W.: Compressed sensing signal detection method based on digital characteristic of sampled value. J. Instrum. Meter **32**(3), 578–581 (2011)
9. Achlioptas, D.: Database-friendly random projections: Johnson-Linden Strauss with binary coins. J. Comput. Syst. Sci. **66**(4), 671–687 (2003)
10. Richman, J.S., Moorman, J.R.: physiological time series analysis using approximate entropy and sample entropy. Am. J. Physiol. **278**(6), 2039–2049 (2000)
11. Sun, K.-H., Tan, G.-Q., Sheng, L.-Y.: Complexity analysis of chaotic pseudo-random sequences based on permutation entropy algorithm. Comput. Eng. Appl. **44**(3), 47–49 (2009)
12. Ahmed, M.U., Mandic, D.P.: Multivariate multiscale entropy analysis. IEEE Signal Process Letters **19**(2), 91–94 (2012)

Feature Representation Based on Improved Word-Vector Clustering Using AP and E²LSH

Hongmei Li[⊠], Wenning Hao, Hongjun Zhang, and Gang Chen

Institute of Command Information Systems,
PLA University of Science and Technology, Nanjing, China
amayli003@sina.com

Abstract. Deep learning model has witnessed its obvious advantage in feature representation and document retrival. However, the model only considered most frequent words as the input to learn latent features, which inevitably ignores lots of useful information contained in documents especially for high-dimensional documents. We introduce a novel method based on word-vector clustering to obtain low-dimensional semantic vectors of documents, as the input of deep learning model to improve the feature representation in the output layer. Firstly, word-vector, a kind of compact and distributed representation of words, is obtained by training neural network language model using word2vec. Then, we present a modified word-vector clustering method based on locality-sensitive hashing and affinity propagation, with a stronger adaptability and scalability for large scale and high dimensionality. Afterwards, each document is represented by the set of cluster centers as the input of deep learning model. Experimental results proved the proposed method improves the ability of feature representation of deep learning model and performs better on document retrieval task compared with traditional methods.

Keywords: Deep learning model · Distributed representation · Word-vector clustering · Affinity propagation clustering · Exact-Euclidean locality-sensitive hashing

1 Introduction

In order to capture low-dimensional feature for representation and discrimination of documents preferably, deep learning model [1] and its contrastive divergence inference mechanism [2] have been introduced in recent years and achieved great performance in the aspect of semantic feature extraction. This model allows to model non-binary data in visible level and get non-binary latent variables in hide level, which represents the semantic representations hidden in documents. In view of the word-count vectors of documents for input, this model is able to produce distributed representations output of the input and perform better than famous models, e.g., LDA. For the input of visible layer, traditional deep learning models only consider proper numbers of most frequent words of the training document set after preprocessing data by removing common stop-words and stemming [3]. This method is simple, but it has certain defects actually. Since it discards the words of low frequency and therefore ignores the useful information contained in

© Springer Science+Business Media Singapore 2016
L. Zhang et al. (Eds.): AsiaSim 2016/SCS AutumnSim 2016, Part IV, CCIS 646, pp. 140–148, 2016.
DOI: 10.1007/978-981-10-2672-0_15

them, and the selected words may have duplicated semantic not hesitate to the independent syntax, which inevitably weakens some latent information contained in documents actually.

To solve these problems, we propose a method based on word-vector clustering, where the word-vector is a kind of distributed representation based on neural network language model [4, 5]. Therefore, a series of words with similar semantic could be clustered into the same concept by measuring the distance between distributed representations. Distributed representation effectively overcomes the drawback of traditional one-hot representation, including high dimension and vocabulary gaps.

However, another problem appears. For a large-scale document set, there exists a list of words with large volume, therefore the distributed representation presents the characteristic of large-scale and high-dimension. Although affinity propagation (AP) [6] is a relatively novel clustering method proposed in recent years famous for its high converging speed and optimal cluster result, its high consumption of memory and computational complexity grow with the rapid growth of volume and dimension. Facing with dynamic incremental data of large volume and high dimensionality, we consider to introduce Exact Euclidean Locality-sensitive Hashing (E^2LSH) [7–11], which is currently the fastest method in solving of approximately neighbored retrieval and clustering, and it is particularly suitable for processing data of large-scale and high dimensionality. E^2LSH provides a randomized solution for the traditional LSH scheme in the Euclidean space with l_2 norm, and achieves good performance especially faced with data of high dimensionality and large scale.

Therefore, this paper proposes a novel word-clustering method based on locality-sensitive hashing and affinity propagation (LSHAP). Firstly, each word is presented as word-vector, which is the distributed representation based on word2vec (Sect. 2). Secondly, E^2LSH method is applied for the initial clustering first, dividing the large set of data into small set of data, and then AP clustering method is used for the further clustering on the small set of data (Sect. 3). Then, experiment is implemented to prove and analyze the proposed method (Sect. 4). Finally, a brief conclusion is given (Sect. 5).

2 Distributed Feature Presentation Based on Neural Network Language Model

In this paper, we choose Skip-Gram model [8] as the training model, which is a kind neural network language model and it predicts the current word by its context. Suppose there is a group of sequence of words as the training corpus, they are w_1, w_2, w_3,..., w_t. Then our goal is to maximize the Skip-Gram model objective function:

$$F = \frac{1}{T} \sum_{i=1}^{T} \sum_{-b \le i \le b, i \neq 0} \log p(w_{t+i}|w_t) \tag{1}$$

Word2vec is a Google' open source tool based on neural network language model, and it can convert words into low-dimensional real-value vectors. And we use word2vec (word to vector) [9] to train distributed representation of words. Before that, document sets are preprocessed by removing punctuations and stopwords, temming, word segmentation (specially for Chinese documents), etc., obtaining large volume of training corpus as the input of word2vec, and then generating the distributed representation of all the words. Then the relation between different words can be measured by the distance of its distributed representation. Specially, the short distance between different words does not necessarily mean the similar synonyms or justice, that is relevant or correlation, which results in statistics training based on word frequency, co-occurrence and so on. In this paper, the size of the window is set as 6, and the hierarchical softmax [10] approach is used to train Skip-Gram model. Finally, we obtain distributed representation vectors of 100 dimension. Those vectors capture large amount of useful syntax and semantics features, and we can determine the correlation of syntax and semantics, according to the distance between the word vectors and cluster according to their correlation.

3 The Improved Word-Vector Clustering Based on E2LSH and AP

We propose an incremental clustering algorithm based on the divide and conquer strategy, which is in combination with E^2LSH and AP algorithm. The main idea is that, first E^2LSH algorithm divides large datasets into amounts of smaller datasets, and each hash bucket is considered as a candidate clusters. Then AP algorithm is applied to clustering on each smaller candidate cluster. Finally, the redundancy data clusters and outliers are further merged.

3.1 The First Clustering Based on E^2LSH

E^2LSH is a method that provides a randomized solution for the traditional LSH schema in the Euclidean space with l_2 norm. E^2LSH uses p-stable distribution for dimension reduction mapping based on the LSH, in order to ensure the similar points have higher probability to be hashed into the same bucket. Recall that each function $g_i(v)$ has to store all possible buckets. Actually only non-empty buckets need to be stored, and k-dimensional vector was remained according to the index of each bucket $(u_1, u_2, \ldots, u_k)$ which may waste large amount of spaces. To this end, E^2LSH uses two associated hash functions h'_1 and h'_2 to hash the bucket. We here define two hash functions: $h'_1 \neg \mathcal{Z}^k \to \{0, 1, \ldots, N\}$ and $h'_2 : r'_i \to \{0, 1, \ldots, C\}$ (each $g_i(v)$ maps from Z^k, N is the size of data sets, and c is an integer) with the following form:

$$h'_1(u_1, u_2, \ldots u_k) = ((\sum_{i=1}^{k} r_i u_i) \bmod prime) \bmod N \tag{2}$$

$$h_2'(u_1, u_2, \ldots u_k) = \left(\sum\nolimits_{i=1}^{k} r_i' u_i\right) \bmod prime \qquad (3)$$

where r_i, r_i' are random integers, and prime is a big prime number $2^{32} - 5$ for the purpose of a faster hash function computation without using module operations. The primary function has the leading role of the index of each point in each hash table with the usual function in a universal hashing scheme. The secondary function was used to store each bucket with a single value $h_2 = (u_1, u_2, \ldots, u_k)$ which identify the buckets in the chains such that decrease the amount of memory space from O(k) to O(1) and the waste of time of looking for a bucket in a hash table.

Then, based on the E^2LSH index, we perform clustering by mapping large-scale documents into hashing buckets of hash tables, and each hash bucket represents an approximate cluster or several clusters. E^2LSH algorithm provides an effective index structure for word vectors to determine the approximate nearest neighbors, and it greatly meets the requirements of near real-time for large-scale data. However, the words of candidate clusters obtained by E^2LSH are similar only with a certain probability, the clustering results are relatively coarse and the clusters can not be directly applied. The better approach is to conduct the secondary clustering based the candidate clusters with smaller scale, obtaining the small and pure clusters.

3.2 The Second Clustering Based on Affinity Propagation

As illustrated above, the candidate clusters obtained by E^2LSH index are usually not the best clustering results, the shapes of such clusters are more complicated and there exist multiple redundant clusters and outliers, it needs a valid clustering algorithm for the next clustering. AP clustering method is a relatively good method, and its clustering results are stable and refined.

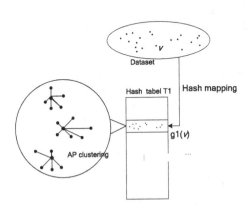

Fig. 1. AP clustering based on LSH

In the process of the secondary clustering based on the initial clustering by E²LSH, we perform clustering for each bucket set using AP clustering algorithm, forming smaller and finer cluster, as shown in Fig. 1.

Affinity propagation takes as input a collection of real-valued similarities between data points, constructing the similarity matrix s where the similarity s(i, k) indicates how well the data point with index k is suited to be t he exemplar for data point i. AP takes as input a real number s(k, k) for each data point k so that data points with larger values of s(k, k) are more likely to be chosen as exemplars. In the clustering process, it needs calculating the degree of attraction of every cluster sample point and all the other sample points, which are mainly described by two indicators: responsibility r and availability a. The "responsibility" r(i, k), sent from data point i to candidate exemplar point k, reflects the accumulated evidence for how well-suited point kis to serve as the exemplar for point i. The "availability" a(i, k), sent from candidate exemplar point k to point i, reflects the accumulated evidence for how appropriate it would be for point i to choose point k as its exemplar. Then the two indicators r and a are iteratively updated according to formula, until the end of clustering.

Before, we have searched each hash bucket in order, and for each of the candidate clusters Ci, we run AP algorithm. Typically, in order to reduce the convergence difficulty for the shock caused by data, we set the damping factor λ, so as to update responsibility r and availability a in each iteration.

$$r_i = (1 - \lambda) \times r_i + \lambda \times r_{i-1}$$
$$a_i = (1 - \lambda) \times a_i + \lambda \times a_{i-1}$$

$$(4)$$

3.3   Merge of Redundancy Clusters

The candidate clusters mapped from E²LSH are further divided into fine clusters based on AP algorithm. Due to the approximately neighbored scheme of E²LSH, there exist large redundancy within each cluster. After fined, some clusters' centers are coincident or approximate.

Generally, Cluster center represents a set of neighbored data, and the coincidence of two clusters' center means that the two clusters belong to the same class, it is necessary to merge them into a common class, eliminating redundancy. The approximation of two clusters center means the high probability they are of a kind, and should treat them as one group. Therefore, only by setting a valid threshold and then measuring the distance between two clusters can we determine whether two clusters are redundant. If the distance is within the threshold range, the two clusters belong to the same cluster to a great extent, and by combining them until all clusters are filtered, the remaining clusters are the final results.

As is shown in Fig. 2, cluster A and B have the coincident center, it indicates the high probability that they are a kind, and they are combined into the bigger cluster C according to merge rules. Due to the merge rule, our algorithm will generate a large group of clusters with various shapes, and incremental clustering performs well with great flexibility and adaptability.

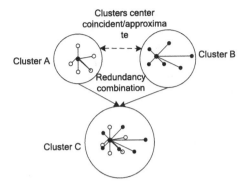

Fig. 2. Merge of redundancy clusters

4 Experimental Results and Analysis

In this section we present experimental results for document retrieval on a document retrieval task of deep learning model with the input based on the two kinds of feature vectors: (1) the low-dimensional concept vector of distributed representation clustering based on LSHAP; (2) the low-dimensional most frequent words vector based on TF.

4.1 Description and Preprocessing of Datasets

The 20-newsgroups dataset contains 18,845 postings taken from the Usenet newsgroup collection. It is partitioned into 20 newsgroups with different topics. The Reuters Corpus is an archive of 21578 newswire stories, we select 10 classes including 9980 newswire stories. We further preprocessed the data by removing punctuations, stop-words, temming, then we only considering the 2000 most frequent words. In addition, before clustering, we should normalize the real-value word vector, transforming them into the range of [0,1].

4.2 Evaluation Criterion and Details of Training

The evaluation criterion contains two aspects: the quality of information retrieval and time complexity. Time complexity is decided by clustering time, and the quality of information retrieval we use Precision-Recall curves, where we define:

$$\text{Recall} = \frac{|S(q) \cap R(q)|}{|R(q)|} \quad \text{Precision} = \frac{|S(q) \cap R(q)|}{|S(q)|} \tag{5}$$

where $|S(q)|$ denotes the total number of retrieved documents, $|R(q)|$ denotes the total number of all relevant documents, $|S(q) \cap R(q)|$ denotes the number of retrieved relevant documents.

For E^{2}LSH algorithm, we perform clustering using E^{2}LSH 0.1 software. For affinity propagation algorithm, preference p is initialized with a mean value of median(s), and the parameters are updated using a damping factor $\lambda = 0.5$, convergence is performed for 50 iterations. For deep learning model, the number of hidden units is set to1000, and the number of visible units is determined according to the actual clusters performed in the clustering algorithms.

4.3   Experiment Results and Analysis

(1) Precision-recall curve of document retrieval performed on two kinds of dataset

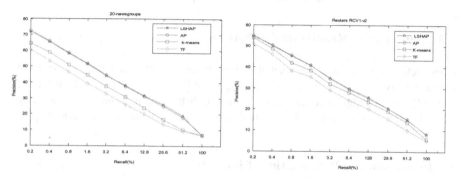

Fig. 3. Precision-Recall   curve   for   the   **Fig. 4.** Precision-Recall curve for the Reuters
20-newsgroups

As is shown in Figs. 3 and 4 above, compared with high-frequency words vector (TF) as the input of Deep learning model, the low-dimensional concept vector obtained by method based on exact-Euclidean locality sensitive hashing and affinity propagation clustering (LSHAP) performs well in feature presentation and clustering experimented on the both datasets. Meanwhile, compared with traditional affinity propagation clustering algorithm (AP), the retrieval accuracy of LSHAP is so closer, while the latter has lower time complexity, as show in Fig. 5, indicating that the proposed algorithm in this paper could greatly improve the clustering speed with the clustering accuracy not less than affinity propagation clustering alone.

It mainly depends on two factors. One is the selection of the parameters of E^{2}LSH algorithm, the other is the structure of dataset. For the former, if parameter k and L are not available enough, the data mapped into the same hash bucket does are not similar enough, and they are less likely to belong to the same class, seriously affecting the clustering quality based on the candidate clusters. For the latter, since AP clustering algorithm is not suitable for data with complex distribution, especially when the data distribution are non-spherical in the feature space, the clustering results based on AP algorithm is not ideal, there will be a large group of small clusters. It involves large amount of time when processing these redundant clusters with similarity computation.

(2) Running time of clustering

As is shown in Figs. 5 and 6 above, with the increase of feature dimension, the running time of k-means and AP clustering algorithm increase with the increases of data volume and feature dimension, and their time complexity is far more higher than LSHAP algorithm. Specially, LSHAP algorithm shows great superiority when the dimension grows, its time complexity changes in sub-linear way, which indicates the outstanding ability in processing high-dimensional data and avoid "dimension disaster".

LSHAP clustering algorithm uses divide and conquer strategy by the large-scale data into multiple small clusters candidate class, avoid direct clustering on large-scale data, but the task will be degraded into a plurality of clusters. Through the divide and conquer strategy of LSHAP clustering algorithm, the massive data are effectively divide into multiple small candidate clusters, to avoid the high computational complexity for directly clustering on the large-scale data, hence the whole complexity is resolved into tiny and simple process, alleviating the traditional computational complexity faced with large-scale corpus with high dimension.

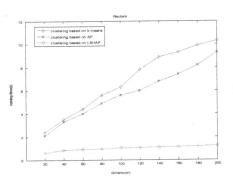
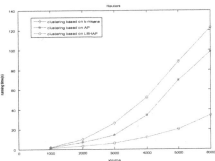

Fig. 5. Running time of clustering of various feature dimensions for 20-newsgroups

Fig. 6. Running time of clustering of various data volume for the Reuters

5 Conclusions

We have demonstrated a fast and effective words clustering strategy through the combination of locality sensitive hash and affinity propagation clustering methods, to achieve the mapping from high-dimensional word frequency vector to low-dimensional concept vector based on distributed representation. Based on the concept vector as the input of deep learning model, our algorithm outperformed traditional method with the most frequent words vector, further improving the capability of document semantic mining. The algorithm, on the one hand, quickly took full advantage of E^2LSH algorithm with quick index and dimensionality reduction. On the other hand, it broke through the limitations of AP clustering method, and improved the accuracy of clustering directly based E^2LSH algorithm. Our method performed good adaptability and scalability in processing data of large-scale and high-dimension. However, the algorithm is sensitive to some parameters, the future work will be focused on the adaptive adjustment of the parameters of E^2LSH algorithm.

References

1. Bengio, Y.: Learning deep architectures for AI. In: Foundations and Trends in Machine Learning (2009)
2. Bengio, Y., Delalleau, O.: Justifying and generalizing contrastive divergence. Neural Comput. **21**(6), 1601–1621 (2009)
3. Salakhutdinov, R., Hinton, G.: Semantic hashing, In SIGIR workshop on information retrieval and applications of graphical models (2007)
4. Paccanaro, A., Hinton, G.: Learning distributed representations of concepts from relational data using linear relation. IEEE Trans. Knowl. Data Eng. **3**, 98–104 (2001)
5. Bengio, Y., Ducharme, R., Vincent, P., et al.: A neural probabilistic language model. J. Mach. Learn. Res. **3**, 1137–1155 (2003)
6. Frey, B.J., Dueck, D.: Clustering by passing messages between data points. Science **315**(5814), 972–976 (2007)
7. Andoni, A., Indyk, P.: Nearest-optimal hashing algorithms for approximate nearest neighbor in high dimensions. Commun. ACM **51**(1), 117–122 (2008). 50th anniversary issue
8. Mikolov, T., Chen, K., Corrado, G.: et al.: Efficient estimation of word representations in vector space[EB/OL], 18 September 2014. http://arxiv.org/abs/1301.3781v3
9. Mikolov, T.: Word2vec project [EB/OL], 18 September 2014. https://code.googlecom/p/word2vec/
10. Mikolov, T., Sutskever, I., Chen, K., et al.: Distributed representations of words and phrases and their compositionality. Adv. Neural Inform. Process. Syst. 3111–3119 (2013)
11. Malcolm, S., Michael, C.: Locality-sensitive hashing for finding nearest neighbors. IEEE Sig. Process. Magzine **8**(3), 128–131 (2008)

The Intrusion Detection Model of Multi-dimension Data Based on Artificial Immune System

Weikai Wang[2], Lihong Ren[1,2(✉)], and Yongsheng Ding[1,2]

[1] Engineering Research Center of Digitized Textile & Apparel Technology,
Ministry of Education, Shanghai, China
{lhren,ysding}@dhu.edu.cn
[2] College of Information Science and Technology, Donghua University,
Shanghai 201620, China
weikai_w@sina.com

Abstract. Facing to the security of the data, this paper proposes a new intrusion detection model in high dimensional data environment based on the artificial immune system. This model pre-processes the high dimensional data to build the data set of self and non-self. In order to make the detectors more efficient and reliable, we improve the existing negative selection algorithm by adding the means of shift mutation and random grouping. Meanwhile, the adaptive learning and dynamic updating of the detectors are realized by introducing the evolutionary computation. The experimental results show that the proposed model can detect the data of non-self and identify the self-data effectively.

Keywords: Data security · Intrusion detection · Shift nutation · Artificial immune system · High dimensional data

1 Introduction

The intrusion detection of computer networks has been studied for a long time, and a number of research results have been obtained. Wang [1] proposed an autonomic intrusion detection framework, which cloud accomplish the online adaptive intrusion detection. Murugan [2] proposed a method to extract unknown activities from the alerts of intrusion detection systems (IDS) by applying data mining technique.

With the rapid development of the biosciences, bio-inspired heuristic algorithms provide us a better solution to some practical problems. Artificial immune system (AIS) is inspired by the natural defense mechanism of biological immune systems, whose characteristics include adaptive, robust and self-organization, and is more suitable for intrusion detection. Negative selection algorithm (NSA) [3] and dynamic clonal selection algorithm (DCSA) [4, 5] are two basic immune algorithms, which constitute the current majority of immune IDS [6–9].

But beyond that, there are a lot of research results that use biological intelligent algorithm to achieve network security. Hui [10] proposed a kind dynamic match algorithm different from traditional affinity match methods, and applied to the intrusion detection model. Kotov [11] proposed an algorithm based on immune model and

L. Zhang et al. (Eds.): AsiaSim 2016/SCS AutumnSim 2016, Part IV, CCIS 646, pp. 149–160, 2016.
DOI: 10.1007/978-981-10-2672-0_16

immune computing, which differed from most methods relied on labeled training data. Moreover, the approach got better performance in detecting new intrusions. Hong [12] compared the differences between the human immune system and intrusion detection systems, and concluded that the intrusion system based on the human immune system is promising for future intrusion detection systems. Kim [13] introduced and investigated the behavior of the dynamic clonal selection algorithm, designed to have such properties of self-adaptation, and demonstrated the abilities to perform incremental learning on converged data and to adapt to novel data. Yan [14] designed a novel dynamic intrusion detection model based on immune evolution by using vaccination and niacin strategy. This model guaranteed the feasibility of the vaccine obtaining and vaccinating.

The pre-process of high dimensional data is very important for the IDS. This paper presents a model of intrusion detection in high dimensional data environment, which involves discrete data serialization, continuous data standardization and normalization, dimensionality reduction, and mass data clustering. In the phrase of data preparation, the method of principal component analysis (PCA) [15] is used to reduce the dimension of high-dimensional data. In order to reduce the computational complexity, the K-means algorithm [16] is used to cluster the data. The improved negative selection algorithm, which is through the way of shift mutation, is used to generate detectors, and the genetic algorithm is used to improve the dynamic clonal selection algorithm to achieve the adaptive learning and dynamic update of detectors. The algorithms proposed in this paper can be used to produce the samples of real value shape space.

The rest of this paper is organized as follows. We introduce the detector generation and the dynamic update strategy in Sects. 2 and 3, respectively. Then, we experimentally evaluate our approach in Sect. 4, and conclude the whole paper in Sect. 5.

2   Detector Generation Strategy

In this paper, the negative selection algorithm and the dynamic clonal selection algorithm are mainly used in the generation and dynamic update of the detectors, respectively. Based on the traditional negative selection algorithm as shown in Fig. 1(a), a method of shift mutation is proposed to improve the efficiency of detector generation, as shown in Fig. 1(b). The method of shift mutation is shown in Fig. 2. Besides, in order to achieve the maximum coverage of the detector for non-self region, we propose a

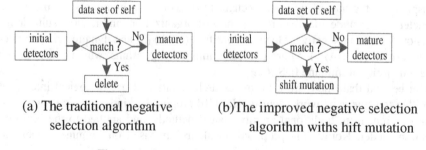

(a) The traditional negative
selection algorithm

(b)The improved negative selection
algorithm withs hift mutation

Fig. 1. An improved negative selection algorithm

strategy of detector cloning with random grouping where the detectors are divided into a certain group and the detector is selected with the highest degree of fitness in every group to clone and proliferate.

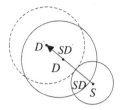

Fig. 2. The way of shift mutation

In Fig. 2, S and D indicates the self and the detector in two dimensions, respectively.

$$\overrightarrow{SD'} = \overrightarrow{SD} + \frac{\overrightarrow{SD}}{|\overrightarrow{SD}|} \times \eta \tag{1}$$

$$\eta = r_s + r_d - \textit{affinity} \tag{2}$$

$$\textit{affinity}(D_i, S_j) = \sqrt{\sum_{k=1}^{n} |D_{ik} - S_{jk}|^2} \tag{3}$$

where, $\overrightarrow{SD}$ is a vector formed of two elements that are, center points of S and D, $|\overrightarrow{SD}|$ is the norm of $\overrightarrow{SD}$, $\overrightarrow{SD'}$ is the vector of $\overrightarrow{SD}$ after shift mutation. In Eq. (2), r_s and r_d are the radius of the self S and the detector D, respectively, and *affinity* is the affinity between the self and the detector, which the computing method is as shown in Eq. (3).

The self is described as.

$$S = (S_1, S_2, \ldots \ldots, S_{N_s}) \tag{4}$$

where N_s is the number of the collected self-samples,

$$S_i = (S_{i1}, S_{i2}, \ldots \ldots, S_{id}) \tag{5}$$

where S_i denotes the i th self-data, $i = 1, 2, 3, \cdots, N_s$.

The detector is described as below

$$D = \{D_1, D_2, \ldots \ldots, D_{N_{det}}\} \tag{6}$$

where, N_{det} is similar to N_s,

$$D_i = (D_{i1}, D_{i2}, \ldots \ldots, D_{id}) \tag{7}$$

The fitness value of the detector in the population determines whether the detector is cloned or mutated, whose calculating formula is shown as follows,

$$fitness = \frac{\omega_1 r_d - \omega_2 d_s - \omega_3 d_d}{num_{det}} \tag{8}$$

where ω_1, ω_2 and ω_3 are the weight values, d_s and d_d represent the distance of detector to the nearest self and the nearest detector, respectively, and num_{det} is the number of the current detector with overlapping detectors in last generation.

In the process of detector generation, the evolutionary computation is introduced to select individuals with high fitness from the way of random grouping. Then, with the operations of crossover, mutation and negative selection a new subset is generated to replace the detectors with low fitness. The strategy of detector generating is shown in Fig. 3.

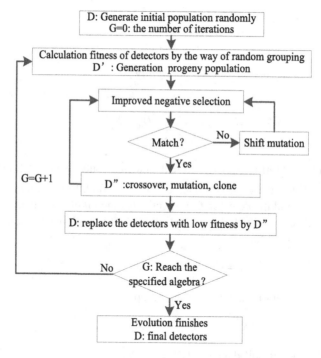

Fig. 3. The strategy of detector generating

3   Dynamic Update Strategy for Detector

In order to be more effective and reliable for the detectors in the IDS under the complex and changeable network environment, it is very important to ensure adaptive learning and dynamic updating of the detector. In this paper, the further definition of detector is given as follows.

$$D_i = (D_{i1}, D_{i2}, \ldots\ldots, D_{id}, rd_i, fitness, age, num) \tag{9}$$

where *age* and *num* are the age and the detected numbers of the *i* th detector, respectively. The dynamic update mechanism is as shown in Fig. 4. In Eq. (9), rd_i, the radius of the detector, would be increased with the detecting efficiency. *fitness*, the unique credentials as the adaptive capacity of the detector, represents the importance in the current generation. While the detector has not detected the illegal invasion in the lifecycle, that is $T \leq age$, it will need to be mutated. Otherwise, the value of *age* should be set to zero, and the value of *num* plus one. The detector will turn into a memory detector while *num* reaching the threshold, which we have set up before. If the accessing is denied, the system will trigger defense mechanism to establish the library of vaccine, which can provide resources for producing the detector of the next generation.

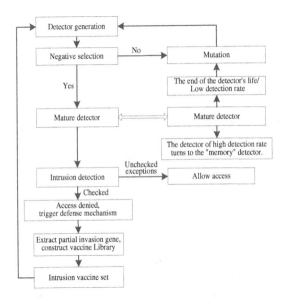

Fig. 4. The dynamic update mechanism

4   Experimental Results

As mentioned in Sect. 1, the proposed model needs to reduce the high-dimension of the data using the PCA algorithm and to cluster the massive data samples for reducing the computational complexity using the K-means algorithm. The data set used in this paper is KDD CUP 1999 [17], which have 41 dimensions in every sample. In order to facilitate the experimental observation of the algorithms proposed in this paper, we do the visualized experiments in two-dimensional (2D) and three-dimensional (3D) space. We reduce the dimension to two and three with PCA to achieve the effect of visualization, and we cluster the new data set to four categories. Figures 5(a) and (b) shows the experimental results of self-data in 2D and 3D space, respectively. In 3D space, the coverage of data is a globe, so the experimental results are not very obvious because of the occlusion between them.

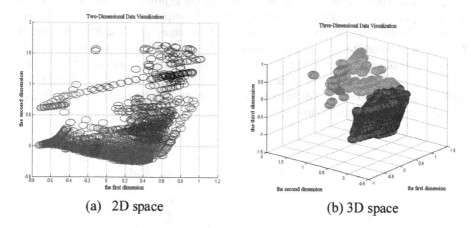

(a) 2D space   (b) 3D space

Fig. 5. The visualized experimental results of self

Based on the proposed fitness function [18], that as shown in Eq. (10), we define a fitness function in Eq. (8). The difference between Eqs. (8) and (10) is that we add a variable, num_{det}, to count the overlapping numbers between current detector and the detectors in the last generation.

$$fitness = \omega_1 r_d - \omega_2 d_s - \omega_3 d_d \qquad (10)$$

In experiment, we set the value of ω_1, ω_2 and ω_3 to 0.45, 0.10 and 0.45, respectively, and the value of r_d is set to 0.1. The experimental results are as shown in Fig. 6, which are all through the process of iterating 50 times. Figure 6(a) shows the results of the detector generating with Eq. (8), which we improved the fitness function based on Eq. (10), and Fig. 6(b) shows the results of the detector generating with Eq. (10). It is obvious that the effect of detector generating in Fig. 6(a) is better than that in Fig. 6(b) in the aspect of coverage rate and dispersing degree.

We define several parameters to evaluate the performance of the IDS, and they are d, l, e, and r. Among them, d represents the detection rate, l represents the missing rate, e represents the mistake rate and r represents the recognition rate, respectively. In general, we calculate these performance parameters using the following variables, and they are FN (number of the abnormal data be detected), FP (number of the abnormal data do not be detected), TP (number of the normal data be recognised), TN (number of the normal data be detected), and whose formulas are shown as follows.

$$d = FN/(FP + FN) \times 100\% \qquad (11)$$

$$l = FP/(FP + FN) \times 100\% \qquad (12)$$

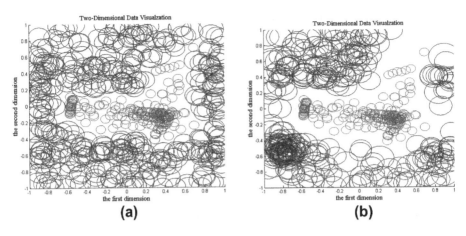

Fig. 6. The results of detector generating with different fitness function

$$e = TN/(TP + TN) \times 100\% \tag{13}$$

$$r = TP/(TP + TN) \times 100\% \tag{14}$$

There are five data sets, which are Normal, DOS attacks, Probing attacks, R2L attacks and U2R attacks. Of course, they will be explained in detail among the following discussion. These data sets are all constituting though the way of randomized extracting in 10 percent corrected data that has 425691 labeled data samples, of KDD CUP 1999. The data set of DOS contains 7000 data samples, which are labeled back, land, nepture, pod, smurf and teardrop. The data set of Probing contains 4000 data samples, which are labeled ipsweep, namp, portsweep and satan. The data set of R2L contains 1125 data samples, which are labeled ftp_write, guess_passwd, imap, multihop, phf, spy, ware-zclient, and warezmaster. Equally, the data set of U2R contains 50 data samples, which are labeled buffer_overflow, loadmodule, perl and rootkit. In addition, the data set of self contains 5000 data samples, which are labeled Normal. In detectors generation, we are also randomized extracting 200 data samples, which are labeled Normal, as self-data to train detectors. In the process of 2D and 3D experiments, we first produce 300 detectors according the 200 data samples. After 100 generations of training detectors, we test the IDS by using four types of attacking data sets. Experimental results are shown in Table 1.

Experimental results show that the detection rates for DOS, Probing, R2L and U2R are satisfactory. As described above, every detector will change its position and detection range constantly and dynamically in the process of every iteration. Figure 7 reveals the distribution situation of detectors after the intrusion detection in 2D space. In experiment, we only exhibit the distribution about 2D space, because of the occlusion between them in 3D space. From these figures we can see that the distribution situation of detectors is different against different data sets of invading. The experimental results show that we can detect illegal invasion effectively, and notwithstanding appearing a small amount of the missing rate.

Table 1. The results of non-self data in 2D and 3D real space

Dimension	Types	DOS	Probing	R2L	U2R
2D	d (%)	99.89	96.38	97.69	98.14
	l (%)	0.11	3.62	2.31	1.86
	e (%)	0.00	0.00	0.00	0.00
3D	d (%)	99.67	96.75	100.00	98.00
	l (%)	0.33	3.25	0.00	2.00
	e (%)	0.00	0.00	0.00	0.00

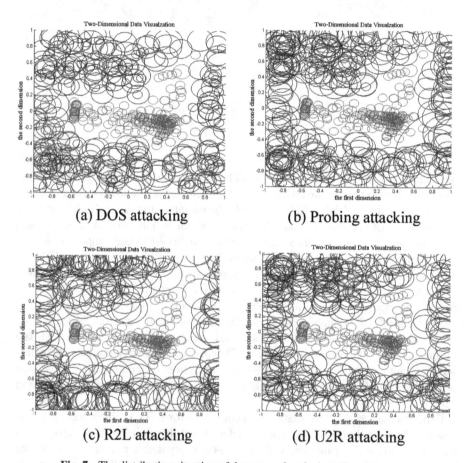

(a) DOS attacking   (b) Probing attacking

(c) R2L attacking   (d) U2R attacking

Fig. 7. The distribution situation of detectors after the intrusion detection

The following will intoduce the instrusion detection model, that proposed in this paper, to recognize self data. The experimental results are shown in Table 2.

Table 2. The results of self data in 2D and 3D real space

Dimension	Times	50	100	200	500
2D	r (%)	94.60	93.40	93.80	92.80
	l (%)	3.20	4.00	3.05	3.00
	e (%)	2.20	2.60	3.15	3.20
3D	r (%)	94.80	94.20	93.80	93.60
	l (%)	3.40	4.20	5.00	4.97
	e (%)	1.80	1.60	1.20	1.43

Table 2 shows that the recognition rate for normal data is satisfactory, while existence a small amount of the missing rate and mistaking rate. Figure 8 reveals the experimental results of self-data testing in 2D space, which are carried out iterations of 50, 100, 200 and 500, respectivly.

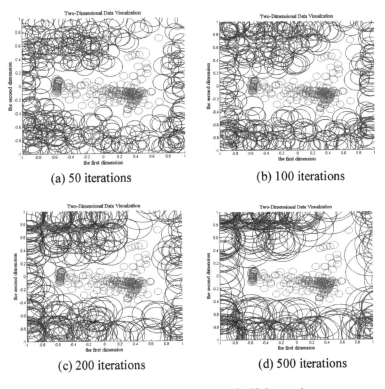

(a) 50 iterations   (b) 100 iterations

(c) 200 iterations   (d) 500 iterations

Fig. 8. The experimental results of self-data testing

We seem to have come to the conclusion that recognition rate is declining with the increasing number of iterations, but all in all, the algorithm that we have proposed can recognise normal data accessing effectively.

As discussed above, we want to prove the validity of this algorithm, which we have improved the traditional negative slection algorithm with shift mutation and radom grouping, and have improved the dynamic clone selection algorithm with genetic algorithm, by visual experiment especially in two-dimensional space. But with normal conditions, the data dimension is higher than 2 or 3 in the IDS.

At the end of this paper, we did a comparative experiment with two other algorithms, that had been proposed in [13, 14]. Certainly, in this experiment we set the data dimension to 10 through readjusting the accumulative contributions ratios of PCA, and this number is more close to the really data dimension in the network environment. The comparative results as shown in Table 3.

Table 3. Comparative results with some other algorithms

Types	Detection Rate (%)		
	DynamicCS in Ref. [13]	IDV in Ref. [14]	DCS-GA
DOS	93.50	97.33	**98.60**
Probing	92.25	96.25	**96.77**
R2L	93.14	93.70	**94.13**
U2R	94.33	**97.50**	90.67

Experimental results show that the performance of DCS-GA, which is proposed in this paper, is better than the other two algorithms in general. However, the detection rate of DCS-GA is lower than the other two when it detects the data set of U2R. One possibility is that the size of the data for detecting is too small, and as illustrated in the previous section that the data set of U2R just contains 50 data samples.

5   Conclusions

In this paper, we propose an intrusion detection model of multi-dimensional data based on the AIS. First of all, we should do the operations of preprocessing the data for building available cubes, which include discrete data continuity, data normalization and data standardization. Secondly, we use the PCA algorithm to reduce the dimensions of the data after pretreatment and use the K-means algorithm to reduce computational complexity. Finally, we improve the traditional negative selection algorithm with the method of shift mutation for increasing the efficiency of generating detectors and use the way of random grouping to keep population diversity. Besides, we improve the dynamic clone selection algorithm using genetic algorithm to realize the dynamic update and adaptive learning of detectors. In order to observe the effectiveness of the proposed algorithm, we do some low dimensional experiments, and then we do a comparative experiment with two other algorithms in muilt-dimensional space to prove the validity.

However, we control the dimensions of data only through readjusting the accumulative contribution ratios of PCA. There are a lot of drawbacks in this approach. Whether having a way of intelligent matching to control data dimensions adaptivly is a wrathful field for research.

Acknowledgment. This work was supported in part by the Key Project of the National Natural Science Foundation of China (no. 61134009), the National Natural Science Foundation of China (nos. 61473077, 61473078), Program for Changjiang Scholars from the Ministry of Education, Specialized Research Fund for Shanghai Leading Talents, and Project of the Shanghai Committee of Science and Technology (no. 13JC1407500).

References

1. Wang, W., Guyet, T., Quiniou, R., et al.: Autonomic intrusion detection: adaptively detecting anomalies over unlabeled audit data streams in computer networks. Knowl.-Based Syst. **70**, 103–117 (2014)
2. Murugan, S., Kuppusamy, D.K.: Intelligent intrusion detection prevention systems. ACM Sigcomm. Comput. Commun. Rev. **42**(4), 285–286 (2012)
3. Ji, Z., Dasgupta, D.: Revisiting negative selection algorithms. Evol. Comput. **15**(2), 223–251 (2007)
4. Du, H., Jiao, L.-c., Gong, M., Liu, R.: Adaptive dynamic clone selection algorithms. In: Tsumoto, S., Słowiński, R., Komorowski, J., Grzymała-Busse, J.W. (eds.) RSCTC 2004. LNCS (LNAI), vol. 3066, pp. 768–773. Springer, Heidelberg (2004)
5. Ulutas, B.H., Kulturel-Konak, S.: A review of clonal selection algorithm and its applications. Artif. Intell. Rev. **36**(2), 117–138 (2011)
6. Mostardinha, P., Faria, B.F., Zúquete, A., Vistulo de Abreu, F.: A negative selection approach to intrusion detection. In: Coello Coello, C.A., Greensmith, J., Krasnogor, N., Liò, P., Nicosia, G., Pavone, M. (eds.) ICARIS 2012. LNCS, vol. 7597, pp. 178–190. Springer, Heidelberg (2012)
7. Luo, W., Cao, X., Wang, J., et al.: Intrusion detection oriented distributed negative selection algorithm. In: Proceedings of International Conference on Neural Information Processing, ICONIP, vol. 3, pp. 1474–1478 (2002)
8. Zhao, T., Li, Z., Wang, Z., et al.: An adaptive intrusion detection algorithm based on improved dynamic clonal selection algorithms. In: Sixth International Conference on Intelligent Systems Design and Applications, ISDA 2006, pp. 1073–1076. IEEE (2006)
9. Yin, C., Ma, L., Feng, L.: Towards accurate intrusion detection based on improved clonal selection algorithm. Multimedia Tools Appl. 1–14 (2015)
10. Hui, Y., Jian-Yong, L.: Intrusion detection based on immune dynamical matching algorithm. In: Proceedings of the International Conference on E-Business and E-Government, ICEE 2010, Guangzhou, China, 7–9 May 2010, pp. 1342–1345 (2010)
11. Kotov, V.D., Vasilyev, V.: Immune model based approach for network intrusion detection. In: International Conference on Security of Information and Networks, Sin 2010, Rostov-On-Don, Russian Federation, pp. 233–237, September 2010
12. Hong, L.: Immune mechanism based intrusion detection systems. In: International Conference on Networks Security, Wireless Communications and Trusted Computing, NSWCTC 2009, pp. 568–571. IEEE (2009)
13. Kim, J., Bentley, P.J.: Towards an artificial immune system for network intrusion detection: an investigation of dynamic clonal selection. In: Proceedings of the 2002 Congress on Evolutionary Computation, 12–17 May, Honolulu, HI, USA, pp. 1015–1020 (2002)
14. Yan, X.H.: An artificial immune-based intrusion detection model using vaccination strategy. Acta Electronica Sinica **37**(4), 780–785 (2009)

15. Jian, Y., David, Z., Frangi, A.F., et al.: Two-dimensional PCA: a new approach to appearance-based face representation and recognition. IEEE Trans. Pattern Anal. Mach. Intell. **26**(1), 131–137 (2004)
16. Hartigan, J.A., Wong, M.A.: Algorithm AS 136: a K-Means clustering algorithm. Appl. Stat. **28**(1), 100–108 (1979)
17. KDD Cup'99 data set. http://kdd.ics.uci.edu/databases/kddcup99/kddcup99.html
18. Weng, G., Yu, S., Zhou, J.: Multimodal evolution approach to multidimensional intrusion detection. J. Southwest Jiao Tong Univ. **14**(3), 212–217 (2006)

Simulation and Analysis of Magnetic Beads Sorting in High Gradient Magnetic Field and Efficiency Study

Wenjun Gao, Wei Tao, and Hui Zhao[✉]

Department of Instrument Science and Engineering, SEIEE,
Shanghai Jiao Tong University, Shanghai, China
huizhao@sjtu.edu.cn

Abstract. Based on the principles of high gradient magnetic field separation, build the model of the separation column, which uses steel balls as magnetic flux gathering matrix. Simulate the distribution of magnetic field and fluid field in the model. Define the magnetic force factor G to measure the magnetic force on magnetic beads, analyze the influences of external magnetic field, the diameter and the relative permeability of steel balls on G, respectively. And calculate magnetic beads movements in the effect of both magnetic field and fluid field, analyze the variation of adsorption rate with external magnetic field, the relative permeability of steel balls, the magnetic beads diameter, the steel balls diameter and the initial fluid velocity. Results indicate that: the magnetic force factor increases with stronger magnetic field, smaller steel balls diameter, and with the relative permeability of steel balls increases, it increases rapidly first, then decreases slightly and becomes steady. Magnetic beads adsorption rate increases with stronger magnetic field, larger magnetic beads diameter, smaller steel balls diameter and lower initial fluid velocity. Among all the factors, the magnetic beads diameter has the greatest influence on the adsorption rate, followed by the initial fluid velocity, the external magnetic field and the steel balls diameter.

Keywords: HGMF · Finite element simulation · Magnetic beads · Adsorption rate

1 Introduction

High gradient magnetic field separation (HGMS) technique is widely used in industry, such as mineral processing, chemical separation and water purification. It aims to generate a high gradient magnetic field (HGMF) with permeable matrix in a uniform magnetic field, and produce a strong magnetic force on the magnetic particles to separate them away from other non-magnetic materials, the matrix can be magnetic mineral powder, steel wool, sponge metal, metal fiber, steel ball, etc. Immunomagnetic beads technique is developed in the basis of HGMS, magnetic beads are superparamagnetic nanoparticles which can combine with biological components specifically, such as cells with specific antigens. When coupled with high gradient magnetic field, components combined with magnetic beads will be adsorbed in magnetic field area and isolated from other non-magnetic components. It has the advantages of fast, good

© Springer Science+Business Media Singapore 2016
L. Zhang et al. (Eds.): AsiaSim 2016/SCS AutumnSim 2016, Part IV, CCIS 646, pp. 161–171, 2016.
DOI: 10.1007/978-981-10-2672-0_17

repeatability, simple to operate and low impact on biochemical compositions, and is widely used in cell sorting, bacteria sorting, biological detection, and drug delivery. Many researches have been conducted in HGMS field so far, and a series of models have been proposed, such as the trajectory model proposed by Watson [1], aggregation model proposed by Nesset and Finch [2], phenomenological model proposed by Watson, Collan and Akoto [3–5], etc. However, most of them are empirical based or semi-empirical based, with few detailed discussion of separation mechanism and dynamic process. Within HGMF produced by permeable matrix, the motions of magnetic beads in fluid are complicated, hard to parse in dynamics perspective.

To clarify the features of magnetic separation, I applied the finite element analysis method to magnetic beads separation model and conducted the simulation, regardless of the theories proposed formerly. First I built the geometrical model for separation column widely used in clinical and research, which uses steel balls as matrix. Then the distribution of magnetic field and fluid field, the particle movements would be calculated with finite element analysis method, and the influence of external magnetic field, the relative permeability of steel balls, the magnetic beads diameter, the steel balls diameter and the initial flow velocity on the magnetic beads' adsorption rate would be discussed according to the simulation results.

2 Principles of HGMS

The separation column uses steel balls as permeable matrix, when apply an external magnetic field, steel balls would be magnetized, a HGMF would be generated in the gaps of the matrix. When fluid containing magnetic beads flows through the column, magnetic beads would be magnetized with a magnetic force, if the magnetic force is strong enough to resist drag force, magnetic beads would be captured in the matrix, as is shown in Fig. 1. After that remove the external magnetic field, steel balls would demagnetize, magnetic force would disappear, thus the magnetic beads could be gathered with eluent.

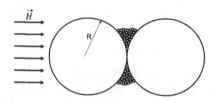

Fig. 1. Schematic of magnetic beads capturing

The main forces act on magnetic beads in the separator are magnetic force, drag force, Brownian force, gravity force and buoyancy force, respectively [6]. We consider the gravity force equals to the buoyancy force for nanoparticles [7], and the Brownian force can be ignored as it's so small compared with other forces. Here we only consider magnetic force and drag force, according to the Newton's second law, the force balance on a moving particle is:

$$m\frac{dV}{dt} = F_m + F_f \tag{1}$$

Where m is the mass of magnetic bead, V is the magnetic bead's velocity, F_m is the magnetic force, and F_f is the drag force.

2.1 Magnetic Force

The force acting on a magnetic bead within a magnetic field is [8]:

$$\mathbf{F}_m = \mu_0\mu_f V_p \frac{3(\chi_p - \chi_f)}{(\chi_p - \chi_f) + 3(\chi_f + 1)}(\mathbf{H} \cdot \nabla)\mathbf{H} \tag{2}$$

Where μ_0 is the permeability of the vacuum, μ_f is the relative permeability of the fluid, V_p is the magnetic bead's volume, H is the external magnetic field intensity and χ_p, χ_f are susceptibility of magnetic beads and fluid, respectively.

Considering $|\chi_f| \ll 1$, $\mu_f \approx 1$, Eq. (2) can be simplified as:

$$\mathbf{F}_m = \mu_0\mu_f V_p \frac{3\chi_p}{\chi_p + 3}(\mathbf{H} \cdot \nabla)\mathbf{H} \tag{3}$$

The equation indicates that when the volume of magnetic bead is certain, the magnetic force $\mathbf{F}_m$ is proportional to the magnetic field intensity and gradient. When the magnetic field gradient is 0, however strong the magnetic field is, $\mathbf{F}_m$ is always 0, that is, when a uniform magnetic field is applied with no matrix, no magnetic force will be acted on particles. Whereas if the magnetic field is weak, we can still increase magnetic force by improving the magnetic field gradient.

Here we define $(\mathbf{H} \cdot \nabla)\mathbf{H}$ as the magnetic force factor, expressed by symbol G. H can be expressed with magnetic scalar potential V_m,

$$\mathbf{H} = -\nabla V_m = -\left(\frac{\partial V_m}{\partial x}\vec{x} + \frac{\partial V_m}{\partial y}\vec{y} + \frac{\partial V_m}{\partial z}\vec{z}\right) \tag{4}$$

We have:

$$\mathbf{G} = (\mathbf{H} \cdot \nabla)\mathbf{H} = \left(\frac{\partial^2 V_m}{\partial x^2}\frac{\partial V_m}{\partial x} + \frac{\partial V_m}{\partial y}\frac{\partial^2 V_m}{\partial x\partial y} + \frac{\partial V_m}{\partial z}\frac{\partial^2 V_m}{\partial x\partial z}\right)\vec{x}$$
$$+ \left(\frac{\partial V_m}{\partial x}\frac{\partial^2 V_m}{\partial y\partial x} + \frac{\partial^2 V_m}{\partial y^2}\frac{\partial V_m}{\partial y} + \frac{\partial V_m}{\partial z}\frac{\partial^2 V_m}{\partial y\partial z}\right)\vec{y}$$
$$+ \left(\frac{\partial V_m}{\partial x}\frac{\partial^2 V_m}{\partial x\partial z} + \frac{\partial V_m}{\partial y}\frac{\partial^2 V_m}{\partial y\partial z} + \frac{\partial^2 V_m}{\partial z^2}\frac{\partial V_m}{\partial z}\right)\vec{z}$$

So we can calculated the three components of G in x, y, z direction as G_x, G_y, G_z.

2.2   Drag Force

For magnetic beads suspending in a fluid flow, a drag force is generated due to the velocity difference between the particles and the fluid. Considering the flow is slow with low Reynolds number, we can estimate the drag force from the Stokes' law [9]:

$$F_f = -6\pi\eta R(v_p - v_f) \tag{5}$$

Where η is the dynamic viscosity of the fluid, R is the radius of magnetic bead, and v_p, v_f are the velocities of magnetic bead and fluid, respectively. The drag force increases with higher velocity and larger magnetic beads diameters.

3   Separation Model

Build the geometric model as shown in Fig. 2. It's a cylinder with symmetry axis parallel to z axis, inside there are three layers of closely packed steel balls in z axis direction. The whole model is surrounded by a large cuboid air domain (not drawn in Fig. 2). Apply an external background magnetic field in x axis direction. The fluid flows into the cylinder from the bottom plane, and flows out from the top plane.

The main parameters involved below are:

(1) Fluid parameters: we use water as carrier liquid, at normal temperature, the dynamic viscosity of water is $\eta = 0.001$ Pa·s, density is $\rho_f = 1000$ kg/m3, suscepti- bility $\chi_f = 7.7 \times 10^{-6}$, relative permeability $\mu_f \approx 1$, the initial velocity v;

(2) Magnetic beads parameters: diameter D (typically nm magnitude), density $\rho_p = 5180$ kg/m3, susceptibility $\chi_f = 0.6377$;

(3) Steel ball parameters: diameter d (typically 0.2 ~ 0.5 mm), relative perme- ability μ_{ball}.

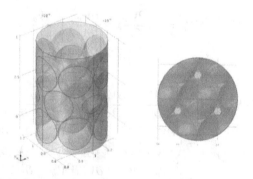

Fig. 2. The geometric model of simulation

4 Magnetic Field Simulation

Figure 3 is the magnetic lines of flux in the midsection of the second steel balls layer when steel balls are not used and used. Set d = 0.5 mm, Fig. 4 is the curve of magnetic force factor G on the transversal shown in Fig. 3b, which is 0.22 mm away from the center of the cylinder in negative y direction.

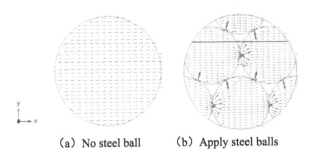

(a) No steel ball   (b) Apply steel balls

Fig. 3. Magnetic field distribution in midsection

As is shown in Figs. 3b and 4, in the gaps of the steel balls, the lines become non-uniform, magnetic force factor increases rapidly, and reaches maximum on the surface and the contact point of the steel balls. With the function of steel balls, the external uniform magnetic field becomes non-uniform, and the magnetic field intensity and gradient increase greatly in the gaps.

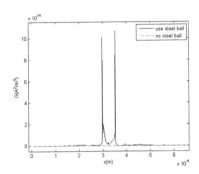

Fig. 4. Magnetic force factor in transversal

According to Eq. (2), to reach a higher adsorption rate, we should increase magnetic force factor G, influenced by external magnetic field H, the relative permeability of steel balls μ_{ball} and the diameter of steel balls d.

In order to measure the magnetic performance of the magnetic separation model, here we uses the average of G in all steel ball gaps as the main indicator, and analyze the impact of each parameter.

4.1   Influence of External Magnetic Field

Set d = 0.3 mm, μ_{ball} = 1000, change H, and calculate the values of G for each H, Fig. 5 shows the variation of G_x, G_y, G_z with H respectively.

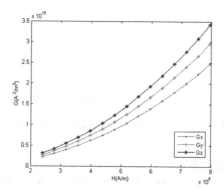

Fig. 5. G versus H

It's obvious that G increases at a growing rate while H increases. This is because G is the secondary power of H actually, hence the slope of G-H curve would increase with H.

4.2   Influence of Steel Balls

When the external magnetic field is certain, G is determined by the parameters of steel balls. Different μ_{ball} and different d would result in different magnetic field gradient. μ_{ball} depends largely on the manufacturing heat process and chemical element composition such as carbon content of steel balls. Here we set H = 400 kA/m, vary μ_{ball} from 1 to 1000, calculate the variation of G with μ_{ball} when d is set to 0.2 mm, 0.25 mm, 0.3 mm, 0.35 mm, 0.4 mm, 0.45 mm and 0.5 mm respectively. Figure 6 shows the curves of Gx versus μ_{ball} for each d, Gy and Gz are similar.

For each d, with μ_{ball} increases, Gx increases rapidly first, and gets to maximum when μ_{ball} is about 45, then Gx decreases slowly and becomes steady after 400.

Compare curves of different d, we can see Gx increases when d decreases, namely, smaller steel balls introduce higher magnetic field gradient.

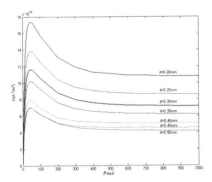

Fig. 6. G versus μ_{ball}

5   Fluid Field Simulation

The fluid flows through the gaps in the steel ball matrix, Fig. 7 shows the fluid field distribution of the inlet and midsection when d = 0.3 mm, v = 0.326 mm/s, respectively. Wherein x, y axis are the position coordinates, z axis is the velocity magnitude. It's shown that velocity of the inlet distributes uniformly, while in the midsection, the fluid velocity increases in the gap, and reaches maximum in the middle of the gap. The fluid field distribution mainly depends on the initial fluid velocity v and steel balls diameter d. It's obvious that flow speed in the gaps increases with a faster inlet velocity and smaller steel balls.

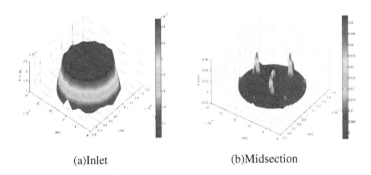

(a)Inlet   (b)Midsection

Fig. 7.   Flow speed distribution

6   Particle Motion Simulation

A number of magnetic beads are released with the fluid in the same initial velocity. Apply magnetic force and drag force to the magnetic beads with the calculated results before, and count the number of magnetic beads in the outlet.

We define the adsorption rate η as:

$$\eta = \frac{N_{in} - N_{out}}{N_{in}} \tag{6}$$

Where N_{in} and N_{out} are the numbers of magnetic beads in inlet and outlet, respectively. We use η as the main indicator of separation efficiency, η is affected by the magnetic force factor $\mathbf{G}$, the magnetic bead diameter D and the inlet fluid viscosity v. As is discussed before, $\mathbf{G}$ depends on μ_{ball}, d and H, whereas when μ_{ball} is larger than 400, its impact on G is little, so we set $\mu_{ball} = 4000$ here, and calculate the variation of η with H, D, v, d.

6.1 Influence of External Magnetic Field

Set D = 8 nm, v = 0.326 mm/s, d = 0.3 mm, vary the value of H, Fig. 8 shows the variation curve of η with H.

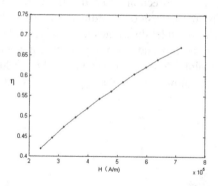

Fig. 8. η versus H

When H increases from 2.39 kA/m to 7.16 kA/m, η increases from 0.42 to 0.67 almost linearly, the increasing range is about 0.25. Vary d and v, η-H curve behaves the same.

External magnetic field is usually provided by permanent magnet, the intensity of H is limited, typically between 200 kA/m and 500 kA/m. We set H equals 400kA/m in the below discussion.

6.2 Influence of Magnetic Beads Diameter

Set d = 0.5 mm, v = 0.326 mm/s, vary the value of D, Fig. 9 shows the variation curve of η with D.

As is shown, when D ranges from 8 nm to 80 nm, η increases from 0.5 to 0.98, and the increasing rate decreases with D. From Eqs. (3) and (5), magnetic force is

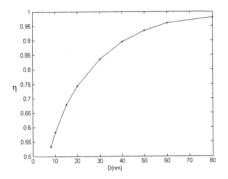

Fig. 9. η versus D

proportional to the third power of D, while drag force is proportional to the first power of D, hence the increasing amplitude of the magnetic force is larger than the drag force, thus η increases with D. In reality, larger magnetic beads have larger mechanical stress to the cells or other biological components, which may cause damage to them.

6.3   Influence of Initial Fluid Velocity

Set D = 8 nm, vary v from 0.1 mm/s to 5 mm/s, calculate the variation of η with v when d is set to 0.2 mm, 0.25 mm, 0.3 mm, 0.35 mm, 0.4 mm, 0.45 mm and 0.5 mm respectively. Figure 10 shows the curves of η versus v for each d.

For each d, η decreases with v, and the decreasing speed slows down while v increases. Higher velocity results in stronger drag force, hence the adsorption rate decreases. The decreasing scale is typically in the range of 0.25 and 0.31.

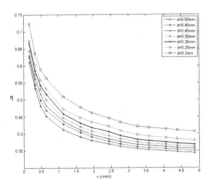

Fig. 10. η versus v

6.4   Influence of Steel Balls Diameter d

From Fig. 10 we can see that for the same velocity, separation model with smaller steel balls has higher adsorption rate. Figure 11 shows the variation of η with d when v is 0.326 mm/s, 0.489 mm/s, and 0.662 mm/s respectively. When d increases from 0.2 mm to 0.5 mm, η decreases in the range of 0.05 and 0.1.

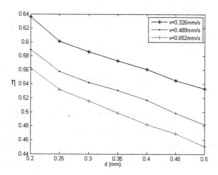

Fig. 11. η versus d

Steel balls diameter d influences both on the magnetic force factor and the fluid velocity in the gaps. Smaller d results in stronger magnetic force and stronger drag force. Through the simulation results, we know that the increase of magnetic force is greater than the drag force, hence the adsorption rate increases with smaller steel balls.

7   Conclusion

For separation columns with steel balls matrix, the adsorption rate depends on the magnetic field H, the relative permeability of steel balls μ_{ball}, the magnetic beads diameter D, the steel balls diameter d and the initial fluid velocity v:

1. The magnetic field H and the relative permeability of steel balls μ_{ball} affect the magnetic force factor G. Stronger H creates stronger magnetic force, thus results in higher adsorption rate. Yet when μ_{ball} increases, G increases rapidly first, then decreases slowly and becomes steady when μ_{ball} is larger than 400.
2. The magnetic beads diameter influences both on the magnetic force and the drag force, larger magnetic beads result in higher adsorption rate.
3. The inlet fluid velocity influence only on the drag force, faster flow results in lower adsorption rate, and the decreasing speed of adsorption rate slows down while v increases.
4. The steel balls diameter influences both on the magnetic force and the drag force, smaller steel balls result in higher adsorption rate.
5. Among all the factors, the magnetic beads diameter has the greatest influence on the adsorption rate, followed by the inlet fluid velocity, the magnetic field and steel balls diameter.

6. In reality, selections of the parameters are limited by experimental conditions: external magnetic field is usually provided by permanent magnet, the intensity of H is limited, typically between 200 kA/m and 500 kA/m; When the magnetic beads are used in cell sorting, larger beads have greater damage to cells; Slower flow can improve the adsorption rate, while it means more time cost. And usually smaller steel ball means higher manufacturing difficulty and higher costs. Balancing of application field, cost and time efficiency should be considered to choose the most suitable parameters.

Acknowledgement. This research was supported by National High Technology Research and Development Program of China (No. 2014AA020701).

References

1. Watson, J.: Theory of capture of particles in magnetic high-intensity filters. IEEE Trans. Magn. **11**(5), 1597–1599 (1975)
2. Nesset, J., Finch, J.: The static (buildup) model of particle accumulation on single wires in high gradient magnetic separation: experimental confirmation. IEEE Trans. Magn. **17**(4), 1506–1509 (1981)
3. Watson, J.H.: Approximate solutions of the magnetic separator equations. IEEE Trans. Magn. **14**(4), 240–245 (1978)
4. Collan, H., Kokkala, M., Ritvos, A.: Analysis of magnetic filter experiments with polydisperse particle suspensions. IEEE Trans. Magn. **15**(6), 1529–1531 (1979)
5. Akoto, I.: Mathematical modelling of high-gradient magnetic separation devices. IEEE Trans. Magn. **13**(5), 1486–1489 (1977)
6. Hejazian, M., Li, W., Nguyen, N.T.: Lab on a chip for continuous-flow magnetic cell separation. Lab Chip **15**(4), 959–970 (2015)
7. Wu, X., Wu, H., Hu, Y.: Enhancement of separation efficiency on continuous magnetophoresis by utilizing L/T-shaped microchannels. Microfluid. Nanofluid. **11**(1), 11–24 (2011)
8. Furlani, E.P.: Magnetophoretic separation of blood cells at the microscale. J. Phys. D Appl. Phys. **40**(5), 1313–1319 (2007)
9. Furlani, E.P., Ng, K.C.: Analytical model of magnetic nanoparticle transport and capture in the microvasculature. Phys. Rev. E Stat. Nonlinear Soft Matter Phys. **73**(6 Pt 1), 061919 (2006)

RUM-TCG: A Test Code Generation Tool for Simulation Model Based on RUM

Tianlin Li[✉], Yiping Yao, Huilong Chen, and Sirui Bao

College of Information System and Management, National University of Defense Technology,
Changsha, Hunan, China
ltl@mail.ustc.edu.cn, {ypyao,chenhuilong}@nudt.edu.cn,
554700702@qq.com

Abstract. As the scale of parallel discrete event simulation (PDES) applications becomes larger, more and more complex simulation models are integrated into those applications. Consequently, integrating and testing these models become quite difficult. Reusable simulation model development Specification (RUM) can make it easier for developers to integrate models into simulation, which accelerates the process of developing simulation applications. However, testing RUM model still relies on writing test code manually by developers, which is very time-consuming. Furthermore, existing test code generation tools cannot be used for testing RUM models directly. To solve this problem, we proposed a customizable test code generation tool for RUM models called RUM-TCG, which can automatically generate executable test code according to models' code files and the configurations of testers. As experiments shows, the code auto-generated by RUM-TCG is able to perform both functional test and automatic regression test for RUM models.

Keywords: RUM · Automated test code generation · Test cases

1 Introduction

As the scale of PDES applications becomes larger and larger, there are many complicated simulation models in one application, and it becomes rather difficult to test these models and integrate them into an application. Reusable simulation model development Specification RUM [1] can reduce the difficulty of model integration and improve the development efficiency of simulation application. The growing complexity of RUM models leads to the continual growth of test cost. According to study [2], test cost often occupies a large part of the total cost of application development. However, testing RUM models still relies on writing test code manually by testers. By executing the test code, testers can observe whether the models' output results are consistent with the expectations. Ideally, the ratio between test code and production code is considered to approach 1:1 [3]. So writing the test code manually is a heavy and laborious work, particularly when application contains many RUM models. Automated generation of test code will be a big help to reduce the testing cost. However, existing test code generation tools cannot be used directly for RUM models.

© Springer Science+Business Media Singapore 2016
L. Zhang et al. (Eds.): AsiaSim 2016/SCS AutumnSim 2016, Part IV, CCIS 646, pp. 172–179, 2016.
DOI: 10.1007/978-981-10-2672-0_18

To solve this problem, this paper proposes a customizable test code dynamic generation tool for RUM models called RUM-TCG, which can automatically generate executable test code according to models' code files and the configurations of testers. By observing the running results of models with these test code, testers can obtain whether there are errors occurred while the models are running. The main section of the test code is used to execute models, including models' instantiation, declaration and assignment of models' parameters, as well as models' calculation. The configurations of testers determine whether the auxiliary code section, which is used to record models' output data to judge whether they are consistent with the expected data, will be added into test code or not. The reason why generated test code is customizable is that auxiliary code is optional. In addition, RUM-TCG can be applied to RUM models developed in C/C++ or Java programming language. The generated test code is executable, so there is no need for testers to edit the code again.

The rest of this paper is organized as follows. The second section describes the background and related work. The third section presents RUM-TCG's architecture and implementation mechanisms in detail. The fourth section is validation of RUM-TCG. Section 5 concludes the whole work of this paper.

2   Background and Related Work

2.1   RUM Specification

Zhu et al. proposed a reusable model development specification called RUM, towards reducing the difficulty of model integration and improving the development efficiency of simulation application. It defines the interface of model including initialization, input data, model process, output data etc. This specification has been applied in a number of simulation applications. In addition, RUM provides a basis for automatic code generation of simulation models.

Figure 1 shows a RUM schematic described in C/C++ language, which can also be applied to models implemented in other object-oriented programming languages such as Java.

2.2   Related Work

After many years development, software and program testing technology has been relatively mature, a variety of program testing tools have been developed [5, 6], such as JUnit, JFCUnit, ISTA and the like. However, the existing tools cannot be directly used to generate test code for RUM model.

Gamma Erich and Kent Beck proposed JUnit [7, 9], a regression testing framework for Java application developers to write unit tests. JUnit can test the interface section with input and output parameters, and provide a package to judge the return parameters. Besides it can return the test results and form a test report automatically. However, it only applies to program written in Java language and cannot be used to test RUM models developed in other languages, such as C, C++ etc.

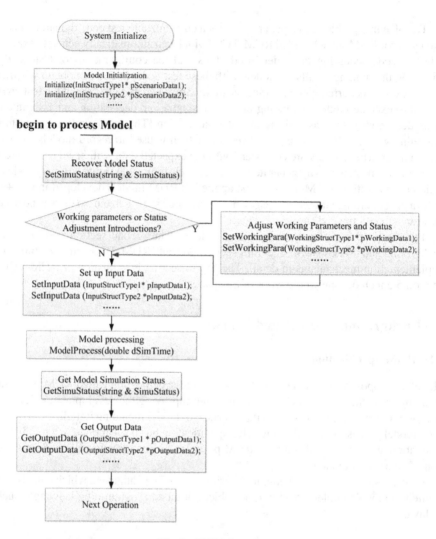

Fig. 1. RUM flow chart

FreeMarker [10] is a code generation engine developed with code generation technology based on template. When used to generate test code of RUM model, the test code template of this model is necessary. Therefore it cannot be directly used for test code generation of RUM model.

Xu [4] proposed ISTA (Integration and System Test Automation), which was a tool for automated generation of executable test code by using high-level Petri nets as finite state test models. However, the input to ISTA should follow MID specification, consisting of a Predicate/Transition net, a MIM (model-implementation mapping), and HC (helper code). Achieving such input for RUM model may cause a lot of additional overhead, so ISTA cannot apply to RUM model directly.

3 Rum-TCG

As Fig. 2 illustrates, RUM-TCG mainly contains four modules, code parser, user interface, test case parser and code generator. By scanning RUM model code files, code parser can extract the important model information, including model custom data structures, model interfaces. User interface can display the model information and provide a configuration module for the assignment of model parameters, and testers can also set the content of generated test code with this module. Test case parser is used to extract test data from the given test cases and assign them to model parameters. In this paper test cases are XML files. Code generator can generate executable test code automatically based on the information from code parser, user interface and test case parser.

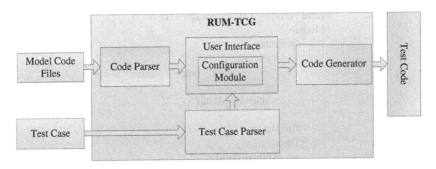

Fig. 2. RUM-TCG architecture

3.1 Code Parser

Test code should contain the call of tested model, to implement the automatic generation of this code section, model interface information must be obtained. According to RUM, models need initialization and input data, achieving them by parameters. Data structures of parameters are necessary for the assignment of these parameters.

In response to these needs, RUM-TCG contains a Code Parser, its function is to scan model code files to extract model information, including custom data structures and interface information. Interface information consists of interface name and data type of parameters. Code Parser mainly contains a lexical analyzer and a lightweight parser, and the parser can locate the custom data structure and interface declaration sections. The reason why the parser is lightweight is that its grammar rules are simple. When locating model data structures, detailed information of these data structures are stored in a dedicated string vector, including data structure name, name and data type of each member of the structure, taking name of data structure as the index. Similarly, for all the declaration section of interfaces, interface name and parameter data types should be stored in another dedicated string vector. Then the two vectors are sent to UI and Code Generator for display and test code generation.

3.2 XML Test Case File

Using test cases to test model is a common method. Test case should include the input data and expected output data of tested object, because the aim of test is to gain a clear idea of the difference between expected results and actual results [8]. For RUM model, the input domain of model are initialization and input data, the output data is the result of model calculations. Given that XML file has a clear hierarchy, using XML file to store test case makes test data easier to extract. A XML test case file specification for RUM model was proposed, as shown in Fig. 3, test case contains three parts, initialization data, input data and expected output data. Initialization and input data are used to configure the model instance, and expected output data are used for comparison with model actual output data. The function of Test Case Parser is to extract test data from the XML test case files.

```
<?xml version="1.0" encoding="UTF-8"?>
<Model>
    <InitData>
        <pScenarioData1>
            <name="" type="" value=""/>
            ...
        </pScenarioData1>
        ...
    </InitData>
    <InputData>
        <pInputData1>
            <name="" type="" value=""/>
            ...
        </pInputData1>
        ...
    </InputData>
    <OutputData>
        <pOutputData1>
            <name="" type="" value=""/>
            ...
        </pOutputData1>
        ...
    </OutputData>
</Model>
```

Fig. 3. XML test case file specification based on RUM

3.3 Code Generator

Code generator is to generate executable test code. Test code mainly includes two parts, main code and auxiliary code. The former contains model instantiation, parameter declarations, parameter assignments and model calculations. The latter is used to record the output data and compare model actual output data with the expected output data in test case. Figure 4 describes the framework of test code.

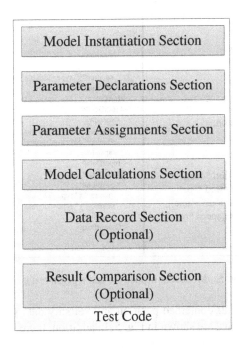

Fig. 4. Test code framework

For the main code section, model instantiation and parameter declarations are generated based on model name and interfaces, extracted from model code files by Code Parser. Parameters assignment code generation needs parameter names, parameter data structures, model initialization data and input data, the data comes from testers input or test case. Model calculation section is generated according to RUM and interface information.

The generation of data record section in auxiliary code needs output parameter names and their data structures. This section is used to write the values of output parameters into files. When testers choose a test case to test the model, result comparison code section can be generated according to output parameters and expected output results in test case. This section can reduce the workload of testers to compare model actual output data with expected output data.

4   Validation

A RUM simulation model called Car written in C++ was tested on RUM-TCG. Car was a simple car model, which is expected to do uniform linear motion. The initialization, input and output data of Car corresponded to starting position, velocity, and current position. The time interval was 1.

Car.h	```xml <?xml version="1.0" encoding="UTF-8"?>

struct position{
    double x;
    double y;
};
struct speed{
    double value;
    double[2] direction;
};
class Car{
  public:
    void Initialize(position *pos);
    void SetInputData(speed *spe);
    void ModelProcess(double time);
    void GetOutputData(speed *result);
    ...
};
	`<Car>`
	  `<InitData>`
	    `<position>`
	      `<name="x" type="double" value="0"/>`
	      `<name="y" type="double" value="0"/>`
	    `</position>`
	  `</InitData>`
	  `<InputData>`
	    `<speed>`
	      `<name="value" type="double" value="10"/>`
	      `<name="direction" type="double[2]"value="1,0"/>`
	    `</speed>`
	  `</InputData>`
	  `<OutputData>`
	    `<position>`
	      `<name="x" type="double" value="10"/>`
	      `<name="y" type="double" value="0"/>`
	    `</position>`
	  `</OutputData>`
	`</Car>`

Fig. 5. Model car header file and a given test case

The header file of Car contained position and velocity data structure declarations, and interface declarations, are shown in Fig. 5. In addition, there was a given XML test case file of Car. In the test case, the starting position was (0, 0), the value of velocity is 10, and the direction is (1, 0), the expected output data is (10, 0). Experiment results showed that RUM-TCG could generate the test code of Car only relying on testers input

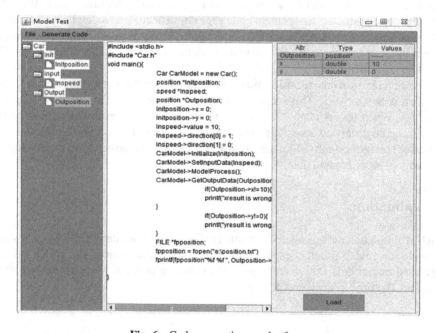

Fig. 6. Code generation result of car

data and the output data of Car was recorded by running the test code. Testers needed to analyze the output data to determine whether the function of Car meet expectations. As Fig. 6 shows, test code could also be generated according to the test case, if the output data is (0, 10), testers could determine that the function of Car did not meet the expectation functions. In addition, if testers chosen to add the result comparison code, the comparison result could be generated automatically by running test code. When Car is changed, RUM-TCG was able to generate the test code again automatically according to the header file, so it support automatic regression test.

5 Conclusion

This article proposed RUM-TCG, a RUM model test code dynamic generation tool. First the importance of RUM for PDES applications and test code generation for RUM model testing were summarized. Then, we listed the limitations of existing test code generation tools when used for RUM model, and concluded that existing tools cannot apply to RUM model directly. Afterwards, we presented the architecture and implementation mechanism of RUM-TCG to describe how test code was generated automatically according to model code files, given test case files and configurations of testers. Besides, the test code framework was presented and each section was explained. Finally, we conclude that RUM-TCG is correct and effective in terms of generating executable test code for RUM model and test code can perform functional test and automatic regression test for RUM model by validating an experimental RUM model.

Acknowledgment. We appreciate the support from State Key Laboratory of High Performance Computing, National University of Defense Technology (No. 201303-05) and Research Found for the Doctoral Program of Higher Education of China (No. 20124307110017).

References

1. Zhu, F., Yao, Y.P., Chen, H.L., Yao, F.: Reusable component model development approach for parallel and distributed simulation. Sci. World J., March 2014
2. Myers, G.J.: The Art of Software Testing, pp. 12–15. Wiley, New York (1979)
3. van Deursen, L., Moonen, A., van den Bergh, G.K.: Refactoring test code. In: Marchesi, M., Succi, G. (eds.) Proceedings of the 2nd International Conference on Extreme Programming and Flexible Processes in Software Engineering (XP2001), pp. 92–95, May 2001
4. Xu, D.: A tool for automated test code generation from high-level petri nets. In: 2011 Proceedings of the 32nd International Conference, PETRi NETS (2011)
5. Garlan, D., Perry, D.E.: Introduction to the Special Issue on Software Architecture. IEEE Trans. Softw. Eng. **21**(4), 269–274 (1995)
6. Kaner, C., Bach, J., et al.: Lessons Learned in Software Testing. John Wiley & Sons (2001)
7. Glassman, P.: Unit testing in a Java project. In: Succi, G., Marchesi, M. (eds.) Extreme Programming Examined, pp. 249–270. Addison-Wesley, Boston (2001)
8. IEEE Std 610.12-1990 IEEE Standard Glossary of Software Engineering Terminology (1990)
9. Erich, G., Beck, K.: Junit version3.8.1 [CP/OL]. http://www.junit.org
10. Radjenovic, J., Milosavljevic, B., Surla, D.: Modeling and implementation of catalogue cards using FreeMarker. Program: Electron. Libr. Inf. Syst. **43**(1), 62–76 (2009)

Simulating Streaming Software Applications Running on Clusters of Processors and Smartphone

Rafael Soto[1], Carolina Bonacic[1], Mauricio Marin[1], and Veronica Gil-Costa[2(✉)]

[1] CeBiB, DIINF, Universidad de Santiago, Santiago, Chile
[2] CONICET, Universidad Nacional de San Luis, San Luis, Argentina
gvcosta@unsl.edu.ar

Abstract. Social software applications devised to process large and intensive streams of data must be usually run on complex computational infrastructure that ranges from clusters of processors to smartphones. The scalability to thousands or even millions of users is a relevant issue to be considered when designing these applications as they are not expected to collapse when they are mostly needed such as in disaster scenarios. In this context, software tools for performance evaluation of social software applications by means of discrete-event simulation have practical benefits, and yet they have not been fully developed in application domains where performance is critically dependent on massive user dynamics. This paper proposes a simulator to address this problem which combines powerful data centers and the computational power provided by mobile devices. We provide experimental evidence that shows a good agreement between actual and simulation performance measures.

1 Introduction

Typically social software applications are based on processing streams of data shared by different users wherein the computational architecture is that of a server hosting the main services and a large set of users accessing them from smartphones. As soon as the number of users scales up the server must be deployed on a cluster of processors to cope with the dynamics and intensity of user workloads. However, practical restrictions of real-life indicates that software developers are expected to test their applications at a small scale rather than test them in demanding scenarios from large number of users. This makes a case for discrete-event simulation as a tool to assist software developers in predicting performance at large scale operation.

The complexity of these applications/systems placed in their operational contexts is evident. Performance is featured by both the dynamics of user behavior and the multiple software and hardware platforms where the applications are expected to be run. The hardware platforms include clusters of processors to large collections of smartphones, with different layers of data communication in between, and multiple software platforms providing services to the application.

© Springer Science+Business Media Singapore 2016
L. Zhang et al. (Eds.): AsiaSim 2016/SCS AutumnSim 2016, Part IV, CCIS 646, pp. 180–190, 2016.
DOI: 10.1007/978-981-10-2672-0_19

To reduce the complexity of our objective we focus on a particular system architecture but our method is extensible to any existing streaming platform. In this work we proposes a simulator for stream processing applications whose performance is hard to estimate at large scale. We develop a java based simulator for performance evaluation of an S4 (simple scalable streaming service) [5] platform running sentiment analysis. The S4 world-view is that streams are passed through a graph (DAG) formed by processing elements (PEs) which are connected to each other in a downstream manner. Each PE performs a given primitive operation on the received stream and generates output streams. User applications are built on top of the streaming platform and are deployed as a graph of PEs. The set of PEs demands computational processing on a cluster of processors, and a subset of these PEs may be also deployed on smartphones which can be used to support ad-hoc networks or work distributing messages in MANET systems. With smartphones, mobile networks characteristics and mobility simulation algorithms have to be included in our proposal.

We compare simulation results with an actual small-scale experiment using twitter data. Results show good agreement (8%) between the simulator and observed experimental results. Then, we apply the simulator to study the execution time for S4 with mobile devices offloading for help with computations. Additionally, we evaluate how replication of PEs can help to reduce the communication saturation between the cluster of PEs and the smartphones.

The remaining of this paper is organized as follows. Section 2 presents the background related to this work. In Sect. 3, we present our proposed simulator. Section 4 presents the results and Sect. 5 summarizes the main conclusions from our work.

2 Background

2.1 Streaming Processing Models

A stream is an unlimited sequence of events of the form $(a_1, a_2, a_3, ..., a_n, t)$ generated continually in time, where a_i ($\forall\ i = 0, 1, 2, ..., n$) is an attribute of the event at time t. In a stream processing motor (SPM), the processing units are generally called "Processing Elements" (PE). Each PE receives information in form of tuples from its "input queues", performs some processing on it, and produces a result in its "output queue". The SPM creates logical networks with the interconnected PEs, forming a directed acyclic graph (DAG). The communication between the PEs takes place according to a "push/pull" model, which means that each element sends information to others PEs, or where the PEs request information from others PEs. Moreover, each PE works independently and only communicates with each other through messages.

Currently, there are various Distributed Stream Processing Systems [5,9,10] that use different programming languages and are focused on different areas and applications, but all of them keep in common the topology of the processing elements.

Stream Processing Platform: S4 S4 is a stream processing platform which allows applications to process data flows continuously without restrictions [5]. This platform uses Adapter applications to convert external stream into stream of S4 events. These events are routed to processing elements (PE) which are the basic units of the platform and messages are exchanged between them. Events are described as a pair (key, attribute). PEs are allocated into processing nodes (PNs) servers. The PNs are responsible for: (a) receiving incoming events, (b) routing the events to the corresponding PEs and (c) dispatching events through the communication layer. The events are distributed using a hash function over the key of the events. To run an application with S4, we need to deploy an Adapter application.

2.2 Mobile Networks

In mobile networks the area with service coverage is divided into cells. Each cell has its own infrastructure offering voice and data service. The cells function as a honeycomb (ideal scheme) in which each cell has a base station and other devices. This scheme is used to keep a good quality of the service, because as the distance between the base station and the mobile devices increases, the signal gets weaker, leading to low quality communications. A mobile device that requests a service is connected with a base station that provides the connecting links to: (1) voice service for phone calls, and (2) data service for access to the Internet. Currently, the main networks are: GSM (2G), UMTS (3G) and LTE (4G). These networks differ one from another on the frequencies at which they operate and the speed they offer.

2.3 Mobility Model and Simulation

Mobility models have been proposed to simulate the movements of participants communicating to each others. Many mobility models, oriented to emulating people's movements on different scenarios, have been proposed in the recent years. The scenario to be simulated is generally a network of "nodes" that have some specific motion pattern. Each motion pattern is represented by models of some related discipline (mathematical, physical, chemical, etc.) by means of which it is possible to calculate the data belonging to the pattern, such as positions (x, y), velocities (v), directions (Θ), etc. There are many research works including the study of the movement of animals [3], vehicles in cities [1], human behavior [6], etc.

3   Proposal

The goal of the proposed simulator is to predict the performance of a large scale application developed with S4 in different hardware scenarios. Due to hardware limitations we can only execute a small set of experiments in a real environment. More precisely, small scale experiments. To evaluate the performance of the application in a larger scale scenario we simulate two cases of study: (1) the application running on the S4 platform on a cluster of distributed processors (baseline), and (2) the application running on the S4 connected to smartphones.

3.1   Baseline

The baseline simulator includes the interconnection of three main processes: (1) the Adapter, (2) the PE, and (3) a new class of PE called lastPE.

Adapter. The Adapter manages the incoming streams and sends them to the corresponding PEs. To simulate this operations the simulator object representing the Adapter uses the "rate of events" (E_{rate}) which depends on the inter-arrival time (t_{ia}). The inter-arrival time and the PE destination are selected by using an empirical probability distribution which was obtained from data of a real small scale execution.

Processing Element (PE) and LastPE. The PEs are continuously waiting for the incoming of new events. When a new event arrives to a given PE, it processes the event and sends a message (event) to the next PE. The processing time (D_{pt}) of the event is simulated by using an empirical probability distribution obtained from a real small scale execution of the application running on the S4 platform.

The next PEs (the ones receiving the new generated events) are selected by using a probability distribution with means D_{send}. This value was also obtained by analyzing the data (traces) obtained from a real execution. The LastPE is a sub-class of PEs, which does not send output messages. Thus, it is a sink PE.

3.2   Simulating Smartphones

The second version of the simulator considers a connection between the LastPE and a new process called *Image* which is located in a mobile device, more specifically in a smartphone. In this case, each LastPE is linked to a single Image process.

Image Process. An Image is a process similar to a PE but located in a mobile device that operates in a 4G network with LTE technology. An Image is considered as a copy of the LastPE. An Image is an additional resource used when the LastPE is overloaded. The Image waits for an event to be processed. When an event arrives, the Image simulates the processing based on the FLOPS received in the event. Then, a new position is obtained according to the Levy Walk mobility model [3]. If the current coverage range is exceeded, it means that the Image must change the network cell, a Handover (HO) random time is selected, according to the mean time given by the LTE technology. A handover consist on transferring an ongoing call or data session from one channel to another channel

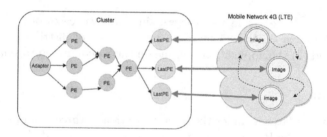

Fig. 1. Interconnection graph between PEs and Images.

(e.g. when the phone is moving away from the area covered by one cell, or when the capacity for connecting new calls of a given cell is used up).

If there is no available cell, the Image chooses the cell that is closest to the new position. If the new closest cell is different from the current one, then the Image evaluates if it is necessary to make a HO, so the propagation loss values are calculated for both cells (current and closest) and the signal power restriction of the decision algorithm of HO is applied. If the HO is necessary, we simulate the time corresponding to the transferring process. Figure 1 shows this process where the segmented lines represent the movement of mobile devices following a Levy Walk mode [3].

3.3 Mobile Network Infrastructure

The infrastructure of the mobile network is based on the fact that each Image will have its own resources (memory, CPU, etc.). They do not share resources between them as the PEs within a cluster. Moreover, the bandwidth (bw) and latency (lat) values are global to all the existing connections between Images and LastPEs. Therefore, there is a bandwidth shared by all the Images, and the mean latency for sending events is a common parameter obtained from the literature for the 4G LTE network. Although the machines of the cluster have a fixed capacity defined by the user and the smartphones have pre-established characteristics. The study presented in this work consider high-end cell phones, mainly because of their high performance, which in many cases does not differ much from that of traditional medium capacity computers.

3.4 Graphic Interface

The graphic interface (GUI), as shown in Fig. 2, was designed with the purpose of showing the characteristic graph of the application and to get some parameters required for the simulation. The parameters that can be defined are mainly related to hardware (number of machines, number of processors per machine, clock speed of the processors), related to the environment (events per second received by the application) and to the replication of the processes (PEs and LastPEs). The trace file is automatically analyzed to obtain the empirical probability distribution of the processing times.

Simulator

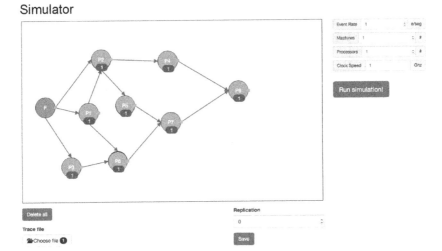

Fig. 2. Graphical interface of the proposed simulator.

The connection (data transferred) between the simulation kernel and the GUI has a negative impact on the execution time of the simulations. Therefore, we propose to set the sample size of the trace by using the formula $n = N/(1+N \times e^2)$ [2], where N is the population size, n is the sample size and e the precision level. In this work, we use a confidence level of 95 % and a degree of variability $\rho = 0.5$.

3.5   Simulation Kernel

Figure 3 shows the architecture and the data flow of our proposed simulator. The simulator was developed using Node.js for the GUI, Java for the simulation kernel, and SimGrid for the simulation of the S4 platform and the smartphones.

We perform a small scale execution of the real application to collect statistical information about the application, the Adapter and the PEs (step 1). This information is stored in a trace file (step 2). Then, in the third step, the GUI reads the trace to obtain the parameters related to the S4 platform which are used to feed the simulation kernel (step 4). The simulation kernel creates two XML files: Platform and Deployment (step 5). These files define how the process is going to be allocated into the machines of the simulated cluster of processors. Afterwards, the simulator named S4Sim is executed (step 6) to produce the results file (step 7) which is read by the simulation kernel. Finally, the simulation kernel sends the data in the appropriate format to the GUI.

Thus, the simulation kernel is a middleware between the GUI and the S4Sim implemented with SimGrid. In this work we used the MSG programming environment which is the most used by the scientific community. MSG provides simple methods for handling processes, virtual machines, message passing, etc.

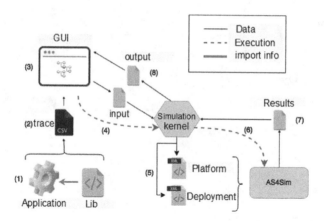

Fig. 3. Architecture and data flow.

4   Experiments

Experiments were performed on a Mac Pro with six physical 3.5 GHz Intel Xeon E5 physical cores and hyperthreading technology. It also has 16 GB of RAM and 256 GB of flash memory storage. The data collection used to evaluate our algorithm has 1.5 millions of tweets. First, we validate our proposed S4Sim using the baseline approach (AppB) and then we evaluate the performance of the application with mobile devices.

S4 Application: Sentiment Analysis (AppB). The application running on the S4 platform is the sentiment analysis presented in [8]. The Adapter receives tweets and then selects the corresponding PE to process them. Then, the sentiment analysis is performed with the arriving tweet considering three classifications: positive, negative and neutral.

The classification process is composed of 4 steps and each one is executed in a single PE: Recollecting, Filter, Relevance and Ranking. The recollecting step retrieves data from the Twitter API. The filter operator exploits a Naive Bayesian model to identify if the tweets are objective or subjective. The relevance step is used to identify whether the information is coming from a trustworthy source or not. During the ranking step a normalization process on the obtained values is performed.

In the baseline approach, the LastPE receives the tweet and performs a reversal of the string. When mobile devices are simulated, the LastPe receives tweets and sends them to the Image. In the following we present experiments with and without replication of the PEs. We present experiments for the test approaches: (1) Base Application (AppB), (2) Application with replication in PE (AppPRep) (3) Application with replication in LastPE (AppLPRep), and (4) Application with replication in PE and LastPE (AppEqRep).

4.1   Validation

The Adapter reads a dataset of tweets used for the sentiment analysis [8]. Then the PE makes a sentiment analysis on the tweet with the Mallet tool [4]. We executed a total of $e = 200.000$ events. Considering that the entire dataset has around of 1.5 millions of tweets, each experiment uses only the 14 % of tweets available selected according to the sample formula presented in the previous section.

The following figures show that our simulator is capable of properly predicting the original curve of the real application. In Fig. 4(a) and (b) we show the execution time reported for each event by the real application and the simulator. The x-axis shows the event identifier and the y-axis show the execution time of the event. The labels "sim 1" ... "sim 5" represent different simulation executions, the values are different for each execution because the random numbers used to simulate the delays (execution times, communication costs, etc.) change. In Fig. 4(a) we show results for the AppLPRep approach with five replicas, in this case the curves are almost identical. Figure 4(b) shows results for the AppB approach, here the curves tend to have similar behavior but with differences of magnitude on the execution time (y-axis).

We also computed the root mean square error (RMSE) measured in seconds. The RMSE is calculated as $\sqrt{\sum_{t=1}^{n}(x_{real(t)} - x_{sim(t)})^2/n}$, where n is the size of the sample, $x_{real(t)}$ is processing time reported by the real application and $x_{sim(t)}$ is the processing time reported by the simulator. The Table 1 shows the result obtained when simulating different replication approaches with different number of replications (5, 10 and 15). Results show that the errors are kept below three seconds (around 8 % absolute error), with an upper bound of 2.77 [s] in AppEqRep(15), and a lower bound of 0.63 [s] in AppB.

4.2   Performance Evaluation with Mobile Devices

In this section we evaluate the performance of the proposed simulator for the S4 platform. To this end, we include the Image process located in smartphones. For lack of space we show results for the AppB and AppLPRep replications approaches. Results obtained with the other replications approaches are very similar. We focus on the AppB because it the baseline approach, and the AppLPRep approach includes replicas in the LastPEs, which are linked to the Image process.

Table 2 shows the parameters used in the following experiments. All the values have been obtained from the technical literature according to experiments reported with 4G LTE networks [7]. The dimensions of area with 4G network coverage is determined by Max [X] Surface and Max [Y] Surface. We define a layout of 14 cells. The HTC One mobile devices with 4 cores, 1,7 GHz and 6,8 Gf is used in the experiments, which are a high gamma of smartphone.

Figure 5(a) shows the results obtained for the simulation of the AppB approach with a mobile device linked to the LastPE (sim 1 ... sim 5) and the Real AppB without connections to mobile devices. We set the probability of sending

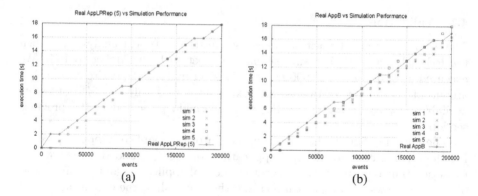

Fig. 4. Real vs Simulations: (a) AppLPRep(5) and (b) AppB.

Table 1. RMSE for different simulations.

RMSE [s]

Application	Sim 1	Sim 2	Sim 3	Sim 4	Event Rate
AppB	1.3758	1.2512	1.2920	**0.6324**	12000
AppLPRep (5)	0.7384	0.7016	0.6917	0.6429	11300
AppLPRep (10)	0.6887	0.6598	0.6918	0.6648	11000
AppLPRep (15)	0.8455	0.7581	0.7951	0.7824	11000
AppPRep (5)	1.4224	1.3457	1.5312	1.3941	11500
AppPRep (10)	1.1247	1.2162	1.1948	1.2203	11000
AppPRep (15)	1.4985	1.1361	1.7168	1.1381	11000
AppEqRep (5)	1.4074	1.7971	1.7464	0.8496	11000
AppEqRep (10)	1.7656	1.2309	1.1551	1.1616	10900
AppEqRep (15)	**2.7729**	2.3163	2.2711	2.2661	10700

Table 2. Mobile network parameters.

Network		
Handover Latency	30	[ms]
Radio Coverage BS	500	[m]
Height BS	30	[m]
Power	46	[dB]
Handover Margin	4	[dBm]
TimeToTrigger	1	[ms]
Frequency	2000	Mhz
Height UE	1.5	[m]
Amount of BS	14	
Max [X] Surface	3600	[m]
Max [Y] Surface	1800	[m]
Average Latency (RT)	10	[ms]
Bandwidth	20	[Mhz]

a request to the Image process $prob = 0.5\%$. We also performed experiments with 1%, 2%, 5% and 5% and all the experiments showed similar behaviors.

Results show that by adding connections to smartphones, the performance of the S4 application is lower. The Real AppB present an execution time of 20[s] at most meanwhile the simulated approach present execution times around 180[s]. This is mainly caused by two factors: (1) the high cost of communication between the LastPE, and (2) the lower computational capacity of the smartphones. Additionally, the execution time is affected if the smartphone performs a Handover.

Table 3 summarizes the results obtained by the simulation of the AppB approach with different probability of sending requests to the mobile devices. Each column of the table represents: (a) PE: Name of the PE. (b) Events: Number of events received during the simulation. (c) PT [s]: Total processing time during the simulation. (d) BW [s]: Waiting time of the PE during the simulation.

Table 3. Simulation results for AppB with cellphones.

AppB (1 %)								
PE	Events	PT	BW	Avg PT	U	T_T	TC	HO
PE	200000	2.9834	1.7546	1.49E-05	62.97 %	4.7380	n/a	n/a
LastPE	200000	0.3323	0.9974	1.66E-06	24.99 %	1.3298	181.407	n/a
Image	2789	0.0574	1.0080	2.06E-05	5.39 %	1.0654	181.407	0
AppB (5 %)								
PE	Events	PT	BW	Avg PT	U	T_T	TC	HO
PE	200000	3.2864	1.7288	1.64E-05	65.53 %	5.0152	n/a	n/a
LastPE	200000	0.3827	0.9993	1.91E-06	27.69 %	1.3821	904.177	n/a

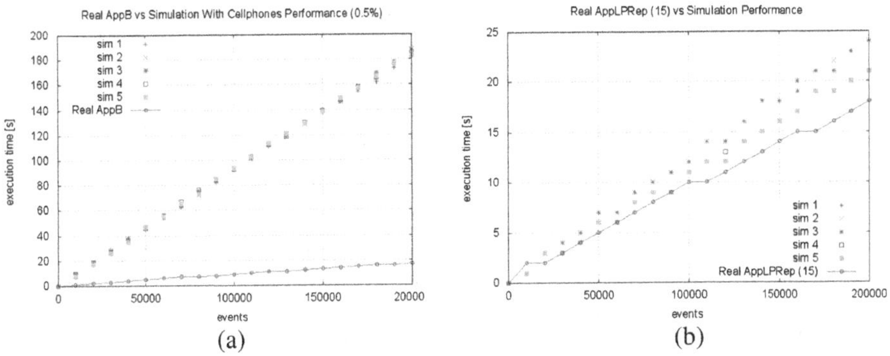

Fig. 5. AppLPRep with smartphones: (a) 5 replicas and (b) 10 replicas.

(d) Avg PT [s]: Average processing time in the simulation. (e) U [%]: Utilization (load work) of the PE during the simulation. (f) T_T: Sum of PT and BW. It does not consider communication time in the case of the LastPE and Images. (g) TC [s]: Communication time in the simulation. It refers to the communication between a LastPE and its Image. (h) HO: Number of handovers carried out during the simulation. In this Table we show that a smartphone requires more time to process events than the average processing time of the LastPEs. It also confirms that the communication cost with mobile devices are very high. It corresponds to 95 % of the total simulation time.

Beside the low performance obtained in the previous experiments, the replication of the LastPEs offers considerable improvements in terms of the performance of the application with mobile devices. Figure 5(b) show that as the LastPEs increase their replication, the execution time reported by the simulations tend to become equal to the curve of the real application without smartphones. This is because there is more parallelization of the communications between the LastPEs and the Images. Moreover, with replication each LastPE receives a smaller fraction of events to send to their corresponding Image.

5   Conclusion

In this work, we proposed a simulator for a stream processing platform connected to mobile devices. In particular, the simulator was designed to emulate the S4 platform when running a sentiment analysis application. The simulated S4 platform connects to mobile devices to distribute the workload of the PEs. A human mobility model and a Handover algorithm were implemented for the 4G network with LTE technology.

The simulator with mobile devices showed that the communication time reported between the LastPEs and the Images decreases the performance of the application as more events are sent to the mobile devices. However, when we replicate the LastPEs, the performance tends to improve with results very close to the real application without mobile devices. Therefore, results show that replication helps to increases the level of parallelism on 4G network.

Acknowledgements. This work has been partially funded by CONICYT Basal funds FB0001.

References

1. Choffnes, D.R., Bustamante, F.E.: An integrated mobility and traffic model for vehicular wireless networks. In: VANET, pp. 69–78 (2005)
2. Israel, G.D.: Determining sample size. UF/IFAS Extension, University of Florida, Agricultural Education and Communication Department (1992)
3. James, A., Plank, M.J., Edwards, A.M.: Assessing lévy walks as models of animal foraging. J. R. Soc. Interface 8(62), 1233–1247 (2011)
4. McCallum, A.K.: Mallet: a machine learning for language toolkit (2002)
5. Neumeyer, L., Robbins, B., Nair, A., Kesari, A.: S4: distributed stream computing platform. In: ICDMW, pp. 170–177 (2010)
6. Rhee, I., Shin, M., Hong, S., Lee, K., Kim, S.J., Chong, S.: On the levy-walk nature of human mobility. Trans. Networking 19(3), 630–643 (2011)
7. Stoke, I.: Latency considerations in LTE (2014)
8. Thinknook: Twitter sentiment analysis training corpus (dataset). www.thinknook.com
9. Toshniwal, A., Taneja, S., Shukla, A., Ramasamy, K., Patel, J.M., Kulkarni, S., Jackson, J., Gade, K., Fu, M., Donham, J., Bhagat, N., Mittal, S., Ryaboy, D.: Storm@twitter. In: SIGMOD, pp. 147–156 (2014)
10. Zaharia, M., Das, T., Li, H., Hunter, T., Shenker, S., Stoica, I.: Discretized streams: fault-tolerant streaming computation at scale. In: SOSP, pp. 423–438 (2013)

Laser Simulation Software: Seelight

Yun Hu[1(✉)], Pin Lv[1], Quan Sun[2], Qiuyan Tang[1], Jing Wang[1], and Changwen Zheng[1]

[1] Science and Technology on Integrated Information System Laboratory,
Institute of Software Chinese Academy of Sciences, Beijing, People's Republic of China
huyuniot@163.com
[2] Optoelectronic Science and Engineering, National University of Defense Technology,
Changsha, People's Republic of China

Abstract. Seelight is a software tool for complex optical system modeling and simulation especially for laser simulation system, and user can build and analyze the complex optical system in a visual environment. This article will describe Seelight in detail. First we will discuss the architecture of the software. Then we give a detailed description of Seelight characteristics such as a rich library of models using for build complex systems, the high-performance computing system, the method of multichannel atmospheric transport, and simulation method of non-ideal light source. Finally we will see the performance of the Seelight through two simple examples.

Keywords: Optical modeling · Adaptive optics · Laser system · Optical simulation

1 Background

Laser is one of the great inventions of mankind in the history of the 20th century. The application of laser is very wide, such as laser radar, optical communications, adaptive optics, laser weapon systems. Sometimes in the field of scientific research, there usually involve a complex optical system, and the optical Instruments in the complex system has characteristics like requiring high precision, expensive, and easily damaged. So the costs associated with scientific experiments is always very high. With the development of computer technology, an optical system simulation software for complex system modeling and simulation can greatly reduce the cost of research and shorten the time of the optical experiments, and develop a more advanced optical systems.

There are agencies in many countries has developed the software used for complex optical system. The well-known software include CAOS (abbreviating for Code for Adaptive Optics System), funded by the European Union and developed by National Observatory from Germany, France, Italy, Spain and other countries. WaveTrain developed by MZA Associates Corporation, and LightPipes developed by the Gleb Vdovin. CAOS build simulation system under low light adaptive optics used for astronomy [1]. CAOS advantage is that code is open, and the disadvantage is that software modeling environment is not perfect, and the running of the system is not very stable [2]. Wave-Train can be used for numerical simulation of light propagation in atmospheric

© Springer Science+Business Media Singapore 2016
L. Zhang et al. (Eds.): AsiaSim 2016/SCS AutumnSim 2016, Part IV, CCIS 646, pp. 191–198, 2016.
DOI: 10.1007/978-981-10-2672-0_20

turbulence and complex adaptive systems [3]. MZA optical simulation provides a solution, which greatly promoted the development of optical simulation software. The general workflow of WaveTrain can be described as follow. First user assembles optical system in the visual design environment, then the system's kernel code analyzes the optical system structure and generate the corresponding simulation program code, finally the whole system can be executed after compiling. WaveTrain's drawback is that the code is not public, and only a small number of US government-related agencies can use the software [4]. LightPipes is written in C language, and it can simulate light propagation in coherent optical apparatus [5], but LightPipes doesn't have specific GUI, and can only run in command line environment.

We combines advantages of CAOS, WaveTrain and LightPipes, and further improve the relevant features, then developed a software named Seelight, which has a more easy to use interface and more powerful function.

2   Software Architecture and Basic Functions

Seelight is an optical simulation software. Software's main interface shown in Fig. 1, the system includes a file menu area, a list of elements area, work area. Software can create a new file in the different subsystems to select the wave optics simulation systems or fiber lasers simulation. Seelight is a graphical system modeling and simulation platform, which can work in WYSIWYG (What You See Is What You Get) style. Users can drag directly from the element area to the workspace. In the work area, user can click the components and enter into the property dialog box which can edit the properties of the components. The components can be connected with the different color line and build a practical optical systems. Different color line represent different data structure.

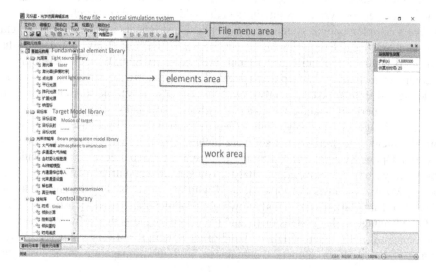

Fig. 1. Software interface

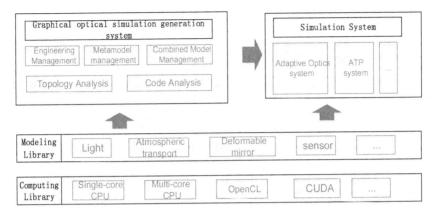

Fig. 2. Software architecture

When a practical optical system has built, user can click the execute button, the system can be executed and the results can be display in visual form.

System architecture shown in Fig. 2. The base of the software is Modeling Library and Computing Library. Modeling Library is used for building the optical system and Computing Library is used for improving the processing speed. When the optical system is built and the software system will analyze the components and the line between the components. There are a lot of complicated system can be built like Adaptive Optics system and ATP system.

Seelight technical implementation process is as follow, first expert in optics should build the mathematical model based on the Optical system, then convert the mathematical model into the software codes. In the final part, we have to compare the simulation result to the actual result, if the results is not similar, we need to go back to the first part. There are a lot of Optical system that the software has realized. These optical systems can be widely used in teaching and research areas, which can represent the function of the software, and the optical systems are as follows,

- Classic optical system, like Michelson interferometer
- Multi-beam lighting system
- Multichannel atmospheric transport simulation system
- Sodium guide star simulation system
- Adaptive optics simulation system (AO system)
- ATP system

3   Advantages

Seelight compared to other optical simulation softwares has three major advantages, rich modeling library, high-performance computing, the method of multichannel atmospheric transport, and Simulation method of non-ideal light source.

3.1 Rich Modeling Library

Model library is the base of the optical system, and the amount of components decide the complexity of the optical system. Up to now, we have 8 type of components.

- Light source library, can simulate continuous light, pulsed light source and so on
- Target Model library, can simulate aircraft, satellites and so on
- Beam propagation model library, can simulate beam propagation in vacuum and Turbulence, scattering absorption, thermal and other halo effect
- Control library, can simulate time, closed-loop feedback and other control module
- Device library, can simulate Newton's rings, deformable mirror and other device
- Detector library, can simulate Hartmann sensor, CCD and other detector device
- Auxiliary library, can help system display and storage
- Fiber laser library, can simulate different fiber laser

3.2 High-Performance Computing

Simulation of complex optical system involves a lot of time-consuming computational problems, and the use of existing high-performance computing systems in simulation can be significance. Up to now, Seelight can run in single-core CPU platform, multi-core CPU platform or CPU-GPU hybrid computing platform. Different platform map to different computing lib. For example, CPU-GPU hybrid computing platform map to CUDA. To enable users to focus on the business of laser simulation and logic design, we propose a parallel processing method based on adaptive hardware. The system can detect the hardware resources of the system, and provide the best lib related to the detected result. If given the best hardware, Seelight can run in style of Multi-user, multi-tasking, multi-core computing.

We will focus on the way that improving performance in using computing lib compared to the original way. Seelight have optimized the system in three level – function level, module level, and system level. In terms of function level optimization, the calculation process has been optimized. For example, we can optimize the convolution process by redesigning, reducing cycle, reducing transmission, optimizing memory access, etc. In terms of module level optimization, we know that the laser system simulation main performance bottleneck concentrated among a few calculation module, such as multi-channel transmission atmosphere, Hartmann sensors. Acceleration for these modules inefficient function can greatly improve the operating speed of the module, and enhance overall system performance. In terms of system level optimization, we can divide tasks and modules combined with the optical system. We can see the preference in different platform in Table 1. The result in Table 1 is run in computer with CPU i7-3770 3.40 GHz, Quad-Core, 4G RAM, CUDA GT620 and the optical system is AO system which will show in part 4.

Table 1. The result of running optical system

Platform/lib	The original	Single-core CPU	Multi-core CPU	CUDA
time	18.32 min	5.172 s	4.381 s	3.880 s

3.3 The Method of Multichannel Atmospheric Transport

Sometimes we need to discuss multi-beam transport in the same atmosphere, and we need create the method of multichannel atmospheric transport in this situation. In Seelight we develop a component named AtmChannelPath to achieve this function. AtmChannelPath can set the amount of the up and down beams and let beams share the atmosphere. The key of the method of multichannel atmospheric transport is the way create the common atmosphere phase screen. We improve the FS method to create the atmosphere phase screen which has better performance than FFT or Zernike polynomials. The improved FS method can get the phase of any point in the space and the number of frequency sampling point is no longer limited by the number of space sampling point.

3.4 Simulation Method of Non-ideal Light Source

The ideal plane-wave or gauss is often used as light source when studying laser system with numerical simulation. The actual light source for laser transmission system does not meet the condition of ideal light, even with poor beam quality, which results in the deviation in the simulation compared with experiments. Starting from the relationship between wave aberration and beam quality β, we came up with the numeric simulation method of nonideal beam and realize the method in Seelight by coding. The initial aberration was equivalent phase screen, which intensity was related with beam quality of the light simulated. According to the setting values of β, the optical field of light was simulated in the method, which was applied in plane - wave and gauss. Compared with setting values, the beam quality of optical field calculated shows that the method can simulate the light with certain beam quality [6].

4 Applications

This chapter will show two simple application examples of Seelight, AO system and simulation of generating a Bessel-Gaussian beam. The application show that we can use Seelight to simulate some complex systems used for the field of science and guide the development of new optical systems.

4.1 AO System

AO (Adaptive optics) system is an important part of optical system and used widely. Figure 3 shows the principle of the AO system. Adaptive optics using a deformable mirror corrects distorted wave front caused by atmospheric, thereby improving the performance of optical systems. Figure 4 shows the optical system in the workspace of software. The light transmit through the atmosphere having turbulence and use the deformable mirror to adjust the phase. We also use the closed loop feedback to make the result more accurate and use the Image display to show the result. Figure 5(a) shows the image before correcting and Fig. 5(b) shows the image after correcting. Figures 5(a) and (b) are in the same size and

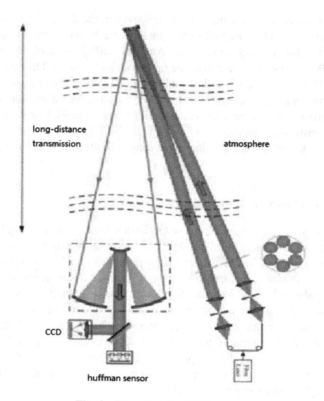

Fig. 3. The principle of AO system

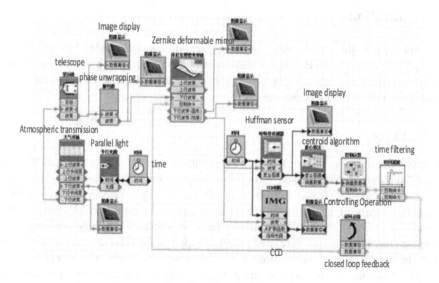

Fig. 4. The AO system

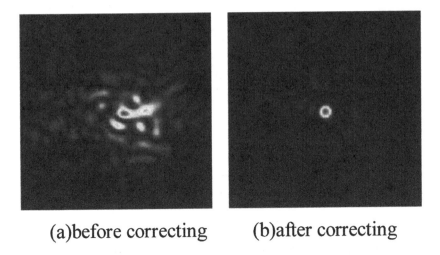

(a)before correcting   (b)after correcting

Fig. 5. The comparison of image before correcting and after correcting

we can see that the beam is more concentrated after correct. From the result of the AO simulation system, we can know that the effect of the atmosphere is perfectly offset and the parameters in the simulation system can use in the true system.

4.2   Simulation of Generating a Bessel-Gaussian Beam

Generating a Bessel-Gaussian beam is a complex work and we can use the Seelight to guide the development of the system. Figure 6 shows simulation result of optical system in Seelight. The actual system of generating 2-order BG beams by fiber lasers is shown in Fig. 7 [7].

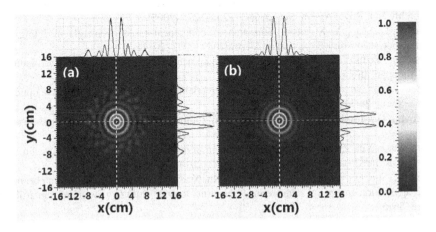

Fig. 6. The result of simulation system

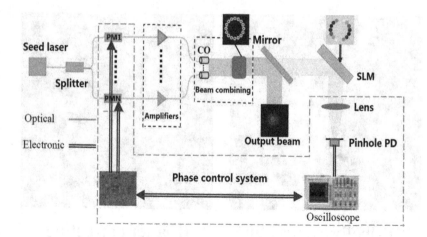

Fig. 7. The actual system of generating a Bessel-Gaussian beam

5 Conclusions and Future Work

We develop a laser simulation software named Seelight based on the optical theories. There are still a lot of work need to do, such as to build a more user-friendly interface, combine more optical system to optimize the system, optimize a number of software modules such as multi-channel atmospheric transport module, and improve the accuracy of the simulation.

References

1. Carbillet, M., Verinaud, C., Femenia, B., et al.: Modeling astronomical adaptive optics. Monthly Not. Royal Astron. Soc. **356**(4), 1263–1275 (2005)
2. Xie, X.-G., Tao, Y.-X., et al.: Research of component-based open-style modeling and simulation software. J. Syst. Simul. **23**(10), 2089–2097 (2011)
3. Mansell, J.D, Jacobs, A.A., Maynard, M.: Development of an adaptive optics test-bed for relay mirror applications. In: SPIE 5894, 1–13
4. Chen, J.-Y., Gan, G.-Y., Tao, Y.-X.: SciAO: modeling and simulation of adaptive optics. J. Syst. Simul. **20**(11), 2864–2884 (2008)
5. Vdovin, G.: LlightPipes: beam propagation toolbox. http://www.okotech.com/software/lightpipes/
6. Jing Wang, Yu., Zhang, P.L., Sun, Q.: Simulation method of non-ideal light source in laser system. Infrared Laser Eng. **43**(11), 3527–3532 (2014)
7. Chu, X., Sun, Q., Wang, J., Lv, P., Xie, W., Xu, X.: Generating a Bessel-Gaussian beam for the application in optical engineering. Scientific Reports. http://www.nature.com/articles/srep18665

Simulation Software

The Design of a Small-Scale Epidemic Spreading Simulation System

Yuyu Luo[1(✉)], Zhichao Song[1], Kai Sheng[2], Hong Duan[1], and Xiaogang Qiu[1]

[1] College of Information System and Management, National University of Defense Technology,
Changsha, 410073, Hunan, China
1533897937@qq.com
[2] Electronic Engineering College, Naval University of Engineering,
Wuhan, 430033, Hubei, China

Abstract. In this paper, we choose H1N1 as the disease research object. On the basic idea of artificial society and considering traffic factors, we use modeling and simulation technology based on agent to build an artificial town which has a population of 1500. In the process of building the small-scale epidemic spreading simulation system, we build epidemic spreading model at first, then we build an artificial town which puts emphasis on traffic model, At last, we integrate the epidemic spreading model into people's daily activities. Based on the system, we design three kinds of experiments to investigate the propagation rules and control measures of H1N1. The experiments are set under three conditions: absence of intervention, closing important places and conducting epidemic surveillance. By analyzing important places of epidemic spreading and the effect of different intervention measures, we can provide powerful auxiliary support for epidemic prevention and control work, and the practicability and effectiveness of the system in controlling epidemic is validated at the same time.

Keywords: H1N1 · Modeling and simulation based on agent · Artificial town · Traffic factors

1 Introduction

An epidemic is an infectious disease which is caused by pathogenic microorganisms and parasites' infection into human body. As a formidable enemy threatening people's health, it influences people's production, living and work badly, and even kills people. It is said that the plague in 600 AD lead to half people's death in Europe; ten percents people lost their lives due to smallpox in 16th in Europe; people suffered a lot during 14th to 18th because of the black death; with the improvement of sanitary condition and development of medical level, threaten of epidemics to people is eased, but the SARS in 2003 and the H1N1 in 2009 still caused many people's death, and brought serious social panic. Thus, it is important to build an epidemic spreading simulation system to research on spread process and control mechanism of epidemics.

Artificial society is a new approach to study social phenomena, it consists of given environment and some entities called Agent. When we set some rules, the entities and

© Springer Science+Business Media Singapore 2016
L. Zhang et al. (Eds.): AsiaSim 2016/SCS AutumnSim 2016, Part IV, CCIS 646, pp. 201–215, 2016.
DOI: 10.1007/978-981-10-2672-0_21

environment will act on each other and cause some complex phenomena. Looking into the overall effect of those entities, we can get basic rules of artificial society and explain macroscopic attributes of real society. Modeling and Simulation based on Agent is the core method to build an artificial society. The Sugarscape model suggested by Josh Epstein and Bob Axtell in 1996 is the most classic artificial society and is used in all fields such as finance, medical, management and so on.

Vehicles especially for public vehicles are very important for people's travels. High population density makes public vehicles to be a high-rate infection place, but at present, the existing epidemic spreading simulation systems which consider traffic factors are little. We only find the "Episims" [1] takes traffic factors into consideration. In the light of "Episims", we build an artificial town, and combine H1N1 spreading model with it to study the disease's propagation rules and control measures. In the process of building the artificial town, we build traffic model which correlates with people's travel activities.

Based on the small-scale epidemic spreading simulation system, we researched the main spreading places and propagation rules of H1N1 in three conditions: in the absence of intervention, closing important places and conducting epidemic surveillance so as to guide the design of disease control measures.

2   The Small-Scale Epidemic Spreading Simulation System

After analyzing the spread mechanism of epidemics, we find that the core factor of epidemic spreading simulation is to build the model of human society and human activities that integrate the epidemic spreading model. Thus, the epidemic spreading simulation system in this paper includes two big parts: epidemic spreading model and artificial town model.

In this paper, we choose the big-influence epidemic Influenza H1N1 which breaks out on a global scale in 2009 to be our research object. This disease has a clear spread mode that people get infected by air droplets produced by infected persons in daily contacts. Besides, the exposed period and infected period is short, and the spread process is obvious and easy to detect and study. So we build related epidemic spreading model for H1N1 according to those characteristics.

As for artificial town, we take a town in real world as prototype and simplify its layout and composition. Considering factors such as layout of the town, individual distribution, individual behaviors, social relationship and travel activities, the artificial town model consists of artificial environment model, individual attribute and behavior model and traffic model. The individual attribute and behavior model include four sub-models which are artificial individual model, artificial social network model, activity schedule model, behavior adjustment model and individual contact model. Artificial individual model describes individual type, residence, work place and epidemic status; social relationship network model explains social relationships such as family, friends and classmates; activity schedule model defines activity type and related probability of daily activities; behavior adjustment model presents people's attribute of changing behaviors when he apperceives outside events; individual contact model defines the epidemic spreading probability in different conditions; traffic model does the planning for individual's travel manner and roads according to path state and outing purpose.

3 Models

The small-scale epidemic spreading simulation system in this paper includes two big models: H1N1 spreading model and "artificial town". Artificial town model consists of environment model, human attribute and behavior model, traffic model those sub-models.

3.1 The Epidemic Spreading Model Based on H1N1

According to the research about H1N1 from medicine investigators, we know that this epidemic's spread approach is similar to common flu, which spreads between sufferers and crowds in a manner of aerosol and air saliva. When people get the disease, symptom doesn't appear at once. People come to infected period after the period of latency. But if a sufferer is cured, he will not be infected during his whole life (Fig. 1).

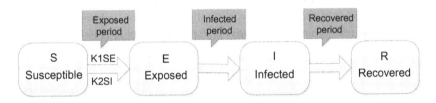

Fig. 1. The infectious mechanism and state transition of H1N1

The figure above is the infectious mechanism and state transition of H1N1. The state transition model of H1N1 includes four kinds of people who are susceptible, exposed, infected and recovered; K1 and K2 represent infection rate of exposed and infected separately, the infection rate starts from the last day of exposed period and has a trend of Gamma distribution as in Fig. 2; the transition of disease state depends on the time during which people are infected. We know that the exposed period of H1N1 is about 1–7 days and submits to Weibull distribution as in Fig. 3 from paper [8].

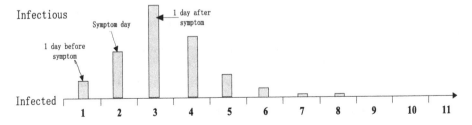

Fig. 2. The infectious distribution of H1N1

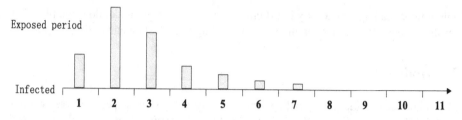

Fig. 3. The exposed period distribution of H1N1

3.2 "Artificial Town" Model

The design and build of "artificial town" is an important part of the process in which we develop the whole simulation platform. And the building and function of the epidemic spreading model is on the base of artificial town. Individuals' contacts are decided by social relationship, distance and activity schedule, thereby based on spreading model we can study how the epidemic spreads. The artificial town consists of those models as below.

Artificial Environment Model. The "artificial town" has a population of 1500 and includes 15 kinds of environment entities such as housing, residential building, restaurant, market, Clinique, hospital, school, office building, mall, bus, administration department, park, bank, factory and many roads. The specific layout is as in Fig. 4.

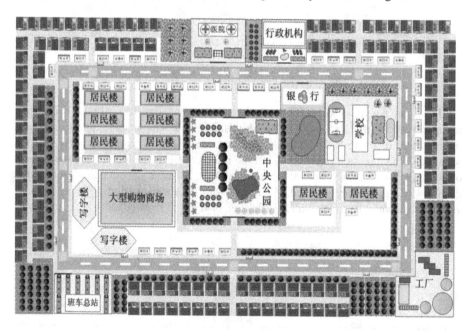

Fig. 4. Composition and layout of the artificial town

Considering the relationship between environment factors and human gathering, rules of going out, disease-spreading control measures, we define the attributes of environment entity as follows.

Environment entity attributes= {environment entity ID, location, max-number, current-number, measures adopted, open state}

As a kind of move entity, bus is special. So we consider it separately:

Bus attributes= {bus ID, location, max-number, passenger ID list, route node list, stop station list, moving speed, at the station or not, arriving time}.

Individual Attribute and Behavior Model.

Artificial individual model. For individual, we must consider those attributes such as type, activity process and social relationship. Besides, in order to study the transmission of infectious disease, attributes related to disease are needed. The model attributes and type of an individual are defined as follows.

Individual model attributes= {Individual ID, type, health state, location, moving speed, moving direction, work/study place, current environment ID, defend measures, time infected, exposed period, infected period, social relationship list};

Individual type= {worker, student, retired senior};

Individual is the smallest unit of society, we assigned resident place, work place and household members to every individual in the model building process. The household number is 515 in the town, in which 127 are located in housing (at periphery) and the others are in residential buildings (at the center of town). The household member distribution can be seen in the follow Table 1).

Table 1. Distribution of household member

Number	Constitute of a household	Number of workers	Number of students	Number of retired elder
15	2 workers+3 students	30	45	0
70	2 workers+2 students	140	140	0
175	2 workers+1 students	350	175	0
75	2 workers	150	0	0
10	1 workers	10	0	0
110	2 retired elders	0	0	220
40	2 workers+1 students+1 retired elder	80	40	40
20	2 workers+2 retired elders	40	0	40

Artificial social network model. In big sites such as mall, outdoor road, factory and school, people only contact with their colleagues, schoolmates or acquaintances in most situation, so we need to build artificial social network model for each person to guide his contact activities.

Social relationship in real world include family, friend, colleague, schoolmate and so on,so when build social relationship network model was, we considered family relationship, neighbourship, colleague relationship and classmate relationship mostly. Family relationship means the relationship among all members in a household; neighbourship can be divided into housing neighbourship and building neighbourship, to be more specific, people living in housing will build relationship with surrounding persons as in Fig. 5, people living in building build relationship stochastically with 8–12 persons in the same building; there are two kinds of colleague relationship: in small working place such as market, clinique and restaurant, because of the small number, colleague relationship is among every individual. But in big working places such as factory, although people work at the same factory, they may be at different workshops, the colleague relationship does not always exist, we choose random network building method to collocate colleagues for each person stochastically; the build of classmate relationship is the same as colleague relationship in factory, we choose 5–25 classmates for each student. Figure 6 presents the social network in this artificial town in which nodes represent persons, lines represent social relationships. Figure 7 is the degree distribution and accumulated degree distribution of social relationship network.

Fig. 5. The sketch map of housing neighborhood relationship

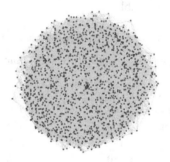

Fig. 6. Social relationship network

Activity schedule model. Individual's daily life is driven by activity schedule model, this model sets individual's activities and related possibility in a given period. When build the system, we set different workday activity schedule and weekend activity schedule for different individual type. Considering that the activities are different for market/restaurant workers and administrative workers, we set them differently. We take the students' activity for example as Table 2. When an individual moves from one place to another, we set the start period for 10–60 min.

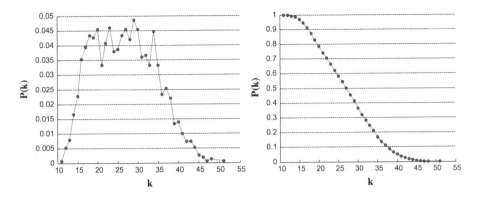

Fig. 7. Degree distribution and accumulated degree distribution

Table 2. The activity schedule of student in working day

Time period	Working day		
	Activity	Place	Probability
00:00–07:00	Rest	Residence	100%
07:00–12:00	Go to school(start time is decided by Agent)	Residence/Route/School	100%
12:00–14:00	Go home after shopping	Market/Route/Residence	20%
	Go home after eating	Restaurant/Route/Residence	15%
	Go home after park	Park/Route/Residence	5%
	Go home	Route/Residence	60%
14:00–18:00	Go to school(start time is decided by Agent)	School	100%
18:00–19:00	Go home after shopping	Market/Route/Residence	20%
	Go home after eating	Restaurant/Route/Residence	15%
	Go home after park	Park/Route/Residence	5%
	Go home	Route/Residence	60%
19:00–24:00	At home	Residence	100%

Behavior adjustment model. Behavior adjustment is that when an individual feels that environment has a bad influence on himself, he will change his own behavior to avoid this influence. For example, when people think the epidemic spreading situation is serious, he will wear respirators, reduce the contact with others, go to hospital and so on. Behavior adjustment model was built to represent this spontaneous behavior. After getting information about the number of infected persons, people change their daily activities to protect themselves from being infected.

Individual contact model. We define the close-distance contact that can arouse the spread of H1N1 as effective contact behavior. It consists of those situations: when people are in the same environment entity, they will make effective contact with persons who have social relationship with them in a given probability; when people are in outdoor roads, the effective contact is produced among persons who has social relationship with each other if the distance is close enough; as for people in bus, because the place is small and contact time is long, we think effective contact will occur stochastically among all people in the bus; for workers in restaurant, market and other big-flow place, they will make contact with every person who enters into this environment entity.

Traffic Model. The small-scale epidemic spreading simulation system is different from most existing epidemic simulation system in that it adds traffic factors into the artificial town. Based on road condition and the purpose of going out, we built traffic model. On the one hand, it can give support to individuals' choice of ways to go out, on the other hand, it will satisfy the need for individual and bus to plan their path.

There are two ways for individual to go out—walking or taking bus. Corresponding to this, the traffic network can be divided into road traffic network and public traffic network as shown in Fig. 8. Road traffic network regards the road intersection, inflexion, end point and exit of environment entity as nodes, and the shortest path between nodes as edge. The traffic network can support the path planning and real time positioning for individuals and buses.

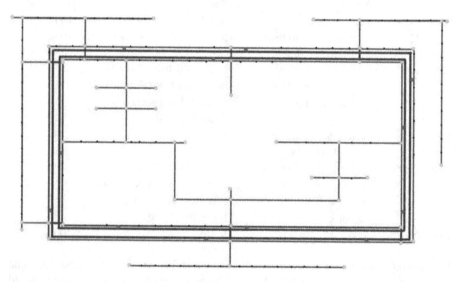

Fig. 8. The traffic network

Because the length of simulation step is short and the amount of calculation is big, in order to meet the need of fast simulation, we calculated the shortest paths of the traffic network in advance using Floyd arithmetic and load them to memory in initialization process. When an individual decides to go out, at first, he judges whether there is a bus running at present (bus runs at 6:00 to 20:00 each day). If there is no bus, he has no choice but to walk to destination, on the contrary, he can choose to walk or take bus in a given probability according to the distance between current location and destination as shown in Fig. 9.

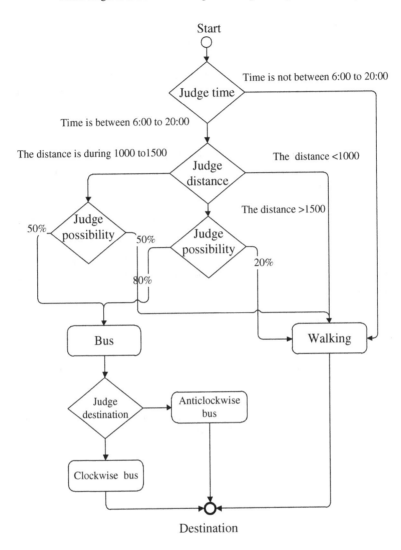

Fig. 9. The way in which people choose to go out

Going out by walking: According to individuals' current locations and destination locations, at first he has to find the related road network nodes (the exit of environment entity) and the roads from pre-calculated shortest paths in memory, then add the result into the individual's outing path node attribute list. An individual leaves environment entity at this simulation time, and will move to destination at his own speed the next simulation time.

Going out by bus: There are two circuits for buses in this artificial town: clockwise circuit and anticlockwise circuit. Individuals choose paths according to the purpose of going out. The process of going out can be divided into three stages. Stage 1: walk to the nearest station (Station A) from current environment entity, then add to the waiting line of station A; Stage 2: wait and take bus to station B which is the nearest station to destination; Stage 3: walk from Station B to destination. In Stage 2, whether there is a bus coming to station have to be judged, if there is, then judge the number of people in the bus and the number of waiting people, if waiting people is less than people the bus can accommodate, the individual can take the bus, else, he has to wait for another bus.

4   Experiments and Analysis

Based on this small-scale epidemic spreading simulation system, we design three kinds of experiments to study the spread of H1N1 and the effect of epidemic control measures in three conditions: the absence of intervention, closing important places and conducting epidemic surveillance.

At first, we do some basic assumptions and set some related parameters for experiments:

1. The sources of infection are a worker and a student from a same family, and the exposed period is 3 days and 2 days, besides, the infected period is 3 days and 4 days respectively.
2. We do not consider the situation in which people die due to H1N1, because most of the infected will be cured.
3. We do not consider the infection when people are in treatment due to people's self-protection and treatment effect.
4. Set exposed period to be 1–4 days, and the infection rate in the last day of expected period is 0.015.
5. When epidemic situation is not serious, that means people under treatment is less than 25, the infected period is 1–3 days. Else the infected period is 1–2 days, the infection rate of infected period is in Table 3.

Table 3. The infection rate of infected period

Time	First day	Second day	Third day	Forth day	Fifth day	Sixth day
Infection rate	0.025	0.05	0.04	0.02	0.01	0.005

4.1   Epidemic Spreading Experiment Under the Absence of Interventions

The purpose of this experiment is to study and analyze main spreading places and nature mechanism of H1N1, and get propagation rules and characteristics of this epidemic so that we can find efficient intervention measures.

After doing many repeated experiments, we can get simulation results as follows.

From Fig. 10 we can get that: if we do not conduct any intervention measures, the final infected people will be as high as 1200 that is over 2/3 of total population in the town. Residence is the main spread place, nearly half of the infected come from this place, the reason might be that people go home every day and contact time is the longest, if one member of the family get infected, there is a high probability for others to be infected, this is the same as actual situation; school is the second high infection place due to the fact that the population density is high in daytime and students contact each other frequently; the next is park, because park is an open place and different kinds of people come here to do exercise every day; besides, mall, market, restaurant and hospital are important spread places; compared with those places, the infected people in main traffic tool—bus is only 11 and the proportion is small, this shows that traffic factors have little influence on the epidemic spreading process.

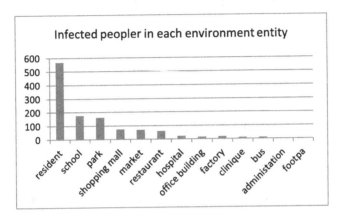

Fig. 10. The infected number in each environment entity

4.2 Epidemic Spreading Experiment Under Closing Important Place

Closing important places is an epidemic spread reducing measure to decreases people's congregating. The important places are those high-density places such as factory, park and school. In the process to control the spread of many kinds of epidemics, such as SARS, hand foot and mouth disease and typhoid fever, the centers for disease control and prevention in China conduct this prevention measure. By analyzing the simulation

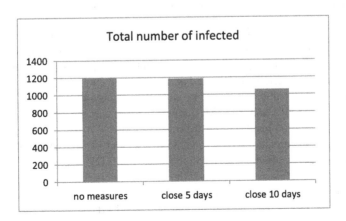

Fig. 11. Total number of infected persons when close important place

results in the experiments without any other interventions, we choose the first inflection point at which the infected number starts to increase quickly to close two kinds of high-infection environment entities—school and park. The inflection point is at the 8th day of the simulation. And we design two simulation cases in which the close period is 5 days and 10 days separately. The simulation results are as follows (Figs. 11 and 12).

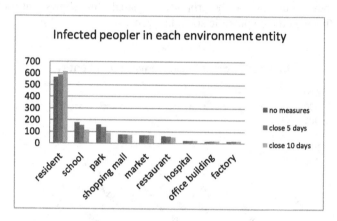

Fig. 12.   Infected number in each environment entity when close important place

According to the simulation results as figures above show, we can find that when we close school and park, though the spread in school and park is reduced, the total number infected nearly has no change. Besides, it is obvious to see that people infected in resident places increase, this may be caused by the fact that people have no choice but to stay at home and the efficient contacts among family members increase. The results illuminate that only taking the measure of closing important place can't control the spread of disease fundamentally, it just transfers the spread place from one to another. Moreover, the effect of increasing the close period is not obvious too.

4.3   Epidemic Spread Experiment Under Conducting Epidemic Surveillance

Conducting epidemic surveillance which is an important measure to reduce the spread of epidemics means to set epidemic surveillance points in residence, factory and school, and use the way such as temperature measurement and inquiry to find infected people during early exposed period and infected period We also choose the inflection point — the 8th day to conduct this measure. The surveillance period is 14 days and monitor strength is set to be 70% and 75%. Monitor strength means the probability to find the infected. The simulation results are as follows.

According to the simulation results as in Figs. 13 and 14, we can find that when we conduct epidemic surveillance measures, the spread of H1N1 is controlled greatly, and the infected number in every eviorment entity has a distinct trend to decrease. Especially when the surveillance strength is increased, the control effect is more and more prominent. When we conduct the surveillance measure for 14 days and set the surveillance strength to be 75%, the total number of infected persons is only 16. So conducting surveillance is a good disease control measure which can find infected people during early period, by taking some measures, the spread of disease will be cut off from source and the effect is obvious.

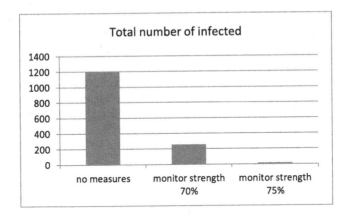

Fig. 13. Total number of infected persons under epidemic surveillance

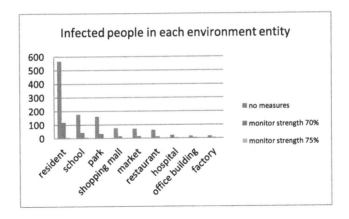

Fig. 14. Infected people in each environment entity under epidemic surveillance

5   Conclusion

On the basic idea of artificial society and considering environment, individual attribute and behavior, traffic factors, as well as the spread mechanism of H1N1, we build a small-scale epidemic spreading simulation system. Because people's travel activities is closely related to traffic factors, in the process of building the system, we put emphasis on traffic model and combine the spread of H1N1 with it. In experiment part, we design three kinds of experiments which are experiments under three conditions (absence of intervention, closing important places and conducting epidemic surveillance) to investigate the spread rule of H1N1 in the artificial town and the effect of intervention measures in controlling disease. The simulation results show that the main spread places are residence, park and school, the population infected in bus is small which means the traffic factors have little influence on the spread of H1N1. Besides, we find that only closing important places can't control the spread fundamentally, it just transfers the infection place from one to another. The epidemic surveillance measure can find infected people in early period and take measures in time, so the spread scale is reduced greatly. If surveillance period and monitor strength is set properly, control effect will be more obvious.

The simulation results not only validate the practicability and effectiveness of the system but also provide powerful auxiliary support for epidemic prevention and control work. What's more, if related parameters are changed, the system can be used to analyze the spread of other similar diseases. In future work, in order to make the system reflects real world better, we will increase the intelligent of artificial individual, consider more detail factors and build social network model which is more close to the actual.

Acknowledgement. The authors would like to thank National Nature and Science Foundation of China under Grant Nos. 61503402 and 71303252.

References

1. Hamer, W.: Epidemic Disease in England. Bedford Press, Harvard (1960)
2. Ross, R.: The Prevention of Malaria. John Murray Albemarle Street, California (1911)
3. Kermack, W., McKendrick, A.: Contributions to the mathematical theory of epidemics. Proc. Royal Soc. A. **115**, 700–721 (1927)
4. Builder, C., Banks, S.: Artificial societies: a concept for basic research on the societal impacts of information technology. Santa Monica 7740 (1991)
5. Zhang, T.: Epidemic and Society during the Period of the Republic of China. Social Sciences Academic Press, Beijing (2008)
6. Sun, R.: Cognition and Multi-Agent Interactions: From Cognitive Modeling to Social Simulation. Cambridge University, Cambridge (2005)
7. Duan, W., Qiu, X.: Fostering artificial societies using social learning and social control in parallel emergency management systems. Front. Comput. Sci. **6**, 604–610 (2012)
8. Duan, W., Cao, Z., Wang, Y., Zhu, B.: An ACP approach to public health emergency management: using a campus outbreak of H1N1 influenza as a case study. IEEE Trans. Syst. Man Cybern. **43**, 1028–1041 (2013)
9. Song, Z., Ge, Y., Duan, H.: The research of influenza H1N1's transmission based on artificial society. Int. J. Model. Optim. **4**, 95–99 (2014)
10. Baidu Encyclopeda. H1N1 Influenza Vaccine
11. Michael, Y., James, S.: Global stability for the SEIR model in epidemiology. Math. Biosci. **125**, 155–164 (1995)
12. Yua, S., Han, L., Ma, Z.: An epidemic model in which epidemic will spread both during exposed period and infected period. Math. Biol. J. **16**, 392–398 (2001)
13. Kermack, W., McKendrick, A.: Contributions to the mathematical theory of epidemics. Proc. Royal Soc. A. **115**, 700–721 (1927)

14. Huang, K., Qiu, X.: System Simulation Technology. National Defense Science and Technology University Press, Beijing (1998)
15. Wang, F., Steve, L.: From artificial life to artificial society—the present situation and prospect of complex social system. Complex Syst. Complex Sci. **1**, 33–41 (2004)
16. Song, X., Shi, W., Ma, Y., Yang, C.: Impart of informal networks on opinion dynamics in hierachically formal organization. Phys. A-Stat. Mech Appl. 436(10), 916–924

Human Behavior Recognition Method Based on Improved Energy Image Species and Pyramid HOG Feature

Lina Liu[1,2], Jiarui Wen[1], Shiwei Ma[1(✉)], and Ling Rui[1]

[1] School of Mechatronic Engineering and Automation, Shanghai University,
No. 149, Yanchang Road, Zhabei District, Shanghai 200072, China
{linaliu-126,wenjiarui2010}@163.com, {masw,ruiling}@shu.edu.cn
[2] School of Electrical and Electronic Engineering, Shandong University of Technology,
Zibo, Shandong, China

Abstract. Since traditional energy image species are easily affected by the motion time and location shift, this paper proposes a human behavior recognition method based on improved energy image species combined with pyramid HOG (PHOG) features. Firstly, Maximum horizontal overlap area method is adopted to match the human body registration. Then, the improved energy image species: average motion energy image (AMEI) and motion entropy image (MEnI) are calculated and PHOG features are extracted as a multi-scale human behavior feature descriptor. Finally, different kernel function support vector machine classifiers are used to identify the human behavior. The results of simulations and performance comparisons on the Weizmann and DHA datasets verify the effectiveness of the proposed method.

Keywords: Human behavior recognition · Energy image species · Average motion energy image (AMEI) · Motion entropy image (MEnI) · PHOG

1 Introduction

Human behavior recognition technology based on computer vision has widely application prospects, such as intelligent monitoring, virtual reality, human-computer interaction, etc. How to extract appropriate features from motion sequences is the key issues of human behavior recognition. According to different feature descriptions, the human motion recognition methods can be divided into four categories: the methods based on silhouette feature, geometric feature description, motion information and spatial-temporal interesting points [1]. In view of the different representation of silhouette feature, the methods based on silhouette can be divided into outer contour method, model method, energy image species method, integration method and tensor method, etc. [2]. Due to the energy image species method can effectively describe the global motion information of the human behavior, and less sensitive to counter noise interference, it has been widely used.

Through putting the human body movement process as a whole object, cumulates all contours according to certain rules, the energy image species can be obtained. In 1997, Davis, etc., proposed motion energy image (MEI) and motion history image (MHI)

© Springer Science+Business Media Singapore 2016
L. Zhang et al. (Eds.): AsiaSim 2016/SCS AutumnSim 2016, Part IV, CCIS 646, pp. 216–224, 2016.
DOI: 10.1007/978-981-10-2672-0_22

to describe the trajectory of human motion [3]. But MEI cannot show the temporal feature of human behavior well, and MHI is sensitive to the influence of the motion time and location shift. In 2006, Weinland, etc. proposed motion history volumes (MHV) template to describe human behavior [4], it extended the MHI to 3D space, and solved the problem of view changes in human behavior recognition better. On the basis of MHI, XuDong Zhang, etc. [5] constructed multilayer MHI to describe the plane motion information of vertical image. OuYang Han [6], etc. proposed the hierarchical model of human behavior by combing MEI with star skeleton. In Gait recognition, Han and Bhanu proposed gait energy image (GEI) to represent the dynamic and static features of pedestrian gait [7]. After that, Khalid etc. proposed gait entropy image (GEnI), and Shannon entropy is used to describe a human behavior period [8]. As the global features in upright walking gait recognition, the above two kinds of energy image species have achieved good results, but because of the characteristic of unchanging with time variance [2], it is difficult to describe other types of human actions as global feature. In addition, before calculating the GEI and GEnI, usually match the contour image sequences by maintaining the center of head gravity position consistent [9], however, the matching method loses the static area easily for larger head range motion. Therefore, the classical energy image species need to be improved so that they can describe the human body movement better.

2 Classical Energy Image Species

The classical energy image species contain MEI and MHI, and MEI is binary image while MHI is gray image. They describe the human motion trajectory through the union of sets of the human motion area and the weight of attenuation area change over time, respectively. The algorithm in details as follows.

Suppose the background is static in the whole motion process and the motion object can be segmented from the background. Let $I(x, y, t)$ be an image sequence, $D(x, y, t)$ is a binary image sequence, expresses the motion area of $I(x, y, t)$, can be obtained by image difference, then MEI can be calculated by Eq. (1).

$$E_\tau(x, y, t) = \bigcup_{i=0}^{\tau-1} D(x, y, t - i) \tag{1}$$

Where, τ is the motion time.

In MHI, pixel intensity is a function of the temporal history of motion at that point, its calculation formulation is

$$H_\tau(x, y, t) = \begin{cases} \tau & D(x, y, t) = 1 \\ \max(0, H_\tau(x, y, t - 1) - 1) & otherwise \end{cases} \tag{2}$$

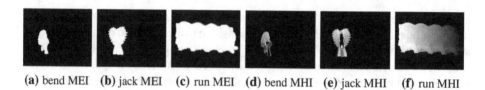

(a) bend MEI   (b) jack MEI   (c) run MEI   (d) bend MHI   (e) jack MHI   (f) run MHI

Fig. 1. Examples of classical energy images species (MEIs and MHIs)

The result is a scalar-valued image where more recently moving pixels are brighter. Examples of some classical energy image species are shown in Fig. 1. From Fig. 1 we can see that the MEI and MHI are all sensitive to the motion time, for the movement of a large position shift, such as run action, the image quality is very fuzzy and not easy to be recognized.

3 Improved Energy Image Species

According to the kinematics, the human body movement is usually expressed as a local body movement in the horizontal direction. When the body center of gravity moves up and down, there is relative motion between the human body and ground, which is a local movement in the vertical direction. While the classical energy image species are susceptible to movement time and position shift, aims to make the energy image species represent the human motion information on the direction of horizontal and vertical better, this paper proposes a body registration method based on the maximum horizontal overlap area principle; constructs the improved energy image species, it contains average energy image (AMEI) and motion entropy image (MEnI). Its calculation procedure contains three steps: selecting the standard image and registration template; image registration and calculating the AMEI and MEnI. The details are as follows.

(a) Using the background subtraction method to obtain the object silhouette images of the image sequence frame by frame, select the middle frame silhouette image as a standard image for matching. Extracting the maximum enclosing rectangle of the other silhouette image as registration template, the region is called as the region of interest (ROI).

(b) Making the registration template slide from left to right on the horizontal direction and take intersection operation with the standard image; replace the current frame image by ROI while the intersected region achieves maximum, and the registration process of one frame image is completed. The matching process need to be done for all the frame images except the standard image.

(c) Calculating the improved energy image species by applying the registration image sequences, that is AMEI and MEnI, expressed by E_{AMEI} and E_{MEnI}, respectively. E_{MEnI} is obtained by calculating the Shannon entropy of E_{AMEI} directly, that is

$$E_{AMEI} = \frac{1}{N} \sum_{t=1}^{N} I(x, y, t) \tag{3}$$

$$E_{MEnI}(x, y) = - E_{AMEI}(x, y) \times \log_2(E_{AMEI}(x, y) + \lambda)$$
$$- (1 - E_{AMEI}(x, y)) \times \log_2(1 - E_{AMEI}(x, y) + \lambda) \tag{4}$$

Where, N is the length of motion sequence; $I(x, y, t)$ denotes the pixel value of the coordinates (x, y) in the t th frame image I; λ is a minimum positive parameter to avoid the occurrence of zero value for the logarithmic function. Examples of some improved energy image species are shown in Fig. 2. The motion is bend, jack and run from left to right in turns.

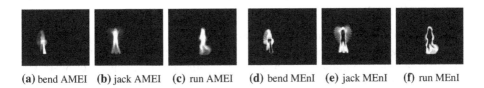

(**a**) bend AMEI (**b**) jack AMEI (**c**) run AMEI   (**d**) bend MEnI (**e**) jack MEnI (**f**) run MEnI

Fig. 2. Examples of improved energy image species (AMEIs and MEnIs)

From Fig. 2 we can see that the white area (the highest energy value) of AMEIs express the fewer magnitude moving parts, such as the legs, torso. And grey areas correspond to the larger magnitude moving parts. And the brighter area of MEnIs represents the moving more areas, its internal area of white outline represent the moving less parts. Obviously, MEnI highlights the limbs or trunk changes during a movement period. Comparing with Fig. 1, we can see that AMEIs and MEnIs can describe the human behavior information better than MEIs and MHIs, especially for large magnitude motion, such as running, the AMEI and MEnI without the big shadow area that are shown in Fig. 2(c) and (f). Thus, they are not easily affected by the movement time.

In addition, there exists large black area without describing any motion information in AMEIs and MEnIs. We cut out the smallest outer rectangle of the object silhouette area by using counter detection method to reduce the image dimension, computational complexity and save storage space. The cropped AMEI and MEnI of hands waving action is shown in Fig. 3.

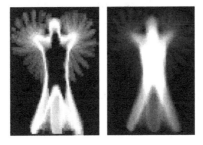

Fig. 3. The cropped AMEI and MEnI of hands waving action

4   Human Behavior Recognition Based on Improved Energy Image Species and Pyramid HOG Features

4.1   Pyramid HOG Feature Extraction

Histograms of oriented gradients (HOG) is an efficient feature descriptor for describing the image shape information [10–13], based on calculating the histograms of oriented gradients of the local area, the human body feature can be constructed. HOG is intensively computed in the so called Cell and Block grid, Cell is composed of a number of pixels, while the Block is composed of a number of adjacent Cells. The computation steps of HOG as follows.

(a) The normalized magnitude of the detection window is used as input, and then computing the horizontal and vertical gradients by applying gradient operator.
(b) Set the gradient amplitude of each pixel as weighting function, statistic the weighted histograms of each Cell's gradient direction to obtain the HOGs of Cell.
(c) Normalize the HOGs of Cell in the same Block to eliminate the effect of illumination, and get the HOGs of Block.
(d) Series all the HOGs of Blocks together in the detection window to constitute the human body feature vector.

The schematic program of HOG computing process is shown in Fig. 4. Obviously, the HOG feature is calculated on dense grid and uniform sized unit Cells, while decomposing the image into multi-layers by using the pyramid model, and extract the image feature under different levels can achieve the purpose of multi-scale analysis of the image. Therefore, aims to analysis the details information of human motion better, pyramid model is used to improve it.

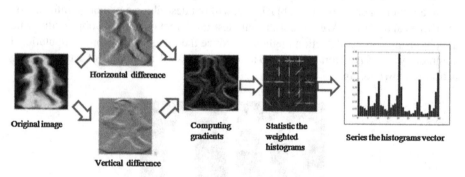

Fig. 4. The schematic diagram of HOG computing process

In order to avoid the different cropped size of AMEIs and MEnIs to effect the feature extraction. Firstly, apply scale normalization operation to the cropped images. Secondly, decompose the normalized AMEIs and MEnIs by pyramid model. Finally, extract the HOG feature of each level's sub-regions and then connect them in series directly to form a PHOG feature for human behavior recognition. Taking the PHOG extraction of MEnI (hands waving action) as example, schematic diagram of the extracting process is shown in Fig. 5.

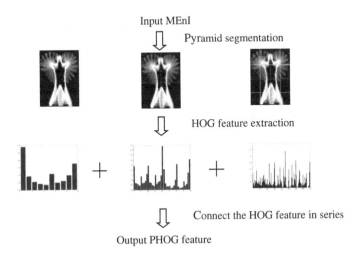

Fig. 5. The schematic diagram of PHOG feature extracting process

4.2   Classifier Design and Evaluation Method

Considering the human action datasets usually have the characteristics of smaller sample number and the video frames is not consistent, and support vector machine (SVM) can efficiently solve the classification problem with small samples, high dimension and nonlinear. The SVM classifier is selected. In the experiments, the kernel functions are radial basis function (RBF) and linear kernel function. Following the common experimental settings, we evaluate our approach by using the leave-one-video-out evaluation strategy.

5   Experiments and Results Analysis

5.1   Introduction of the Used Human Behavior Datasets

In order to verify the effectiveness of the human action recognition method based on improved energy image species and PHOG feature, the relevant recognition experiments and performance comparisons have been done on the classical human motion datasets Weizmann and the challenging datasets DHA [14]. Weizmann datasets includes 10 kinds of human behavior, such as bend, Jack, jump, run, etc., every action is completed by 9 performers under similar background, the action video sequences have different length, and 9 behaviors are involved in the recognition experiments. DHA datasets including bend, Jack, jump, kick and Taichi etc. 17 categories of human behavior, every action contains 12 male performers and 9 female performers, the length of action video sequences is not consistence, and 14 group actions are chosen for the recognition experiments.

5.2   The Performance Comparison of Improved Energy Image Species and PHOG Features

To verify the effectiveness of improved energy image species and PHOG features describe for the description of human motion information, we compare the proposed method with different combination features, contains improved energy image species and R transform, the traditional energy image species and PHOG, traditional energy image species and R transform, respectively. The specific parameters in the experiment are set as follows: pyramid structure with 2*2 and 4 layer, thus, the number of layers in PHOG is 4, the range of gradient direction is[$0° \sim 360°$], the gradient direction of histograms is divided into 10 bins, and the dimension of the PHOG feature is $\sum_{i=1}^{4} 4^{i-1} \times 10 = 850$; the angle interval of R transform is $2°$, and the characteristic dimension is 90. The testing results on the Weizmann and DHA datasets are shown in Tables 1 and 2 respectively.

Table 1. The testing results on the Weizmann datasets

Combination features	Correct recognition rate (%)	
	SVM(Linear kernel)	SVM(RBF kernel)
AMEI+PHOG	**96.3**	**95.1**
MEnI+PHOG	**95.1**	**93.8**
AMEI+R	82.7	75.3
MEnI+R	**95.1**	92.6
MEI+PHOG	82.7	87.7
MHI+PHOG	**92.6**	88.9
MEI+R	86.4	81.5
MHI+R	81.5	86.4
MEI(without registration) +PHOG	74.1	84.0
MHI(without registration) +PHOG	86.4	86.4
MEI(without registration)+R	81.5	80.4
MHI(without registration)+R	74.1	74.1

Table 2. The testing results on the DHA datasets

Combination features	Correct recognition rate (%)	
	SVM(Linear kernel)	SVM(RBF kernel)
AMEI+PHOG	**94.2**	**90.1**
MEnI+PHOG	**92.9**	**89.5**
AMEI+R	79.6	73.5
MEnI+R	87.1	78.6
MHI+PHOG	86.7	80.6
MEI+PHOG	**89.0**	87.4
MHI+R	77.9	70.7
MEI+R	82.3	76.2

Trough Tables 1 and 2 we can see that the proposed algorithm has achieved the best recognition results on the two datasets. In the Weizmann datasets, for the linear kernel SVM classifier, the recognition of AMEI+PHOG feature combination can reach 96.3 %, and MEnI+PHOG feature combination is 95.1 %, which are higher than the other feature combinations. On the challenging DHA datasets, the correct recognition rate of AMEI+PHOG feature combination in the linear kernel SVM classifier can be as high as 94.2 %, and MEnI+PHOG feature combination up to 92.9 %, they also higher than the other features. Meanwhile, the feature combinations MEnI+R and MHI+PHOG also have achieved good recognition results.

In addition, in order to reflect the proposed registration scheme can better describe the human behavior information, in view of classical energy image species after registration, the recognition testing is done in the Weizmann datasets by combining them with R transform and PHOG feature. The testing results are shown in Table 1. As it can be seen from Table 1, the proposed registration method can improve the recognition rate of traditional energy image species to a certain extent, in which the feature combination MHI+PHOG can be improved from 86.4 to 92.6 %.

Therefore, the improved energy image species AMEI and MEnI can describe human motion information better than the classical method. By applying PHOG features, better recognition effects can be achieved by using linear kernel and RBF kernel SVM classifiers, and linear kernel function is better than RBF kernel function.

6   Conclusion

In this paper, the human body registration method based on maximum horizontal direction overlap area is used to improve the traditional energy image species, the AMEI and MEnI are calculated, and their PHOG features are extracted for human behavior recognition. The proposed method has the following characteristics: compared with the traditional energy image species, the improved energy image species (AMEI and MEnI) can reflect the global shape and local detail features of human behaviors, they can not only describe the dynamic area, but also reflect the static region, which is very useful for the human behavior recognition.

The effectiveness of the proposed method has been verified by the experimental research and performance comparison experiments on classical human action datasets Weizmann and challenging human action datasets DHA. Next step we will construct the human behavior model with depth information to improve the robustness of the algorithm, and use more datasets for performance testing.

References

1. Zhao, H.Y., Liu, Z.J., Zhang, H.: Human action recognition using the image contour. J. Optoelectron. Laser **21**(10), 1547–1551 (2010)
2. Ben, X.Y., Xu, S., Wang, K.J.: Review on pedestrian gait feature expression and recognition. Pattern Recogn. Artif. Intell. **25**(1), 71–81 (2012)
3. Bobick, A.F., Davis, J.W.: The recognition of human movement using temporal templates. IEEE Trans. Pattern Analysis Mach. Intell. **23**(3), 257–267 (2001)
4. Weinland, D., Ronfard, R., Edmond, B.: Free viewpoint action recognition using motion history volumes. Comput. Vis. Image Underst. **104**(2–3), 249–257 (2006)
5. Zhang, X.D., Yang, J., Hu, L.M., et al.: Human activity recognition using multi-layered motion history images with Time-Of-Fligh (TOF) camera. J. Electron. Inf. Technol. **5**, 1139–1144 (2014)
6. Ouyang, H., Fan, Y., Gao, L., et al.: Hierarchical human action recognition based on normalized R-transform. Comput. Eng. Des. **34**(6), 2170–2174 (2013)
7. Han, J., Bhanu, B.: Individual recognition using gait energy image. IEEE Trans. Pattern Anal. Mach. Intell. **28**(2), 316–322 (2006)
8. Bashir, K., Xiang, T., Gong, S.: Gait recognition using Gait entropy Image. Crime Detect. Prev. Int. Conf. on **2**, 1–6 (2009)
9. He, Y.F.: Research on gait recognition algorithm via random subspace method. South China University of Technology, Guangzhou (2013)
10. Dalal, N., Triggs, B.: Histograms of oriented gradients for human detection. In: CVPR (2005)
11. Zeng, C., Li, X.H., Zhou, J.L.: Pedestrian detection based on HOG of ROI. Comput. Eng. **12**(24), 182–184 (2009). 35
12. Yang, X.M., Yan, B.Y., Li, K.L., et al.: An image classification based on pyramid model. Comput. Digit. Eng. **43**(4), 704–706 (2015)
13. Shen, X.X., Zhang, H., Gao, Z., et al.: Human behavior recognition based on Kinect and pyramid feature. J. Optoelectron. Laser **25**(2), 357–363 (2014)
14. Lin, Y.C., Hu, M.C., Cheng, W.H., et al.: Human action recognition and retrieval using sole depth information. In: Proceedings 20th ACM Int'l Conference Multimedia (MM 2012), Nara, Japan (2012)

Locality Constrained Dictionary Learning for Human Behavior Recognition: Using AMEI and EMEI

Lina Liu[1,2], Shiwei Ma[1(✉)], Ling Rui[1], and Jiarui Wen[1]

[1] School of Mechatronic Engineering and Automation, Shanghai University,
No.149, Yanchang Road, Shanghai 200072, China
{linaliu-126,wenjiarui2010}@163.com,
{masw,ruiling}@shu.edu.cn
[2] School of Electrical and Electronic Engineering,
Shandong University of Technology, Zibo, Shandong, China

Abstract. In this paper, a human behavior recognition method based on locality constrained dictionary learning (LCDL) is proposed, the average motion energy image (AMEI) and enhanced motion energy image (EMEI) are utilized to describe the human behavior features. Using the LCDL algorithm to train sub-dictionary for each category of human behavior, and then cascading all the sub-dictionaries together to form a structured dictionary, the dictionary is discriminative. The sparse representation errors of the testing samples are used for recognition. Compared with existing methods, the proposed methods can reduce the storage space and calculation quantity through the normalization treatment of AMEIs and EMEIs. And the locality constrained conditions can enfore the inner-class distance and improve the discriminative ability of the structured dictionary. The human beavior recognition experiments on Weizmann and DHA datasets have proven the validity of the proposed method.

Keywords: Locality constrained dictionary learning (LCDL) · Average motion energy image (AMEI) · Enhanced motion energy image (EMEI) · Structured dictionary · Human behavior recognition

1 Introduction

Human behavior recognition has been an active research topic in computer vision and pattern recognition for more than two decades. The applications in many areas have promoted the development of this technology, such as video surveillance, human computer interaction, video retrieval, sports event analysis, etc. [1]. But due to the individual differences and external environment change, a large number of variables may be produced to make the problem complex and difficult to solve, such as gesture, clothing, camera motion, occlusion, complex scene degree, etc. Therefore, how to improve the accuracy and robustness of human behavior recognition is still a challenging problem.

The framework of human behavior recognition has two parts, the human behavior feature extraction and behavior pattern recognition. There exists two representation

© Springer Science+Business Media Singapore 2016
L. Zhang et al. (Eds.): AsiaSim 2016/SCS AutumnSim 2016, Part IV, CCIS 646, pp. 225–232, 2016.
DOI: 10.1007/978-981-10-2672-0_23

methods of the human behavior feature, methods based on global features and local features [2]. The commonly used global features include contour silhouette, skeleton, optical flow and energy image species, etc. [3]. And the energy image species has been widely used because it can describe the global human behavior feature effectively, and not sensitive to the contour noise. It contains motion energy image (MEI) and motion history image (MHI) [4], gait energy image (GEI) and gait entropy image (GEnI) [5], etc.

In recent years, sparse coding has become a hot research topic in the field of signal processing and computer vision. The dictionary learning method based on integrated sparse model has been widely used in image classification, image denoising, image super-resolution and so on [6]. Currently, human behavior recognition method based on sparse representation is mostly based on spatial-temporal characteristics of video, such as space-temporal interest points [7], space-temporal volume [8], which needs to extract the complex interest points and tracking operation, and is sensitive to noise.

Different from the existing methods, this paper proposes a framework based on local constrained dictionary learning (LCDL) algorithm for human behavior recognition. This method extracts the global features as the human behavior description, including average motion energy image (AMEI) and enhanced motion energy image (EMEI). And then, the LCDL algorithm is used to learn sub-dictionary for each motion category. After that, a discriminative structured dictionary is obtained by cascading all the sub-dictionaries together, and the sparse representation errors of the testing samples are used for recognition. The human behavior recognition experiments and performance analysis have been done on Weizmann and DHA datasets.

2　Human Behavior Feature Description

Through viewing the human motion process as a whole object, and cumulating all the silhouettes together according to certain rules, the energy image species can be obtained. In this paper, AMEI and EMEI are constructed as the human behavior description, and background subtraction method [4] is applied to extract the target contour images.

2.1　Calculation of AMEI

AMEI is obtained by averaging the binary silhouettes over whole motion sequence [5], its computation formula is

$$E_{AMEI}(x, y) = \frac{1}{N} \sum_{t=1}^{N} I(x, y, t) \tag{1}$$

Where, N is the length of motion sequence, $I(x, y, t)$ expresses the pixel value at candidate (x, y) of t th frame image. Obviously, the influences of motion cycle and some random noise are eliminated in the average process.

The AMEI of walk behavior is shown in Fig. 1(a), we can see that there exist three different brightness regions: region A, represents the background; region B, its brightness is highest, represents the relatively static area (i.e., torso area); region C, its gray changes significantly, expresses the high frequency movement parts, such as limbs swing parts.

2.2 Calculation of EMEI

In order to highlight the dynamic parts, it is necessary to enhance the high frequency movement parts in AMEI and eliminate the relatively static region. Thus, the EMEI is extracted, defined as:

$$E_{EMEI}(x, y) = \frac{1}{N} \sum_{t=1}^{N} ||I(x, y, t) - E_{AMEI}(x, y)|| \tag{2}$$

The EMEI of walk action is shown in Fig. 1(b), it can be seen that compared with AMEI, EMEI has obvious difference in region B and C: the lighter region C denotes the movement region; black region B which insides the white contour is the relatively static part.

In order to reduce computation cost solve, the AMEI and EMEI are unified and scaled to 64×64, and the normalized image is shown in the upper left corner.

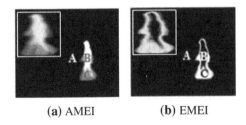

(a) AMEI   (b) EMEI

Fig. 1. AMEI and EMEI of walk behavior (Normalized AMEI and EMEI is shown in the upper left corner, respectively)

3 Locality Constrained Dictionary Learning

3.1 The Algorithm Description

Suppose there exists a diffeomorphism mapping g, such that we can predict the low embeddings $Y = [y_1, \cdots, y_N] \in \Re^{d \times N}$ of the high dimensional data points $X = [x_1, \cdots, x_N] \in \Re^{n \times N}$, where $d < n$. According to the sparse representation, if the dictionary D is confirmed, the data points x_i and its embeddings $y_i = g(x_i)$ can be approximately represented by the linear combination of the atoms d_j and its embeddings $g(d_j)$, respectively, i.e.

$$x_i = \sum_{j=1}^{K} c_{ji} d_j, \quad y_i = \sum_{j=1}^{K} c_{ji} g(d_j) \tag{3}$$

Where, c_{ji} is the j-th element of the sparse coding c_i.

In order to determine the dictionary D and its coding C, the above two linear representation errors need to be minimized, i.e., the following two items need to be minimized simultaneously.

$$\sum_{j=1}^{N} \left\| g(x_i) - \sum_{j=1}^{K} c_{ji} g(d_j) \right\|^2, \quad \sum_{j=1}^{N} \left\| x_i - \sum_{j=1}^{K} c_{ji} d_j \right\|^2 \tag{4}$$

The sparse coding should satisfy two constrained conditions, i.e., $\forall i, \sum_{j=1}^{K} c_{ji} = 1$ and $\|c_i\|_0 = \tau$. Thus, the local geometry property of the neighborhood of x_i is preserved, the dictionary learning algorithm is called as locality constrained dictionary learning (LCDL) algorithm. This problem can be solved by the object function as follows

$$<D, C> = \underset{D,C}{argmin} \|X - DC\|_F^2 + \lambda \sum_{i=1}^{N} \sum_{j=1}^{K} c_{ji}^2 \|x_i - d_j\|^2 + \mu \|C\|_2^2$$

$$s.t. \quad \begin{cases} \mathbf{1}^T c_i = 0, & \forall i = 1, 2, \cdots, N \\ c_{ji} = 0, & \text{if } d_j \notin \Omega_\tau(x_i) \end{cases} \tag{5}$$

Where, the elastic item $\mu \|C\|_2^2$ is introduced to ensure the stability of least square method; $\mathbf{1}$ is a column vector of all ones; $\Omega_\tau(x_i)$ denotes the τ neighborhood of x_i, we express $\Omega_\tau(x_i)$ as Ω_τ for brevity in the following parts; λ and μ are trade-off parameters.

The optimization problem can be solved by the iterative method.

3.2   Optimization of LCDL

Although the objective function in Eq. (5) is not jointly convex to (D, C), it is convex with respect to each of D and C when the other is fixed. Thus, we adopt an alternative minimization scheme.

Update C by fixing D. Suppose D is fixed, it is initialized or set from previous iteration. The objective function is reduced to a sparse coding problem, the i-th column c_i in C can be computed by the following equation which should satisfy the constrained conditions in Eq. (5).

$$<c_i> = \underset{c_i}{argmin} \|x_i - Dc_i\|_2^2 + \lambda \sum_{j=1}^{K} c_{ji}^2 \|x_i - d_j\|^2 + \mu \|c_i\|_2^2 \tag{6}$$

Let $\hat{c}_i$ express a compact sub-vector which only contains the nonzero elements of c_i, by applying Lagrange multiplier method [9], the analytical solution of $\hat{c}_i$ can be calculated as:

$$\hat{c}_i = \frac{(Q + \lambda F(Q) + \mu I)^{-1} \cdot 1}{1^T (Q + \lambda F(Q) + \mu I)^{-1} \cdot 1} \tag{7}$$

Where, I is a unit matrix; $Q = (\Omega_\tau - x_i 1^T)^T (\Omega_\tau - x_i 1^T)$, is a τ dimensional locality covariance matrix; $F(Q)$ is a τ dimensional diagonal matrix, its diagonal elements is the diagonal elements of Q.

Update D by fixing C. After obtained the optimal coding C, we can optimize D atom by atom. Letting d_j is the j-th column of D and c_j is the j-th row in C, once C and all other atoms of D are fixed, the optimizing problem of d_j can be obtained as

$$<d_j> = \underset{d_j}{\arg\min}\, Dic(d_j) = \left\| X - \sum_{k \neq j} d_k c_k - d_j c_j \right\|_F^2 + \\ + \lambda \left\{ \sum_{i=1}^N c_{ji}^2 \|x_i - d_j\|_2^2 + \sum_{i=1}^N \sum_{k \neq j}^K c_{ki}^2 \|x_i - d_k\|_2^2 \right\} \tag{8}$$

Denote as $E = X - \sum_{k \neq j} d_k c_k$, we can yield the optimal solution by setting its gradient about d_j to be zero, and the analytical solution of d_j is

$$d_j = \frac{1}{(1 + \lambda)(c_j c_j^T)} (E c_j^T + \lambda X [c_{j1}^2, \cdots, c_{jN}^2]^T) \tag{9}$$

4   LCDL for Human Behavior Recognition

The dictionary learning based recognition method can be divided into two kinds. One way is to construct a discriminative structured dictionary directly, which needs to training sub-dictionaries for each class. Another way is to make the dictionary representation coefficient have discriminative ability, which only needs to train a whole dictionary, without having to clear the sub-dictionaries of all categories [6]. In this paper, based on the first way, we learn a structured dictionary for recognition.

Define the structured dictionary as $D = [D_1, \cdots, D_C]$, where D_i, $i = 1, \cdots, C$ denotes the sub-dictionary of class i. Each sub-dictionary can be obtained by applying the LCDL algorithm. The local constrained conditions can enforce the intra-class distance. After the discriminative dictionary is constructed, the sparse reconstruction errors can be used for recognition, the details are as follows.

(a) Calculate the sparse coding. Denote by $\hat{\alpha} = [\hat{\alpha}_1, \cdots, \hat{\alpha}_C]$, and $\hat{\alpha}_i$ is the coefficient vector associated with sub-dictionary D_i. For a testing sample y, its sparse coding $\hat{\alpha}$ over the whole dictionary D can be solved by

$$<\hat{\alpha}> = \arg \min_{\alpha} \left\{ \|y - D\alpha\|_2^2 + \gamma \|\alpha\|_1 \right\} \tag{10}$$

Where, γ is a scalar constant.

(b) Recognition. The recognition can be done via the reconstruction error as

$$\text{identity}(y) = argmin_i \{e_i\} = argmin_i \{\|y - A_i\hat{\alpha}_i\|_2\} \tag{11}$$

The procedure of the proposed method for recognition is given in Fig. 2.

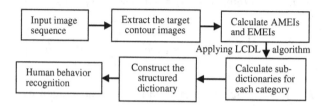

Fig. 2. The procedure of the proposed method for recognition

5 Experiments

In order to verify the validity of the proposed method, we have done some recognition tasks on classical datasets Weizmann and challenging datasets DHA [10]. Following the common experimental settings, our approach is evaluated by leave-one-video-out evaluation strategy. The extracted AMEIs and EMEIs as the motion feature descriptions. The proposed LCDL method is compared with 2DPCA and K-SVD [11]. For each datasets, we give the parameter setting, accuracy and average running time.

5.1 Parameter Selection

Before recognition, we first introduce the parameter selection of LCDL, K-SVD and 2DPCA. For LCDL, there are five parameters $(K, \tau, \lambda, \mu, \gamma)$ need to be tuned. The parameter τ, λ and μ are evaluated by 5-fold cross validation, where $\tau = 2$, $\lambda = 0.2$ and $\mu = 0.001$. The dictionary size K is set equal to the number of training samples. In the training stage, the iterative number and the reduction dimensionality will impact the computation complexity and running time. And the experimental results indicate that iterative 30 steps will minimize the objective function. We set the reduction dimensionality equal to 50 and 300 for Weizmann and DHA, respectively. In order to compare with K-SVD, the reduction dimensionality, iterative steps and dictionary size are set the same as LCDL. For 2DPCA, its reduced dimensionality is set for obtaining the highest recognition rate.

5.2   Performance Analysis of the Proposed Method

Weizmann datasets. The Weizmann datasets consists of 10 kinds of human behavior, such as bend, jack and jump, etc., each behavior is completed by 9 performers under similar background. About the extracted AMEIs and EMEIs, each has 9 images per behavior, therefore we have 90(9 × 10) AMEIs and EMEIs respectively. According to leave-one-video-out method, the dictionary size K is fixed as 80(8 × 10). The accuracy and average running time are summarized in Table 1. From Table 1, we can observe that LCDL gives the highest accuracy 98 % for EMEI and AMEI, and 2DPCA has the least running time.

Table 1. The testing results on the Weizmann datasets

Methods	Correct recognition rate (%)		Running time (s)	
	EGEI	GEI	EGEI	GEI
2DPCA	95	97	**0.3431**	**0.3501**
K-SVD	92	95	8.0227	8.061
LCDL	**98**	**98**	1.147	1.550

DHA datasets. The DHA datasets includes bend, jack, jump, kick and taichi, etc. 17 categories of human behavior, every action contains 12 male performers and 9 female performers. For the extracted AMEIs and EMEIs, each has 21 images per behavior, therefore we have 357(17 × 21) AMEIs and EMEIs, respectively. And the dictionary size K is 340(17 × 20) here. The accuracy and the average running time are summarized in Table 2.

Table 2. The testing results on the DHA datasets

Methods	Correct recognition rate (%)		Running time (s)	
	EGEI	GEI	EGEI	GEI
2DPCA	88.82	87.05	**4.345**	**4.033**
K-SVD	83.82	87.65	40.677	41.239
LCDL	**94.71**	**92.64**	24.479	23.672

We can observe that LCDL gives a significant improvement compared to the other methods, its accuracy of EMEI and AMEI is 94.71 % and 92.64 %, respectively, which is higher than the other two methods.

6 Conclusion

In this paper, the AMEI and EMEI are extracted as the human behavior description, the normalization size 64×64 is smaller than the original size of the target contour image, thus the storage space and computation load are reduced much. The LCDL method is used for recognition, the locality constrained condition can preserve the intra-class distance; a structured dictionary is constructed with its sub-dictionaries correspond to each category; the sparse reconstruction error of testing sample is used for recognition.

The effectiveness of the proposed method has been verified by the experiments on Weizmann and DHA datasets. However, we need to construct sub-dictionaries for each category, this process is time-consuming. Next step we will learning a whole dictionary without having to clear the sub-dictionaries of all categories.

References

1. Guo, G.D., Lai, A.: A survey on still image based on human action recognition. Pattern Recogn. 47(04), 3343–3361 (2014)
2. Cai, J.X., Feng, G.C., Tang, X., et al.: Human action recognition by learning pose dictionary. ACTA OPTICA SINICA 34(12), 1–12 (2014)
3. Ben, X.Y., Xu, S., Wang, K.J.: Review on pedestrian gait feature expression and recognition. Pattern Recogn. Artif. Intell. 25(1), 71–81 (2012)
4. Bobick, A.F., Davis, J.W.: The recognition of human movement using temporal templates. IEEE Trans. Pattern Anal. Mach. Intell. 23(3), 257–267 (2001)
5. Han, J., Bhanu, B.: Individual recognition using gait energy image. IEEE Trans. Pattern Anal. Mach. Intell. 28(2), 316–322 (2006)
6. Lian, Q.S., Shi, B.S., Chen, S.Z.: Research advances on dictionary learning models, algorithms and applications. ACTA Autom. SINICA 41(2), 240–260 (2015)
7. Niebles, C., Wang, H.C., Li, F.F.: Unsupervised learning of human action categories using spatial-temporal words. Int. J. Comput. Vis. 79(3), 299–318 (2008)
8. Liu, J.G., Ali, S., Shah, M: Recognizing human actions using multiple features. In: Computer Vision and Pattern Recognition, pp. 1–8. Anchorage (2008)
9. Boothby, W.M.: An Introduction to Differentiable Manifolds and Riemannian Geometry, 2nd edn. Academic, New York (2003)
10. Lin, Y.CH., Hu, M.CH., Cheng, W.H., et al.: Human action recognition and retrieval using sole depth information. In: Proceedings of the 20th ACM Int'l Conference Multimedia (MM 2012), Nara, Japan (2012)
11. Aharon, M., Elad, M., Bruckstein, A.: K-SVD: an algorithm for designing overcomplete dictionaries for sparse representation. IEEE Trans. Signal Process. 54(11), 4311–4322 (2006)

Social Simulations

Pedestrian Navigation Using iZES Framework for Bounding Heading Drift

Liqiang Zhang, Zhong Su$^{(\boxtimes)}$, and Qing Li

Beijing Key Laboratory of High Dynamic Navigation Technology,
Beijing Information Science and Technological University,
No. 35, Beisihuan Middle Road, Chaoyang District, Beijing 100101, China
zlq_bistu1407@163.com, {sz,liqing}@bistu.edu.cn

Abstract. In this paper, we describe an EKF-based framework called iZES (improved ZUPT-EKF-SINS) which is used to estimate the position and attitude of a person while walking. ZES framework consists of Zero velocity Updating algorithm, an Extended Kalman Filter and Strap-down inertial system. There is no observable variables for ZES to estimate heading and its drift, which will lead to inaccurate positioning. Therefore, on the basis of ZES, Zero Angular Rate Updating (ZARU) algorithm and Magnetic Correction (MC) methodology are considered into the framework, which is called iZES (improved ZES). The iZES PDR method was tested in several real indoor and outdoor environment with a foot-mounted IMU. Compared with ZES, iZES has a better performance that its horizontal positioning error is about 1.7 % of the total travelled distance.

Keywords: Pedestrian navigation · Heading drift · Magnetic correction · Extended Kalman Filter · iZES

1 Introduction

In the field of pedestrian navigation, GNSS (Global Navigation Satellite System) is widely used as an essential positioning method. But in the field, urban canyon or indoor environment, the accuracy of GNSS positioning becomes lower due to the signal attenuation, interference and shade. In order to get continuous positioning results, further research in sensor complementation and diversified positioning technology is required. Local Positioning System (LPS) is being investigated by using ultrasound, radio or vision technology [1]. However, in some cases, infrastructure-free solutions are preferred because they do not need any extra equipment and are economic. IMU-based navigation methods are now hot research points due to lower cost, high reliability, as well as no infrastructure needed.

At the end of last century, Draper lab in US firstly proposed the method of foot-mounted IMU to achieve positioning. Due to the accumulated errors of MEMS inertial sensors, especially the heading drift caused by gyroscope errors, the

This work is supported by The National Natural Science Foundation of China (Grant No. 61471046) and Beijing Municipal Commission of Education (Grant No. TJSHG 201510772017).

© Springer Science+Business Media Singapore 2016
L. Zhang et al. (Eds.): AsiaSim 2016/SCS AutumnSim 2016, Part IV, CCIS 646, pp. 235–244, 2016.
DOI: 10.1007/978-981-10-2672-0_24

development of pedestrian navigation system is restricted. To improve the accuracy of positioning, domestic and foreign scholars do a lot of work. Foxlin [2] proposed the framework of ZUPT-EKF-SINS to calculate the position of pedestrian. But there is no observable variables to estimate the heading and its drift. S. Rajagopal [3] added ZARU algorithm to the ZES to bound the heading drift. Following Foxlin's work, Chinese scholar Wei-Xing Qian [4] made use of three-axis magnetometer for initial alignment, which will still lead to heading drift because of no reduction of gyroscope biases.

In this paper, in order to overcome these limitation, we proposes iZES framework which is based on ZES (ZUPT-EKF-SINS) by using a foot-mounted IMU. ZARU and MC algorithms are integrated into ZES. Instead of gyroscope data, the accelerometer data of stance phase is used to calculate the attitude of IMU, which leads to better magnetic heading information. Finally, iZES was tested in several real indoor and outdoor environment and had a good performance.

2   ZES Framework

We use EKF-based PDR algorithm proposed by Foxlin [2] to estimate position and attitude of a strap-down inertial navigation system. While walking, the velocity of foot is nearly zero when it is attached on the ground. The EKF is updated with velocity measurements by ZUPT. 15-element error state vectors are considered into EKF: $\delta \mathbf{x} = \left[\delta \varphi, \delta \omega^b, \delta \mathbf{r}, \delta \mathbf{v}, \delta \mathbf{a}^b \right]^T$ which contain the biases of gyroscope and accelerometer $\delta \omega^b$ and $\delta \mathbf{a}^b$, as well as the error vectors of attitude $\delta \varphi$, position $\delta \mathbf{r}$ and velocity $\delta \mathbf{v}$. We call this framework ZES. The main blocks are as showed in Fig. 1.

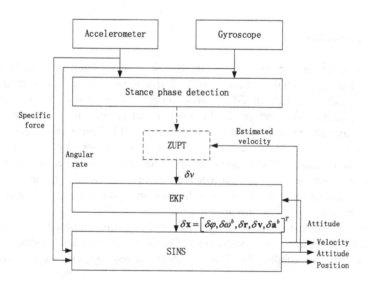

Fig. 1. Main blocks of ZES framework

3   Improved ZES Framework

In the traditional ZES framework, yaw angle $\delta\psi$ and biases of gyroscope $\delta\omega^b$ are not observable to estimate the heading and its drift. We integrate ZARU and MC algorithms into the EKF-based framework to form the improved ZES framework, or iZES for short. Figure 2 shows the main blocks of iZES.

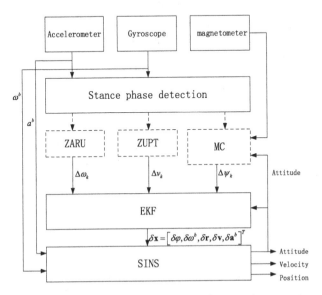

Fig. 2. Main blocks of iZES framework

3.1   Stance Phase Detection

The EKF is triggered only when the foot is detected to be absolutely still, or in stance phase while walking. Most algorithms for stance phase detection rely on single sensor signal with accelerometer [5] or gyroscope [10]. According to [6], we implement a multi-sensor algorithm by using both accelerometers and gyroscopes signal to make the detector robust enough.

Stance detection problem can be formalized as a binary hypothesis testing problem. The two hypotheses H_0 and H_1 can be defined as follows:

$$H_0 : \text{IMU is moving}$$
$$H_1 : \text{IMU is stationary} \tag{1}$$

There are different models of IMU [7–9] for different applications. When IMU is used in pedestrian navigation, its output can be described as follows:

$$y_k = s_k(\theta) + v_k \tag{2}$$

Where

$$s_k(\theta) = \begin{bmatrix} s_k^\theta(\theta) \\ s_k^\omega(\theta) \end{bmatrix} \text{ and } v_k = \begin{bmatrix} v_k^a \\ v_k^\omega \end{bmatrix} \tag{3}$$

Here, $s_k^a(\theta) \in \mathbf{R}^3$ and $s_k^\omega(\theta) \in \mathbf{R}^3$ donate the specific force and angular rate measured by IMU, respectively. $v_k^a \in \mathbf{R}^3$ and $v_k^\omega \in \mathbf{R}^3$ donate the noise associated with the accelerometer and gyroscope, respectively. We assume that the noise is white Gaussian noise with covariance matrix

$$C = E\{v_k v_k^T\} = \begin{bmatrix} \sigma_a^2 I_3 & 0_3 \\ 0_3 & \sigma_\omega^2 I_3 \end{bmatrix} \tag{4}$$

Where I_3 and 0_3 donate a 3×3 identity matrix and 3×3 zero matrix, respectively. $E\{\}$ denotes the expectation operation. Further, $\sigma_a^2 \in \mathbf{R}^1$ and $\sigma_\omega^2 \in \mathbf{R}^1$ denote the accelerometer and gyroscope noise variance, respectively.

When IMU is stationary, the detector chooses the hypothesis H_1. It will satisfy the equation as follows:

$$T(z_n) = \frac{1}{W} \sum_{k=n}^{n+W-1} \left(\frac{1}{\sigma_a^2} \left\| y_k^a - g \frac{\bar{y}_n^a}{\| \bar{y}_n^a \|} \right\|^2 + \frac{1}{\sigma_\omega^2} \| y_k^\omega \|^2 \right) < \xi \tag{5}$$

where $z_n = \begin{bmatrix} z_n^a \\ z_n^\omega \end{bmatrix}$ donates the sequences measured by IMU at time n. $T(\ )$ donates the GLRT function. Further, $z_n^a = \{y_k^a\}_{k=n}^{n+W-1}$ and $z_n^\omega = \{y_k^\omega\}_{k=n}^{n+W-1}$ donate accelerometer and gyroscope measurement sequences within sample window W, respectively. g donates the local acceleration of gravity. $\bar{y}_n^a = \frac{1}{W} \sum_{k=n}^{n+W-1} y_k^a$ and $\bar{y}_n^\omega = \frac{1}{W} \sum_{k=n}^{n+W-1} y_k^\omega$ donate the mean values of specific force and angular rate sequences, respectively. We can comprehend Eq. (5) like this: The mean square error of fitting a vector of magnitude g with the direction of the average specific force vector to the accelerometer data in combination with the energy in the gyroscope signal are weighed each by the quality of the measurements. If the result of their fusion falls below the threshold ξ, the detector chooses the hypothesis H_1 that the IMU is stationary. Logical "1"s represent the stance or still phase when the velocity of foot is nearly zero. "0"s represent the swing phase which means the pedestrian is walking. Detecting results are as shown in Fig. 3.

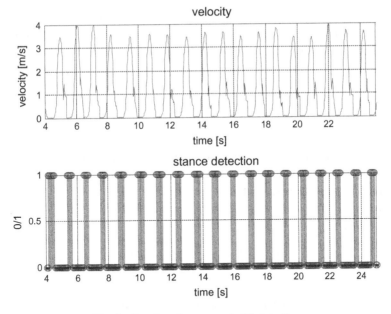

Fig. 3. Results of stance and still detection

3.2 Zero Angular Rate Update

The velocity and angular rate of foot are nearly zero when it touches the ground while walking [3]. During the period, the EKF is fed with the error measurement vector of angular rate. Thus, the error measurement vector is as follows:

$$\mathbf{z}_k = \Delta\omega_k^b = \omega_k^b - [0,0,0] \tag{6}$$

Its measurement matrix must be:

$$\mathbf{H} = \begin{bmatrix} \mathbf{0}_{3\times3} & \mathbf{I}_{3\times3} & \mathbf{0}_{3\times3} & \mathbf{0}_{3\times3} & \mathbf{0}_{3\times3} \end{bmatrix} \tag{7}$$

3.3 Magnetic Correction

This compensation algorithm can be normally used in outdoor environment where magnetic perturbation are gentle. But indoors, the magnetic perturbation may be severe and variable. In spite of this, we still believe magnetic field is a valid reference for heading and make an assumption that the magnetic field indoor is stable.

In order to use the magnetometer to calculate the heading angle, the sensor body frame readings $\mathbf{B}_k^b$ must be transformed into the readings $\mathbf{B}_k^n$ under the navigation frame using the roll angle ϕ_k and pitch angle θ_k:

$$\mathbf{B}_k^n = \mathbf{R}_{b_{k|k}}^n \mathbf{B}_k^b \tag{8}$$

where $\mathbf{B}_k^b = \begin{bmatrix} B_{kx}^b & B_{ky}^b & B_{kz}^b \end{bmatrix}^T$. $\mathbf{R}_{b_{k|k}}^n$ donates the corrected rotation matrix that transforms from the body frame (b) to the navigation frame (n. defined to be North-West-Up). Hence, we can calculate the horizontal vectors of magnetic intensity as follows:

$$\begin{cases} B_{kx}^n = B_{kx}^b \cos\theta_k - B_{ky}^b \sin\theta_k \sin\phi_k - B_{kz}^b \cos\theta_k \sin\phi_k \\ B_{ky}^n = B_{ky}^b \cos\phi_k - B_{kz}^b \sin\phi_k \end{cases} \qquad (9)$$

In the frame of body, gravity vector can be described as $\mathbf{g}^b = \begin{bmatrix} g_x^b & g_y^b & g_z^b \end{bmatrix}^T$. When IMU is still, or in the stance phase during walking, gravity vectors in the navigation frame can be described as $\mathbf{g}^n = \begin{bmatrix} 0 & 0 & g \end{bmatrix}^T$.

Hence,

$$\mathbf{g}^b = \mathbf{R}_{n_{k|k}}^b \mathbf{g}^n = \begin{bmatrix} -g\sin\theta \\ g\sin\phi\cos\theta \\ g\cos\phi\cos\theta \end{bmatrix} \qquad (10)$$

The roll angle ϕ_k and pitch angle θ_k can be calculated as follows:

$$\begin{cases} \phi_k = \arctan(g_y^b / g_z^b) \\ \theta_k = \arcsin(-g_x^b / g) \end{cases} \qquad (11)$$

Since magnetic north does not coincide with geographical north, we define B_d as the declination at a given point on the earth surface. So the heading angle is:

$$\psi_{compass_k} = \arctan\left(\frac{B_{ky}^n}{B_{kx}^n}\right) + B_d \qquad (12)$$

The error measurement vector $\mathbf{z}_k$ for the EKF is

$$\mathbf{z}_k = \Delta\psi_k = \psi_k - \psi_{compass_k} \qquad (13)$$

Its measurement matrix is

$$H = \begin{bmatrix} [001] & 0_{1\times3} & 0_{1\times3} & 0_{1\times3} & 0_{1\times3} \end{bmatrix} \qquad (14)$$

3.4 Extended Kalman Filter

The state model of pedestrian navigation system is a nonlinear function of the state vectors, which can be linearized according to [2, 10]. A classical INS mechanization was implemented, including some modification provided by the EKF using the error state vector: $\delta\mathbf{x}_{k|k} = \delta\mathbf{x}_k = \begin{bmatrix} \delta\varphi_k, \delta\omega_k^b, \delta\mathbf{r}_k, \delta\mathbf{v}_k, \delta\mathbf{a}_k^b \end{bmatrix}^T$ which contains the biases of gyroscope and accelerometer $\delta\omega_k^b$ and $\delta\mathbf{a}_k^b$, as well as the error vectors of attitude $\delta\varphi_k$, position $\delta\mathbf{r}_k$ and velocity $\delta\mathbf{v}_k$.

Then, the linearized state transition model is:

$$\delta\mathbf{x}_{k|k-1} = \mathbf{\Phi}_k\delta\mathbf{x}_{k-1|k-1} + \mathbf{w}_{k-1} \tag{15}$$

where $\delta\mathbf{x}_{k|k-1}$ donates the prior error state vector at time k, $\delta\mathbf{x}_{k-1|k-1}$ is the posterior error state vector at time $k-1$ and $\mathbf{w}_{k-1}$ donates the process noise with covariance matrix $\mathbf{Q}_{k-1} = E(\mathbf{w}_{k-1}\mathbf{w}_{k-1}^T)$, as well as $\mathbf{\Phi}_k$ is the 15×15 state transfer matrix:

$$\mathbf{\Phi}_k = \begin{bmatrix} \mathbf{I}_{3\times3} & \Delta t\mathbf{C}_{b_{k|k-1}}^n & 0 & 0 & 0 \\ 0 & \mathbf{I}_{3\times3} & 0 & 0 & 0 \\ 0 & 0 & \mathbf{I}_{3\times3} & \Delta t\mathbf{I}_{3\times3} & 0 \\ -\Delta t[\mathbf{a}_k'^n\times] & 0 & 0 & \mathbf{I}_{3\times3} & \Delta t\mathbf{C}_{b_{k|k-1}}^n \\ 0 & 0 & 0 & 0 & \mathbf{I}_{3\times3} \end{bmatrix} \tag{16}$$

where $[\mathbf{a}_k'^n\times] = \begin{bmatrix} 0 & -a_{z_k} & a_{y_k} \\ a_{z_k} & 0 & -a_{x_k} \\ -a_{y_k} & a_{x_k} & 0 \end{bmatrix}$ is the skew symmetric matrix for acceleration,

$\mathbf{a}_k'^n$ is the bias-corrected acceleration under the navigation frame, and Δt donates the sample interval.

The measurement equation is:

$$\mathbf{z}_k = \mathbf{H}\delta\mathbf{x}_{k|k} + \mathbf{n}_k \tag{17}$$

where $\mathbf{z}_k$ is the error measurement vector, $\mathbf{H}$ is the measurement matrix, $\delta\mathbf{x}_{k|k}$ is the posterior error state vector at time k, and $\mathbf{n}_k$ donates the measurement noise with covariance matrix $\mathbf{R}_k = E(\mathbf{n}_k\mathbf{n}_k^T)$.

The Kalman update equation is:

$$\delta\mathbf{x}_{k|k} = \delta\mathbf{x}_{k|k-1} + \mathbf{K}_k(\mathbf{z}_k - \mathbf{H}\delta\mathbf{x}_{k|k-1}) \tag{18}$$

where $\mathbf{K}_k$ is the Kalman gain.

We integrate ZARU and MC algorithms into the ZES framework. Thus, its measurement matrix is:

$$\mathbf{H} = \begin{bmatrix} [001] & \mathbf{0}_{1\times3} & \mathbf{0}_{1\times3} & \mathbf{0}_{1\times3} & \mathbf{0}_{1\times3} \\ \mathbf{0}_{3\times3} & \mathbf{I}_{3\times3} & \mathbf{0}_{3\times3} & \mathbf{0}_{3\times3} & \mathbf{0}_{3\times3} \\ \mathbf{0}_{3\times3} & \mathbf{0}_{3\times3} & \mathbf{0}_{3\times3} & \mathbf{I}_{3\times3} & \mathbf{0}_{3\times3} \end{bmatrix} \tag{19}$$

and the measurement vector is:

$$\mathbf{z}_k = [\Delta\psi_k, \Delta\omega_k^b, \Delta\mathbf{v}_k]^T \tag{20}$$

4 Experiment

In order to evaluate the performance of iZES framework, we did a lot of experiments in real scenarios with a foot-mounted IMU. The IMU used for test is IG-500 N product of SBG Company and it contains 3-axis accelerometer, 3-axis gyroscope and 3-axis magnetometer as standard sensors. The performance of each individual sensor is shown in Table 1.

Table 1. Performance of each individual sensor

Parameter	Specifications		
Output frequency	100 Hz		
Sensor	Accelerometer	Gyroscope	Magnetometer
Range	±5 g	±300/s	±1.2 Gauss
nonlinear	<0.2 % of FS	<0.05 % of FS	<0.2 % of FS
Random drift	±5 mg	±0.5/s	±0.5 m Gauss
Bandwidth	250 Hz	240 Hz	500 Hz

Tests were performanced in No. 2 building of BISTU campus. The tester started from point A inside the building, walked outside and returned to point A. Figure 4 shows the estimated trajectories for a path 169 meters long.

We calculated the positioning errors (difference between starting point and end point) with respect to the total travelled distance (TTD). 2D positioning error of the proposed method is improved from >8 % (ZES framework) to 1.5 %–1.9 %. Figure 5a shows that the biases of gyroscope converge to the true value rapidly in iZES framework compared with ZES. Without measurements, ZES framework cannot

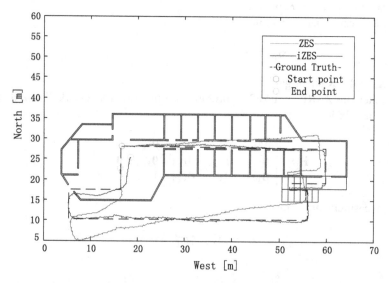

Fig. 4. Estimated 2D trajectories using ZES and iZES framework

predict the biases of gyroscope exactly as it shows in Fig. 5b. The estimation covariance of position, velocity and heading converge to lower values by using iZES framework, as is shown in Fig. 6a and b, which means that iZES framework can offer more precise results.

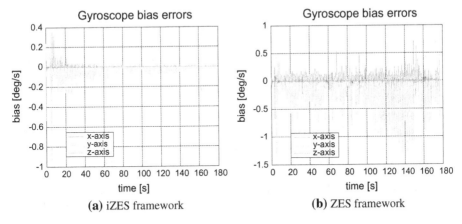

(a) iZES framework   (b) ZES framework

Fig. 5. Biases of gyroscope estimated by EKF in different frameworks

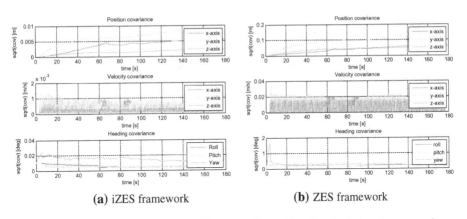

(a) iZES framework   (b) ZES framework

Fig. 6. Estimation covariance of position, velocity and heading in different frameworks

5 Conclusion and Future Work

We implemented and compared ZES and iZES PDR algorithms with foot-mounted IMU for pedestrian navigation. We use single IMU sensor to do our research instead of using any external infrastructure such as GPS, Wi-Fi, Bluetooth or building-maps to bound the heading drift.

The presented result shows iZES PDR algorithm has a better performance than ZES. Its 2D positioning error is about 1.7 % of the total travelled distance compared with ZES.

However, there may be magnetic perturbation under indoor and outdoor environment. Future work will be focused on correcting the positioning errors due to magnetic distortion.

References

1. Jiménez, A.R., Seco, F., Prieto, C., Roa, J.: Tecnologías sensorialesde localización para entornos inteligentes. In: I Congreso español deinformática - Simposio de Computación Ubicua e Inteligencia Ambiental, UCAmI2005 (Granada), pp. 75–86 (2005)
2. Foxlin, E.: Pedestrian Tracking with shoe-mounted inertial sensors. IEEE Comput. Graph. Appl. **25**(6), 38–46 (2005)
3. Rajagopal, S., Rajagopal, S.: Personal Dead Reckoning System with Shoe Mounted Inertial Sensors. Master of Science Thesis (2008)
4. Qian, W.-X., Zhu, X.-H., Yan, S.: Personal navigation method based on foot-mounted MEMS inertial/magnetic measurement unit. J. Chin. Inertial Technol. **20**(5), 567–572 (2012)
5. Stirling, R.G.: Development of a pedestrian navigation system using shoe-mounted sensors. Library and Archives Canada = Bibliothèque et Archives Canada (2005)
6. Skog, I., Händel, P., Nilsson, J.O., et al.: Zero-velocity detection—An algorithm evaluation. IEEE Trans. Biomed. Eng. **57**(11), 2657–2666 (2010)
7. Titterton, D., Weston, J.L.: Strapdown inertial navigation technology. IET (2004)
8. Skog, I., Händel, P.: Calibration of a MEMS inertial measurement unit. XVII IMEKO World Congress, pp. 1–6 (2006)
9. Sabatini, A.M.: Quaternion-based strap-down integration method for applications of inertial sensing to gait analysis. Med. Biol. Eng. Compu. **43**(1), 94–101 (2005)
10. Schumacher, A.: Integration of a gps aided strapdown inertial navigation system for land vehicles. Master of Science Thesis, Stockholm, Sweeden, pp. 1–57 (2006)

Research on Step-Length Self-learning Pedestrian Self-location System

Hui Zhao[✉] and Qing Li

Beijing Key Laboratory of High Dynamic Navigation Technology,
Beijing Information Science and Technology University, Beijing 100101, China
843071809@qq.com, liqing@bistu.edu.cn

Abstract. Pedestrian navigation in a non beacon environment is a difficult problem and a hot research topic in the field of navigation. This paper introduces a design which implement the pedestrian dead reckoning based on the characteristics of human gait,and the MIMU is fixed on the waist behind. The traditional step-length model can't adapt to all kinds of moving forms, so a new self-learning step-length estimated model is proposed by the combination of SINS and PDR. The speed is introduced from SINS to estimate the step-length at the beginning. And the step-length is used to train the step-length model based on frequency and acceleration variance. After a period of time, the speed begin to divergence and we use the trained model to estimate the step-length. Tests have been done in the indoor and outdoor. The test results show that the TTD error is less than 2 %,and most of results are around 1 %.

Keywords: Pedestrian self-navigation · Wearable · MIMU · Step-length estimation · Self-learning

1 Introduction

In recent years, with the rapid development of the Internet, location-based services (LBS) more and more appear in people's lives, such as travel map navigation, search the surrounding store information, as well as a lot of group buying activities [1]. Most location-based services are based on the use of GNSS to obtain location information, but for indoor, underground and Canyon where GNSS can't work under such circumstances, the acquisition of location information has become a problem.

The pedestrian navigation and positioning system based on MEMS inertial sensor (MEMS IMU) has the advantage of not being restricted by the environment, flexibility and the positioning robustness. And the PNS(pedestrian navigation system) has important application value in the emergency relief, anti-terrorism security, military operations command and daily navigation and so on. Therefore, using MEMS IMU for pedestrian navigation has become a hot research topic.

The current mainstream algorithm framework is mainly divided into two types: strapdown inertial navigation system(SINS) and pedestrian dead reckoning (PDR) [2]. In one side, the SINS integration operation will bring the cumulative error with the drift of time, and although there is a corresponding zero velocity update algorithm to modify it, the

© Springer Science+Business Media Singapore 2016
L. Zhang et al. (Eds.): AsiaSim 2016/SCS AutumnSim 2016, Part IV, CCIS 646, pp. 245–254, 2016.
DOI: 10.1007/978-981-10-2672-0_25

determination of zero velocity state will introduce a lot of problems. In the other side, in this paper the MIMU is fixed on the waist behind. It is difficult to detect the zero velocity of the waist, so that the integral error of SINS can't be corrected by zero velocity update algorithm. So in order to avoid introducing the cumulative error, this paper chooses the pedestrian dead reckoning program to implement personal self-navigation and positioning.

At present, the main step length estimation model from simple to complex, can be divided into constant/pseudo constant step length model, linear step length model, nonlinear step length model and artificial intelligence step length model [3]. The constant/pseudo constant step length model is to set the step length as a fixed value. Although it can realize a simple walking distance estimation, the accuracy is too low and it doesn't adapt to a long distance travel and high accuracy navigation applications. The complex model is mostly based on the statistic correlation between the velocity and the acceleration of the pedestrian. The relevant features has step frequency, maximum acceleration and minimum acceleration during each step, and acceleration variance in each step.

The linear step length model proposed by Swiss Federal Institute of Technology Quentin Ladetto et al. is as follows [4].

$$SL = A + B \times SF + C \times SV \tag{1}$$

where SL is step length, SF is step frequency, SV is acceleration variance in each step, A, B, C is regression coefficients. This model use a linear combination of frequency and acceleration variance to approximate the step length. It is simple and flexible, but the error is relatively large.

The nonlinear step length model proposed by The United States University of Notre Dame P.J. Antsaklis, M. Lemmon et al. is as follows [5].

$$SL = K \times \sqrt[4]{A_{max} - A_{min}} \tag{2}$$

where SL is step length, A_{max} and A_{min} is maximum acceleration and minimum acceleration during each step respectively. K is correlation coefficient. Since only one parameter is used, this model has the accesses to carry out real time step length estimation. However, the extreme value of the acceleration in one step is greatly influenced by the noise, the estimation error would be relatively large.

A more complex step length estimation model is artificial intelligence step length model proposed by Seoul National University Seong Yun Cho et al. [6]. The main advantage is that there is no need to establish the mapping relationship between the step length and the statistical characteristics of acceleration. It uses feed forward back propagation network which has 16 nodes in hidden layer, and adopts the 'tansig' transfer function. The input parameters of four nodes in the input layer are: frequency, acceleration variance in each step, the extreme value of acceleration in each step. Through a large number of experiments to collect data. The network is trained by the sample data and then the mapping relationship between the step length and the acceleration statistic characteristic can be obtained. Once we get the trained network, we can estimate the step length based the input parameters. The artificial intelligence step length model can be more accuracy then the above methods. But it need large number of experiments and has a poor real-time performance.

The above step length estimation models need to be trained to get the correlation coefficients and the network before the actual use. And they have a poor real-time performance. Once the train is completed, the model wouldn't be modified so that it can't adapt to various environments and different users. In view of the above problems, this paper proposes a step length self learning model to improve the real-time performance and adaptability of the step length estimation.

This paper takes the STM32F429 as the platform and use the waist measurement scheme, as shown in Fig. 1. The acceleration signal is processed in the vertical direction. A threshold method is used to carry out the counting step. The speed information is introduced to estimate the step length and train the step length model. Using the gyro information to update the quaternion, so as to get the heading angel. If the initial position is known, the real-time position information can be obtained by integrating the heading and the step length information, and then the goal of the pedestrian navigation and positioning is achieved.

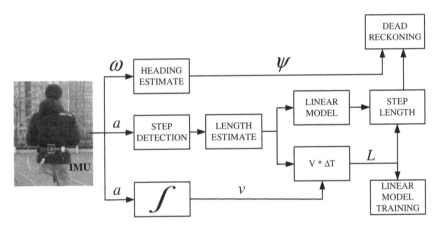

Fig. 1. Pedestrian Dead Reckoning Architecture

2   Gait Detection and Step Length Estimation

2.1   Threshold Method Gait Detection

While man is walking, the state of waist and foot is different. The foot has a short transient when zero velocity update algorithm (ZUPT) can be introduced to control the cumulative error [7]. But it is difficult to find the same feature on waist, so the ZUPT can't be applied on waist. From the point of view of the motion characteristics of the human body, the center of gravity of the waist will produce displacement in the vertical direction while the man is walking. The acceleration signals in the vertical direction is shown in Fig. 2. As the figure shows, the signal cycles of the three axis is very obvious, so the signals can be processed to carry out the step counting.

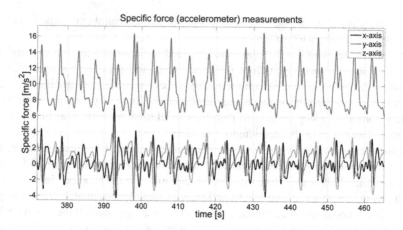

Fig. 2. Acceleration signals

The acceleration signals of the three axis are processed by the following formula:

$$T(i) = \sqrt{\frac{a_{xi}^2 + 4 \times a_{yi}^2 + 2 \times a_{zi}^2}{6}} \tag{3}$$

Where $T(i)$ is the synthesis acceleration of sampling point at the time i, a_{xi}, a_{yi}, a_{zi} are the x axis acceleration, y axis acceleration and z axis acceleration respectively at the time i. As can be seen in the above formula, the weight of y axis acceleration is 4 for the purpose of highlighting the periodicity of the y axis signal. After treated by the above formula, the synthesis acceleration can be obtained. Then low-pass filtering. The processed signal is shown in Fig. 3.

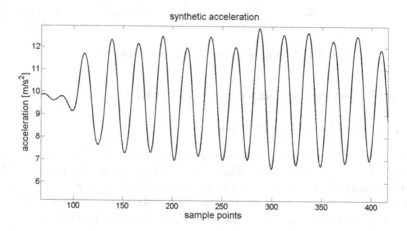

Fig. 3. Synthetic acceleration

As the Fig. 3 shows, we can set a threshold, such as 60, if the synthetic accelera-tion is greater than 60, it stands the pedestrian move a step forward and the step number plus 1. In this way, we can get the number of pedestrian moving. The threshold method is as follow:

$$Z = \begin{cases} 1 & if \ T \geq th \\ 0 & if \ T < th \end{cases} \tag{4}$$

where T is synthetic acceleration, th is threshold, Z is the state of pedestrian, 1 stands for moving a step, 0 stands for static. In real test, a pedestrian moved 70 steps, the threshold method detected 70 steps. The counting experiments show the threshold method is effective.

2.2 Step Length Estimation

When the IMU is fixed on the waist, the acceleration waves is corresponding to each single steps. Single step length is the distance between one foot to the other. A person's step length would be influenced by the height, road condition and mood et al. Every step length of the same person is not the same. Obviously, different people's step length are not the same, either. At present, the main step length estimation model from simple to complex, can be divided into constant/pseudo constant step length model, linear step length model, nonlinear step length model and artificial intelligence step length model. The main input variables are frequency, leg length, acceleration extreme values and acceleration variance et al. The above step length estimation models need to be trained to get the correlation coefficients and the network before the actual use. And they have a poor real-time performance. Once the train is completed, the model wouldn't be modified so that it can't adapt to various environments and different users. In different walking environments and for different users, it will produce large errors.

In the view of above problems, we proposed a self-learning step length estimation methods to improve the system's adaptability and real time performance. Within a short period of time the system has just started, we introduced the speed information from the SINS(strap-down inertial navigation system) to estimate the step length. Calculate the duration of each step, and then use single step time and single step speed to get the single step length. At the same time, the single step length can be used to train the model based on frequency and acceleration variance. After a period of time, speed begins to diver-gence as a result of drift of the inertial devices. At this time, we begin to adopt the trained step length model to estimate the step distance instead of using the speed and the single step duration time. The algorithm avoids the trouble of collecting a lot of data to train model in advance. What's more, for different users and various moving forms, it can get a good performance in adaptability.

However, it is difficult to accurately determine a single step duration time. Under normal circumstances, to determine a step time, we need to know the beginning and end of the step time and take the difference as the single step time. But according to the acceleration signals, it is very difficult to accurately find the corresponding time points.

Taking a simple way, we consider the time interval between two steps as the single step time. As shown in Fig. 4.

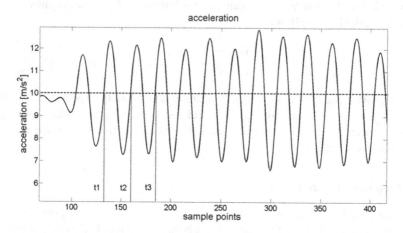

Fig. 4. Step time

We use the 10 as the threshold. If the synthetic acceleration is greater than 60, it stands for a step moving, and we record the time point as t_1, then record the next step time point as t_2. If the average speed during t_1 and t_2 is $\bar{v}$, the single travel distance L can be obtained through the following formula:

$$L = \bar{v} \times (t_2 - t_1) \tag{5}$$

At the beginning, we take the above formula to estimate the step length, and use the length to train the model based step frequency and acceleration covariance. Here we adopt the multiple linear regression method to get the adaptive coefficients of the step length model. When the speed information begins to divergence because of the drift of the inertial devices, we use the trained model to estimate the step length, the model is as follows[8].

$$L = a_1 \times f + a_2 \times \text{var}(T) + b \tag{6}$$

where L is step length, f is step frequency, $\text{var}(T)$ is synthetic acceleration variance, a_1, a_2, b is the coefficients. The coefficients are obtained through the linear regression method.

3 Heading Estimation

Once we get the single step length, if we know the heading angles and the initial position, the next position can be calculated. This paper takes the quaternion to get the course and the heading. With the application of flight carrier navigation control system and the rapid development of the digital computer in the motion control, control system requirements the navigation computation can describe the body motion reasonably in rigid space. The research of the quaternion method has received extensive attention.

Firstly, use the initial attitude angels to determine the initial quaternion. The formula is as follows.

$$
\begin{bmatrix} \lambda(0) \\ p_1(0) \\ p_2(0) \\ p_3(0) \end{bmatrix} = \begin{bmatrix} \cos\dfrac{\psi_0}{2}\cos\dfrac{\theta_0}{2}\cos\dfrac{\gamma_0}{2} + \sin\dfrac{\psi_0}{2}\sin\dfrac{\theta_0}{2}\sin\dfrac{\gamma_0}{2} \\ \cos\dfrac{\psi_0}{2}\cos\dfrac{\theta_0}{2}\sin\dfrac{\gamma_0}{2} - \sin\dfrac{\psi_0}{2}\sin\dfrac{\theta_0}{2}\cos\dfrac{\gamma_0}{2} \\ \cos\dfrac{\psi_0}{2}\sin\dfrac{\theta_0}{2}\cos\dfrac{\gamma_0}{2} - \sin\dfrac{\psi_0}{2}\cos\dfrac{\theta_0}{2}\sin\dfrac{\gamma_0}{2} \\ \sin\dfrac{\psi_0}{2}\cos\dfrac{\theta_0}{2}\cos\dfrac{\gamma_0}{2} - \cos\dfrac{\psi_0}{2}\sin\dfrac{\theta_0}{2}\sin\dfrac{\gamma_0}{2} \end{bmatrix}
\tag{7}
$$

Where $\psi_0, \theta_0, \gamma_0$ is the initial attitude angles.

Next in order to update the quaternion, we use the two order Runge Kutta method to solve the Quaternion Differential Equation. The formula is as follows.

$$
\frac{dQ}{dt} = \frac{1}{2}\begin{pmatrix} 0 & -\omega_x & -\omega_y & -\omega_z \\ \omega_x & 0 & \omega_z & -\omega_y \\ \omega_y & -\omega_z & 0 & \omega_x \\ \omega_z & \omega_y & -\omega_x & 0 \end{pmatrix} \cdot \begin{pmatrix} q_0 \\ q_1 \\ q_2 \\ q_3 \end{pmatrix}
\tag{8}
$$

where $\omega_x, \omega_y, \omega_z$ is angular velocity.

After real time computation of quaternion, we can get the rotation matrix. The formula is as follows.

$$
C_E^b = \begin{bmatrix} \lambda^2 + p_1^2 - p_2^2 - p_3^2 & 2(p_1 p_2 + \lambda p_3) & 2(p_1 p_3 - \lambda p_2) \\ 2(p_1 p_2 - \lambda p_3) & \lambda^2 + p_2^2 - p_1^2 - p_3^2 & 2(p_2 p_3 + \lambda p_1) \\ 2(p_1 p_3 + \lambda p_2) & 2(p_2 p_3 - \lambda p_1) & \lambda^2 + p_3^2 - p_1^2 - p_2^2 \end{bmatrix}
\tag{9}
$$

In the final, we can calculate the attitude angels through the rotation matrix. The attitude angel can be obtained by the following formulas.

$$
\begin{cases} \theta = -\arcsin\left(T_{13}(n)\right) \\ \psi = \arctan\left(\dfrac{T_{12}(n)}{T_{11}(n)}\right) \\ \gamma = \arctan\left(\dfrac{T_{23}(n)}{T_{33}(n)}\right) \end{cases}
\tag{10}
$$

Where T_{12} denotes the first line, second column element. The same as other.

Through the above formulas, we can get the pedestrian heading. Next, we can integrate the step length and the heading to calculate the pedestrian's position.

4 Pedestrian Dead Reckoning and Experiments

4.1 Pedestrian Dead Reckoning

The pedestrian dead reckoning can be implemented by the following formulas.

$$\begin{cases} E_k = E_{k-1} + L_k \times \sin(\varphi_k) \\ N_k = N_{k-1} + L_k \times \cos(\varphi_k) \end{cases} \tag{11}$$

Where L_k is the step length, φ_k is the heading angels. When $k = 0$, it denotes the initial position (E_0, N_0).

4.2 Experiments

The MIMU is fixed on the waist behind by the belt. It connect to the PC through the serial port to collect the inertial data. And then we draw the travel path on the PC according to the pedestrian dead reckoning. The test environments include indoor and outdoor. Both the indoor and outdoor travel path is a rectangle. During test we record the number of steps and the total travel distance to compute the positioning accuracy at the end. Both indoor and outdoor have three groups of tests. The results are as follows.

Indoor and outdoor actual walking track and heading chart are shown below:

From the results of the above tests can be seen, both indoor and outdoor have a high accuracy in counting steps. As the Table 1 shows, all the tests accuracy can meet the international standard 2 % total travel distance. The minimum error can be 0.6 % total travel distance. From the actual walking trajectory can be seen, the LINEAR + SINS(this paper proposed) has a higher accuracy than the normal linear length model. All the above results indicate that the system designed by this paper has a high positioning accuracy in the autonomous navigation and positioning field and has high practical value (Fig. 5).

Table 1. Results of walking tests

		Number of circles	Counting steps	Real steps	Travel distance	Error	Accuracy(%)
Indoor	1	1	36	36	20 m	0.187 m	0.9 %
	2	2	71	70	40 m	0.545 m	1.4 %
	3	3	106	106	60 m	0.362 m	0.6 %
Outdoor	1	1	96	96	54 m	0.676 m	1.3 %
	2	2	197	196	108 m	1.16 m	1.0 %
	3	3	289	288	162 m	3.5 m	2.2 %

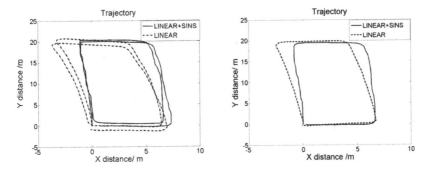

Fig. 5. Indoor and Outdoor walking trajectory

5 Conclusion

This paper designed a low cost, wearable pedestrian self-navigation and positioning system which has a certain positioning accuracy. The MIMU is fixed on the waist behind by the belt. Human body's gait characteristics are used to count steps and estimate the step length. The Heading information is updated by the quaternion. The heading and the step length are integrated to calculate the pedestrian's real time position.

This paper proposed a new step length estimation method which combined the strapdown inertial navigation system and the pedestrian dead reckoning system. That is to introduce the speed information to estimate the length at the beginning, and use the length to train the step length model based on the step frequency and the acceleration variance. When the speed begins to divergence because of the drift of the inertial devices, the system adopts the trained linear step length model to estimate the travel distance. The method can adapt to different users and various environments.

This system has advantages of small size, wearable and high accuracy, and has certain practical application value. In order to further improve the positioning accuracy, next step we consider adding external reference information, such as map [9] and vision information [10].

References

1. Sun, Y., Wu, H., Schiller, J.: A step length estimation model for position tracking. In: International Conference on Localization and GNSS (ICL-GNSS). IEEE (2015)
2. Yuan, X., Yu, S., Zhang, S., et al.: Quaternion-based unscented Kalman Filter for accurate indoor heading estimation using wearable multi-sensor system. Sensors **15**(5), 10872–10890 (2015)
3. Ruotsalainen, L.: Vision-aided pedestrian navigation for challenging GNSS environments. Kirkkonummi (2013)
4. Kourogi, M., Ishikawa, T., Kurata, T.: A method of pedestrian dead reckoning using action recognition. In: Proceeding of Plans Indian, pp. 85–89 (2010)

5. Zhao, K., Li, B.H., Dempster, A.G.: A new approach of real time step length estimation for waist mounted PDR system. In: International Conference on Wireless Communication and Sensor Network (WCSN), 2014, pp. 400–406. IEEE (2015)

6. Goyal, P., Ribeiro, V.J., Saran, H., et al.: Strap-down Pedestrian Dead-Reckoning system. In: International Conference on Indoor Positioning and Indoor Navigation (IPIN), 2011, pp. 1–7. IEEE (2011)

7. Lan, K.C., Shih, W.Y.: Using simple harmonic motion to estimate walking distance for waist-mounted PDR. In: Wireless Communications and Networking Conference (WCNC) 2012, pp. 2445–2450. IEEE (2012)

8. Ladetto, Q.: On foot navigation: continuous step calibration using both complementary recursive prediction and adaptive Kalman filtering. Ion Gps Salt Lake City Utah USA, pp. 1735–1740 (2000)

9. Fang, L., Antsaklis, P.J., Montestruque, L., et al.: Design of a wireless assisted pedestrian dead reckoning system - the NavMote experience. IEEE Trans. Instrumen. Meas. 54(6), 2342–2358 (2005)

10. Lachapelle, G., Godha, S., Cannon, M.E.: Performance of integrated HSGPS-IMU technology for pedestrian navigation under signal masking. In: Proceeding European Navigation Conference, Manchester, UK (2006)

Optimal Allocation of Resources by Interest Groups

A Mathematical Model

Max-Sebastian Dovì[1,2P(✉)]

[1] University of St. Andrews, St. Andrews, UK
dovi@startmail.com
[2] Yenching Academy of Peking University, Beijing, China

Abstract. When trying to influence legislators, interest groups can either try to persuade them by informative signalling or exert an indirect pressure by mobilizing voters through the launch of appropriate campaigns. Both activities require substantial efforts and the use of financial resources. Their allocation between the two strategies can be optimized as a function of the parameters contained in the mathematical model presented in this article. The sensitivity of the resulting allocation of resources with respect to the parameters can also be approximately estimated.

Keywords: Optimal allocation · Lobbying · Interest groups · Sensitivity analysis

1 Introduction

In this article, I shall consider the broadest definition of lobbying, i.e. any attempt to influence the decisions of a government or administrative branch, including efforts to influence public opinion [1], even if legal definitions of lobbying may be limited to a subset of the whole range of these. However, the lobbying activities considered do not include policy information and/or political intelligence, which can be regarded as a form of legislative subsidy [2]. It is further assumed that opposing interest groups try to influence legislators' preferences over policies by lobbying for antithetical programs.

Lobbying groups can optimize the impact of their financial resources by allocating them between costs related to direct contacts with decision makers and costs related to public campaigns that are expected to influence the electorate and consequently to increase the bargaining power of the lobbyists. Indeed, like direct contacts with decision makers, the mobilization of the electors requires a considerable financial effort; thus the problem arises of how to optimally allocate the resources available among the two strategies. In addition to providing a mathematical model for the solution of the allocation problem, this article derives an expression for the sensitivity on the parameters contained in it. Indeed, due to the uncertainties in their estimations, a proper sensitivity analysis can be crucial in the overall allocation process.

© Springer Science+Business Media Singapore 2016
L. Zhang et al. (Eds.): AsiaSim 2016/SCS AutumnSim 2016, Part IV, CCIS 646, pp. 255–262, 2016.
DOI: 10.1007/978-981-10-2672-0_26

The paper is organized as follows: the first section describes the methodology employed to construct the theoretical model. The second section carries out a simplified sensitivity analysis for the identification of the most influential parameters. The conclusions are contained in the last section.

2   Mathematical Model

2.1   Interactions of Interest Groups with Decision Makers

The lobbying movement is supposed to be able to use an amount of financial resources up to r_0 for lobbying, the actual amount used being indicated by r_0-r, (the evaluation of the optimal value of r is precisely the goal of this article). The potential utility for the decision maker is a function that depends on the amount of financial resources spent by the movement, i.e. $\Gamma(r_0-r)$. The goal it lobbies for is the attainment of a specific target c being close to zero. Obviously, if a different target c' is campaigned for, the new variable $c-c'$ is considered.

Opposing interest groups can use an amount of financial resources s which provides a utility $\Psi(s)$ to the policy decisor. Their goal is the attainment of a target as close to $q > 0$ as possible, the value of q best corresponding to their particular interests.

The political decisors' preference in the absence of lobbying is a value of the target equal to $c*$ $(0 < c* < q)$, which provides a utility $F(c*)$. The value of $c*$ is a function of the general orientation of the electorate and depends on the particular issue considered.

Since the utility for decision makers coincides with their chances of being re-elected, $c*$ would correspond to the median voter's attitude in a Downsian approach [3]. The results obtained can be generalized to a polarised environment using suitable models for voting behaviour. If its final decision c_0 is different from $c*$ because of lobbying, its overall utility will be $F(c_0) < F(c*)$ plus either $\Gamma(r_0-r)$ or $\Psi(s)$.

The solution of a similar one-stage game is provided by De Figuereido and De Figuereido [4] as a Nash equilibrium.

2.2   Solution of the Nash Equilibrium for Given (R_0-R)

Let us indicate the policy decisor by P, the stronger of the two lobbyists (according whether $\Phi(r_0-r) \leq or \geq Y(s)$) by L1 and the weaker of the two by L2, replacing the two symbols Φ and Ψ by U. L2 knows that he'll be beaten by L1 in any case. On the other hand, the larger the difference between $c*$ and his required value (c_{L2}), the lower the utility P receives and consequently the larger the value of c that L1 might require. Consequently L2 will lobby for $c_{L2} \to *$ offering all its utility $U(L2)$. The value of c_0 actually obtained by L1 by offering all his resources $U(L1)$ is the value that makes P better off than it would be either accepting L2 or rejecting any lobbying altogether, i.e.

$$F(c_0) + U(L1) = F(c*) + U(L2) \tag{1}$$

$$c_0 = F^{-1}[F(c*) + U(L2) + - U(L1)] \tag{2}$$

If the interest group under scrutiny is indeed the weaker of the two (which is often the case when grassroots movements oppose powerful vested interests), Eq. (2) can be rewritten as

$$c_0 = F^{-1}\left[F(c*) + \Gamma(r_0 - r) - \Psi(s)\right] \tag{3}$$

By moving part of its resources to litigation, the grassroots movement reduces the value of $\Gamma(r_0-r)$, but it can still attain a more favourable value of c_0, provided the expected campaign modifies the electorate's orientation $c*$ and consequently $F(c*)$.

Thus, by optimally breaking down the amount of resources into lobbying activities and campaign costs the interest group or the grassroots movement can maximize its influence over the decision makers. Obviously, a fraction of campaign resources equal to zero implies a rejection of the electoral mobilization option.

2.3   Modelling the Campaign Effectiveness and the Electoral Mobilization

Two issues are to be taken into account when the launch of a campaign is considered:

- Campaign effectiveness
- Electoral mobilization

The former of the two issues implies the determination of the campaign outreach, which hinges on a number of factors and is heavily dependent on the amount of resources used. It can be safely assumed [5] that the number of actual recipients is subject to a non-uniform probability distribution function. The most parsimonious assumption is to consider a truncated Gaussian distribution of the type

$$\varphi(n) = \frac{\frac{1}{\sqrt{2\pi}\sigma}e^{-\frac{(n-n_0)^2}{2\sigma^2}}}{\Phi\left(\frac{N-n_0}{\sigma}\right) - \Phi\left(\frac{-n_0}{\sigma}\right)} \qquad 0 \le n \le N \tag{4}$$

where N is the maximum number of recipients and Φ is the cumulative gaussian distribution from negative infinity to 0 and 1 respectively. The two parameters n_0 and σ are functions not only of the resources r allocated to the awareness raising campaign, but also of other factors such as the experience gained in previous campaign and the development of alliances and networks with other interest groups. The decision on the opportunity of launching a campaign does not depend on the exactness of the predictions by the lobbying movements, but rather on the confidence placed by them in the estimated values of n_0 and σ and on the possibility of affecting these values using part of their financial resources. Thus, the information provided by the algorithm could be interpreted as a likelihood function that multiplied by the prior distribution function (i.e. the preliminary level of confidence) gives the posterior probability density from which the most likely values of n_0 and σ can be calculated [6].

The latter depends on the significance of the issue for the voters, but generally not on the financial efforts made during the campaign. Furthermore, the mobilization of voters is roughly proportional to the number of targeted recipients that have been made aware of the content of the proposal [7, 8]. In other words, the impact of the campaign on public opinion shifts the median voter's position from c_0^* to c^* according to the linear relation

$$c_0^* - c^* = k\bar{c} \tag{5}$$

where k is a proportionality factor, $\bar{c} = \frac{1}{\bar{n}}$ and $\bar{n}$ is the expected average value of n, which can be calculated as

$$\bar{n} = \int_0^N \left(\frac{\frac{1}{\sqrt{2\pi}\sigma} e^{-\frac{(n-n_0)^2}{2\sigma^2}}}{\Phi\left(\frac{N-n_0}{\sigma}\right) - \Phi\left(\frac{-n_0}{\sigma}\right)} \right) n \, dn \tag{6}$$

Equation (6) can be easily computed in terms of the Error Function [9]. With a view to stressing its dependence $\bar{n}$ on r, both $\bar{n}$ and $\bar{c}$ will be rewritten as $\bar{n}(r)$ and $\bar{c}(r)$.

A rough estimate of the proportionality factor k can be obtained using the reports of public opinion polls and/or surveys carried out by specialized companies on analogous issues. One minor difficulty with this procedure is that the reports generally provide dichotomous data only, such as the number of respondents who are favourable/unfavourable to the issue considered. This difficulty can be overcome if the percentage attitude change Δ resulting from the survey is assumed to be equal to the difference between the values of the cumulative distribution function corresponding to the old and new median values. This assumption makes it possible to evaluate c^* and, since the slope of the initial cumulative distribution function is known, to calculate an approximate value of k (see Fig. 1).

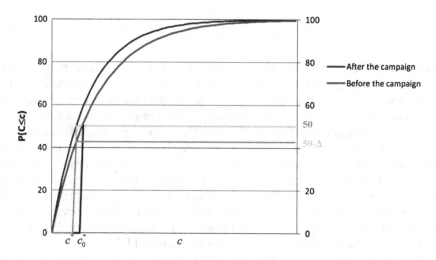

Fig. 1. Variation of median voter orientation

2.4   The Overall Model

The interest group can now determine the optimal amount of resources r to be dedicated to direct lobbying by minimizing the value of

$$c_0 \quad \textit{with respect to } r$$
$$\textit{subject to}$$
$$F(c_0) = F\left[c_0^* - k\bar{c}(r)\right] + \Gamma(r_0 - r) - \Psi(s) \tag{7}$$

the equality constraint being the outcome of the game established by De Figuereido and De Figuereido [4].

Practically, this task can be accomplished by dividing the range $0 \leftrightarrow r_0$ into a reasonable number of intervals and repeating the procedure using a value of r equal to the middle value of each interval. The optimal value is obviously the one that leads to a minimal value of c_0.

However, some additional insight can be gained by considering an approximation to the functions Γ, Ψ, and F. While linear approximations to Γ and Ψ can be employed, at least a quadratic function (centred about the median voter's position) must be used for F, because both positive and negative deviations from this position would reduce the corresponding utility function. In other words, I have used the relations:

$$\Phi(r_0 - r) = \eta(r_0 - r)$$
$$\Psi(s) = \theta s \tag{8}$$
$$F(c) = \mu - \lambda\left[c - \left(c_0^* - k\bar{c}(r)\right)\right]^2$$

where η, θ, μ and λ are positive constants. Using this approximation, the previous constraint gives the following solution:

$$c_0 = \left(c_0^* - k\bar{c}(r)\right) + \sqrt{\beta s - \alpha(r_0 - r)} \tag{9}$$

where $\alpha = \eta/\lambda$ and $\beta = \theta/\lambda$. Thus, the optimization task takes the form

$$\frac{dc_0}{dr} = \frac{d\left[\left(c_0^* - k\bar{c}(r)\right) + \sqrt{\beta s - \alpha(r_0 - r)}\right]}{dr} = 0 \tag{10}$$

and the optimal value of r can be obtained by solving the equation

$$\frac{d\bar{c}}{dr}(r) = \frac{\sqrt{\beta}A}{k\sqrt{s - A(r_0 - r)}} \quad A = \alpha/\beta \tag{11}$$

This approximate solution can be used for a preliminary order-of-magnitude estimation of the likely outcome of the target c_0 when the variables s, r_0 and c_0^* are known, the parameters k, α, β can be reliably estimated and the model for $\bar{c}(r)$ can be adequately constructed.

3 Sensitivity Analysis

A sensitivity analysis with respect to k (i.e. verifying how the minimal value of c_0 changes when the parameter is modified) can provide an approximate risk analysis, i.e. an evaluation of the variations of c_0 if the value of k is different from the one predicted. Similarly, a sensitivity analysis with respect to r_0 gives an indication of how beneficial for the reduction of c_0 an attempt to increase the overall budget r_0 could be.

The sensitivity analysis with respect to both parameters can be carried out by calculating the sensitivity factors $\frac{Dc_0}{Dk}, \frac{Dc_0}{Dr_0}$. This can be accomplished by simply repeating the numerical optimization procedure with different values of k and r_0, and evaluating the corresponding variations of c_0 or using the approximate analytical solution. In the latter case we can use the two relations

$$\begin{cases} c_0 = \left(c_0^* - k\bar{c}(r)\right) + \sqrt{\beta}\sqrt{s - A(r_0 - r)} \\ G(r|k, r_0) = \frac{d\bar{c}}{dr}(r) - \frac{\sqrt{\beta A}}{k\sqrt{s - A(r_0 - r)}} = 0 \end{cases} \tag{12}$$

to evaluate $\frac{Dc_0}{Dk}, \frac{Dc_0}{Dr_0}$

The sensitivity with respect to s can be obtained from that with respect to r_0, noting that the problem is invariant with respect to an interchange of s with $-Ar_0$.

To calculate the derivatives $\frac{Dc_0}{Dk}, \frac{Dc_0}{Dr_0}$, it is necessary to remember that when either parameter changes, so does the corresponding optimal value of r. In other words, it is necessary to regard them as total derivatives that account for variations in both the parameters and the variables r. The chain rule provides the relations:

$$\begin{aligned} \frac{Dc_0}{Dk} &= \frac{\partial c_0}{\partial k} + \frac{\partial c_0}{\partial r}\frac{dr}{dk} \\ \frac{Dc_0}{Dr_0} &= \frac{\partial c_0}{\partial r_0} + \frac{\partial c_0}{\partial r}\frac{dr}{dr_0} \end{aligned} \tag{13}$$

While the terms containing the partial derivatives can be obtained directly from the expression of c_0 (i.e. the first equation of the system), the two derivatives $\frac{dr}{dk}$ and $\frac{dr}{dr_0}$ must be computed from the second equation using Dini's theorem on implicit functions, i.e.

$$\frac{dr}{dk} = -\frac{\frac{\partial G}{\partial k}}{\frac{\partial G}{\partial r}} \qquad \frac{dr}{dr_0} = -\frac{\frac{\partial G}{\partial r_0}}{\frac{\partial G}{\partial r}} \tag{14}$$

The following result can be obtained after somewhat lengthy but straightforward algebra:

$$\frac{Dc_0}{Dk} = -\bar{c}(r) + \frac{d\bar{c}}{dr}\frac{A\sqrt{\beta}}{k\rho\left[\frac{d^2\bar{c}}{dr^2} + \frac{A^2\sqrt{\beta}}{2k\rho^3}\right]} - \frac{A^2\beta}{2k\rho^2\left[\frac{d^2\bar{c}}{dr^2} + \frac{\sqrt{\beta}}{2k\rho^3}\right]}$$

$$\frac{Dc_0}{Dr_0} = -\frac{\alpha}{2\rho} + \left[k\frac{d\bar{c}}{dr} - \frac{\alpha}{2\rho}\right] \frac{A^2\sqrt{\beta}}{2k\rho^3\left[\frac{d^2\bar{c}}{dr^2} + \frac{A^2\sqrt{\beta}}{2k\rho^3}\right]} \tag{15}$$

where $\rho = \sqrt{s - A(r_0 - r)}$

If it can be assumed that $\frac{d^2\bar{c}}{dr^2} \approx 0$ (i.e. $\bar{c}(r)$ is approximately linear)

$$\frac{Dc_0}{Dk} = -\bar{c}(r) + \frac{d\bar{c}}{dr}\frac{2\rho^2}{A} - \sqrt{\beta}\rho$$
$$\frac{Dc_0}{Dr_0} = -\frac{\alpha}{\rho} + k\frac{d\bar{c}}{dr} \tag{16}$$

Since $\frac{d\bar{c}}{dr}$ is negative (increasing the resources on campaigning increases $\bar{n}$ and consequently reduces $\bar{c}$) both $\frac{Dc_0}{Dk}$ and $\frac{Dc_0}{Dr_0}$ are, as expected, negative and depend strongly on both the outreach process and the direct lobbying contacts.

4 Conclusions and Future Work

In this article I have presented a mathematical model capable of evaluating a concurrent combination of direct lobbying and resort to electoral pressure, using a modified version of the algorithm proposed by De Figuereido and De Figuereido [4]. Furthermore, the sensitivity analysis discussed in the previous section can furnish the necessary guidance to carry out an approximate risk analysis and consequently to evaluate the overall convenience of mobilizing voters.

While a two-tier approach is well recognizable in the strategy of several interest groups (for instance when initiating national referendums or campaigning in them), there is not enough evidence for assessing whether any rational criterion for the identification of optimal strategies has already been employed in the past. However, as more and more reliable decision tools become available, a growing interest for the possibilities and advantages provided by them can be expected.

An obvious extension of the work is the inclusion of further activities in the overall optimization procedure. In particular lobbying groups can start lawsuits with a view to using the outcome of the judiciary process as an instrument of political pressure and as a further means of influencing the public opinion [10]. The relevant model, which optimizes the impact of financial resources by allocating them between direct lobbying, awareness raising campaigns and litigation proceedings, is presently being developed.

References

1. Baumgartner, F.R., Leech, B.L.: The Importance of Groups in Politics and in Political Science. Princeton University Press, Princeton (1998)
2. Hall, R.L., Deardorff, A.V.: Lobbying as legislative subsidy. Am. Polit. Sci. Rev. **100**, 69–84 (2006)

3. Downs, A.: An Economic Theory of Democracy. Harper, New York (1957)
4. De Figueiredo, J., De Figueiredo, R.J.P.: The allocation of resources by interest groups: lobbying, litigation and administrative regulation. Bus. Politics **4**, 161–181 (2002)
5. Rosset, S., Neuman, E., Eick, U., Vatnick, N., Idan, I.: Evaluation of prediction for marketing campaigns. In: Proceedings of KDD-2001, pp. 456–461. AAAI Press, Menlo Park (2001)
6. Bard, Y.: Nonlinear Parameter Estimation. Academic Press, New York (1974)
7. Huckfeldt, R., Sprague, J.: Political parties and electoral mobilization: political structure, social structure, and the party canvass. Am. Polit. Sci. Rev. **86**, 70–86 (1992)
8. Wielhouwer, P.W.: In search of lincoln's perfect list: targeting in grassroots campaigns. Am. Politics Res. **3**, 632–669 (2003)
9. Abramowitz, M., Stegun, I.A.: Handbook of Mathematical Functions. Dover Books, Mineola (1965)
10. Solberg, R.S., Waltenburg, E.N.: Why do interest groups engage the judiciary? Policy wishes and structural needs. Soc. Sci. Q. **87**, 558–572 (2006)

Modeling and Simulation of Organizational Routines Deliberately Designed by Management

Dehua Gao[1], Xiuquan Deng[2(✉)], Yan Xu[3], and Bing Bai[4]

[1] School of Management Science and Engineering,
Shandong Institute of Business and Technology, Yantai, China
dhuagao@gmail.com
[2] School of Economics and Management, Beihang University, Beijing, China
dengxiuquan@buaa.edu.cn
[3] College of Business Administration, Shandong Institute of Business and Technology,
Yantai, China
xuyan3456@163.com
[4] Business School, Jiangsu Normal University, Xuzhou, China
szzxbb@163.com

Abstract. Artifacts play an important role in organizational routines deliberately designed and implemented by management. In this paper, we regarded creating and/or planning artifacts as an effective approach for the formation of the designed routines in practice, and treated the formation process from a game theory-based perspective and put forward a CG-MABS model for coping with this problem. Our simulation results show that game theory can provide us an effective tool for researching this type of organizational routines quantitatively. In addition, multi-agent based simulation offers a useful way of concretely observing the routines' formation process.

Keywords: Organizational routines · Artifacts · Coordination game · Multi-agent based simulation

1 Introduction

It is widely accepted that organizational routines are indeed some 'recognizable, repetitive patterns of interdependent actions, carried out by multiple actors' [1]. Many scholars treated individual habits as 'fundamental, individual level building blocks' of organizational routines [2, 3], and focused on the dynamic mechanisms that underpinning the evolution of organizational routines from an emergence-based perspective [3–6]. Nevertheless, Pentland and Feldman [7, 8], Witt [9] pointed out that in addition to spontaneously emerging from repeated interactions that individual actors engage in on an increasingly habitual basis, organizational routines can also be deliberately designed and implemented by management. In such cases, the routines and the typical behaviors underlying them involve 'detailed directives that prescribe how to pursue particular tasks or how to proceed in particular situations' [9]. However, Cohen and Bacdayan [10] argued that these formal directives alone do not automatically translate into routines in practice. The reasons are that even when the directives from management

© Springer Science+Business Media Singapore 2016
L. Zhang et al. (Eds.): AsiaSim 2016/SCS AutumnSim 2016, Part IV, CCIS 646, pp. 263–270, 2016.
DOI: 10.1007/978-981-10-2672-0_27

are highly appropriate, individual actors may still resort to behavior that deviates from or even conflicts with them due to conflicting interests or other factors.

In this paper, we put the complex phenomenon addressed above in game- theoretical terms. From this perspective, Winter [11] pointed out that routine performance at the individual level can be considered as equilibrium play. Although there is still little literature about behavioral game theory dealing explicitly with the notion of organizational routines [6, 12], it has been confirmed that [13], by concerning multi-agent decision problems, the game theory offers a formal means of analyzing strategic interactions among rational but heterogeneous individuals that often behave strategically. Thus, Narduzzo and Warglien [14] claimed that many experimental game settings often concern behavior in repeated interactive situations, and clearly 'provide interesting ground for the emergence of routinized behaviors'.

A coordination game and multi-agent based simulation (CG-MABS) model of the implementation process of organizational routines deliberately designed by management is proposed in the paper. Our simulation results show that the initial proportion of individual actors with different behavioral strategies should be considered, and a balance of profits of individual actors with different strategies is needed for the formation of organizational routines. Furthermore, a broader field of vision for individual actors is helpful to accelerating the routines' formation process.

The rest of this paper is structured as follows. In the second section, we provide a brief overview of literatures related to our work. Based on a summary of their crucial role, we put artifacts at the center of organizational routines, and present an approach for creating new routines through deliberately design of the artifact systems. In the third section, we consider organizational routines as some of the evolutional equilibrium states, and depict their formation processes by a coordination game model on graphs. On the basis of this game model, we build up a multi-agent based simulation of organizational routines through a 'bottom-up' approach. Next, we present the simulation results for variant concrete situations, and discuss some factors that do have impacts on the formation process of organizational routines. The last section includes our conclusion.

2 Theoretical Foundations

2.1 Organizational Routines Deliberately Designed by Management

According to Feldman and Pentland [1], organizational routines are some repetitive patterns of interdependent actions that are carried out by multiple individual actors. Witt [9] argued that there are mainly two absolutely different approaches for organizations to establish these 'patterns of actions'. One is of spontaneously emerging from repeated interactions between individual actors that are involved in on an increasingly habitual basis. The other one is of being deliberately designed and implemented by management. For the former situation, while these routines are established, all the individual actors involved should comply with them due to their spontaneous and informal nature [9]. Many scholars have yet focused on the fundamental role of these individual actors and their connections that contribute to the performance of routines in practice [10, 15–18].

For the latter case, however, much more input of managerial resources is needed. Even so, Cohen and Bacdayan [10] confirmed that these formal routines alone can not automatically be translated into real practices. No matter whether behavioral regulations from the routines are highly appropriate or not, conflicts of interests are often existed. Besides, there may be lack of adequate information for individual actors to deal with an assigned task. Thus, Witt [9] concluded that whether the routines deliberately designed by management is spontaneously optimized or, to the contrary, whether they are watered down, depends on both the appropriateness of the design and the attitude of individual actors when they start to improvise.

2.2 The Role of Artifacts in the Design of Organizational Routines

According to Pentland and Feldman [19], artifacts are some 'physical manifestations' of the performance of organizational routines that may take many different forms, from written rules and procedures to general physical settings such as layout of a factory, etc.

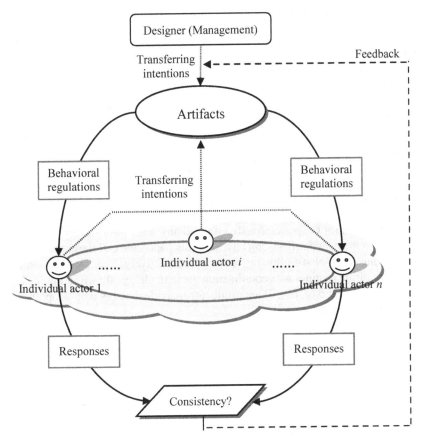

Note: amended based on the work of Bapuji et al [20]

Fig. 1. Artifacts as intermediaries in performance of organizational routines

These artifacts are differentiated from both specific performances and abstract patterns [8], and they offer a unique environment for individual actors to live in and play important roles as intermediaries [6, 20].

Bapuji, et al. [20] and D'Adderio [21] asserted that artifacts are indeed some explicit expressions of organizational knowledge. On one hand, artifacts can provide a guideline for individual actors to act in a standardized way so as to reduce their decision-making spaces and maintain the consistency and efficiency of the organizational internal behaviors. On the other hand, artifacts can transfer specific intentions between individual actors, and/or even help to coordinate interactive activities of individual actors involved in the routines. Based on literature [20, 21], we can depict the role of artifacts and their internal mechanisms in the performance of organizational routines as shown in Fig. 1.

Figure 1 gives us an effective approach for the management staff to create new routines through deliberately planning their artifacts and endow them with some of their specific intentions.

2.3   Re-considering of Organizational Routines from a Game-Based Perspective

When new routines are deliberately designed by management through the planning of the related artifacts, the success of these routines' implementation mostly depends on the attitude of individual actors that involved in the routines. Nevertheless, in the game-theoretical terms, we can consider the routine as an equilibrium state that resulted from the interactive activities of individual actors. It is a good fit for introducing game theory (GT) into studies of the phenomenon addressed here, because GT can be regarded as concerning multi-agent decision problems [13], and it offers a formal means of analyzing strategic interactions among rational but heterogeneous individual participants [6, 12].

In this paper, we only consider a simple situation as shown in the following. For a given scenario consists of certain artifacts that are created and/or planned by management, there are mainly two choices for each individual actor involved in the routines to choose. That is, they may choose to follow the behavioral regulations inherited in the artifacts, or search for or spontaneously establish any other informal but new routines, so as to obtain their own selfish-objectives. In this paper, we call these two choices as the 'Following' and 'Non-Following' strategy, respectively. Then, we can depict the performance of the routines as a coordination game model, as shown in Fig. 2. Where, the coefficients a and b ($a, b \geq 0$) are profits for individual actors who adopt these two strategies above, respectively.

		Individual actor y	
		Following	Non-Following
Individual actor x	Following	(a, a)	(0, 0)
	Non-Following	(0, 0)	(b, b)

Fig. 2. Payoff matrix of the coordination game model of organizational routines

That is, if both the individual actors choose to adopt the 'Following' strategy, a consistent pattern may be formed as a result. Then, each of the individual actor would earn a profit a ($a \geq 0$). While in the contrary, all the individual actors may ignore the existing artifacts and turn to adopt the 'Non-Following' strategy for their own purposes. In this situation, they may earn a profit b ($b \geq 0$), respectively. However, when there are differences between the two individual actors, i.e., one individual actor adopts the 'Following' strategy and the other one individual actor adopts the 'Non-Following' one, then, there is not any consistent patterns emerged, and both the two individual actors ultimately earns nothing.

3   Simulation and Discussion

3.1   Development of the CG-MABS Model

The coordination game model shown in Fig. 2 provides us an effective approach for analyzing organizational routines quantitatively. However, in the real world, there are often more than two individual actors involved in the routines and they only hold limited field of vision and have limited computational capacities. In other words, they can only interact with their nearest neighbors. For coping with this scenario, in this paper, we put all the individual actors in an artificial community, and develop a coordination game & multi-agent based simulation (CG-MABS) model, as described in the following.

We suppose that there are 2500 individual actors that distributed on a 50 × 50 regular lattices. We consider each of the individual actors as one of active agents that can only interact with their nearest neighbors because of their limited field of vision and limited computational capacities. In this paper, we use the Moore neighborhood, and let the coefficient K represent the agent's real field of vision in their interactive activities ($K \geq 0$). For example, as shown in Fig. 3, for any given agent (the black lattice), there may be 8 nearest neighbors (the grey lattices) for it when K equals to 1, and 24 ones when K equals to 2.

Let n represent the total number of the nearest neighbors of an agent. At each simulation tick t, we suppose that there are s ($0 \leq s \leq n$) such neighbors that adopt the 'Following' strategy, and ($n - s$) neighbors that adopt the 'Non-Following' strategy. Thus, according to the coordination game model shown in Fig. 2, we can calculate profits that the agent would gain with its own choices of either the 'Following' or 'Non-Following' strategies,

$$P_F = sa/n \tag{1}$$

$$P_{NF} = (n - s)b/n \tag{2}$$

Then, we have the strategy updating rule for this agent as that: If $P_F \geq P_{NF}$, it would adopt the 'Following' strategy at the $t + 1$ tick. Or otherwise, it would adopt the 'Non-Following' strategy as its future choice in the next round.

We construct this CG-MABS model using Swarm package [22], and do some verification & validation activities so as to guarantee effectiveness and accuracy of the program codes.

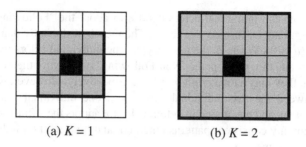

(a) $K = 1$ (b) $K = 2$

Fig. 3. The Moor neighborhood used in simulation

3.2   Simulation Results

In our simulation study, there are four input parameters to consider: the initial proportion of the agents that adopt the 'Following' strategy (*initProportion*), the coefficient K, and the profit parameters a and b. In scenarios of different combination of these four parameter values, we execute the simulation model with 65 simulation ticks (representing 65

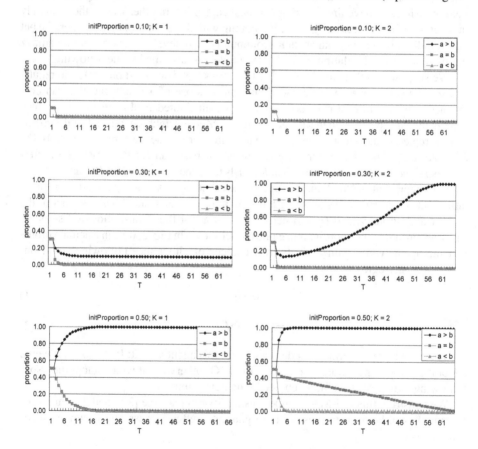

Fig. 4. Simulation results with different scenarios

performances of the routine, iteratively), successively, arriving at the simulation results shown in Fig. 4.

From the simulation results shown in Fig. 4, we can state that:

First, if the initial proportion of agents that adopt the 'Following' strategy is small (*initProportion* = 0.10), both the values of K and the profit parameters a and b have little impacts on the formation process of the routine.

Second, when there are enough number of agents that adopt the 'Following' strategy (*initProportion* = 0.30), a balance of values of the profit parameters a and b is crucially important. Furthermore, a broader field of vision ($K = 2$) may be helpful in accelerating the formation process of the routine, or the creation of some other new routine, – as it contributes to the transfer of behavioral information between near-located agents.

4   Conclusions and Future Work

In this paper, with a brief review of the crucial role of artifacts in organizational routines, we considered the routines deliberately designed and implemented by management. We regarded creating and/or planning artifacts as an effective approach for the formation of the designed routines in practice, and treated the formation process from a coordination game-based perspective. We built up a CG-MABS model and provided the simulation results, as well. Our conclusions are that game theory can give us an effective tool for studies of this type of organizational routines quantitatively. In addition, multi-agent based simulation offers a useful way of concretely observing the routines' formation process.

However, the authors only put forward a fundamental model for theoretical researches. Much more details such as profits of the designer of the routines (namely, the management), costs for individual actors to search for or spontaneously establish any other new routines, the connection network topologies between individual actors, and so forth, should be considered in the future work.

Acknowledgements.   The work for this work is supported by National Natural Science Foundation of China (under Grant No. 71272122 and 71501113), Beijing Natural Science Foundation (under Grant No. 9142013), Humanities and Social Sciences Research Planning Project of the Education Department of Shandong Province (under Grant No. J12WF04), Doctoral Foundation of Shandong Institute of Business and Technology (Under Grant No. BS201606).

References

1. Feldman, M.S., Pentland, B.T.: Reconceptualizing organizational routines as a source of flexibility and change. Adm. Sci. Q. **48**(1), 94–118 (2003)
2. Hodgson, G.M.: The concept of a routine. In: Becker, M.C. (eds.) Handbook of Organizational Routines, pp. 15–30. Cheltenham, Edward Elgar (2008)
3. Knudsen, T.: Organizational routines in evolutionary theory. In: Becker, M.C. (eds.) Handbook of Organizational Routines, pp. 125–151. Edward Elgar, Cheltenham (2008)
4. Becker, M.C.: Organizational routines: a review of the literature. Indus. Corp. Change **13**(4), 643–677 (2004)

5. Pentland, B.T., Feldman, M.S., Becker, M.C., et al.: Dynamics of organizational routines: a generative model. J. Manage. Stud. **49**(8), 1484–1508 (2012)
6. Gao, D., Deng, X., Bai, B.: The emergence of organizational routines from habitual behaviours of multiple actors: an agent-based simulation study. J. Simul. **8**(3), 215–230 (2014)
7. Pentland, B.T., Feldman, M.S.: Narrative networks: Patterns of technology and organization. Organ. Sci. **18**(5), 781–795 (2007)
8. Pentland, B.T., Feldman, M.S.: Designing routines: on the folly of designing artifacts, while hoping for patterns of action. Inf. Organ. **18**(4), 235–250 (2008)
9. Witt, U.: Emergence and functionality of organizational routines: an individualistic approach. J. Inst. Econ. **7**(2), 157–174 (2011)
10. Cohen, M.D., Bacdayan, P.: Organizational routines are stored as procedural memory: evidence from a laboratory study. Organ. Sci. **5**(4), 554–568 (1994)
11. Winter, S.G.: Habits, deliberation, and action: strengthening the microfoundations of routines and capabilities. Acad. Manage. Perspect. **27**(2), 120–137 (2013)
12. Gao, D., Deng, X., Bai, B.: An Evolutionary Game Model of Organizational Routines on Complex Networks. In: Tan, Y., Shi, Y., Mo, H. (eds.) ICSI 2013, Part I. LNCS, vol. 7928, pp. 548–555. Springer, Heidelberg (2013)
13. Myerson, R.B.: Game Theory: Analysis of Conflict. Harvard University Press, Cambridge, MA (1991)
14. Narduzzo, A., Warglien, M.: Conducting experimental research on organizational routines. In: Becker, M.C. (ed.) Handbook of Organizational Routines, pp. 301–324. Cheltenham, Edward Elgar (2008)
15. Feldman, M.S., Rafaeli, A.: Organizational routines as sources of connections and understandings. J. Manage. Stud. **39**(3), 309–331 (2002)
16. Lazaric, N.: Routines and routinization: an exploration of some micro-cognitive foundations. In: Becker, M.C. (ed.) Handbook of Organizational Routines, pp. 205–227. Cheltenham, Edward Elgar (2008)
17. Turner, S.F., Fern, M.J.: Examining the stability and variability of routine performances: the effects of experience and context change. J. Manage. Stud. **49**(8), 1407–1434 (2012)
18. Gao, D., Deng, X., Zhao, Q., et al.: Multi-agent based simulation of organizational routines on complex networks. J. Artif. Soc. Soc. Simul. **18**(3) (2015). http://jasss.soc.surrey.ac.uk/18/3/17.html
19. Pentland, B.T., Feldman, M.S.: Organizational routines as a unit of analysis. Ind. Corp. Change **14**(5), 793–815 (2005)
20. Bapuji, H., Hora, M., Saeed, A.M.: Intentions, intermediaries, and interaction: examing the emergence of routines. J. Manage. Stud. **49**(8), 1586–1607 (2012)
21. D'Adderio, L.: Artifacts at the centre of routines: performing the material turn in routine theory. J. Inst. Econ. **7**(2), 197–230 (2011)
22. Swarm Development Group [SDG]. A tutorial introduction to Swarm (2000). http://www.swarm.org

Large-Scale Pedestrian Evacuation Modeling During Nuclear Leakage Accident

Sihang Qiu, Zhen Li, Liang Ma, Zhengqiu Zhu,
Bin Chen[✉], Xiaogang Qiu, and Xingbing Li

College of Information System and Management,
National University of Defense Technology,
Changsha 410073, Hunan, People's Republic of China
nudtcb9372@gmail.com

Abstract. Studying large-scale pedestrian evacuation is essential to nuclear leakage incident, since nuclear incidents have brought great loss to mankind. This paper models the large-scale evacuation under nuclear leakage incident via atmospheric dispersion model and pedestrian evacuation model. Based on this, an synthetic Fukushima accident is given to analyze simulation results. Research findings are helpful for risk assessments and emergency management.

Keywords: Nuclear leakage incident · Atmospheric dispersion model · Pedestrian evacuation model · Fukushima accident

1 Introduction

Nuclear accidents have brought huge damage to human beings. The Fukushima Daiichi Nuclear Power Plant (FDNPP) accident caused 200-thousand people escaping from their home [1]. Therefore, studying emergency management under nuclear accident is increasingly important.

Atmospheric dispersion is a very common phenomenon. The dispersion process of nuclide is similar to that of normal particle. Currently, researchers have proposed many models for diffusion simulation. NOAA established a HYbrid Single-Particle Lagrangian Integrated Trajectory (HYSPLIT) model [14,17], which was extensively applied all over the world. Andrews et al. [2] proposed a radionuclide dispersion model based on Gaussian plume model. Moreover, RIMPUFF is also an extensively used Gaussian-based atmospheric dispersion simulation tool [3]. In this paper, a simulation tool based on Gaussian puff model (KD-ADSS) is implemented to model atmospheric dispersion.

In terms of evacuation simulation, cellular automaton (CA) is the most common model used in evacuation simulation [4,15]. Besides, Reynolds [13] modeled individual escaping by establishing rules of movement. Helbing [5,6] proposed social force to model evacuation. This model regards individuals as particles in physics system and abstract social force from social interaction between each individual. Social force model is a pretty appropriate model for micro escaping

© Springer Science+Business Media Singapore 2016
L. Zhang et al. (Eds.): AsiaSim 2016/SCS AutumnSim 2016, Part IV, CCIS 646, pp. 271–281, 2016.
DOI: 10.1007/978-981-10-2672-0_28

reproducing. However, the scale of evacuation under nuclear accident usually is quite large. The efficiency of social force cannot satisfy this situation. Song et al. [16] proposed selfishness- and selflessness-based models of pedestrian room evacuation, which make indoor evacuation more accurate.

The target of this paper is to model large-scale pedestrian evacuation of nuclear leakage accident. In order to complete this target, KD-ADSS is applied to evaluate the effects of nuclear accident. After evaluation, CA model is implemented to establish a large-scale pedestrian evacuation model with a corresponding algorithm to program escaping route.

This paper is organized as follows. Section 2 describes the methods of modeling radioactive atmospheric dispersion, measurements of radioactive effects, and pedestrian evacuation simulation. Section 3 presents the experiments based on a synthetic situation of 2011 Fukushima Daiichi nuclear power plant. The conclusion is given in Sect. 4.

2   Methods

In this paper, location of source l, release rate $q(t)$, properties of radioactive material p, and wind field W are used to analyze tendency of atmospheric dispersion. Wind speeds and directions recorded in W are time-variant, which dominate the movements of radioactive particles. We denote the parameters of diffusion as $\theta = \{l, q, p, W\}$, so that the theoretical concentration of location x at time t can be expressed as Eq. (1).

$$c_x(t) = f(x, t, \theta) + e, \tag{1}$$

where observation error e follows a Gaussian distribution with standard deviation σ_e, i.e. $e~N(0, \sigma_e^2)$. In order to solve Eq. (1), KD-ADSS is used to calculate the function f.

After obtaining the distribution of radioactive concentration, the effects of pedestrian can be estimated by calculated concentration. In terms of evacuation, this process can be realized by CA model. In order to implements CA model, evacuation space is divided into a grid, where escaping route is presented by cells in this grid. Because of the serious radioactive influence of some cells, shortest escaping route may not represent optimal route. This paper proposed methods to model radioactive dispersion, to obtain proper escaping route, and to simulate pedestrian evacuation.

2.1   Atmospheric Dispersion Modeling Based on KD-ADSS

In order to simulate atmospheric dispersion process of radioactive material, KD-ADSS (KD Atmospheric Dispersion Simulation System) is used to model nuclide diffusion in atmosphere. KD-ADSS is a Gaussian-model based simulation system for particle atmospheric dispersion developed by National University of Defense Techonology. It uses a series of puffs to approximate a radioactive plume. Wind field is also feasible to generate through KD-ADSS with meteorological data collected from monitoring stations. This simulation tool generates wind field using Inverse Distance Weighted (IDW) method. Besides, the radioactive materials usually have obvious radioactive decays. Therefore, theoretical dispersion function described in KD-ADSS $f(x, t, \theta)$ can be improved by a decay term $d(t)$, which is shown as follows:

$$f'(x, t, \theta) = d(t) f(x, t, \theta), \tag{2}$$

where decay term $d(t)$ is an exponential function relates to the half-life of radioactive material. If the half-life of dispersion material is h, the expression of $d(t)$ in presented following equation.

$$d(t) = \exp\left(\frac{\ln 0.5}{h} t\right). \tag{3}$$

2.2   Measurements of Radioactive Effects

High radioactivity is definitely able to cause huge damage to human beings. However, most dangerous radioactive materials are invisible and of no smell, which means people usually cannot feel them. Therefore, most radioactive materials are different from some typical toxic gas such chlorine and sulfur dioxide. People can feel many kinds of toxic gas and take some actions to protect themselves, while radioactive materials chronically influence people. In former study, we proposed an effect model to evaluate the influences of hazardous gas via a logarithmic normal distribution. This model is able to estimate the healthy state of human through measured concentration. Not like toxic gas, although it is difficult to evaluate healthy state caused by radioactive material, we can still use the similar method to approximately estimate their effects.

In this study, it is necessary to assume that the person standing in a high radioactive concentration place is influenced more seriously than the person standing in a relative low radioactive concentration place. Thus, the integration of concentration along the escaping route can measure the total effect caused by nuclear accident. Denoting this integration as I, the expression of I of person i is shown as follows:

$$I_i = \int c_{x_i(t)}(t) dt, \tag{4}$$

where I_i represents integrated concentration of person i, t represents time, and $x_i(t)$ is the function of escaping route of person i about time t. Besides, the expression of c is already shown in Eq. (1).

2.3   Large-Scale Pedestrian Evacuation Model

The evacuation model should have large-scale modeling ability since nuclear accident has huge influences in both spatial and temporal domains. The number of individuals in evacuation area may higher than one million, which demands that the model should have high efficiency. Social force model is a common escaping simulation model. However, social force model usually applied in micro-scale situation in order to emphasize individual activity, and it does not have enough computational efficiency. Considering individual activity is not so important in large-scale evacuation, this study uses CA to model escaping process since it can reflect macro evacuation tendency and its efficiency is pretty high.

A typical CA model splits evacuation space into grid with equally sized cells. Each cell contains one individual, while each individual occupies one cell. During the simulation, each individual moves one cell towards its target at each step. In terms of its moving direction, it usually depends on path programming method or predefined emergency plan. In large-scale evacuation simulation, if each individual occupies one cell, most computers cannot satisfy this demand. Therefore, in this paper, CA model is modified through upgrading population upper limit of each cell for supporting huge number of people. For example, assuming the population upper limit of a cell is 100, if the number of individuals of this cell is less than 100, it is feasible to get in or walk through this cell. However, if the number of individuals of this cell reaches 100, this cell becomes unwalkable until someone leave. Upper limit depends on size and type of the cell, e.g. a water cell accommodates fewer individuals than a ground cell.

Initializing population distribution is the precondition of evacuation modeling. Obviously, cities and towns have relatively high-density population, while forests and rivers have low-density population. If it is difficult to obtain real population density data, estimating population density via map and general demography data is also acceptable. Typical BFS algorithm is able to find shortest paths. It classifies all cells into two categories: walkable and unwalkable. The weight of a walkable cell (i, j) is $w(i, j) = 1$, while the weight of an unwalkable one is $w(i, j) = \infty$. Paths with least weight sum to escaping targets of all cells can be easily found via BFS algorithm. Because most individuals are considered as locals, it is reasonable to assume they escape within the shortest paths found by BFS. But in real condition, following situations may cause individual walk without the shortest paths:

1. Different cells may have different extents of "walkability". For instance, cells representing road are easy to walk through, while cells in the sea can hardly contain individuals.
2. Individuals can determine the dangerous area according to their experiences. For example, they would try to find an escaping route away from nuclear power plant.
3. Intervention of emergency departments may influence escaping routes.

To solve this problem, weight of each cell can varies from 1 to infinity. Cells that easy to walk trough have low weights; cells near the nuclear power plant have high weights; cells that emergency departments forbid people walk have high weights, etc. Finding paths in this condition needs a modified Dijkstra algorithm. In contrast to BFS algorithm, Dijkstra algorithm uses a priority queue instead of normal queue. The priority queue, where the cell with minimum distance is the head, is implemented with a heap. However, typical Dijkstra cannot settle the multi-sources problem. Therefore, an extra point linking with all evacuation target cells (safety cells) could be added. Then apply Dijkstra algorithm using this extra point as the source.

3   Synthetic Situation Study

This paper uses a synthetic situation to analyze atmospheric dispersion model and evacuation model. The background of this situation is Fukushima Daiichi Nuclear Power Plant (FDNPP) accident in 2011. First, FDNPP accident is recovered by KD-ADSS, where release rate is estimated by Katata et al. (ref), and wind data is collected from NOAA. After that, simulation results are compared with concentration data of MEXT. Then, population distribution and evacuation grid are generated according to map of Fukushima. Individuals finally escape along escaping routes obtained by path programming method based on Dijsktra algorithm.

3.1   Recovering FDNPP Accident

In this synthetic FDNPP accident, we try to use real hazard parameters to recover this nuclear accident. Wind direction and speed data are collected from NOAA. Meteorological stations around FDNPP are used in this situation since the dispersion model is suitable for regional simulation. Wind field is generated via corresponding model in KD-ADSS and collected meteorological data. Thus, the speeds and directions of radioactive puffs depend on calculated wind field.

After obtaining wind field, it is essential to determine source term which contains location, start time, duration, and release rate. The location of FDNPP is (37.42N, 141.02E), and release started at 0:00, 12th March, 2011. The release rate of FDNPP is difficult to measure and obtain. Fortunately, many a researcher has done some significant work about this issue. In this study, the release rate estimated by Katata et al. [7,8] is used for nuclear accident simulation. The duration of this case is set to be 24 h, and the radioactive material that studied in this case is ^{137}Cs. Figure 1a shows the cumulative concentration of ^{137}Cs after dispersion. Figure 1b shows the cumulative concentration of ^{137}Cs depositing to ground. As we can seen in these figures, after 24 h, south-east-direction is influenced most seriously in this nuclear accident, while relative north and west areas are little effected by ^{137}Cs dispersion.

It is necessary to verify simulation results by real ^{137}Cs observation data since the recovered accident is regarded as real accident in this study. Because of insufficient ^{137}Cs data during 11th March to 14th March in 2011. We examine the simulation results from 15th March to 31st March. Real concentration data is collected from JAEA [12] and MEXT [9–11], where JAEA has one monitoring station collect concentration data nearly all these days in Tokai. MEXT set several monitoring stations around FDNPP. The simulation results are calculated by Eq. 2. As we can seen in Fig. 2, calculated concentrations have acceptable agreements with the observations.

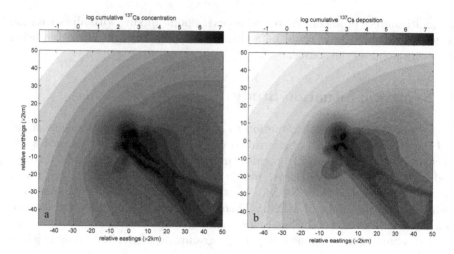

Fig. 1. Cumulative concentration (unit: Bq · min · m^{-3}). (a) Cumulative air concentration at elevation 1.7 m after 24 h; (b) cumulative concentration depositing to ground after 24 h.

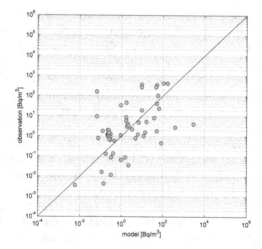

Fig. 2. Comparison of modeled concentrations and observations

3.2 Evacuation Initialization

Evacuation initialization determines the key constant parameters including evacuation area, grid partition, population distribution, walkability of each cell, escaping velocities, release rate, and other settings about evacuation simulation.

This study considers evacuation area from longitude 140.6E to 141.4E, latitude 37.2N to 37.6N. This area is partitioned into a grid with 100 × 100 cells. According to the satellite map from Yahoo (shown in Fig. 3a), it is not difficult to find villages or towns in this area. Assume each cell in village or town is expected to

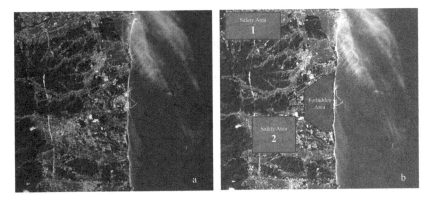

Fig. 3. Satellite map of FDNPP. (a) Original map from Yahoo; (b) Evacuation plan based on map.

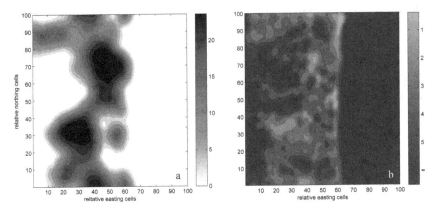

Fig. 4. (a) Estimated population density around FDNPP; (b) Walkability of evacuation space.

accommodate 30 individuals. Therefore, at daytime, it is reasonable to simply distribute individuals around the cell that they live in following a 2-D gaussian distribution. Then set the number of individuals in unwalkable place equals to zero. The total population density is shown in Fig. 4a. Similarly, walkability of each cell also depends on the satellite map, which is determined according to terrain type of the relative cell, as shown in Fig. 4b. Extent of walkability is classified into five types, and the weights of them are 1 to 5 from easy to difficult.

In terms the parameters about individuals, this study assume all people have the same properties because individual differences can only cause tiny influences in large-scale evacuation simulation. The basic escaping velocity of each person is 3 m/s, and the actual velocity during escaping is $3/w$ m/s, where w is the weight of current cell. The height of each person is 1.7 m. Moreover, The release rate equals to 10^{15} Bq/s, which is not key parameter for evacuation modeling.

3.3   Controlled Variables

In order to obtain varied simulation results, it is essential to control some important variables, which is also determined by emergency manager in real accident. Firstly, expected wind speeds and directions should be determined, which is the basis of evacuation management since wrong judgment may cause huge casualty. After that, safety cells should been pointed. Safety cells are the places that individuals expect to get first-aid and escape by public transportation. Therefore, safety cells should not only avoid being set in dangerous area, but also avoid far from most individuals. Another important controlled variable is the forbidden area. In order to prevent individuals from escaping to potentially dangerous area, relevant departments are responsible to set forbidden area in evacuation space.

Thus, these variables are varied in synthetic experiments. Eight cases are applied to test evacuation model. These cases are shown in Table 1 and corresponding explanation map is illustrated in Fig. 3b. Evacuation model will be implemented through all these cases to find out relatively reasonable evacuation plan.

Table 1. Experiment cases. Column "Safety cells" represents plan ID illustrated in Fig. 3b. The unit of wind directions and speeds is m/s.

Case	Wind direction	Wind Speed	Safety cells	Forbidden area
C01	300	3	1	No
C02	270	3	1	No
C03	300	3	1	Exists
C04	270	3	1	Exists
C05	300	3	2	No
C06	270	3	2	No
C07	300	3	2	Exists
C08	270	3	2	Exists

3.4   Evacuation Results

Path programming algorithm is firstly applied in obtain the appropriate escaping path to safety cells. As shown in Fig. 5, safety area of plan 1 is in the northwest corner, which is determined since radioactive materials may dispersion to south with wind. However, individuals from southern area have to walk very long distances to safety place. Safety area of plan 2 is nearly in the center of evacuation, which makes individuals easier to arrive. Figure 6a shows the number of individuals who arrive the safety area of each test case. Individuals in plan 2 can arrive safety area about one-hour quickly than plan 1 because average distance of each cell in plan 1 is obviously longer than that in plan 2. Moreover,

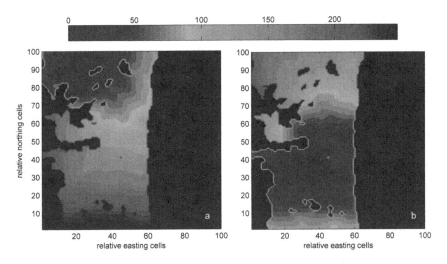

Fig. 5. Evacuation path programming results, figure shows the distance to safety area of each cell. (a) Results based on plan 1; (b) Results based on plan 2.

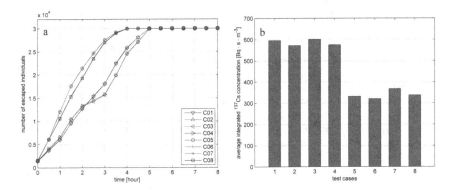

Fig. 6. Experiment results. (a) Number of evacuated individuals; (b) Average integrated ^{137}Cs concentration of each test case

forbidden area makes individuals walk more than normal plan. Therefore, the evacuation duration is little longer than normal plan.

As can be seen in Fig. 6b, average integrated ^{137}Cs concentration of each individual of C05-C08(plan 2) is significantly less than that of C01-C04(plan 1) although safety area is really close to FDNPP in plan 2. Shorter exposure time causes individuals in C05-08 have less integrated concentration. Besides, it is found that forbidden area cannot help individuals avoid contacting with ^{137}Cs. Actually, it makes individuals take more time to escape, and exposure time seems to be the most important parameter in this experiment. Therefore, setting forbidden area may not have positive effects, while it perhaps cause more risks.

4   Conclusion

This paper focuses on modeling large-scale evacuation during nuclear accident. Atmospheric dispersion model and large-scale evacuation model are proposed in this study to settle this problem. Moreover, Fukushima accident is recovered to test atmospheric dispersion model and evacuation model. In the future, detailed radioactive effect on human beings will be studied in order to establish nuclear hazard model, and multi-transportation will be considered.

Acknowledgements. This study is supported by the National Natural Science Foundation of China under Grant Nos. 71303252, 61503402, 61403402, 61374185, 91024032.

References

1. Akahane, K., Yonai, S., Fukuda, S., Miyahara, N., Yasuda, H., Iwaoka, K., Matsumoto, M., Fukumura, A., Akashi, M.: The Fukushima nuclear power plant accident and exposures in the environment. Environmentalist **32**(2), 136–143 (2012)
2. Andrews, W.S., Ham, M.E.J., Bennett, L.G.I., Grandmaison, E.W.: Modeling the dispersion of radionuclides released during reactor accidents aboard nuclear-powered vessels. J. Radioanal. Nuclear Chem. **248**(3), 657–662 (2004)
3. Connan, O., Smith, K., Organo, C., Solier, L., Maro, D., Hbert, D.: Comparison of RIMPUFF, HYSPLIT, ADMS atmospheric dispersion model outputs, using emergency response procedures, with 85Kr measurements made in the vicinity of nuclear reprocessing plant. J. Environ. Radioact. **124**, 266–277 (2013)
4. GwizdaHa, T.M.: Some properties of the floor field cellular automata evacuation model. Physica A Stat. Mech. Appl. **419**, 718–728 (2015)
5. Helbing, D., Farkas, I., Vicsek, T.: Simulating dynamical features of escape panic. Nature **407**(6803), 487–490 (2000). doi:10.1038/35035023
6. Helbing, D., Molnr, P.: Social force model for pedestrian dynamics. Phy. Rev. E **51**(5), 4282–4286 (1995). PRE
7. Katata, G., Chino, M., Kobayashi, T., Terada, H., Ota, M., Nagai, H., Kajino, M., Draxler, R., Hort, M.C., Malo, A., Torii, T., Sanada, Y.: Detailed source term estimation of the atmospheric release for the Fukushima Daiichi nuclear power station accident by coupling simulations of an atmospheric dispersion model with an improved deposition scheme and oceanic dispersion model. Atmos. Chem. Phys. **15**(2), 1029–1070 (2015). ACP
8. Katata, G., Ota, M., Terada, H., Chino, M., Nagai, H.: Atmospheric discharge and dispersion of radionuclides during the Fukushima Dai-ichi nuclear power plant accident. part i: Source term estimation and local-scale atmospheric dispersion in early phase of the accident. J. Environ. Radioact. **109**, 103–113 (2012)
9. MEXT. Information on the location including lat/long of the reading point
10. MEXT. Readings of dust sampling, 20 March 2016 (2011)
11. MEXT. Readings of dust sampling by mext, 20 March 2016 (2011)
12. Ohkura, T., Oishi, T., Taki, M., Shibanuma, Y., Kikuchi, M., Akino, H., Kikuta, Y., Kawasaki, M., Saegusa, J., Tsutsumi, M., Ogose, H., Tamura, S., Sawahata, T.: Emergency monitoring of environmental radiation and atmospheric radionuclides at nuclear science research institute, JAEA following the accident of Fukushima Daiichi nuclear power plant. Report 2012–010, Japan Atmomic Energy Agency, 20 March 2016 (2012)

13. Reynolds, C.W.: Steering behaviors for autonomous characters. In: Proceedings of the Computer Game Developers Conference, pp. 763–782 (1999)
14. Rolph, G.: Real-time envrionmental application and display system (ready) website (2016)
15. Song, W., Yu, Y., Fan, W., Zhang, H.: A cellular automata evacuation model considering friction and repulsion. Sci. China Ser. E Eng. Mater. Sci. **48**(4), 403–413 (2005)
16. Song, X., Ma, L., Ma, Y., Yang, C., Ji, H.: Selfishness- and selflessness-based models of pedestrian room evacuation. Physica A Stat. Mech. Appl. **447**, 455–466 (2016)
17. Stein, A., Draxler, R., Rolph, G., Stunder, B., Cohen, M.: Noaa's hysplit atmospheric transport and dispersion modeling system. Bull. Amer. Meteor. Soc. **96**, 2059–2077 (2015)

The Geographical Characteristics of WeChat Propagation Network

Chuan Ai[1], Bin Chen[1(✉)], Lingnan He[2], Yichong Bai[3], Liang Liu[1], Xingbing Li[1], Zhichao Song[1], and Xiaogang Qiu[1]

[1] College of Information System and Management, National University of Defense Technology, 410073 Changsha, China
nudtcb9372@gmail.com
[2] The School of Communication and Design, Sun Yat-Sen University, 510275 Guangzhou, China
[3] Fibonacci Consulting Co. Ltd., Hong Kong, China

Abstract. WeChat is one of the most popular social media applications, its characteristics of using easily and privacy make it accepted by the majority of Chinese. Because of the feature of privacy, public opinion in WeChat is difficult to monitor. We can build the WeChat social network simulation system to study how to monitor it. Studying the propagation feature of WeChat-messages is of great significance for establishment of the system. Due to the difficulty in obtaining data, current researches hardly study on the WeChat-messages' propagation characteristics. This paper get the geographical interaction activity network (GIAN) from history records of HTML5 webpages propagation in WeChat, and analyze the GIAN with the methods and techniques in the field of complex network. We have preliminary exploration on the relationship between the threshold and geographical characteristics of information propagation in WeChat, then we find that there are several geographical regions that are stable in community detection results of GIAN.

Keywords: Wechat · HTML5 webpage · Geographic characteristics · Threshold · City community

1 Instruction

Today, we use the mobile phone terminal to not only make phone calls and send text messages, but also take it as an important platform for the dissemination of information and interpersonal communication. It is more and more important in our lives.

Chinese Internet users is very diverse and complex in education degree, income levels, hobbies, geographical distribution, and other aspects of media literacy. Therefore, the false information such as rumors and false news are easy to spread in the Internet. WeChat has some difference from other online social media applications, such as privacy and widely using, which make the network supervision more difficult. Through analysis of the WeChat network, we can have detailed and deep understanding of propagation characteristics. Then we can provide theoretical and technical support for the supervision of online public opinion, and WeChat social network simulation system.

© Springer Science+Business Media Singapore 2016
L. Zhang et al. (Eds.): AsiaSim 2016/SCS AutumnSim 2016, Part IV, CCIS 646, pp. 282–292, 2016.
DOI: 10.1007/978-981-10-2672-0_29

At this stage, researches hardly study on WeChat propagation networks based on real data, for the data is hard to get. To our best known, this paper for the first time analyzes the geographical characteristics of the information propagation in WeChat network.

We find that the threshold is related to geographical characteristics of WeChat in this paper, and analyze this relationship. Then, we take cities as nodes instead of users, and take interactions of users in different cities as the links between cities. We construct the geographical interaction activity network (GIAN) from the history click records of HTML5 web pages spreading in WeChat network. The remainder of this paper is organized as follows. Section 2 introduces the related works in the field of OSN. Section 3 introduces the HTML5 dataset while Sect. 4 proposes a method to construct the GIAN. Section 5 gives detailed analysis of the relationship of the threshold and geographical characteristics of WeChat network. In Sect. 6, we focus on the geographical characteristics. In the end, this paper is concluded in Sect. 7.

2 Related Works

In real life, communication with others is a major personal behavior, people will always be connected to each other by some relationships, and all the relationships form a social network.

Analysis of social network is an important branch of sociology, work on it can be traced back to the study of Auguste Comte (1798–1857) and Georg Simmel (1858–1918). It takes society as a set of relationships, which is different from taking society as a collection of individuals usually. This breaks the tradition of focusing on individual psychology and behavior, it pay close attention to the relationship between people instead.

The social media network formed by users of social websites is referred to online social networks (OSN). Academic study of OSN has already started for a long time. Study of OSN focused on static topology [1] at beginning. Modern concepts and methods of social network analysis came from the work of Jacob Moreno in 1934 [2]. After that, people improved and systematized Moreno's work gradually and formed today's social network analysis theory.

OSNs such as Sina Weibo, Facebook, Flicker and WeChat have become the main platforms for information dissemination nowadays. Users in OSNs communicate and share information by building unidirectional or bidirectional relationship.

Measurement and analysis of OSN is mining and extracting structural features and user behavior characteristics of OSN. We collect and sort raw data with theory and technology in complex networks, social networks and data mining [3].

In recent years, the academic study of OSN is deepening [4, 5] but content is varies, including network topology, user behavior [6], user privacy and security [7], system architecture [8], community mining [9] and information dissemination [10].

3 Dataset and Topic

HTML5 is one of web programming language that support multimedia on mobile terminal.

The dataset comes from Fibonacci Consulting Co. Ltd. The HTML5 webpages propagate in Moments (a function of WeChat, which we can use to show all friends pictures and sentences), Official Accounts, and friends. Each time the webpage is clicked, a record will be generated and saved by the server. The records include information in five aspects, that is, clicker's ID, sharer's ID, time, webpage's ID, and clicker's IP. A user has only one unique ID, when he click a webpage, the ID is regard as ViewID, and when the webpage he shared was clicked by others, the ID is regard as SourceID to write in the record. Fibonacci Consulting Co. Ltd. collects the history records of these HTML5 webpages as the dataset.

$$Record = < SourceID, ViewID, PageID, IP, Time > \tag{1}$$

The dataset in this paper is the history records of 29 days, which is in four periods of time. The details are shown in Table 1.

Table 1. Dataset detail

Time period	Start time	End time	Duration(days)
1	2015.04.22	2015.04.25	4
2	2015.05.08	2015.05.14	7
3	2015.05.16	2015.05.26	11
4	2015.05.29	2015.06.04	7

A record from the dataset is illustrated as follows:

INFO - b6a2abbd-f2bf-4920-9dde-b1bea2b0dd1f@null@e239db59-550e-4461-bd3e-df36f1d920d3@null@552aa8c7a1a16ca07094f28c@119.1.91.8@2015-04-22 00:00:00

Table 2 gives detailed explanations of each part of the record. We use the PageID to find the content of webpage, and then we can choose pages of different categories to study.

Table 2. Explanation of each part of the record.

Name of parts	Explanation	Parts of record
SourceID	Sharer's ID	b6a2abbd-f2bf-4920-9dde-b1bea2b0dd1f
ViewID	Clicker's ID	e239db59-550e-4461-bd3e-df36f1d920d3
PageID	ID of HTML5 webpage	552aa8c7a1a16ca07094f28c
IP	Clicker's IP	119.1.91.8
Click time	Time when clicker view the HTML5 webpage	2015-04-22 00:00:00

We select 500 HTML5 webpages, of which click volume break through 1000 up to the first day when it starts to propagate. Then we classify the webpages into four categories due to titles and contents, which are important events, advertisements, feelings, and festival wishes.

Firstly, we select three webpages that focus on Eastern Star Shipwreck(Eastern Star was a river cruise ship that operated in the Three Gorges region of inland China. On June the First 2015, the ship was traveling on the Yangtze River in Jianli, Hubei Province with 454 people on board when it capsized in a severe thunderstorm.) to analyze in the category of important events. Then we select one webpage in each rest category to do more comparisons and analysis.

4   Methods

We analyze the click volume of every webpage in total and that in every province to find the relationship between them. We construct GIAN from the history records of HTML5 webpages when propagating in WeChat network. Then we use the theory and methods of complex network to analyze the GIAN taking cities as nodes in network.

4.1   Threshold

This paper focus on the threshold of the webpages propagating in WeChat. We get the total click volume and each province's click volume, and then analyze the changes of them by time.

Let the total click volume of a webpage be $N(t)$, and click volume of each province be $N_i(t)$. The change rate of total click volume is $N'(t)$, and $P_i(t)$ is the percentage of click volume of each province. We pay close attention to the time that the total click volume grow most rapidly T_1, which is the time that the $N'(t)$ increase to a high level from a low one.

In order to objectively measure the change trend of provincial click volume overall, we propose an index to describe that trend:

$$CR = \sum_{i=0}^{30} P_i'(t) \tag{2}$$

If CR is large, it means that the percentage of click volume of each province changes rapidly, and if CR is small and close to zero, it means that the percentage of click volume of each click volume remain constant on the whole. Let T_2 be the time point that CR get close to zero. Here we do not take data from Hong Kong, Macao and Taiwan into consideration, so, there are 31 provincial administrative units.

4.2 Network Definition

The friend relationship between two users in OSN does not guarantee the interaction activity between them. Cameron et al. [11] find that in Facebook, though a user has many friends, only ten to forty friends he keeps in touch with.

The network constructed by the interaction activities of different users is named as activity network [12] apart from the network of friend relationship, the topological structure is named activity topology [3].

Therefore, we construct activity network as follows in this paper. We regard users as nodes. A directed edge $i \rightarrow j$ from i to node j represent that user i has an action targeting on user j. The set of users and the set of edges together make the individual interaction activity network (IIAN). It is described as follows:

$$G =< V, E > \tag{3}$$

V is the set of nodes, which represents the set of users. E is the set of edges, which represents the interaction activity among the users

$$V = \{v_i | i \in [0, n-1]\} \tag{4}$$

$$E = \{e_{ij} | i, j \in [0, n-1]\} \tag{5}$$

n is the number of users in the whole network. Each v_i represent a user and each e_{ij} represent an interaction activity, which means that user j has clicked the HTML5 webpage shared by user i, and has a corresponding record in dataset.

The network G represents the network of information propagating in WeChat essentially. Each node v_i in the network has not only the unique identification (SourceID or ViewID), but also has another attribute, which is the user's address because we can get the user's IP, and it reflects the user's geographic location.

$$v_i =< ID, AD > \tag{6}$$

Take all the nodes of the same addresses (a city or a province for example) as a node set, then all the nodes in the network that represents all the users can be divided into a number of node sets. As in Fig. 1(a), the nodes with the same color are in the same city and the same node sets. Then we take each node sets as a special node in Fig. 1(b), with the same color with the nodes in Fig. 1(a). Take the interaction activities between users from different original nodes sets as new edges between the nodes in (b), which represents the interactions. The network in Fig. 1(b) is the GIAN developed from the activity network in Fig. 1(a). We describe the geographic interaction activity network as follow.

$$GIAN =< V_{ad}, E_{geo} > \tag{7}$$

In this network, each node represents an address (a city), and V_{ad} is the set of the nodes. We suppose that there are m cities in the network.

$$V_{ad} = \{v_{ad_i} | i \in [0, m-1]\} \tag{8}$$

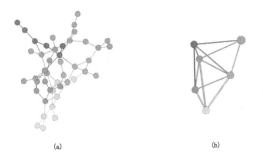

(a)   (b)

Fig. 1. (a) A simple activity network, nodes with the same color are from the same city. (b) A GIAN created from the activity network in (a), one node in (b) represent a node set that contains all the nodes in (a) with the same color. (Color figure online)

$$E_{geo} = \left\{ e_{ad_i ad_j} \right\} \qquad (9)$$

E_{geo} represents the set of the edges, each edge represents that the users in the two cities have interactions.

5   Propagation Threshold

At first, we take provinces as nodes to construct the GIAN, we count the number of times that users click the webpage in each province. We select and analyze three webpages about the same topic of Eastern Star Shipwreck.

Figure 2 shows the changes of $P_i(t)$ of each province by time of each webpages. The horizontal axis shows the delay time from the time that the webpage starts to propagate in WeChat. In the figure, each color represents a province, the width of the each color bar represents the $P_i(t)$ of each province at a time.

In Fig. 3, we show the change of the total click volume of three H5 webpages. We find that $N'(t)$ of the webpages is small at beginning, and become lager suddenly at a time point which it is the T_1 mentioned in Sect. 4.1.

T_1 and T_2 represent the state that webpages start to propagate rapidly, and the state that the webpages spread widely and click volume become stable geographically. We analyze the T_1 and T_2 of three H5 webpages about different topics, and find the connections between the two time points.

In Fig. 4, we find that the time that CR becomes zero is close to the time that $N'(t)$ becomes large suddenly. It is not coincidental. CR becoming zero means that the rate of click volume of each province become stable, it is a state that the H5 webpage spreads widely enough geographically. $N'(t)$ becoming large suddenly means that the click volume increase rapidly, it is the best state that can lead to great number of click times. It can be conclude that, there is connection between wide spreading geographically and a large number of clicks.

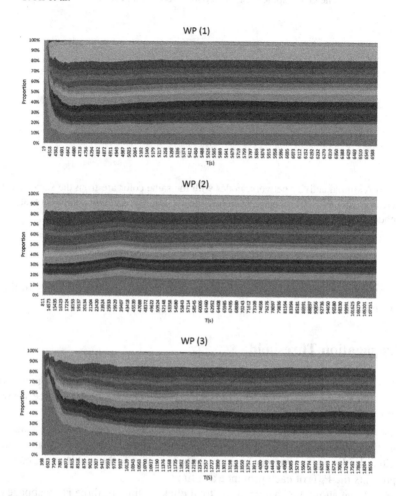

Fig. 2. The change of the click volume rate of each province Three H5 webpages about the topic Eastern Star shipwreck

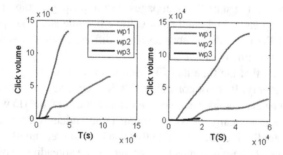

Fig. 3. The total click volume of three webpages about Eastern Star with time delay from the beginning of the propagation

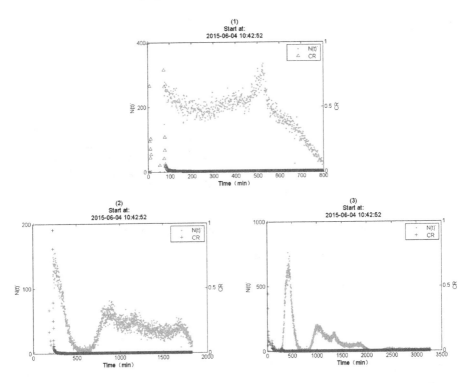

Fig. 4. CR and N'(t) change with time, and we find that the time point that CR become close to zero is nearly the same to the time that N'(t) become large suddenly

6   Geographical Characteristics

In this section, we take all the cities as nodes, and take all the interactions among users in different cities as edges to construct new GIAN.

We fuse the GIAN of three H5 webpages together, and analyze the GIAN. Weighted degree of each node in GIAN reflects the click volume of the users in the city, and also reflects the degree of concern about the event of Internet users in the city. Weighted out degree is the number of times that the H5 webpages shared by the citizens were reviewed, reflecting the influence of the city.

And it can be seen from Fig. 5 that the weighted degree, weighted out degree and weighted in degree of Shanghai, Beijing, Hangzhou and Chongqing were really large. They are followed by Tianjin, Nanjing, Guangzhou, Changsha, Wuhan and Shenzhen. These cities are the capital cities or municipalities, they are much more developed, and the citizens have more access to the Internet, and care more about the important events.

Betweenness centrality of a node refers to the number of the shortest paths that get through the node in the network. This reflects the central status of a node in the network. It can be seen from the analysis of Fig. 6 that Beijing is the city that has largest betweenness rather than Shanghai.

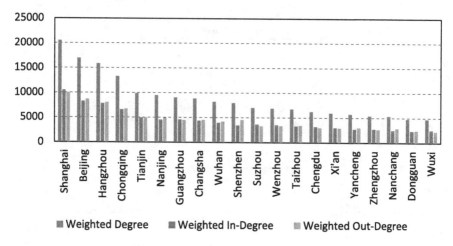

Fig. 5. Weighted degree of top 20 city nodes

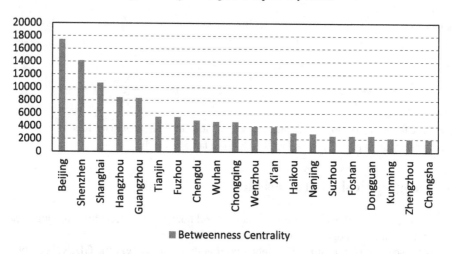

Fig. 6. Cities that betweenness centrality rank top 20 Conclusion

It is interesting that Shenzhen ranks tenth in weighted degree, but ranks second in betweenness centrality. This phenomenon shows that the city's concern on the event is not particularly outstanding, but the betweenness centrality is high. There are several possibilities about that.

- First, as frontier zone of Reform and Opening, Shenzhen is development, and the media literacy of the citizens is relatively higher.
- Then, Internet giants such as Tencent and Xunlei are in Shenzhen, and a large number of Internet-related enterprises have settled in Shenzhen, so that the city is in the center position of information dissemination.
- At last, while the Shenzhen has small local population, and big migrant population, which is concentric relatively high important reason.

7 Conclusion

At first, we focus on the connection between width of spreading geographically and trend of propagation in total such as click volume in total. And we find that the time that the time that CR becomes zero is close to the time that $N'(t)$ becomes large suddenly. We conclude that there is connection between the two time points, and the threshold of the propagation of H5 webpage in WeChat is related to the geographical propagation of WeChat network.

Then we analyze the geographical characteristics of WeChat network by constructing the GIAN taking cities as nodes. We find that the cities which care the important event most are most developed, and they also have highest central status.

Research on WeChat social network is of great significance. Though we cannot get the origin social network data from WeChat itself at present, by analyzing from the history record of HTML5 webpages, we can also get the propagation characteristic of WeChat. In this paper, we regard the cities as nodes, the interactive activities among users in different cities as edges to build the geographical network and we get valuable results in the final. In the future, we will try to study WeChat transmission network with more methods from different aspects, and get better results.

Acknowledgement. The authors would like to thank the National Natural Science Foundation of China under Grant Nos. 71303252, 61503402, 61403402, 91024032. We also thank Fibonacci Consulting Co. Ltd. for the big dataset.

References

1. Ni, Q., Yin, X., Tian, K., et al.: Particle swarm optimization with dynamic random population topology strategies for a generalized portfolio selection problem. Natural Comput. 1–14 (2016)
2. Moreno, J.L.: Who shall survive? A new approach to the problem of human interactions. Bull. Chem. Soc. Japan **9**, 402–409 (1934). Nervous and Mental Disease Publishing Company, Washington, DC
3. Xu, K., Zhang, S., Chen, H., et al.: Measurement and analysis of online social networks. Chin. J. Comput. pp. 29–42 (2014)
4. Song, X., Zhang, S., Qian, L.: Opinion dynamics in networked command and control organizations. Physica A Stat. Mech. Appl. **392**(20), 5206–5217 (2013)
5. Song, X., Shi, W., Ma, Y., et al.: Impact of informal networks on opinion dynamics in hierarchically formal organization. Physica A Stat. Mech. Appl. **436**, 916–924 (2015)
6. Benevenuto, F., Rodrigues, T., Cha, M., et al.: Characterizing user behavior in online social networks. In: Proceedings of the 9th ACM SIGCOMM Conference on Internet Measurement Conference, pp. 49–62. ACM (2009)
7. Zhang, C., Sun, J., Zhu, X., et al.: Privacy and security for online social networks: challenges and opportunities. IEEE Network **24**(4), 13–18 (2010)
8. Gao, W., Li, Q., Zhao, B., et al.: Multicasting in delay tolerant networks: a social network perspective. In: Proceedings of the tenth ACM international symposium on Mobile adhoc networking and computing, pp. 299–308. ACM (2009)

9. Yang, B., Cheung, W.K., Liu, J.: Community mining from signed social networks. IEEE Trans. Knowl. Data Eng. **19**(10), 1333–1348 (2007)

10. Cornand, C., Heinemann, F.: Optimal degree of public information dissemination. Econ. J. **118**(528), 718–742 (2008)

11. Marlow, C., Byron, L., Lento, T., et al.: Maintained relationships on Facebook, vol. 15 (2010)

12. Chun, H., Kwak, H., Eom, Y.H., et al.: Comparison of online social relations in volume vs interaction: a case study of cyworld. In: Proceedings of the 8th ACM SIGCOMM Conference on Internet Measurement, pp. 57–70. ACM (2008)

A Novel Real-Time Pedestrian Detection System on Monocular Vision

Aiying Guo[1,2(✉)], Meihua Xu[1], and Feng Ran[3]

[1] School of Mechatronical Engineering and Automation,
Shanghai University, Shanghai, China
{gayshh,mhxu}@shu.edu.cn
[2] Department of Electrical Engineering,
Shanxi Light Industry Vocational and Technical College, Shanxi, China
[3] Microelectronics Research and Development Center,
Shanghai University, Shanghai, China
ranfeng@shu.edu.cn

Abstract. Accuracy and speed are the two important keys in pedestrian detection. In order to balance these two indexes well, this thesis presents a novel pedestrian detection system, ROIs cascaded Uniform LBP and improved HOG, for real-time pedestrian detection in monocular vision. Two contributions are made in this system. First contribution is that Uniform LBP (Local Binary Pattern) cascaded improved HOG (Histograms of Oriented Gradients) are the novel structure for pedestrian detection, which can improve detection speed. Second contribution is that this pedestrian detection system is evaluated by many methods and algorithms. Experiment shows that this system can deal with 31 fps, which can be used as the real time pedestrian detection system.

Keywords: Real-time · Pedestrian detection · (Local Binary Pattern) LBP · Improved (Histogram of Oriented Gradient) HOG · (Support Vector Machine) SVM

1 Introduction

Every year, the number of pedestrians who are killed in the traffic accident is incredible. These accidents cause the huge economic losses on the government and people. So, many researchers and institutions invest huge economic and humans to study the pedestrian detection in Automobile Driver Assistance System (ADAS). Pedestrian Detection (PD) gradually becomes the key technology of ADAS. The particular interest in PD has dramatically increased with the improvement of hardware technology.

Although the development of PD has achieved many good results, there still doesn't have the mature products in the market for PD with the high accuracy and speed. There are some reasons to prevent this function as the vehicle equipment. So, PD is the big problem for being embedded into the vehicle equipment.

At the same time, the performance of PD is improved through more complex algorithms or the better hardware platform. Such as, Integral Channel feature [1],

© Springer Science+Business Media Singapore 2016
L. Zhang et al. (Eds.): AsiaSim 2016/SCS AutumnSim 2016, Part IV, CCIS 646, pp. 293–303, 2016.
DOI: 10.1007/978-981-10-2672-0_30

Deformable Parts Model (DPM) [2], Conventional Neural Network (CNN) [3], Color Self Similarity (CSS) [4], Deep Learning [5], Semantic Segmentation [6] and so on [7–10] are the excellent algorithms for pedestrian detection on high accuracy. But these systems detect pedestrians too slowly on the PC. Benenson's fast pedestrian detection system based on the GPU with CPU can process about 100 fps [11]. The hardware overload of this system is so huge, which can't be embedded into the vehicle equipment. Others, most of the papers about pedestrian detection are realized by the OPENCV or MATLAB based on the PC [12–14]. But the drawback is that these systems can't be used on the vehicle equipment as real-time detection system.

Based on the above problems, this thesis proposes a novel pedestrian detection system. This thesis makes some contributions on the theory. Regions Of Interest (ROIs) are firstly extracted from original frames based on the camera parameters. Inherits from Boosting, the Uniform LBP cascaded improved HOG are used as the two stage classifier to detect pedestrians. Through these process, it can be decreased about $70 \sim 80$ % calculation and accelerated by $5 \sim 7x$ of the whole detections system.

This thesis is listed as follows: Sect. 2 will introduce the relative theory in the pedestrian detection system; Sect. 3 explains the whole structure; Sect. 4 makes the evaluation the performance of pedestrian detection system. At last section, the conclusion is made.

2 Related Algorithms

Recently years, the institutes and researchers exhibit many useful pedestrian detection algorithm and structure. Dalal's HOG is the perfect descriptor for pedestrian feature compared with the other feature descriptors since 2005 [15]. But drawback is that HOG has the feature redundancy and isn't suitable to be used in the real-time pedestrian detection system. If these algorithms are realized on the hardware, the overload and speed can't be balanced very well. Based on these, the Uniform LBP cascaded improved HOG based on the camera parameters are cascade as the novel structure of pedestrian detection system. When scanning the frames, the Uniform LBP detection window slides overall the frames and replaces the improved HOG detection window. This operation can decrease the computational about $70 \sim 80$ % and promote the $5 \sim 7x$ speed compared with the traditionally method.

2.1 Uniform LBP

LBP (Local Binary Pattern) is the effective texture descriptor with low complexity and gray invariant [16, 17]. The LBP feature is improved into many other variant LBP features for different scene. In this paper, detection window is 64×128 pixels. One detection window is divided into many blocks, which are 16×16 pixels. One block can generate 256 LBP features. Then the LBP histograms in one block can't exhibit the information of texture and lost the main information because of sparse histogram. Based on these, the Uniform LBP is adopted as the pedestrian descriptor. Uniform LBP is defined as follows: if the change numbers from 0 to 1 or 1 to 0 in the LBP binary code isn't larger than 2, the Uniform LBP is the LBP binary code. If not, the other all LBP features will be grouped into one feature, called 59th Uniform LBP feature as function (1) shows. In function (1) and (2), g_p stands for the pixel value.

$$LBP_{P,R} = \begin{cases} \sum_{p=0}^{P-1} s(g_p - g_c), & if(U(LBP_{P,R}) \leq 2 \\ P+1, & otherwise \end{cases} \quad (1)$$

While:

$$U(LBP_{P,R}) = |s(g_{p-1} - g_c) - s(g_0 - g_c)| + \sum_{p=1}^{P-1} |s(g_p - g_c) - s(g_{p-1} - g_c)| \quad (2)$$

The number of Uniform LBP is 59. So, one cell in one block generates 59 kinds of LBP features at most. Experiments shows that the 58 kinds of LBP feature can cover above 90 % the number of LBP features. In this system, one pedestrian detection window is 64 × 128 pixels. One block can have 59 LBP features. Then, the sliding step of block is 16 pixels and one detection window has 32 blocks as Fig. 1 showed. So, the one detection window can generate 1888 dimension LBP features.

Fig. 1. Relationship between block and detection window

2.2 Improved HOG

The classic thought of HOG is that the feature of pedestrians is described with the orientation and magnitude of gradients. The main parameters for HOG algorithm are detection window, block and cell. In this detection system, the detection window is 64 × 128 pixels, cell is 8 × 8 pixels and block is 2 × 2 cells. When extracting HOG features, the first step is to calculate the gradients of one pixel. The second step is to give the magnitude and orientation through gradients. The third step is to calculate the trilinear interpolation through function (3) to combine the histogram. The last step is to normalize the HOG features. The 64×128 pixels detection window can generate 3780 dimension feature.

$$h(x_1,y_1,\theta_1) \leftarrow h(x_1,y_1,\theta_1) + M(x,y)\left(1 - \frac{y-y_1}{dy}\right)\left(1 - \frac{x-x_1}{dx}\right)\left(1 - \frac{\theta(x,y)-\theta_1}{d\theta}\right) \quad (3)$$

$$h(x_1,y_1,\theta_2) \leftarrow h(x_1,y_1,\theta_2) + M(x,y)\left(1 - \frac{y-y_1}{dy}\right)\left(1 - \frac{x-x_1}{dx}\right)\left(1 - \frac{\theta(x,y)-\theta_2}{d\theta}\right) \quad (4)$$

In function (3), $M(x,y)$ stands for the magnitude of (x, y) of pixel; $\left(1 - \frac{x-x_1}{dx}\right)$ and $\left(1 - \frac{y-y_1}{dy}\right)$ for the distance to the center of block; $\left(1 - \frac{\theta(x,y)-\theta_2}{d\theta}\right)$ and $\left(1 - \frac{\theta(x,y)-\theta_1}{d\theta}\right)$ for the distance to the center of corresponding bin, $h(x_1,y_1,\theta_1)$ for the hog histogram value of (x_1,y_1,θ_1). According to function (3) and (4), the traditionally HOG calculates trilinear interpolation related with the location and orientation. That means that the magnitudes of one pixel will be divided into the corresponding bins with projection factors from location and orientation. To complete the whole trilinear interpolation of one pixel, there exists other 7 functions, which are similar to function (1), to generate the HOG features. The huge calculation and memory makes it to be difficultly realized in the hardware platform. Others, the calculation time is also the restrict part to satisfy the real-time. In order to protect the accuracy of HOG algorithm, the improved HOG still calculate trilinear interpolation. But the projection method is reviewed.

The location and orientation projections are explained separately. About the orientation projection, the orientation doesn't be projected into the 2 bins, just 1 bin. Let's suppose the orientation of one pixel is as the Fig. 2 showed, $[50°]$ locates in $[40°,60°]$ bin. According to the function (3) and (4), the projection factors are 0.75 and 0.25. In the improved HOG, $[50°]$ is projected into the bin of $[40°,60°]$.

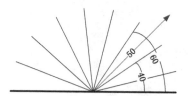

Fig. 2. Orientation projection

The location projections are changed with the corresponding distance to block center Let's suppose one cell is divided into A zone and B zone as Fig. 3(a) showed. Figure 3(b) exhibits the block with A zone and B zone.

If one pixel locates in the A zone, then the function (3), (4) is changed to the function (5), (6). The magnitude will make contributions to the other three cells in one block. If one pixel locates in the B zone, then the function (3), (4) is changed to the function (7), (8). They just make contributions to their own block, which it is located.

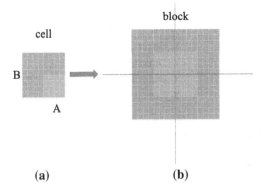

Fig. 3. Different zone in one block

$$h(x_1, y_1, \theta_1) \leftarrow h(x_1, y_1, \theta_1) + M(x, y)\left(1 - \frac{y - y_1}{dy}\right)\left(1 - \frac{x - x_1}{dx}\right) \qquad (5)$$

$$h(x_1, y_1, \theta_2) \leftarrow h(x_1, y_1, \theta_2) + M(x, y)\left(1 - \frac{y - y_1}{dy}\right)\left(1 - \frac{x - x_1}{dx}\right) \qquad (6)$$

$$h(x_1, y_1, \theta_1) \leftarrow h(x_1, y_1, \theta_1) + M(x, y) \qquad (7)$$

In the function (5) and (6), the location factor can be calculated offline. The A zone in one block can combine the location factors parameter array. When calculate the trilinear interpolation, the function (5) and (6) will use the look up table to generate the HOG features. If the pixels are located in the B zone, the magnitude just needs to be added without other calculation.

3   Structure of Pedestrian Detection

3.1   Pedestrian Detection System

The theory is realized by Visual Studio 2012 with C language and the PC is Dual-Core 3.00Ghz CPU. The whole structure of pedestrian detection system is divided into two groups: ROIs Extraction and Object Recognition.

This detection system uses the graying function (8) based on the human physiology.

$$H(x, y) = 0.11B(lue) + 0.59G(reen) + 0.3R(ed) \qquad (8)$$

In the ROIs Extraction module, the images are dealt with the 0.75 parameter at the Table 1 showed.

Table 1. Scaling factor

Factor	0.75
X_Direction	0
Y_Direction	138
X_Direction	192
Y_Direction	480

Figure 4(a) is the original image; Fig. 4(b) is the graying image and Fig. 4(c) is the scaling image compared with the original image; Fig. 4(d) is the image which is the ROIs for detecting pedestrians in the next step.

(a) Original image   **(b)** Graying image

(c) Scaling image   **(d)** ROIs image

Fig. 4. Different images

Figure 5 shows the process of pedestrian detection system. In the Object Recognition module, Uniform LBP cascaded improved HOG based on the linear SVM are the two classifier to be used in the pedestrian detection system. The Uniform LBP is the first classifier and the improved HOG the second classifier. The sliding of Uniform LBP detection window scans the whole image and replaces the detection window of improved HOG. The sliding step of detection window is according to "coarse-to-fine". If the result from the Uniform LBP with linear SVM based on the Uniform LBP is true, the sliding step is fine, 8 pixel. If not, the sliding step is coarse, 16 pixel. The Uniform LBP is the first classifier to detect whether pedestrians or not.

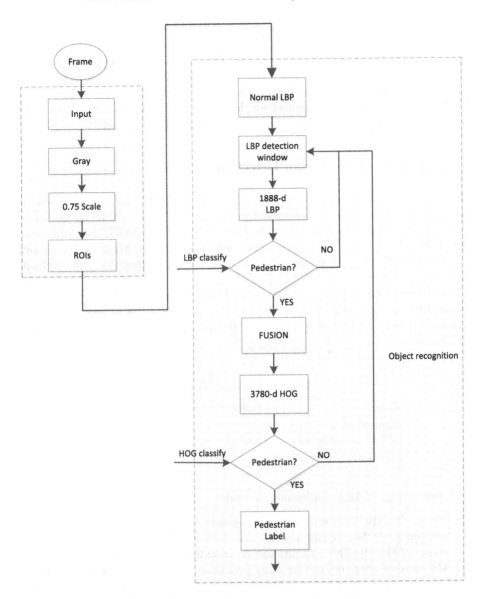

Fig. 5. Flow chart of pedestrian detection system

At the same time, the linear SVM based on the Uniform LBP will be processed to give the results. If the results is true, that means this detection window may be exist pedestrians. Then, this detection window will be processed in the second classifier. If the results is false, it means that this detection window don't exist any pedestrians and won't be processed in the second stage.

When sliding the detection windows, the pixel will be calculated many times because of the overlapping data in the corresponding window. So, in order to satisfy the real-time, time for space is used to process the data. The Uniform LBP features are stored in the memory. If the Uniform LBP feature are used, then it be read from the memory not real-time calculated. Before the first classifier is process in the second classifier, the window fusion will be used to make one pedestrian one detection window. The fusion method is explained in Sect. 3.2. The improved HOG with linear SVM is the second stage to determine whether pedestrians or not. If true, this window is the pedestrian zone. If false, this detection window will be disposed.

4   Evaluation of Pedestrian Detection System

This thesis uses the cascaded Uniform LBP and improved HOG based on the camera parameters as the structure of pedestrian detection system. Table 2 shows the detection time from the improved HOG, cascade LBP and improved HOG, cascaded Uniform LBP and improved HOG based on the camera parameters after all of images are scaled with 0.75. Figure 6 exhibits the detection results of three structures without mixture.

In Table 2, the detection time of HOG is almost $3 \sim 4X$ compared Uniform LBP. That means that the effective of LBP is almost $3 \sim 4X$ to HOG. So, in the pedestrian detection, the LBP is used as the first classify to promote the efficiency of whole system.

Table 2. Processing Time

Method	Figure 6(a) (ms)	Figure 6(b) (ms)
Improved HOG	686	713
LBP, Improved HOG	249	337
ROIs, LBP, Improved HOG	21	30

From the Fig. 6, three conclusions are made.

(1) There still exist many errors when using the LBP or HOG to detect pedestrians independently. So, the cascaded Uniform LBP and HOG can be used as the two stages of classify. This structure can decrease the detection error effectively.
(2) One third of image doesn't have any pedestrians. So, the ROIs extractions based on the camera parameters can reduce the effective scanning zones without sacrifice of detection accuracy.
(3) One pedestrian is annotated many times. The false error detection windows are scattered in the whole detection image and the pedestrian windows are intensive segment. So the detection window must be fusion and make some threshold to make only one pedestrian to one label window. Others, the fusion window can decrease the detection error. Figure 7 shows the fusion result.

Figure 7 just shows the visual results of pedestrian detection. Based on the above analysis, the cascaded Uniform LBP and improved HOG can accelerate the detection speed through sliding LBP detection window replace the HOG detection window. The

Fig. 6. Detection results of different algorithms combination

Fig. 7. Window fusion

ROIs based on the camera parameters can reduce the false warning and promote the detection efficiency. This system can detect pedestrians 31 fps (720 × 480 pixels) and satisfy the detection speed.

5 Conclusion

This thesis proposes a novel structure of pedestrian detection system and can be used as the real time hardware pedestrian detection.

Acknowledgement. This work is supported by the National Natural Science Foundation of China (Grant: 61376028).

References

1. Miyamoto, R., Yu, J., Onoye, T.: Normalized channel features for accurate pedestrian detection. In: International Symposium on Communications, Control and Signal Processing, pp. 582–585 (2014)
2. Chuang, M.C., Hwang, J.N., Ye, J.H., et al.: Underwater fish tracking for moving cameras based on deformable multiple kernels. IEEE Trans. Syst. Man Cybern. Syst. 1–11 (2016)
3. Xiao, L., Liao, B.: A convergence-accelerated Zhang neural network and its solution application to Lyapunov equation. Neurocomputing (2016)
4. Zeng, B., Wang, G., Lin, X.: Color self-similarity feature based real-time pedestrian detection. Journal of Tsinghua University (2012)
5. Schulz, H., Behnke, S.: Deep learning. KI - Künstliche Intelligenz 26(4), 357–363 (2012)
6. Benenson, R., Omran, M., Hosang, J., Schiele, B.: Ten years of pedestrian detection, what have we learned? In: Agapito, L., Bronstein, M.M., Rother, C. (eds.) ECCV 2014 Workshops. LNCS, vol. 8926, pp. 613–627. Springer, Heidelberg (2015)
7. Lakshmi, A., Faheema, A.G.J.: Dipti Deodhare. Pedestrian detection in thermal images: an automated scale based region extraction with curvelet space validation. Infrared Phys. Technol. **76**, 421–438 (2016)
8. Varga, D., Szirányi, T.: Robust real-time pedestrian detection in surveillance videos. J. Ambient Intell. Humanized Comput. 1–7 (2016)
9. Lee, C.-H., Kim, D.: Improvement of processing time for stereo vision-based pedestrian detection. In: Proceedings of HCI Korea. Hanbit Media, Inc. (2016)
10. Tayb, S., Azdoud, Y., Amine, A., et al.: HOL, GDCT and LDCT for pedestrian detection. In: International Conference on Signal, Image Processing and Pattern Recognition (2016)
11. Van Gool, L.: Pedestrian detection at 100 frames per second. In: IEEE Conference on Computer Vision & Pattern Recognition, pp. 2903–2910 (2012)
12. Bauer, S., Köhler, S., Doll, K., et al.: FPGA-GPU architecture for kernel SVM pedestrian detection. In: IEEE Computer Society Conference on Computer Vision and Pattern Recognition Workshops (CVPRW). IEEE, pp. 61–68 (2010)
13. Martelli, S., Tosato, D., Cristani, M., et al.: FPGA-based pedestrian detection using array of covariance features. In: ACM/IEEE International Conference on Distributed Smart Cameras, pp. 1–6 (2011)

14. Hahnle, M., Saxen, F., Hisung, M., et al.: FPGA-based real-time pedestrian detection on high-resolution images. In: 2013 IEEE Conference on Computer Vision and Pattern Recognition Workshops (CVPRW). IEEE Computer Society 629–635 (2013)
15. Dalal, N., Triggs, B.: Histograms of oriented gradients for human detection. In: IEEE Conference on Computer Vision & Pattern Recognition, pp. 886–893 (2005)
16. Werghi, N., Tortorici, C., Berretti, S., et al.: Boosting 3D LBP-based face recognition by fusing shape and texture descriptors on the mesh. IEEE Trans. Inf. Forensics Secur. 11(5), 964–979 (2016)
17. Yang, Y., Yang, J., Liu, L., et al.: High-speed target tracking system based on a hierarchical parallel vision processor and gray-level LBP algorithm. IEEE Trans. Syst. Man Cybern. Syst. 5(1), 1–15 (2016)

Improvement of Non-maximum Suppression in Pedestrian Detection Based on HOG Features

Qi Wang[1], Meihua Xu[2(✉)], Aiying Guo[2,3], and Feng Ran[1]

[1] Microelectronics Research and Development Center,
Shanghai University, Shanghai 200072, China
[2] School of Mechatronic Engineering and Automation,
Shanghai University, Shanghai 200072, China
mhxu@shu.edu.cn
[3] Department of Electrical Engineering, Shanxi Light Industry Vocational
and Technical College, Taiyuan 030013, China

Abstract. Pedestrian detection is a hot topic in the field of computer vision in recent year. But the current studies about pedestrian detection mainly focus on feature extraction, training and classifier model and pay little attention to non-maximum suppression (NMS). This thesis uses the information like ratio of detection scores, neighborhood window to improve NMS based on HOG-SVM algorithm, solving the problems that alone windows in detected images arise false detection rate and the suppression windows surrounded by inhibited windows arise false detection rate and missing detection rate. Experiment results on the INRIA pedestrian database show that the improved non-maxima suppression can solve the above problems, reducing the false detection rate and missing detection rate in pedestrian detection.

Keywords: HOG-SVM algorithm · Pedestrian detection · Non-maximum suppression

1 Introduction

Recently, pedestrian detection has a wide range of applications in the field of driver assistance and becomes a challenging task in the field of computer vision. Currently, several main pedestrian detection algorithms including HOG-SVM [1, 2] algorithm, LBP [2, 3] algorithm, DPM [4] algorithm and the relatively popular superpixel segmentation [5] algorithm. Due to the high degree of accuracy, HOG-SVM algorithm has been widely used and there are a lot of algorithms improved based on HOG-SVM algorithm, for example, the LBP algorithm. However, the present improvements always focus on feature extraction and classifier model, the studies about NMS are not many. This work improves the NMS inspired by Chen Jinhui et al. [6] based on HOG-SVM algorithm and mainly against the problems caused by alone windows and the suppression windows which surrounded by inhibited windows. Through the ratio of detection scores and the neighborhood windows to solve the above problems so that false detection rate and missing detection rate will be decreased. For simplicity and

L. Zhang et al. (Eds.): AsiaSim 2016/SCS AutumnSim 2016, Part IV, CCIS 646, pp. 304–310, 2016.
DOI: 10.1007/978-981-10-2672-0_31

speed, we use linear SVM as a baseline classifier throughout the study. The experiment of pedestrian detection is on the INRIA pedestrian test set.

2   Detection Scores

In the work of Chen Jinhui *et al.* [6], the initial detection windows are measured by detection scores which are obtained by the Adaboost classifier. However, this work uses HOG-SVM algorithm, the classifier is SVM(Support Vector Machine) so that it is hard to get detection scores as Adaboost. After some researches, we decides to use "dec_values" as detection scores.

In this work, SVM is the LIBSVM which chooses linear kernel function. LIBSVM's multiple classification strategy uses one-against-one strategy, establishing $\frac{N \times (N-1)}{2}$ classifiers for N classes data. This work divides the prediction samples into two classes, so it only needs to build one classifier. Specifically, after extracting the prediction samples' features, the characteristic matrix is substituted into the decision function of LIBSVM, if the result is greater than the threshold, the sample is a positive sample, otherwise, the negative one. The decision function is as follows:

$$f(x) = \sum_{i=1}^{K} \partial_i y_i x_i \cdot x + b \tag{1}$$

Where in, K indicates the number of training samples, ∂_i indicates the Lagrange multiplier, y_i indicates the label of sample, x_i indicates a characteristic matrix for the training sample, b indicates the offset. If $\partial_i = 0, x_i$ is not a support vector, so the front of formula (1) calculates the sum of the product of characteristic matrix of support vectors and the other items. The default decision function threshold of Linear LIBSVM is 0. For a prediction sample, "dec_values" is one of the return values of decision function, if it is greater than 0, positive samples' vote value plus one, otherwise the negative samples plus one. Since only one classifier, one vote process is needed, "dec_values" decides if the sample is a positive sample. Suppose that the threshold value is a number greater than 0, the larger the value of "dec_values", the more likely a positive sample it is, so this work regard "dec_values" as the detection scores.

3   Non-maximum Suppression Algorithm

NMS is the key process in many fields of computer vision application [7], it also plays an important role in pedestrian detection. If somewhere in the sample image exits a pedestrian, we can find that there are many windows which have different sizes and locations after obtaining initial detection windows with sliding window detector, it will have a great influence on the subsequent window fusion. Felzenszwalb *et al.* [7] only retains a pair of intersecting windows that have the highest detection scores when meeting the minimum intersected area condition, this method is called paired maximum suppression (PMS). Mean shift [9] non-maximum suppression is also a related method, it needs to project the detection windows into 3D space and through kernel density estimate to get the final detection results. The greedy NMS is the most commonly used NMS [6], through greedy strategy to carry out pairwise comparison of detection windows, once a detection window is suppressed, it can't suppress the worse detection window. Specific steps are as follows:

First of all, rank the initial detection window from low to high according to the detection scores.

Make the first window as the suppression window, the other as inhibited windows.

Calculate the overlap area of suppression window and inhibited window, if the ratio of the overlap area between the two: $\frac{overlap\,area}{union\,area}$ is greater than the threshold, delete the inhibited window.

Make the next window as the suppression window until the last window.

4 Improved Non-maximum Suppression

Brown *et al.* [10] propose Temporal Non-maximum Suppression (TNMS), using time information to find several maximum points in pedestrians' overlap area to reduce the false detection rate. In order to calculate the NMS more efficiently, Neubeck [8] uses partial maximum sequences (PMS) and modular processing. However, it is rare to improve the NMS in our country, Chen Jinhui *et al.* [6] improve the NMS based on ACF algorithm and have a good result. This work carries out improvements based on HOG-SVM algorithm which uses the greedy NMS, introducing information like score ratio, neighborhood window and so on. Compared to PMS and TNMS, this work has higher speed and is efficient in some simply case. Compared to greedy NMS, this work is more accurate. And this considers some problems that paper [6] has not been solved.

4.1 Suppress Alone Window Strategy

HOG-SVM algorithm through sliding window to detect pedestrians, the result windows tend to congregate in the areas where exit pedestrians or suspected exiting pedestrians in the obtained image which is not dealt with NMS. But in some situations, like image is so small that there are few detection windows or SVM occurs a false detection, it will appear alone windows in the image, in other words, the window do not overlap with other windows.

These windows are false detection windows in majority and difficult to be suppressed because they do not have overlaps with other windows, following the increase of false detection rate. As shown in (Fig. 1a), on the left of image exists an alone window which is an obvious false detection window, it can be seen in (Fig. 1b) that the former NMS algorithm that only uses the information of overlaps can not suppress this window.

This work introduces the detection window scores to suppress the alone windows. Due to the alone windows always contain no pedestrians and only in rare cases substantially complete pedestrians, we can conclude two aspects: The first is the case of relatively low detection scores, indicating a false detection; the second is the case of

(a) Original NMS detection window   (b) Original NMS result   (c) Improved NMS result

Fig. 1. Suppress alone window NMS result

relatively high detection scores, indicating a correct detection. The detection scores of two cases have a big difference, so using average or median detection score as a threshold value can suppress or retain alone window simply and effectively. This work uses average score of all detection windows as threshold, if the score of the alone window is higher than the threshold, it is supposed that the alone window contains a pedestrian, so we retain the alone window; if the score of the alone window is lower than the threshold, suppressing this window. The experiment results are shown in (Fig. 1c), the algorithm reduces the number of false detection windows and decrease the false detection rate.

4.2 Periphery Window Strategy

During the process of pedestrian detection, due to the use of sliding window when searching with a certain step, a lot of initial detection windows will surround the pedestrian, these windows may become useful neighborhood information to NMS. Dalal [9] uses the neighborhood information to operate Kernel Density Estimate and searches mode with mean shift algorithm.

Original algorithm uses greedy strategy to suppress windows, which only through detection scores and overlap area information and uses the highest score window to suppress the other windows. In fact, because of variable appearance of pedestrians, blocking and some other factors, the lower detection score window may be more suitable to match the real pedestrian. For example as shown in (Fig. 2a), the score of dotted line window is 0.2325, while the solid line window is 0.2205, it is evident that the solid line window covers more pedestrian area and matches the pedestrian. Although the score of dotted window is higher, it covers only the head and chest of the pedestrian and differs greatly from the entire pedestrian area.

On the basis of the original NMS algorithm, this work proposes a method for solving the above problem. Here consider only a special case: when suppression window is surrounded by the inhibited window. In this case, we can consider in two aspects. At first, when the scores of suppression window and inhibited window are close, retaining only the peripheral inhibited window, while the inhibited window inherits the score of suppression window and becomes the new suppression window as

(a) Original NMS result   (b) Retain peripheral
window NMS result

Fig. 2. Result when the scores of two window are close

shown in (Fig. 2b). Because when the two scores are close, indicating that the two windows both are relatively good coverage of some pedestrian area, but due to the factor like scale, position or the size of covered area, they have some difference. Of course, if blindly choose the peripheral window, the final detection window may be too big so that lower the performance of the algorithm. Therefore, we must consider the second aspect, when the scores of the inhibited window and the suppression window have big difference. As shown in (Fig. 3a), the score of dotted line window is 0.8326, and the score of solid line window is 0.1724, it seems that the solid line window is a bad window, a lot of grass contained in the solid line window. However, we can't ignore that the solid line window contains an entire pedestrian. So either only suppressing the inhibited window or just retaining the peripheral window is one-sided. The scheme is to fuse the two windows based on the normalized scores of the two, the score of the fused window is the score of the suppression window. The dotted line window is the result of fusion as shown in (Fig. 3b), it matches the pedestrian better than the original suppression window clearly. The following formulas can summarize the above scheme:

(a) Original NMS result   (b) Window fusion
NMS result

Fig. 3. Result when the scores of two window are not close

$$[sx_f \; sy_f \; sw_f \; sh_f] = \begin{cases} [sx_d \; sy_d \; sw_d \; sh_d], & \frac{s_d}{s_u} \geq thr \\ [sx_d \; sy_d \; sw_d \; sh_d] * Pd + [sx_u \; sy_u \; sw_u \; sh_u] * Pu, & \frac{s_d}{s_u} < thr \end{cases} \quad (2)$$

$$Pd = \frac{s_d}{s_d + s_u} \tag{3}$$

$$Pu = \frac{s_u}{s_d + s_u} \tag{4}$$

$[sx_f \; sy_f \; sw_f \; sh_f], [sx_d \; sy_d \; sw_d \; sh_d], [sx_u \; sy_u \; sw_u \; sh_u]$ represent the latitude, longitude, width, height of the output window, the inhibited window and the suppression window. Pd represents the score of the inhibited window after normalized, Pu represents the score of the suppression window after normalized. thr is the threshold of score ratio, it is appropriate to make the value of thr 0.85 according to the experiment result, if the score ratio is greater than 0.85, retaining the peripheral window, otherwise fusing.

Using the peripheral window strategy can not only reduce the number of missing detection windows, but also reduce the number of false detection windows, as shown in (Fig. 2a), the value of $\frac{overlaparea}{union\ area}$ between the retained window (the dotted window due to the greedy strategy) and the real pedestrian area is lower than 0.5, the retained window can only be regard as false detection window. But due to the score radio of the two windows is higher than 0.85, after using the peripheral window strategy the retained window becomes the solid line window, reducing the false detection rate. If the peripheral window is too large, it may cause new false detection window, so the constrains of score ratio are made and this case can be avoided.

5 Conclusion

This work carries out two improvements for the greedy NMS which is most commonly used in the field of pedestrian detection based on HOG-SVM algorithm, introducing "dec_values" of the decision function as detection score and making full use of the information includes overlaps, ratio of detection score, neighborhood window. Experiment results show that both suppress alone window strategy and peripheral window strategy are useful and can reduce the missing detection rate and false detection rate of pedestrian detection.

Acknowledgement. This work is supported by the National Natural Science Foundation of China (Grant: 61376028).

References

1. Dalal, N., Triggs, B.: Histograms of oriented gradients for human detection. In: IEEE Computer Society Conference on Computer Vision and Pattern Recognition, CVPR 2005, vol. 1, pp. 886–893. IEEE (2005)

2. Hurney, P., Waldron, P., Morgan, F., et al.: Night-time pedestrian classification with histograms of oriented gradients-local binary patterns vectors. Intell. Transport Syst. IET **9** (1), 75–85 (2015)

3. Li, W., Chen, C., Su, H., et al.: Local binary patterns and extreme learning machine for hyperspectral imagery classification. IEEE Trans. Geosci. Remote Sens. **53**(7), 3681–3693 (2015)

4. Wan L, Eigen D, Fergus R. End-to-end integration of a convolution network, deformable parts model and non-maximum suppression[C]//Proceedings of the IEEE Conference on Computer Vision and Pattern Recognition. 2015: 851–859

5. Liu, S., Zhang, L., Zhang, Z., et al.: Automatic cloud detection for all-sky images using superpixel segmentation. IEEE Geosci. Remote Sens. Lett. **12**(2), 354–358 (2015)

6. Chen, J., Ye, X.: Improvement of non-maximum suppression in pedestrian detection. Nat. Sci. **41**(3), 371–378 (2015). East China University of Technology

7. Felzenszwalb, P.F., Girshick, R.B., McAllester, D., et al.: Object detection with discriminatively trained part-based models. IEEE Trans. Pattern Anal. Mach. Intell. **32**(9), 1627–1645 (2010)

8. Neubeck, A., Van Gool, L.: Efficient non-maximum suppression. In: 18th International Conference on Pattern Recognition, ICPR 2006, vol. 3, pp. 850–855. IEEE (2006)

9. Dalal, N.: Finding people in images and videos[D]. Institut National Polytechnique de Grenoble-INPG (2006)

10. Brown, L.M., Feris, R., Pankanti, S.: Temporal non-maximum suppression for pedestrian detection using self-calibration. In: 22nd International Conference on Pattern Recognition (ICPR), pp. 2239–2244. IEEE (2014)

Social Spatial Heterogeneity and System Entrainment in Modeling Human and Nature Dynamics

Zining Yang[✉], Mark Abdollahian, and Patrick deWerk Neal

Claremont Graduate University, Claremont, CA 91711, USA
{zining.yang,mark.abdollahian}@cgu.edu, patrick.d.neal@gmail.com

Abstract. In the context of sustainable development, a complex adaptive systems framework can help address the coupling of macro social, environmental and economic constraints and opportunities with individual agency. Using a simple evolutionary game approach, we fuse endogenously derived socio-economic system dynamics from human and nature dynamics (HANDY) theory with Prisoner's Dilemma, spatial intra-societal economic transactions. We explore the potential of spectral information from the social network adjacency matrices to predict synchronization dynamics and see how behavioral social spatial heterogeneity entrain with wealth, carrying capacity and population.

Keywords: Sustainable development · Complex adaptive systems · Network analysis · Agent-based modeling · System dynamics · Game theory

1 Introduction

Social scientists have long identified dynamic linkages between economic development, population dynamics, and environment [8, 6, 11]. Starting in ecological economics, the human and nature dynamics (HANDY) perspective is a quantitative, trans-disciplinary approach to understanding modernization and development through interdependent economic and social forces at the aggregate society level. Here we extend previous work by Motesharrei's [11] novel systems dynamic representation of societal level theory towards integrated macro-micro scales in a complex adaptive systems framework using an agent-based approach. As macroscopic structures emerging from microscopic events lead to entrainment and modification of both, co-evolutionary processes are created over time [13]. Similar to Abdollahian et al. [1–3] and Yang [15], we posit a new, approach where agency matters: individual game interactions, strategy decisions and historical outcomes determine an individual's experience. These decisions are constrained or incentivized by the changing macro economic, cultural, social and political environment via human and nature dynamics theory, conditioned on individual attributes at any particular time. Emergent behavior results from individuals' current feasible choice set, conditioned upon past behavior, event history and macro societal outcomes. Conversely, progress on economic development, the formation of cultural mores, societal norms and democratic preferences emerge from individuals' behavior interactions.

To explore potential real-world applications of this analysis, we consider the potential explanatory power of information contained in the eigenspectrum of the Laplacian

© Springer Science+Business Media Singapore 2016
L. Zhang et al. (Eds.): AsiaSim 2016/SCS AutumnSim 2016, Part IV, CCIS 646, pp. 311–318, 2016.
DOI: 10.1007/978-981-10-2672-0_32

matrix describing the dynamic adjacency matrices of the underlying social network of relationships between competing agents. This approach, borrowed from the theoretical physics literature, allows potential mean-field style analysis of an otherwise intractably complex game.

2 HANDY Background

HANDY postulates a development process in which inequality and use of resources play a critical role. Brander and Taylor [5] developed an ancestor model of population and renewable resource dynamics and demonstrated that reasonable parameter values can produce cyclical feast and famine patterns of population and resources. Their model shows that a system with a slow-growing resource base will exhibit overshooting and collapse, whereas a more rapidly growing resource base will produce an adjustment of population and resources toward equilibrium values. However, this approach does not include a central component of population dynamics: economic stratification and the accumulation of wealth.

Inspired by a Lotka-Voltera model at the core, Motesharrei et al. [11] develop a human population dynamics model by adding accumulated wealth and economic inequality. They develop and measure "carrying capacity" and show it to be a potentially practical means for early detection of societal collapse. When a population surpasses the carrying capacity, starvation or migration can threaten to significantly impact population levels and rates of change. However, humans can also accumulate wealth and then draw down resources when production cannot match consumption needs. Empirically, they posit that accumulated surpluses are not evenly distributed throughout society. As elites control resources normally, they could leave the mass of the population, while producing a portion of generated wealth, with only a small portion of it usually at or just above subsistence levels [4,7]. While the Brander–Taylor model has only two equations, Motesharrei et al.'s model supplements an additional two equations to predict the evolution of nature, accumulated wealth, elites and commoners as an interdependent, asymmetric first order system. Their HANDY equations are given by:

$$\begin{cases} \dot{\chi}_C = \beta_C \chi_C - \alpha_C \chi_C \\ \dot{\chi}_E = \beta_E \chi_E - \alpha_E \chi_E \\ \dot{y} = \gamma y (\lambda - y) - \delta \chi_C y \\ \dot{w} = \delta \chi_C y - C_C - C_E. \end{cases}$$

In this system, the total population is divided between the two variables, χ_C and χ_E, representing commoners and elites respectively. The population grows at a birth rate β and decreases at a death rate α. In their model, β is assumed to be constant for both elites and commoners but α depends on wealth. The equation for nature includes a regeneration or gain term $\gamma Y(\lambda - Y)$, and a depletion or loss term $-\delta \chi_C Y$. Technological change can make the use of resources more efficient, but it also tends to raise both per capita resource consumption as well as resource extraction scales. Thus accumulated wealth increases with production, $\delta \chi_C Y$, and decreases with the consumption of the elites and the commoners.

3   An Agent-Based, Complex Adaptive Systems Approach

While innovating a formal a systems approach for HANDY theory, a limitation of Motesharrei et al.'s [11] work lacks coupling and interdependence across human scales, from individuals to institutions and finally the societal outcomes they generate. Inspired by Motesharrei et al., our agent-based, complex adaptive systems HANDY model uniquely combines the interactive effects and feedbacks between individual human agency as well as the macro environmental constraints and opportunities that change over time for any given society. Decisions by individuals, including both elites and commoners, are affected by other individuals, social context, and system states, including accumulated wealth and resources. These decisions have variegated first and second order effects, given any particular system state, individual attributes or spatial heterogeneity. Such an approach attempts to increase both theoretical and empirical verisimilitude for some key elements of complexity processes, emergence, connectivity, interdependence and feedback [10] found across all scales of human development.

We specifically model socio-economic transaction games as producing either positive or negative values to capture both upside gains or downside losses. Subsequently, A^{ij} games' V^{ij} outcomes condition agent W_{t+1}^i values, modeling realized costs or benefits from any particular interaction. The updated $W_{t+1}^i = W_t^i + A^{ij}$ game payoff for each agent subsequently gets added to the individual's attributes for the next iteration. We then repeat individual endogenous processing, aggregated up to society as a whole and repeat the game processes for $t + n$ iterations.

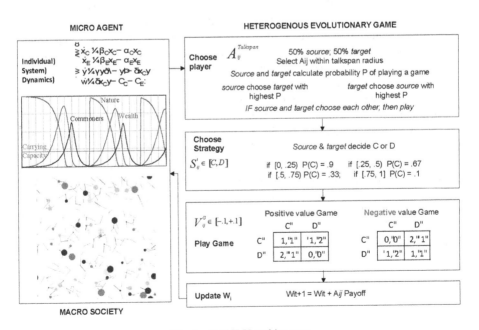

Fig. 1. HANDY architecture

Aggregated wealth gets transformed into macro-society levels and impacts nature consistent with standard ecological economics as involving both inputs from, and outputs to nature, through depletion of natural sources and carrying capacity. The sum of all prior individual behavioral histories, evolutionary through iterations, does contribute to each individual and societal current states as an initial effort at a scale integrated framework. Thus agents simultaneously co-evolve as strategy pair outcomes at t to impact W^i at $t + 1$, thus driving both positive and negative feedback process through $t + n$ iterations. These shape A^i attributes that spur adaptation to a changing environment. Feedback into subsequent A^{ij} game selection networks and strategy choice yields a complex adaptive system representation across multiple scales. Figure 1 shows our high level architecture and agent processing.

We instantiate a non-cooperative, socio-economic Prisoner's Dilemma (PD) trans-action game given agent i's attribute vector (A^i) of individual agent attributes similarity to agent j (A^j) for any A^{ij} pairs. The motivation behind this is that individuals are more likely to interact, engage and conduct transactions with other agents of similar norms [14] and produce different co-evolutionary behavior via frequency and rate dynamics [9]. To capture complex, nonlinear and emergent behavior, we first randomly choose 50 % of spatially proximal agents as sources who can choose a partner at each iteration t. The remaining targets are chosen by other agents based on symmetric preference rankings and asymmetric neighborhood proximity distributions. Following Abdollahian et al. [1–3] and Yang [15], we explore communications reach, social connectivity and technology diffusion that constrains the potential set of A^{ij} game pairs through talk-span.

The resulting networks provide a rich simulation dataset ripe for spectral analysis. By considering spectral gap metrics, the characteristic times between stable periods can be regressed against predictive qualities of the socio-economic transaction games networks. Following Neal [12], specifically this analysis proceeds on the basis of using mean values of the maximum eigenvalue gap max for a given t, the average eigenvalue gap mean, and the median eigenvalue gap median, averaged over the proceeding period of disorder. This is as opposed to using the maximum value of any of these measures observed during the disorder period, as doing so would bias longer disorder $n(t)$ periods towards higher maximum observations simply by means of more draws.

We detail a generic example of the type of information and results such analysis can provide, examining whether or not the eigenspectrum of the Laplacian matrix of the system under examination is able to predict the sequence of synchronization over the examination period. Figure 2 [12] gives two such examples of thresholds which generate a monotonically decreasing number of separate components over time. The top row of Fig. 2 examines the time evolution Phase of synchronization of GDP for two networks, defined by thresholds of 0.976, 0.99, respectively. The second row displays the index of eigenvalues from the Laplacian, in ascending order, against the inverse of the eigen-values themselves, from the Laplacian matrix derived from the adjacency matrix.

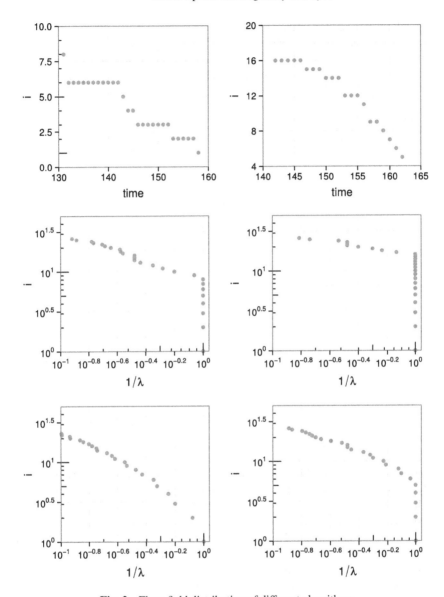

Fig. 2. Floor field distribution of different algorithms

4   Results

A sample one-simulation result is visualized below in Fig. 3, with number of agents initialized at 200 and talkspan social space compression parameterized at 15 indicating medium high social connectivity. The time series plot in the center of the figure shows the level of commoner and elite populations with natural carrying capacity over time. For selected iterations t, we then sampled the particular agent social space to the corresponding summed time series plot. Agent size represents wealth, color represents carrying capacity ranging from darker brown indicating lower and bright green higher capacity. Edges indicate the cumulative sum of agent pairs engaged in a socio-economic transaction games from $t = 0$ to t, which could be either coercive or cooperative.

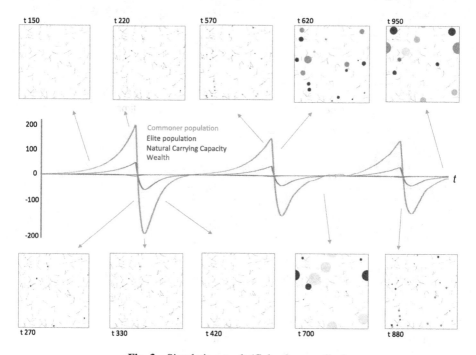

Fig. 3. Simulation result (Color figure online)

Consistent with our HANDY system dynamic equations *a priori* expectation, we can see that in the time series plot cycling with strong, sharp phase transitions occurs. Both the number of commoners and elites entrainment persists although amplitude dampens over time. Levels of carrying capacity oscillate slowly, decreasing over time while wealth responds inversely, increasing marginally over time with the same frequency. In each of the agent social space plots at t, first we can observe that edges are consistent over time indicating the rate of socio-economic transaction games is relatively stable, regardless of population, wealth or carrying capacity concerns. When either population is positive and increasing, the carrying capacity is relatively high indicated by green agents and the converse is true with negative and decreasing series. This supports our hypotheses for high levels of carrying capacity, population and wealth increases until thresholds where there are short, sharp phase transitions, until equilibrium recovery of society where wealth continues to accumulate. Regardless of wealth levels or carrying capacity, agent interactions are likely to continue and help drive recovery phases.

5 Discussion

In the context of sustainable development, a complex adaptive systems framework can help address the coupling of nature constraint and opportunity with population dynamics and individual agency. Our work demonstrates the theoretical importance of individual agency entrainment with macro-social and environmental outcomes; how societal phase shifts and tipping points result from, and recover to, human behavior. By taking our previous research a step further with the introduction of spectral analysis on simulated social network fabrics, we contribute both to the understanding of complex, strategically driven economic societies, as well as to the understanding of the value of theoretical physics methods in a new domain. The benefit is a potentially substantial, computational cost savings in the pursuit of understanding complex games and could represent a significant advance in the practice of artificial economics.

References

1. Abdollahian, M., Yang, Z., Coan, T., Yesilada, B.: Human development dynamics: an agent-based simulation of macro social systems and individual heterogeneous evolutionary games. Complex Adapt. Syst. Model. **1**(1), 1–17 (2013)
2. Abdollahian, M., Yang, Z., Neal, P.W.: Human development dynamics: an agent based simulation of adaptive heterogeneous games and social systems. In: Kennedy, W.G., Agarwal, N., Yang, S.J. (eds.) SBP 2014. LNCS, vol. 8393, pp. 3–10. Springer, Heidelberg (2014)
3. Abdollahian, M., Yang, Z., Neal, P.W., Kaplan, J.: Human development dynamics: network emergence in an agent-based simulation of adaptive heterogeneous games and social systems. In: Nakai, Y., Koyama, Y., Terano, T. (eds.) Agent-Based Approaches in Economic and Social Complex Systems VIII, pp. 3–14. Springer, Japan (2015)
4. Banerjee, A., Yakovenko, V.M.: Universal patterns of inequality. New J. Phys. **12**(7), 075032 (2010)
5. Brander, J.A., Taylor, M.S.: The simple economics of easter island: a Ricardo-Malthus model of renewable resource use. Am. Econ. Rev. **88**(1), 119–138 (1998)
6. Chua, A.: World on Fire: How Exporting Free Market Democracy Breeds Ethnic Hatred and Global Instability. Anchor, New York (2003)
7. Drăgulescu, A., Yakovenko, V.M.: Exponential and power-law probability distributions of wealth and income in the United Kingdom and the United States. Phys. A: Stat. Mech. Appl. **299**(1), 213–221 (2001)
8. Feng, Y., Kugler, J., Zak, P.J.: The politics of fertility and economic development. Int. Stud. Q. **44**(4), 667–693 (2000)
9. McKelvey, B.: Avoiding complexity catastrophe in coevolutionary pockets: strategies for rugged landscapes. Organ. Sci. **10**(3), 294–321 (1999)
10. Miller, J.H., Page, S.E.: Complex Adaptive Systems: An Introduction to Computational Models of Social Life. Princeton University Press, Princeton (2009)
11. Motesharrei, S., Rivas, J., Kalnay, E.: Human and nature dynamics (HANDY): modeling inequality and use of resources in the collapse or sustainability of societies. Ecol. Econ. **101**, 90–102 (2014)
12. Neal, P.W.: Policy Implications of Econophysics: Oscillators. Coupling and Causality. Claremont Graduate University, Claremont (2016)

13. Nowak, M.A., Sigmund, K.: Evolution of indirect reciprocity by image scoring. Nature **393**(6685), 573–577 (1998)
14. Redman, C.L., James, S.F., Paul, D.R.J. (eds.): The Archaeology of Global Change: The Impact of Humans on Their Environment. Smithsonian Books, Washington, D.C. (2004)
15. Yang, Z.: An agent-based dynamic model of politics, fertility and economic development. In: Proceedings of the 20th World Multi-Conference on Systemics, Cybernetics and Informatics (2016)

Global Community Connectivity of Complex Networks

Jun Jia[✉], Xiao-feng Hu, and Xiao-yuan He

National Defense University, Beijing 100091, China
samurasun@gmail.com, xfhu@vip.sina.com,
binglingl922@sina.com

Abstract. We defined and generated the community mapping network by the original network and its community structure, and we gave the definition of global community connectivity, which can measure the connectivity among all the communities of the original network at first. This metric can be built by the adjacency matrix of the community mapping network. Then in order to measure the node's effect on the community connectivity, we defined a new property of node and give its calculating method. After that, we do the invulnerability experiment on three computer generate networks' and three real networks' in four different situations separately. The results prove that the global community connectivity is a monotonic and valid index for measuring the situation of network's community connection. The connectivity among all the communities mainly depends on a few nodes in the original network which have the high value of node's connecting number of community and the community's connectivity represents both robustness and vulnerability in different node's removal procedures.

Keywords: Community structure · Global community connectivity · Node's connecting number of community · Network's invulnerability

1 Introduction

Our world is composed of different types of networks. These networks present opposite fragile or robust features in different situations. Researching of these's networks invulnerability is to grasp and take advantage of these features and play its active role in the actual networks. Starting from the Albert's work on the WWW [1], the network invulnerability has become an ongoing focus in complex networks' research areas. Although there is still lack of a uniform definition of network's invulnerability in the strict sense, it didn't affect the widely used of its research results in many fields, such as computer, biology, sociology and etc [2–5]. Quantitative description of invulnerability is one of the most basic and important work in complex network's research. It mainly consists of two aspects. The one is the quantitative description of the network's capabilities or features, such as the diameter of the network, the efficiency, the average inverse geodesic length or the size of largest connected subgraph. The other is the quantitative description of the network's damage, for example, the policy or the ratio of the nodes' or links' removal [6]. The combination of these two aspects can measure the

© Springer Science+Business Media Singapore 2016
L. Zhang et al. (Eds.): AsiaSim 2016/SCS AutumnSim 2016, Part IV, CCIS 646, pp. 319–329, 2016.
DOI: 10.1007/978-981-10-2672-0_33

network survivability through the changing of the network's capabilities or feature in varying of damages.

The traditional metrics of network invulnerability mostly measure the changing of the network's capabilities or features from the macroscopic or microscopic level, such as the cohesion degree, the natural connectivity [7] and so on. But there is little research of the invulnerability from the meso level, especially the community of the network. The communities refer to the sets of nodes in the network which the internal connections are dense and the connections between them are sparse [8]. Finding the community structure in network and the communication or synchronization based community are also the hotspots in complex network's research [9–18]. In the researching area of the community-based invulnerability, the work of Brain Karrer has the largest influence. He successful measured the quality of the divided community by changing the connections in network [19]. Lemmouchi studied the community-based invulnerability in computer communication networks and social networks by changing the node's parameters [20–22]. The traditional ways of studying the invulnerability of community are generally to measure the changing of the nodes or links in community from the perspective of the community's structure [19, 23], recent studies have defined the community-based invulnerability from the network's connectivity, but are actually considering the connectivity between nodes [24]. The connectivity between communities has played an important role in network's communication, synchronization and etc which based community structure. But these are rarely involved and seldom studied in the existing literatures.

Therefore, this paper chooses the connectivity between communities as the subject and studied its changing under four different node's failure modes. The experiments' results show that the global community connectivity, which presented in this paper, is a monotonic changed metric and it can effectively measures the connection situation between communities which are overlapped or non-overlapped. The quantified concept of node's community connection number, which presented in this paper too, can effectively measure the node's importance in community connection.

2 Definitions

The connections are dense in community and sparse between communities. This particular structure means that the less external connections between communities play a more important role in network. So taking the connection situation between communities as the measure of the communities' connectivity will be the foundation of researching the community-based invulnerability from the meso level.

Thus, an undirected and unweighted network can be denoted as $G(V, E)$. The nodes set of this network is $V = [v_1, v_2, \cdots, v_N]$ and the sum of the nodes is $N = |V|$; The links set of this network is $E = [e_1, e_2, \cdots, e_M]$ and the sum of the links is $M = |E|$. The adjacency matrix of this network is $A = \{A_{ij}\}$.

Suppose the network had been divided into R communities. All the communities can be denoted as $C = \{C_1, C_2, \cdots, C_R\}$ and the nodes set of every single community is V_{C_r}, and the links set is E_{C_r}. Then it can be concluded that the nodes sets of different community have following relationship which can be denoted as $V_{C_r} \cap V_{C_s} = \Phi$ and the links sets also can denoted as $E_{C_r} \cap E_{C_s} = \Phi$ when the communities in the network are non-overlapped. If the communities are overlapped, the nodes sets' relationship won't change but the links sets' intersection, which are denoted as $E_{C_r} \cap E_{C_s}$, may be null or non-null. No matter the communities in network overlap or not, all communities' nodes sets' union will meet following equation which is $\bigcup\limits_{r=1}^{R} V_{C_r} = V$ and the links set's union also is $\bigcup\limits_{r=1}^{R} E_{C_r} = E$. Now we give standardized definitions of the relevant concepts which will be used in follow-up studies.

Definition 1: (Community mapping network) a new undirected weighted network $G^*(V^*, W^*)$ can be built based on the already divided community $C = \{C_1, C_2, \cdots, C_R\}$ of network G. The nodes set of network G^* is $V^* = [v_1^*, v_2^*, \cdots, v_R^*]$. Every single node represents the community C_r; The weight of link between node r and s is ω_{rs}, it represents the sum of connections between community C_r and community C_s. The weight ω_{rs} can be get from the adjacency matrix of network G, the equation is $\omega_{rs} = \sum\limits_{v_i \in C_r} \sum\limits_{v_j \in C_s} A_{ij}$. The constructing network G^* can be called the community mapping network of the original network G.

The original network G and the generated community mapping network G^* are shown in the Fig. 1:

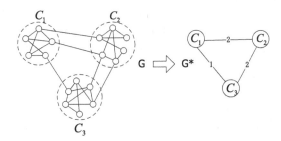

Fig. 1. Network G and its community mapping network G^*

According to the Definition 1, the community mapping network G^* can be generated from any network G and its already divided community structure. The adjacency matrix of community mapping network G^* can be denoted as $A^* = \{A_{rs}^*\}$. Every element in matrix equals to the link's weight ω_{rs}. After this definition, we give the definition of the metric which could measure the situation of connection between communities in network.

Definition 2: (Global Community Connectivity) if we construct the community mapping network G^* with the original network G and its community structure C, the global community connectivity η_C of the original network G, which is under the community structure C, can be get from the adjacency matrix of community mapping network G^*, the equation is shown as below:

$$\eta_C = \sum_{r=1}^{R} \sum_{s=1}^{R} \frac{A_{rs}^*}{R(R-1)} \tag{1}$$

The parameter $R = |C|$ is the sum of the communities in network G.

It can be seen from the Eq. 1 that the global community connectivity is actually the ratio of the total number of links between communities to the sum of the communities. It is the quantitative description of the situation of connection between communities from the holistic perspective. The larger the metric's value, the denser the connection between communities; whereas if the smaller, the sparser. The different between the global community connectivity and the Newman's modularity is that the former describes the average connection between communities, while the latter is examining the quality of divided communities through the relative relationship between internal and external links of community.

3   Attack Strategies

For the study of the global community connectivity, the attack experiment is a good choice. If the metric varies monotonically during the removal procedure, it can prove the global community connectivity's effectiveness in measuring the community's connection situation. The removal procedure, which also can be called attach strategy, can be divided into two aspects depending on whether random. For the non-random attacking experiment, Holme's work is the most comprehensive. He studied the attacking vulnerability systematic based on node's and link's four different attacking strategies respectively [25]. As we can see, the mature non-random attacking strategies on nodes just use the node's properties, such as degree or betweenness. This paper gives a new property of node which can quantitative descript the node's connecting number of different community. This property can be used as a new attacking strategy. Along with the three existing strategies which are random, "RD" and "RB", we can fully test the global community connectivity. Now, we give the relevant definition at first.

Definition 3: (Node's Connecting Number of Community) for any node v_i in network, the neighbor set of this node is $\Gamma(v_i)$. For any community C_r in network, we give a parameter $c(v_j, C_r)$ for every node $v_j \in \Gamma(v_i)$ in neighbor set $\Gamma(v_i)$, when $v_i \in C_r$ and $v_j \notin C_r$, the parameter's value equals to one $c(v_j, C_r) = 1$, otherwise it equals to zero $c(v_j, C_r) = 0$. Then the node's connecting number of community $Cb(v_i)$ is the sum of its neighbor which does not belong to the same community, it can be shown as the equation below:

$$Cb(v_i) = \sum_{C_r \in C} \sum_{v_j \in \Gamma(v_i)} c(v_j, C_r) \tag{2}$$

The $C = \{C_1, C_2, \cdots, C_R\}$ are the divided community structure of network.

We can derive the node's connecting number of community's $Cb(v_i)$ value interval is $0 \leq Cb(v_i) \leq (R-1)|\Gamma(v_i)|$ from the Eq. 2. When the node's all neighbors $v_j \in \Gamma(v_i)$ and the node itself v_i belong to the same community, the node's connecting number of community take the minimum value $Cb(v_i) = 0$; and when they belong to different community, it can take the theoretic maximum value $Cb(v_i) = (R-1)|\Gamma(v_i)|$.

It can be seen from the definition 3 that this new property of node is totally different with the betweenness. The betweenness is considered from the overall connection situation of network, not from the community structure of network. But the node's connecting number of community can truly reflect the node's importance of community connection in network. The higher the node's connecting number of community's value, the more important the node of community connection. After all the definitions, we do the experiments on different networks with four different node removal strategies which are random, recalculated degree, recalculated betweenness and node's connecting number of community.

4   Experiment and Analysis

In order to demonstrate that the global community connectivity has the extensive applicability, we choose two groups, a total of six networks to do the experiments.

4.1   Computer Generated Networks

There're two computer generated benchmark graphs which are most used in researching the community of complex network. The one is used by Girvan and Newman's at first and is called GN network. This network has 128 nodes, they are evenly divided into four communities and each community has 32 nodes. Every node in this network almost has the same degree and Girvan and Newman set the degree equals to 16 [26]. Then Andrea Lancichinetti, Santo Fortunato and Filippo Radicchi extend the GN network, they create a set of new benchmark networks for community which more closely match the networks in real world. They're called LFR network. The LFR network can adjust the generate parameters so that the generated networks could present power-law degree distributions in different scales of community [27].

This paper uses the LFR program, which is provided in Santo Fortunato's home page, to generate three different networks. The first is GN network (GN); the second is LFR network (LFR-1000) which has 1000 nodes, the average degree is 15 and the maximum degree is 50, each community has at least 20 nodes and not more than 50; the third network (LFR-500-overlapping short as LFR-O) has overlapped community, it has 500 nodes, the average degree is 15 and the maximum degree is 30, the community's scale is the same with the second and each overlapped part probably has 5 nodes and each nodes may be belong to 3 communities. These three networks' basic parameters are show in the Table 1:

Table 1. The value of basic parameters of computer generated networks

Network name	Nodes	Links	Density	Average clustering	Power exponent	Assortativity	Efficiency
GN	128	1024	0.126	0.346	–	–	0.49
LFR-1000	1000	7692	0.015	0.533	2.57	−0.169	0.315
LFR-O	500	3779	0.03	0.436	3.21	−0.124	0.35

These are the three computer generate networks' basic parameters' value. With the Santo Fortunato's LFR program, we can get every network's community structure. They are shown in the Table 2:

Table 2. The community structure of computer generated networks

Network name	Sum of community	Community's scale and amount (scale: amount)	Global community connectivity
GN	4	(32:4)	17.7
LFR-1000	28	(22:1)(23:2)(24:2)(25:1)(27:2)(28:1)(29:1) (30:1)(33:1)(34:1)(35:1)(38:2)(39:1)(41:2) (43:2)(45:1)(47:1)(48:3)(49:1)	2.02
LFR-O	16	(20:1)(22:1)(23:2)(24:2)(25:1)(31:1)(35:1) (36:4)(41:1)(46:1)(52:1)	4.46

PS: the community scale means the total number of nodes in the community

Based on the divided community structure of these three computer generated networks, we do the attacking invulnerability experiment separately. The specific invulnerability metric is the global community connectivity which we defined before. The first step of experiment is determining the attacking strategy. Then we remove one node each time with the attacking strategy and calculate the value of global community connectivity and then delete the node from the network until all the nodes are deleted. If the strategy is random, we choose one node random and record the value, and then we repeat this procedure for 50 times and calculate the average value. If the strategy is RD or RB or node's connecting number of community, we choose the node with biggest value of it each time and calculate the value of global community connectivity. At last we record all the value's change. They are all shown in the figure below:

These three figures are the attacking results of the three networks. In each figure, all the curves indicate the changes of global community connectivity of the network. Different shape in each curve means different attacking strategy. The cross represents the result of random, the circle represents the result of RD, the star represents the result of RD and the diamond represents the result of the node's connecting number of community. The big figure shows the results of global community connectivity in different node's removal ratio which is 0 to 1, the small figure shows the results too but the ratio is just 0 to 0.2. The results of network LFR-1000 is too many, so in order to make the figure more clearly, we process the results with mean interval sampling.

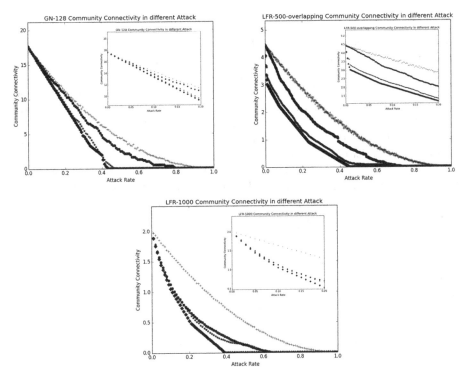

Fig. 2. The results of attacking vulnerability experiment on three computer generated networks

We can see from the Fig. 2 that the value of global community connectivity changes monotonically under different attacking strategies in different networks. No matter the communities in network are overlapped or not. Meanwhile, we can see from the small figure that when the node's removal ratio is low, the network's global community connectivity is robustness under random attack but vulnerability under non-random attack especially under the attacking strategy of RB or the node's connecting number of community. This is all because of the characteristic of the network's community structure. This contradiction between robustness and vulnerability just means that the connection between communities depends on a small set of nodes which has low value of node's connecting number of community.

We can also find out that the value of global community connectivity will finally turn to 0 when the node's removal ratio is too high. But these ratios are different under different attacking strategies. When the attacking strategy is random, the final ratios are always beyond 80 %. The RD's final ratios are 60 %, the RB's final ratios are about 50 %, and the node's connecting number of community's final ratios are always lower than 40 %. It means that this property could effective measure the importance of nodes in network's community connection. The bigger the value, the more important the node.

4.2 Real Networks

Now we choose three real networks as objects and verify the conclusions which we got from the previous experiments. These three real networks datasets are most widely used in researching the community of complex network. The dataset dolphins was first used by Dr. Lusseau in 2003, it describe the communities in bottlenose dolphins [28]. The dataset polbooks record the sales data of political books in Amazon during the period of Presidential election of US in 2004. The nodes represent the books and the links mean two books are brought by same person. The communities in this network actually describe the behavior of buying [29]. The dataset football was first used by M. Girvan and M. Newman in 2002. It mainly describes the competition's situation of all the American college football team during the whole season in the autumn of 2000. The nodes represent the team and the links mean two teams compete once [26]. All these three networks' basic parameters are show in the Tables 3:

Table 3. The value of basic parameters of real networks

Network name	Nodes	Links	Density	Average clustering	Power exponent	Assortativity	Efficiency
Dolphins	62	159	0.084	0.25	5.13	−0.04	0.379
Polbooks	105	441	0.08	0.49	2.92	−0.13	0.397
Football	115	613	0.09	0.4	75.7	0.16	0.45

The communities of these three networks are shown in the Table 4:

Table 4. The community structure of real networks

Network name	Sum of community	Community's scale and amount (scale: amount)	Global community connectivity
Dolphins	4	(7:1)(16:1)(18:1)(21:1)	5.5
Polbooks	5	(3:1)(8:2)(42:1)(44:1)	4.3
Football	11	(6:1)(8:1)(9:2)(10:2)(11:1)(12:2)(13:1)(15:1)	3.36

PS: the community scale means the total number of nodes in the community

Then we do the attacking invulnerability experiment on these three networks too and the procedures are same with previous experiment. The results are shown in the table below:

We can see from the Fig. 3 that the results of real network's experiment are same with the experiment on computer generated networks. So we can get the following conclusions: first, the global community connectivity could effective measure the connection's situation between communities in network. Second, the node's connecting number of community could reflect the importance of node in network's community connection. The bigger the value, the more important the node. Third, the connection

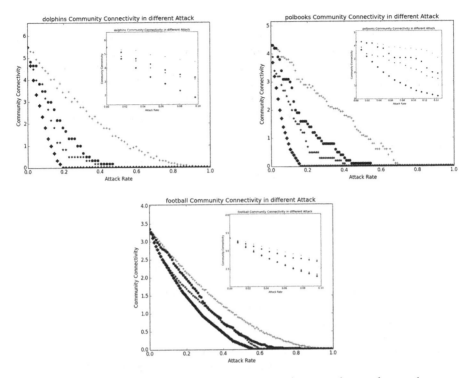

Fig. 3. The results of attacking vulnerability experiment on three real networks

between communities is robustness when facing the random removal of nodes, but is vulnerability when the removal is non-random especially removing the high value of betweenness or the node's connecting number of community. These three conclusions are more obvious in the real networks. In Fig. 3, if the node's removal strategy is the node's connecting number of community, the real network's global community connectivity will turn to 0 when the node's removal ratio is just 20 %. But when the strategy is RD or RB, the ratio will be 40 % or more. It means that there are very few nodes with high value of node's connecting number of community in real networks, but they play a very important role in the network's community connection.

5   Conclusions

The traditional researching of network's connectivity is mainly focused on the whole network or the node pairs. This article gives a new metric of measuring the network's connectivity from the meso level which is community. Based on this metric, it define a new property of node which could reflect the node's importance in network's community connection. Then it proves that the network's community connectivity is robustness when facing the random removal of nodes, but vulnerability especially when removal of the nodes with high value of node's connecting number of community.

The future research can be carried out from the following aspects: first, the global community connectivity measure the whole connection situation of all the communities in network, it requires the knowledge of whole network structure. We can find new metrics of measuring some specified communities connectivity based on incomplete information of the network. Second, the network's community connectivity mainly influence the communication or synchronization of network, we can study the community connectivity's effect on these even use the related connectivity to control them.

Acknowledgement. This research is supported by the fund of the Natural Science Foundation of China (The number of the NSFC are U1435218, 61174035, 61273189, 61374179, 71401168 and 61403401) and we greatly appreciate their helping.

References

1. Albert, R., Jeong, H., Barabási, A.L.: Error and attack tolerance of complex networks. Nature **406**(6794), 378–382 (2000)
2. Newman, M.E.J., Forrest, S., Balthrop, J.: Email networks and the spread of computer viruses. Phys. Rev. E **66**(3), 035101 (2002)
3. Jeong, H., Mason, S.P., Barabási, A.L., et al.: Lethality and centrality in protein networks. Nature **411**(6833), 41–42 (2001)
4. Dunne, J.A., Williams, R.J., Martinez, N.D.: Network structure and biodiversity loss in food webs: robustness increases with connectance. Ecol. Lett. **5**(4), 558–567 (2002)
5. Latora, V., Marchiori, M.: Vulnerability and protection of infrastructure networks. Phys. Rev. E **71**(1), 015103 (2005)
6. Holme, P., Kim, B.J., Yoon, C.N., et al.: Attack vulnerability of complex networks. Phys. Rev. E **65**(5), 056109 (2002)
7. Jun, W.U., Barahona, M., Yue-Jin, T., et al.: Natural connectivity of complex networks. Chin. Phys. Lett. **27**(7), 078902 (2010)
8. Radicchi, F., Castellano, C., Cecconi, F., Loreto, V., Parisi, D.: Defining and identifying communities in networks. Proc. Natl. Acad. Sci. U.S.A. **101**, 2658–2663 (2004)
9. Girvan, M., Newman, M.E.J.: Community structure in social and biological networks. Proc. Ntl. Acad. Sci. **99**(12), 7821–7826 (2002)
10. Newman, M.E.J., Girvan, M.: Finding and evaluating community structure in networks. Phys. Rev. E **69**(2), 026113 (2004)
11. Clauset, A., Newman, M.E.J., Moore, C.: Finding community structure in very large networks. Phys. Rev. E **70**(6), 066111 (2004)
12. Newman, M.E.J.: Fast algorithm for detecting community structure in networks. Phys. Rev. E **69**(6), 066133 (2004)
13. Capocci, A., Servedio, V.D.P., Caldarelli, G., et al.: Detecting communities in large networks. Phys. A: Stat. Mech. Appl. **352**(2), 669–676 (2005)
14. Newman, M.E.J.: Finding community structure in networks using the eigenvectors of matrices. Phys. Rev. E **74**(3), 036104 (2006)
15. Arenas, A., Díaz-Guilera, A., Pérez-Vicente, C.J.: Synchronization reveals topological scales in complex networks. Phys. Rev. Lett. **96**(11), 114102 (2006)
16. Reichardt, J., Bornholdt, S.: Statistical mechanics of community detection. Phys. Rev. E **74**(1), 016110 (2006)

17. Bagrow, J.P.: Evaluating local community methods in networks. J. Stat. Mech. Theor. Exp. 49(5) (2008)
18. Newman, M.E.J., Peixoto, T.P.: Generalized communities in networks (2015). arXiv preprint arXiv:1505.07478
19. Karrer, B., Levina, E., Newman, M.E.J.: Robustness of community structure in networks (2007). arXiv preprint arXiv:0709.2108
20. Lemmouchi, S., Haddad, M., Kheddouci, H.: Robustness of emerged community in social network. In: Proceedings of the International Conference on Management of Emergent Digital EcoSystems, vol. 78. ACM (2009)
21. Lemmouchi, S., Haddad, M., Kheddouci, H.: Study of robustness of community emerged from exchanges in networks communication. In: Proceedings of the International Conference on Management of Emergent Digital EcoSystems, pp. 189–196. ACM (2011)
22. Lemmouchi, S., Haddad, M., Kheddouci, H.: Robustness study of emerged communities from exchanges in peer-to-peer networks. Comput. Commun. 36(10), 1145–1158 (2013)
23. Massen, C.P., Doye, J.P.K.: Thermodynamics of community structure (2006). arXiv preprint cond-mat/0610077
24. Li, H.J., Wang, H., Chen, L.: Measuring robustness of community structure in complex networks. EPL Europhys. Lett. 108(6), 68009 (2014)
25. Holme, P., Kim, B.J., Yoon, C.N., et al.: Attack vulnerability of complex networks. Phys. Rev. E 65(5), 056109 (2002)
26. Girvan, M., Newman, M.E.J.: Community structure in social and biological networks. Proc. Ntl. Acad. Sci. 99(12), 7821–7826 (2002)
27. Lancichinetti, A., Fortunato, S., Radicchi, F.: Benchmark graphs for testing community detection algorithms. Phys. Rev. E 78(4), 046110 (2008)
28. Lusseau, D., Schneider, K., Boisseau, O.J., et al.: The bottlenose dolphin community of Doubtful Sound features a large proportion of long-lasting associations. Behav. Ecol. Sociobiol. 54(4), 396–405 (2003)
29. Krebs, V.: Unpublished. www.orgnet.com

Optimization of Public Transit Network Caused by Adjustment of Land Use

Jinli Wei[✉], Shengyou Wang, Shouhui Duan, and Chen Qi

Collage of Automobile and Traffic, Qingdao University of Technology,
Qingdao 266520, Shandong, China
wjl827025@163.com

Abstract. The optimization problem of the urban Public Transit Network has been caused by the adjustment of land use during the process of urbanization in China. Combined with the system analysis method (ISM), two core issues have been solved in this paper: (1) how to generate the theory of optimal line network and (2) how to adjust the original line. The improved "ant colony algorithm" method has been used in accordance with the principle that: "one by one wiring and optimization is needed to develop a network". This introduced the optimal bus network theory, comparing the new and the old network, using the "pruning" line adjustment method. The optimization scheme of transit networks, verified the feasibility of the method through the instance and provided reference for urban road network optimization that caused by adjustment of land use.

Keywords: Public transit network · Land use · ISM · Ant colony algorithm · The "pruning" line adjustment method

1 Introduction

With the increased level of urbanization and the necessary expansion, many cities are in a period of readjustment. This expansion has included the adjustment of zoned areas and the transformation of old cities, which has resulted in direct infrastructure problems, where the cities have had to reintegrate and adjust the present transport resources. In order to meet the metropolitan traffic demand, many bus lines have needed to expand their existing lines, which has been difficult to plan and organize. In some instances the existing lines have needed to be re-generated to a new line. Considering this context, I have selected the "urban public traffic network adjustment optimization theory" for the adjustment of land used as the study aim. In this report we have analyzed the synergy amongst the public transport system and the land used in urban development. The study has avoided the waste of existing public traffic resources and has established the optimization model of the public traffic network. Most importantly it has promoted the city's public traffic system effectively.

At present, there are 3 methods, which used to optimize the current bus network both domestically and internationally. The first method considers that the whole network is optimal [1–3], the second that one by one wiring optimized the network [4, 5] and the third that combined with the present public transportation network to prefer-eliminate line [6–9]. The function of whole network optimal method is complex.

L. Zhang et al. (Eds.): AsiaSim 2016/SCS AutumnSim 2016, Part IV, CCIS 646, pp. 330–339, 2016.
DOI: 10.1007/978-981-10-2672-0_34

Multiple objectives and constraints appear in the optimization target at the same time and it has generated many influencing factors and constraints. The solution method is cumbersome and once applied in practice, can be much more difficult, especially if the network is relatively large. These multi-factors can interfere with each other, which often make the method of solving even become impossible. The latter two-optimization methods (one by one wiring and combination of present system) combined with routes merge, retain a reasonable part of the present network and are a simple and practical public transportation network optimization method. Therefore, this paper has combined and developed this optimization theory to its research. The combination of planning and the optimization method analyses the following information. The research begins at the land use to analyze the passenger flow at present and in future, combing with the first and the end station analysis. The optimization method is used to generate the optimal theory network, and is then contrasted with the present road network. One by one optimization alongside the line adjustment method is used to form the final optimal solution.

2 Analysis of Related Factors of City Public Traffic Network Layout

There are many factors, which affect the layout of urban public traffic network. These include passenger flow distribution, the structure and distribution pattern of urban land use and the urban nature and spatial extension form. We need to consider also the economic level of the city, the urban road network, engineering factors, and urban cultural and geographical conditions. Interpretative Structural Modeling Method [10] (ISM) was used to analyze the numerous factors in the relationship and hierarchy, as shown in Fig. 1.

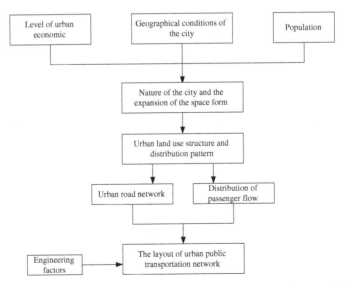

Fig. 1. Impact factor hierarchical relationship of urban public traffic network layout

As demonstrated in Fig. 1, the public traffic network and the land used for urban development must develop a cooperative relationship. This will be the most effective way to improve the public transport system and ensure that it runs efficiently and effectively. Distribution of passenger flow and urban road network are two direct factors influencing the network optimization, and are also the basis of parameter selection in optimization modeling.

3 The Optimized Process of Urban Public Transit Network for the Adjustment of Land Use

The outstanding problems (existing in connective band of public traffic network) are caused by the adjustment of land use. Issues such as low coverage, blind spot, lack of systematic operation, inconvenient transfer and large coefficient transfers all play a factor in the analysis. We need to investigate the present situation of the urban bus network and then generate the future distribution of passengers, combined with a passenger demand forecast. The wire mesh and optimization objectives and the first and last stop, and the use of improved ant algorithm are used to generate the theoretical optimal line network. The research will then compare the analysis of the original bus network, optimizing network through method of "pruning" line adjustment to adjust one by one to generate the final optimization program, finally verifying the feasibility of the final through the evaluation and illustrations authentication method. The specific optimization process is shown in Fig. 2.

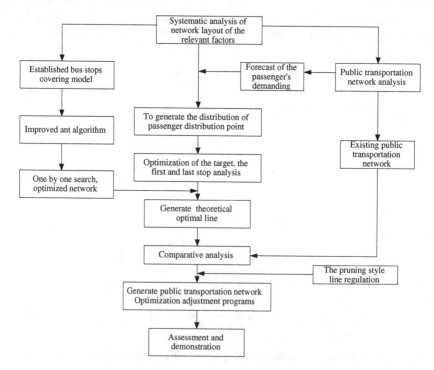

Fig. 2. Optimization process of public transportation network

3.1   Optimization Objective Analysis

This generally includes two adjusting ways: improving traffic accessibility and covering passenger flow. In order to improve the efficiency of the public traffic system and to reduce transit coverage holes, this paper combined the two ways simultaneously.

3.2   First and Last Stop Analysis

This analysis mainly include the size match with all levels of bus lines, as well as the existing first and last stop resource priority. Investigate the full use of the first and last station (existing resources) combined with the future passenger flow distribution to adjust bus line.

3.3   Improved "Ant Colony Algorithm"

"Ant colony algorithm" [11, 12] using the distributed parallel operation mechanism, is easy to combine with other methods. It is robust and is widely applied to combinatorial optimization problems. The traditional "ant algorithm" have to search for a long time and is easy to be restricted into local optimum solution. To solve this problem, this paper used the improved "ant algorithm" to generate an optimal line network.

Optimization ideas: place an artificial ant in each line of the existing bus start (final), according to "taste" [13] (traffic) and "pheromone" [13] (density) to determine the transition probability of ants from the site to the adjacent public site, and according to the transition probability decided to the next bus station. Continue to use this, until all the ants arrived with the origin-destination pair site, as shown in Fig. 3. In the process of optimization, dynamic direct passenger flow in unit time is the objective function, one by one search, and optimization into the net.

Using average passenger flow density [14] to initialize the pheromone matrix, as shown in Fig. 1.

$$\bar{\tau} = \frac{\sum\limits_{i,j \in N} P_{ij}}{\sum\limits_{i,j \in N} l_{ij}} \tag{1}$$

In formula: $\bar{\tau}$ is the pheromone matrix, and $\tau_{ij}(t)$ represents the number of pheromone on the time t path (i, j);

P_{ij} is the transition probability of site i to site j ;

l_{ij} is the length of the distance from the site i to the site j.

Ants transferred to other neighboring nodes, a node will try to transfer from their distance and the direction of the largest concentration of pheromone, the probability [15] is shown in Fig. 2.

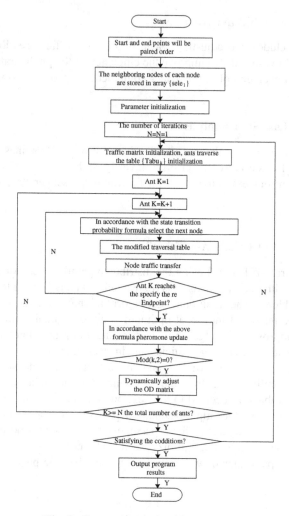

Fig. 3. Improved ant algorithm processes

$$
P_{ij}^k = \begin{cases} \dfrac{[\tau_{ij}^k]^\alpha \cdot [\eta_{ij}^k]^\beta}{\sum\limits_{s \in allowed_{i,k}} [\tau_{is}^k]^\alpha \cdot [\eta_{is}^k]^\beta} & if\ j \in allowed_{i,k} \\[4ex] 0 & the\ other \end{cases} \tag{2}
$$

In formula:

$allowed_{i,k} = \{sele_i - tabu_k\}$ means that the ant k Next is allowed to select the site, wherein: $sele_i$ indicates the i-th site adjacent to the site, which means ant k has reached the site;

f_{ij} is the amount of information of the ant k on the path (i, j);

α is the Information heuristic factor, reflecting the relative importance of the ant colony residual amount of information in the course of the campaign;

β is the Expectations heuristic factor, reflecting the the expectations relative importance degree;

η_{ij}^k is the ant k transferred by the site i to site j desired degree, known as heuristic function, the paper selected objective function that dynamically direct traffic heuristic function.

At the same time, in the correction rule of the pheromone, let best around the ant's release "pheromone", to ensure that the ants in excellent parents around the field complete more search. This improved "ant algorithm" can be used to improve convergence rate, and is more in line with the actual situation of the ant movement. It can be better used in the actual public traffic network optimization problem. Specific search process is shown in Fig. 3.

3.4   Line Regulation Way of "Pruning"

In the process of comparative analysis of the theoretical optimal network with the original public transportation network, there need to be some adjustments to the original line alignments according to the relationship between the public transportation network and the traffic demand [16]. This includes line reserving, line canceling, line extension, line truncating, line diversions and line consolidation type.

- Line reservation

Preserved line which meets the following characteristics of the generated optimal line. Line assumes large passenger flow with various points along the flow more uniformed and familiar with the residents. The accepted traditional line; proper length contact of the city peripheral area or the suburbs (important township) and the central area of the line; line density smaller region for communication line etc.

- Line cancellation

For passengers with less demand, the operation is poor, and is inconsistent with the passenger flow in the main direction of line. Needs to be considered or cancelled. On line adjustment, needs to determine the sequence of analysis circuit.

- Line extension

When the extension of lines is required, this can eliminate bus service areas, expand transit service scope and completely replace some shorter lines. This would reduce the duplication of routes however connecting rail transit; large transport hubs or bus stop is not ideal. Can consider to extend the line; adjusting mode as shown in Fig. 4.

- Line truncation

For the lines that contact the periphery area of city suburbs including the city center. If it is too long, and into the city center area, we may need to consider the operation management and prevent driver fatigue. The general choice in public transit

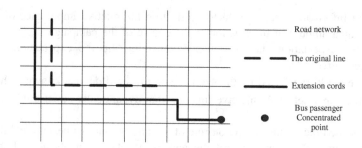

Fig. 4. Chart of bus line extension

hub is truncated at the city center and passengers can transfer to other lines from the central area.

- Line diversion

Too intensive bus lines in the city center on the road to consider diversion, take the other parallel lines; speed or bus routes through high requirements, can be diverted to fill the blank area of expressway transit or peripheral bus coefficient smaller area; for the rural poor road conditions, on and off staff less lines may also consider diverse road, diversion conditions better and travel more along the way.

- Line combination

For the road line overlap coefficient large, can consider to merge some can completely replace the line, in order to facilitate the operation, reduce the operation cost, improve operation efficiency. The adjustment method as shown in Fig. 5.

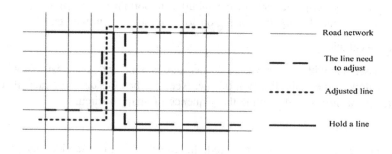

Fig. 5. Chart of bus line consolidation

4 The Example Analysis

In accordance with the approval of the State Council in 2012, Qingdao part of administrative division adjustment; the administrative region of Huangdao District and the county Jiaonan city as the new administrative area of Huangdao District. With the establishment of the new district, the bus integration trend is imperative, especially considering the current bus problems, which exist in two districts. These include connecting regional and rural, whilst considering the existing blind area, high transfer rate, the phenomenon of line settings duplicating and multiple site settings being unreasonable. This is shown in Fig. 6.

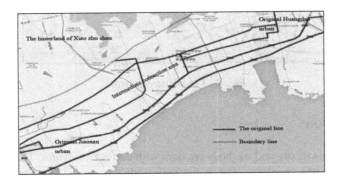

Fig. 6. The present situation of public transit network in Huangdao

Through forecasting the bus transit demand, generated the passenger flow distribution of 2035, as shown in Fig. 7. Using the method of improved "ant algorithm" to generate theory optimal bus network, compared with the existing road network, used the "pruning" line adjustment technology to adjust the bus line, obtained adjusted network, as shown in Fig. 8.

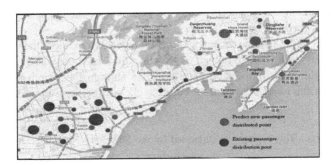

Fig. 7. The passenger distribution of new Huangdao in 2035

Using the selected evaluation index, such as the line density, the rate of line repetition, the unbalanced coefficient of direction, transfer coefficient, to establish evaluation index system to evaluate the optimized network. Compared with the original network, the length of the optimized line increased by 101.7 km, the average line density increased to 3.13 km/km2, has reached the requirement of the specification, the rate of line repetition is 1.88, the number of duplicated lines is reduced, the efficiency of line use has been improved.

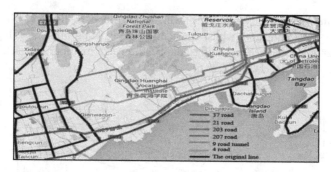

Fig. 8. The adjusted network

5 Conclusions

The study of this theory and methods are born with current hot issues. Through out the urban development, problems, such as the zoning adjustment and the transformation of the old city, have become universal phenomenons in the process of urbanization. Accordingly, we take the system analysis methods which combined with the macro and micro approaches in this paper, proceed from the adjustment of urban land-use, to form the future passenger flow distribution. Combining this with the graph theory and utilizing the combination of planning forms a new public transportation network. Optimization ideas combined with the actual subject of the Huangdao District verifies the reliability and usefulness of the theory and provides the new ideas. The method of the public transportation network optimization for the city, faces the adjustment of land-use and maximizes the use of existing resources to solve the bus problem. This enables us to obtain the greatest social and economic benefits, and to realize the intensive "green travel".

With respect to the search efficiency of the ant algorithm method, the improvements can be listed as follows: Combined with allocation methods, such as simulated annealing, genetic algorithms, tabu algorithms, to shorten the search path, and The improvement of the objective function. Future work will be focused on improving the above aspects.

Acknowledgments. This research is supported by the Shandong Natural Science Foundation (ZR2014EEP023).

References

1. Hong, L., Qu, S.Y.: The ranking of optimization schemes of public traffic line network based on set-pair and entropy analysis. Adv. Mater. Res. **790**, 484–487 (2013)
2. Bar-Yosef, A., Martens, K., Itzhak, B.: A model of the vicious cycle of a bus line. Trans. Res. Part B Methodological **54**, 37–50 (2013)

3. Xu, J., Yang, J., Yao, L.: Transportation structure analysis using sd-mop in world modern garden city: a case study in china. Discrete Dynamics Nat. Soc., **2012** (2012), Article ID 710854

4. Chen, M., Niu, H.: A model for bus crew scheduling problem with multiple duty types. Discrete Dyn. Nat. Soc., **2012** (2012), Article ID 649213

5. Euchi, J., Rafaa, M.: The urban bus routing problem in the Tunisian case by the hybrid artificial ant colony algorithm, Swarm and Evolutionary. Computation **2**, 15–24 (2012)

6. Wang, J., Zhu, R.: Efficient intelligent optimized algorithm for dynamic vehicle routing problem. J. Softw. **6**(11), 2201–2207 (2011)

7. Moura, J.L., Borja, A.: A two-stage urban bus stop location model. Net. Spat. Econ. **12**(2), 403–420 (2012)

8. Umapathy, P., Venkataseshaiah, C., Senthil Arumugam, M.: Application of interval arithmetic in the evaluation of transfer capabilities by considering the sources of uncertainty. Discrete Dyn. Nat. Soc. **2009** (2009), Article ID 527385

9. Hacker, J.F., Krykewycz, G.R., Meconi, J.M., Dashes, D.: Transit planning outreach and education in a board game format. Trans. Res. Record **12**, 127–134 (2009)

10. Shivraj, K., Bhatnagar, V.V.: Beyond generic models for information system quality: the use of interpretive structural modeling (ISM). Syst. Res. Behav. Sci. **19**(6), 531–549 (2002)

11. Xingguo, C., Nanfeng, X.: Parallel implementation of dynamic positive and negative feedback ACO with iterative. J. Inf. Comput. Sci. **10**(8), 2359–2370 (2013)

12. Yong, L., Sheng, W., Fangmin, D., Dong, R.: A two stage method for VRP based on the improved ant colony algorithm. Int. J. Model. Ident. Control **18**(2), 174–181 (2013)

13. Poorzahedy, H., Farshid, S.: An ant system application to the bus network design problem: an algorithm and a case study. Public Transp. **6**(2), 165–187 (2011)

14. Wang, Y.: Constraint cellular, ant algorithm for the multi-objective vehicle routing problem. J. Softw. **8**(6), 1339–1345 (2013)

15. Zhang, J., Liu, S., He, Z., Cai, Z.: A physical topology-aware chord model based on ACO. J. Comput. **6**(12), 2711–2718 (2011)

16. Piwonska, A., Jolanta, K.: Evolutionary algorithms find routes in public transport network with optimal time of realization. Commun. Comput. Inform. Sci. **104**, 194–201 (2010)

A New Method of Evacuation Under Fire Environment

Jing Zhou[1,2], Xiao Song[1,2(✉)], and Zenghui Zhang[1,2]

[1] School of Automation Science and Electrical Engineering,
Beihang University, Beijing, China
[2] Engineering Research Center of Complex Product Advanced
Manufacturing System, Ministry of Education, Beijing, China
{zhoujing10365,609098664}@qq.com,
songxiao@buaa.edu.cn

Abstract. Fire is one of the most deadly disaster in human life. Large quantities of people lose their life every year. Recently, researchers have carried out a great number of studies and simulations, however, few of which focus on evacuation in fire environment, let alone the impact on human health of fire's products. This paper proposes an improved social force model for fire situation. A method for outputting data from Pyrosim and inputting data to Anylogic was introduced. The visibility and toxic gas dose at are used to determine the motion speed, direction and health condition of pedestrian. The social force model is implemented in pedestrian modeling, which makes simulation real and intelligent.

Keywords: Evacuation · Social force model · Anylogic · Pyrosim

1 Introduction

The research of pedestrian evacuation in fire environment has guiding significance to design on building fire protection, the establishment of personnel safety evacuation plan and fire rescue work, etc. Computer simulation is a more economical and effective way of research according to the actual phenomenon and the general law of pedestrian movement.

The most typical evacuation model is the social force model proposed by Helbing [1, 2]. It is used to quantify the physical effects between a person and environment and psychological effects among people into repulsive force, attractive force and self-driving force, described by Newton's second law. AnyLogic [3] is a widely used modeling and simulation tool which supports discrete, continuous, system dynamics, multi-agent and hybrid systems modeling. Its pedestrian library adopts social force model, accurately simulating the influence of environment and surrounding people to one's action.

In actual fire environment, the spread of smoke is key factor affecting the safety evacuation of personnel. On the one hand, the ability of pedestrian under fire smoke atmosphere to choose the correct evacuation and the movement speed would be lowered due to reduced visibility. On the other hand, inhaling much smoke, poison gas or lacking oxygen can cause death. According to statistics, about 75 %–85 % of the

© Springer Science+Business Media Singapore 2016
L. Zhang et al. (Eds.): AsiaSim 2016/SCS AutumnSim 2016, Part IV, CCIS 646, pp. 340–348, 2016.
DOI: 10.1007/978-981-10-2672-0_35

deaths building fire are caused by smoke. At present, most evacuation research in fire environment are based on smoke toxicity evaluation model (such as Fractional Effective Dose) [6] and conduct general evaluation of evacuation. Fire Dynamics Simulator (FDS) is a computational fluid dynamics (CFD) model of fire-driven fluid flow, developed by VTT Technical Research Centre of Finland and National Institute of Standards and Technology (NIST), can predicts smoke, temperature, carbon monoxide, and other substances during fires [6]. Smokeview is a software tool designed to visualize numerical calculations generated by FDS. It visualizes smoke and other attributes of the fire using traditional scientific methods such as displaying tracer particle flow, 2D or 3D shaded contours of gas flow data [7]. PyroSim is a graphical user interface for the Fire Dynamics Simulator (FDS), integrating FDS (version 5 and 6) and Smokeview. Its biggest feature is the visual construction of the model, freeing the user from tedious and complex command lines in FDS modeling [8].

This paper is organized as follows: Improved pedestrian evacuation model is described in Sect. 2. Section 3 explains the method to construct Anylogic evacuation model based on output data of FDS. It contains introduction of FDS model, how to get FED and visibility. Simulation and result discussion are described and analyzed in Sect. 4. We simulates the fire in friendship palace of Karamay in 1994. Finally we conclude our conclusion and future work in Sect. 5.

2 Improved Pedestrian Evacuation Model

2.1 Classical Social Force Model

According to the social force model, the change of velocity in time is given by the acceleration Eq. (7) [1].

$$m_i \frac{dv_i}{dt} = m_i \frac{v_i^0(t)e_i^0(t) - v_i(t)}{\tau_i} + \sum_{j(\neq i)} f_{ij} + \sum_W f_{iW} \qquad (1)$$

Where $m_i \frac{dv_i}{dt}$ is the sum of the social forces influencing pedestrian i.

e_i^0 is the direction to the desired target. Pedestrian tends to adapt the actual velocity v_i with a certain characteristic time τ_i.

$\sum_{j(\neq i)} f_{ij}$ and $\sum_W f_{iW}$ are the repulsive forces to keep safety distance to other pedestrians and obstacles respectively.

2.2 Improved Social Force Model for Fire Situation

The classical social force model doesn't consider the impact of fire on pedestrians. In fire situation, the smoke visibility influences the evacuation routes choice and evacuation speed of pedestrians.

In general, the greater the smoke concentration is, the worse the visibility is. Thus, the pedestrians are more inclined to conduct blind action. So we use the weighted average of the random motion and the deterministic motion to determine the motion direction:

$$e_i(t) = (1 - \gamma_i)e_i^0(t) + \gamma_i e_i^R(t) \tag{2}$$

Where $e_i^0(t)$ is the correct direction; $e_i^R(t)$ is random direction; γ_i is weight coefficient, determined by the visibility of current location. When visibility is low, γ_i should be close to 1. Otherwise, γ_i should be close to 0. In view of this, we use the hyperbolic tangent function to describe it:

$$\gamma_i = \frac{1 + \tanh(-\xi(S_v - S_0))}{2} \tag{3}$$

Where ξ is an attenuation coefficient, S_0 is a threshold of visibility, determined according to the fire scene. British national standard BSDD240 [4] suggested that in large space the criterion of dangerous state is that visibility is less than 10 m. Babrauskas [5] thought that if the individual is familiar with the evacuation route in a small space, the visibility that can leads successful evacuation is just 1.6 m.

Additionally, under the smoke environment, low visibility will slow down the evacuation speed. FDS provides the calculation formula of the velocity variation under smoke environment [6]:

$$V_i^0(K_s) = Max\left\{ V_{i,min}^0, V_i^0\left(1 + \frac{\beta}{\alpha}K_s\right)\right\} \tag{4}$$

Where K_S is extinction coefficient, which can be obtained from Pyrosim slice, associated with visibility. $V_{i,min}^0 = 0.1 \cdot V_i^0$, V_i^0 is initial desired speed. Frantzich and Nilsson [9] conducted experiment to determine $\alpha = 0.706$ m/s, $\beta = -0.057$ m²/s.

Personnel casualties in the fire environment are mainly due to the inhalation of smoke and toxic gases. At present, the most widely used gas toxic evaluation model is FED proposed by Purser [10]. FED is calculated by measured exposure time and concentration of main toxic gas and comparing mixed gas FED. If the cumulative value of FED is greater than 1, it is considered that the individual is incapable of safely escaping. According to different composition of the gas, there are many kinds of calculating formula of FED. FDS uses the gas O2, CO2, and CO concentrations to calculate FED. Total FED value is calculated as follows [10].

$$FED_{tot} = FED_{CO} \times HV_{CO2} + FED_{O2} \tag{5}$$

Because the individual gas toxicity load is an accumulation process, we construct an iterative model of gas toxicity load:

$$L_i(t + \Delta t) = L_i(t) + FED_{tot}(i, j, t + \Delta t) \tag{6}$$

Where $L_i(t)$ represents the gas toxicity load of person p at integer time t. $FED_{tot}(i,j,t +\Delta t)$ is the value of cell or vertice person on at integer time t+Δt. If $L_i(t)$ is greater than 1, the person is viewed as incapacitation, whose social force is set to be 0.

Therefore, according to Eqs. (2), (4), (5), and (6), the improved acceleration equation is as follows:

$$\left\{ \begin{array}{l} m_i \dfrac{dv_i}{dt} = m_i \dfrac{Max\left\{ V_{i,min}^0, V_i^0\left(1 + \frac{\beta}{\alpha}K_s\right)\right\}\left[(1 - \gamma_i)e_i^0(t) + \gamma_i e_i^R(t)\right] - v_i(t)}{\tau_i} \\[2ex] \qquad + \displaystyle\sum_{j(\neq i)} f_{ij} + \sum_W f_{iW}(L_i(t) < 1) \\[2ex] m_i \dfrac{dv_i}{dt} = 0(L_i(t) \geq 1) \end{array} \right\} \tag{7}$$

3 FDS Based Evacuation Simulation

In this section, we mainly introduce a method to output the fire data and input it to AnyLogic.

3.1 Preprocessing of FDS Output Data

In this paper, we mainly investigate smoke toxicity effective dose FED and visibility of smoke environment in FDS simulation results. As smoke affects people by eyes and nose, we measure the relative data of smoke at an average height of 1.4 m. Thus, we add a horizontal slice with the height of 1.4 m as follows:

As shown in Fig. 1, the slice can obtain visibility, carbon monoxide volume fraction, carbon dioxide volume fraction, oxygen volume fraction and extinction coefficient at Z = 1.4 m plane. More specifically, considering that FDS computational region is grid, the slice, in fact, output the data of four points of each grid on plane. Thus, in AnyLogic, we continue to use the XY plane mesh method in FDS. For example, the horizontal calculation area is $[x_1, x_n] \times [y_1, y_n]$. $x_1...x_n$ and $y_1...y_n$ are the grid points on X axis and Y axis. Therefore, each rectangular area becomes a cell, such as $[x_i, x_{i+1}] \times [y_j, y_{j+1}]$, we regard it as Cell(i,j). The smoke data of Cell(i,j) at a certain time is the average value of its four vertices (x_i, y_j), (x_{i+1}, y_j), (x_i, y_{j+1}), (x_{i+1}, y_{j+1}). FED value of Cell(i,j) at time t is recorded as FED(i,j,t). Equally, visibility value is V(i,j,t). When a person goes into some Cell, if the time t is integer, he can get the smoke data of this Cell. As Fig. 2 shows, the green person can obtain the smoke date of the green cell at integer time t. It should be pointed out that if one happens to be on a vertice of a cell at integer time t, just like the red person on (x_{i+2}, y_j) in Fig. 2, he just gets the smoke data of this point.

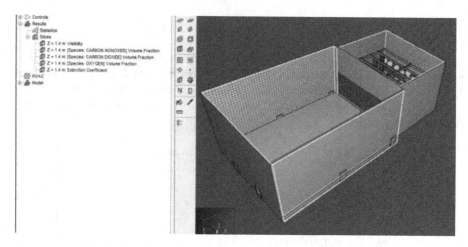

Fig. 1. The 1.4 m slice (pink) in pyrosim (Color figure online)

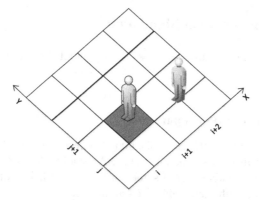

Fig. 2. Grid division (Color figure online)

3.2 Data Transfer from Pyrosim to Anylogic

Firstly, you should set up a proper fire scene including various parameters of building, Meshes, Reactions, and Materials. Here we don't mention the specific functions of parameters. If you want to build a more accurate fire model, which is the key point to the simulation, please refer to document [8].

Secondly, running model for a period of time, the result can be visualized in Smokeview. There is an executable file "fds2ascii" in FDS root directory "X:\... \PyroSim 2016(your edition)\fds", which is used to convert the slice files into .csv files in the model directory. Copying "fds2ascii.exe" to the model directory. You must make sure that the model has finished running before run the program. You will be asked a series of questions about which type of output file to process, what time interval to time average the data, and so forth.

However, the program has an extremely inconvenient disadvantage that it will be closed after output a file. That is to say, we must input the same options other than the different integer time t each time we run the program, which is impossible in several minutes long model because time unit is second. After programming to realize automatically outputting csv file, each output file has the following form (Fig. 3):

X	Y		SOOT VISIBILITY	CARBON DIOXIDE	CARBON MONOXIDE	OXYGEN VOLUME	SOOT EXTINCTION COEFFICIENT
m	m	m	mol/mol	mol/mol	mol/mol	1/m	
3.00E+00	3.00E+00	3.00E+01	3.87E-04	0.00E+00	2.08E-01	0.00E+00	
3.50E+00	3.00E+00	3.00E+01	3.87E-04	0.00E+00	2.08E-01	0.00E+00	
4.00E+00	3.00E+00	3.00E+01	3.87E-04	0.00E+00	2.08E-01	0.00E+00	
4.50E+00	3.00E+00	3.00E+01	3.87E-04	0.00E+00	2.08E-01	0.00E+00	

Fig. 3. The form of output files

As we can see, the first two columns are the coordinates of cell vertices. Each cell is a square with the side length 0.5 m. The third column is used to describe the spread of smoke, which we will introduce later. And the fourth, fifth, sixth and seventh columns correspond to Eq. (5).

Finally, we create several three-dimensional arrays in AnyLogic to save the csv data. The three dimensions are X coordinate, Y coordinate and time t. The time t should be in accordance with the t of output files.

4   Experiment

In this section, we simulate the big fire in The Friendship Palace of Karamay in 1994. Almost 200 of 710 students died by suffocation and poisonous gas.

Because the fire happened on the stage, we only simulate the audience area in Anylogic. The auditorium is a 25.5 m long, 20.9 m wide rectangular with six evacuation doors, however, according to the accident report [11], two of which were locked. Circles represent students, whose diameter is uniform distribution from 0.3 m to 0.34 m and desired speed is uniform distribution from 0.8 to 1.2 m/s. If someone inhales excessive toxic gas (FED > 1), the color of circle will turns red and actual speed changes to 0. Figure 4 shows the Anylogic simulation at 41 s.

According to the accident report [11], the fire was because the 1000 W lamp (surface temperature 600–800°C) above the stage was too close to curtain on the wall, causing the curtain burning and spreading to other 12 curtain quickly. We reproduce this scene in Pyrosim. The spread of smoke (visibility), FED and extinction coefficient are measured at horizontal slice Z = 1.4 m. Figure 5 shows the visibility of Pyrosim simulation at 41 s.

Through comparison between Figs. 4 and 5, it is obvious that we have succeeded in reproducing the fire condition in AnyLogic. Next, we conduct four experiments and the result is as Table 1 shows:

Table 1. Experiment setting and result

	No smoke		Smoke	
Four doors	Experiment1		Experiment3	
	Evacuation time	127 s	Evacuation time	152 s
	Average evacuation time	57 s	Number of incapacitation students	197
Six doors	Experiment2		Experiment4	
	Evacuation time	88 s	Evacuation time	132 s
	Average evacuation time	41 s	Number of incapacitation students	49

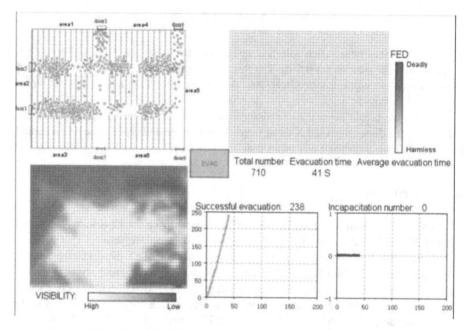

Fig. 4. AnyLogic simulation at 41 s. (Color figure online)

Fig. 5. Visibility of Pyrosim simulation at 41 s.

4.1 Analysis

Smoke appears at 1.4 m horizontal plane at 36 s. At the beginning of the smoke, the gas is not so toxic. There are still many students surviving during 50 s to 100 s. However, as the fire spread, FED value gradually increases, especially near door3 and door4, causing many students incapacitated.

From experiment 1 and 2, we can see the influence of four exits and six exits on evacuation without smoke. Table 1 shows that evacuation time is 127 s and average evacuation time is 57 s. Table 1 shows that evacuation time is 88 s and average evacuation time is 41 s. The two extra exits can significantly reduce the evacuation time and the average evacuation time, which is in line with actual situation.

From experiment 1 and 3, we can see the influence of smoke in four exits condition. Table 1 shows that evacuation time is 152 s, 25 s more than the time without smoke. This is because smoke slow down the pedestrian speed. Average evacuation time is meaningless because of there are 197 incapacitation students, close to the actual died students.

From experiment 3 and 4, we can see the influence of four exits and six exits on evacuation under smoke environment. Table 1 shows that evacuation time is 132 s, 20 s less than the time of four exits. More importantly, the incapacitation student number is 49, far less than the number in experiment 3.

5 Conclusion and Future Work

In this paper, we establish an evacuation model considering the fire and smoke environment. The evacuation utilizes the advantage of social force model, which avoids the complex movement rules of discrete model.

Fire dynamics simulation software FDS was used to simulate smoke spread. The staff smoke load and smoke density parameters are coupled to the AnyLogic pedestrian movement model. Smoke visibility determines the desired speed and motion direction of pedestrian under fire. And toxic gas load (FED) determines whether a person is incapacitated or not, so as to simulate the casualties under fire environment.

Some phenomena that are consistent with actual situation also appeared in the simulation cases. Such as: the staff crowded into a bow shape at the exit; Congestion will reduce the escape speed and so on. These verifies the rationality of the model.

In future work, we also want to consider following conditions into model: Increase individual differences, optimize the path selection and so on.

References

1. Helbing, D., Molnár, P.: Social force model for pedestrian dynamics. Phys. Rev. E (S1539-3755) **51**(5), 4282–4286 (1995)
2. Helbing, D., Farkas, I., Vicsek, T.: Simulating dynamical features of escape panic. Nature (S0028-0836) **407**(6803), 487–490 (2000)

3. Borshchev, A.: The Big Book of Simulation Modeling: Multimethod Modeling with Anylogic 6. AnyLogic North America, Chicago (2013)
4. British Standards Institution. Draft British standard BSDD240 fire safety engineering in building, Part 1: Guide to the application office safety engineering Principles (1997)
5. Babrauskas, V., Levin, B.C., Gann, R.G., et al.: Toxic potency measurement for fire hazard analysis. Fire Technol. (S0015-2684) **28**(2), 163–167 (1992)
6. McGrattan, K., McDermott, R., et al.: Fire Dynamics Simulator User's Guide. NIST Building and Fire Research Laboratory, Gaithersburg Maryland USA, NIST Special Publication 1019-5, April 2016
7. Forney, G.P.: Smokeview (Version6) - A Tool for Visualizing Fire Dynamics Simulation Data, vol. 1. User's Guide. NIST Special Publication 1017-1, April 2016
8. Thunderhead Engineering, PyroSim: A Model Construction Tool for Fire Dynamics Simulator (FDS), PyroSim User Manual. Thunderhead Engineering, Manhattan (2016)
9. Frantzich, H., Nilsson, D.: Utrymning genom tät rök: beteende och föflyttning, Report 3126, 75 p., Department of Fire Safety Engineering, Lund University, Sweden (2003)
10. Purser, D.A.: Toxicity assessment of combustion products. In: SFPE Handbook of Fire Protection Engineering, 5th edn. National Fire Protection Association, Quincy, Massachusetts (2016)
11. Jiang, A.H.: Karamay fire disaster. Zhejiang Firefighting **2**, 7–8 (1995)

A Review of Opinion Dynamics

Ziping Xie[1,2], Xiao Song[1,2(✉)], and Qiyuan Li[1,2]

[1] School of Automation Science and Electrical Engineering,
Beihang University, Beijing, China
ziping15@qq.com, songxiao@buaa.edu.cn
[2] Engineering Research Center of Complex Product Advanced
Manufacturing System, Ministry of Education,
Beijing, China

Abstract. Opinion dynamics utilize mathematical and physical models and agent-based computational modeling tools to describe the interactive features and rules among individuals, reduction and explain the opinion formation and evolution in the real life. Based on the analysis of the basic ideas and methods of the modeling of opinion dynamics, the main contents, characteristics and achievements of classical model and extended model of opinion dynamics are reviewed, and discussed the current research status. Finally, the main problems and challenges of opinion dynamics are analyzed, correspondingly, shed light on its future directions.

Keywords: Opinion dynamics · Modeling · Agent-based

1 Introduction

In recent years, the studies on opinion dynamics have attracted wide attention, especially in the statistical physics community; and many interesting outcomes have been reported. The studies on opinion dynamics cover a wide range of social phenomena, e.g. minority opinion survival and spreading, consensus building, emergence of political parties, emergence of fashions and fads, diffusion of rumor, expansion of extremism. These phenomena are the persisting topics of interest in many areas of social sciences.

The study of opinion dynamics is helpful to reveal the essential characteristics of the phenomenon of opinion and the deeper reasons and rules that behind the features. The study also has important significance for the further understanding and explanation of the generation and evolution of the complex group behavior of human beings.

As a cross-disciplinary field, the opinion dynamics has been studied by the scholars in the fields of statistical physics, social dynamics, social psychology and so on, drawing a number of classic theoretical model, which has a profound accumulation and a profound impact on the subsequent research.

© Springer Science+Business Media Singapore 2016
L. Zhang et al. (Eds.): AsiaSim 2016/SCS AutumnSim 2016, Part IV, CCIS 646, pp. 349–357, 2016.
DOI: 10.1007/978-981-10-2672-0_36

2 Modeling and Analysis Method

The modeling of opinion dynamics focusing on describing the information interaction process between individuals, namely the exchange of views between agents and the formation of opinion, therefor in the modeling, most of the mathematical modeling methods are agent-based modeling [2].

This kind of models usually assume that the agent involved in the interaction is composed of a group of individuals with a network of interpersonal relationships, and the individual's point of opinions represented by continuous or discrete values. In certain primary initial condition, the individual's perspective began to evolve. In the interaction of each view, some individuals of a group exchange their views according to the rules define by the model, to determine whether to change their views and the special value of changed. After repeated interaction of opinion, it is usually observed that the consensus, phase change, split and other macro phenomena of opinion occur in the group, and accompanied by the spring up phenomenon.

Compared to the analysis model, the majority model of opinion dynamic pay attention on the definition and description of individual characteristics, rules of inter-action between individual and local interaction characteristics. And often employ probabilistic or stochastic process characterization of individual heterogeneity and non rational characteristics, these discussions is difficult to calculate the evolution result of the model through analysis method. For this kind of model, the computer simulation and the observation and statistical processing of the simulation results are usually the most important methods, and the Monte Carlo method has been applied in a large number of applications.

An additional important aspect always present in opinion dynamic is topology, which describing who is interacting with whom, how frequently, and the intensity. So in the topology graph the vertexes represents the agents, and the edges define the possible interaction patterns [2], and the study of the effect of their nontrivial topo-logical properties on models of opinion dynamics is a hot topic.

The rise of complex networks has greatly stimulated researchers to improve and revise the classical model, and considering the heterogeneity of individual makes the model closer to reality. So the following of this paper will first introduce the basic network of complex network, then introduce the classical model of dynamic and outline the key work on opinion dynamics in terms of these models.

3 Basic Network Topology

The network is an important part of opinion dynamics researches. Using different network with the same rules of interact may end up with different results [5]. The simplest network is just lattice. Each nod has four neighbors, just like the lattice on a surface. The most obvious advantage of lattice is the simplicity. It is wildly used for researches could use it to eliminate independent variables, make sure the key points stand out [6], especially for innovating rules which has unknown effect of the network. The other advantage of lattice is it can visualize the spread of opinion in a simple way [7]. Instead of the data you get from a complex network, you can see your result clearly from a lattice by coloring the nods base on their opinion. It's not only good for popular science, but also give researchers a direct feeling of what is going on and what might happen, inspiring them to find the essential factor.

It has been a while since the complex network has been related to our society and used to study different social behavior such as the well-known research of six degree separation in 1967 [8]. Those early researches can be seen as initial tentative works of explaining our society in a mathematical way. Some outstanding models that are wildly considered as reflecting some critical features of real life social network such as NW [9]/WS [10] small world model or the BA scale free network model [11].

Those networks make a balance between randomness and organization, reflecting features of reality relationship network such as the small-worldness. Choosing the network related to the main parameter may give you more useful data and compare the influence of different network is still an open topic [12]. We list the basic network in the Table 1 and number these networks.

Table 1. Basic Network

Regulation Network	Lattice [13–17]	One-dimensional (One dimensional chain)
		Two-dimensional (square lattice)
		Three-dimensional (space lattice)
	One dimensional ring	
	Ring nearest neighbor regulation network	
	Complete graph [18]	
	Star-shaped network	
Random graph [19]		
WS-small world [20,21]		
NW-small world [9,22]		
BA-scale free [9, 23–26]		
Randomized group Network		

4   Classical Opinion Dynamics Model

Comprehensive using the modeling methods of social dynamics, complexity science, statistical physics and other disciplines, combined with the conclusions drawn from the study of social psychology that how individuals form and change their opinions, researchers proposed many models of opinion dynamics. And some of these models have had a profound impact on the following studies.

4.1   Ising Mode

Ising model, the physicist Emst ising created in the 1920s [27], the first is used as a model to explain the phase transition of ferromagnetic material. The model uses the discrete variables (+1, −1) to represent the magnetic poles to carry out the study of the physical phase transition. The abstract model was wise used because it has two kinds of characteristics: a simple expression and rich connotation. Only in the field of social science, it has been applied to the stock market, apartheid, political elections, etc.

Because in the opinion dynamics, the opinion of individuals can also be binary, such as +1 represent support, −1 represent opposition, and the individual's opinion correction by the influence of neighboring individual and the entire social trends. So the Ising model was introduced into the research of opinion dynamic. Pekalski simulate the finite temperature phase transition of Ising model on the NW Small world network [28]. Bartotozzi use the Ising model to study the opinion dynamic on the scale-free network, and it is considered that the distribution of the system's opinion is close to the Gauss distribution [29].

4.2   CA Model (Cellular-Automaton)

Cellular-Automaton (CA), also known as cellular automaton, is a kind of discrete mathematical model, which consists of space discrete cellular components, the state of each cellular component is determined by it' s own value, and is updated according to certain rules. The model was first used to study the biological reproduction. Sakoda first applied the model in the field of social science, to study the interaction process of a relocation center's staff [30]. Alves established a stochastic cellular automaton computer simulation model of democratic voting process [31]. In this model, voters will update their voting intentions according to their ideology and social influence which mainly includes the interaction between voters, the film degree of maintaining the original choice and the influence of the media.

The characteristics of cellular automaton are that the state of the individual is explicit, and the interaction rules are simple. These features, what make it the most popular research model in the early stage of theoretical development, also make it impossible to a more in-depth study the individual interaction in a complex state. So the model is used to test the characteristics of network structure. Tomassini compared the cellular automaton model in the structure of standard lattice and small world network, and found that the difference was significant, the small world network is more efficient and has strong robustness, and is less affected by random noise [32].

4.3   Voter Model

Voter model was first propose by Clifford and Sudbury (1973) and was used to study the competition of species and named "Voter model" by Holley and Liggtee in 1975. The model concerns the evolution process of opinion on particular issue and the individuals are in a specific space, suppose that the individual opinions are influenced by the neighboring individuals, and randomly select one of the neighbor's opinion as their own. It is a cellular automaton model with probability, and is equal to one dimension Ising model in the one dimensional lattice structure.

Although the voter model is a rather crude when describing the real process, it soon attract much attention for its simplicity. After the gradually rise of theory of complex network, the voter model with different network structure has become a hot research topic. The voter behavior on networks is dramatically different from that on lattices, which stated by Sood and Tendner (2001) [33]. Stellano applied the voter model in the WS small world network, and the results show that for a finite population, the time required to complete an interaction sort in the WS small world network is small than the one-dimensional lattice [34]. On the other hand, the study of survival rate shows that the voter dynamics will not make the system orderly. And Suchecki also applied this model to the BA scale-free network [35].

4.4   Majority Rule Model

Majority rule model, derived from the psychology of the "herd phenomenon", the basic rule is that the minority is subordinate to the majority in local group. In the model, at each iteration, a group of r agents is selected at random (a local group): as a consequence of interaction, all agents take the majority opinion inside the group. That is, the probability that an agent chooses to select an opinion in the iteration is proportional to the number of neighbors who hold the opinion. The model is usually applied to group discussions or debates, and it can be used to reveal the propagation and evolution of public opinion under the majority rule.

In the model that uses majority rule, the Galam model is the most famous. Galam used the Ising model to simulate the local majority principle in the election process and then proposed the Galam model [36]. The basic rule of Galam model is Local Majority Rule, that is, in a local group, individuals always reach consensus in the principle that the minority subordinate to the majority. The study of Galam model shows that in the evolution process of opinion, the public preference of the initial state has a decisive influence on the final polarization direction of the group. The impact of public preference on individuals' opinion comes from the exchange of opinions between individuals. So it can control the effect of public preferences by stopping or enhancing the communication between individuals [37]. Galam use the improved model and found that some opponents who always hold minority opinions will play an important role in the evolution of opinion [38–39]; when the proportion of the opponents is very small, the consensus can be reached in most individuals and the equilibrium of majority and minority is reached, but the evolution to the equilibrium state will be longer; when the proportion of opponents is greater than a certain limit, there will be two kinds of opinions take advantage by rotation. In addition, Galam et al. also studied the influence of the stubborn [40] and the extremists [41] on the evolution process. The relevant research work on the Galam model and its extension is introduced in detail in the literature [38].

4.5   Szanjd Model

The Sznajd model is based on the Ising model which describes the ferromagnetic phase transition in physics [42]. We know that convincing somebody is easier for two or more people than for a single individual. This is the basic principle behind the Sznajd model. The model first defines simple interaction rules between individuals and the basic essence is "united we stand, divide we fall": interaction leads to some of the particles are completely by the influence of other particles, and accept the opinions of those particles, give up their own point of opinion. The running results of the model show that there are only two possible states in a closed system: dictatorship and deadlock; the individuals that have changed their opinion will further change his opinion; a group that hold consistent opinion can make the system into a state of deadlock; but the group which want to has 50 % winning probability is required to contain more than 70 % of the individual, rather than only more than half which is usually thought.

5 Comparison

The opinion dynamics models that described above look completely different, but there are some common characteristics between them, so they can be divided into several categories. Essentially, the aforementioned models all follow the bottom-up modeling approach to study the evolution of opinion. The bottom-up modeling approach, that is, by investigating the micro, individual, simple, local, nonlinear interactions to investigate the emergence of abnormal complex and the macro behavior of a group. This kind of model is the focus of academic research, and from the Ising model to Cellular-Automaton model, Sznajd model and the most of the models evolved later are this kind of model, which can reflect the development and evolution of opinion by setting the individual state and interaction rules. For the opinion dynamics model, there are several key modeling elements: the representation of an opinion (discrete or continuous), the local interaction rulesand the environment of interaction. These three elements determine the characteristics of the opinion dynamics model, which is to form a special opinion dynamics model. In addition to these three basic modeling elements, there are other factors, such as the impact of zealots, the impact of external forces and considering individual heterogeneity and so on. The Table 2 summarizes and compares the aforementioned models under the consideration these modeling elements.

6 The Development Trend of Opinion Dynamics Research

6.1 The Relative Simplicity of Statistical Physics Model and the Complexity of the Network Public Opinion Still Need to Be Coordinated

On the one hand, applying statistical physics model to social science, simplifying the individual interaction of multi levels as a series of mathematical rules, we can gain insight into the change process of the relationship between the micro (psychological, individual) and the emergence of macro (social, cultural) properties. The interaction of individual opinion in the opinion dynamics can be based on the interaction of particles in the field of physics, and the interpersonal relationship network is also consistent with the characteristics of small world and scale-free of complex network, so the use of statistical physics model to simulate the opinion evolution can reflect the microscopic generation mechanism.

The future research should pay more attention to the intersection of disciplines, fully integrating the natural system and social system, closely combining the evolvement mechanism of opinion dynamics model and the real event of public opinion, at the same time considering the social and cultural factors.

Table 2. The summarizes and compares of models

model		Environmental structure	the number of interacting neighbors	randomly select neighbors	interaction rules	final result	Application	reference basic model	reference Extended model
Ising		①	2	✗	individual opinions is influenced by the neighbors and the trend of whole society (external stimulation T_s)	if T>TC ,there is an abrupt disappearance of dominant opinion in the community (phase transition)	stock market, election,pu blic opinion research	[27] [67]	[23] [68] [69] [31]research the dynamic on BA
		②	4	✗					
		③	8	✗					
		④	determined by the degree of each node	✗					[28]
		⑤(BA)	determined by the degree of each node	✗					[29]
CA(Cellular-Automata)	②	①	define radius r to determine neighbors	✗	the dynamics function which determine the cellular state of the next moment according to the current state of the cell. $S(t+l)=f(S_{t-t}, S_{t}, ..., S_{t}, ..., S_{t+t})$ the dynamic function is the core of cellular automata, which make the evolution of CA to be ever changing	the random initial states with different approval rate wil reach the corresponding stable final state with time. But the final approval rate are in different phase with the different of initial approval .And the ranges of the parameters of each phase are different because of different neighborhood	biological reproducti on,voting,p ublic research,co mmunicati on,transpor tation	[30]	[70] [74]based on fuzzy cellular automata rules
		4-neighborhood	4	✗					
		8-neighborhood	8	✗					
		extended-neighborhood	24	✗					
		③	l	✗					
		②	determined by the degree of each node	✗		in the small world network,cellular automata model is more efficient and has stronger robustness			[29]
Voter		①	two choose one	✓	the selected neighbor's opinion as their own opinion	$t_s \propto N^2$	election, voting	[71]	[12] [72] [73] [14]add zealots [77] add noise [80]take the heterogeneous of individuals into account [82]the single-type zealotry voter model (using the makovian property of voter dynamics)
		②	four choose one	✓		$t_s \propto NlnN$			
		③	eight choose one	✓		$t_s \propto N$			
		②	choose one from D, (D, represents the degree of i)	✓		After a period of time ,the system convergence	the ordering process takes a time shorter than on a regular lattice of the same size		[74],[75] [76]
		④(BA)	choose one from D, (D, represents the degree of i)	✓			the size of an ordered domain is sensitive to the network disorder and the average degree,decreasing with both.		[35]
Majority rule(Galam model)		①	choose 3 neighbors from N	✓	(1)The G near neighbors of a singular continuous local area is randomly selected from a N-system with a finite number of dimension D, where G=2*D+1. (2)the state of the G neighbors is changed according to the majority state of G.	After a period of time ,the system convergenc (The only system that has the potential to develop into a consistent approval state from a minority approval)	election, voting, public opinion research	[36]	[5] [38] [78]-[85] [78]-[85]descripe the hierarchical voting theory
		②	choose 5 neighbors from N	✓		the initial approval density p=0.5 is a transition point.when p<0.5,the system finally reaches a stable state of opposition; when p>0.5,the system finally reaches a stable state of approval			
		③	choose 7 neighbors from N	✓					
		②	choose r neighbors from N to form a small group	✓	update the selected groups of nodes adopt the state of the majority inside the group				
Sznajd		④		✗			economi c, polotical market finance	[42] [49]	[87],[19], [88]-[92], [42]introduce a random noise to the Sznajd model
		①		✗	if $S_i * S_{i+1}=1$, $S_{i-1}=S_i=S_{i+1}=S_{i+1}$ if $S_i * S_{i+1}=-1$, $S_{i-1}=S_{i+1},S=S_{i+1}$ (now,the model does not consider the second rule)	there are noly two possible states in a close system: dictatorship and deadlock. the probability that all opinions are +1(or -1) is 1/4; the probability of confrontation is 1/4(the number of +1 and -1 is the same)			
	2	②		✗					
		③		✗					[87]join the leader
		②		✗					[43]
		②		✗					[47]
		⑩		✗					[93],[94]

Continuous	bounded confidence	Deffuant (inspired by the Axelrod model)	② four choose one	✔	base on the principle of bounded confidence, if $\|o_i - o_j\| < \varepsilon$	If t >0.5, the system will converge, the opinion tends to consistent; If t <0.5, the system will not converge, and will produce a certain number of opinion culters	poloitical, public opinion research, emergence of extremism	[95]	[97] [96]	[17]the role of threshold and network scale in the evolution of network public opinion
			⑧ N-1 choose one	✔						
			② randomly choose one from the neighbors	✔						
			⓪ randomly choose one from the neighbors	✔	$o(t+1) = o(t) + \mu*(o(t) - o(t))$ $o(t+1) = o(t) + \mu*(o(t) - o(t))$	when t >0.4 a full consensus is reached ,For smaller t no consensus is reached and the number F of fixed opinions increase with decreasing t .when the number N of people increase, the F small t also increases ∝N for large N.(diffemt with the random version)			[96]	
		H-K (similar to Deffuant when the average degree of the graph is low)	② r	✗	each node interacts with all its neighbors	the number of opinion cluste will increase with the decrease of t .And when the t is greate than a certain threshold,there will be only opinion cluster. There are only two possible values for the consensus threshold 3n4	poloitical, public opinion research, emergence of extremism	[60]	[59]	[59]a survey about no unde confidence model
			⑧ N-1	✗						
			⑧ determined by the degree of each node	✗	$o(t+1) = \frac{\sum_{\|o(t)-o(t)\|<\varepsilon} o(t)}{N}$					
			⓪ determined by the degree of each node	✗						
	CODA		① 2	✗	Agents never observe the value of p, of other agents, only the choices made by agents the interact with,after observing other agents choices,each agent update its own probabilities using a simple Bayesian calculation. $u = \ln(\frac{p_i}{1-p_i})$ U can be translate back to p_i	Increasing contact between different opinions teng to make agents less extreme	advertising	[63]	[13],[14] [18],[99][64]	[64]effect of different networks on extremism
			② 4	✗						
			⑧ 8	✗						
			⑧ N-1	✗						
			② determined by the degree of each node	✗						

6.2 The Cooperative Evolution of Network Topology and Opinion Need to Be Studied in-Depth

The topology of complex networks has a variety of evolutionary types: the evolution of network components, the evolution of network weights, the different evolution mechanism of network, whether the network form changes, these development and evolution may play a role in the evolution of opinion.

In the evolution of network structure, there are some research results about the directed and weighted network. As the *World Wide Web*, the paper citation network, the spreading and evolution of opinion is also directed. However, most of the current evolution models ignore the directed of network, and how to design the opinion dynamics model with directed is worth studying in the future [69]. Weighted network can reflect the topology and the dynamic characteristics of real network. Although there have been some representative models such as DM model [70], but the weighted network will still be one of the key research directions in the future[72]. And in real world, there are many factors to determine the weighted and the factors are dynamic changed, so the weighted network of research is a complex and arduous task.

6.3 Establish Unified Standard for Opinion Dynamics

The development of opinion dynamics is the result of the joint endeavors of many disciplines. However, the related endeavors are largely uncoordinated, so there is phenomena of "re-discovery" and the chaos of measures that used in different branches continue to grow, which is not conducive to its further development. These are problems left over by history but have to be fixed. For this flaw, it's hard to compare the result of different works or build a structure of subject for the use of word is not rigorous. So bridging works for opinion dynamics are needed desperately, it could be a painful process but it has to be done. And some work has been done [73], which is a good start.

References

1. Xia, H., Xuan, Z.: Opinion dynamics: a multidisciplinary review and perspective on future research. Int. J. Knowl. Syst. Sci. 2(4), 72–91 (2011)
2. Castellano, C., Fortunato, S., Loreto, V.: Statistical physics of social dynamics. Rev. Mod. Phys. 81, 591–646 (2009)
3. Fudenberg, D., Tirole, J.: Game Theory. China Renmin University Press, Beijing (2002)
4. Weibull, J.: Evolutionary game theory. Shanghai People's Publishing House, Shanghai (2006). Wang, Y., Translation
5. Ding, F., Liu, Y., Shen, B., Si, X.-M.: An evolutionary game-theory model of-binary opinion formation. Phys. A 389, 1745–1752 (2010)
6. Wen, L.S., Liang, X., Zhong, J., Long, B.: Oscillation-of-the-NCO-model. Phys. A 391, 3300–3307 (2012)
7. Balankin, A.S.: Miguel Ángel Martínez Cruz. Effect of initial concentration and spatial heterogeneity of active agent distribution on opinion dynamics. Phys. A 390, 3876–3887 (2011)
8. Karinthy, F.: Chain-Links. Translated from Hungarian and annotated by A. Makkai and E. Jankó
9. Newman, M.E.J., Watts, D.J.: Renormalization group analysis of the small-world network model. Phys. Lett. A 263, 341–346 (1999)
10. Watts, D.J., Strogatz, S.H.: Collective dynamics of small-world networks. Nature 393, 440–442 (1998)
11. Barabási, A.-L., Réka, A.: Emergence of scaling in random networks. Science 286, 509–512 (1999)
12. Javarone, M.A.: Social influences in opinion dynamics: the role of conformity. Phys. A 414, 19–30 (2014)
13. Martins, A.C.R.: Discrete opinion models as a limit case of the CODA model. Phys. A 395, 352–357 (2014)
14. Deng, L., Liu, Y., Xiong, F.: An opinion diffusion model with clustered early adopters. Phys. A 392, 3546–3554 (2013)
15. Diao, S.-M., Liu, Y., Zeng, Q.-A., Luo, G.-X., Xiong, F.: A novel opinion dynamics model based on expanded observation ranges and individuals social influences in social networks. Phys. A 415, 220–228 (2014)
16. Kurmyshev, E., Juárez, H.A., González-Silva, R.A.: Dynamics of bounded confidence opinion in heterogeneous social networks: concord against partial antagonism. Phys. A 390, 2945–2955 (2011)
17. Luo, G.-X., Liu, Y., Zeng, Q.-A., Diao, S.-M., Xiong, F.: A dynamic evolution model of human opinion as affected by advertisin. Phys. A 414, 254–262 (2014)
18. Weimer-Jehle, W.: Cross-impact balances Applying pair interaction systems and multi-value Kauffman nets to multidisciplinary systems analysis. Phys. A 387, 3689–3700 (2008)

Simulation-Based Population Dynamics Analysis: Korean Population Aging

Jang Won Bae$^{(\boxtimes)}$, Euihyun Paik, and Karandeep Singh

Department of Big Data Intelligence Research,
Electronics and Telecommunications Research Institute, Daejeon, Korea
jwbae@etri.re.kr

Abstract. Many countries have experienced demographic problems. Population aging in Korea is, for example, considered as the representative and severe one. To analyze such population changes, this paper applied modeling and simulation method from the micro-level perspective. Specifically, this paper introduce Korean population dynamics model, and this model was designed with micro population data and population statistics in Korea. Using the developed model, we performed virtual experiments to estimate future population dynamics. Through the result analyses, this paper presents how the future Korean population would move and suggests socio-economic factors that are related with the progress of Korean population aging.

Keywords: Simulation-based analysis · Population aging · Demographic analysis · Korean population aging

1 Introduction

As social and economic advances in modern times, many countries recently have experienced various demographic problems. One representative problem is *population aging*. Population aging is a shift in the distribution of a country's population towards older ages due to increasing life expectancy and decreasing fertility rate. This population problem has been widely spread in and Europe regions, and it would affect the form of work, families, health, education, and technology of the world's population [1].

In particular, population aging in Korea has been rapidly progressed: Korea became an aged society (over 65 years population takes 7 % of the overall population) in 2000 and is predicted to become an aging and a super-aging society (over 65 years population takes 14 % and 20 % of the overall population) before 2020 and 2030. Moreover, the period of transferring aging to super-aging society in Korea is estimated as 23 years, which is even faster than other advanced countries (e.g., France, and Sweden took 115 and 85 years). To alleviate Korean population aging, Korean government established economic and welfare policies, yet their effectiveness has been hardly seen.

To tackle population problems, many demographic researchers have been studied about population dynamics. Population dynamics helps to see the future

© Springer Science+Business Media Singapore 2016
L. Zhang et al. (Eds.): AsiaSim 2016/SCS AutumnSim 2016, Part IV, CCIS 646, pp. 358–367, 2016.
DOI: 10.1007/978-981-10-2672-0_37

population and establish political strategies for dealing with future population problems [2]. One approach for the population dynamics analysis is modeling and simulation. In particular, micro-level modeling and simulation provides individual features about how population structures were developed and how they would be evolved in the future. It also means that the micro-level modeling and simulation could also deliver key information for mitigating the population aging problem.

This paper introduces Korean population dynamics model, and the developed model describes behaviors and interactions of individuals in Korean population, i.e., from the micro-perspective. Behaviors and Interactions of an individual are modeled by stochastic process and rule-based interaction based on real-data, such as micro-population data and population statistics. We utilized also the real-data in the model development and initialization.

Using the developed model, virtual experiments were conducted. The virtual experiments were designed with varying parameters of behavioral models and rule-based interactions, and the experiment results are measured by demographic indexes for population aging, such as aging index, elderly dependency ratio, and median age of the population [3]. The result analysis shows Korean population aging has been progressed since 2010, and it becomes far worse after 2030. Also, we performed meta-modeling analysis on the experiment results to investigate significant factors that lead to the population aging. We expect those factors would be used to mitigate or hold Korean population aging.

This paper is organized as follows: Sect. 2 illustrates previous research about population dynamics and analysis; Sect. 3 introduces the developed model, Korean population dynamics model; Sect. 4 and 5 presents the design and results of virtual experiments; Sect. 6 concludes this paper.

2   Related Works

Population dynamics has been analyzed using analytical and simulation models. One famous example of the analytical models is Thomas Malthus's model [4]. There has been several methods for the analytical models of population dynamics, such as differential equation, matrix-based model, and the optimization model. Based on these methods, more complex analytical models have been invented for resolving current population problems.

Simulation-based analysis on population dynamics has been also widely used. It is considered as an important method for studying natural population dynamics [5]. The classic method for simulation-based population dynamics analysis is microsimulation model invented by Orcutt [6]. Microsimulation model describes a population by the aggregation of individuals, and each individual is modeled using micro population data, e.g., Census data in US. Another simulation method is agent-based model. Agent-based model is also based on the bottom-up approach for modeling population dynamics, yet it rather focuses on the interaction among individuals in the population. Such simulation methods have been applied to estimated the future population changes and public policies.

There are several studies for the analysis on population aging using the above methods: Prettner investigated the population aging from long-run economic growth perspectives by incorporating endogenous growth models and semi-endogenous growth models [7]. Börsch-supan et al. developed a simulation model describing general equilibrium model for population aging and pension reform [8]. Auerbach et al. presented a simulation model for demographic changes of aging population with respect to bequest behavior, technological change, and economic policy [9]. These previous works dealt with population aging and its derived problems, but they were limited in applying real-data from the population of interest and performing the analysis in various situations.

3   Korean Population Dynamics Model

We developed Korean population dynamics model to estimate future population changes and investigate social factors associated with the aging society. Korean population dynamics model is developed by the combined modeling approach of microsimulation and agent-based model, which means the agent behaviors are expressed as stochastic process and rule-based interactions [10]. The future population changes are estimated by the aggregation of individual changes as the simulation executes. The following subsections introduce the details of Korean population dynamics model.

3.1   Individual Modeling

Korean population dynamics model consists of a large number of agents that are corresponded with individuals in the population. The individual agents would conduct their behaviors during simulation execution, and their collective behaviors produce the population changes (e.g., the population size and age distribution). This section explains how we developed the individual agents.

We designed individual agent to hold attributes (or states) and behaviors (refer to individual in Fig. 1). Their behaviors are selected by the consideration of the relationship of Korean population size and age distribution, and the attributes are successively determined by the relationship of the selected behaviors. Specifically, we defined agent behaviors as mortality, fertility, education, economy, matrimony, and migration. Mortality and fertility directly affects the population changes, and other behaviors are related with the mortality and fertility behaviors (e.g., a wealthy and married individual lives longer than a poor and single individual).

There are two considerations on identifying agent attributes: (1) relationship to agent behaviors and (2) obtainable real data. Unifying the two considerations, we selected agent attributes from Korean micro-population data [11]. Korean micro-population data is same as the Census data in US, so individual information of the resident population (e.g., age, sex, education level, children, employment status, etc.) is described. We also categorized agent attributes into

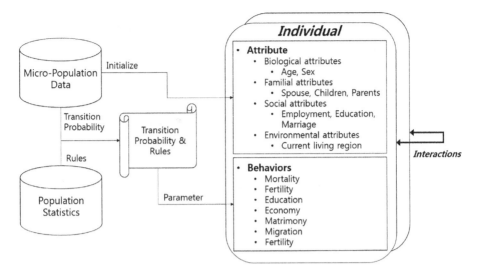

Fig. 1. Initial population of Korean population dynamics model utilizing micro-population data and population statistics

biological, familial, social, and environmental factors. Such categorizations are convenient for us to associate the agent behaviors with attributes.

Agent behaviors are described as stochastic process and rule-based interactions. The stochastic process uses transition probabilities of the agent behaviors, and the transition probabilities $(P_{i}j)$ are mathematically defined as Eq. 1.

$$P_{ij} = Pr\{X_t = j | X_{t-1} = i\}, \tag{1}$$

where P_{ij} is a transition probability and X_t is a set of agent attributes at time t

Most of agent behaviors are described by the stochastic process, but matrimony behavior holds interaction modules. Figure 2 illustrates how the matrimony behavior proceeds. If an individual agent is not in the married status, the agent decides whether it marries now or not using the stochastic process. When it decides to marry, it should find its spouse (see *Makecouple()* in Fig. 2), and the stochastic process is not proper to express this procedure because it needs the information of other unmarried agents. Hence, we designed this procedure as rule-based interactions.

Rule-based interactions for selecting a spouse can be derived from domain knowledge, population statistics, and social norms. In this research, we developed the rules with respect to age and education level difference between marriage couple. One example of the age difference rule is "Men of marriage couples cannot be five years older than their spouse". When we applied the example rule to the developed model, male individual agents seek a 5-year-younger female agents in their searching window. If failed, their marriage states do not changed to the married state.

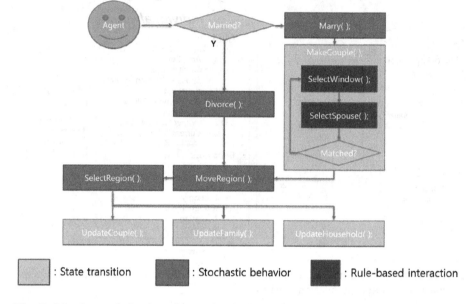

Fig. 2. Matrimony behavior of an individual model in Korean population dynamics model

Before simulating the developed model, the virtual society consisting of the modeled individuals is required. At the initial population of individual agents, we used 2 % sample of Korean micro-population data to characterize attributes of each individual (see Fig. 1).

3.2   Simulation Execution Procedure

To simulate the developed model, we applied event-based discrete time simulation execution algorithm. Specifically, the simulation proceeds with a yearly step, and each individual updates its attributes and exchanges events with other individuals.

Figure 3 illustrates the life event structure of an individual agent. Similar as the model design, an individual conducts mortality, education, economy, matrimony, migration and fertility at every simulation tick sequentially. However, there is an exception case: when the mortality behavior decides to be dead, the rest behaviors are not activated. Most of blocks in agent behaviors are stochastically performed, and two blue blocks in the matrimony are rule-based interactions because marriage requires another individual.

Simulation
Tick : *t-1*

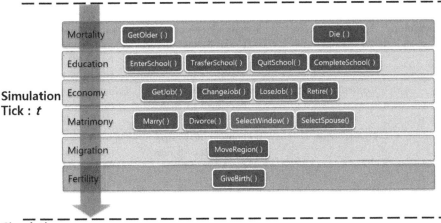

Simulation
Tick : *t*

Simulation
Tick : *t+1*

Fig. 3. Life Event Structure of an individual model in Korean population dynamics model at every simulation tick

4   Virtual Experiments

Using the developed model, we conducted virtual experiments for analyzing population dynamics in Korea. We varied the parameters and rules of an individual related with the matrimony and education behaviors. The simulation results then provided demographic indexes using the inidividual information.

4.1   Demographic Indexes

The developed model abstracts behaviors and interactions related with the population dynamics, especially the size and distribution of Korean population. Hence, The experiment results would show how the Korean population dynamics would change by the model parameter setting. To see the population changes of experimental cases, we defined several indicators that are currently used in demographics [3].

  Four demographic indicators are utilized in the virtual experiments: *population growth rate, aging index, elderly dependency ratio and median age*. *Population growth rate* indicates the increase of the number of individuals in a population, and is defined as as the ratio of the difference between current and previous population size to the previous size. *Aging index and elderly dependency ratio* illustrates how close a population reach to the aging society, and the average of global aging index and elderly dependent ratio was recorded as 39.7 and 12.3 in 2014 [12]. Aging index and elderly dependency ratio are calculated

Table 1. Virtual experimental design with varying parameters and rules of individual behavioral models (e.g., matrimony and education behavior models).

Behavior	Variables	Cases	Implications
Matrimony	Age difference	5 years older man (5M), 3 years older woman (3W) (2 cases)	Man (Woman) of the marriage couple is not 5 (3) years more than the partner
	Education difference	don't care, one level, two level (3 cases)	Education level difference between the couple
	Divorce rate	no change, 30 % up, 30 % down (3 cases)	Changing a divorcing probability with 30 % up/down or no change
Education	Entrance rate	no change, 15 % up, 15 % down (3 cases)	Changing an entrance probability with 15 % up/down or no change
Total cases	$2 \times 3 \times 3 \times 3 = 54$ cases		Each case is repeated by 10 times

as the number of persons 65 years old or over per hundred persons under age 15 and age 15–64, respectively. Last indicator is *median age* of a population, which is defined as the age that divides a population into two groups of the same size.

We calculate these indexes from the simulation results, and they are utilized to estimate the current status of Korean population aging and predict its future.

4.2   Experimental Design

We developed an experimental design for the virtual experiments. The design explains which and how parameters and rules of individual behaviors would be varied. Specifically, the design considered age difference and education level between a marriage couple as rules of matrimony behavior and divorce rate as its parameter. Also, entrance rate is defined as parameters of the education behavior, respectively. With the full-factorial design method, we defined 162 cases and each case is repeated by 10 times. Table 1 presents the experimental design details.

5   Result Analysis

This section shows simulation results from the virtual experiments and meta modeling analysis on the results

5.1 Simulation Results

Following the above experimental design, we obtained simulation results from various settings of individual behavior models. Simulations are started from 2010 Korean demographic status and continued until 2110 to estimate yearly demographic changes. The number of individuals in the virtual experiments is 89M, which is 2 % of Korean total population, and 2 % sample of Korean micro-population data and 2010 population statistics.

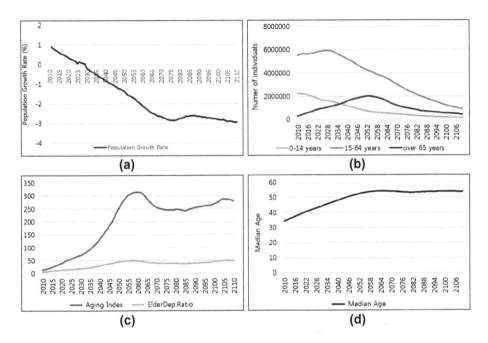

Fig. 4. Simulation results according to (a) population growth rate, (b) age distribution (c) aging index, elderly dependency ratio, and (d) median age of the future Korean population (*age difference: 5M, education difference: don't care, divorce rate: no change, education rate: no change* case)

Figure 4 shows the demographic indexes from the simulation results from one experimental case (i.e., *age difference: 5M, education difference: don't care, divorce rate: no change, education rate: no change* case). The figure represents that Korean population growth rate is decreased from 2010, and it becomes negative value around 2030, which means the overall population size decreases from 2030. Also, aging indexes of future Korean population increases and its median age is also increased. Such trends indicate that Korean population would reach at an aging society in the near future. Actually, Korean currently experiences low fertility and population aging problems [12], and the simulation results represents the same problems as well.

Table 2. Standardized coefficients of the linear regression models: dependent variables are number individuals of population, aging index, elderly dependency ratio, and median age; independent variables are parameters and rules of marriage and education behavior models (bold figures indicate p-value < 0.05)

	Num. Population	Aging Index	Elder Dependency Ratio	Median Age
Age Difference	**0.017**	**-0.107**	**-0.038**	**-0.054**
Education Diff	**0.024**	**-0.141**	**-0.051**	**-0.072**
Divorce Rate	**0.019**	**-0.051**	**-0.026**	**-0.036**
Education Rate	**0.039**	**-0.109**	**-0.056**	**-0.079**
R square	0.003	0.046	0.008	0.015

To resolve such problems, Korean government conducted political treatments, but it is hard to figure out key factors to these situations. In that sense, the developed model would support to investigate factors associated with the population changes from the micro-level perspective. This paper presents a simple example of those investigations using meta-modeling analysis.

We developed linear regression models where dependent variables are defined as the demographic indexes and independent variables are as the experimental variables. Table 2 shows standardized coefficients of the linear regression models and their p-values. The regression results illustrate that education state of individuals are most significant factor to increasing population size and reducing aging indexes. Therefore, to avoid the aging society, we may argue that Korean government would develop political treatments for encouraging education level of individuals. Also, we emphasize that such insights are provided by the virtue of micro-level population dynamics model.

6   Concluding Remarks

Korean population dynamics model describes individuals in the population and shows future population changes by the aggregation of the individuals. With the developed model, we conducted virtual experiments for estimating future population changes, especially about Korean aging society. Though the experiment results, this paper provides demographic indexes that tells how close Korea comes to the aging society and suggests meta-modeling analysis to investigate significant factors to the aging society. In particular, we expect that finding significant factors would be helpful to establish polices for mitigating the progress of the aging society.

To this end, the developed model should be validated and calibrated for the robust and credible estimation and prediction. Also, we consider to adopt machine learning techniques to efficiently figure out the significant factors.

Acknowledgement. This research was supported by the Korean ICT R&D program of MSIP/IITP (R7117-16-0219, Development of Predictive Analysis Technology on

Socio-Economics using Self-Evolving Agent-Based Simulation Embedded with Incremental Machine Learning).

References

1. Keeling, S.: Ageing societies: myths, challenges and opportunities. Australas. J. Ageing **25**(4), 223–223 (2006)
2. Royama, T.: Analytical Population Dynamics, vol. 10. Springer, Heidelberg (2012)
3. Department of Economic, Social Affairs United Nations. World population ageing: 1950–2050. UN (2002)
4. Malthus, T.R.: An essay on the principle of population, as it affects the future improvement of society, vol. 2 (1809)
5. Deng, H., Wang, L., Wang, F.L., Lei, J. (eds.): Artificial Intelligence and Computational Intelligence. Lecture Notes in Artificial Intelligence, vol. 5885. Springer, Heidelberg (2009)
6. Orcutt, G.H.: A new type of socio-economic system. Rev. Econ. Stat. **39**, 116–123 (1957)
7. Prettner, K.: Population aging and endogenous economic growth. J. Popul. Econ. **26**(2), 811–834 (2013)
8. Börsch-supan, A., Ludwig, A., Winter, J.: Ageing, pension reform and capital flows: a multi-country simulation model. Economica **73**(292), 625–658 (2006)
9. Auerbach, A.J., Kotlikoff, L.J., Hagemann, R.P., Nicoletti, G.: The dynamics of an aging population: The case of four oecd countries (1989)
10. Bae, J.W., Paik, E., Kim, K., Singh, K., Sajjad, M.: Combining microsimulation and agent-based model for micro-level population dynamics. In: 2016 International Conference on Computational Science. SDSC (2016)
11. Korean statistical information service. http://kosis.kr/eng/, Accessed 30 Jan. 2016
12. World demogrpahics profile (2014). http://www.indexmundi.com/world/demographics_profile.html, Accessed 29 May 2016

Opinion Formation Using the Gür Game

Shu-Yuan Wu[1](✉) and Theodore Brown[1,2]

[1] Department of Computer Science, Graduate Center, City University of New York,
365 Fifth Avenue, New York, NY 10016, USA
`swu2@gradcenter.cuny.edu, tbrown@gc.cuny.edu`
[2] Department of Computer Science, Queens College, City University of New York,
65-30 Kissena Blvd., Queens, NY 11367, USA

Abstract. Opinion leaders with different degrees of influence may lead to different outcomes when seeking support from their followers. In this paper, we present the opinion leaders with high trustworthiness or the effective persuasion tactics will gain the desired proportion of support from followers sooner in the Gür game framework. The composition of followers in a group affects the time to achieve the target proportion of support as well. The Gür game is a self-organized artificial game associating players with finite state automata and a moderator with a reward function. We regard each follower as a player associating with a finite state automaton to reflect their states of mind. An opinion leader, considered as a moderator, has a reward function to reflect his/her degree of influence and to predict the probability of followers changing their state of mind after he/she delivers a speech or comments on a topic or a product.

Keywords: Opinion formation · Gür game · opinion leader

1 Introduction

With the proliferation of social medias and the development of Web 2.0 platforms, people interact with celebrities, friends, people with the same interests, etc. over the Internet to form friendships, share their opinions on various topics from politics to restaurants, new products and so on. These opinions can be from their experience, influenced by peers, or a group leader.

Opinion formation has attracted a great set of research in statistical physics. In most of these opinion formation models, individuals adjust their opinions when two individuals interact with each other. Nevertheless, with the two-step flow communication model, a hypothesis based on empirical studies, proposed by Katz and Lazarsfeld [7] and widely studied in the research communities of diffusion and marketing research [20], the importance and influence of opinion leaders have been shown in various decision-making scenarios ranging from political campaigns to movie-going, fashion etc. With the analysis of Twitter data, Wu et al. [21] found that the two-step flow model can be validated by the Twitter data as well.

© Springer Science+Business Media Singapore 2016
L. Zhang et al. (Eds.): AsiaSim 2016/SCS AutumnSim 2016, Part IV, CCIS 646, pp. 368–377, 2016.
DOI: 10.1007/978-981-10-2672-0_38

In this paper, we extend the prior proposed opinion formation model [22] in which individuals adjust their opinions when the followed opinion leaders update or comment on a topic. Specifically the model will take the degree of influence of opinion leaders and followers' states of mind into account. In order to reflect an opinion leader's trustworthiness and the effectiveness of persuasion tactics, and a follower's states of mind, we take advantage of the Gür game, an artificial game, associating followers with finite state automata and an opinion leader with a reward function and seek to conduct a series of simulation to validate the model.

In the next section, related work on opinion formation and the Gür game paradigm are shown. The opinion formation model using the Gür game paradigm is followed by the preliminary simulation results. The paper ends with conclusions.

2 Related Work

2.1 Opinion Formation

Opinion formation has been widely studied by the statistical physics community [1]. Generally, most opinion formation models can be categorized into either the models with binary opinions (e.g. voter models [13] and Sznajd models [14,15]) or the continuous opinion models under bounded confidence. In these models, each individual adjusts their opinion when two individuals interact with each other. In the binary opinions models, each individual is associated with a binary opinion variable $s = \pm 1$. However, there are some real scenarios that are not restricted the choices to extreme left or right but in between such as strength of political selection. Continuous opinions under bounded confidence [9] (e.g. Deffuant models [2,3], Hegselmann-Krause models [4,5] and Song et al. [11,12]) thus were proposed and the opinions were represented using real numbers. Each individual in these models is capable of gradually adjusting their opinion when two individuals interact with each other and their opinions are close within a certain bound of confidence. Usually the continuous opinion models are analyzed by using agent-based simulation.

2.2 Gür Game

The Gür game was introduced by Tsetlin [17], which has two types of players in the game: a moderator and a set of voters. Voters are only aware of the moderator; voters can not know each other's vote. On each round of the game, the moderator asks voters to vote yes or no, simultaneously followed by the moderator counting the fraction of yes votes, f. The moderator decides whether to reward or penalize a voter based on f and a generated reward function $r(f)$ which is only known by the moderator. The reward function is assumed to be $0 \le r(f) \le 1$. At the end of each round, every voter is independently rewarded (with probability $r(f)$) or penalized (with probability $1 - r(f)$) one unit regardless what he/she votes. Each voter decides what to vote on the next round based on their current state. After enough rounds, approximately f^* of voters vote yes no matter how many voters there are. f^* is where the maximum of the reward function occurs. Note that a reward function can be any function. It can be unimodal, discontinuous, multi-modal, etc. A typical reward function is shown in Fig. 1. Furthermore, Tsetlin [17] associated each voter with an automaton $L_{2, 2n}$ of $2n$ states or said it has a memory size of n as shown in Fig. 2.

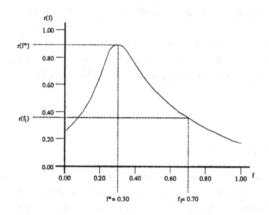

Fig. 1. A typical reward function. Figure extracted from [18].

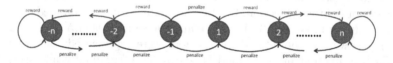

Fig. 2. Automata design of $L_{2, 2n}$. Figure redrawn from [17].

If a voter's current state is a negative numbered state, the automaton gives output of A_0; otherwise A_1 is given. If an automaton is rewarded, it moves from state i to $i+1$ if i is positive or from i to $i-1$ if i is negative. If the automaton is penalized, it moves from state i to $i-1$ if i is positive or from i to $i+1$ if i is negative. The $L_{2, 2n}$ automaton follows the following state transition rules:

if an automaton is rewarded **then**
    if its current state, $i = n$ or $-n$ **then**
        stay in the current state
    else if $1 \leq$ current state, $i < n$ **then**
        next state $= i + 1$
    else if $-n <$ current state, $i \leq -1$ **then**
        next state $= i - 1$
    end if

else
    if current state, $i = -1$ **then**
        next state $= 1$
    else if current state, $i = 1$ **then**
        next state $= -1$
    else if current state, $i > 1$ **then**
        next state $= i - 1$
    else if current state, $i < -1$ **then**
        next state $= i + 1$
    end if
end if

Note that only the behaviors of a single automaton has been described above. Since the analysis of multiple automata, actually non-homogeneous Markov chains, is far from trivial, we summarize the asymptotic behaviors of the Gür game below, which have been proved or shown by simulations by Tung and Kleinrock [18,19].

1. Suppose that each automaton has only two states. As the number of automata, N and time, $t \to \infty$, $f(t) \to 1/2$.
2. For any number of N, the system will spend a desired proportion of time in optimal configurations when the number of states for each automaton is high enough.
3. Given a fixed memory size of n, an increasing number of automata of N will lead the system to spend more time on $f \approx 1/2$.

With the further studies by Tung and Kleinrock [18,19], the Gür game started to gain increasing interest in some research communities such as wireless sensor networks [6,8,10,16,23], etc. Due to the nature of the Gür game, it mostly applied in the research area of wireless sensor networks to achieve self-organizing battery life control of sensors and optimal QoS. And most research employs only one moderator in a system. However, the Gür game is not restricted to have only one moderator in a system. Wu and Brown [22] applied the Gür game in opinion formation while two opinion leaders have followers in common and investigated how an opinion leader's degree of influence, group sizes, the role of overlapped followers and opinion convergence speed in each group affect the final result of opinions.

In the next section, we will present how to integrate the Gür game in opinion formation to profile an opinion leader and followers.

3 Opinion Formation Model in the Gür Game Framework

In this paper, we extend our prior work [22] that an opinion leader is considered as a moderator and followers are regarded as voters in the Gür game. Different from the most opinion formation models proposed by the statistical physics community, where each individual gradually adjusts their opinion when two individuals interact with each other, individuals in the model we proposed [22] adjust their opinions while their opinion leaders update or comment on an issue instead. We assume that an opinion leader is able to know how well followers are convinced by him/her (followers do not necessarily agree on the leader) through conducting survey or a long-term observation. On the basis of this assumption, an opinion leader is associated with a reward function to reflect his/her degree of influence and to predict the probability of followers changing the states of mind after he/she delivers a speech or comments on an issue. Followers are associated with finite state automata representing the followers' states of mind. Each follower changes the state after his/her group leader updates the status or comments on an event or issue. If a follower is currently in the positive numbered state, it means he/she agrees with his/her opinion leader op_i's opinion; if the current state is negative, he/she disagrees with op_i. The more positive the current state is, the more the follower is convinced by op_i. Likewise the more negative the current state is, the less the follower is convinced by op_i. A follower's states of mind can be represented by an automaton as shown in Fig. 3.

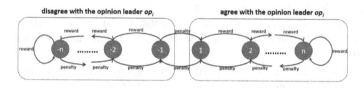

Fig. 3. Using a finite state automaton to represent a followers states of mind. Figure redrawn from [22].

Although our prior work [22] analyzed that two opinion leaders with opposite opinions on an issue and some followers in common in terms of group sizes, the roles of overlapped followers, and opinion leaders' degree of influence under the assumption that one group gets to the equilibrium state faster than the other, we eager to explore how a reward function can reflect an opinion leader's degree of influence or trustworthiness and effectiveness of persuasion tactics and how finite state automata can represent a follower's characteristics.

We present when two opinion leaders with the same reward function have different compositions of followers, in which one opinion leader has a collection of followers that adjust their opinions easily or more open-minded but the other with followers that are conservative or single-minded in the Gür game framework. To present the difference, the single-minded followers are associated with longer finite state automaton as their states of mind. Contrarily, the open-minded followers are associated with shorter finite state automaton to reflect they are more willing to change their beliefs or decisions in contrast to the conservative ones.

Additionally, we present how a reward function can represent an opinion leader with high trustworthiness or the effective persuasion tactics gaining support from the followers sooner in the paper. We propose that a narrow function (e.g. $r1(f)$ in Fig. 4) can be used to represent an opinion leader with higher trustworthiness or the effective persuasion tactics who gains a desired support speedily. An opinion leader with less trustworthiness or the less able persuasion tactics can be represented by a wide function (e.g. $r3(f)$ in Fig. 4).

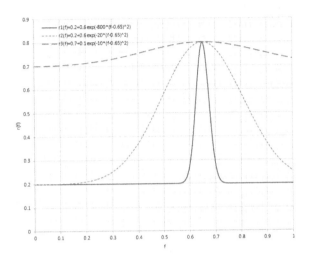

Fig. 4. Reward functions used to represent trustworthiness and the effectiveness of persuasion tactics of opinion leaders.

In the next section, we conduct a series of simulations to show the effects of followers' states of mind and an opinion leader' degree of influence in terms of the system configuration.

4   Simulation

To validate the proposed model by simulation, we assume that we have one opinion leader with 20 followers and followers are not necessary to agree with the opinion leader in the following discussions. Each follower picks a random state as its initial state of mind. We assume that the opinion leader desires an average of 13 followers agreeing with him/her at each time. The simulation was run for 1,000,000 time steps, and each point averages 100 runs.

4.1   Effect of Number of States

To validate our model and discuss the effect of number of states assigned for followers, the reward function $r(f) = 0.2 + 0.6e^{-800.0(f-0.65)^2}$ ($r1f$ in Fig. 4) will be used in the simulation. For each run, each follower is associated with 4 or 12 states. As shown in Figs. 5 and 6, the followers associated more states is much more stable after the optimal configuration has been achieved. Fewer states for followers result in approximately 1/2 followers agreeing with the opinion leader instead of the desired 13 followers. In other words, when there are more open-minded followers in a group, the opinion leader would need more efforts to convince followers. Although the open-minded individuals are more willing to adapt a new idea or new product, for a long term they change minds easily when other ideas or new products come up. In contrast, the single-minded followers are more faithful once they adapt an idea or a product.

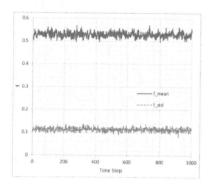 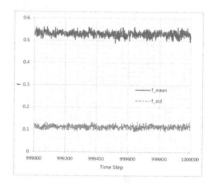

Fig. 5. Y-axis is the average fraction of the followers agreeing with their opinion leader in each time step observed from 100 Gür games. 20 followers participate in each game and each is associated with an automaton of 4 states. Reward function, $r(f) = 0.2 + 0.6e^{-800.0(f-0.65)^2}$ where $\max r(f) = 0.8$ with $f^* = 0.65$.

4.2   Reward Functions for Opinion Leaders

We use two different shapes of reward functions and followers are assigned the same number of sates to study the influence of opinion leaders' trustworthiness and the effectiveness persuasion tactics. The reward functions $r(f) = 0.7 + 0.1e^{-10.0(f-0.65)^2}$ ($r3f$ in Fig. 4) and $r(f) = 0.2 + 0.6e^{-800.0(f-0.65)^2}$ ($r1f$ in Fig. 4), representing the opinion leader with lower trustworthiness or the useless persuasion tactics and the opinion leader with higher trustworthiness or the effective persuasion tactics respectively, are studied for each follower with 12 mind states. As shown in Figs. 6 and 7, an opinion leader with high trustworthiness or the effective persuasion tactics can attract a desired fraction of followers agreeing with him/her speedily and stay in the optimal configuration for a long time. However, the opinion leader with lower trustworthiness or the less able persuasion tactics has to spend a longer time to gain followers agreeing with him/her and may not have the desired number of supporters.

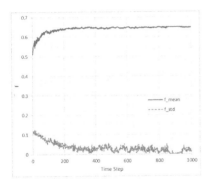
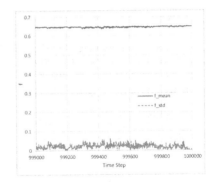

Fig. 6. Y-axis is the average fraction of the followers agreeing with their opinion leader in each time step observed from 100 Gür games. 20 followers participate in each game and each is associated with an automaton of 12 states. Reward function, $r(f) = 0.2 + 0.6e^{-800.0(f-0.65)^2}$ where max $r(f) = 0.8$ with $f^* = 0.65$.

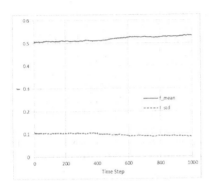
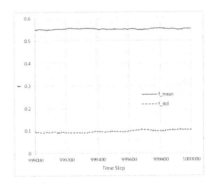

Fig. 7. Y-axis is the average fraction of the followers agreeing with their opinion leader in each time step observed from 100 Gür games. 20 followers participate in each game and each is associated with an automaton of 12 states. Reward function $r(f) = 0.7 + 0.1e^{-10.0(f-0.65)^2}$ where max $r(f) = 0.8$ with $f^* = 0.65$.

5   Conclusion

Opinions are usually modeled as a binary variable or represented in a real number and determined by social interactions in opinion formation models. The mechanism of social interaction is usually that each individual adjusts their opinions while two individuals interact with each other. In this paper we presented a model using the Gür game paradigm that allowed to reflect the degree of influence of opinion leaders and reactions of followers on a topic. In this paper we have demonstrated the preliminary results of the power of the Gür game in the opinion formation area, many future studies remain open to explore.

References

1. Castellano, C., Fortunato, S., Loreto, V.: Statistical physics of social dynamics. Rev. Mod. Phys. **81**(2), 591 (2009)
2. Deffuant, G., Amblard, F., Weisbuch, G., Faure, T.: How can extremism prevail? a study based on the relative agreement interaction model. J. Artif. Soc. Soc. Simul. 5(4) (2002)
3. Deffuant, G., Neau, D., Amblard, F., Weisbuch, G.: Mixing beliefs among interacting agents. Adv. Complex Syst. **3**(01–04), 87–98 (2000)
4. Hegselmann, R., Krause, U.: Opinion dynamics driven by various ways of averaging. Comput. Econ. **25**(4), 381–405 (2005)
5. Hegselmann, R., Krause, U., et al.: Opinion dynamics and bounded confidence models, analysis, and simulation. J. Artif. Soc. Soc. Simul. **5**(3), 1–33 (2002)
6. Iyer, R., Kleinrock, L.: Qos control for sensor networks. In: IEEE International Conference on Communications, ICC 2003, vol. 1, pp. 517–521. IEEE (2003)
7. Katz, E., Lazarsfeld, P.F.: Personal influence; the part played by people inthe flow of mass communications. Free Press, Glencoe, Ill (1955)
8. Liu, C., Hui, P., Branch, J., Yang, B.: Qoi-aware energy management forwireless sensor networks. In: 2011 IEEE International Conference on Pervasive Computing and Communications Workshops (PERCOM Workshops), pp. 8–13. IEEE (2011)
9. Lorenz, J.: Continuous opinion dynamics under bounded confidence: a survey. Int. J. Mod. Phys. C **18**(12), 1819–1838 (2007)
10. Nayer, S.I., Ali, H.H.: A dynamic energy-aware algorithm for self-optimizing wireless sensor networks. In: Hummel, K.A., Sterbenz, J.P.G. (eds.) IWSOS 2008. LNCS, vol. 5343, pp. 262–268. Springer, Heidelberg (2008). doi:10.1007/978-3-540-92157-8_23
11. Song, X., Shi, W., Ma, Y., Yang, C.: Impact of informal networks on opinion dynamics in hierarchically formal organization. Phys. A **436**, 916–924 (2015)
12. Song, X., Zhang, S., Qian, L.: Opinion dynamics in networked command and control organizations. Phys. A **392**(20), 5206–5217 (2013)
13. Sood, V., Antal, T., Redner, S.: Voter models on heterogeneous networks. Phys. Rev. E **77**(4), 041121 (2008)
14. Sznajd-Weron, K.: Sznajd model and its applications. arXiv preprint physics/0503239 (2005)
15. Sznajd-Weron, K., Sznajd, J.: Opinion evolution in closed community. Int. J. Mod. Phys. C **11**(06), 1157–1165 (2000)
16. Tsai, R.G., Wang, H.L.: A coverage-aware qos control in wireless sensornetworks. In: 2010 International Conference on Communications and Mobile Computing (CMC), vol. 3, pp. 192–196. IEEE (2010)
17. Tsetlin, M.: Automaton theory and modeling of biological systems: by ML Tsetlin. Translated by Scitran (Scientific Translation Service), vol. 102. Academic Press (1973)
18. Tung, B., Kleinrock, L.: Distributed control methods. In: Proceedings the 2nd International Symposium on High Performance Distributed Computing, pp. 206–215. IEEE (1993)
19. Tung, B., Kleinrock, L.: Using finite state automata to produce self-optimization and self-control. IEEE Trans. Parallel Distrib. Syst. **7**(4), 439–448 (1996)
20. Watts, D.J., Dodds, P.S.: Influentials, networks, and public opinion formation. J. Consum. Res. **34**(4), 441–458 (2007)

Opinion Formation Using the Gür Game   377

21. Wu, S., Hofman, J.M., Mason, W.A., Watts, D.J.: Who says what to whom on twitter. In: Proceedings of the 20th International Conference on World Wide Web, pp. 705–714. ACM (2011)
22. Wu, S.Y., Brown, T.: Opinion formation under the two-step flow model and the gur game framework. In: The Sixth Annual Asian Conference on the Social Sciences (ACSS 2015). IAFOR (2015)
23. Zhao, L., Xu, C., Xu, Y., Li, X.: Energy-aware qos control for wireless sensor network. In: 2006 1ST IEEE Conference on Industrial Electronics and Applications, pp. 1–6. IEEE (2006)

Can a Buffering Strategy Reduce Workload Related Stress?

An Exploration Using an Agent Based Model

Harshal Hayatnagarkar, Meghendra Singh, Suman Kumar, Mayuri Duggirala, and Vivek Balaraman[✉]

Human Centric Systems, TCS Research, Hadapsar, Pune, 411013, India
{h.hayatnagarkar2,meghendra.singh,suman.kumar4,mayuri.duggirala, vivek.balaraman}@tcs.com

Abstract. The support services industry remains a competitive business operating on very stringent budgets, metrics, and milestones. Given the heavy and varying workloads that are characteristic in this business, stress is a common all-too-common phenomenon and emerges from different sources. In this context, we use an agent based approach to examine whether using a workload buffering strategy based loosely on the Leaky Bucket Algorithm can help to manage workload-related stress. We use our workplace stress model to see the implications of such a buffering approach on workload related stress at an individual level and on macro indicators such as turn-around time (TAT). The experiments show that the strategy can help not only reduce the stress but also provide knobs to the operations managers to manage workload and to ensure compliance. We conclude with implications for future research and practice.

Keywords: Human behavior modeling · Behavior factors · Stress · Agent-based modeling and simulation

1 Introduction

The support services industry is known to be a highly knowledge-based competitive work environment where the teams face challenges associated with high workload, long working hours, tight budgets, and strict milestones [1, 2]. In addition, the performance of the teams and individuals is monitored on regular basis across various metrics, such as individual productivity per unit of time and quality of services [3]. In the support services context, these metrics can be both quantitative (such as average handling time) and qualitative (such as rapport) in nature [4]. The challenge to sustain business performance is compounded when there is variance in the workload [5]. These factors are known to cause work-related stress to individuals and it is also known that stress negatively affects their productivity [6]. In an earlier work [7], we explored this relationship between stress and productivity while in a later one [8] we explored the impacts of different sources of stresses. For example, fatigue develops from long working hours, event stress with workload arrival and time-pressure emerges from backlog. Models of

© Springer Science+Business Media Singapore 2016
L. Zhang et al. (Eds.): AsiaSim 2016/SCS AutumnSim 2016, Part IV, CCIS 646, pp. 378–388, 2016.
DOI: 10.1007/978-981-10-2672-0_39

stress show that stress is bi-polar with respect to productivity, i.e. stress can help to both increase and decrease productivity. There is also an optimal band of stress that maximizes productivity. Lower levels of stress lead to suboptimal levels of productivity. Among the various sources of stress, fatigue and time-pressure do not vary a lot but event stress does because of its association with workload (or demand). We can therefore surmise that a work environment with unpredictable and high variation in workload would lead to high variation in productivity. We therefore hypothesize that a demand management strategy that smoothens jitter in workload would similarly help us to reduce variation in individual stress and consequently individual and group productivity. The exploration of this hypothesis is therefore the focus of the current paper.

2 Related Work

Past research in support services has primarily adopted quantitative and mathematical approaches to study various aspects of managing work in this context. A quick search of past research on this topic identifies sub-areas of research, such as process management, inventory and warehouse management, skill-based routing and performance to name just a few [9–11]. A related stream of research focuses on developing models for establishing the link between workload and performance and its associated tradeoffs [12]. Thus we can see how past has focused more on the tangible or measurable aspects of work in support services, such as in terms of changing the level of workload on a team and alternative models of work allocation, for example in call centers [13]. In this study, we focus on work-related stress and how this can be controlled through demand management. In this research domain, past work on reducing work stress has articulated four common forms of social support [14] namely, emotional support, tangible support, information support and companionship support. Our paper focuses on the construct of informational support which is described in terms of providing advice, guidance, suggestions or useful information to someone [14] in a way that reduces the latter's uncertainty or confusion regarding the specific situation they are faced with [15]. A related process is that of information filtration in organizations where only select information is conveyed [16]. Our study examines a strategy for informational support via filtration in a support services context. We explore how a strategy for systematically filtering or moderating workload-related information at various levels of workload for a team helps mitigate the negative impact of workload related stress among employees in the support services organization. The challenges associated with variance in the demand are not new and have been seen in many situations such as computer networks, supply chain management, support services [17], and e-commerce [18]. Higher variance typically makes model predictability difficult, and hence a standard technique is to smoothen jitter in the demand as much as possible. In case of computer networks, network protocols and the architecture employ a traffic shaping strategy such as the Leaky Bucket [19] and Token Bucket [20]. In this work, we use a variation of a specific case of leaky bucket namely 'Leaky bucket as a queue', which is typically used to remove jitter from the incoming traffic by regulating outgoing flow and by discarding traffic when the bucket overflows. However, in case of the support services, one cannot discard the incoming workload and hence we need to devise a variation of this strategy such that in case of overflow, the additional workload is not discarded but pushed out. This decision does not remove the jitter completely, but reduces its intensity. In our work we use an agent based model to examine how such a strategy may help service engineers to better cope with demand/workload variations and mitigate the negative impact of workload related stress.

3   The Support Services Workflow

In support services organizations, tasks originate from a client's business processes. Within the organization, each task is allocated to a specific team. Each task is independent of other tasks in a team's task pool. For example, in a claims team, a specific task could be the creation of a new customer claim file, which requires verification of the customer's details. For the claim file to be created, individual team members are required to review these for accuracy and validity. Task assignment can be either voluntary or by a supervisor or by an automated process. The team size is planned by considering the mean time to complete a typical task, and a typical task volume. When the regular team cannot deal with the volume, the operations manager can make use of an auxiliary team called the bench strength, which works together with the regular team to deal with the excess tasks. Any task left unfinished at the end of a work day becomes the backlog for the next working day's operations.

4   Field Study and Model Development

4.1   Definitions

We define some terms specific to the support services domain in the interest of clarity:

Task arrival rate: Rate at which new tasks arrive at the beginning of each work day
Backlog: Unfinished tasks for an employee at the end of each work day
Unplanned absenteeism: Unplanned leave taken by an employee
Productivity: Capacity of an employee to do work related tasks per hour
Turn-around-time: Time duration in hours for a task from arrival to completion
Bench strength: A pool of employees that is assigned work in case of absenteeism or increased workload, and calculated as a percentage of original team size
Bucket: A temporary buffer or storage for holding incoming tasks
Bucket size: Maximum number of tasks that can be stored in the bucket

4.2   Model of Stress in Services Environment

We conducted a field study at a support services organization to capture various contextual details from employees and the organization [7, 8]. After analyzing the field study data, we extracted relationships between relevant behavioral factors, especially drivers for variables of interest such as performance and stress induced unplanned leaves. These relationships were composed together into an integrated model of behavior along with other relations obtained from past work in behavioral sciences literature. Although we have already presented this model in [7, 8], we briefly describe it here for the sake of clarity. Based on the field study, we found three most significant stress inducing factors (stressors) namely; long work hours, increase in the daily task arrival rate, and accumulating backlog. To integrate these different stressors into a single model, we refer to the 'PMFServ' framework, which demonstrates that stress is composed of three main components – Effective fatigue (EF), event stress (ES), and time pressure (TP) [21].

In our context we map our study findings to these three components as: Long work hours $\rightarrow$ Effective fatigue, Increase in the daily task arrival rate $\rightarrow$ Event stress, and Accumulated backlog $\rightarrow$ Time pressure. These components which individually vary between 0 and 1, are assumed to be additive in nature and to carry an equal weightage. Thus, the integrated stress is computed as – Integrated stress = $\sum$(EF, ES,TP)/3. As a result, integrated stress also varies from 0 to 1. To explain impact of stress on productivity, 'PMFServ' framework combines 'Inverted-U' model by 'Yerkes-Dodson' [22] with the 'Janis-Mann' taxonomy of stress coping strategies [23]. In our context, we reinterpret this approach by considering integrated stress as a predictor of productivity of an individual, as shown in the right hand side figure in Fig. 1, where integrated stress is plotted against the productivity multiplier (M) for various levels of stress.

Table 1. Composed behaviour model (Sourced from [8])

Relation	Model	Description
Effective Fatigue (EF) $\leftarrow$ Number of work hours	EF = 0.01054 * (Work Hours) + 0.4536;	Effective fatigue increases with number of hours an agent works for in a day.
Event stress (ES) $\leftarrow$ Volume of task arrival	ES = (Task Arrival Today/2)/ Mean Task Arrival	Increase in volume of task arrival is perceived as increase in event stress.
Time pressure (TP) $\leftarrow$ Backlog	TP = (Current Backlog/2)/Mean Task Arrival	Increase in backlog adds to the time pressure component of stress.
Integrated stress $\leftarrow$ EF + ES + TP	Stress = (EF + ES + TP)/3	Integrated Stress is a composite of the three components (EF, ES and TP)

Productivity $\leftarrow$ Stress	**Productivity = $\underline{M}$ * Base Productivity**
	 If (Stress <= 0.2) then M = 0.5
	 If (Stress > 0.2 && <= 0.4) then M = 1.0
	 If (Stress > 0.4 && <= 0.6) then M = 1.25
	 If (Stress > 0.6 && <= 0.8) then M = 1.0
	 If (Stress > 0.8) then M = 0.5
		Coping strategy for stress has an impact on agent productivity.

P(Absenteeism) $\leftarrow$ Stress	If stress > 0.8 then N(0.1, 0.1)	High stress (>0.8) was correlated with high absenteeism

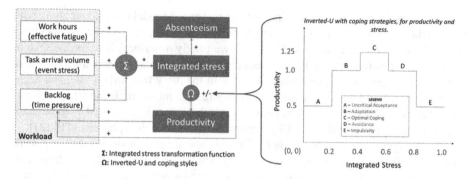

Fig. 1. Composed model of stress, productivity and absenteeism

The computation of coping strategies, productivity and other relationships are detailed in our previous work [8]. Table 1 has details about the composed model.

4.3 Simulated Process Model

We model the support services process to closely match the real world support services workflow as described in Sect. 3, although with few assumptions shared in Sect. 4.4.

The support service organization maintains a team of employees that work on tasks arriving at the beginning of a business day. The number of tasks arriving on a particular day is determined from a Gaussian distribution. These tasks are queued up in a task pool and are evenly distributed among individual team members. A member can work on assigned tasks for eight work hours, which can be extended to a maximum of two more work hours in a day. Unfinished tasks go back to the task pool, to be redistributed on the next day. A team member's behavior in terms of productivity and absenteeism is driven by the integrated stress which is affected by workload as shown in Fig. 1. An

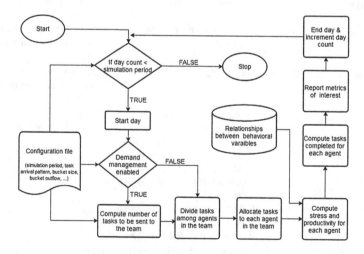

Fig. 2. Flow chart of simulation model

individual's behavior in turn affects the simulated team's outcome metrics of interest, such as the average TAT, backlog and absenteeism. Figure 2 shows the flow chart of the simulation model.

As discussed in earlier sections, we intend to mitigate effect of high variance of task arrival rate on event stress, and subsequently on productivity of an individual team member. Therefore we implement a demand management strategy in our simulation model by taking a cue from the leaky bucket analogy, as shown in Fig. 3.

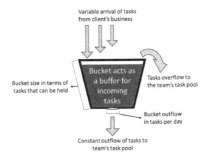

Fig. 3. Demand management strategy in the simulated model, using leaky bucket

In this strategy, tasks arriving from the client's business are first routed to a bucket which acts as a temporary storage of incoming tasks. This bucket tries to maintain a constant outflow of tasks to the task pool at the beginning of each work day. The bucket has a limited capacity (or size) to hold number of tasks, and overflowing tasks are pushed forward to the task pool. However, when bucket ends up having fewer tasks than for the desired constant outflow, the entire bucket is emptied in to the task pool. This strategy helps to smooth out sudden spikes and troughs in the incoming task traffic and help to maintain optimal productivity for the simulated team.

4.4 Assumptions

In the simulation model which we have discussed above, we emphasize on retaining only the most necessary contextual behavioral factors in the models and then incrementally adding complexity. This requires us to make some assumptions. We simulate tasks associated with a single process. All tasks arriving as part of work do not have a deadline by which they need to be completed and are assumed to be similar in terms of complexity, priority and time for processing. Daily task arrival rate is assumed to follow the Gaussian distribution. All people have uniform professional skills, competence levels and base productivity, and are driven by a common behavioral model. In future, we may do away with one or more of these assumptions. Next, we discuss the experimental scenarios and results in detail.

5   Experiments and Results

We conduct several experiments on the simulated team, with a constant mean arrival of 1000 tasks per day, while using different variance values from the Gaussian distribution of task arrival rate. We vary the standard deviation (SD) of the task arrival rate as shown in Fig. 4, from 0 tasks (no variation in task arrival) to 500 tasks (very high variation in task arrival), and observe its effect on the average TAT.

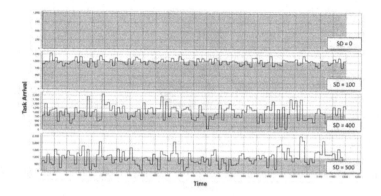

Fig. 4. Sample task arrival patterns generated for various SD values

Next, we repeat the experiments by deploying the demand management strategy to deal with variance in task arrival rate. We vary bucket sizes and outflows to estimate their optimal values. In a second set of experiments, we employ different bench strength values and make observations on the average TAT for different bucket sizes, in the case of high variance (SD = 500) in task arrival.

Each simulation experiment in a set was repeated 10 times for every parameter combination. The results are reported as averages for each set of experiments. To simulate the proposed model, we chose GIS and Agent-based Modelling Architecture (GAMA) [24] because it has a powerful specification language, good visualization features, and good extensibility. In GAMA, team members become instances of a species, which embeds our behavioral model, implemented using a combination of GAMA's behavior constructs such as 'reflex' and 'actions'.

5.1   Without Demand Management

Higher SD in the task arrival rate leads to higher peaks and deeper valleys. The peaks induce event stress in individual team members [8]. This increased stress reduces productivity levels which result in greater TAT per task for an individual. This results in an increased average TAT for the simulated team. Consequently, the collective lower productivity builds up the backlog, which further adds up as the time pressure component of the integrated stress for team members.

In Fig. 5, we can observe that for SD greater than 300, TAT increases rapidly, suggesting that high variance causes more stress in individual team members, and forces them to remain in the impulsivity coping strategy.

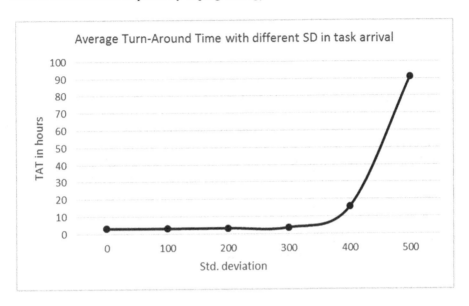

Fig. 5. Average TAT without demand management

5.2   With Demand Management

Next, we deploy the demand management strategy described in Sect. 4.3. The strategy offers two parameters to control its behavior namely bucket size and bucket outflow. The bucket's size and outflow introduce a barrier for an individual to experience the event stress. Smaller bucket size causes frequent task overflows, and as a result higher event stress, leading to lower productivity, leading to higher TAT. Figure 6(a) shows that the bucket sizes of 1500 and 2000 are able to maintain an optimal TAT even for high values of SD in task arrival.

Earlier we fixed bucket outflow at 1200 tasks and varied bucket sizes, to discover 1500 is able to maintain a low TAT. Now we vary bucket outflow to find an optimal value, for a constant bucket size of 1500.

As seen in Fig. 6(b), if we increase the bucket outflow from 1000 to 1600, we observe that an outflow of 1000 (equal to the mean task arrival) leads to high TAT for high variance (SD = 500) in task arrival. This happens because the outflow of 1000 tasks leads to greater number of tasks being held in the bucket. This causes the bucket to overflow frequently leading to greater workload for the agents thereby causing higher levels of stress and thereby increased average TAT for the team. As we increase the outflow up to 1400 tasks, the average TAT remains low as the bucket rarely overflows and the workload is small enough for the simulated team to cope with it. When the outflow reaches 1600 tasks, the bucket outflow itself becomes large enough to increase

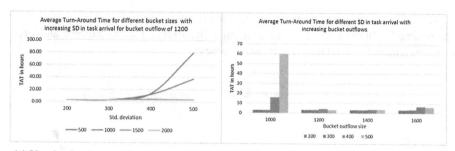

(a) Varying bucket size (overflow = 1200) **(b)** Varying bucket outflow (bucket size = 1500)

Fig. 6. TAT with demand management strategy

stress levels in the agents leading to lower productivity, thereby slightly increasing the average TAT for the team. Thus, we observe that, the outflows of 1200 and 1400 are optimal.

Next, we wanted to understand if demand management strategy has an effect on bench strength. As discussed, the organization maintains a bench strength as a percentage of the actual team size (6 % in our field study). So we conducted additional experiments by varying bench strengths, as rendered in Fig. 7.

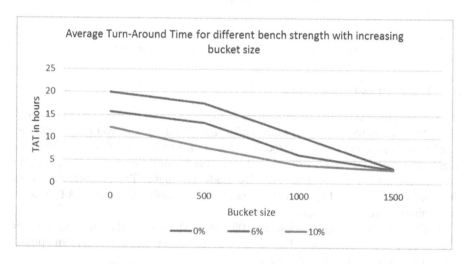

Fig. 7. Effect of bench strength on Turn-around time

Figure 7 shows the average TAT for three different bench strengths (0 %, 6 % and 10 %) and four bucket sizes for a constant bucket outflow of 1200 tasks. The SD for task arrival in this case is fixed at 500 tasks. We observe that bench strength plays an important role when bucket size is sub-optimal. However, for the optimal bucket size of 1500 tasks the bench strength does not impact the TAT of the simulated team as the bucket keeps the workload on individual agents in check, thereby obviating the need for the bench.

6   Conclusions and Future Work

In this paper, we study effect of variance in workload on the productivity of individual team members. This impact emerges from the task arrival rate to stress to productivity chain of relations because higher variation in arrival rate affects stress, and then the 'Inverted-U' pattern of the coping strategies pushes the productivity down whenever stress reaches suboptimal zone. We further discuss how this variation in the task arrival rate can be smoothened by using a traffic shaping strategy based on the 'Leaky Bucket' approach. With this strategy, the bucket outflow is regulated as much as possible, thus altering the perception of task arrival rate by team members and reducing their event stress. The strategy provides two knobs to the operations managers: Bucket size and bucket outflow. By tweaking these knobs, the managers can strike a balance between demand variance, workload stress and SLA compliance. Further, we suggest that the Leaky Bucket strategy acts as a buffer to maintain team productivity and prevent adverse effects to team performance when faced with spikes in workload. The buffering effects of organizational communication have been extensively documented in past research [25]. In future, we intend to explore fine-tuning of this strategy at individual level, such that under stress few individuals may perform better with lesser workload and few others with more. This distribution may help achieve anti-fragility against variance in the workload [26].

References

1. Budhwar Pawan, S., Arup, V., Virender, S., Rohin, D.: HRM systems of Indian call centres: an exploratory study. Int. J. Hum. Res. Manage. **17**(5), 881–897 (2006)
2. David, H., Chissick, C., Peter, T.: The effects of performance monitoring on emotional labor and well-being in call centers. Motiv. Emot. **26**(1), 57–81 (2002)
3. https://en.wikipedia.org/wiki/Service-level_agreement
4. Peter, B., Aileen, W., Gareth, M., Phil, T., Gregor, G.: Taylorism, targets and the pursuit of quantity and quality by call centre management. New Technol. Work Employ. **17**(3), 170–185 (2002)
5. Witt, L.A., Andrews Martha, C., Carlson Dawn, S.: When conscientiousness isn't enough: emotional exhaustion and performance among call center customer service representatives. J. Manage. **30**(1), 149–160 (2004)
6. Bakker Arnold, B., Evangelia, D., Wilmar, S.: Dual processes at work in a call centre: an application of the job demands–resources model. Eur. J. Work Organ. Psychol. **12**(4), 393–417 (2003)
7. Singh, M. et al.: Multi-agent model of workgroup behavior in an enterprise using a compositional approach. In: 2nd Modeling Symposium (ModSym 2016). ISEC (2016)
8. Duggirala, M., Singh, M., Hayatnagarkar, H., Patel, S., Balaraman, V.: Understanding impact of stress on workplace outcomes using an agent based simulation. In: Simulation Multiconference 2016 (Summer, forthcoming) (Manuscript is available on request)
9. Hasija, S., Pinker, E.J., Shumsky, R.A.: Call center outsourcing contracts under information asymmetry. Manage. Sci. **54**(4), 793–807 (2008)
10. Aksin, Z., Armony, M., Vijay, M.: The modern call center: a multi-disciplinary perspective on operations management research. Prod. Oper. Manage. **16**(6), 665–688 (2007)

11. http://www.wired.com/2014/06/inside-amazon-warehouse/
12. Robert, G., Hockey, J.: Compensatory control in the regulation of human performance under stress and high workload: a cognitive-energetical framework. Biol. Psychol. **45**(1), 73–93 (1997)
13. http://www.stern.nyu.edu/om/faculty/armony/research/CallCenterSurvey.pdf
14. https://en.wikipedia.org/wiki/Social_support
15. Paula, C., Mila, L.: A model for the influence of social interaction and social support on female expatriates' cross-cultural adjustment. Int. J. Hum. Res. Manage. **13**(5), 761–772 (2002)
16. O'Reilly Charles, A., Roberts Karlene, H.: Information filtration in organizations: three experiments. Organ. Behav. Hum. Perform. **11**(2), 253–265 (1974)
17. Jack Eric, P., Bedics Tom, A., McCary Charles, E.: Operational challenges in the call center industry: a case study and resource-based framework. Managing Serv. Qual. Int. J. **16**(5), 477–500 (2006)
18. Crandall Richard, E., Markland Robert, E.: Demand management-today's challenge for service industries. Prod. Oper. Manage. **5**(2), 106–120 (1996)
19. https://en.wikipedia.org/wiki/Leaky_bucket
20. https://en.wikipedia.org/wiki/Token_bucket
21. Silverman Barry, G.: More realistic human behavior models for agents in virtual worlds: emotion, stress, and value ontologies (2001)
22. Yerkes Robert, M., Dodson John, D.: The relation of strength of stimulus to rapidity of habit-formation. J. Comp. Neurol. Psychol. **18**(5), 459–482 (1908)
23. Janis Irving, L., Leon, M.: Decision Making: A Psychological Analysis of Conflict, Choice, and Commitment. Free Press, New York (1977)
24. Grignard, A., Taillandier, P., Gaudou, B., Vo, D.A., Huynh, N.Q., Drogoul, A.: GAMA 1.6: advancing the art of complex agent-based modeling and simulation. In: Boella, G., Elkind, E., Savarimuthu, B.T.R., Dignum, F., Purvis, M.K. (eds.) PRIMA 2013. LNCS, vol. 8291, pp. 117–131. Springer, Heidelberg (2013)
25. Jiang, L., Probst, T.M.: Organizational communication: a buffer in times of job insecurity? Econ. Ind. Democracy **35**(3), 557–579 (2014)
26. https://en.wikipedia.org/wiki/Antifragile

Shandong Sports Industry Resources Trading Platform's Construction and Operation Research

Licai Zhang[1(✉)] and Yimin Liu[2]

[1] Shandong Sport University, Jinan, China
1101458696@qq.com
[2] Shandong Administration of Sport, Jinan, China
1594886455@qq.com

Abstract. The author participated in the related work of Shandong sports industry resources trading platform, by using the method of expert interview, literature review and logical analysis, etc. To analyze the platform from the angle of the construction and operation mechanism. Starting from the analysis of these two aspects, the author analyzes its existing problems and difficulties in the operation of the trading platform, thus puts forward their own opinions.

Keywords: Shandong sports industry resources trading platform · Construction · Operation mechanism

1 Introduction

1.1 Policy Background

In October 2014, issued by the state council "Opinions of the State Council on accelerating the development of sports industry and promoting sports consumption" ("nation [2014] No. 46") (hereinafter referred to as "nation No. 46") clearly pointed out: "developing sports industry resources trading platform, innovation market operation mechanism, promoting the host, as well as the rights of the event and the development of intangible assets which meets trading conditions fair, just and opening the flow of resources" [1]. In June 2015 to September 2015, the provinces have issued on the implementation of the nation No. 46, Shandong implementation opinion about nation No. 46 [2], clearly put forward to setting up provincial sports industry resources trading platform. According to statistics, in the implementation opinion has been introduced, in addition to a total of 4 provinces and cities in Shandong province, Tianjin, Hebei, Sichuan, Shanxi, respectively, will be made clear in 2016 to complete the construction of the sports industry resources trading platform, the sports industry resources trading platform has entered a stage of rapid growth.

1.2 Purpose Significance

Shandong sports industry resources trading platform is the first provincial sports industry management department and provincial property right transaction center to build the

© Springer Science+Business Media Singapore 2016
L. Zhang et al. (Eds.): AsiaSim 2016/SCS AutumnSim 2016, Part IV, CCIS 646, pp. 389–395, 2016.
DOI: 10.1007/978-981-10-2672-0_40

platform, trading platform will become an important platform of Shandong sports industry resources' circulation. Sports industry resources trading fair is advantageous to the liberation of resources, stimulating vitality, fully giving play to the role of market mechanism, promoting the common social forces to run the sports industry, speeding up the formation of effective competition in the market and expanding sports supply products and services. Establish the meaning of the sports industry resources trading platform is more important under the environment of open and transparent transactions, the greatest degree to preventing and putting an end to corruption "black-box". It can give full play to the market value of evaluation function at the same time, to improve efficiency of resource allocation.

2   Trading Platform Construction Scheme Analysis of Shandong Sports Industry Resources

2.1   The Establishment of Organizations

Shandong sports industry resources trading platform sets up the organization structure reference to property rights trading center trading platform, on the basis of property right transaction integrity, balancing the industrial characteristics of the sports industry. The planning department has decided its divided into function. Specific institutions for setting up as Fig. 1.

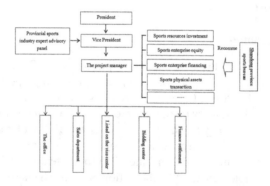

Fig. 1. Shandong sports industry resources trading platform organization chart

2.2   Function Orientation

After establishing the sports industry trading platform, sports industry resources trading will be fair, conducive to liberating resources, stimulating vitality, fully giving play to the role of market mechanism, promoting the common social forces to run up the sports industry, speeding up the formation of effective competition market structure, expanding the sports products and services supply, justly and openly. In addition to attracting more social capital into the sports industry, the more important meaning of the sports industry resources trading platform establishing is, under the environment of open and transparent transacting, doing the greatest degree to preventing and putting an end to corruption "black-box". Also giving full play to the market of evaluation function at the same time, it is promoting the efficiency of the allocation of resources. [3] For the establishing of resource trading platform, sports industry can give full play to the market in the allocation of resources and decisive role, for the sports industry in Shandong province and even the whole country to provide an open, transparent resources flow platform.

2.3 Establishing of the Rules and Regulations

Shandong sports industry resources trading platform mainly implementing the market circulation of Shandong province sports industry resources, maximizing the value of industrial resources through the marketing operation to overflow. Through its will is to achieve the goal that the basic mode of operation, on the basis of meeting all the rules and regulations of property right transaction, objective to follow the special requirements of sports industry, and thus improving the rules and regulations should be covered by the regulations. Therefore, sports industry resources trading platform should include trading rules and measures for the implementation of the rules of operation and capital operation rules, dynamic pricing, enterprises to increase their investment projects operating rules, auction implementation measures, physical assets, trading rules and other common property right transaction rules and regulations based on. Inclusion the declaration of joint development of the resources, the measures for the financial management of the cross industry transactions, and the measures for the management of sports industry members to complete the special requirements of the sports industry profession. Efforts should be made with the sports sector to implement the administrative measures for sports industry resources, quality resources collection methods and other soft regulations auxiliary platform operation demand.

2.4 Business Operation Process

Sports industry resources trading platform has the characteristics of sports industry, so in the business, process is different from other resources. Platform invests is for advertisers and sports event operators with event operation experience, which also collects

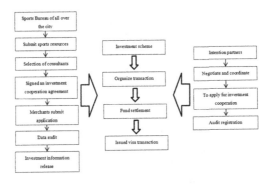

Fig. 2. Trading platform business process

event planning operation plan. The main contents is including the title sponsor rights, the right to use the image of clothing, advertising rights, products provide rights, logo right and other investment business rights. After the release of information, trading platform will be organized, coordinative and promoted greatly. Specific projects will be carried out to discuss from the investment side (Figs. 2 and 3).

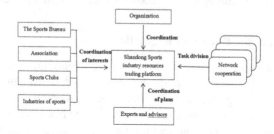

Fig. 3. Diagrammatic drawing of coordination mechanism

3 Research About Trading Platform Operation Mechanism of Shandong Sports

3.1 Coordination Mechanism

Trading platform operation mechanism of Shandong sports, which should ensure fair principles at first, mainly aims to promote the development of sports' industry of Shandong province, and to realize the maximum value of resource in our province. Besides, it can also help to unit the interests of different branches. So trading platform should firstly build its coordination system that can realize the communication between the sports office of Shandong and the other units.

3.2 Guarantee Mechanism

The construction of sports ecological model based on event operation content platform + Intelligence + value added service, which aims to build the platform from four aspects of events, services, content and terminals. The resources trading platform of sports industry in every subsystem, complement each other in good ways. In order to fully mobilize the enthusiasm of each subsystem, the platform should produce the linkage safeguard mechanism, maintain the balance of each subsystem, and work to realize the effective balance of the whole business ecosystem.

Guarantee mechanisms require the formation of a highly efficient environment for individual subsystems, and strive to maintain the stability and effectiveness of the subsystem, which requires a single subsystem to be simple, to form a professional, clustering. According to the modern project management theory, the use of project management knowledge system, theory, methods and the application of subsystems' work-time, cost, quality and risk management, strictly control the subsystems information management, team organization and human resource management.

3.3   Resource Audit Mechanism

Shandong sports industry resources trading platform resources to solicit early, sports industry resources projects are submitted to the Provincial Sports Bureau, through the cities of Shandong Province Sports Bureau. The provincial sports bureau in conjunction with experts, will sort out, screen, assess, audit the resources, and then choose the better ones.

Nowadays, high quality resources are defined as a high degree of concern, higher social awareness, broad market prospects, and sports resources available for market operation. Trading platform for sports industry in Shandong Province resources sets up advisory group of sports industry development, which is composed of the well-known sports industry experts and senior practitionersin our province. They have higher grasp and understand the sports resources in the province. Sports resources will be choosen by the Provincial Sports Bureau to trading platform, the expert advisory group give corresponding market operation opinions for trade. For the failed resources, advisory group will give advice on the development of proposed development views, which help to promote the development of Shandong sports industry.

3.4   Distribution and Supervision Mechanism

Trading platform upholds the Shandong sports industry development concept, although the market operation, not to profit for the purpose.

Transaction platform operating expenses and service member units are divided into the percentage of sports resources in the turnover of the platform, which can eliminate the wrong mode that need pay charge firstly. Shandong Province Sports Bureau will oversee the development direction of the platform, the financial operation mode of supervision, to prevent any form of fund "covert operation".

3.5   Propaganda Mechanism

Shandong sports industry resources trading platform regards the property rights trading center in Shandong Province as parent and sets up a trading platform for the official website to enhance trading platform prestige and recognition. Sports industry resources trading platform with high strength of the policy. Society pays close attention to the development trend of trading platform, the major mainstream media attention to the development trend of trading platform, which are trading platform provides a unique promotional capital. Sports industry in Shandong Province resources trading platform makes full use of advantageous resources, integrates various media, which forms the network propaganda, and continues to the next line of the interactive industry, enhances the trading platform in the sports industry and other industry awareness, credibility.

3.6   Evaluation Mechanism

Healthy development can not be separated from the evaluation. Shandong sports industry resources trading platform thinks provincial sports industry advisory group for evaluation mechanism, so that can promote the development of sports industry in Shandong Province. It forms evaluation system, which contains the annual transaction volume, the transaction amount, the development of related industries, attracting industry investment and financing amount, incubation of new industries such as the number of for specific evaluation indicators, and trading platform development evaluation.

4 Difficult Point Analysis During Running Platform

4.1 Traditional Platform Promoting Way

Even the sports industry resource trading platform came out with policy, people are not familiar to, believing and recognizing it. Trading platform needs some successful stories to enhance the affinity of enterprise and yearning degree of source. Enforcement won't follow the industry developing if only relying on media coverage and traditional thought to popularize.

4.2 Be Difficult to Resource Integration

Platform is "fourth-party", which is independent of buyer, seller and neutral. Even platform is set up by Shandong Provincial Sports Bureau and Shandong Provincial Sports property rights trading company together, it doesn't have fundamental force for the disposal of Sports Resource in Shandong Province. In enlistment resource in the initial operation platform sports, the local Sports Bureau needs to coordinate the Municipal Sports Bureau and Subordinate units, and put high-quality resource on resource industry trading platform by marketing way, in which it doesn't show credibility and effect of marketization.

Besides, most sports resource belong to period of separation and management, the market operation is not high and can't control the resource in fact. It's easy to collect resource tedious or fail.

4.3 Original Pattern of Profit Will Be Broken

Sports Resources units own resource, whether it is the invitation of tender of Sports project or transaction of assets or not, it is mostly done one by one in ways. The market participation is not good and information is not enough, bargaining ability of sports industry resource is a little worse. There are "black box" phenomenons in many projects because of non-standard trading and lacking of supervision. Setting up trading platform will change the current pattern of profit, some units which have special resource errors. The ways in solving the problem profit is the first thing for similar trading platform.

4.4 Lack of Compound Professional Talent

Sports resource trading platform is new industry with pushing from industry policy and developing demand. How to mobilize the enthusiasm fully and coordinate with every department and every industries will be to set up resource trading platform with managing experience of similar projects. Industry can't develop without talents. Sports industry is fusion industry. Compound talents join it to promote development in talent patterns.

5 Conclusion

Shandong sports industry resources trading platform is at the beginning of the construction, the relevant operating mechanism is not perfect, which needs actual combat experiences to enrich and improve its experience. Meanwhile, it needs to break the existing institutional constraints, and positive integration other industries. Implementation and operation of the platform can not do without the professional operation, the trading platform needs to be added to compound talents who have a specific understanding of the sports industry and are full of confidence and passion.

References

1. The State Council: Opinions of the State Council on accelerating the development of sports industry and promoting sports consumption (Nation [2014] No. 46) (2014)
2. Shandong Provincial People's Government: Shandong Provincial People's Government on the implementation of Document No. 46, 2014, accelerate the development of the sports industry to promote the implementation of the views of sports consumption (Lu [2015] No. 19) (2015)
3. Yang, L., Rui, Z.: 8 days 3 sports industry resources trading platform was established. Beijing Business Daily (12) (2014)
4. Kong, W.: Internet plus sports pattern seeking change. China Economic Information Network (12) (2015)

Hierarchical Analysis Model of Human Motion

Xiangchen Li[1], Tianyu Huang[2(✉)], and Jihai Sun[3]

[1] China Institute of Sport Science, Beijing, China
lixiangchen@ciss.cn
[2] School of Software, Beijing Institute of Technology, Beijing, China
huangtianyu@bit.edu.cn
[3] College of Physical Education, Shandong University, Jinan, China
sunjihai@sdu.edu.cn

Abstract. A joint-based hierarchical analysis model of human motion was proposed to solve the problem of the movement intent and quantitative description in human body postures. In this paper, a statistical observation was made on about 181 h video data to be summarized as 31 basic activities, which are defined by genera and species. A four-level hierarchical model with posture-activity- motion- style was proposed in this paper, which is specified formally by PDM (Point Distribution Models). At the final, the model validations were given by the experiments and applications.

Keywords: Human motion · Hierarchically modeling · Joint-based hierarchical analysis models · Point distribution models

1 Introduction

Human motion not only has the characteristics of complexity and diversity, but also can do flexibility and variability characteristics that any mechanical can not finish that. Human motion analysis is a challenging topic. It plays an important role in promoting the development of bionic engineering, medical engineering, sport competitions and animation games. Though tracking and analyzing human motion parameters, human motion analysis achieves the recognition and classification of human behavior, which is the basis of human behavior understanding, and explore the effective method of human motion analysis has important practical significance [1]. Traditional human motion analysis always obtains the human motion information from image sequence or video. With the development of micro sensors, human motion analysis based on MEMS has also been widely focused, but whether it is video based or MEMS based, people are often concerned about only one or a few moves, the object of study is relatively single, also does not have the corresponding theoretical system. In addition, in the process of looking through relevant documents we found that there is no strict division and clear definition about motion, and there are three concepts about posture, activity, motion be confused.

This paper presents a joint-based hierarchical theory and model of human motion, as the theoretical foundation for human motion analysis system. Establishing the human motion hierarchical model has a positive role in quantitative description of human motion and establishing the human motion database.

L. Zhang et al. (Eds.): AsiaSim 2016/SCS AutumnSim 2016, Part IV, CCIS 646, pp. 396–405, 2016.
DOI: 10.1007/978-981-10-2672-0_41

2 Related Works

In recent years, hierarchical model [4] has gradually become a kind of behavior representation method. Hierarchical definition of human motion first proposed by Nagel in 1988 [5], he defined the human motion as 4 layers: change, event, verb, history, 'change' represents change, i.e., the change in addition to the noise, 'event' represents a pre-defined activity, i.e., the basis for description of complex motion, 'verb' represents an act, 'history' is the entire understanding of the whole motion, at this level, not only need to know human's motion, but also must understand the human's environment.

Moeslund et al. [6] made a comprehensive review and summary about the progress of human motion from 2000 to 2006, in this paper, we also used the hierarchical definition method to define the human motion, the motion in accordance with the semantic description is divided into 3 levels: activity/motor primitives, activity and activity. 'Activity/motor primitives' refers to the basic unit of 'activity'; 'activity' is the orderly combination of 'motor primitives'; 'activity' is formed with much 'activity' after a logical combination.

The motion is divided by such a hierarchy according to posture, activity, activity/motion and it is the current more used model, these levels are in accordance with the time scale and the realization of the algorithm from easy to difficult. They put the activity as the basic unit of human motion, but did not notice the role of gesture in human motion analysis, the activity is divided into several more helpful postures to analysis of human activity better, and then to analysis the human motion.

Therefore, this paper will make a systematic analysis of the posture, activity and motion.

3 Statistical Analysis

Although human motion is protean, both in daily life and sports, complex activity or behavior is composed of several basic activity. In order to find out exactly what are the basic activity of the human motion, We studied by watching a total of 28.4G video, that the total duration of 181 h and 31 min, covering the 5 daily behaviors and 119 sports fitness programs, a total of 124 items consisting of the video data, which summarized the 31 basic activities: bowing (106, 0.0306), turning to the side (268, 0.0773), walking forward (632, 0.1822), turning backward (30, 0.0087), retreating (108, 0.0311), running forward (530, 0.1528), jumping up (244, 0.0704), squatting (158, 0.0456), sliding (359, 0.1035), jumping forward (144, 0.0415), sitting (44, 0.0127), kicking (26, 0.0075), cross steps (150, 0.0433), running backward (76, 0.0219), one knee kneeling down (6, 0.0017), lunges (106, 0.0306), horse-riding steps (50, 0.0144), lying (2, 0.0006), somersaults (54, 0.0156), dropping to the ground (38, 0.0110), lying prone (2, 0.0006), rolling over (2, 0.0006), knees kneeling down (4, 0.0012), crawling forward (1, 0.0003), riding (22, 0.0063), splits (4, 0.0012), turning and crawling (1, 0.0003), up the stairs (66, 0.0190), down the stairs (80, 0.0231), side shoveling (6, 0.0017), piaffing (149, 0.0430). The values in the brackets are separately the number of occurrences and the frequency of each activity. The statistics pie chart is illustrated in the Fig. 1. Shown in figure, walking forward is the most common activity in human

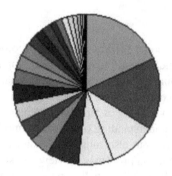

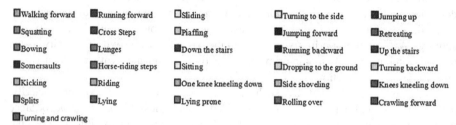

Fig. 1. The proportion of the basic activity

motion, whether in daily life or physical exercise, walking forward is the most basic human activity, which is consistent with the rules of human motion, in the later study we will study on walking emphatically.

Through analyzing the video, we can get conclusions that any complex behaviors are the combination and repetition of these 31 kinds of activities, and therefore they are the most common activities of the human motion. For example, the motion of playing basketball is repeated by walking, running, jumping and other activities.

4 Activity Definition

We used the plus differentia definition method to define the activities [5]. In general, all kinds of elements in a given genus share the certain attributes. These attributes make them become the elements of this genus. However, any kinds of elements share some further attributes, and these attributes make them separate with any other elements of this genus. This attribute used to distinguish them called differentia.

When we define the activity, the human body can be divided into three parts that are upper limbs, trunk, lower limbs, each activity is a combination of the three parts, in which the activity of lower limbs and trunk is relatively simple, such as the trunk can be straight and curved, lower limbs can interactive step, bend the knees and unbend. The activity of upper limbs is relatively complex, but in the definition of activity, we only define it as the auxiliary activity, including the upper limbs drooping and swinging naturally, and the upper limbs bending and swinging naturally. The specific activities are defined as shown in Table 1, in the analysis of human motion, when we describe

Table 1. The table of activity definitions

	Activity (genera)	Definition	Differentia	Activity (species)	Differentia
1	Walking	Legs cross steps and the arms droop and swing naturally, having a displacement toward the direction of the body moving (the displacement can be 0)	There must be one leg on the ground during The process of walking, there must be temporary suspension and high speed during the process of running, legs apart rarely and the displacement of up and down is big during the process of jumping	Walking forward	The direction of displacement is different, the side sliding is moving crosswise(in the frontal plane), the displacement of piaffing is 0
2				Retreating	
3				Side sliding	
4				Cross steps	
5				Up the stairs	
6				Down the stairs	
7				Piaffing	
8	Running	Legs cross forward quickly, the arms bend and swing naturally		Running forward	The direction of displacement is different
9				Running backward	
10	Jumping	Feet off the ground and the body forward or upward		Jumping up	Jumping forward has the forward displacement
11				Jumping forward	
12	Turning	Change the direction of the body		Turning to the side	The variation of human body heading angles is different
13				Turning backward	
14	Kneeling	Knees touch the ground and the shanks are straight		One knee kneeling down	The number of knees touching the ground is different
15				Knees kneeling down	
16	Riding	The activity of riding a bike		Riding	
17	Bowing	Keeping the lower limbs still and the upper limbs bending forward in the sagittal plane		Bowing	
18	Kicking	One leg touches the ground and the other leg keeps away		Kicking	

(Continued)

Table 1. (*Continued*)

	Activity (genera)	Definition	Differentia	Activity (species)	Differentia
		from the frontal plane			
19	Crawling	Hands and feet touch the ground and moving together	There is a displacement of crawling and there is no displacement of lying	Crawling forward	The direction of displacement is different
20				Turning and crawling	
21	Lying	The process of sitting to lying and then to sitting		Lying	
22	Sitting	The process of standing to sitting and then to standing	the downward displacement of squatting is bigger than sitting	Sitting	
23	Squatting	The process of standing to squatting and then to standing		Squatting	
24	Rolling over	Changing the body direction while lying		Rolling over	
25	Lying prone	The body is lying prostrate on the ground		Lying prone	
26	Dropping to the ground	The body touches the ground first after jumping	The difference with jumping is the legs touch the ground first during jumping	Dropping to the ground	
27	Side shoveling	The body falls to the ground and legs extend after running		Side shoveling	
28	Somersaults	The body turns over in the air and then returns to the original state		Somersaults	
29	Lunges	One leg goes one step forward and the knee is straight after bending		Lunges	

(*Continued*)

Table 1. (*Continued*)

	Activity (genera)	Definition	Differentia	Activity (species)	Differentia
30	Horse-riding steps	Legs keep apart and squat	The angle of legs apart is larger	Horse-riding steps	
31	Splits	Legs are apart into 180 degrees and parallel to the ground		Splits	

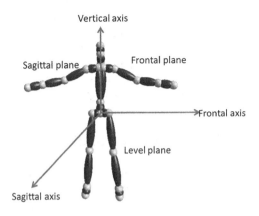

Fig. 2. The schematic of human axial plane

the motion it also involves the body's axial surface and axial direction, from the anatomical point of view, on the basis of the standard posture, often as three kinds of mutually perpendicular sections and axes [6], as shown in Fig. 2, where the frontal plane divided the human body into the frontal part and the reverse part, the sagittal plane divided the human body into the left part and the right part, the level plane divided the human body into two upper part and the lower part.

5 A Joint-Based Hierarchical Model Framework

Through observation, we found that the human motion has the following four key principles:

(1) Human's posture is measurable
(2) Human's activity is limited
(3) Human's motion is unlimited
(4) Human's style is personality

The hierarchical theory of human motion is the combination of Pose, Activity, Motion, and Style. The description of a transient state of a frame (a certain number of sampling points) is called a pose; the continuous pose from one pose after moving back to the pose is called an activity; the combination of a series of activities for a meaningful activity is called a motion. The human body is a hinge structure, the essence of human motion is the transformation of space pose, i.e., the pose is the most basic unit of human motion, which can be quantitatively measured and described by space joint angle [7]; human activity is the result of continuous pose transformation, and it is a periodic change; motion is a series of activities by the random combination with unpredictability. Each person's motion is personalized, which means different people doing the same activity shows his own unique style.

An activity is composed of many poses, but not all poses contain useful information of motion analysis, if all poses are to be studied, which not only spend a lot of time, but also have no significance. In the process of motion analysis, we are concerned about the characteristics of the pose, i.e., the key pose that has a clear distinction with other poses. Activities are the most frequently mentioned in people's daily life, that is the most significant aspects of description of human motion, the same can also introduce the concept of key activities for the motion analysis.

6 Hierarchical Modeling of Human Motion

Pose, activity, motion all can be described, there are clear definitions about the three in the human motion hierarchical model, and the system describes the relations between the three. Pose characterizes the basic unit of human motion, which is described by the original data. Activity characterizes the most representation unit of human motion, which is described by poses. Motion characterizes the most meaningful activity, which is described by activities. There are some blind spots while determining people's pose when used acceleration alone or pose angle exists, and the recognition rate is not high. Therefore, in the hierarchical model of human motion, when the human pose is determined the acceleration data and the attitude angle can be fused to achieve a higher recognition rate.

We apply PDM (Point Distribution Models) [8] to human motion analysis which is abstracted as a rigid body, through the establishment of PDM, a series of poses in the process of human activities are modeled, through the reasonable additional constraints, the poses are not expressed in the activities will be removed off.

PDM-based hierarchical model of human motion describes a series of regular deformation, each shape is defined as a vector:

$$X_s = (x_1, y_1, \cdots, x_n, y_n)^T \tag{1}$$

The vector represents a series of coordinate values that can describe the shape, and is normalized. These deformations are represented by the shape deviation from the median, and the covariance is expressed as follows:

$$\sigma = \frac{1}{n} \sum_{i=1}^{n} (x_i - \bar{x})(x_i - \bar{x})^T \tag{2}$$

Among them,

$$\bar{x} = \frac{1}{n} \sum_{i=1}^{n} x_i \tag{3}$$

To solve the feature vector eigenvalue:

$$\lambda_i e_i = \sigma e_i \tag{4}$$

Each feature vector corresponds to a deformation model, the corresponding eigenvalue and the eigenvector change related. Select the best characterize of the deformation from eigenvalues, therefore the shape after every change is presented as:

$$x' = \bar{x} + Eb \tag{5}$$

Among them, $E = (e_1, \cdots, e_m)$ represents eigenvector, b is the weight vector. Each weight is within a proper limit, so that the shape is similar to the beginning:

$$-3\sqrt{\lambda_k} \le b_k \le 3\sqrt{\lambda_k} \tag{6}$$

In the model of this paper, the pose is presented as

$$P_s = (Y_1, P_1, R_1, \cdots, Y_{11}, P_{11}, R_{11})^T \tag{7}$$

An activity consists of a series of poses, i.e.,

$$A = \{P_1, \cdots, P_n\} \tag{8}$$

Among that, P_i represents the No. i pose in the series of poses. After figuring out $\bar{x}$, we put

$$A' = \{x_1 - \bar{x}, \cdots, x_n - \bar{x}\} \tag{9}$$

as a covariance

$$\sigma = A'A'^T \tag{10}$$

According to the above covariance to solve the eigenvector and the eigenvalue, the eigenvector e_i expresses the pose change, each pose indicate by the formula (5), the final activity can be expressed as

$$A = (E, \bar{x}) \tag{11}$$

After the above steps to complete the mathematical modeling of the activity, the relationship between activity and pose was described mathematically, that is better for the further utilization and analysis of poses, such as we can extract poses from different activities to form a new activity.

7   Experiments and Applications

7.1   Activity Definition

Table 1 gives the 31 basic activity definitions. The meta activity is defined bygenera and species. The differentia is used to distinguish the attributes between genera and species.

7.2   Quantitative Description and Simulation

From the kinematic point of view, the human body is composed of a variety of material forms of various segments, which through the joint link to form a complete system. To facilitate quantitative analysis of poses in human motion, we abstract it into a multi-link rigid system. As long as measuring the velocity, acceleration and other kinematic parameters of each joint angle in the human motion, we can roughly determine the pose of human space motion. According to the hierarchical model of human motion, posture as the bottom layer is not dependent on the sequence context, and the original data is collected directly from the sensor as the information of human motion, according to Hanavan rigid model of the human body [8], ignoring the hands and feet that impact human motion little, the human body model is simplified to the waist, chest, left arm, left forearm and right arm, right forearm, left thigh, left shank and right thigh, right shank, head of 11 parts, in this way, the pose angle and acceleration value of each part can be collected as the frame data for data description. An application of human motion simulation is shown in Fig. 3.

Fig. 3. An application of human motion modeling and simulating

7.3 Data Format

According to the hierarchical model of human motion, posture, activity, motion, style form, in the data storage we need to take into account this hierarchy, which also provides a convenient of data retrieval. XML format enables the information to be encoded in a meaningful structure, computers and human can understand this encoding to a certain extent [9], it also can accurately describe the level relation of posture, activity, motion, and can be directly stored in the database in XML format.

8 Conclusion

A joint-based hierarchical analysis model of human motion was proposed to solve the problem of the movement intent and quantitative description in human body postures. In this paper, a statistical observation was made on about 181 h video data to be summarized as 31 basic activities, which are defined by genera and species. A four-level hierarchical model with posture- activity- motion- style was proposed in this paper, which is specified formally by PDM (Point Distribution Models). It is a preliminary exploration, further research will continue in the classification and definition of the activity, and further improve the hierarchical model [10] of human motion.

References

1. Lara, O.D., Labrador, M.A.: A survey on human activity recognition using wearable sensors. Commun. Surv. Tutorials IEEE **15**(3), 1192–1209 (2013)
2. Niebles, J.C., Fei-Fei, L.: A hierarchical model of shape and appearance for human activity classification. In: Computer Vision and Pattern Recognition, pp. 1–8 (2007)
3. Nagel, H.H.: From image sequences towards conceptual descriptions. Image Vis. Comput. **6**(2), 59–74 (1988)
4. Moeslund, T.B., Hilton, A., Kr, V.: A Survey of advances in vision-based human motion capture and analysis. Comput. Vis. Image Underst. **104**(3), 90–126 (2006)
5. Ni, Y.: New insights on the concept of the object and its definition. J. Anhui Univ. Philos. Soc. Sci. **28**(1), 18–23 (2004)
6. Mao, B., Liu, M.: Anatomic measurement and kinematic analysis of the lower joint. J. Chinese Orthop. **16**(1), 50–52 (1996)
7. Feng-Shun Lin, J., Karg, M., Kulić, D.: Movement primitive segmentation for human motion modeling: a framework for analysis. IEEE Trans. Hum. Mach. Syst. **46**(3), 325–339 (2016)
8. Nair, P., Cavallaro, A.: 3-D face detection, landmark localization, and registration using a point dictribution model. IEEE Trans. Multimedia **11**(4), 611–623 (2009)
9. Youkang, H.: Hanavan rigid model and calculation of the human body. J. Wuhan Sports Coll. **4**, 81–88 (1983)
10. Huang, T., Li, F., Zhan, S.-y., Min, J.: Variable duration motion texture for human motion modeling. In: Yang, Q., Webb, G. (eds.) PRICAI 2006. LNCS (LNAI), vol. 4099, pp. 603–612. Springer, Heidelberg (2006)

An Approach for Analysis of Magnetic Disturbance Based on Maxwell Modeling for the Load of Simulation Turntable

Feng Yue, Tao Lv[✉], and Shuang Wang

The Research and Development Center of Infrared Detection Technology of China Aerospace
Science and Technology Corporation, Shanghai Institute of Spaceflight Control Technology,
Shanghai, China
Lvtao913@163.com

Abstract. When a simulation turntable is delivered to users, the general
magnetic analysis method is applied to test the magnetic field intensity on the
fitting surface of load by using some special instruments (e.g. Gauss meter). This
paper proposes an approach for analysis of magnetic disturbance by modeling
and simulation based on Ansoft Maxwell, considering the disturbances can not
be determined before the simulation turntable is used with load, such as the gyro.
By modeling the simulation turntable and the load, calculating the magnetic
distribution around them, we can realize whether the simulation turntable inter-
feres with load is validated and the interference magnitude is also reflected. By
comparing the simulation analysis and experimental results, the proposed method
can accurately analyse the magnetic filed generated by the simulation turntable
to avoid the test error which may influence or damage the product.

Keywords: Maxwell · Magnetic disturbance · Simulation turntable · Modeling

1 Introduction

The rotational symmetry of a gyro component has a great influence on output signal
quality. This gyro component, conducted in the five-axis simulation turntable flight
test (such as Fig. 1), once appeared rotational symmetry instability by unknown
causes. The instability affected the quality of output signal of gyro component. After
the test, the possibilities of impacts caused by target axis light parallelism of five-
axis simulation table, load installation alignment and position control precision were
excluded. It is noticed that the output signal of gyro component changed because of
inner magnetic materials and the different axial installation position of load. In order
to determine the influence factors which may cause the signal disturbance of the
simulation turntable at run time, the effects on the surrounding magnetic field should
be analyzed,

In order to meet the bandwidth index, simulation turntable usually requires characteristic of fast response to control commands. Thus, the drive system's power, especially
the electrical simulation turntable's power, is high generally. It is easy to produce muta-
tive magnetic and electric field in the turntable body and the surrounding space.

© Springer Science+Business Media Singapore 2016
L. Zhang et al. (Eds.): AsiaSim 2016/SCS AutumnSim 2016, Part IV, CCIS 646, pp. 406–419, 2016.
DOI: 10.1007/978-981-10-2672-0_42

Fig. 1. Flight test & five-axis simulation turntable

The load of simulation turntable is usually put in this area, which may generate force to coil or metal parts of the load. The magnetic force may affect the normal operation of the load, resulting in some erroneous testing results of the simulation and even damaging the product.

Institutions in different countries developed over test equipments, such as three-axis simulation turntable, "flight motion simulator" or simply "turntable". But for various reasons, they did not consider the magnetic interference from the components of the flight simulator [1]. Thus, at present it is not common to consider the magnetic field environment during the design stage of simulation turntable.

Due to the compact structure of simulation turntable and working in the high-frequency vibration state, it is difficult to install space magnetic field detection equipment. Before delivery, users usually detect the magnetic field only in the static case with a Gauss meter and other special instruments on load installation position. However, such detection cannot determine the dynamic rotary magnetic field generated by the drive system. To test the dynamic field, sensors need to be installed on the turntable and load. But because of the lack of precise, continuous rotation, ultra-low magnetic interference automatic test and calibration equipment [2], the cost of testing is high, even impossible. This paper introduces a more flexible approach for analysis of magnetic disturbance based on the Ansoft Maxwell software modeling and simulation method. Magnetic interference can be obtained in a relatively short period of time. Magnetic interference from simulation turntable can be quickly excluded or easy to determine the impact on the measured products. The paper is organized as follows. In Sect. 2, the simple principle of magnetic field analysis based on Maxwell is given. In Sect. 3, we focus on the description of the simulation analysis of turntable space magnetic field. As a case study, a model of turntable bracket and the load which implements the proposed method is also presented. In Sect. 4, experimental analysis of turntable space magnetic field is discussed. Finally, in Sect. 5, the conclusion and future work are outlined.

2   The Simple Principle of Magnetic Field Analysis Based on Maxwell

Generally, load mounting bracket of inner axis made of metal materials, is driven by high power motor. Products loaded in bracket tend to be composed of magnetic materials in the moving parts. In the use of simulation turntable test, the load bracket may affect magnetic components of product, especially the movement of the gyroscope. Usually the causes of the magnetic field disturbances to surrounding space of load are as follows. (1) Winding coil in drive motor create space of magnetic flux leakage and magnetic pollution while working. (2) The rotary metal bracket cutting magnetic induction line generate induced current. (3) Control electrical signals of inner axis generate space radiation. These factors may cause different magnetic noise to load while simulation turntable is running, and the effects are superimposed. If calculation is made item by item, especially in irregular space superposition calculation, it will lead to huge computational complexity. The model of the magnetic space needs to be simplified. Thus, the detection efficiency will not be high enough, and the simplified model will lead to the lower calculation precision.

It is known by Lorentz force formula (1) that the relationship between the magnetic induction intensity and the forces between objects is:

$$F = q \cdot v \cdot B \cdot \sin \theta \tag{1}$$

Where, the magnetic force F between objects is determined by magnetic induction B and the relative velocity vector $v \cdot \sin \theta$ between objects. q is the amount of charge, a constant.

When using the simulation turntable, the product is measured in the load bracket, the motion relationship between the product and simulation turntable load bracket is constant. It is easy to determine whether the simulation turntable load bracket affects product movement, by testing whether the surrounding magnetic induction lines (magnetic induction B) distribution is changed in different gyro assembly installation location. According to the changing magnitude of magnetic induction line, the magnetic influence on moving parts of the product caused by load bracket can be confirmed.

The force is generated by magnetic field superposition of interaction force, which can be analyzed through the space magnetic induction intensity B. By back stepping disturbance quantity of this space, interference which may be caused by some parts of turntable can be calculated. Ansoft Maxwell software is based on the finite element analysis. With high accuracy solution of magnetic induction B, this software can be used to reasonably divide the finite element according to the spatial dimension finite element model, Therefore, this paper presents the analysis based on Maxwell's field modeling method to determine whether the simulation turntable generate magnetic interference to the load.

3   Simulation Analysis of Turntable Space Magnetic Field

Modeling and simulation are important processes in perspective of design, test, and also in this case.

A. The establishment of turntable and load simulation model

The establishment of turntable and load simulation model mainly includes three steps: load mounting bracket and load of turntable's model structure, model material set, physical boundaries set of constraints.

(1) Establish a model of turntable load installation structure and load. Built the model of turntable and load in Maxwell software platform, which is consistent with the real dimensions of the load and mounting bracket. According to the actual size of turntable load mounting bracket and the load, model is shown in Fig. 2.

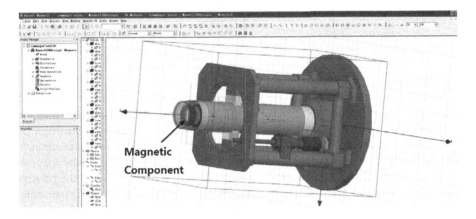

Fig. 2. Model of turntable bracket and the load

(2) Set up the material parameters used in the simulation model. After establishing the model, the material parameters need to be set according to the actual turntable and load materials. In the magnetic analysis, the model parameters of ferromagnetic material and the conductor with current should be considered. Load mounting bracket is made of metal material. If necessary, the magnetic coercive force coefficient parameters needs to be set by testing the actual material used in the model.

As shown in Fig. 2, there is an internal composition of magnetic components made of AlNiCo5 in measured product. In addition to setup the regular parameters, the initial magnetic pole direction of magnetic materials also needs to set. Figure 3 is showing the Maxwell software material parameters settings and some options can be seen from the picture. AlNiCo5 space magnetic induction intensity of the material is anisotropic and nonlinear. Space magnetic induction intensity settings need to fit different directions with different data [3]. While material parameters are setting up in the simulation model, the initial direction of the magnetic materials and space magnetic induction intensity variation are important parameters in the simulation. The precision of these two parameters has a great effect on reliability of simulation results.

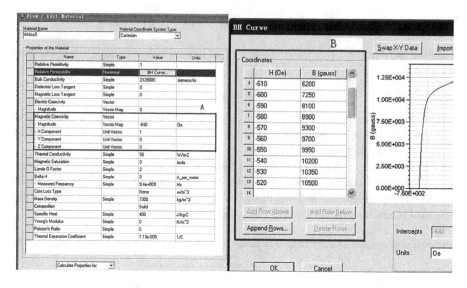

Fig. 3. Related parameter of AlNiCo5 magnets

In Maxwell software, the magnetic pole direction of the magnetic material AlNiCo5 is set as a vector and points to N pole. By setting the three-axis direction in the rectangular coordinate system, vector components can synthesize the final direction of the magnetic vector. Part A in the red box body in Fig. 3, Maxwell software defines the component values of magnetic pole in three-axis direction. Default parameters of software are positive, then the direction of the magnetic vector component in the axis and the positive direction of the axis is in the same direction. Otherwise, if the corresponding parameter is set to a negative number, indicating vector component in the axis and the positive direction of the axis is in the opposite direction.

The Z axis coincides with the rotation axis. The rotation axis is the perpendicular to the plane which is formed from rotation of the magnetic pole of the material. The pole direction is determined at two typical positions during simulation: pole N points parallelly to the X-axis; pole N points parallelly to the Y-axis.

In setting up the direction of material's pole, three axial component composes N pole, pointing to the direction of the vector of material. However, the vector modulus values do not represent the space magnetic induction intensity of the material. Most of the magnetic induction intensity surrounding magnetic materials decreases non-linearly with the increase of distance space, and most of them cannot be described as a function accurately. So when we set up the magnetic induction around space of magnetic material, curve fitting method is used in Maxwell software. As shown in Part B in the red box body of Fig. 3, the space distribution of magnetic induction of the material is set by input mode and using the measured data. While the discrete data input into software, fitting magnetic induction continuous curve of magnetic space is formed automatically in Maxwell. So the more experimental data, the more accurate of curve fitting.

(3) Excitation loading and simulation boundary settings. Related parameters of electromagnetic valve and motor winding must be set with necessary constraints of

insulating boundary, because there exist electromagnetic valve and motor winding in the load mounting bracket of inner axis. If current does not flow along the bracket, electric current loop and magnetoelectric incentives will not generate, and the error simulation results are not exited. In excitation settings, motor and electromagnetic valve are simplified to an equivalent coil. They are loaded with the corresponding excitation current to realize the actual electromagnetic characteristics of the motor and the electromagnetic valve, and effectively reduce the complexity of the algorithm at the same time.

In the simulation boundary setting, we need to set up the zero vector space boundary. The simulation stops on this border to reduce the computational complexity of the computer. At the joint of different material surface, some parts of surface get treatment, such as oxalic acid oxidation. This layer of surface treatment is very thin and far less than the size of model space. It is not necessary to be drawn in model. In order to guarantee the insulation effect, insulating boundary need to be set at the joint in different parts of the model to make sure the current blocking performance. The boundary effect of oxalic acid oxidation is shown in Fig. 4:

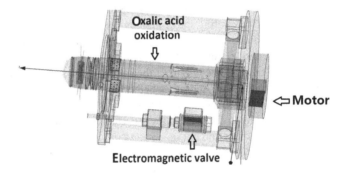

Fig. 4. Effect of excitation loading and boundary settings. *Green color* is boundary effect of oxalic acid oxidation, *Purple color* is excitation effect of motor and electromagnetic valve settings. (Color figure online)

The internal state of electrical components of turntable changes at run time, and these changes often lead to the change of surrounding space magnetic field. To make the simulation more realistic, excitation signal on a charged object should be set to ensure these parts reflect real electromagnetic characteristics. Excitation effect of motor and electromagnetic valve settings are also shown in Fig. 4.

B. Simulation model calculating and result interpretation

After the construction of the simulation model, model calculating parameters need to be determined according to the requirements of the simulation precision and computing ability. Because Maxwell is a kind of finite element analysis software, after the settings of the overall dimensions, the excitation and the boundary, the model needs to be split into grid. In order to ensure the accuracy of the simulation, the tetrahedral grid side length should be less than or equal to tenth of split side. However, too small split grid makes computation increase sharply. Thus, taking the computer operation ability into account, maximum length of the grid tetrahedron side is defined as one over ten of the divided side length. Specific grid split results as shown in Fig. 5:

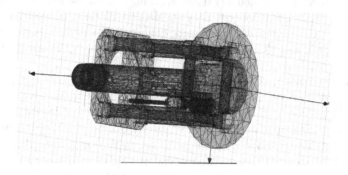

Fig. 5. Effect of grid model

After the model grid, we need to set up the simulation steps and parameters related to the tolerance precision. Considering the computer operation ability, the tolerance is set to 5 % [4]. The results can be seen in Fig. 5. The software does not use uniform grid size in different part of the model during split process to reduce the calculation amount [5]. Split size depends on the specific length of the different parts in this model.

After the simulation model calculating, whether the turntable bracket producing magnetic interference to load can be interpreted by the following three methods: drawing of the magnetic induction intensity envelope; the establishment of the observation surface; rendering magnetic induction curve.

(1) Mapping the surrounding space magnetic induction intensity envelope of model to observe the distribution and extension state of the actual magnetic induction line of load. When the model of turntable load rotates at different location, magnetic induction intensity from internal of the load are calculated. Different magnetic induction envelopes are generated by the magnetic material AlNiCo5, and the outermost layer envelope is the magnitude of 10e−4 T.

Normally, when we set in the software, the default non-magnetic metal surface magnetic induction is 10e−4 T magnitude. Within this magnetic induction space, the

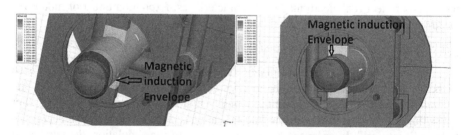

Fig. 6. Zero magnetic induction envelope of magnets in different positions. Left Fig, pole in the x-axis, Right Fig, pole in y-axis.

magnetic field between two objects should be zero. So the envelope is also known as "zero magnetic induction envelope". Because the gyro component needs to rotate, the symmetry of the space magnetic induction envelope of the magnetic parts, usually as axisymmetric, needs improvement. The rotational symmetry of magnetic components is guaranteed by manufacturing process. If the rotation of the rotating magnetic part is disturbed and the rotational symmetry is degraded, it must be realized through the perturbation on the distribution of the peripheral magnetic line of magnetic part. The disturbance causes changes of space magnetic induction envelope of magnetic components. When the changes are greater than 10e−4 T magnitude, they will make the "zero magnetic envelope" deformation and generate asymmetry. Figure 6 shows the envelope of magnetic induction, which is not affected by the load bracket. Thus it can be initially determined that the load mounting bracket does not generate magnetic disturbance on loaded product.

(2) Establish the observation surface, check reduction situation of magnetic induc-tion in and around the magnetic components. Estimating magnetic force between objects through the zero magnetic envelope is more accurate while the geometry object is regular. However, structure of the turntable load mounting bracket is not central symmetric, (only an axisymmetric geometry), and the actual simulation drawings of zero magnetic induction envelope are also axisymmetric graphics. It is difficult to distin-guish whether the zero magnetic induction envelope occurs deformation during the rotating situation. Meanwhile, the method of drawing the magnetic induction intensity envelope can only be observed through zero magnetic induction intensity envelope. It is unable to effectively observe descent of magnetic induction intensity around the magnetic material. So we need to "open" envelope and check the actual magnetic induc-tion descent gradient. As shown in Fig. 7, the observation surface is established in the

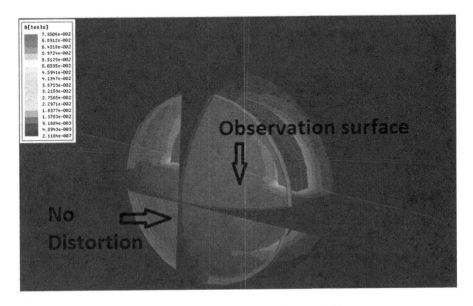

Fig. 7. Magnetic induction intensity nephogram inside magnets

model of magnetic materials. The magnetic induction intensity descent situation can be effectively observed around the magnetic materials. By observing the magnetic induction intensity descent gradient, the envelope distortion cannot be found inside. Then it can further determine that the load bracket does not affect the spatial magnetic induction line of magnetic components during the rotating state.

(3) Drawing of quantitative magnetic induction intensity curve. In order to determine the magnetic influences more accurately, which are tiny in magnetic space of turntable load, the magnetic induction intensity changing surrounding space need to be calculated quantitatively. By establishing the observation curve, we can check the distribution curve of the magnetic induction intensity in different position at different time. The changes of magnetic induction intensity of motional magnetic material in space can be interpreted. Magnetic observation lines of magnetic induction intensity curve are established along the direction of the pole. As shown in Fig. 8 (above and below), magnetic pole is in different position.

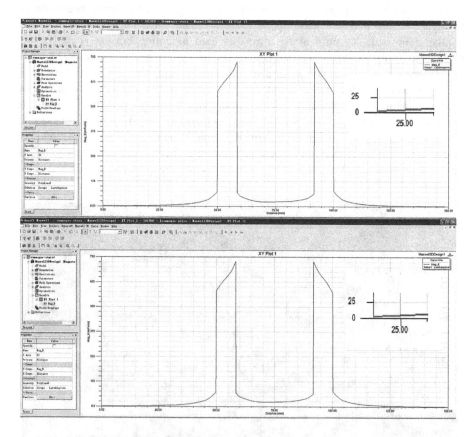

Fig. 8. Magnetic induction intensity distribution of magnetic materials in different position. The above and below are hardly the same.

According to the actual model, load mounting bracket and observation line intersect at 25 mm of the abscissa in Fig. 8.

By setting magnetic material at two different pole positions, the magnetic induction intensity of bracket (abscissa, 25 mm) is partial enlarged to figure in the upper right corner (ordinate for milli-tesla, 10e−3 T). It is shown that magnetic induction intensity is less than 250 Gauss in this part. In actual cases, the magnetic force comes from inter-action between peripheral electrons of atom of objects. Since some of the magnetic induction intensity on the surface of the metal are in scale of 2000 Gauss, the metal is considered to be non-magnetic [6]. Some commonly used non-magnetic metals are given in literature [6]. The range is between 1500–2000 Gauss of the magnetic induction intensity on the surface. Different metal surface magnetic induction intensity is influ-enced by different factors, such as various processing technology. The distributions of the magnetic induction line are also highly irregular. In Maxwell, the magnetic induction intensity on the surface of nonmagnetic metal is set to 0 gauss [4]. So according to above situation, the magnetic induction intensity of bracket (abscissa, 25 mm, in Fig. 8) should be in the magnitude of 1750–2250 Gauss.

We can draw magnetic induction intensity curve along different symmetrical axis of the magnetic components. By comparing the change of the magnetic induction intensity of the two symmetrical axis, two curves are almost completely coincident, as shown in Fig. 8 (above and below). This phenomenon shows that in the process of rotation, magnetic induction intensity has no obvious fluctuation within the magnetic space during load movement. The turntable has no interference to the magnetic field.

4   Experimental Analysis of Turntable Space Magnetic Field

In order to verify the simulation results, the load was installed in load mounting bracket, the same type of magnetic sensors was installed in different location of the load. The output of sensors array under different working conditions of turntable were acquired via digital system (AD sampling). By analyzing changes of magnetic induction intensity surrounding the load, whether the turntable caused the magnetic interference to the magnetic parts of load during operation can be judged. As shown in Fig. 9, sensors were placed at the position of the same distance relative to the symmetry center of magnetic component. They were marked as 1–4.

In the experiment, turntable was set as power off, return zero completion and running status respectively to test the actual output of sensors. Through the acquisition of sensors output signal at the same condition, no uniformity of space magnetic induction intensity of the bracket can be detected. Sensors array output signal sampling curve of the three situations are shown in Fig. 10 below.

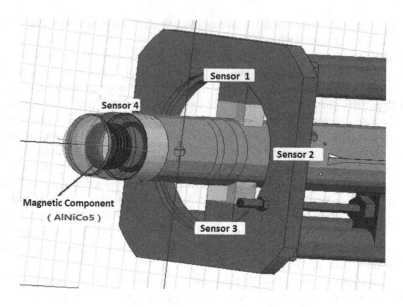

Fig. 9. Sensor placement in space magnetic field experiment.

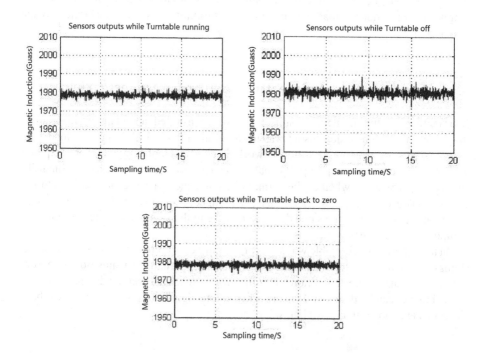

Fig. 10. Sensors sampling curves in space magnetic field experiment.

The sampled magnetic induction intensity range does not exceed 20 Gauss, and all the sensors array outputs magnitude are within 2000 Gauss. It can be determined that the turntable under different working condition did not lead to sharp fluctuations in space magnetic field surrounding the turntable load. By observing the different sensors' output of the turntable in the same condition, the space magnetic induction intensity symmetry center of the turntable load bracket is the rotation center of the turntable load. From the center of rotation to different locations on the load (the sensors mounting position 1–4), the average variation of magnetic induction is not more than 20 Gauss with the same distance. That is the magnetic induction lines at equidistant positions to the center of rotation load are uniform. In this case, the load mounting bracket rotates did not cut uneven magnetic induction line, or produced induced magnetic fluctuations from metallic bracket.

Average outputs of sensors at different location are shown in Fig. 11 below (ordinate for Gauss [7], transverse four points for average output of different label sensors) under different condition of turntable. Through the observation of curves, obvious variation tendency of outputs cannot be found in different condition. That is in the space surrounding the turntable load, magnetic induction intensity did not change with the position and working condition of the turntable.

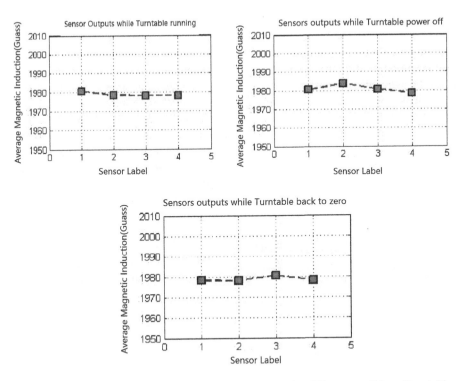

Fig. 11. Average output of sensors at different location under different condition of turntable

Table 1 lists the average outputs of sensors at different location under different condition of turntable. The data in Table 1 shows that even though turntable is in different states, the sensor outputs were substantially the same, and the range was between 1980 ± 10 Gauss.

Table 1. Average Output of sensors at different location under different condition of turntable

Turntable status	Sensor label 1	Sensor label 2	Sensor label 3	Sensor label 4
Power off	1979.6	1981.7	1978.5	1977.7
Running	1978.1	1982.8	1983.2	1978.5
Return zero	1978.1	1984.9	1983.1	1980.2

The output values of the same sensor under different conditions were compared, showing that the changes under different working conditions were small. They did not exceed 20 Gauss magnitude. The magnetic interference around the space can be considered negligible. Change of turntable work status caused no disturbance to the magnetic induction surrounding space, and the experiment results are consistent with Maxwell simulation.

5   Conclusion

According to the method described herein, by Maxwell modeling and simulation software, together with data interpretation, the analysis of spatial magnetic field surrounding the load on the turntable has high credibility. It is a new method to study turntable spatial magnetic field distribution without depending on special magnetic field measuring instrument. It is proved that the testing with this simulation turntable does not produce magnetic interference to the gyro component of load. Through this simulation method, products with strong magnetic sensibility can be measured in turntable. It will provide prejudgment before test and reduce the probability of damage to product. The proposed method can improve the reliability of the experimental data during product testing and provide the basis for accurate validation of the product performance.

This kind of magnetic simulation also provides a low cost and high reliability analysis method for the magnetic field environment impact of test equipments during the scheme design phase.

Limited to computing ability, the tetrahedral grid side length is defined tenth of split side length in this paper. As future work the follow-up will study the relationship between the finite element grid and the simulation accuracy, to improve confidence level of the simulation.

References

1. Wang, X., Dai, Y., Tao, J., Zeng, J., Li, F.: The magnetic analysis and structure design of tri-axial non-magnetical turntable. Chin. J. Mech. Eng. **13**, 21 (2008)
2. Li, F.: The magnetic properties analysis and experimental research of the non-magnetic turntable. Shanghai Jiao Tong University (2011)

3. Li, X., Chen, H.: An illusion effect of MAXWELL's fish-eye lens. Sci. China (Inf. Sci.) **12**, 154–158 (2013)
4. Honecker, A., Mila, F., Troyer, M.: Magnetiztion plateaux and jumps in a class of frustrated ladders a simple route to a complex behavior. Eur. Phys. J. B **2**, 227–233 (2000)
5. Truong, D.Q., Ahn, K.K.: Force control for hydraulic load simulator using self-tuning trey predictor—fuzzy PID. Mechatronics **2**, 233–246 (2008)
6. Lin, R.M., Zhu, J.: Model updating of damped structures using FRF data. Mech. Syst. Signal Process. **8**, 2200–2218 (2006)
7. Kang, C.-I., Kim, C.-H.: An adaptive notch filter for suppressing mechanical resonance in high track density disk drives. Microsyst. Technol. **8**, 638–652 (2005)

Evaluation of Process Simulation Model Based on a Multi-level Test Case Method

Lili Jia[✉], Beike Zhang, and Yangyang Song

Information Science and Technology College,
Beijing University of Chemical Technology, Beijing, China
jll_diligent@163.com

Abstract. The credibility of process simulation model is one of the most important indicators that evaluate whether the simulation is success. However, up to now, the assessment methods for simulation model depend too much on the experts' subjective opinions and there is not a complete assessment mechanism that can be used to perform chemical engineering assessment easily. In this paper, an assessment method based on multi-level test cases for chemical process simulation model was proposed. The evaluation was divided into five levels. We took the evaporator simulation model as an example to establish multi-level test cases, which accomplished the credibility evaluation of simulation system effectively and improved the work efficiency greatly.

Keywords: Credibility · Model evaluation · Process simulation

1 Introduction

With the development of industry intellectualization, application fields of process simulation model for flow enterprises have become more widely and been extended to some other fields such as education and training, project design, auxiliary production, auxiliary study and so on. At the same time, the requirements for the credibility of simulation model under various working conditions have become more and more strict. So the value of the simulation depends on the credibility of simulation model that meets the requirements of system [1]. There are three main assessment methods for the credibility of simulation model at present. They are qualitative method, quantitative method and fuzzy comprehensive evaluation method.

- Qualitative method

This method is mainly rely on the external performance of the system and the experience of experts, taking a certain subjective analytical approach like Turing test, Graphic comparison to evaluate the credibility of simulation and make a qualitative conclusion. Hermann proposed a surface validation method, which means domain experts can intuitively determine the effectiveness of simulation model according to their experiential knowledge [2]. Hong Zehua used the Turing test to assess the credibility of the aircraft hardware-in-the-loop simulation system [3].

Although qualitative method is practical and easy to learn and master, it suffers the weakness that the evaluation highly depends on the subjective assessment of experts.

L. Zhang et al. (Eds.): AsiaSim 2016/SCS AutumnSim 2016, Part IV, CCIS 646, pp. 420–431, 2016.
DOI: 10.1007/978-981-10-2672-0_43

- Quantitative method

The quantitative method mainly aims at consistency analysis of input and output data of the system and the data from model. It depends on the statistical analysis methods or mathematical analysis method such as Parameter estimation, Hypothesis test and Spectrum analysis, etc. Balci proposed a method that increases the model validation workload by increasing the sample size in order to reduce the risk for the use of Hypothesis test method [4]. Liu Shikao achieved the credibility evaluation using similarity to compare actual output and model output [5].

Quantitative methods depend on the data support from real system test. However, it has limitation in the situation that lack of data, which makes it difficult to effectively evaluate the model.

- The fuzzy comprehensive evaluation method

Fuzzy evaluation method fuse the qualitative method and quantitative method, and it unify the opinions from estimator and then express the opinions by a certain algorithm. However, there are too many factors that affect the credibility of the model besides the fuzzy factors. Only relying on the subjective judgment of staff will reduce the objectivity [6]. Zhao Caishan used hierarchy analysis method based on triangular fuzzy number and fuzzy comprehensive evaluation method to evaluate the credibility in rural distribution simulation training system, which provides an approach for the study of simulation system [7]. But the experts' subjective experience still has a significant impact on the results.

2   Multi-level Assessment Cases Method

In the process of chemical production, the application fields of simulation software have been extended wider. The credibility of the simulation model is needed. Then multi-level assessment cases method that performed engineering evaluation easily is proposed, which combines the qualitative and quantitative knowledge based on system mechanism to assess the credibility of the model. The evaluation is divided into five levels, not only includes the evaluation of the start and stop operation in chemical process, but also abnormal conditions and equipment failure and other assessments. And in this paper, verification and validation techniques are applied to each level. When model passes through different levels' testing, it represents that the model is with varying degrees of credibility.

2.1   Validation, Verification and Testing Techniques

There are 75 validation, verification and testing techniques that Balci [8] have presented. We next present some techniques.

Parameter Variability – Sensitivity Analysis is a technique that consists of changing the values of the input and internal parameters of a model to determine the effect upon the model and its output. Those parameters that are sensitive, i.e., cause significant changes in the model's behavior, should be made sufficiently accurate prior to using the model.

Historical Data Validation where part of the data is used to build the model and the remaining data are used to determine if the model behaves as the system does if historical data exist.

Face Validity is the subjective judgment of domain experts who asked whether the model behavior is reasonably and whether the model is sufficiently accurate.

Traces if a technique that involves determining if the logic of the model is correct when the behaviors of different types of entities in the model is traced.

2.2   Multi-level Evaluation System

In this paper, Parameter Variability was used to each level of evaluation system. And the proposed five levels are as follows:

- Grade-A: tendency evaluation with single factor

The grade-A only concerned with the trend of a single variable in the system and only focus on direct outcome that variables caused. Once the trend of variables accord with system working principles, it can be confirmed that the simulation model passed through grade-A test and would has a credibility of grade-A. For example, in the feed pipe of evaporator system, the relationship between feed flow F_1 and valve opening A_1 can be expressed as follows:

$$F_1 = A_1 * C_{v1} * \sqrt{P_{in} * (P_{in} - P)} \tag{1}$$

In Eq. (1), F_1 denotes the feed flow, A_1 is the valve opening, C_{v1} is the flow coefficient, P_{in} is the feed pressure, and P represents the pressure in the evaporator. If the valve opening A_1 of feed valve V_1 (see in Fig. 2) was changed form 20 % to 50 %, whether the growth rate of feed flow F_1 is increased should be observed.

- Grade-B: semi-quantitative evaluation with single factor (steady state evaluation)

The grade-B only concerned with the value of variable in a steady state. When the steady-state value of the variable varying within the desired range, it can be considered that the simulation model has passed through grade-B test. For example, a open tank with a certain amount of water is heated under normal atmospheric pressure, and the temperature of the water will always be steady at 100°C.

- Grade-C: quantitative evaluation with single factor

The grade-C mainly focused on the degree and feature points of curves' that variables vary with time, such as inflection points, maximum points, and minimum points and so on. It can be considered that the simulation model has passed through grade-C test when the degree and feature points of variables are coincide with the real system.

For feature point, consider the evaporator tank. Open the feed valve V_1 and the feed flow F_1 is kept constant, after one minute, close valve V_1 and open the outlet valve V_2 to make the outlet flow F_2 constant. During the process, the variable of evaporator level is increased at the beginning, and then decreased linearly. The relationship between level and flow (inlet and outlet) can be expressed as follows:

$$\frac{dL}{dt} = \frac{F_1 - F_2}{\pi * r * r} \tag{2}$$

In Eq. (2), L denotes the level of the evaporator tank, and r represents the radius of tank bottom.

Obviously, the curve of the evaporator level exist a feature point which can be calculated accurately. So, if the feature points of liquid level curve derived from the simulation model in accordance with the calculated feature points, it can be confirmed that the simulation model has passed through grade-C test.

For curve's degree, however, data on the real system may be unavailable, so differential equation analysis can be applied to find out whether the model is correct. For example, the liquid holdup m of evaporator is changed by inlet flow F_1 and outlet flow F_2 (see in Fig. 2), which can be expressed by differential equation as follow:

$$\frac{dm}{dt} = F_1 - F_2 \tag{3}$$

If the changing of the difference between inlet flow F_1 and outlet flow F_2 is close to the changing of the curve slope of liquid holdup at the same time, then it will be considered that the simulation model has passed through grade-C test.

- Grade-D: interaction evaluation

One case is the competition between multi-factors, that is, two or more factors with the same trend but different slope affect a single variable. Then as long as the degree and feature points of the variable curve are consistent with the real system, it can be considered that the model has D grade reliability. For example, Evaporator system is heated by two streams (Q_{first}, Q_{second}), and its temperature T is influenced by two shares of the heating steam temperature (T_{first}, T_{second}). When $T_{first} > T_{second}$ ($Q_{first} > Q_{second}$), the stream one has greater impact on the evaporator temperature; when $T_{first} < T_{second}$ ($Q_{first} < Q_{second}$), the steam two has greater impact on the evaporator temperature. Differential equation is expressed as follows:

$$\frac{d}{dt}(mcT) = UA(T_{first} - T) + UA(T_{second} - T) - q(v) \tag{4}$$

After the reduction:

$$\frac{d}{dt}(mcT) = UA(T_{first} + T_{second} - 2T) - q(v) \tag{5}$$

In Eq. (3), m is the evaporator liquid holdup, c is the specific heat capacity, $q(v)$ is the vapor heat.

The other case is the negative effects offset between several factors. That is, two or more factors with opposite trend affect a single variable the same time. As long as the order and feature points of the variable curve are consistent with the real system, it will be considered that the model has D-grade reliability. For example, an evaporator is affected by heating steam and cooling water (T_{heat}, T_{cool}). When $T_{heat} > T_{cool}$, the stream one has greater impact on the evaporator temperature, and the evaporator temperature may be increased; when $T_{heat} < T_{cool}$, the steam two has greater impact on the evaporator temperature and the evaporator temperature may be decreased; when $T_{heat} = T_{cool}$, the evaporator temperature remains unchanged.

- Grade-E: multi-fault mode evaluation

Grade-E emphasized equipment failure, and the impact on technological process that external disturbance caused. Model analysts need to consider many kinds of fault that system may exist, and then write the evaluation case. In this way, if the simulation model passed the grade-E test, it will be considered that the simulation model positively simulates the state of real system under fault conditions and has E grade reliability. For example, there may be many abnormal problems, such as pipe blockage, pipeline leakage and suddenly increased heat, etc. in the evaporator simulation system [10].

2.3   The Application for Multi-level Evaluation System

In the chemical production process, the application fields of simulation software have become more and more widely. However, the credibility requirements for simulation model in different fields are different. The main differences are as follows [9].

- Operator training. Simulation software can be used in the chemical process to train operators and help them memorize operation steps.
- Verification tool. The simulation software with high precision can provide a basis for verification of complex control system, which can not only save money, but accelerate the acquisition for analog data.
- Process design. Simulation model can better simulate the dynamic changes of the system, which can help technological design personnel design operation scheme and operation steps.
- Production optimization. Applying simulation software in the production optimization can directly avoid the dangers in the device test and economic losses.
- Model prediction. Simulation models with high quality have good predictability and can predict long-time phenomenon in a relatively short period of time, which benefit the trouble-free operation of production.

In this paper, multi-level evaluation system was proposed and the corresponding relation between simulation software and evaluation system was described. The different requirements for the credibility of simulation software in different application fields are as follows (Table 1).

Table 1. Requirements for the credibility of simulation software

Application fields	Credibility requirement
Operator training	Achieve grade-A, B
Verification tool	Achieve grade-A, B, C, D, E
Process design	Achieve grade-A, B, C
Production optimization	Achieve grade-A, B, C
Model prediction	Achieve grade-A, B, C

2.4   The Establishment of Assessment Case

The purpose of establishing the credibility of simulation model is to test whether the simulation model can achieve the expected goals, and then replace the real system. Therefore, we established assessment cases based on the five-level evaluation system. Through different levels of assessment cases, model would show its different degrees of credibility [10].

In this paper, according to the multi-levels evaluation system, assessment cases are designed for the simulation model. The specific steps are as follows:

• Normative analysis for assessment cases

Through the analysis of system simulation model, extract object for simulation model evaluation. For example, in the process of running evaporator simulation model, many objects need to be analyzed and tested, such as evaporator pressure and temperature, vapor composition and liquid composition, etc.

• Determine the assessment cases according to system

After the objects were determined, assessment cases needed established for every test object according to the specific content of five-level evaluation system. The assessment cases are divided into five modules and each module has a level. Each level should include case number, operating condition, reference condition and expected result. Case number can be used to count the number of assessment cases and to identify whether the case was executed. Operating condition is the start trigger condition of assessment cases. As the comparison basis, reference condition is the executive results that real system should have.

• Perform and record the results

Write and generate assessment cases for each module, and connect the model through the interface of simulation engine. Then complete the automatic evaluation of model and record the failed cases.

• Output analysis and evaluation

Analyze and examine the failed cases and figure out the reason of failure. If the error of evaluation case is the reason, then modify the evaluation case and carry it out again. Moreover, when the case meets the evaluation requirements, the credibility of simulation model can be confirmed.

3 Design and Implement of Evaluation System for Multi-level Test Cases

In this paper, the evaluation system was applied in a simulation model of evaporator which inlet stream is the miscible fluid components formed by methanol and water. Figure 2 is the evaporation simulation model and the initial values of variables are given in Table 2 (Fig. 1).

Table 2. The initial values of variables

Name of variables	value	means
P_{in}	100 kPa	Feed pressure
P	101 kPa	Evaporator pressure
P_o	101 kPa	Outlet pressure
T_{in}	30°C	Initial feed temperature
T_{heat}	350°C	The temperature of heating stream
x_1	75 %	Feed composition for component methanol
x_2	25 %	Feed composition for component water
y_1	0 %	Vapor composition for component methanol
y_2	0 %	Vapor composition for component water
L	0 m	Initial level
T	30°C	Evaporator temperature
v_E	0 m³/s	Outlet vapor flow

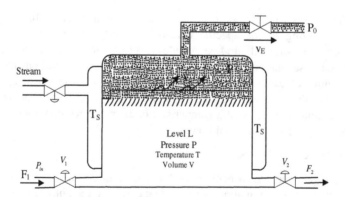

Fig. 1. Evaporator simulation model

Use mesh equations [11] (material balance equation, phase equilibrium equation, the mole fraction normalized equation, energy balance equation) to establish the mathematical model, and obtained the evaporator simulation model (Table 3).

Table 3. Test cases with grade-A for evaporator simulation model

Number	Operating conditions	Contrast conditions
101	Increase the inlet valve opening A_1	F_1 was increased
102	Increase inlet flow F_1	L was increased
103	Increase the outlet valve opening A_2	F_2 was increased
104	Quantity of heat $Q_{heat} > 0$	T was increased
105	Vapor flux v > 0	P was increased
106	Vapor flux v > 0	v_E was increased
107	Vapor flux v > 0	x_i was decreased, y_i was decrease

To implement cases, assessment case 102 can be used as an example. Giving two different inlet flow values ($F_1 = 0.4$ m^3/s, $F_1' = 0.2$ m^3/s), then observe whether evaporator level L is increased differently. See Fig. 3, case 102 was passed (Table 4).

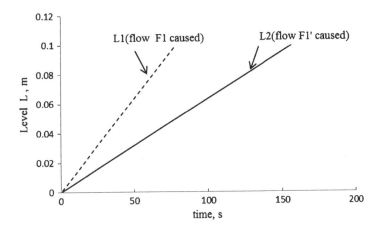

Fig. 2. Influence of flow on level

Table 4. Test cases with grade-B for evaporator simulation model

Number	Operating condition	Contrast condition
201	Steady state	Temperature T was 80°C
202	Steady state	Pressure P was 120 kPa
203	Steady state	Methanol vapor composition y_1 was 0 %
204	Steady state	Water vapor composition x_1 was 0 %
205	Steady state	Methanol liquid composition y_2 was 100 %
206	Steady state	Water liquid composition x_2 was 100 %

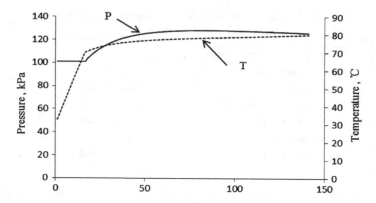

Fig. 3. Temperature and pressure of evaporator simulation model

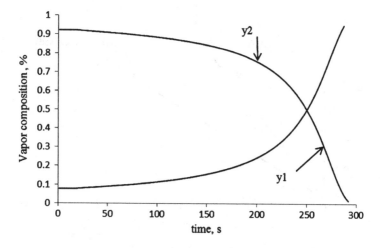

Fig. 4. Methanol and water vapor composition

Figure 4 is temperature and pressure curve of evaporator simulation model and Fig. 5 is Methanol vapor composition and Water vapor composition curve. Figure 6 is Methanol liquid composition and Water liquid composition curve. By contrast, grade-B assessment cases was passed that simulation model had grade-B credibility (Table 5).

Figure 6 is the implement for assessment case 303. Firstly, make $F_1 = 0.4$ m^3/s, $F_2 = 0$, until level L reached half height of evaporator, then make $F_1 = 0$, $F_2 = 0.2$ m^3/s until level L becomes 0. Obviously, as long as the values of feature points of the simulation model' level is same as values that we calculated, it can be considered that the assessment case 303 has passed (Tables 6 and 7).

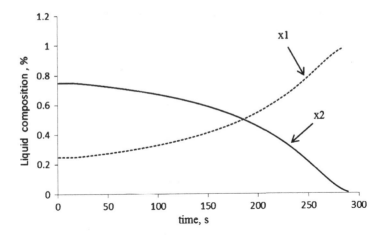

Fig. 5. Methanol and water liquid composition

Table 5. Test cases with grade-C for evaporator simulation model

Number	Operating condition	Contrast condition
301	Heating quantity Q first-order increased	T gradient was increased
302	Vapor flux first-order increased	P gradient was increased
303	$F_1 > 0, F_2 = 0$ then $F_1 = 0, F_2 > 0$	Observe Levle's feature points

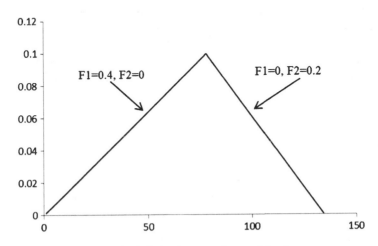

Fig. 6. Relation between flow and level

Table 6. Test cases with grade-D for evaporator simulation model

Number	Operating Condition	Contrast Condition
401	F_1 equals to F_2	Level L was unchanged
402	Q_{heat} equals to Q_{cool}	Temperature T was unchanged
403	$Q_{heat} > Q_{cool}$	T was increased but slower than T_{heat}
404	$Q_{heat1} > Q_{heat2}$	T was increased but faster than T_{heat1}

Table 7. Test cases with grade-E for evaporator simulation model

Number	Operating condition	Contrast condition
501	Inlet pipe blockage	Inlet flow becomes 0
502	The holdup becomes 0	F_1 was increased, F_2 was 0
503	Pressure is too large	Add a safety valve
504	Liquid tank full	F_1 was 0, F_2 was increased

4 Conclusion and Future Work

The study of credibility for simulation system model has always been the key issue in the field of system simulation. Although many engineering technical personnel that at home and abroad have done a great amount of work in theoretical research and exploitation of model assessment tools, with the widely application of the system simulation technology and the increasing complexity of system, the requirements for model credibility have been more and more rigid. In this paper, we combined the qualitative method and quantitative method and proposed a complete set of evaluation system for simulation model based on the assessment of process simulation model. We divided the evaluation system of chemical process simulation model into five-level tests and then designed test cases to form the automatic testing and evaluation for simulation model. This system contained not only the open parking operation in chemical process and steady tests, but also the tests for unusual service condition and equipment failure. In short, this evaluation system comprehensive effectively provided a new method for the further research of model assessment and achieved a certain theoretical reference value and practical application value.

References

1. Wei, Z., Wang, X.: Credibility of simulation. J. Syst. Simul. Acta **13**(3), 312–314 (2001)
2. Hermann, C.F.: Validation problems in games and simulations with special reference to models of international politics. Behav. Sci. **12**(12), 216–231 (1967)
3. Hong, Z., Pan, H., Lu, Z., et al.: The comparative study for the credibility evaluation method of hardware-in-the-loop system. Electronics R & D (9) (2015)
4. Balci, O., Sargent, R.G.: Some examples of simulation model validation using hypothesis testing. In: Proceedings of the 1982 Winter Simulation Conference, San Diego, USA, pp. 621–629 (1982)

5. Liu, S., Liu, X., Zhang, W.: Fixed quantity evaluation to reliability of simulation system with similar degree. J. Syst. Simul. **14**(2), 143–145 (2002)
6. Wei, Z., Wang, X.: Fuzzy judgment to Simulation Credibility. J. Syst. Simul. **13**(4), 473–475 (2001)
7. Zhao, C., Sun, G., Liang, D., et al.: Research on simulation credibility assessment of rural distribution simulation training system. China Rural Water Hydropower **12**, 169–172 (2014)
8. Balci, O.: Verification, validation and testing. In: Handbook of Simulation: Priciples, Methodology, Advances, Applications, and Practice. Wiley, New York (1998)
9. Yu, B.: Study on dynamic modeling and simulation of general plate distillation column towards automatic system validation. Beijing University of Chemical Technology (2011)
10. Wang, Y.: Safety engineering management books - safety system engineering. Tianjin University Press (1999)
11. Franks, R.G.E.: Modeling and simulation in chemical engineering. Comput. Chem. Eng. **21**(10), S805–S809 (1972)

Research on Test Technology of Security and Stability Control Technology of UHVDC Based on Real-Time Digital Simulation

Lei Fu[✉], Fenqing Wei, and Yuehai Yu

State Grid Electric Power Research Institute, Nanjing, China
`fulei@sgepri.sgcc.com.cn`

Abstract. A real-time digital simulation research and closed-loop testing platform for the security and stability control devices is built based on RTDS in this paper, which includes the simulation models for Lingzhou-Shaoxing (Lingshao) ±800 kV UHVDC transmission system, and the 3-level functions of the master control, pole control, and valve control is simulated. Based on the research and testing platform, the security and stability control strategies for N-2 faults occurring in AC transmission lines and other DC system faults of the Lingshao UHVDC system are tested. The research and testing results verify the accuracy of the control strategies and the accuracy of the simulation models. And the new research and testing method need no access to actual UHVDC control and protection system, which saves the testing cost and time significantly.

Keywords: UHVDC · The security and stability strategies · Real-time digital simulation (RTDS) · Testing platform

1 Introduction

Lingzhou to Shaoxing (Lingshao) UHVDC transmission project, beginning in the west from Lingzhou converter station in Lingwu City of Ningxia Province, and ending in the east at Shaoxing converter station in Zhuji City of Zhejiang province, passes through six provinces and regions in Ningxia, Shaanxi, Shanxi, Henan, Anhui, Zhejiang, with a total line length of 1720 km. The engineer is planed to put in operation in June of 2016 with the low-end of two polars, and will be in full operation mode to September of 2016. Its rated DC voltage of is ±800 kV, rated current is 5000 A, minimum DC current of 500 A, and the scale of power transmission is 8 million kilowatts.

The security and stability control system (control system) on receiving side of Lingshao consists of Shaoxing UHVDC control host, AC control host of Shaoxing converter, and control system in Yongchao station. Through the acquisition of analog quantity and protection tripping signal, the control system judges the conditions of in or out of operation. The stability control device in AC system sends the control orders to stability control devices in DC part to reduce DC power, according to security and stability control strategies. The control system on sending side of Lingzhou converter station consists of Lingzhou UHVDC control host, AC control host of Lingzhou converter and

© Springer Science+Business Media Singapore 2016
L. Zhang et al. (Eds.): AsiaSim 2016/SCS AutumnSim 2016, Part IV, CCIS 646, pp. 432–441, 2016.
DOI: 10.1007/978-981-10-2672-0_44

Ningxia generation-tripping station. According to the DC fault information and running status information of 750 kV AC system, AC control station sends the instructions to generation-tripping station, and carry out emergency control to reduce DC power.

At present, a series of achievements have been made in the research of real time digital simulation and the construction of experimental platform of security and stability control strategies. References [1, 2] carry out test research on the dynamic characteristics of Yunnan-Guangzhou UHVDC system under islanded condition based on RTDS, while various of faults occur. References [3, 4] design and construct the control technology experiment platform of the safety and stability technologies based on RTDS, and carry out the test and research of based of the three lines of grid defense. Reference [5] proposed and implemented a testing device based on RTDS on UHVDC stability control system and strategy table verification and system response test method. References [6–12] introduce other research achievements about HVDC system and control methods. However, all the simulation test methods above need to access the actual DC control protection system, which greatly increase the research and development costs and test cycle, which is difficult to achieve universal promotion and application. This paper simulates various modes of operation and control mode of UHVDC system based on RTDS, establishes a three-level multi domain DC control and protection system model, based on which a safety and stability control device test platform is set up, and real-time simulation research and closed-test AC system and DC system of Lingshao UHVDC transmission system is carried out.

2   Basic Principle UHVDC Control and Protection System

The connection between DC transmission system and AC systems at both ends of UHVDC is very closely. The AC system on sending side provides the power source for DC power transmission, meanwhile, the AC system on receiving side operates as load, receiving and consuming the power delivered by the DC transmission line. And the use of the land as the circuit realizes the operation of HVDC transmission system reliably and flexibly, DC transmission system also needs to be equipped with the grounding electrode and the electrode lead composition of grounding system. Therefore, in addition to the rectifier and inverter station and DC lines, a complete two terminal UHVDC system also consists of grounding system and an adaptation system control and protection system.

The control and protection system of UHVDC transmission system is usually divided into three levels: the main control layer, the pole control layer and the valve group control layer. The main control layer includes power modulation and fast power change control module. The pole control layer contains a constant current controller, voltage controller and other control devices. Valve control layer mainly completes the acquisition synchronization signal and generates the trigger pulses for valves. Main control layer receives instructions of the DC transmission power value from dispatching center, and then send DC current command to the control electrode layer after control algorithms, and finally send a firing angle order to valve group control layer after signal-processing modulation.

The Fig. 1 describes the control process of master control level: the "POWERSET" is instructions of the DC transmission power value from dispatching center. And the corresponding DC Current Reference value equals "POWERSET" divided by DC voltage reference. And the command value of DC current is switched to expected current value if the control system adopts constant current control.

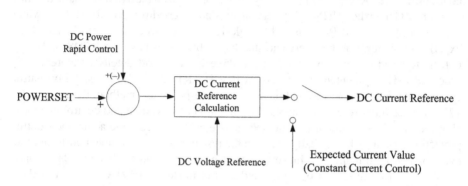

Fig. 1. Master control level control function

Figure 2 illustrates the control process of pole control level: the "DC Current Reference" is get through DC control modulation and rapid current control, considering the margin value of DC current and VDCOL control. The minimum of the outputs of constant voltage controller, constant current controller and constant γ controller is the command valve of α, which is thyristor's trigger delay angle.

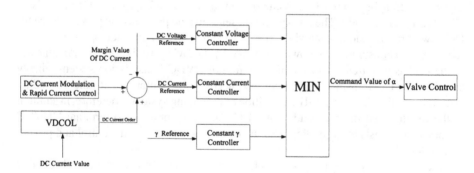

Fig. 2. Pole control level control function

Valve group control mainly completed two functions: (1) to take the synchronization signal of the trigger pulse. Usually synchronization signal of trigger pulse is obtained from PLL Frequency Multiplier. The input signal of the PLL frequency multiplier is taken directly from AC bus voltage of the converter. The output signal of the synchronous signal should be strictly keep the multiple relationship with frequency of the bus voltage of and converter. Since the synchronization signal is the base of the control angle, and the quality of the synchronous signal is directly related to the precision of the

DC transmission control, UHVDC PLL frequency multiplier requires not only fast tracking speed, but also to work normally as serious faults occur in the system and the converter AC bus voltage drops significantly. (2) to produce a trigger pulse series to meet the requirements to trigger thyristor valve.

3   System Modeling of UHVDC on RTDS

3.1   Equivalent System Model and Parameters of AC System on Rectifier Side and Inverter Side

For ease of modeling and simulation, as validating the security and stability strategies of one side (sending or receiving side), the equivalent simplification of contralateral AC system is necessary: using constant potential equivalent voltage source to simulate the AC grid, and using the equivalent impedance to reflect the actual system strength. The system impedance on the rectifier side is 7.011 Ω, and the one of the inverter side is 4.674 Ω. The voltage on both sides of the equivalent AC system changes in the range below: 750 kV–800 kV on rectifier side, and 490 kV–525 kV on inverter side.

3.2   Model and Parameters of Converter Transformer

The converter transformer and converter valve is packaged into a module in RTDS (Fig. 3). The regulating range of the rectifier side includes −6~18 taps, and the inverter side position adjustment range is −8~16, and the voltage regulation of each tap is 2.5 % of the rated voltage.

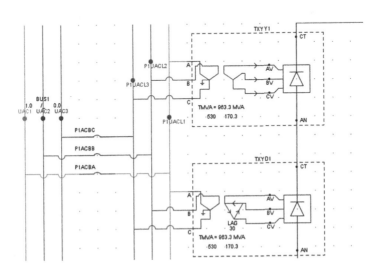

Fig. 3. RTDS model of 12-pulse valve group on rectifier side

The parameters of converter transformer is shown in Table 1.

Table 1. The parameters of converter transformer

Parameter name	Lingzhou station	Shaoxing station
Capacity (MVA)	1236.9	1152.69
Voltage on grid side (kV)	765	520
Voltage on valve side (Y/Y connection) (kV)	$175/\sqrt{3}$	$163/\sqrt{3}$
Voltage on valve side (Y/D connection) (kV)	175	163
Short circuit impedance	21 %	16 %

3.3 Model and Parameters of DC Lines

Lingshao ±800 kV DC transmission system of the RTDS model adopts dual 12-pulse valve groups in series model. Both the of pole line and neutral bus of Lingzhou and Shaoxing converter stations are equipped with 150 mH flat wave reactor. The total length of UHVDC line is 1712 km, and the rated current is 5000 A, with the resistance of conductor is 0.0233411 Ω per km.

3.4 Model and Parameters of AC Filters

The converter stations on both sides are equipped with substantial reactive power compensation equipments. Is of layout, The filters and shunt capacitors installed in rectifier station consist of a total of 16 groups (4 groups of 11th/13rd harmonic filters, 4 groups of 24th/36th harmonic filters, 3 group of 3rd harmonic filters and 5 groups of shunt capacitors), which is divided into four groups and with a total capacity of 4720 MVar;

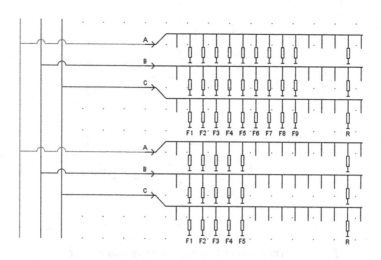

Fig. 4. RTDS model of AC filters of rectifier station

The filters and shunt capacitors installed in inverter station also consist of a total of 16 groups (9 groups of $12^{th}/24^{th}$ harmonic filters, 7 groups of shunt capacitors), which is divided into two groups and with a total capacity of 4820 MVar. The model diagram of AC filter of rectifier station is given in Fig. 4.

3.5 Modeling of DC Control and Protection System

The simulation models of DC control and protection system includes constant current control, minimum trigger angle control, constant extinction angle control, constant voltage control, CEC and VDCOL control, and the control logic to switch the multi control modes, to complete the regulation and control functions. Under normal operating conditions, constant DC current controller on rectifier side controls DC current and constant DC voltage controller on inverter side controls DC voltage. When DC voltage on the inverter side drops, the extinction angle (γ) will be reduced to raise DC voltage, and if α reduces to 17°, which is the minimum extinction angle, then the inverter side changes into the constant γ control. When DC voltage on the rectifier side drops, the constant DC current controller will send out the command to reduce the trigger angle (α), in order to raise the DC current, however, the rectifier side has a minimum trigger angle limit, generally 5°. If the trigger angle is reduced to the minimum limit, the rectifier side will changed into a constant α control. At this time, control of DC current switches to the inverter side.

4   Simulation and Test of Stability Control System for UHVDC System

For modeling Lingshao ±800 kV UHVDC simulation system on RTDS, 2 racks is needed to simulate UHVDC transmission system of the rectifier side and the inverter side, and the two racks are connected through DC transmission lines. The main control module of DC control and protection system sets the bipolar/one polar operation mode, DC transmission power, and generates the DC current command to the pole control module. Pole control module encapsulates the two parts of the rectifier and the inverter control models. The rectifier module includes constant DC current control, minimum α control, and the inverter module including constant DC voltage control, constant γ control and constant DC current control mode. Valve control module takes the synchronization signal of the trigger pulse, and modulates the trigger pulse series to meet the requirements to trigger thyristor valves.

In this paper, the stability control system of receiving side of Lingshao UHVDC system is taken as example to carry out the research on RTDS modeling and closed-loop test. The stability control system of Shaoxing converter station consists of Shaoxing DC control host, AC control host and Yongchao stability control system. The stations are connected through optical fiber channel. Shaoxing Station DC control host acquisites the analog signals of the high-end valves and low-end valves of bipolar, and communicate with DC pole controller, judging the conditions of valves such as in operation or blocking. Shaoxing station AC control host acquisites the analog signals of 6 500 kV

AC lines, including Shaoxing-Yongchao double-circuit lines (5847/5848), Shaoxing-Lanting double-circuit (5453/5454), and Shaoxing-Shunjiang double-circuit (5849/5850), and also protection tripping signal, judging operational maintenance of 500 kV transmission lines. And Yongchao station acquisites the analog signals of Yongchao-Qiaosi double-circuit (5493/5494).

When it's needed to implement measures to reduce DC power according to the control strategies, the AC stability control devices in Shaoxing station send the order to DC stability control devices in Shaoxing station. The RTDS test platform for Lingshao stability control system is shown in Fig. 5. And the action strategies for Shaoxing-Yongchao N-2 fault under operation mode 1 is illustrated in Table 2.

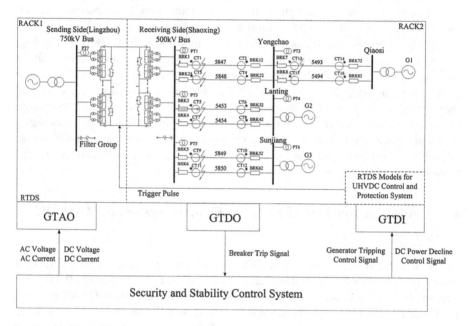

Fig. 5. The Closed-loop simulation platform of UHVDC transmission system based on RTDS

Table 2. Action strategies for Shaoxing-Yongchao N-2 fault under operation mode 1

Operation model 1	Transmission power flow	Setting value of action (MW)	Fault types	Action strategies
Mode 1	Shaoxing-Yongchao	1200	Shaoxing-Yongchao N-2 faults	To decrease the DC power to 800 MW

As shown in Fig. 6, before the fault occurs, the DC transmission power of Shaoxing-Yongchao was 500 MW. 0s Line 5847 fault occurred and tripped, and 2s Line 5848 fault occurred and tripped. Due to the DC transmission power value did not meet the strategies table settings, security devices did not act. As is shown in Fig. 7, before the fault occurs, the DC transmission power of Shaoxing-Yongchao was 700 MW. 0s Line 5847 fault occurred and tripped, and 2s Line 5848 fault occurred and tripped. Due to the DC transmission power of Shaoxing-Yongchao double-circuit was 1400 MW, the devices acted, and RTDS system received the order (variable "ZHILING" in the waveform) to decrease the DC power back to 800 MW.

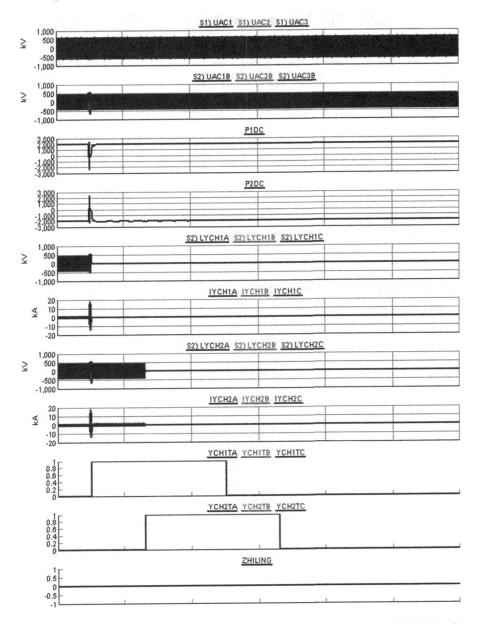

Fig. 6. Action waveform of line Shaoxing-Yongchao (5847/5848) N-2 Fault (ZHILING = 0)

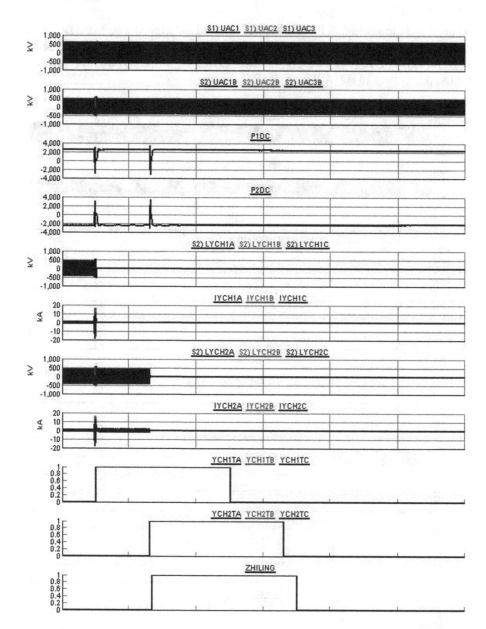

Fig. 7. Action waveform of line Shaoxing-Yongchao (5847/5848) N-2 Fault (ZHILING = 1)

5   Conciusion and Future Work

Based on the Lingshao ±800 kV UHVDC project as an example, the RTDS closed-loop simulation test platform for security and stability control system is set up, and action strategy of the control system is verified for N-2 faults occurring in AC system. The model integrates the main control, the pole control and the valve control of the actual HVDC control and protection system, with excellent accuracy and efficiency, significantly simplifies the test process of UHVDC transmission system stability control devices.

References

1. Hu, M., Jin, X.-M., Gao, P., et al.: Stability control strategies for ±800 kV DC transmission system from Yunnan to Guangdong under islanded operation. Power Syst. Technol. **33**(18), 5–8 (2009)
2. Li, Z.-Y., Han, W.-Q., Huang, L.-B.: Construction and analysis of the RTDS testing platform for islanding operation of Yunnan – Guangdong UHVDC system. South. Power Syst. Technol. **4**(2), 47–51 (2010)
3. Guo, Q., Han, W., Zeng, Y.: Security and stability control technology test and research platform based on real-time simulation: part one framework and characteristics. Autom. Electr. Power Syst. **36**(20), 1–5 (2012)
4. Guo, Q., Han, W.-Q., Zeng, Y.-G.: Security and stability control technology test and research platform based on real-time simulation: part two application examples. Autom. Electr. Power Syst. **36**(21), 19–23 (2012)
5. Guo, Q., Han, W.-Q., Jia, X.-D.: Study on the RTDS simulation test of the system stability control of Yunnan – Guangdong ±800 kV DC transmission project. South. Power Syst. Technol. **4**(2), 43–46 (2010)
6. Cigre Workshop Group 14.32. HVDC Converter Stations for Voltage Above ±600 kV (2002)
7. Esmersldo, P.C.V.: New HVDC projects under study in Brazil. In: Power Grid HVDC Workshop, New Delhi (2005)
8. Maruvada, P.S.: ±800 kV HVDC transmission systems. In: Transmission and Distribution Conference and Exposion, pp. 1–2. T&D, IEEE/PES, 21–24 April 2008 (2008)
9. Liu, K.-Z., Shu, H.-C., Chen, Y., et al.: Analysis on fault of Yun-Guang hybrid AC/DC power transmission system. In: 2008 Joint International Conference on Power System Technology and IEEE Power India Conference, 12–15 October 2008, pp. 1–6 (2008)
10. Zhao, W.-J.: HVDC Transmission Engineering Technology. China Electric Power Press, Beijing (2004)
11. Chen, Q., Zhang, Y., Zhong, Q., et al.: Simulation of ±800 kV UHVDC system under different operation modes. Power Syst. Prot. Control **35**(16), 27–32 (2007)
12. Liu, W., Zhao, Y., Zhou, J.-Q., et al.: Comparison and research on the reliability between the 12-pulse and 2 × 12 pulse HVDC transmission system. Power Syst. Prot. Control **36**(9), 29–34 (2008)

Verification, Validation and Accreditation (VV&A) of M&S

Performance Analysis of Enhanced AODV Protocols in a Mobile Ad Hoc Network Environment

Hwa-Mok Lee, Sun-Hong Kim, Da-Woong Jung,
and Seong Yong Jang[✉]

Information and Industrial Systems Engineering,
Seoul National University of Science and Technology, Seoul, Korea
{siam8526,kshsmr,jdw7040}@naver.com,
syjang@seoultech.ac.kr

Abstract. The objective of this study is to enhance the Ad hoc On-demand Distance Vector (AODV) routing protocol, a representative mobile ad hoc network environment routing protocol. In the existing AODV protocol, dynamic topology changes due to node mobility cause frequent route failures and network instability. We herein propose a local repair scheme to re-establish routes when links are broken and a dual-path routing scheme to improve network stability by employing alternate routes. After comparing the total data processing volumes, average packet end-to-end delays, numbers of connection pairs, energy consumptions, and numbers of generated packets of the enhanced AODV protocols, we discuss the optimal operating conditions for each scheme. We also investigated the performance variations resulting from changing the number of nodes and node mobility, using an NS-2 simulator. The results revealed that the dual-path protocol generally performs the best and improves the packet end-to-end delay by up to 45 %.

Keywords: AODV · Protocol · NS-2 · Simulation · Dual path

1 Introduction

A mobile ad hoc network (MANET) is a wireless communication network consisting of wireless mobile nodes without fixed infrastructure. Since the mobile nodes are connected without wired infrastructure and instead communicate by themselves, each node acts as a router and performs multi-hop communications. Due to the nature of the wireless environment, such as its use of wireless channels, transmission range and bandwidth restrictions, and signal interference, the routing protocols that determine and maintain the data transmission routes in wireless networks are different from those in wired networks.

This study was supported by the Research Program funded by the Seoul National University of Science and Technology.

L. Zhang et al. (Eds.): AsiaSim 2016/SCS AutumnSim 2016, Part IV, CCIS 646, pp. 445–454, 2016.
DOI: 10.1007/978-981-10-2672-0_45

In a MANET, since the network range is not limited, data can be transmitted regardless of distance. When there are more than two communication terminals, a network can be easily built without any complex advance setup. The Internet Engineering Task Force MANET working group currently proposes ad hoc routing protocols largely based on either of two approaches: a table-driven method in which the mobile nodes maintain all of the route information and can perform changes at any time and an on-demand method in which the mobile nodes perform route discovery only when a specific destination's route is requested.

The Ad hoc On-demand Distance Vector (AODV) protocol, which was taken as a representative on-demand ad hoc routing protocol in this study, forms a network of nodes without the assistance of a fixed access point [1]. However, due to the nature of wireless links and node mobility, each link is unstable and unreliable. In a MANET, if the nodes on a transmission path move during data transmission and link failure occurs, routes must be re-established between the source and the destination, resulting in data loss and increased transmission delay [2]. Moreover, the new control packets that are necessary to re-establish the routes can cause to generate an excessive number of packets, which is known as a flooding problem.

This paper proposes an enhanced local repair AODV (LR-AODV) protocol in which, when a link failure occurs closer to the destination than the source, the node at the point of link failure performs a route request. This report also proposes a dual-path AODV (DP-AODV) protocol for faster route repair using an alternate route upon link failure. We used an NS-2 simulator to evaluate the performances of the proposed protocols relative to the AODV protocol in terms of their total data processing volumes, packet end-to-end delays, and total numbers of control packets generated.

2 Related Work

With recent wireless network technology research, which is actively proceeding, the communication protocols used in the MANET environment have advanced considerably. Instead of the table-driven routing protocols used in wired communication environments, on-demand or reactive routing protocols such as the TORA, ABR, DSR, and AODV protocols have been proposed. The study discussed in this paper was focused on enhancing the AODV protocol.

2.1 AODV

The AODV protocol is an ad hoc on-demand routing protocol, which communicates hop-by-hop via a routing table maintained by each node. When a source needs a route to a destination, it initiates a route search process. The source sends a Route Request (RREQ) packet to find the route to the destination. Upon receiving an RREQ packet, a node examines whether it is the intended destination of the packet. If the node is not the destination, the node sends the RREQ packet again toward the destination; otherwise, the node generates a Route Reply (RREP) packet toward the source. Once the source receives an RREP packet, a forward path to the destination is established and data transmission begins along the route.

Route maintenance in the AODV protocol is as follows. If a node detects a link failure when it sends data to the next hop, it sends a Route Error (RERR) packet to the source. The RERR packet propagates toward all of the traffic sources and erases all of the broken routes in the routing tables along the way. Upon receiving the RERR, the source initiates a new route search if it still needs the route.

2.2 LR-AODV Protocol

In the LR-AODV protocol, when a route fails, the node prior to the broken link sends an RREQ packet toward the destination to re-search the route. This mechanism is able to re-establish routes faster than the existing route maintenance method and can immediately re-send along a new route data packets that could not be sent due to the route failure [3]. Figures 1 and 2 show the operation theory of the local repair mechanism. If, while the source node S and destination node D are connected over an active data transmission route, node C leaves the route, causing a link break, the node upstream from the broken link, node B, detects the route failure. Unlike in the existing mechanism, in which an RERR message is sent to the source, when the link break occurs closer to the destination than the source, node B directly broadcasts when it

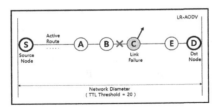

Fig. 1. Local repair operation 1

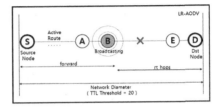

Fig. 2. Local repair operation 2

detects the link break. The decision to broadcast is made by comparing the hop count that the packet passed by ("forward") and the hop count remaining to reach the destination ("rt_hops"). After a link break, if the reverse route in the routing table is still valid, the upstream node B compares the "forward" and "rt_hops" values and repairs the local route. If the "forward" value is greater than the "rt_hops" value, node B directly broadcasts a route request. If this route request fails, node B generates an RERR message and sends it to the source [4].

2.3   DP- AODV Protocol

While the existing AODV routing protocol uses a single path, the proposed DP-AODV protocol employs multipath routing. If data transmission is needed, the DP-AODV protocol selects the most end-to-end reliable route as the primary route and additionally selects an alternate route for quick replacement in case the primary route fails. This mechanism enables data loss reduction and controls the packet traffic involved in new route establishment [5].

Multipath routing protocols discover multiple paths between the source and the destination and offer load balancing, fault tolerance, and higher bandwidths in the frequently varying and unpredictable MANET environment. The presence of multiple paths improves the traffic distribution and load balance and reduces the traffic congestion and bottleneck problem. Furthermore, when multiple paths exist between the source and the destination, data can be transmitted via an alternate route even if one route fails, reducing data transmission failure and delay [6].

To maintain the routes continuously, the routes are repaired when they fail in single-path routing. Therefore, data transmission stops until a new route is established, resulting in data transmission delay. On the contrary, routes are maintained when one or all of the routes fail in multipath routing. If the routes are repaired before all of the routes fail, multiple routes are always available, so data transmission delay due to route failures can be reduced. If route maintenance is performed whenever any of the routes fails, the transmission of RREQ and RREP packets increases, causing the routing overhead to increase as well [7].

Figures 3 and 4 depict the operation theory of the DP-AODV protocol.

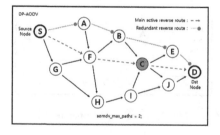

Fig. 3. Dual-path operation 1

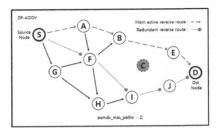

Fig. 4. Dual-path operation 2

3   Simulation Scenarios and Model Design

3.1   Experimental Conditions

In this study, we evaluated the performances of the existing AODV, LR-AODV, and DP-AODV protocol scenario using the NS-2 network simulator.

We performed independent experiments to investigate the effects of varying the number of nodes and the node velocity. Each protocol scenario was prepared based on the NS-2 Linux source. As shown in Table 1, the experiments were performed with five different numbers of nodes in the traffic range (100, 150, 200, 250, and 300) and four different node velocities (5, 10, 15, and 20 m/s). Each experiment was repeated five times, and the results were averaged. The number of simulation repetition is set to 5 times because this paper deals with the big network with maximum 300 nodes requiring large amount of computation time.

Table 1.   Experimental cases for simulation

	Number of nodes	Node velocity	Total replication
AODV	100/150/200/250/300	5/10/15/20	100
LR-AODV	100/150/200/250/300	5/10/15/20	100
DP-AODV	100/150/200/250/300	5/10/15/20	100

The total time for each simulation was 20 s, and data transmission started as soon as the simulation began. Among the nodes, 10 source nodes and 10 destination nodes were randomly chosen. Each connected pair exchanged data continuously. The constant bit rate (CBR) traffic model was employed; five packets were sent each second, and each packet had a size of 1024 bytes. The simulation was performed five times using each of the protocols (AODV, LR-AODV, and DP-AODV), and then the simulation results were averaged for each protocol (Table 2).

Table 2. Simulation parameters for case study

Experimental variable	Value
Routing protocol	AODV, LR-AODV, DP-AODV
Dimensions of simulated area	1000 m × 1000 m
Simulation time (s)	20
Traffic type	CBR 5 pkts/s
Number of nodes	100, 150, 200, 250, 300 for random velocity
Node velocity (m/s)	5, 10, 15, 20
Transmission range (radius)	100 m
Packet size (bytes)	1024
Agent type	UDP
Connections	10
Replication	5
Mobility model	Random waypoint

3.2 Protocol Algorithm

The simulation models were developed using the protocol scripts and commands within NS-2 simulator. Proposed simulation models consist of protocol algorithm, data packet structure, schedule, implementation command, mobility model and animation. Overall protocol structure and core algorithm are included in header file "AODV.h". Core algorithms for LR-AODV and DP-AODV are shown in Fig. 5.

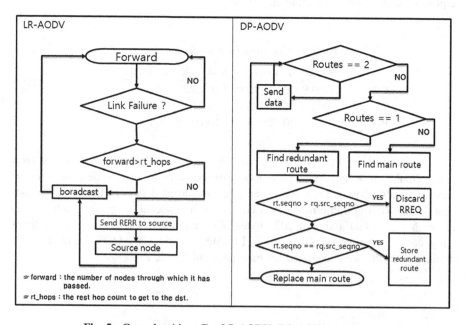

Fig. 5. Core algorithms For LP-AODV, DP-AODV protocols.

In LR-AODV, when link failure is found during packet forwarding process, the algorithm determines if new broadcasting must be done at the failure link comparing the current and passed hop count or rebroadcasting must be done at the source node after sending RERR packet to source node. In DP-AODV, algorithm determines if the main route or redundant route must be explored using the active route number 1 or 2 stored in routing table. When redundant route is selected, RREQ packet is discarded if the sequence number of arrived RREQ packet is less than that stored in routing table. The reverse route of arrived RREQ packet is set as redundant route if two sequence numbers are the same, and main route is replaced as a current route if the sequence number of RREQ packet is greater than that stored in routing table.

3.3   Performance Evaluation Metrics

We used the following five metrics to evaluate the performances of the AODV, LR-AODV, and DP-AODV protocols:

(1) Packet Delivery Ratio (PDR): the ratio of the data packets successfully delivered from the source to the destination;
(2) End-to-End Delay: the total time for a data packet to travel from the source to the destination;
(3) Connections: the number of successful connections between 10 randomly chosen source nodes and 10 randomly chosen destination nodes;
(4) Control Packets: the total number of control packets generated during the simulation time, which is the sum of the numbers of RREQ, RREP, RERR, and HELLO control packets;
(5) Energy Consumption: the total energy consumption during the simulation, which is calculated by summing the energy differences of all of the nodes between the start and end of the simulation.

4   Analysis of Simulation Results

4.1   Experimental Results

Table 3 presents the simulation results for the newly proposed DP-AODV model. These results show that the numbers of connections in the 100- and 150-node groups are relatively low. In the 200-, 250-, and 300-node groups, the total amount of data delivered decreases as the node velocity increases, and the average energy consumption and total number of control packets increase as the number of nodes increases.

The fact that the source and destination nodes were randomly selected in the simulation affected the results, which do not always exhibit consistent patterns even within the same scenario and occasionally deviate from the general patterns.

In the 100- and 150-node simulations, the transmission field of 1000 m × 1000 m, which is relatively large for such small numbers of nodes, resulted in inefficient communication among the nodes. We consider this inefficient communication to have been caused by both the random designation of the coordinates for each node and the

Table 3. Simulation results for DP-AODV protocol

Number of nodes	DP-AODV performance				
	PDR	End-to-end delay	Connections	Energy consumption	Control packets
100	22.92	0.6346	5.45	9924	0.0569
150	25.50	0.4960	7.75	22726	0.0784
200	32.56	0.3720	8.95	37007	0.0839
250	29.67	0.4215	8.8	64883	0.0892
300	30.35	0.3756	8.75	81767	0.0964
Average	28.20	0.4599	7.94	43261	0.0809

low node density. Table 3 shows that the PDR decreased as the node velocity increased, for the same number of nodes. We consider that the fast node velocities caused link breaks and affected the performance of the entire network.

The average performances of the AODV, LR-AODV, and DP-AODV protocols are compared in Table 4. The LR-AODV protocol exhibits improvements in the PDR, end-to-end delay, number of connections, and energy consumption compared to the existing AODV protocol. Meanwhile, as HELLO packets were added, the total number of control packets increased slightly. The DP-AODV protocol shows remarkable improvements in the end-to-end delay, number of connections, number of control packets, and energy consumption compared to the existing AODV protocol. It is considered to be even more efficient than the LR-AODV protocol.

Table 4. Comparison of AODV, LR-AODV, and DP-AODV protocol results

Criteria	AODV	LR-AODV	DP-AODV
PDR	0.4784	0.6399	0.2820
%	100 %	134 %(+34 %)	59 %(−41 %)
End-to-end delay	0.8014	0.7909	0.4599
%	100 %	98.7 %(−1.3 %)	57.4 %(−32.6 %)
Connections	6.88	7.2	7.94
%	100 %	104.7 %(+4.7 %)	115.4 %(15.4 %)
Energy consumption	0.1000	0.0981	0.0809
%	100 %	98.1 %(−1.9 %)	80.9 %(−19.1 %)
Control packets	179380	208910	43261
%	100 %	116.5 %(+16 %)	24.1 %(−75.9 %)

Table 4 also shows that the LR-AODV protocol exhibits higher performance than the existing AODV protocol does except in terms of the energy consumption and the number of control packets, i.e., its PDR, end-to-end delay, and number of connections are about 34 %, 1.3 %, and 4.6 % higher, respectively, than those of the AODV protocol. Meanwhile, the energy consumption and number of control packets for the LR-AODV protocol are 1.9 % and 16 % lower, respectively, than the corresponding values for the AODV protocol. We consider these differences to have resulted from the enhanced local route repair method, which can carry out more route searches and enables more efficient route repair.

Comparison of the LR-AODV and DP-AODV results shows that most of the metrics, except for the PDR, which slightly decreases, are remarkably improved by the DP-AODV protocol. Specifically, the end-to-end delay, number of connections, energy consumption, and number of control packets are improved by about 32.6 %, 15.4 %, 19.1 %, and 75.9 %, respectively, by the DP-AODV protocol. In conclusion, among the three protocols, the DP-AODV protocol exhibits the best performance.

4.2 Recommendation of Optimal Operating Environments

The simulation results in Table 4 demonstrate that the performances of the protocols vary with the node mobility and the number of nodes. Therefore, we determined the operating conditions that optimize each protocol's performance by normalizing the simulation results and via the Analytical Hierarchy Process (AHP) technique. Table 5 shows the final weighted averages of the metrics, as determined by AHP analysis.

Table 5. AHP results

Division	Weighted average
PDR	0.249870917
End-to-end delay	0.370086393
Connections	0.140019335
Energy consumption	0.13000612
Control packets	0.110017236

Based on the simulations and AHP analysis, we recommend the following optimal operating conditions: 200 nodes and a node velocity of 10 for the LR-AODV protocol, and 300 nodes and a node velocity of 5 for the DP-AODV protocol.

5 Conclusions and Future Work

This paper has examined enhanced versions of the AODV protocol, which was taken as a representative MANET protocol, and compared their performances by discussing the results of simulations conducted using each protocol. Among the investigated protocols, the DP-AODV protocol, which is based on the use of multiple paths, exhibited the best performance. It was superior to the existing AODV protocol in each of the examined metrics and notably achieved a 75.9 % reduction in the number of control packets compared to the AODV protocol.

The simulation results indicated that the number of nodes, node velocity, and simulation environment affect the protocol performance. We also observed that optimal operating conditions exist for each protocol.

Since a large variety of cases were simulated in this study, we could not perform the individual experiments with sufficient replication. In future research, we plan to conduct the same simulations with greater replication to obtain more accurate results. In addition, the relationship between the protocol mechanism and the network environment needs to be investigated by performing correlation studies and sensitivity analyses.

References

1. Perkins, C.E., Royer, E.M., Das, S.R.: Ad Hoc On-Demand Distance Vector (AODV) Routing. IETF Internet Draft (2002). http://www.ietf.org/internet-drafts/draft-ietf-manet-aodv-10.txt
2. Pan, M., Chuang, S., Wang, S.: Local repair mechanisms for on-demand routing in mobile ad hoc networks. In: Proceedings of the 11th Pacific Rim Internet Symposium on Dependable Computing, pp. 317–324 (2005)
3. Seo, H.G., Kim, G.H., Seo, J.H.: AFLRS: An AODV-based fast local repair scheme in ad hoc networks. J. KIISE: Inf. Commun. 31(1), 81–90 (2004)
4. Ahn, S.G., Cheon, S.J., Ahn, S.H.: Improvement of the AODV routing protocol for an efficient local repair. In: Proceedings of the KIISE Fall Conference, vol. 30(2), pp. 38–40 (2003)
5. Marina, M.K., Das, S.R.: Ad hoc on-demand multipath distance vector routing. Wirel. Commun. Mob. Com. 6(7), 969–988 (2006)
6. Qq, Marina, M.K., Das, S.R.: On-demand multi path distance vector routing in ad hoc networks. In: Proceedings of the 9th International Conference on Network Protocols, pp. 14–23 (2001)
7. Kwon, H.C.: The optimal inventory modeling and the cost sensitivity analysis with reducing inventory investment. J. Digit. Pol. Anal. Ma. 11(12), 265–274 (2013)
8. Jang, Y.M.: Understanding of NS-2 Network Simulator. Hongleung Science Publishers (2008)

Simulation Validation Technology of the C⁴ISR System Based on Component-Oriented Development Platform

Wenyuan Xu[✉], Li Guo, Shengxiao Zhang, Dongmei Zhao, and Hao Li

Systems Engineering Research Institute of China State Shipbuilding Corporation,
Beijing, China
xwy0987@sina.com

Abstract. In view of these problems such as the poor reliability of the validation environment for C⁴ISR system, the difficulties of model sharing between the pilot projects, and the low development efficiency of the validation environment, and according the characteristics of multi-domain, multi-function, alternately frequent interaction and real time of C⁴ISR system, we designs an open, scalable, and extensible system structure of the simulation and validation environment (S&VE). In this paper, we mainly describe some key techniques such as the combat protocol interfacing based on XML, data analysis and interacting based on memory database, and dynamic composition of business model. The paper also presents the case and operation of the S&VE. The S&VE has been applied successfully in several projects.

Keywords: Dynamic business model composition · Simulation and validation environment · C⁴ISR system

1 Introduction

Command information system, that is command automatic system, which is called C⁴ISR by U.S. army [1, 2], is the nerve center of networking and informationize combat, and is the force multiplier. The quality of it will directly affect the result of a war to a large degree. C⁴ISR is a distributed, heterogeneous, and complicated military information system which involves many military resources including command and control, intelligence and reconnaissance, early warning and detection, communication and navigation, electronic counter measures, integrated support, and combatant [3]. It has the characteristic of multi-domain, structure complicated, various function, frequently information interaction, and high real-time requirement. Besides, as the rapid development of computer technology and the complication of international environment, C⁴ISR development has the characteristic of rapid update of equipment, many types of test, and high simultaneously. These characteristics bring an unprecedented challenge to the development of S&VE, and some simulation and validation requirements, such as plug and play, frequently sharing, fast response, and joint operation, are hard to meet. U.S. army has developed several co-simulation platforms and systems which cover equipment completely process and support argument analysis, design, development,

© Springer Science+Business Media Singapore 2016
L. Zhang et al. (Eds.): AsiaSim 2016/SCS AutumnSim 2016, Part IV, CCIS 646, pp. 455–462, 2016.
DOI: 10.1007/978-981-10-2672-0_46

validation and evaluation of C⁴ISR system [4]. The platforms and systems include JSIMS [5], JWARS [6], JSEM [7], etc., characterized by sharing, reusability and interoperability. In respect of simulation and validation techniques of C⁴ISR, the domestic has been done some researches on this. Related institution also set up S&VE of C⁴ISR, and studied on related critical technology, but these works are not systematic and kind of homogeneous compared with foreign countries. When studying and set up S&VE, some problems have existed, including less sharing, badly duplicate research and development, cycle of R&D long, uncontrollable of processing, and can not guarantee process and quality of trial under the condition of trial project with high concurrency.

2   Design of C⁴ISR Simulation and Validation Environment

C⁴ISR validation environment structure is facing requirements of non-sharing between multiple trial projects, can not rapidly response to various requirements, long cycle of R&D, uncontrollable of processing, can not adapt to high concurrency and requirement of validation environment cross platform, and the credibility of validation can not be guaranteed [3]. To solve these problem, we should follow the following principles when designing the architecture of C⁴ISR simulation and validation environment:

- The development of validation environment should take the way of component-based, to assemble and deploy each function module flexibly, thus set up the validation environment quickly according to validation requirements, reuse the function module and improve sharing.
- Validation environment should encrypt the module under the way of component-based and systematic, offer a unified management and maintain to module.
- Validation environment should record and store data in a unified way, offer data access interface, in order to applicable analysis and evaluation.
- It should be portable for validation environment, support Windows and Linux operating system, satisfy various trial requirements, improve the trial credibility.
- Validation environment can scale down the environment according to various trial requirement, in order to meet the process requirement and quality requirement of the trial.
- Architecture design should not only utilize the existed fruit, but also take into account the development requirement of modeling and simulation technique in the future.

A scalable validation environment architecture which oriented multi specialized domain has been set up in the basis of component-based architecture design method and C⁴ISR validation requirement. See in Fig. 1.

The architecture consists of 4 layers, from bottom to top, they are resource layer, middleware layer, platform layer, and application layer, respectively.

Among which, resource layer mainly used to store and manage model and data, provide resources for applications in upper layer. Middleware layer mainly used to encrypt each function module, provide interface for encrypted model component and UI model, and provide protocol conversion, component information interaction, and

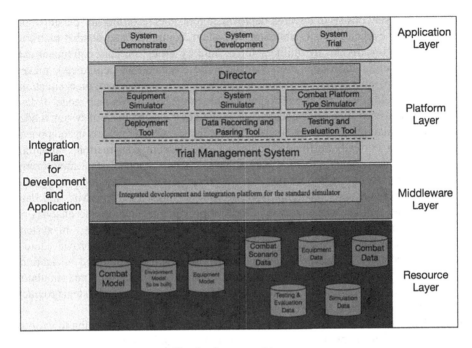

Fig. 1. System architecture

component dispatch management. Platform layer mainly based on integrated development and integration platform for the standard simulator, formulate the specialized function and generalized function which orient domain, offer validation function set for application layer. Application layer utilize the model and tool provided by platform layer, scale down the environment adaptively and carry on simulating work in system demonstration, system development, and system trial according to system validating requirement. The integration specification for development and application in the left of Fig. 1. is a standard specification which used to build the S&VE, standardize the component development, system integration, model assemble, environment deploy and other work. The composition and function of each layer in system architecture is shown in the follows:

- Resource layer is used to store and manage model and data, including combat model, equipment model, environmental model, combat scenario data, equipment data, combat data, evaluation data and simulation data.
- Middleware layer involves integrated development and integration platform for the standard simulator, provides component interface development, component data interaction, component dispatch management; provide user management, UI arrangement, UI component dispatch and common table, situation, radar, dialog and other public component.

- Platform layer consists of director, deployment tool, data recording and parsing tool, testing and evaluating tool, simulator of system, equipment and combat platform type. Director provides the military force, military group, military equipment and armament, initial location and state attribute, these can edit the belligerents; makes combat plan, edits operation of typically military task, shows chart, plots situation, sets battlefield environment; environment deployment tool allows each model or data deployed on each simulation node rapidly, validates the correctness of system model and the availability of running environment, validates whether models in component are running correctly, including validating environment construction, validating process control, input activation data edition, system or model state monitoring, deploying plan, and system resource management; data recording and parsing tool provides network data recording, storing, data parsing based on XML, and data display and edit; testing and evaluating tool provides evaluation and analysis of accuracy and order response time based on collected data; simulator of system provides direct and control functional simulator; equipment simulator provides intelligence reconnaissance, early warning detection, communication and navigation, electronic countermeasure and other equipment simulators; platform type simulator provides air, surface, undersea platform simulator; trial management system provides trial process planning, monitoring and quality management.
- Application layer mainly scale down and select various model according to various stage of system demonstrate, system development and system trial, formulate a deployment plan which satisfy this trial.

3   Critical Technique of System Validation Environment

3.1   Combat Protocol Interfacing Technique Based on XML

One of important work of C^4ISR simulation and validation is message interface interfacing, but because of the difference of equipment, the difference of development period of identical equipment, the difference of combat protocol format, and the difference of checking code of different equipment, check message by hard coding can lead problems of coding duplicated, hard maintaining multi versions, and low efficiency. In order to address this, combat protocol interfacing based on XML has been proposed, implement the requirement of adapt to the change of protocol through configuration file, and the relationship between code and specific message format is transparent. First of all, due to the fixed length of first N bytes of protocol, we can obtain information including IP address of sender and receiver, protocol type used to locate, and whether subpackage by analyzing these N bytes. Then abstract data behind these N bytes, including field name, type, size, and attribute information. Type includes int, char, discrete, BCD, control word, and other types; attribute information includes significant bits and unit. Last, in the basis of abstract type, define the protocol as XML file, parse data by recorded binary file and abstract type, to complete interfacing. The combat message abstract model instance is as follows:

```
<Protocol Name=TimeMessage>
    <Element name=NUMBER, Type=unsigned int, Length="1"/>
    <Element name=ID, Type= unsigned int , ValidValue="128"Length="1"/>
    <Element name=LENGTH, Type= unsigned int , ValidValue="88"Length="2"/>
    <Element name=TIME, Type= unsigned int , Length="4">
        <BasicInfo LSB="0.1" Unit="MS"/>
    </Element>
    <Element name="Control1",Type="CONTROL" Length="4">
        <subelement name="spair", Begin="0", End="0" Type="spair"/>
        <subelement name="OperationType", Begin ="1", End="2" Type="Code">
            <EncodeItem Type ="COMMON", Value="0" Content="one"/>
            <EncodeItem Type ="COMMON", Value="1"Content ="two"/>
            <EncodeItem Type ="COMMON", Value="4" Content="custom"/>
        </subElement>
    </Element>
</Procotol>
```

3.2 Data Analysis and Exchanging Based on the Memory Database

The application layer communication protocol is the format of message communication between application process on different client system that defined by program developer. Data in simulation software are communicated in the basis of application protocol, data analysis and exchanging based on the memory database can parse the communication protocol of application layer automatically, and offer interactive data cache based on memory database. This technology has format define tool based on memory data, support user revises communication message format between application process dynamically, has the function of message format dynamic parsing, it can automatically parse the message format defined by user to identifiable and communicable format. The data interactive cache based on memory database provided by it is a shared memory set for data receiving and sending. The cache has following functions: when application processing module receiving information from other system, it first stores the raw information (string) into information cache, then informs application processing module get the information that need to be addressed from information cache; when application need send information, it first converts formatted data into string and store the string into cache, then informs information sending module get the data from cache and sent it. Data analysis and exchanging based on the memory database provides a set of high-efficiency, high-reliability management mechanism for simulation software data analysis and real-time data storage.

3.3 Dynamic Business Model Composition

A lot of processing model, which complete different business, existed in simulator, and these business model need to play a role in different simulator [6]. The raw business model development technology can not support the reuse of these model and automatic composition. Dynamic business model composition technique develops the independent processing model into the independent processing module, then complete independent model reuse and model new composition reuse by module dynamic dispatch technology. This reduces development cost of simulator, improves development efficiency. Dynamic business model composition technique can set up relationships between trigger and model while implementing model reuse and automatic composition. To support the setting up of relationship, dynamic business model composition technique also provides business application register and application dispatch interface for the development of simulation software. When develop simulation software based on the above technology, the reuse of model, automatic composition, timing call business application, and business application called by external event all can be implemented by dynamic configuration, this can improve the flexibility of model composition and call to a large degree, then improves software development efficiency.

4   C⁴ISR Validation Environment Application Instance

In the system trial stage, validating function, interface, operation and performance that support C⁴ISR including correctness validation of system devices/software implementation and system interface; function implementation correctness validation; information flow and running correctness validation; performance quota satisfy degree validation, development platform based on component-based, build C⁴ISR validation application instance, shown in Fig. 2.

C⁴ISR validation environment is composed of director, data recording and parsing tool, deployment tool, testing and evaluating tool, platform simulator of air, surface and undersea, time simulator, navigation simulator, radar simulator and command simulator. The network deployment of this system use multi-layer net structure, implement communication between simulators and the verified system. Among them, equipment simulator and command simulator communicating with the verified system through wired network; air, surface and undersea platform communicating with the verified system through the wireless simulated network; simulation environment communicating with simulator and the verified system through simulated network; and divide several VLAN. The adaption of multi-layer net structure design makes various combat and simulation data isolated mutually, makes data keep pure, improves the accuracy of system verification.

During verification, director insert situation information into verification system and simulator through simulated network, the verified system need feed back command to director through platform type simulator, control the running data of entity equipment; equipment and command simulator interact with command information, intelligence information, and combat state of equipment through weird network; platform type simulator interact with command information, intelligence information and combat state

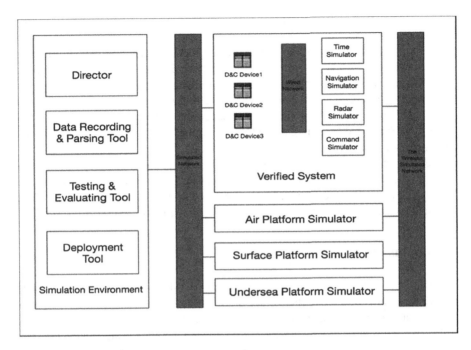

Fig. 2. Application example of the C⁴ISR system validation environment

through wireless simulated network and verification system; recording and parsing tool record and store the network data during running, used to test and evaluate.

The build step of C⁴ISR validation environment including requirement analysis on the trial, design, S&VE development, data preparation for the trial, S&VE validation, S&VE trial, and analysis of the trial. The rationality and validity can refer to literature build evaluation model and evaluate it. Mainly content of each activity is as follows:

- Carrying out requirement analysis and design according to trial plan. First, make requirement analysis from S&VE composition, function, interface, quality, document and schedule; clarify the requirement of resource reuse, function composition, internal & external interface, data, computer resource, UI; meanwhile carry out plan design, including S&VE composition, function dispatch, interface protocol, deployment design, network design, running operation, and software architecture, formulate plan design report as the basis of environment development.
- According to reuse situation analysis chart in plan design report, select directly reuse or revised component from model base, build S&VE through integrated development and integration platform for the standard simulator.
- It is required to prepare basic data and combat scenario before trial start. Basic data is the data support the verified system and S&VE, including map data and communication parameter; combat scenario clarify the scope of study on military problem of combat simulating system, and clarify the objective of simulating, give the simulation boundary condition and corresponding constraint, describes each entity took

part in simulation and each entity's basic attribute, presents situation data for the whole trial running.

- Before using S&VE, according to plan design report, organizing the confirmation test of whether S&VE can running normally, version and function performance satisfaction by the quality party, provide credibility of verification result.
- After S&VE has been verified, according to the test instance designed by trial, carry out function, interface, flow, and performance quota verification trial in S&VE. During verification, according to evaluation requirement, record and store network running data, evaluate and analysis related quota.
- After trial, according to the data record during trial process, analysis whether this trial has been through on the basis of trial pass evaluation principle. Summing up and analyzing the problem exist in trial, proposing equipment revision requirement and existed problem, presenting experience for trial in the future and other projects.

5   Conclusion

As the last checkpoint before system delivered, C^4ISR simulation validation need improve the quality and credibility of S&VE, in order to guarantee function, performance, interface integrity, reliability, availability, and usability of C^4ISR, reduce the actual combat risk. This paper proposes S&VE build method, network design and interfacing design real equip based on integrated development and integration platform for the standard simulator according to the requirement of low sharing, low credibility of S&VE, hard to control R&D cycle and can not meet high-concurrency of trial. Repeat design-development-validation constantly, thus improve the efficiency of environment development, reduce the R&D cycle, improve the credibility of validation. Besides, this paper proposes a C^4ISR validation application instance, and describes C^4ISR operation, provide reference for actual application.

References

1. Fu, J.P., Wang, J.Q., Zhang, S.F.: Software testing method for integrated electronic information system. Command Inf. Syst. Technol. **6**(1), 87–91 (2015)
2. Sun, X.G., Fu, J.P., Lu, L.F., et al.: Software testing method for integrated electronic information system. Command Inf. Syst. Technol. **5**(4), 75–79 (2014)
3. Zhang, S.F., Cai, D.H., Yang, L.P.: Construction of evaluation model for software testing process of C^4ISR system. Command Inf. Syst. Technol. **5**(3), 82–86 (2014)
4. Men, X.H., Yu, K.Y., Zhen, L.: Simulation test technology of the C^4ISR system. Command Control Simul. **36**(1), 94–98 (2014)
5. Wang, W.P., Liu, G.Y., Yang, H., et al.: Theory and process of validation for C3I. Command Control Simulation **36**(6), 88–91 (2014)
6. Wang, F., Guo, J.J.: Design and implementation of the hardware-in-the-loop simulation system for target missile test. Tactical Missile Technol. **3**, 103–107 (2013)
7. Peng, H., Wang, P., Zhang, X.: Research of C^4ISR system warfare simulation test technology in battlefield environment. Fire Control Command Control **38**(8), 158–162 (2013)

Research on Reuse Modeling for C4ISR Simulation Verification System

Hao Li[✉], Wenyuan Xu, Shengxiao Zhang, Li Guo, and Dongmei Zhao

China Shipbuilding Industry Systems Engineering Research Institute, Beijing, China
choupangpang@163.com

Abstract. The process of research and development of C4ISR (Command, Control, Communication, Computer, Intelligence, Surveillance, Reconnaissance, C4ISR) system is a multiple cycle iterative, function continuously improved, evolution process, thus the simulation model and system supporting C4ISR system at different stages must be with multi granularity, phase correlation characteristics. The focus of this paper is how to use system simulation model and system correlation reasonably and efficiently, improve reusability and interoperability of simulation model between various simulation applications, and make the various simulation applications no longer fragmented, uncorrelated. In this paper, the modeling methods of the reuse based on the unified modeling simulation language (UMSL), the reuse based on model framework, the reuse based on component model (Library), the reuse based on general model, the reuse based on unified simulation platform is studied, the reuse modeling techniques used often or developed at present on a warship fleet C4ISR system are introduced.

Keywords: Reusability · UMSL · Model framework · Modularization · General model · Simulation platform

1 Introduction

C4ISR is an electronic information system integrated command, control, communications, computers, intelligence, surveillance and reconnaissance, which can support commanders to plan, command and control the army in all military operations; it is also an important weapon equipment. It has characteristics of involving many elements, complex information, complex combat style and complex process, and a wide range of combat resources. Therefore, the process of research and development of C4ISR system is a multiple cycle iterative, function continuously improved, evolution process, which includes the phases of project demonstration, scheme design, technical design, system development, integrated verification and system delivery. At present, system simulation is usually available to verification, the simulation models are operated repeatedly to do all kinds of test, including the concept demonstration, key technologies verification, technical architecture verification, conventional function performance test, some risk test, boundary condition test and fault reappearance test, in order to analyze and determine the appropriate technical index, verify and optimize the system design solution, find out and solve technical bottlenecks, analyze and judge the reason of fault, predict

© Springer Science+Business Media Singapore 2016
L. Zhang et al. (Eds.): AsiaSim 2016/SCS AutumnSim 2016, Part IV, CCIS 646, pp. 463–471, 2016.
DOI: 10.1007/978-981-10-2672-0_47

the characteristics of the system. So as to promote communication and cooperation between the personnel of the research and development of C4ISR system, military personnel, and users of the system, make different people to reach a consensus on the same problem, so that different people who have different knowledge backgrounds can communicate effectively, and providing a strong support for function of continuous improvement, loop iterations of C4ISR system.

The simulation model and system supporting C4ISR system at different stages has multi granularity, phase correlation characteristics. The simulation model becomes deepen and refine continuously with the advancement of C4ISR system development phase, but the simulation verification framework is basically the same. And the simulation model of different types of C4ISR system has the characteristic of function comparability, that different C4ISR system although have a lot of changes in functions, but the requirements for simulation verification environment are similar, especially to the function of the test system especially are often very close to each other. How to use system simulation model and system correlation reasonably and efficiently, improve reusability and interoperability of simulation model between various simulation applications, and make the various simulation applications no longer fragmented, uncorrelated, is an important research content of C4ISR system simulation verification technology.

2   Model Reuses Type Partitioning

Model reuse is to achieve multiple application purpose through one time modeling; main idea is to use the mature model to avoid repeated modeling as much as possible, so as to reduce the development cost of simulation. Simulation model reuse technology is a method supporting simulation model reuse in multiple simulation application. According to the focus of model reuse and different main features, the current simulation model reuse technology is roughly divided into the following 5 categories:

The reuse based on Unified Modeling and simulation language (UMSL). Characteristics of UMSL consist in sufficient expression and platform independent, so that the description of the complex system is not limited to specific computing/simulation platform, such as simulation reference markup language (SRML), simulation modeling language (SML) and so on.

The reuse based on model framework. Model framework is a standard, consistent description of the elements of the model and their relations, generally includes composition of the model, structure and interface, the different application requirements model has the same framework, different business logic/algorithm.

The reuse based on the component model (Library). This is a much popular model reuse technology, and its role is to provide consistent high cohesion and low coupling function model for different applications.

The reuse based on general model. The general model are models of the basic type's simulation objects. When the new application requirements appear, the basic model can construct a new model quickly by adjusting the parameters.

The reuse based on the unified simulation platform. For the whole simulation process, the unified simulation platform provides visualization description and definition, the consistent methods of call and integration, running monitoring, analysis and evaluation of models. Therefore, simulation model reuse is generally easier in the simulation platform in which it is developed, such as COSIM, SIM 2000 etc. At the same time, the platform also provides the model base of the basic model and professional model, which can reduce the workload of modeling, such as joint operations simulation software JTS (Fig. 1).

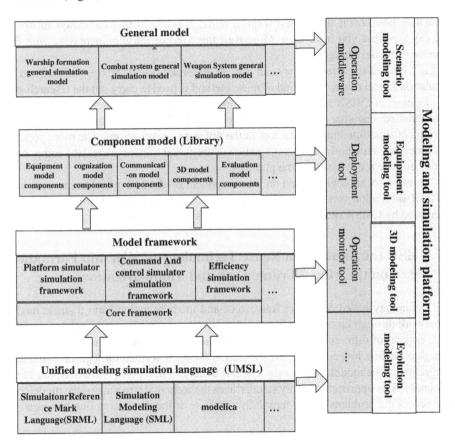

Fig. 1. The structure of the types of the model reuse

In the 5 kinds of reuse technology, the reuse of the unified modeling language is the most basic reuse technology. It has a wide application range, but requires a higher simulation model. The reuse based on framework model can transform specific modeling languages into the language that the public is familiar with to model and reduce the difficulty of modeling, and achieve the reuse of the model framework through making the specification of the structural relations of different types of business model and unifying the technical architecture of model. The reuse based on component model goes a step even further than the code framework reuse, by not only is the reuse of model structure, including direct reuse of interface, communication, business logic and functional model, but component granularity requirements of this kind of reuse is higher, the reuse rate is correlative to the component division method and the size of the component and the reuse technology is often used together with the model frame. With respect to the other reuse technology, the reuse based on the general model adapts to the smaller range, and must be used to the simulation system in the specific application fields. But it has the highest degree of reuse, just need to adjust some parameters of the model to form a new model, it can implement the reuse of models quickly. The reuse of the unified simulation platform is the highest form of reuse. It is one of the reuse ways in which you can see what you have seen. Moreover, this kind of reuse is increasing with the increase of model library.

Each kind of reuse technology can play an important role in solving the problem of simulation model reuse, what kind of reuse method is used to carry out the research and development of C4ISR simulation verification system, depends entirely on the situation of simulation resource accumulation, Technology ability of simulation personnel, investment situation and other factors in the different organizations. The more popular and widely used method are the combination of the model framework and the component model, and the reuse based on the platform.

The reuse technologies based on the component model and model framework, and a C4ISR simulation verification support platform will be introduced bellow, which are offen used by C4ISR simulation and verification system for a naval ship formation.

3   C4ISR the Simulation Reuse Technology of Warship Formation Based on the Model Framework and Modularization

The technology based on model framework and modularization form a stable model framework through layering the functions of models, abstracting and modularizing the basic content of different layers; the business model is modularized with the principle of high cohesion, low coupling, the simulation model is formed through invoking and integration of the model framework, which is of certain functions, and can be run independently. This approach not only standardizes the technical structure of the model, but also solves the problem of low reusability because of the direct coupling between the application codes.

The technology based on the model framework and modularization is divided into six layers: communication layer, message distributing and processing layer, business logic layer, memory data layer, human-computer layer and model scheduling engine. The communication layer, message distribution layer, memory data layer, human-computer interaction layer and the model scheduling engine belong to the model framework. The business logic layer is relevant to the simulation application, form different components according to the different simulation requirements. At the same time, in order to standardize the use of the framework model and the subsequent expansion, the method provides the corresponding standard for different layer.

The communication layer which encapsulates the existing means of communication provides the unified communication call interface to the upper layer, including initialization interface, sending interface and receiving interface, and the layer is responsible for initializing and creating a communication interface, in order to achieve the ability of communication to multiple network domains by one simulation model.

The message distributing and processing layer receives messages from the network, format messages to the format which can be identified, and provides the messages to the corresponding logical business processing module. At the same time, the module accepts the message which is submitted by the upper layer, and transmits the message to the communication package layer.

The memory data layer is used to receive and dispatch the data periodically, or store the data in the memory database. It is the basis of interaction between different layers. It is recommended to use the memory database or other components that can provide standard access interface.

The human-computer interface layer realizes the human-computer interaction function of the business process, and interacts with the business model layer and the communication layer through the memory data layer.

The model scheduling engine provides interfaces of the whole framework, including the external message trigger interface, timer trigger interface and human-computer interaction interface. This layer responds to the external trigger, and calls

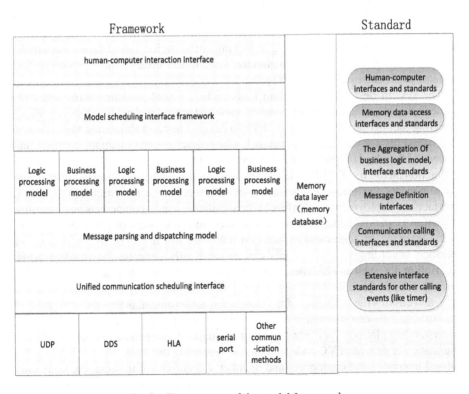

Fig. 2. The structure of the model framework

the model of business process and logic processing, and completes the function of the whole simulation model.

Business logic model is the core function layer of the simulator, mainly include time system components, navigation component, radar components, sonar module, communication system components, formation level command and control components, the ship level command and control components, the platform motion components (Fig. 2).

4 The Simulation and Verification Platform for C4ISR of Warship Formation

The reuse technologies based on model framework and component provide code level reuse for the model constructor, and The simulation and verification platform for C4ISR of warship formation provides a way to reuse in which you can see what you have seen, not only for the model constructor, but also for the model designer.

The simulation and verification platform for C4ISR of warship formation is based on the multi-view and multi-granularity modeling and simulation method theory of complex system, provides functions of the system design and verification, the development of standard model, storage model management, deployment of model, multi-protocol system integration, operation management and online data acquisition and evaluation, supports top-down design patterns of combat command system virtual prototype, supports the development pattern of prototype system from simple into the complex, model reuse and rapid reconfiguration of the system. The platform mainly includes system design and modeling tools, simulation engine, model deployment tools, operation management tools, evaluation tools and model library. The composition and application processes as shown in Fig. 3.

The system design and modeling tools include visual modeling tools and code framework generation tool, based on multi-view and multi-level modeling theory, visual modeling tool divides the system model into design view and simulation view. Design view is mainly for the domain personnel, which describes the function, interface and process of the physical prototype according to system, equipment, and the relationship of function hierarchy. The simulation view is mainly for simulation designer, according to components, the hierarchy relationship of members to describe simulation functions, interface and deployment. According to the simulation needs, equipments and functions of platform can be flexibly deployed to the specified component or personnel, in order to the interface of equipment or function automatically deployed to components or members accordingly, finally, tools can automatically generate the required XML description file, such as FED files, and a member of the component description file etc. The separation of two kinds of view ensures that the consistency of the physical prototype, and ensures the flexibility of the simulation achievement, makes the separation of the business between simulation designer and domain personnel, provide a consistent understanding platform for the two kinds of personnel. Code generation framework tool automatically generates VC code framework by reading the XML file, provides encapsulated interfaces and component and member's management information, users only need to fill the function algorithm in the designated location, and the tool also provides

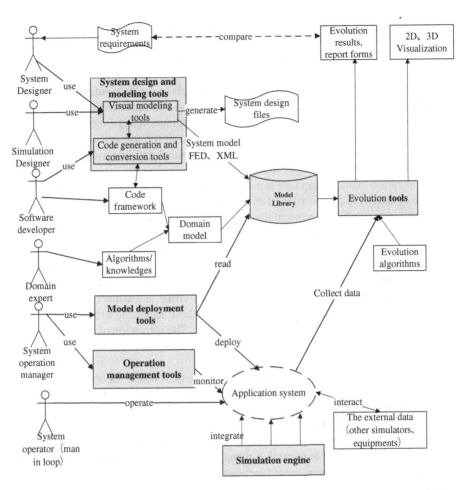

Fig. 3. The composition and application processes of the simulation and verification platform for C4ISR of warship formation

a automatic mapping function between code and visualization model, that ensures the consistency between them.

Simulation engine is the core of the supporting platform of virtual prototype of combat command system. It provides flexible model integration mechanism, multi-protocol, distributed system integrated mechanism and flexible architecture and support services. Model integration mechanism mainly includes components, scripting, hook function, source code; distributed system integration mechanism mainly includes HLA/ RTI, CORBA and TCP/IP; flexible architecture is mainly to achieve through simple, the component interface (API) easy to use. The interface defines: (1) components are how to use the underlying platform service; (2) components are how to be extended; (3) how to control platform or "glue" components through the modeling language, in order to reduce coupling of business model and simulation engine to the fullest extent, reduce the difficulty of model development and system integration; simulation engine also provides declaration management, object management, time management and other services.

The model deployment tool is a visualization tool which can manipulate and manage various resources centrally in the distributed environment, to realize virtual prototype system conveniently formed through integrating models in the distributed environment. The tool realizes remote host file upload and download and start running of the remote file by specifying the deployment file, deployment destination and executable file path. Model deployment tools greatly reduce the workload of the integration of the virtual prototype system, and realize the centralized deployment and integrated operation of the distributed system in one node mode.

The operation management tool is mainly used to monitor and control each simulation node operation in the distributed environment, mainly including the virtual prototype system state control, process management, system resource condition monitoring.

Evaluation tools include data acquisition, data analysis and assessment center, data acquisition collects the original data through deploying the probe to the acquisition point, in the case without affecting the network traffic. Data analysis carries out the analysis mainly according to the data structure defined by users, and stores the analysis results in the center database. Assessment center provides visual assessment modeling environment, and automatically reads the data in the database according to the defined interface relationship, in order to drive the model solution. The separation of data acquisition, data analysis and evaluation center is use of carrying out the three jobs in different places asynchronously.

Multi granularity model library provides management functions of size model and the multiple model system, and meets the needs of a variety of model management system of different particle size and different classification criteria through the edit generation of model classification method to. In a certain model system, it can be used of the effective management and reuse of the model. Multi granularity model library mainly provides the model information management, model entity management, user management and other management functions.

5   Conclusions

The simulation verification system provides a kind of non-destructive method for the C4ISR system, which can be used repeatedly, can be controlled, and can be reused. It also plays an important role in the practical work. The reuse of simulation model, model framework and simulation system has become the important content of the research of simulation verification system. That is because of the evolution process of C4ISR system development, which is multiple cycles iterative, and the continuous improvement of the function. Therefore, system reuse technology and reuse level will be improved continuously to the highest reuse level, the specification of the simulation model and system, rapid development will be realized, and finally to promote the C4ISR simulation system to be mature. At the same time, the reliability of the model can be improved by reusing and consummating continuously.

References

1. Su, W., Luo, X., Zhang, Y.: Research on design methods and support environment based on simulation for C4ISR. Comput. Simul. **8**, 6 (2003)
2. Yu, B., Zhang, Y., Chen, H., Huang, L.: The component-based system effectiveness simulation environment for C4ISR. Mil. Oper. Res. Syst. Eng. **1** (2002)
3. Guo, L., Jiang, J., Lv, B.: The study of modeling and simulation environment in the C4ISR system. Inform. Technol. **11** (2005)
4. Bai, X.-L., Yi, X.-Q., Luo, X.-S., Bai X.-H.: Study on simulation model description for C4ISR systems development. J. Natl Univ. Defense Technol. **33**(2) (2011)
5. Liu, C., Huang, Y.-Y., Li, Q., Wang, W.-P.: Extending SRML schema based on DEVS: a foundation for simulation model representation and reuse. J. Syst. Simul. **17**(10) (2005)
6. Liang, Y.-Z., Zhang, W.-S., Kang, X.-Y., Zhang, G.: A survey of model reuse methods. Comput. Simul. **25**(8) (2008)
7. Liang, Y.-Z., Zhang, W.-S., Kang, X.-Y., Zhang, G.: Warship combat simulation model frameworks supporting model reuse. J. Syst. Simul. **21**(4) (2009)
8. Liu, C., Wei, H.-T., Li, Q., Wang, W.-P.: A new simulation language for supporting model integration and reuse. Comput. Simul. 23(5) (2006)

Application Development of Monitor and Diagnosis System Based on Simulation Platform

Qicai Wu[1] and Haibin Yuan[2(✉)]

[1] Beijing Institute of Space Launch Technology, Beijing, China
gensome@sina.com
[2] Beihang University, Beijing, China
yuanhb@buaa.edu.cn

Abstract. In industry automation, fault monitor and diagnosis play vital role in ensuring on demand operation of complex system with safety and reliability. Simulation platform is useful way for researchers to design and develop application-based system monitor and diagnosis, especially in the field of engineering-based vehicle. A method using modular design is presented in this paper to achieve information synthesis, distributed control and supervisory management based on the field bus simulation platform. With the simulation platform is proposed, method of design and development for engineering vehicle supervisory management system is proposed and implemented. The system is divided into separate functional modules and each module is designed in the form of dynamic link library encapsulation in order to achieve the goal of high cohesion and low coupling. Furthermore, the module is loaded on demand so that operation resource requirement is optimized in the system. At last, detail analysis and research work are carried out regarding design and implementation plan according to a case study from equipment monitor and diagnosis system. The proposed design method can improve compatibility and adaptability of the monitor and diagnosis system, and operation efficiency is improved as well.

Keywords: Simulation platform · Hardware-in-the-loop · Fault · Diagnosis · Software design · Vehicle

1 Introduction

With the tendency toward multi-system synthesis and automation in the field of industry, it is becoming more and more complicated for exchange and transmission among different information and energy, information comes in the form of digital signal, analog signal, continuous pulse, sequence pulse. This information is characterized working condition of complex plant. It is one of the important ways to evaluate and improve performance and parameters of the system process according to obtained information. Usually in this process, different design projects have to be tested and verified to produce optimal result for practical purpose. Simulation platform is ideal way in dealing with design and development of monitor and diagnosis prototype for industry automation [1–3]. Especially for application of monitor and fault diagnosis toward engineering vehicle, the hardware-in-the-loop platform is setup, and control system is developed on

© Springer Science+Business Media Singapore 2016
L. Zhang et al. (Eds.): AsiaSim 2016/SCS AutumnSim 2016, Part IV, CCIS 646, pp. 472–481, 2016.
DOI: 10.1007/978-981-10-2672-0_48

the simulation platform at first, with the hardware function and software development, the prototype platform that simulates plant operation is implemented, which has interface with actual control unit. As a result, integrated development platform for algorithm research and information processing with monitor, diagnosis, manipulation, control and analysis function can be achieved.

Along with simulation platform setup, software development is another issue regarding proper operation flow of the system. That is to say, both hardware and software are important in developing functional modules, with the simulation hardware is confirmed, software package is the only concern. Usually for early development or simple development, task demand for monitor and diagnosis is unified and easy to achieve. Un-structured framework is taken as module design and development routine. With more and more complex task is added to the system development plan, functions for monitor and diagnosis are different and sophisticated, a unified development framework is defined for better design. Although the method is easy to take, disadvantage of compatibility and expandability problem is hardly overcome because of strong function coupling and data information overlap. Once the developed prototype is put into practice, all the function modules are loaded to memory simultaneously; the performance is bad because the system resources are occupied too much. It is also difficult to plant from one platform to another especially in a distributed and network environment. By comparison, method of function segmentation and separate design is better in realizing system function independently, and some practical applications are studied as well [4–6]. In this paper, simulation platform is presented and method of function segmentation and modular isolation is proposed. The proposed method can improve compatibility and adaptability of the monitor and diagnosis system, and operation efficiency is improved as well.

2   Framework for Prototype Development

2.1   Network Topology for Simulation Platform

Nowadays simulation technology has applied to many application fields such as national defense, aerospace, chemical engineering, traffic control, industry automation and software engineering [7–9]. Simulation method on automobile engineering and internal combustion engine has been studied by many researchers and engineers. Software-in-the-loop simulation, rapid-control-prototyping and hardware-in-the-loop are typical technologies that are used for simulation. Software-in-the-loop (SIL) is more like distributed computing environment, in which real-time data interchange is produced, software package that simulates system dynamics is run on the platform, with control algorithm is developed and verified. Issues of distributed control, network transmission, task schedule, data sampling, process synchronize are taken into account. The simulation platform is easy to deploy and model a prototype. While rapid control prototyping (RCP) is based on the function test and performance evaluation between simulated control unit, in which different signals transmission are produced from hardware interface and input to control unit as simulate, the response is analyzed to make decision on system working condition. Hardware-in-the-loop (HIL) is found in the aviation industry and is becoming more prevalent in all industries. HIL is a technique that is used in development and test of complex systems. It provides an effective platform by adding the complexity of the plant under control to the development and test platform. The complexity of the plant under control is included in test and development by adding a mathematical representation (model) of all related dynamic systems.

Considering the requirement for engineering vehicle development, control area network (CAN) field bus network is taken as simulation topology, with field devices that represent different part of the system are connect to the network. In this way, it is very useful to develop and test a controller function with a simulated process before the controller is applied to the physical plant. All the researches can be done without damaging equipment of the physical plant. Figure 1 show the field bus network topology used for application design and development.

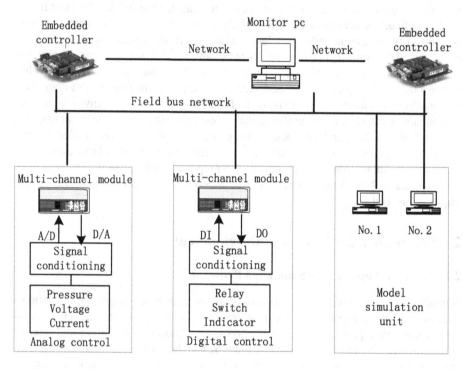

Fig. 1. Network topology for simulation platform

The main purpose is to develop integrated monitor and diagnosis system for a kind of engineering vehicle management. CAN based field device signal processing and test is carried out, and software function that can configure working condition and schedule operation mode is studied. Simulation system is setup on monitor pc as main node, software function development, model database and schedule management are run. Multi-channel modules act as prototype system to simulate field device of the physical system. Devices that are embedded to the multi-channel module is used to receive information of plant work condition, such as speed, pressure, switch, lift leverage, pedal threshold, indicator and wheel angle. Model simulation unit is used as platform to setup control and monitor process by means of graphical interface. Figure 2 shows one of the modules on the platform.

Fig. 2. Multi-channel module and hardware platform

2.2 Module Based Software Function Architecture

Main purpose of software function for application is to monitor physical plant working condition. Visual user interface has to be developed to show system dynamics such as waveform, indicator, and instrument meter and trend line. So that users can understand current state of the system working condition and make decision on future working performance. Once alarm is triggered and received by software function, fault diagnosis process is underway and subsequent decision is made. Each module represents each function according to physical equipment. Method of modular based design is taken into consideration [10–12]. With this method, one task can be divided into several separate sub-tasks, with teach sub-task is developed in the form of function module. With each module is programmed to provide same design standard and interface. The efficiency is improved greatly because each module can be designed and debugged separately. The function module can be further divided into smaller sub- function module according to practical application.

Interface is designed to transmission data between function modules, and it is implemented by means of developing link library. Static link library and dynamic link library are used more often, and both share code in the memory. Static link library is compiled to final execution file of the developed software package, and only one static link library is included. Execution code of dynamic link library includes many functions that have been compiled and linked. Dynamic link library is stored separately from running process of the main file. Once reference interface is set up, dynamic library is loaded and unloaded dynamically. In this way, problem of heavy system resources occupation is overcome and performance is improved as well.

Figure 3 shows function architecture, Fig. 4 shows data interface and data flow between different function module, the function module is developed separately. Based on the design method, three main function modules are developed, which are fault

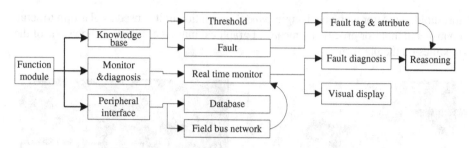

Fig. 3. Function architecture of the module

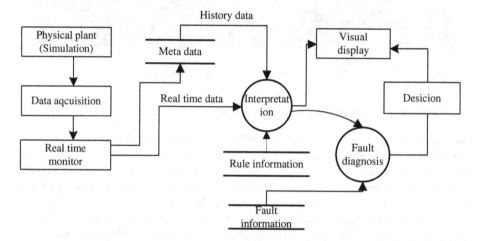

Fig. 4. Data flow of function module

knowledge module, monitor and diagnosis module, interface module. Fault knowledge module act as fault data processing and analysis. Users can perform fault knowledge input, store, and update and delete operation. The module is at the bottom of the function module, there is no need for further classification. Monitor and diagnosis module is in the core of the developed system, and the module can be classified into real time monitor module, history data analysis module, fault diagnosis module and peripheral interface module. Real time monitor module and history data analysis module performs data interpretation, processing and display according to rules stored in the database. Once alarm information is interpreted, fault diagnosis module is loaded and fault diagnosis and fault location is performed. The reference interface for the module is implemented by library function, and the parameters that denote fault tag are included. Peripheral interface implements data acquisition. Initialization function that is used to control device open port and close port is included in this module.

2.3 Peripheral Interface Implementation

Based on the control area network field bus as network topology, the peripheral interface means communication between computer host and field device such as CAN PCI card and USB-CAN. Dynamic link library is developed to encapsulate network configuration. The parameters for network configuration includes baud rate, mask code, frame format and frame type. A function module name CANModule.dll developed. Function module can be added or updated on demand. Network l as follows:

```
[DllImport("dynamic link library name")]
static extern function return type  function
name(parameter type parameter ,…);
```

To exemplify configuration in order to open CAN for sending and receiving message over the network, the function is loaded as follows:

```
Uint32 openReturn = OpenDevice(4, 0);
```

Other modules that in the form of dynamic link library are developed besides dynamic link library developed for CAN configuration purpose. The load procedure is to exemplify the function and return value. Some others are InferModule.dll, Monitor-Module.dll, which is load as follows:

```
MonitorModule. MonitorRealTimeForm monitorForm = new
MonitorModule. MonitorRealTimeForm();
```

3 Application Development Based on Simulation Platform

3.1 Configuration of the Hardware Device

It is important for control unit of engineering vehicle to add monitor and diagnosis system in order to improve working performance and operational mode. Due to restriction of physical environment, the design and test is not fit to perform on site. Simulation platform is a useful way to simulate real plant of the target at early stage. The function of the controller can be tested and modified before it is applied to real plant. Based on the proposed network topology and simulation method, the design cycle of the typical system is performed. The first step is to define the signals that will be used to represent information about working condition. As shown in Fig. 1, the signals are produced from the nodes, while each node is in the form of multi-channel module and is added to the network of the simulation platform.

Software configuration tools that runs operation environment configuration and integrated data flow management is developed. Software package that was developed and tested can be planted to physical embedded system. Control nodes within the network have the function of data processing and transmission in order to provide the real time condition of prototype simulation plant. Decision can be made based on the simulation result. All nodes are added or removed on demand according to simulation requirement.

Table 1 shows node definition and signal for physical layer. Information from pedals, switches, sensors, relays and others is obtained and processed, and finally, the information is then transmitted to the network for further management.

Table 1. Node signal type

Signal	Name	Parameters	Module	Channel
Analog input	Pump pressure	Pressure	K8512	CH1
	System pressure	Pressure	K8512	CH2
	Airbag pressure	Pressure	K8512	CH3
	Front beam level	Angle	K8512	CH4
	Back beam level	Angle	K8512	CH5
	Lift level	Angle	K8512	CH6
Analog output	Control panel	Voltage	K8516	CH1-CH6
	Servo valve	Voltage	K8516	CH7-CH8
Digital input	Oil filter	Switch	K8522	DIN1
	Reset	Switch	K8522	DIN2
	Pump reset	Switch	K8522	DIN3
	Latch reset	Switch	K8522	DIN4
Digital output	Relay	Switch	K8522	DOUT1-DOUT4
	Indicator	Switch	K8522	DOUT5-DOUT8
Pulse	Speed	Frequency	K8514	CH1-CH2

3.2 Design of Software Function Module

Based on the module classification and engineering practice, software function modules that represent different simulation operation are developed on the simulation platform and capsulated into dynamic link library. It can be seen in Fig. 5 that the developed system has hierarchical structure. On top level, fault tree is first defined, this module is used to create fault tree and as a reference for further monitor and diagnosis. On bottom level, peripheral interface is defined, and these modules are used to implement database interface and network communication interface. So that operation of data sending, receiving and storing process is achieved. There are 6 main module developed on the simulation. These modules are named as FaultTreeManager, DrawTree, Parameter, HistoryModule, Infermodule, MonitorModule and CANModule, with each module can be classified into sub-modules. Taken FaultTreeManager as example, this module includes two sub-modules, that is FEMABOM and FEMASYS, both module are inherited from the top module. CANModule is first configured prior to other modules, this module is used to start network configuration and initialize frame transmission. During simulation test, the module is loaded on demand according to operation function switch. The module is unloaded from simulation running environment after operation function is finished.

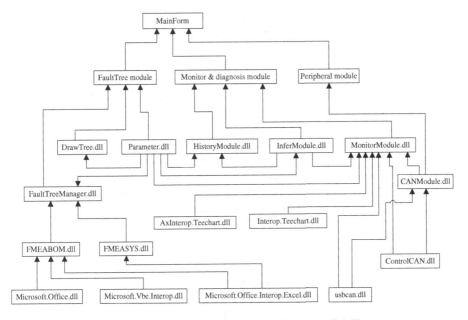

Fig. 5. Function call procedure module of dynamic link library

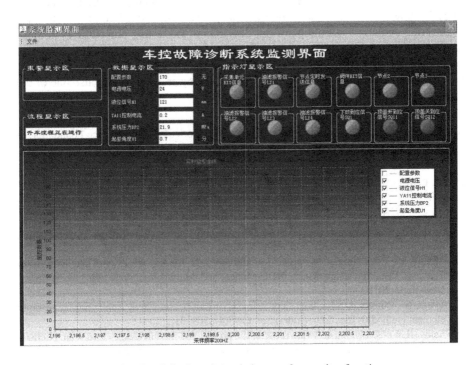

Fig. 6. Visual display of simulation test for monitor function

Figure 6 shows one of the realization function interface on the simulation platform. The function components of hardware device and software are tested and verified before applied to the real physical plant. The first version has been embedded to the real physical plant. In the future, the developed package can be included to physical plant as one part of the prognostic health management system project.

The proposed simulation platform is advantageous in prototype development for engineering application. The framework of hardware can be applied to many industry applications, with software configuration, the simulation platform can be used for specific engineering development. For example, with the signals from the hardware modules are redefined and configured, the message that used to be defined as vehicle pressure can then be used to stand for a pump pressure in fire system. As a result, one simulation platform can be used to development many different engineering application. The cost of research and development is reduced greatly.

4   Conclusion

Simulation is becoming more prevalent in all industries for development and test of engineering application. Different part of the system function can be tested individually to make sure it works as planned before the developed hardware and software is connected to the real physical plant. In this paper, the simulation platform for application design and development is presented. The simulation platform is used for hardware and software function test and development for monitor and diagnosis system. The case study is shown to present application development on integrated control system for engineering vehicle. With the platform, developing and testing procedure is in close parallel with the development of the hardware and software, as a result. Reliability and quality will be increased and procedure for development is more efficient. However, it is noted that the method is need to be verified in many case study, it is also one of the future work.

Acknowledgement. The research of the paper was supported by Aero-Science Foundation of China 2014ZD51047.

References

1. Youjun, Y., Xiang, L., Zongqiang, W., et al.: Design and realization of multi-function car-carry fault diagnosis system. In: 2011 International Conference on IEEE Transportation, Mechanical, and Electrical Engineering (TMEE), pp. 1949–1952 (2011)
2. Navabi, Z.: Fault simulation application and methods. In: Navabi, Z. (ed.) Digital System Test and Testable Design: Using HDL Models and Architectures, pp. 103–142. Springer, New York (2010)
3. Tyagi, S., Panigrahi, S.K.: Transient analysis of ball bearing fault simulation using finite element method. J. Inst. Eng. (India) Ser. C **95**(4), 309–318 (2014)
4. Selby, R.W.: Analyzing software reuse at the project and module design levels. In: Nichols, H., Simpson, D. (eds.) ESEC '87. LNCS, vol. 289, pp. 212–220. Springer, Heidelberg (2005)

5. Ma, J., Wang, Z., Li, Y., Yu, L.: Analysis and design of automotive body control module. In: SAE-China, FISITA, (eds.) Proceedings of the FISITA 2012 World Automotive Congress: Volume 6: Vehicle Electronics. LNEI, vol. 194, pp. 25–32. Springer, Heidelberg (2013)

6. Aleti, A., Buhnova, B., Grunske, L., Koziolek, A., Meedeniya, I.: Software architecture optimization methods: a systematic literature review. IEEE Trans. Softw. Eng. **39**(5), 658–683 (2013)

7. Liu, W., Li, Y., Jia, J., Ling, L.: Construction method and implementation of hardware-in-the-loop real-time dynamic simulation platform for airborne environment control system. In: 2015 IEEE International Conference on Mechatronics and Automation (ICMA), Beijing, pp. 1368–1373 (2015)

8. Shi, J., An, W., Liu, K.: A design of simulation and analysis platform of BIT false alarm considering stochastic characteristics. In: 2014 Prognostics and System Health Management Conference (PHM-2014 Hunan), Zhangiiaijie, pp. 456-459 (2014)

9. Li, X., Yu, F., Jin, H., Liu, J., Li, Z., Zhang, X.: Simulation platform design for diesel engine fault. In: 2011 International Conference on Electrical and Control Engineering (ICECE), Yichang, pp. 4963–4967 (2011)

10. Wang, Y., Zhang, Z., Qiu, W.: Development of software module for model reference adaptive control simulation based on the LabVIEW. In: Xiao, T., Zhang, L., Fei, M. (eds.) AsiaSim 2012, Part I. CCIS, vol. 323, pp. 240–249. Springer, Heidelberg (2012)

11. Sozer, H., Tekinerdogan, B., Aksit, M.: Optimizing decomposition of software architecture for local recovery. Software Qual. J. **21**(2), 203–240 (2013)

12. Aleti, A.: Designing automotive embedded systems with adaptive genetic algorithms. Autom. Softw. Eng. **22**(2), 199–240 (2015)

Design Method of FCM Representation with Optimization Algorithm

Haibin Yuan[1(✉)] and QiCai Wu[2]

[1] Beihang University, Beijing, China
yuanhb@buaa.edu.cn
[2] Beijing Institute of Space Launch Technology, Beijing, China
gensome@sina.com

Abstract. A design method of Fuzzy Cognitive Map (FCM) model is simulated and verified with both PSO algorithm and SA algorithm based on computational intelligence. The aim is to develop the design method of FCM effectively and concentrate on the algorithmic way of forming the FCM model while overcome the involvement of subjective factors from the manual or user-driven interference in the case of real world application. Simulation experiment of information granules representation for time series analysis is carried out to evaluate the behavior of the proposed method and algorithm performance. With data sample is given, connection matrix is generalized using supervised training process in a reasonable way. The parameters of node number and transmission function are introduced and discussed to assess performance and quality of candidate FCM configuration for further analysis and representation. The proposed approach is alternative way for FCM model based application.

Keywords: Fuzzy cognitive map · Simulation · Optimization · Time series · Fuzzy systems · Prediction

1 Introduction

The Fuzzy Cognitive Map was proposed by Kosko [1] to depict the relationships between the elements (also refer to as concepts, events etc.) and to analyze it's gross behavior or dynamics based on computational theory of fuzzy logic and improved model of cyclic weighted signed digraphs. Despite the fact that it is developed from fuzzy logic, FCM has evolved in many ways. FCM model is also developed to express complex systems in order to overcome difficult reasoning process and precise mathematical model. FCM model offer alternative way to reason knowledge, moreover, the cause-effect relationships can be emulated to imitate the cognitive process that is similar to intelligent systems and the setup of the element in a FCM can be configured in accordance to practical demand with flexibility. The reasonable attribute of abstraction, flexibility and adaptability have appealed to researchers in the last decade and many different applications of FCM have been developed in a much wider range of scientific fields [2–5].

© Springer Science+Business Media Singapore 2016
L. Zhang et al. (Eds.): AsiaSim 2016/SCS AutumnSim 2016, Part IV, CCIS 646, pp. 482–492, 2016.
DOI: 10.1007/978-981-10-2672-0_49

In general, the main approaches than are used to develop FCM model are divided into two groups. One is expert based development and the other is automated or semi-automated based development [6–8]. The former approach uses an expert knowledge to describe application field, which has the drawbacks of domain knowledge restrictions, subjective inclination and overhead in modeling complex system in which a significant number of nodes are included [9]. When it comes to the latter approach, two learning algorithms are involved, the first one is based on artificial neural network, and the second one is based on optimization technique such as evolutionary optimization, simulated annealing and particle swarm optimization [9, 10]. In this case, the weights are optimized by the minimization of the absolute error between all actual output and all calculated output at each state.

Although much progress have been made with regard to the development of FCM model, few attention has been paid to both the inherent investigation of FCM with fully connected topology and comprehensive criteria using optimized method. As a result, a comprehensive investigation of design methodology and algorithm suitable for FCM model is of great necessity especially applied to analysis of time series representation. In this paper, we first aim at finding data samples representation to make it fall within the dynamic scope of the FCM model, and then make a further step toward the method of constructing an FCM model that mainly utilizing PSO and SA algorithm-based learning mechanism in order to obtain essential numerical data and carry on simulation test. Exploration is made to understand the efficacy of FCM model to be used for the dynamics representation of data or knowledge. Design and validation of FCM model is made based on simulation test to explore the usefulness of proposed FCM design method.

In short, FCM has been used in many fields for reasoning process, the construction method of FCM is of great concern in order to achieve better result, optimization is useful way to improve FCM model. As a result, research on FCM representation with optimization method is necessary.

2   General Model for FCM

FCM is regarded as the extension of cognitive map, into which the combined principle of fuzzy logic and neural networks is incorporated to provide modeling methodology of knowledge representation for complex system. In graph theory, FCM structure is a graph topology and can be observed directly. A general graphical topology of FCM model is shown in Fig. 1. There are some elements included in a FCM model, and two basic elements are node and connection, and these elements are fundamentals to form FCM model. A node stands for different meaning, such as concept, event, action, goal or trend of the system. At each time state, characteristic of the system in the FCM model is depicted by node. A connection is also named as weight, edge, arc or interaction between nodes. The connection is used to define cause-effect relationship of adjacent node. Nodes and connections are named in different way according to practical application. Nodes and connections are added or reduced according to different application requirement. In what follows, we use the term "node" and "weight" to denote two basic elements in the FCM model. The relationship between two nodes can be defined as positive causality, negative causality or neutral causality. The relationship is defined as weight and put value in $[-1, 1]$, the value shows the strength of the corresponding causality. Maximum value 1 denotes the strongest cause-effect relationship in a positive way. Minimum value -1 denotes the strongest cause-effect relationship in a negative way. Neutral vale denotes no cause-effect relationship. The positive, neutral and negative are in accord with the range in $[-1, 1]$. In Fig. 1, cause-effect relationship from source node i to node j is denoted as w_{ij}, which holds some conditions. If value of node i and node j increase in the same direction or decrease in the same direction, then weight value $w_{ij} \in (0, 1]$. If value of node i and node j increase in a opposite direction decrease in a opposite direction, then weight value $w_{ij} \in [-1, 0)$. If change of node i value does not affect node j value, then weight value $w_{ij} = 0$.

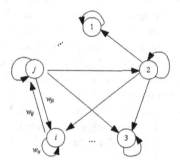

Fig. 1. Overview of FCM topology

In the FCM model, the weights are defined in a weight matrix. Each cell in the weight matrix indicates the strength of cause-effect relationship in the form of float number that falls into interval $[-1, 1]$. The weight matrix can be represented as below.

$$\mathbf{W} = \begin{pmatrix} w_{11} & \cdots & w_{1n} \\ \vdots & \ddots & \vdots \\ w_{n1} & \cdots & w_{nn} \end{pmatrix}_{n \times n} \tag{1}$$

where $\mathbf{W}$ can be marked as $\mathbf{W} = (w_1, w_2, \ldots, w_i, \ldots, w_n)' \cdot w_i = (w_{i1}, w_{i2}, \ldots, w_{ii}, \ldots, w_{in})$. The state of nodes in value for a FCM model can be described as vector:

$$\mathbf{v}(t) = (v_1(t), v_2(t), \cdots, v_i(t), v_n(t))' \tag{2}$$

where t denotes the iteration step, $vi(t)$ denotes the state value of node i, and $v(t)$ denotes FCM state at iteration step t. At each time step, reasoning process and state update of FCM model is depicted according to the following equation:

$$v_i(t+1) = f\left(\sum\nolimits_{j=1}^{n} v_i(t) \times w_{ij}(t)\right)$$

$$i,j = 1, 2, \cdots, n; \ n = 1, 2, \cdots, k.$$

(3)

where f means threshold (activation) function. A threshold function is applied to map the resulting sum into active level of the nodes in the range of [0, 1]. At each step, each node value is computed and updated. The node value is also called activation level. Activation level of all nodes are combined together to form dynamic behavior and characteristics of FCM model.

In this paper, we are interested in developing the universal FCM model by improving the procedure of FCM formation with theoretical approach, and at the same time, using most recent learning method in order that the scheme of constructed architecture is able to analyze trend of a time series. The data sample is used to form times series, behavior of time series is analyzed, and the feature is captured. The data sample is produced by simulation.

3 FCM Architecture with Learning Method

Simulation of time series behavior is studied by input produced data set from FCM model, and features of time series is captured to observe how well the state of the FCM model can describe time series. FCM should be as objective as possible, so as to overcome subjective affect from manual intervene, and the learning algorithm is used to validate the configuration after simulation.

3.1 Design of Candidate FCM Module Procedure

At first step, FCM prototype has to be setup, with connected weights are not zero, and each node has cause-effect relation to itself, by producing data with the existing FCM prototype, the capability of the data representation is simulated by changing the node number of the candidate FCM prototype. Diversified data is produced to check the robustness while using the learning method to train the prototype. Figure 2 shows simulation procedure of FCM reconstruction and validation.

As shown in Fig. 2, a FCM prototype (marked as F) is built firstly, the initial weight matrix and initial state vector is randomly specified at iteration, and the total node number in F is defined. Simulation data is then produced according to Eq. (3), the data set is then organized in order to form the time series, which illustrates the patterns of the FCM prototype. Next step is to reconstruction of new FCM model (namely candidate FCM) using the data set from the generated time series, the number of the nodes in the candidate FCM model is equal to existing FCM prototype node number. The formation of the weight is carried out by taking advantage of most recent learning method. Typical fitness functions are defined to check validation process. If the objective function reaches the desired minimum, the process can also be regarded as convergence. By compare the data value produced from existing FCM prototype with the data value produced from candidate FCM model. Performance validation is

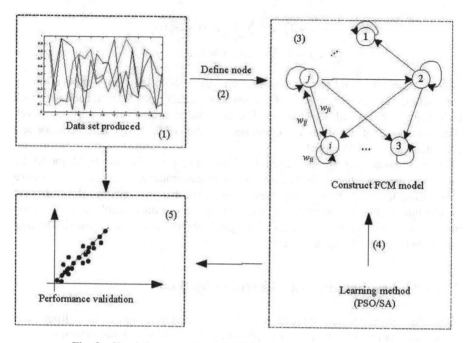

Fig. 2. Simulation procedure of FCM reconstruction and validation

obtained by changing node number of candidate FCM model. In order to justify the formation of FCM model, self-feedback is taken into account for each node. More specifically, the state of each node $v_i(t + 1)$ is effected not only by the last states of other nodes $v_j(t)(j, i)$, but also by the last state of the node $v_i(t)$ itself. Furthermore, data source should be more diversified in the range [0, 1] so as to validate all the state of the FCM model as fully as possible. In addition, the fully connected weight allows for the interactive relationship in a more general way and all the nodes and connections are employed to function actively at the most extent, as a result, the setup of the candidate FCM model will be more universal.

3.2   Parameters of Training Method

In the training method, weight matrix is key parameter, which has to be optimized in a FCM model. Learning process also plays vital rule in the procedure of FCM design. Evolutionary strategy, particle swarm optimization, simulated annealing are dominate optimization algorithm, whereas some improvements can be made to enhance the efficiency. After the data sample is provided, the first algorithm to be used is supervised learning method. In the paper, particle swarm optimization and simulated anneal are adopted. The determination of the weights is very important for candidate FCM model, therefore the performance index that is used to decide the process toward optimized values of weight matrix is put forward, in this case, the objective function is setup so that proper weights that are able to depict the system will be met. The objective function can be described as follows.

$$F_{obj} = \frac{1}{n(k-1)} \sum_{t=1}^{k} \sum_{i=1}^{n} ||\hat{v}_i(t+1) - \hat{v}_i(t)||^2 \tag{4}$$

more specifically, Eq. (4) can be written in detail, as follow.

$$F_{obj} = \frac{1}{n(k-1)} \sum_{t=1}^{k} \sum_{i=1}^{n} ||f\left(\sum_{j=1}^{n} v_i(t) \times \hat{w}_{ij}(t)\right) - \hat{v}_i(t)||^2 \tag{5}$$

where k denotes the length of data points that are taken from data set, n denotes node number in the candidate FCM model. The objective function value is computed and updated. At each iteration step, $\hat{w}_{ij}$ is replaced by new one, and iteration will continue until the goal is achieved. Let $n \times n$ be the search space, objection function F_{obj}: $\hat{W} \to R$.

Without loss of generosity, the FCM prototype is first given prior to performing a comprehensive analysis. By changing the parameters regarding the existing FCM prototype, diversified data points are produced at each iteration step, and the data points are collected together to form data set. A candidate FCM model is then designed and the training process is performed by using the data set. At current iteration step, the node acts as input, at next iteration step, the node acts as output. Node output has the form of numerical value or linguistic value, which is based on application requirement. There are many activation functions for Eq. (3), in this paper, activation function is denoted as $f(x) = 1/(1 + exp(-\sigma x))$ and $\sigma = 1$.

The data set is also an important factor to be considered. Here, two kinds of FCM prototype are taken into consideration to produce diversified data set, the first FCM prototype F_1 is generic model, and the value of each node in this model evolves from the initial state vector according to Eq. (3), it is apparently that the total data length comes from each node value will be $L_1 = l$, where l denotes data length to be created, whereas the second FCM prototype F_2 is more diversified with initial state vector is set by a sequence of ordered vector, and the value of each node is calculated based on each initial state vector according to Eq. (3), and then these data are combined together to form a data set. To make it clear, assume FCM prototype F_2 has n nodes, and then n ordered sequences are set as initial state vector, which is marked as matrix $V_0 = I_{n \times n}$, where I denotes unit matrix, with each column implies initial state vector. The total data length comes from each node value will be $L_2 = l \times n$, where l denotes data length to be created for each initial state vector. Apparently, the data set is synthetic with diversified values.

Table 1 shows the formation of synthetic data produced to train the candidate FCM model. For each sequence, the initial values of all nodes begin with Data 1, which are taken as input of existing FCM prototype, and output is produced as Data 2 according to Eq. (3), at the next iteration, the input will be taken as Data 2, and the output is produced as Data 3, the same process is repeated until all data are produced. It is noted that in this respect, the same number of nodes is set for both FCM prototype and

Table 1. Synthetic data as input of candidate FCM model F_2

Sequence No.	Sequence 1	Sequence 2	$\cdots$	Sequence n
Data 1	$[\overbrace{10\ldots0}^{n}]$	$[\overbrace{01\cdots0}^{n}]$	$\cdots$	$[\overbrace{00\ldots1}^{n}]$
Data 2	$[\overbrace{v_1^2 v_2^2 \cdots v_n^2}^{n}]$	$[\overbrace{v_1^2 v_2^2 \cdots v_n^2}^{n}]$	$\cdots$	$[\overbrace{v_1^2 v_2^2 \cdots v_n^2}^{n}]$
$\cdots$	$\cdots$	$\cdots$	$\cdots$	
Data l	$[\overbrace{v_1^l v_2^l \cdots v_n^l}^{n}]$	$[\overbrace{v_1^l v_2^l \cdots v_n^l}^{n}]$	$\cdots$	$[\overbrace{v_1^l v_2^l \cdots v_n^l}^{n}]$

candidate FCM model. We focus on the quality of data representation by constructing candidate FCM model from data that are produced by FCM prototype. We can anticipate the result of data representation when the number of nodes in the FCM is increasing gradually.

3.3   Simulation and Statistical Result of Validation

Figures 3 and 4 show the validation for FCM prototype F_1, data length $L_1 = 7$ and node number $n = 5, 10$ respectively. Figures 5 and 6 shows the validation for FCM prototype F_2, and the node number $n = 5, 10$ respectively, and the data length is set to $l = 10$ for each initial state vector, therefore, the total data length is $L_2 = 50$ and 100 respectively. In the Figure, the horizontal axis stands for the data set from FCM prototype, which is called original node value, and the vertical axis stands for the data set from candidate FCM model $\hat{F}$, which is called target node value. The solid line in the figure means $vi\,(t) = \hat{v}_i(t)$, and the dashed line at each side of solid line in the figure means the absolute error threshold $|vi\,(t) - \hat{v}_i(t)| < 0.25$. Some results are shown in Figs. 3 and 4. For FCM prototype F_1, the target node value is in good accordance with the original node value when the PSO algorithm and SA algorithm are applied. It is also can be seen that if the node number increase as shown from Figs. 3 to 4, the result will still remains stable along the solid line, which means the optimization is effective in representing the data set that comes from FCM prototype, as a result, the recon-struction of the candidate FCM model is capable of imitating the behavior of FCM prototype.

When it comes to validation of FCM prototype F_2, as shown in Figs. 5 and 6, the result shows different performance for PSO and SA separately. Figures 5 and 6 show other results as well. PSO algorithm is superior to SA algorithm for the diversified data representation, as we can find that the points are more close to the center line for PSO algorithm. The original node value and the target node value pairs $(vi, \hat{v}_i)$ center around solid line, the same performance is shown for PSO and SA algorithm when the number of points to be simulated is less, and PSO algorithm is superior to SA algorithm when the node number increases from 5 to 10, for both case, the absolute error is less than

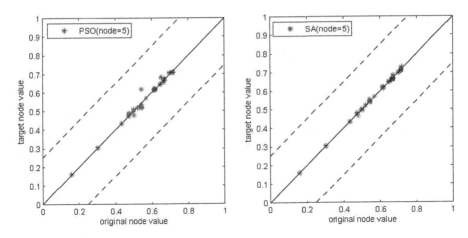

Fig. 3. Validation of FCM prototype F_1 versus candidate FCM model $\hat{F}_1$, $n = 5, L_1 = 7$

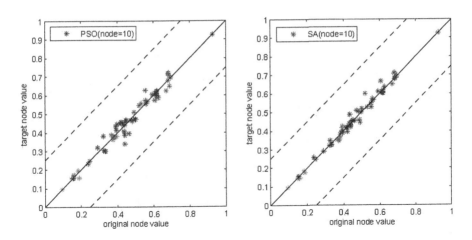

Fig. 4. Validation of FCM prototype F_1 versus candidate FCM model $\hat{F}_1$, $n = 10, L_1 = 7$

0.25 for many data points. By comparison, FCM prototype F_2 is more generally data representation than FCM prototype F_1 because the data series is more diversified. Nevertheless, the better result can be achieved based on proper optimization algorithm.

Performance index is also shown regarding the candidate FCM model $\hat{F}_i$, $i = 1, 2$. By comparison, It can be see that for both PSO algorithm and SA algorithm, the error of candidate FCM model is becoming high with the increasing number of node, as the performance index is increasing. The performance is affected by node number greatly for candidate FCM model. If number of nodes is more than the length of the data points

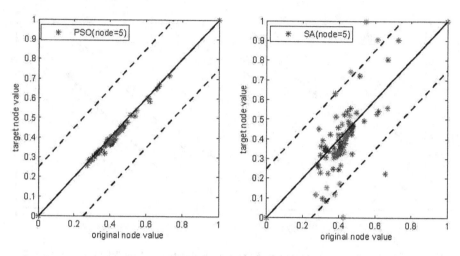

Fig. 5. Validation of FCM prototype F_2 versus candidate FCM model $\hat{F}_2, n = 5, L_2 = 50$

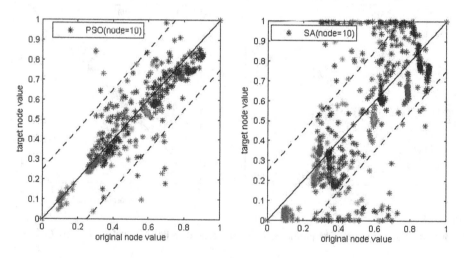

Fig. 6. Validation of FCM prototype F_2 versus candidate FCM model $\hat{F}_2, n = 10, L_2 = 100$

to be represented. The upper part in Fig. 7 shows the performance index versus node number. PSO is slightly better than SA in this case, and FCM model 2 with fewer nodes can be used to represent the dynamics of the FCM prototype F_2, the trend of each node in FCM prototype F_2 can be represented by candidate FCM model 2. The lower part in Fig. 7 shows the performance index versus node number for candidate FCM model 2.

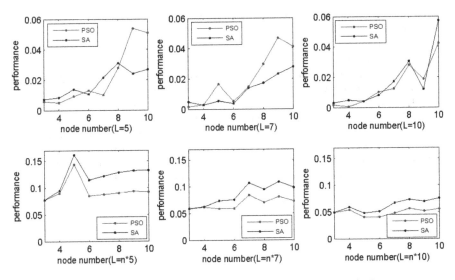

Fig. 7. Performance index for PSO and SA learning method

4 Conclusion

Comprehensive investigation of design methodology and algorithm suitable for FCM model is of great necessity especially applied to analysis of time series representation. Simulation experiment is studied to explore the usefulness of proposed FCM design method as a way to analysis time series representation. The performance metrics that are used to evaluate the result is based on statistical analysis and the standard statistical measures of performance index was put forward. Configuration of diversified parameters is taken into consideration thoroughly and subsequent impact that results from configuration is analyzed and discussed. Further study can be made on application evaluation. It is also noted that future work should be made on practical application.

Acknowledgement. The research of the paper was supported by Aero-Science Foundation of China 2014ZD51047.

References

1. Kosko, B.: Fuzzy cognitive maps. Int. J. Man Mach. Stud. **24**, 65–75 (1986)
2. Groumpos, P.P., Stylios, C.D.: Modelling supervisory control systems using fuzzy cognitive maps. Chaos, Solitons Fractals **11**, 329–336 (2000)
3. Pelez, C.E., Bowles, J.B.: Using fuzzy cognitive maps as a system model for failure modes and effects analysis. Inf. Sci. **88**, 177–199 (1996)
4. Papakostas, G.A., Boutalis, Y.S., Koulouriotis, D.E., Mertzios, B.G.: Fuzzy cognitive maps for pattern recognition applications. Int. J. Pattern Recogn. Artif. Intell. **22**, 1461–1486 (2008)

5. Rod, T.: Knowledge processing with fuzzy cognitive maps. Expert Syst. Appl. **2**, 83–87 (1991)
6. Stach, W., Kurgan, L., Pedrycz, W.: A divide and conquer method for learning large fuzzy cognitive maps. Fuzzy Sets Syst. **161**(18), 2515–2532 (2010)
7. Song, H., Miao, C., Shen, Z., Miao, Y.: Fuzzy cognitive map learning based on multi-objective pso. Int. J. Comput. Cogn. **6**, 51–59 (2008)
8. Petalas, Y.G., Parsopoulos, K.E., Vrahatis, M.N.: Improving fuzzy cognitive maps learning through memetic particle swarm optimization. Soft Comput. **13**, 77–94 (2008)
9. Pedrycz, W.: The design of cognitive maps: a study in synergy of granular computing and evolutionary optimization. Expert Syst. Appl. **37**, 7288–7294 (2010)
10. Papageorgiou, E.I., Parsopoulos, K.E., Stylios, C.S., Groumpos, P.P., Vrahatis, M.N.: Fuzzy cognitive maps learning using particle swarm optimization. J. Intell. Inf. Syst. **25**, 95–121 (2005)

Research on Simulation System Design for Vulnerability/Lethality Analysis

Bin Tan[✉], Liangwen Shi, Zilong Cong, and Yuheng Wang

Northwest Institute of Nuclear Technology, Xi'an, 710024, China
tbonln@163.com

Abstract. In this paper, a Vulnerability/Lethality (V/L) analysis process with seven levels is given, and a HLA- based collaborative simulation of V/L analysis is introduced, where the adapter approach method is presented. With the V/L process, the operational process is divided into several sub processes and a construction method for federate member based on the sub process is given. The different sub processes are serial or parallel, and need to be completed by complex weapon subsystem functions. The ability model for sub process is set up, as a core to build a federal member. This method realizes the unification of the V/L analysis process and the simulation realization, which can reduce the difficulty of the V/L analysis based on modeling and simulation.

Keywords: Vulnerability/Lethality analysis · Modeling and simulation · HLA

Vulnerability and lethality (V/L) are defined to describe the same physic progress of weapon system from contrary points of view. Vulnerability generally refers to the assessment of damage and dysfunction when the specific target is under attack. By contrast, lethality generally refers to the assessment of damage and dysfunction on the target by specific weapon system. Vulnerability/Lethality analysis in assessment of weapon system operational efficiency covers a complex, multidisciplinary field including weapon system, target and their encountering environment. Each subject has its own research method which could be applied by specific simulation tools. These tools are often very effective whether they were developed by commercial company or not. Collaborative simulation technology can be used as effective method to integrate these simulation tools into a single simulation platform. Thereby all related information and data can be achieved and used from these different subjects and simulation tools.

1 V/L Analysis Framework

On V/L analysis theoretic research, the concept of V/L analysis space was first used in the late 1980s. V/L analysis space divided the V/L analysis progress into four different levels [1]: space one refers to the initial characteristic parameters collection of weapon system, target and their encountering condition; space two refers to details of the damage to the target; space three refers to engineering capability of the target; space four refers to operational capability of the weapon system. From then on, V/L analysis has been

© Springer Science+Business Media Singapore 2016
L. Zhang et al. (Eds.): AsiaSim 2016/SCS AutumnSim 2016, Part IV, CCIS 646, pp. 493–499, 2016.
DOI: 10.1007/978-981-10-2672-0_50

greatly expanded [2–6]. One of the main outspread is using V/L analysis method to assess survivability and effectiveness for weapon systems. That is, V/L analysis progress can be separated into more than the presented four levels, which should be redefined in need, by adding cause (level 0, −1, ...) and effect (level 5, 6, ...). The V/L analysis framework in this paper is a seven-levels progress with the dimension of time. Figure 1 depicts the detailed progress.

[level −2]: weapon deployment conditions, consisting of weapon systems deployment, tactical deployment and encounter environment parameters.

[level −1]: weapon detection-identification conditions, including detection environment conditions, target identification conditions and weapon system detection capability.

[level 0]: weapon tracking-launch condition, consisting of launch initial conditions, navigation controlling conditions and launch environment parameters.

[level 1]: threat-target (or platform) initial condition, consisting of interaction parameters of weapon system and target, such as engage geometry, target mechanic and engineering characteristics.

[level 2]: target (or platform) damaged components. Level 2 outcome represents the list of platform components either killed or not.

[level 3]: Measurement Performance, measuring dysfunction caused by physical damage.

[level 4]: Measurement Effectiveness, the final assessment goal.

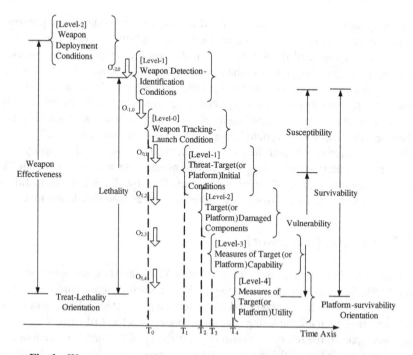

Fig. 1. Weapon system V/L analysis framework with seven-levels progress

Arrows in Fig. 1 refer to mapping relations between different levels.

$O_{-2,-1}$: confirming target and operational effectiveness for weapon system, deciding whether to use specific weapon system or not.

$O_{-1,0}$: deciding whether to launch or not and launching initial conditions.

$O_{0,1}$: deciding physic characteristics of threat-target initial conditions.

$O_{1,2}$: deciding status of platform physic damage. For each condition in level 1, there are two or more mapping conditions. That is, $O_{1,2}$ is not one-to-one mapping.

$O_{2,3}$: mapping components damage status to target dysfunction. As users are concerned with different performances because of the different targets or missions, the mapping space consists of different subspaces. As defined, $O_{2,3}$ are mathematically many-to-one mapping.

$O_{3,4}$: mapping target dysfunction to measurement effectiveness.

Time dimension:

T_0: Launching time; T_1: Encountering time; T_2: Components damaging time; T_3: Dysfunction begin time;

As Fig. 1 shows, V/L analysis framework divides operational progress into several different levels, sorts the levels effective time, establishes relations of the different models, data and information, and eventually decides measurement effectiveness from physic damage status, dysfunction and operational effectiveness. In general, level 0 condition is easily known. Mapping relations from level 0 to 1, 1 to 2, 2 to 3 and 3 to 4 should also be achieved. Mathematically speaking, if the certain numerical formulas or experience expressions have been gained, level 3 and 4 statuses could be calculated to accomplish V/L assessment. The mapping relations can be achieved by theoretic analysis, lab or field experiment and modeling and simulation.

2   HLA-Based Collaborative Simulation

Collaborative simulation is typically collateral and distributed. It provides collaborative virtual environments, which makes it possible that developers from different

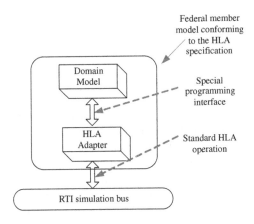

Fig. 2. HLA adapter

professional fields model and simulate the whole system simultaneously by collaterally modeling and simulating the subsystems using their professional information and skills. Collaborative simulation can transparently, conveniently and effectively connect the subsystems to accomplish modeling and simulation of the whole system [7].

Using HLA adapter to encapsulate models from different fields into HLA/RTI is one of the frequently used methods in collaborative simulation. Figure 2 shows the HLA adapter schematic diagram.

Data and information from models in different fields are exchanged indirectly by communicating through HLA RTI bus. As models in different fields are run in specific simulation software, interfaces between RTI and the specific software are needed. HLA adapter can be used as RTI interface data buffer for the communication between RTI bus and specific simulation software. In HLA-based collaborative simulation, federation should be designed according to simulated objectives.

3   Operational Progress Oriented Federation Design

3.1   Operational Progress Analysis

Operational effectiveness of weapon systems is related to operational progress. The precise measurement of operational effectiveness depends on cognition degree of operational progress from mission arranging to withdraw. Figure 3 depicts decomposition of operational progress according to different operational phases: first deciding their main missions; then deciding needed functions to accomplish these missions; and then analyzing the parameters of the functions.

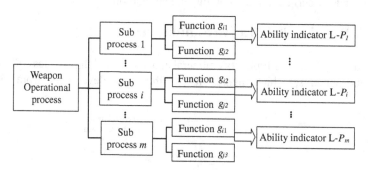

Fig. 3. Weapon operational process

There, in fact, does not exist a model that could depict or solve all related problems in operational progress for its complexity. Instead, a model that could depict the key aspects is often used. For each operational sub-progress, its key functions are identified and modeled. In different operation phases, all related sub-models are used collaboratively. Figure 4 shows the decomposition of function structure of weapon system. The decomposition is indeed a progress identifying all unitary capacities of the weapon system and establishing the mapping relation between mission targets and weapon functions.

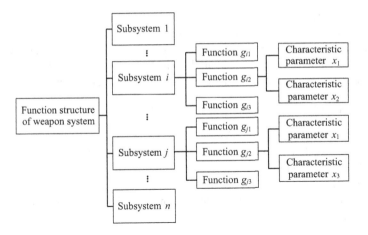

Fig. 4. Function structure of weapon system

The complex weapon system is decomposed into several subsystems according to its function structure. Each subsystem is able to accomplish some independent

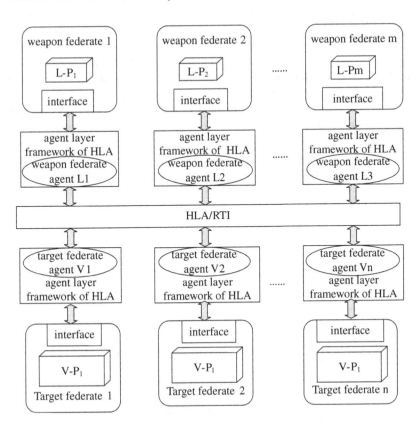

Fig. 5. HLA-based framework for V/L analysis

operational function, which are supported by corresponding characteristic parameters. Operational function depends upon surrounding environment and target characteristic parameters. Different operational functions of subsystems could be affected by the same surrounding parameter. Weapon system decomposing progress is indeed a progress to identify operation related factors and to model weapon system functions.

3.2 Federation Designing Based on Progress Phases

The federations are designed according to different operation progress phases. Figure 5 gives a HLA-based framework for V/L analysis. The index L-Pi is calculated by Federate 1, which is the degree of completion of the sub process. Figure 4 shows that Function gi2 and function gj2 are used in the calculation and parameters x1, x2, x3 are needed. The weapon agent member L1 is responsible for the parameters transfer.

4   Conclusion

The V/L analysis method is based on the engagement process of weapon and target. The engagement process is divided into a number of sub processes in series or parallel, and the states and state transitions of sub processes are need to be described. Three effects are distinguished such as Component damaging, ability reducing and utility decline, and operational time, models, data, information relationships are recognized. With the single V/L analysis process, the Operational effectiveness of weapons and targets is obtained, and the V/L analysis method is an operational effectiveness evaluation method based on the condition of confrontation.

Based on HLA the V/L analysis method can be realized. The federate agent is constructed by adapter, and federate models with different software developing are linked to RTI by the federate agents, then the domain experts can focus on domain models research. The weapon operational process is divided into a number of sub processes in series or parallel, and each process is modeled as a federate, which can realize the unification of the V/L analysis process and the simulation realization, constructing the federation rapidly and improving efficiency of the HLA system building.

References

1. Deitz, P.H., Ozolins, A: Computer simulation of the abrams live-fire field testing, ADA209509 (1989)
2. Klopcic, J.T., Starks, M.W., Walbert, J.N.: A taxonomy for the vulnerability/lethality analysis process, ADA250036 (1992)
3. Deitz, P.H., Starks, M.W.: The generation, use and misuse of "PKs" in vulnerability/lethality analysis, ADA340652 (1998)
4. Klopcic, J.T.: The vulnerability/lethality taxonomy as a general analytic process, ADA250036 (1992)
5. Deitz, P.H., Sheehan, J., Harris, B., et al.: A general framework and methodology for analyzing weapon systems effectiveness, ADA405473 (2001)

6. Deitz, P.H., Starks, M.W.: The generation, use and misuse of "PKs" in vulnerability/lethality analysis, ADA340652 (1998)
7. Su, Y., Ma, J.Z., Liu, Y., Zhai, Z.: Research and implementation of integration-based HLA cooperative simulation system. Aeronaut. Comput. Technol. **39**(2), 68–71 (2009)
8. Zhan, Y., Liu, H., Li, J.: HLA and it's application in the collaborative simulation research based on conventional simulation software. In: System Simulation Technique and Application, HeFei, China, pp. 281–285, August 2006

A Method of Virtual Reliability Test for Complex Structure and System Based on Simulation Data

Pengfei Chen[1(✉)], Yuxin He[2], and Shurong Sun[2]

[1] School of Mechanical Engineering,
Changchun University of Technology,
Changchun, China
chenpengfei@ccut.edu.cn
[2] School of Engineering Technology,
Changchun Vocational Institute of Technology,
Changchun, China

Abstract. Because complex structures and systems in engineering are usually implicit limit state equations and the change range of variation coefficients are larger, the paper put forward a method of virtual reliability test for complex structures and systems based on simulation data. The proposed method based on the reliability analysis method of first order second moment and important sampling method according to Taylor formula. It is shown that the proposed method has less number of iterations and high precision compared with previous methods by the numerical and engineering examples given in the paper. So the proposed method is especially suitable for the reliability analysis of large-scale complicated implicit structures and systems.

Keywords: Simulation data · Reliability index · Most probable point · Reliability sensitivity analysis

1 Introduction

Random factors generally exist in engineering systems and it is very necessary to regard the engineering system as a random system to study when the variation coefficients of influence factors are large [1, 2]. On the other way the functions of systems model generally have implicit characteristics due to the complexity of the engineering systems [3]. So it is one of the focus areas of reliability analysis that how to determine the reliability and sensitivity of the implicit structures and systems.

The paper combines first order second moment method and important sampling method of reliability to put forward a method of virtual reliability test for complex structures and systems based on simulation data. The final examples show that the proposed method has high computational efficiency and accuracy compared with previous methods.

L. Zhang et al. (Eds.): AsiaSim 2016/SCS AutumnSim 2016, Part IV, CCIS 646, pp. 500–507, 2016.
DOI: 10.1007/978-981-10-2672-0_51

2   Reliability of Normal Random Space

Supposing the vector $x = [x_1, x_2, \ldots, x_n]$ contains n normal distribution random variable independently, its limit state equation is [1]

$$z = g(x) = 0 \tag{1}$$

Formula (1) represents a hyper-surface in normal random space. Stochastic variable x can be transformed to standard normal stochastic variable y [3]

$$y = \mathbf{T} \times x + b \tag{2}$$

In the above matrix $\mathbf{T}$ and vector b are expressed as

$$\mathbf{T} = \begin{bmatrix} 1/\sigma_{x_1} & 0 & \cdots & 0 \\ 0 & 1/\sigma_{x_2} & \cdots & 0 \\ 0 & 0 & \ddots & 0 \\ 0 & 0 & \cdots & 1/\sigma_{x_n} \end{bmatrix} \tag{3}$$

$$b = \left[-\mu_{x_1}/\sigma_{x_1}; \ -\mu_{x_2}/\sigma_{x_2}; \cdots \ ; -\mu_{x_n}/\sigma_{x_n} \right]^{\mathrm{T}} \tag{4}$$

Here μ_{x_i} is the means of variable x_i ($i = 1, 2, \ldots, n$); σ_{x_i} is the standard deviation of x_i. So the stochastic variable x_i and y_i are suitable for the relationship equation of

$$F_i(x_i) = \Phi(y_i) \tag{5}$$

Here $F_i()$ express the probability distribution function of the variable x_i and $\Phi()$ express the standard normal distribution function. According to formula (5)

$$x_i = F_i^{-1}[\Phi(y_i)] \tag{6}$$

So the state function in the $\mathbf{Y}$ space can be expressed as

$$\begin{aligned} z &= g\left(F_1^{-1}[\Phi(y_1)], F_2^{-1}[\Phi(y_2)], \ldots, F_n^{-1}[\Phi(y_n)]\right) \\ &= G(y_1, y_2, \ldots, y_n) = G(y) \end{aligned} \tag{7}$$

Then the failure probability of structure is

$$\begin{aligned} P_f &= P\{x : g(x) \leq 0\} = P\{y : G(y) \leq 0\} \\ &= \int\limits_{G(y) \leq 0} f_Y(y)dy = \int\limits_{G(y) \leq 0} (2\pi)^{-\frac{n}{2}} \exp\left(-\tfrac{1}{2} y \cdot y^{\mathrm{T}}\right) dy \end{aligned} \tag{8}$$

In the above $f_Y(y)$ express the joint probability density function in $\mathbf{Y}$ space. According to the formula (8) the reliability index β^* can be achieved [2]

$$\beta^{*2} = \min_{G(y)=0} \left(y \cdot y^{\mathrm{T}} \right) = y^* \cdot y^{*\mathrm{T}} \tag{9}$$

3 Bisection Method of Sampling

3.1 Reliability Analysis of Second Moment

According to Taylor expansion method the limit state equation which expressed by formula (7) is linearized at the most probable point y^*

$$z_{\mathrm{L}} = G(y^*) + \sum_{i=1}^{n} \frac{\partial G}{\partial y_i} (y_i - y_i^*) \tag{10}$$

Here z_{L} is normally distributed because it is linear combination of the vector y. So the mean and standard deviation of z_{L} are [1]

$$\mu_{z_{\mathrm{L}}} = G(y^*) - \sum_{i=1}^{n} y_i^* \frac{\partial G}{\partial y_i} \tag{11}$$

$$\sigma_{z_{\mathrm{L}}} = \left[\sum_{i=1}^{n} \sum_{j=1}^{n} \frac{\partial G}{\partial y_i} \frac{\partial G}{\partial y_j} \right]^{1/2} \tag{12}$$

Thereupon the failure probability is also approximately expressed as

$$P_{\mathrm{f}} \approx P\{z_{\mathrm{L}} \leq 0\} = \Phi(-\beta_{\mathrm{L}}) \tag{13}$$

In the above β_{L} is the reliability index of the limit state equation after linearization. Here,

$$\beta_{\mathrm{L}} = \mu_{z_{\mathrm{L}}} / \sigma_{z_{\mathrm{L}}} \tag{14}$$

According to Eqs. (11), (12) and (14) it can be derived that the coordinate values of point y^* are

$$y_i^* = -\frac{\beta_{\mathrm{L}}}{\sigma_{z_{\mathrm{L}}}} \sum_{i=1}^{n} \frac{\partial G}{\partial y_i} \bigg|_{y=y^*} = \beta_{\mathrm{L}} \cos \theta_{y_i} \tag{15}$$

Here $\cos \theta_{x_i}$ is expressed as

$$\cos \theta_{y_i} = -\frac{1}{\sigma_{z_{\mathrm{L}}}} \sum_{i=1}^{n} \frac{\partial G}{\partial y_i} \bigg|_{y=y^*} \tag{16}$$

3.2 Bisection Sampling of Reliability Index

It is difficult to ensure the convergence of iterative process according to the formula (16) [4, 5]. Bisection method is a numerical method based on the intermediate value theorem which is characterized by simple structure and reliable convergence. So the paper uses Bisection sampling method to bisect the reliability index of limit state equation after linearization.

After sampling step of $(t + 1)$ each interval length of reliability index β is the half length of previous interval to ensure that $\beta^{(t)}$ and $\beta^{(t+1)}$ converge to β^*. So the error is expressed as

$$\left|\beta^{(m)} - \beta^*\right| \leq \frac{\left|\beta^{(m)} - \beta^{(m-1)}\right|}{2} = \frac{\left|\beta^{(t)} - \beta^{(t+1)}\right|}{2^{m-t+1}} = \frac{\Delta\beta}{2^{m-t+1}} \tag{17}$$

4 Calculation of Partial Derivatives Based on Sampling Data

Calculation of partial derivative is a key link to study the changing rate of multivariate function [6]. According to the definition of partial derivative we can determine the partial derivative of implicit function $g(x)$ by the Forward difference method and the Central difference method based on sampling data. Here the Forward difference method and the Central difference method are expressed as [7]

$$\frac{\partial g(x)}{\partial x_i} \approx \frac{\Delta g_{\Delta x_i}}{\Delta x_i} = \frac{g_{x_i + \Delta x_i} - g_{x_i}}{\Delta x_i} \tag{18}$$

$$\frac{\partial g(x)}{\partial x_i} \approx \frac{\Delta g_{2\Delta x_i}}{2\Delta x_i} = \frac{g_{x_i + \Delta x_i} - g_{x_i - \Delta x_i}}{2\Delta x_i} \tag{19}$$

In the above $g_{x_i} = g(x_1, \ldots, x_n)$, $g_{x_i + \Delta x_i} = g(x_1, \ldots, x_i + \Delta x_i, \ldots, x_n)$, and $g_{x_i - \Delta x_i} = g(x_1, \ldots, x_i - \Delta x_i, \ldots, x_n)$.

5 Calculation Examples

Case 1: It is the nonlinear function $g(x) = x_1^3 + x_1^2 \times x^2 + x_2^3 + x_3^3 - 80$ that the variables x_1, x_2 and x_3 are independent each other and obey normal distribution. The means of variables x_1, x_2 and x_3 are respectively $\mu_{x_1} = 4.5$, $\mu_{x_2} = 2$, $\mu_{x_3} = 1$. When the variation coefficient C_v take different values (C_v are taken 0.05, 0.1, 0.3 and 0.5 in Table 1), the failure probability P_f are calculated by the Monte Carlo method (MCM), the Importance Sampling method (ISM), the Response Surface method (RSM) and the proposed method (PM) in the paper. The calculation results of P_f are listed in Table 1. In the Table 1 xw represents the relative error of failure probability compared with the true value calculated by the Monte Carlo method (MCM) and jw represents the

Table 1. Statistics table of the calculation results and the number of sampling

C_v	0.05				0.1			
	P_f	N^*	xw	jw	P_f	N^*	xw	jw
MCM	2.27000×10^{-5}	10^7	0	0	2.10899×10^{-2}	10^7	0	0
ISM	2.82123×10^{-5}	5000	0.243	5.51×10^{-6}	2.20217×10^{-2}	5000	4.42×10^{-2}	9.32×10^{-4}
RSM	3.35316×10^{-4}	13	13.8	3.12×10^{-4}	3.98236×10^{-2}	13	0.888	1.87×10^{-2}
PM	2.58989×10^{-5}	100	0.141	3.20×10^{-6}	2.15015×10^{-2}	88	1.95×10^{-2}	4.12×10^{-4}

C_v	0.3				0.5			
	P_f	N^*	xw	jw	P_f	N^*	xw	jw
MCM	0.240909	10^7	0	0	0.323622	10^7	0	0
ISM	0.241181	5000	1.13×10^{-3}	2.72×10^{-4}	0.324602	5000	3.03×10^{-3}	9.80×10^{-4}
RSM	0.226954	13	5.79×10^{-2}	1.39×10^{-2}	0.402007	13	0.242	7.83×10^{-2}
PM	0.240722	80	7.73×10^{-4}	1.86×10^{-4}	0.336368	96	3.94×10^{-2}	1.27×10^{-2}

absolute error compared with the true value calculated by the Monte Carlo method (MCM) and N^* represents the number of sampling.

It is shown in Table 1 that the accuracy of the Importance Sampling method (ISM) is high compared with the true value calculated by the Monte Carlo method (MCM) but the number of sampling is large. It is also shown that the Response Surface method (RSM) has high computing efficiency but the results of RSM are inaccurate. So the proposed method (PM) in the paper has high accuracy and computational efficiency compared with previous methods in conclusion.

Case 2: When transmission mechanism of M12-20/43 type reciprocating compressor is working, the bearing liner size and crankshaft diameter influence formation of hydrodynamic lubricating oil film seriously [8]. Because of existing machining errors these dimensions are all regarded as random variables obedient to normal distribution, its means and standard deviations are listed in Table 2.

Table 2. The means and standard deviations of dimension variables

Dimension variables	Means $\bar{x}$	Standard deviations s_x
Inner diameter D/mm	200.115	0.04
Width B/mm	110	0.05
Shaft diameter d/mm	199.545	0.04

The paper regards a turning circle of crankshaft as a period of virtual test and builds the virtual simulation platform using ANSYS/LS-DYNA shown as Figs. 1 and 2. It is the dynamic stress contour plot of all parts in transmission mechanism when time is 0.029 s shown in Fig. 1 and it is the contour plot of bearing liner at the time shown in Fig. 2. If limit pressure-bearing capacity of hydrodynamic lubricating oil film in bearing liner $P_{\lim} = 500$ MPa [9], please analyze wear life reliability and size parameters sensitivity of sliding bearing.

The paper based on the simulation data of compressor to analysis the reliability and the sensitivity of sliding bearing using the method of virtual reliability test. Table 3 shows the results about the reliability of wear life and the sensitivity of each dimension parameters on sliding bearing. The sensitivity of random parametric means indicates that wear life reliability of bearing is improved if the inner diameter of bearing liner D,

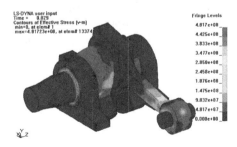

Fig. 1 The dynamic stress contour plot of transmission mechanism by ANSYS

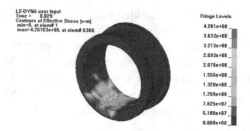

Fig. 2. The dynamic stress contour plot of bearing liner by ANSYS

Table 3. The results about reliability sensitivity of sliding bearing

Terms	Inner diameter D/mm	Width B/mm	Shaft diameter d/mm
Sensitivity of means ($\times 10^{-5}$)	2.563	4.942	1.238
Sensitivity of standard deviation ($\times 10^{-6}$)	−6.795	−8.247	−3.649
Reliability (%)	99.8655		

width B, and main diameter of crankshaft d increase and the influence of bearing liner width B is more powerful. The sensitivity of random parametric standard deviations indicates that the reduction of standard deviations will increase reliability. The sensitive parameters of reliability should be controlled seriously during design.

Above calculation results mainly accord with common qualitative analysis and provide theoretical quantitative basis for design of sliding bearing in reciprocating compressor.

6 Conclusions

(1) The paper proposes a method of virtual reliability test for complex structures and systems based on simulation data with high accuracy and low sampling frequency. It is especially suitable for large-scale and complex structures and systems with heavy calculation in engineering.

(2) According to the process of derivation in the paper the theoretical error of failure probability is mainly due to the linearization of limit state equations. Therefore the proposed method is only suitable for non-strongly nonlinear structures and systems.

References

1. Zhao, Y.-G., Ono, T.: Moment methods for structural reliability. Struct. Saf. **23**(1), 47–75 (2001)
2. Huang, B., Du, X.-P.: Probabilistic uncertainty analysis by mean-value first order saddle point approximation. Reliab. Eng. Syst. Saf. **93**(2), 325–336 (2008)
3. Du, X., Chen, W.: A most probable point based method for efficient uncertainty analysis. J. Des. Manuf. Autom. **4**(1), 47–66 (2001)
4. Richard, J.-F., Zhang, W.: Efficient high-dimensional importance sampling. J. Econometrics **141**(2), 1385–1411 (2007)
5. Au, S.-K., Beck, J.-L.: A new adaptive importance sampling scheme for reliability calculations. Struct. Saf. **21**(2), 135–158 (1999)
6. Au, S.-K.: Reliability-based design sensitivity by efficient simulation. Comput. Struct. **83**(14), 1048–1061 (2005)
7. Sudret, B., Defaux, G., Pendola, M.: Time-variant finite element reliability analysis application to the durability of cooling towers. Struct. Saf. **27**, 93–112 (2005)
8. Longo, G.-A., Gasparella, A.: Unsteady state analysis of the compression cycle of a hermetic reciprocating compressor. Int. J. Refrig. **26**(6), 681–689 (2003)
9. Cho, J.-R., Moon, S.-J.: A numerical analysis of the interaction between the piston oil film and the component deformation in a reciprocating compressor. Tribol. Int. **38**(5), 459–468 (2005)

Credibility Evaluation of Simulation Models Using Group Analytic Hierarchy Process Based on Priority Probability Conversion

Gengjiao Yang[1,2], Yuanjun Laili[1,2], Lin Zhang[1(✉)], and Xiaolin Hu[3]

[1] School of Automation Science and Electrical Engineering,
Beihang University, Beijing 100191, China
`yanggengjiao@126.com`
[2] Engineering Research Center of Complex Product Advanced Manufacturing
Systems, Ministry of Education, Beijing 100191, China
`llyj0721@sina.com,johnlin9999@163.com`
[3] Department of Computer Science, Georgia State University,
Atlanta, GA 30314, USA
`huxiaolin@gmail.com`

Abstract. The credibility evaluation of models has attracted extensive attention in Modeling and Simulation (M&S). With increasingly complex models, multiple domain experts are required to jointly assess the credibility of a model. Group analytic hierarchy process (GAHP) is a method by many experts to make decision. In GAHP, the preference aggregation of group members is a critical procedure. However, the impact of expert number and indicator priority order on the evaluation results has not been well considered in previous preference aggregation procedure yet. In this paper, we first propose a novel preference aggregation procedure, priority probability conversion (PPC), to enhance the effectiveness of GAHP, named PPC-GAHP. Then, we introduce a commonly used evaluation criteria for such procedures. Finally, a numerical example is provided to elucidate the details of the proposed procedure and is compared with other aggregation procedures in GAHP to further demonstrate its validity.

Keywords: Model credibility evaluation · Group analytic hierarchy process · Preference aggregation

1 Introduction

Nowadays, Modeling and Simulation (M&S) technology becomes more and more important in various fields, such as communication, transportation and manufacturing. With multiple connected models, many complex objects which can not be represented in mathematical ways are able to be directly described and analyzed in computer. In M&S of complex system, model credibility, defined to evaluate whether the model can correctly represent the real states and situations of system, is the most important thing. It is concerned with developing in

© Springer Science+Business Media Singapore 2016
L. Zhang et al. (Eds.): AsiaSim 2016/SCS AutumnSim 2016, Part IV, CCIS 646, pp. 508–515, 2016.
DOI: 10.1007/978-981-10-2672-0_52

(potential) users the confidence they require in order to use a model and in the information derived from that mode [1]. A simulation model and its results are credible if the decision maker and other critical project personnel accept them as "correct" [2]. Therefore, the credibility evaluation of simulation models can actually be considered as a subjective decision problem [3]. Due to the complexity of simulation models, single domain experts are often unable to complete the assessment work independently. So multiple experts who have different knowledge structure and domain knowledge to complete jointly the evaluation work under the same indicators system are required in the credibility evaluation of simulation models.

In this aspect, GAHP based on the analytic hierarchy process is one of the most widely used group decision making methods [4,5]. At present, research of GAHP can be divided into three categories: preference aggregations [6–8], group consensus [9,10] and expert weight [11]. This paper mainly focuses on preference aggregations.

In practical decision, evaluation opinions provided by experts in various fields are often inconsistent due to the complexity of models as well as the limitation of the expert cognition. The group opinion obtained by various preference aggregations is different. In the past decades, many preference aggregations have been proposed [6–8], which can be mainly classified as the aggregation of individual judgments (AIJ) and the aggregation of individual priorities (AIP) [12,13]. However, these two kinds only focus on the integration of the quantity of the indicators weight and ignore of the impact of expert number and indicator priority order on the evaluation results. Furthermore, even if the indicator weights provided by the experts are very close in quantity, they are not necessarily consistent in the priority order. To make the evaluation result more objective, we put forward a new preference aggregation procedure based on expert number and indicator priority order. Combining the two, we construct a probability matrix by probability transition to determine the indicator weight appropriately.

The structure of this paper is as follows. In Sect. 2, preference aggregations procedure in the GAHP, two main aggregation procedures and a new aggregation procedure, are introduced in detail. In Sect. 3, two evaluation criteria are described. In Sect. 4, the calculation method of credibility value is briefly displayed. In Sect. 5, an illustrative example for simulation model credibility is provided to show that the proposed procedure is reasonable compared with other two aggregation procedures. Finally, main conclusion is concluded in Sect. 6.

2   Preference Aggregations in GAHP

Two traditional preference aggregations in GAHP, AIJ and AIP, are introduced briefly. After that, a new aggregation is introduced in detail.

2.1   Brief Introduction of AIJ

Let individual judgment matrix be $A_k = (a_{ij}^{(k)})_{n \times n}(k = 1, 2, \cdots, m)$ and expert weights be $\lambda_i(i = 1, 2, \cdots, m)$, the integrated judgment matrix $\bar{A} = (\bar{a}_{ij})_{n \times n}$

can be calculated by the following formula $\bar{a}_{ij} = \prod\limits_{k=1}^{m} \left(a_{ij}^{(k)}\right)^{\lambda_k}$, and then indicator weight is obtained by eigenvector method (EV) [14] in this paper.

2.2 Brief Introduction of AIP

Let $w^{(k)} = [w_1^{(k)}, w_2^{(k)}, \cdots, w_n^{(k)}]$ be the individual priority vector for each expert, and then the group priority vector $\bar{w} = [\bar{w}_1, \bar{w}_2, \cdots, \bar{w}_n]$ can be calculated by AIP, which is as follows.

$$\bar{w}_i = \sum_{k=1}^{m} \lambda_k w_i^{(k)}, i = 1, 2, \cdots, n \tag{1}$$

where, m is the number of experts. $\lambda_k (k = 1, 2, \cdots, n)$ is the weight of the kth expert and $\sum\limits_{k=1}^{m} \lambda_k = 1$.

2.3 Priority Probability Conversion

Assume that m experts make decisions on the priority of n indicators under some criterion. Let weight vectors of these experts be $\lambda = [\lambda_1, \lambda_2, \cdots, \lambda_n]$.

Step 1: Construct individual judgment marix.

Expert individual judgment matrix is usually obtained by pairwise comparisons on system indicators according to 1–9 scale [15]. Let expert individual judgment matrix be $A_k = (a_{ij}^{(k)})_{n \times n} (k = 1, 2, \cdots, m)$.

Step 2: Calculate indicators weight and construct weight matrices.

Indicators weight vector is calculated from expert individual judgment matrix by EV. Let us assumed that indicators weight vector given by k th expert is $x_k = [x_{k1}, x_{k2}, \cdots, x_{kn}]$, $k = 1, 2, \cdots, m$, and then based on which the weight matrix $X = [x_1, x_2, \cdots, x_m]_{m \times n}^T$ is constructed.

Step 3: Construct order matrices.

Convert weight matrix $X = (x_{ij})_{m \times n}$ into order matrix $R = (r_{ij})_{m \times n}$, where r_{ij} represents the order of the element x_{ij} in the i th row of matrix $X_{m \times n}$.

Step 4: Construct probability matrices.

Probability matrices $P = (p_{ij})_{n \times m}$ are constructed by the following formula:

$$p_{ij} = \frac{n_{ij}}{m} \tag{2}$$

where, n_{ij} is the occurrence number of r_{ij} in the j th column of the order matrix, m represents the total expert number.

Step 5: Construct the matrix $S = (s_{ij})_{m \times n}$.

The matrix $S = (s_{ij})_{m \times n}$ based on $P = (p_{ij})_{n \times m}$ is constructed by the following formula:

$$s_{ij} = x_{ij} p_{ij}, \quad i = 1, 2, \cdots, m, \ j = 1, 2, \cdots, n \tag{3}$$

Step 6: Construct the matrix $Z = (z_{ij})_{m \times n}$.

Combined with the expert weight, the matrix $Z = (z_{ij})_{m \times n}$ is constructed by the following formula:

$$Z = \lambda S \tag{4}$$

Step 7: Calculate final indicators weight vector.
The final indicators weight vector determined by expert group is calculated using row sum normalization method.

3 Evaluation Criteria

In order to illustrate the validity of the proposed method, we should evaluate it by certain criteria. Two main evaluation criteria available and acceptable are ED and MV [14,16]. In this paper, these criteria are used in the group text, namely GMV and GED. The following is a brief description of the two evaluation criteria.

3.1 Group Minimum Violation (GMV)

GMV sums up all local violations associated with the group priority vector, which is described as follows.

$$GMV = \sum_{k=1}^{m} \sum_{i=1}^{n} \sum_{j=1}^{n} I_{ij}^{(k)} \tag{5}$$

where,

$$I_{ij}^{(k)} = \begin{cases} 1 & if \ \bar{w}_i > \bar{w}_j \ and \ a_{ji}^{(k)} > 1 \\ 0.5 & if \ \bar{w}_i = \bar{w}_j \ and \ a_{ji}^{(k)} \neq 1 \\ 0.5 & if \ \bar{w}_i \neq \bar{w}_j \ and \ a_{ji}^{(k)} = 1 \\ 0 & otherwise \end{cases} \tag{6}$$

where, $\bar{w} = [\bar{w}_1, \bar{w}_2, \cdots, \bar{w}_n]$ is the final indicators weight and $a_{ij}^{(k)}$ is the element in the individual judgment matrix A with $a_{ji}^{(k)} = 1/(a_{ij}^{(k)})$.

3.2 Group Euclidean Distance (GED)

GED sums up all difference between the input (individual judgments) and output (the final indicators weight vector $\bar{w} = [\bar{w}_1, \bar{w}_2, \cdots, \bar{w}_n]$). GED is represented by the total distance between each element in all individual judgments and related ratios of the weights contained in some prioritization method. The smaller the GED is, the more effective the resulting group priority vector becomes. GED is described as follows.

$$GED = \left[\sum_{k=1}^{m} \sum_{i=1}^{n} \sum_{j=1}^{n} \left(a_{ij}^{(k)} - \frac{\bar{w}_i}{\bar{w}_j} \right) \right]^{1/2} \tag{7}$$

where, m is the total number of experts and $\sum_{i=1}^{n} \bar{w}_i = 1$.

4   The Calculation Method of Credibility Value

Combined indicator weights, a credibility value is calculated based on weighed sum method from the bottom to the top. A specific formula is described as follows.

$$v = \sum_{i=1}^{n} w_i \xi_i \tag{8}$$

where, v is a credibility value. $w_i(i = 1, 2, \cdots, n)$ is the weight of the ith indicator, $\xi_i(i = 1, 2, \cdots, n)$ is quantitative value of the ith indicator.

5   Example

Take the simulation model of XX air defense system as an example to verify the effectiveness of the proposed method. Establish the credibility evaluation indicator system of the simulation model, as shown in Fig. 1. This example is only used to verify the effectiveness of the proposed method. Therefore, the indicator system is no longer refined.

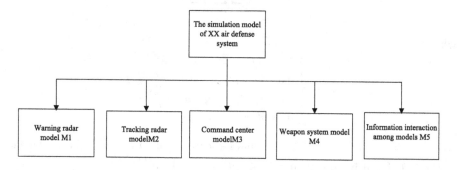

Fig. 1. The indicator system of the simulation model credibility evaluation

Invite four experts to assess the credibility of the simulation model, and assume expert weight vector $\lambda = [0.5\ 0.2\ 0.2\ 0.1]$. The judgment matrices are as follows.

$$A_1 = \begin{bmatrix} 1 & 1 & 1/4 & 1/3 & 1/2 \\ 1 & 1 & 1/2 & 1/3 & 1/2 \\ 4 & 2 & 1 & 1/2 & 2 \\ 3 & 3 & 2 & 1 & 2 \\ 2 & 2 & 1/2 & 1/2 & 1 \end{bmatrix}, A_2 = \begin{bmatrix} 1 & 2 & 1/3 & 1/4 & 1/3 \\ 1/2 & 1 & 1/3 & 1/3 & 1/3 \\ 3 & 3 & 1 & 1 & 1/2 \\ 4 & 3 & 1 & 1 & 1/2 \\ 3 & 3 & 2 & 2 & 1 \end{bmatrix},$$

$$A_3 = \begin{bmatrix} 1 & 1/3 & 1/3 & 1/2 & 1/4 \\ 3 & 1 & 1/2 & 1/2 & 1/3 \\ 3 & 2 & 1 & 1 & 1 \\ 2 & 2 & 1 & 1 & 1/2 \\ 4 & 3 & 1 & 2 & 1 \end{bmatrix}, A_4 = \begin{bmatrix} 1 & 1/2 & 1/4 & 1/3 & 1/4 \\ 2 & 1 & 1/3 & 1/2 & 1/3 \\ 4 & 3 & 1 & 2 & 1 \\ 3 & 2 & 1/2 & 1 & 1/3 \\ 4 & 3 & 1 & 3 & 1 \end{bmatrix}.$$

All the judgment matrices have passed the consistency test.

Let weight vector of indicators be $\xi = [\xi_1, \xi_2, \xi_3, \xi_4]$, and the final weights of indicators calculated by the proposed method are as follows.

$$\xi_1 = 0.0895, \quad \xi_2 = 0.1248, \quad \xi_3 = 0.3019, \quad \xi_4 = 0.1464, \quad \xi_5 = 0.3382$$

Quantified reliability values of bottom indicators given by expert group are shown in Table 1.

The final model credibility obtained by the weighted sum method is 89.6950. The weight vectors of indicators obtained by AIJ-EV and AIP-EV respectively are as follows.

$$w_{AIJ-EV} = [0.0834, 0.1085, 0.2747, 0.2432, 0.2902]$$

$$w_{AIP-EV} = [0.0877, 0.1064, 0.2614, 0.2867, 0.2578]$$

Based on the weighted sum method, the final credibility values of the system simulation model obtained by AIJ-EV and AIP-EV respectively are 89.8167 and 89.8644. Comparing the proposed procedure with two classical procedure, the comparison results are shown in Table 2.

From Table 2, it is seen that the weight values calculated by AIJ-EV and AIP-EV are very close, but importance sorting of indicators obtained by AIJ-EV

Table 1. Quantified credibility of bottom indicators

Warning radar model	Tracking radar model	Command center model	Weapon system model	Information interaction among models
88	90	85	92	93

Table 2. Method comparison results

	The proposed method	AIJ-EV	AIP-EV
The weight of M1	0.0795	0.0834	0.0877
The weight of M2	0.1231	0.1085	0.1064
The weight of M3	0.2830	0.2747	0.2614
The weight of M4	0.1396	0.2432	0.2867
The weight of M5	0.3748	0.2902	0.2578
Importance sequence of indicators	$5 > 3 > 4 > 2 > 1$	$5 > 3 > 4 > 2 > 1$	$4 > 3 > 5 > 2 > 1$
The credibility of the system simulation model	89.8296	89.8167	89.8644

and AIP-EV are different, therefore it is necessary that considering importance sorting of indicators in evaluation result. The weight value calculated by the proposed procedure is different from that by other two classical procedures, but the importance sorting of indicators calculated is identical. The proposed procedure in this paper is evaluated through general and applicable evaluation criteria to further illustrate the effectiveness of the method. The method evaluation results are shown in Table 3.

Table 3. Method evaluation result

	The proposed method	AIJ-EV	AIP-EV
GMV	9	11	11
GED	11.4765	15.3271	15.2236

From Table 3, it is seen that GMV and GED on the proposed procedure in this paper are all smallest. Therefore, the proposed method is valid.

6   Conclusion and Future Work

With the developing of computer and information science, simulation technology has been widely used in various fields. The simulation model credibility evaluation determined by multiple experts is a very important topic. In this paper, a new preference aggregation in GAHP, priority probability conversion, was proposed. We first constructed probability matrix based on expert number and indicators priority order. After that, combined with the experts' weights, the indicators' weights were obtained by row sum normalization method. And then the credibility value of the simulation model was calculated with the weighted sum. Compared with the traditional reference aggregations, the proposed aggregation took into account the impact of expert number and indicators priority order on the evaluation results, which is closer to practical decision making. A numerical example was used to illustrate the effectiveness of this method.

Many uncertain factors exist in the practical decision making. In order to make the evaluation result more objective, we will pay more attention to the impact of uncertainty factors in decision making on evaluation results in the future research.

Acknowledgments. Authors gratefully acknowledge the support of National Natural Science Foundation of China under Grant No. 61374199, Natural Science Foundation of Beijing under Grant No. 4142031 and National High-Tech Research and Development Plan of China under Grant No. 2013AA041302.

References

1. Sargent, R.G.: Verification and validation of simulation models. In: 2005 Winter Simulation Conference, pp. 130–143. IEEE Press, New York (2005)

2. Law, A.M.: How to build valid and credible simulation models. In: 2008 Winter Simulation Conference, pp. 39–47. IEEE Press, New York (2008)

3. Balci, O.: How to assess the acceptability and credibility of simulation results. In: 2008 Winter Simulation Conference, pp. 62–71. IEEE Press, New York (1989)

4. Shi, S.G., Cao, J.C., Feng, L., Liang, W.Y., Zhang, L.Q.: Construction of a technique plan repository and evaluation system based on AHP group decision-making for emergency treatment and disposal in chemical pollution accidents. J. Hazard. Mater. **276**, 200–206 (2014)

5. Jiang, C.Z., Bian, Z.Y., Yuan, J.X., Xu, F., Cheng, H.: Mineral reserves optimization based on improved group AHP. Intell. Autom. Soft Comput. **20**, 587–597 (2014)

6. Cho, Y.G., Cho, K.T.: A loss function approach to group preference aggregation in the AHP. Comput. Oper. Res. **35**, 884–892 (2008)

7. Xu, Y.J., Wang, H.M., Sun, H., Yu, D.J.: A distance-based aggregation approach for group decision making with interval preference orderings. Comput. Ind. Eng. **72**, 178–186 (2014)

8. Dong, M., Li, S., Zhang, H.: Approaches to group decision making with incomplete information based on power geometric operators and triangular fuzzy AHP. Expert Syst. Appl. **42**, 7846–7857 (2015)

9. Herrera-Viedma, E., Martinez, L., Mata, F., Chiclana, F.: A consensus support system model for group decision-making problems with multigranular linguistic preference relations. IEEE Trans. Fuzzy Syst. **13**, 644–658 (2005)

10. Wu, Z., Xu, J.: A consistency and consensus based decision support model for group decision making with multiplicative preference relations. Decis. Support Syst. **52**, 757–767 (2012)

11. Yue, Z.: Deriving decision maker's weights based on distance measure for interval-valued intuitionistic fuzzy group decision making. Expert Syst. Appl. **38**, 11665–11670 (2011)

12. Forman, E., Peniwati, K.: Aggregating individual judgments and priorities with the analytic hierarchy process. Eur. J. Oper. Res. **108**, 165–169 (1998)

13. Escobar, M.T., Aguarlón, J., Moreno-Jimíenez, J.M.: A note on AHP group consistency for the row geometric mean priorization procedure. Eur. J. Oper. Res. **153**, 318–322 (2004)

14. Kou, G., Lin, C.: A cosine maximization method for the priority vector derivation in AHP. Eur. J. Oper. Res. **235**, 225–232 (2014)

15. Saaty, T.L.: How to make a decision: the analytic hierarchy process. Eur. J. Oper. Res. **48**, 9–26 (1990)

16. Blagojevic, B., Srdjevic, B., Srdjevic, Z., Zoranovic, T.: Heuristic aggregation of individual judgments in AHP group decision making using simulated annealing algorithm. Inf. Sci. **330**, 260–273 (2016)

Simulation and Algorithm Verification for Polar Region Inertial Navigation Based on Low Latitude Test Sailing

Jing Lei[✉] and Wenqi Wu

College of Mechatronic Engineering and Automation,
National University of Defense Technology, Changsha, China
598919521@qq.com, wenqiwu_lit@sina.com

Abstract. Simulation and algorithm verification is very important for the technique research of inertial navigation in polar region due to the high expenditure for field experiments in polar region. The limitation of the traditional pure mathematical simulation method lies in that the simulated trajectory is not so coincident with the real vehicle kinematics especially for a shipborne rotational INS (Inertial Navigation System). In this paper, a new 6-DOF simulation trajectory generating method for polar region is proposed. Navigational parameters from an actual single-axis rotational INS including attitude, velocity and position in a test sailing are converted from low latitude area to the polar region by frame rotation and transformation. Sampling data of gyroscopes and accelerometers from the IMU (Inertial Measurement Unit) in the test sailing is adjusted to match the new generated trajectory in polar region. Simulation results show that the trajectory is accurate enough for simulation and algorithm verification of an INS designed for the use in polar region. The angular and linear motions of the INS in the trajectory are coincident with the kinematics of a practical shipborne rotational INS, in this way, performance and error characteristic evaluation can be achieved effectively through simulation.

Keywords: Inertial navigation of polar region · 6-DOF simulation trajectory generating · Wander azimuth frame · Frame rotation and transformation

1 Introduction

Navigation techniques in polar region have been getting more and more concern due to the potential commercial values of polar routes for air/sea transport with advantages of time and cost saving. Harsh conditions, such as highly convergent longitude lines and magnetic lines, as well as the unstable ionosphere affecting the transmission of radio or satellite signals, make inertial navigation a core technique for polar region navigation [1, 2]. What's more, it is hard to get actual offline data of inertial navigation in polar area, as field experiments in polar area are prohibitively expensive, which makes simulated data important for the research.

Traditionally, the pure mathematical simulation methods are most applied in polar navigation algorithm research. The pure mathematical simulation works well with uniform motion, uniform acceleration motion or other types of ideal motion [3].

© Springer Science+Business Media Singapore 2016
L. Zhang et al. (Eds.): AsiaSim 2016/SCS AutumnSim 2016, Part IV, CCIS 646, pp. 516–523, 2016.
DOI: 10.1007/978-981-10-2672-0_53

However, when dealing with inertial navigation in polar area, it is rather hard to reflect the real dynamic situation. As we all know, the motion of aircrafts and vessels is more than ideal motion. And it is also hard for the pure mathematical methods to simulate the attitude of body, which is important for navigation. Besides, all error models of gyroscopes and accelerometers can't be realized by simulation. Thus, conclusions reached from polar navigation research based on pure mathematical simulation are lacking in comprehensiveness and persuasiveness. Special methods are needed in data simulation to provide a more effective environment when testing inertial navigation at high latitude.

In this paper, the frame rotation method as a new idea will be used to get high-quality simulated experimental data of polar area, then use inertial navigation based on the wander azimuth frame to calculate the results. Instead of pure mathematical method, this method is based on actual navigation data obtained at low latitudes, which makes it possible to overcome the problems above, and get simulated data which is less ideal and more practical.

2   The Simulation Thought of the Frame Rotation Method

Suppose the longitude and latitude coordinates of some point p_0 on (or nearby) the original track are (λ_{p0}, L_{p0}). The original Earth-Centered Inertial (ECI) coordinate i_0 and the original Earth-Centered Earth-Fixed (ECEF) coordinate e_0 coincide with each other. Rotate λ_{p0} of both the coordinate systems i_0 and e_0 clockwise about z-axis. Then rotate them $(\pi/2 - L_{p0})$ clockwise about y-axis to get the new ECI coordinate system i and the new ECEF coordinate system e. The progress of the rotation method is shown as the following direction cosine matrix:

$$\mathbf{C}_{i_0}^i = \mathbf{C}_{e_0}^e = \begin{bmatrix} \sin L_{p0} & 0 & \cos L_{p0} \\ 0 & 1 & 0 \\ -\cos L_{p0} & 0 & \sin L_{p0} \end{bmatrix} \begin{bmatrix} \cos \lambda_{p0} & \sin \lambda_{p0} & 0 \\ -\sin \lambda_{p0} & \cos \lambda_{p0} & 0 \\ 0 & 0 & 1 \end{bmatrix} \tag{1}$$

During this rotation of these two coordinates, the track itself never rotates and the direction of Body Frame (BF) b never changes. Now the new polar axis coincides with the local vertical through the point. Therefore the rotation makes p_0 the North Pole and converts the actual track to a simulated one through the North Pole. The method of the frame rotation is showed in the Fig. 1 and the diagram of the frame rotation method with the earth is an oblate spheroid is showed in Fig. 2.

Because the track never changes, the relationship between the position vectors of the track in the ECEF coordinate systems before and after the rotation is:

$$\mathbf{r}^e = \mathbf{C}_{e_0}^e \mathbf{r}^{e_0} \tag{2}$$

Suppose the reference frame of the earth's rotation as the initial frame, the earth's rotation is the same as the rotation of the ECI coordinate system relative to the ECEF coordinate system. There is relative motion between i_0 and i, but no between e_0 and e. Thus the velocity of the body on the track relative to the ECEF never changes

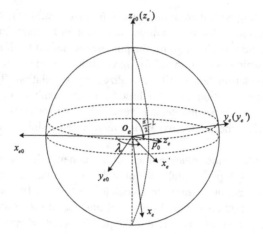

Fig. 1. The frame rotation method

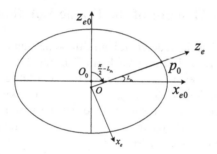

Fig. 2. The frame rotation method of earth as an oblate spheroid

during the rotation. The relationship between the velocity vectors in the ECEF coordinate systems before and after the rotation is:

$$\mathbf{v}^e = \mathbf{C}_{e_0}^e \mathbf{v}^{e_0} \tag{3}$$

Likewise, the relationship between the attitude matrix of the body on the track relative to the ECEF before and after the rotation is:

$$\mathbf{C}_b^e = \mathbf{C}_{e_0}^e \mathbf{C}_b^{e_0} \tag{4}$$

The Earth's shape is not quite a sphere but approximates an oblate spheroid, slightly flattened in the direction of its axis. That means, when the ECEF rotates, the track moves from low latitude area to polar area, and from the earth surface to the air, which also changes the shape of its projection on the earth. Thus, in order to guarantee the accuracy during the calculation, while converting the data, accurate position vectors describing the track position should be applied and then we can derive out the accurate longitude, latitude and altitude figures. Do high latitude or high longitude calculations as little as possible.

3   Coordinate Rotation of Actual Track

3.1   The Conversion of the Initial States

The conversion of the initial states is to change the attitude, the velocity and the position at low latitude to the simulated ones in polar at the initial time of the experiment. The conversion can be described by equations same to Eqs. (1), (2), (3) and (4). Meanwhile, we calculate out the value of the gravity acceleration for later processing like data simulation and navigation solution.

3.2   The Simulation of Gyroscopes Data

Before the coordinate system conversion, the attitude differential equation of the BF relative to the ECEF is:

$$\dot{\mathbf{C}}_b^{e_0} = \mathbf{C}_b^{e_0}[\boldsymbol{\omega}_{e_0b}^b \times] = \mathbf{C}_b^{e_0}[(\boldsymbol{\omega}_{i_0b}^b - \mathbf{C}_{e_0}^b\boldsymbol{\omega}_{i_0e_0}^{e_0}) \times] \tag{5}$$

After the rotation, it changes to:

$$\dot{\mathbf{C}}_b^e = \mathbf{C}_b^e[\boldsymbol{\omega}_{eb}^b \times] = \mathbf{C}_b^e[(\boldsymbol{\omega}_{ib}^b - \mathbf{C}_e^b\boldsymbol{\omega}_{ie}^e) \times] \tag{6}$$

We already know that there is no relative motion between the e_0 and e, so the parameter matrix $\mathbf{C}_{e_0}^e$ is a constant one. Differentiating Eq. (4), and one new equation is got:

$$\dot{\mathbf{C}}_b^e = \mathbf{C}_{e_0}^e\dot{\mathbf{C}}_b^{e_0} \tag{7}$$

Substitute Eq. (5) and Eq. (6) into Eq. (7):

$$\boldsymbol{\omega}_{ib}^b - \mathbf{C}_e^b\boldsymbol{\omega}_{ie}^e = \boldsymbol{\omega}_{i_0b}^b - \mathbf{C}_{e_0}^b\boldsymbol{\omega}_{i_0e_0}^{e_0} \tag{8}$$

That is, after the coordinate system rotation, the theoretical sampled value of the gyroscope is:

$$\boldsymbol{\omega}_{ib}^b = \boldsymbol{\omega}_{i_0b}^b + \mathbf{C}_e^b\boldsymbol{\omega}_{ie}^e - \mathbf{C}_{e_0}^b\boldsymbol{\omega}_{i_0e_0}^{e_0} = \boldsymbol{\omega}_{i_0b}^b + \mathbf{C}_{e_0}^b[\mathbf{C}_e^{e_0}\boldsymbol{\omega}_{ie}^e - \boldsymbol{\omega}_{i_0e_0}^{e_0}] = \boldsymbol{\omega}_{i_0b}^b + \mathbf{C}_{e_0}^b[\mathbf{C}_e^{e_0} - I]\boldsymbol{\omega}_{i_0e_0}^{e_0} \tag{9}$$

Integrating the equation above, we get the sampled value of the gyro integral angular range in high latitudes:

$$\int_t^{t+T} \boldsymbol{\omega}_{ib}^b dt = \int_t^{t+T} \boldsymbol{\omega}_{i_0b}^b dt + \int_t^{t+T} \mathbf{C}_{e_0}^b[\mathbf{C}_e^{e_0} - I]\boldsymbol{\omega}_{i_0e_0}^{e_0} dt \tag{10}$$

In Eq. (10), the value of $\int_t^{t+T} \mathbf{C}_{e_0}^b[\mathbf{C}_e^{e_0} - I]\boldsymbol{\omega}_{i_0e_0}^{e_0} dt$ can be calculated out by trapezoid numerical integration.

3.3   The Data of Accelerometers

Before the coordinate system rotation, the velocity differential equation of the BFS relative to the ECEF is:

$$\dot{\mathbf{v}}_0^{e_0} = \mathbf{C}_b^{e_0}\mathbf{f}_0^b - (2\boldsymbol{\omega}_{i_0e_0}^{e_0}) \times \mathbf{v}_0^{e_0} + \mathbf{g}_0^{e_0} \tag{11}$$

After the rotation, it becomes:

$$\dot{\mathbf{v}}^e = \mathbf{C}_b^e\mathbf{f}^b - (2\boldsymbol{\omega}_{ie}^e) \times \mathbf{v}^e + \mathbf{g}^e \tag{12}$$

Differentiating Eq. (3):

$$\dot{\mathbf{v}}^e = \mathbf{C}_{e_0}^e\dot{\mathbf{v}}_0^{e_0} \tag{13}$$

Substitute Eq. (11) and Eq. (12) into Eq. (13):

$$\mathbf{C}_b^e\mathbf{f}_0^b - \mathbf{C}_{e_0}^e(2\boldsymbol{\omega}_{i_0e_0}^{e_0}) \times \mathbf{v}_0^{e_0} + \mathbf{C}_{e_0}^e\mathbf{g}_0^{e_0} = \mathbf{C}_b^e\mathbf{f}^b - (2\boldsymbol{\omega}_{ie}^e) \times \mathbf{v}^e + \mathbf{g}^e \tag{14}$$

That is, after the coordinate system rotation, the theoretical sampled value of the accelerometer is:

$$
\begin{aligned}
\mathbf{f}^b =& \mathbf{f}_0^b - \mathbf{C}_{e_0}^b(2\boldsymbol{\omega}_{i_0e_0}^{e_0}) \times \mathbf{v}_0^{e_0} + \mathbf{C}_{e_0}^b\mathbf{g}_0^{e_0} + \mathbf{C}_e^b(2\boldsymbol{\omega}_{ie}^e) \times \mathbf{v}^e - \mathbf{C}_e^b\mathbf{g}^e \\
=& \mathbf{f}_0^b - \mathbf{C}_{e_0}^b(2\boldsymbol{\omega}_{i_0e_0}^{e_0}) \times \mathbf{v}_0^{e_0} + \mathbf{C}_{e_0}^b\mathbf{g}_0^{e_0} + \mathbf{C}_{e_0}^b\mathbf{C}_e^{e_0}(2\boldsymbol{\omega}_{ie}^e) \times (\mathbf{C}_{e_0}^e\mathbf{v}^{e_0}) - \mathbf{C}_{e_0}^b\mathbf{C}_e^{e_0}\mathbf{g}^e \\
=& \mathbf{f}_0^b + \mathbf{C}_{e_0}^b\{\mathbf{g}_0^{e_0} - (2\boldsymbol{\omega}_{i_0e_0}^{e_0}) \times \mathbf{v}_0^{e_0} + \mathbf{C}_e^{e_0}[(2\boldsymbol{\omega}_{i_0e_0}^{e_0}) \times (\mathbf{C}_{e_0}^e\mathbf{v}^{e_0}) - \mathbf{C}_e^{e_0}\mathbf{g}^e]\}
\end{aligned} \tag{15}
$$

Integrating the equation above, we get the sampled value of the integral range of the specific force:

$$\int_t^{t+T} \mathbf{f}^b dt = \int_t^{t+T} \mathbf{f}_0^b dt + \int_t^{t+T} \mathbf{C}_{e_0}^b\{\mathbf{g}_0^{e_0} - (2\boldsymbol{\omega}_{i_0e_0}^{e_0}) \times \mathbf{v}_0^{e_0} + \mathbf{C}_e^{e_0}[(2\boldsymbol{\omega}_{i_0e_0}^{e_0}) \times (\mathbf{C}_{e_0}^e\mathbf{v}^{e_0}) - \mathbf{C}_e^{e_0}\mathbf{g}^e]\}dt \tag{16}$$

As above analysis, for the sake of the accuracy after the rotation, we don't calculate $\mathbf{g}^e$, the projection of the gravity acceleration in the ECEF, through its altitude and latitude. Instead, we take it as a function of its position vector. The function is as followed:

$$\mathbf{g}^e = \boldsymbol{\gamma}_{ib}^e + \omega_{ie}^2 \begin{bmatrix} 1 & 0 & 0 \\ 0 & 1 & 0 \\ 0 & 0 & 0 \end{bmatrix} \mathbf{r}_{eb}^e \tag{17}$$

In this equation, $\boldsymbol{\gamma}_{ib}^e$ is the gravitational acceleration, and it can also be taken as a function of the position vector [5]. $\mathbf{g}_0^{e_0}$ and $\mathbf{g}^e$ share the same calculation method. Other parameters can be calculated out by trapezoid numerical integration.

4 Simulation and Discussion

It can be tested out by experiments whether this simulation method works or not by comparing the results calculated by the original data and simulated data. But before the comparison we need to put them into the same reference coordinate system. Because the altitude channel is divergent, we don't calculate the altitude and the vertical velocity during the navigation solution, which makes the vertical result inaccurate. Therefore, we should avoid comparing results relative to the altitude and the vertical velocity. Thus, we convert the results to the attitude in pseudo-geographic coordinate system, the velocity in pseudo-north direction, the velocity in pseudo-east direction and the lateral longitude and latitude. Then the results for comparison don't include altitude, vertical velocity or their components, which makes sure that the test is accurate and reliable.

The original actual experimental data at low latitude shows the position: 28.22° as latitude, and 112.99° as longitude, 54.89 m as altitude. After converted into the ECEF coordinate system, the position vector can be represented as $(-2.20 \times 10^6, 5.18 \times 10^6, 3.00 \times 10^6)$ in meters. The zero bias stability of the gyroscope is 0.01 deg/h, while that of the accelerometer is $5 \times 10^{-5} g$. And it takes 4.67 h in total. The sampling frequency is 100 Hz. We use linear interpolation method to increase the sampling frequency to 400 Hz, and increase the attitude update frequency and the data conversion frequency to 200 Hz.

The Fig. 3 shows that the result of latitude and longitude calculated by simulated data in polar region. It proves that the track is successfully transferred from low into the polar region.

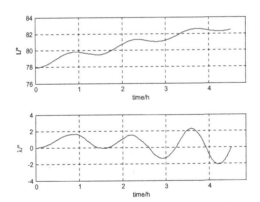

Fig. 3. The simulated track

From the error curves in Fig. 4, we can tell that before and after the rotation, the errors of three rotation angles of pitch, roll and yaw are all on the order of 10^{-70}. Thus the attitude error is so small that can be ignored, which means the simulation method is good at reflecting the practical attitude of body during the motion.

In Fig. 5, it can be found that the errors of latitude and longitude between the two tracks are both on the order of 10^{-30}, which is small enough to show that two tracks is

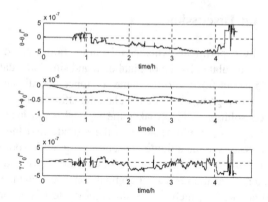

Fig. 4. The error of attitude angles between two tracks

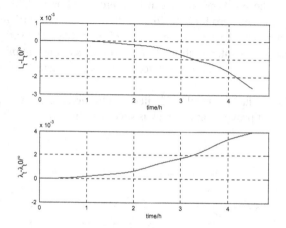

Fig. 5. The comparison of two track

almost in the same shape. This means the simulated data can effectively reflect the actual motion.

As is known to all that the earth is actually an oblate spheroid and the latitude isn't uniform, so small deformation is certainly to appear when the track is transferred from the low latitude to polar, which causes these small errors. But it doesn't matter as the errors are small enough. Because we aim to get a navigation track of polar which can be good at reflecting the real circumstances instead of get a track which is considerably similar to another track. In summary, for all results of the simulation experiment mentioned above proves the frame rotation method is feasible.

In this paper, we have deduced a new algorithm to simulate the output data of gyroscopes and accelerometers in polar area. This has made it possible to simulate high-latitude experimental data based on actual low-latitude experiments instead of the traditional pure mathematical method. The contrast test, between the results calculated from the original low-latitude data and simulated data in polar region, shows that the error of the traces before and after the rotation is small enough within the error allowance, which has verified the correctness and the validity of the algorithm. So we can do navigation experiment at low latitude to sample data and transfer the actual data into polar region through the simulation method. And we can control the motion of body at low latitude to get the polar navigation data of the motion needed.

References

1. Zhao, C.-L., Wu, W.-Q., Lian, J.-X.: Research on rotating modulation inertial navigation system error characteristics simulation method in polar area. In: Guidance, Navigation& Control Conference, pp. 2790–2794. IEEE, Chinese (2014)
2. Wang, J., Li, B.-P.: Analysis and countermeasures for condition of navigation in north pole. Sci. Technol. Inform. **20**, 126 (2012)
3. Qin, Y.-Y.: Inertial Navigation. Science Press, Beijing (2013)
4. Department of the Air Force. Air Navigation (US. Air Force Pamphlet 11-216). CreatSpace Independent Publishing Platform (2013)
5. Groves, P.D.: Principles of GNSS. Inertial and Multisensor Integrated Navigation Systems (2011)
6. Gao, Z.-Y.: Inertial Navigation System Technology. Tsinghua University Press, Beijing (2012)
7. Hu, X.-P., et al.: Autonomous navigation technology. In: College of Mechatronic Engineering and Automation, NUDT (2014)
8. Liu, W.-C., Bian, H.-W., Wang, R.-Y.: A calculating method of polar navigation parameters for inertial navigation system. J. Shanghai Jiao Tong Univ. **48**(4), 539–543 (2014)
9. Skopeliti, A., Tsoulos, L.: Choosing a Suitable Projection for Navigation in the Arctic. Taylor & Francis, London (2013)
10. Wang, Z.H., Chen, X.J., Zeng, Q.H.: Ship's inertial navigation system rotating modulation based on navigation coordinates. J. Harbin Eng. Unv. **30**(7), 921–926 (2011)

Research on Uncertainty Analysis Method of Aircraft's HWIL Simulation

Huapin Geng[✉], Wenhua Kong, and Yingkang Wang

Beijing Electro-Mechanical Engineering Institute, Beijing 100074, China
geng_sky@163.com

Abstract. Uncertainty exists in simulation modeling, simulation running and simulation evaluation. The HWIL simulation's credibility has been affected by the complicated uncertainty factors existing in the HWIL simulation's process. Based on uncertainty main factors analysis of HWIL simulation, the uncertainty analysis methods are put forward. Application is made of the uncertainty analysis methods. It is proved that the uncertainty methods is suited, and provides an effective way to improve the credibility of HWIL simulation.

Keywords: HWILS (hardware-in-the-loop simulation) · Uncertainty analysis method · Simulation model · Simulation device

1 Introduction

Generally, uncertainty refers to the inherent variability of the physical system and its environment, the incompleteness of human knowledge of the physical system and its environment. Specifically in aircraft HWIL, uncertainty includes various manifestations of unrecognized or incompletely unrecognized and not measurable factors, which leading to the phenomenon that the simulation results estimated in a way are inconsistent with the real simulation results.

Aircraft HWILS uncertainty lies in the different stages of simulation modeling, simulation running, the analysis and evaluation of HWILS system. Uncertainty will seriously affect the robustness and reliability of the aircraft HWILS system, reducing the aircraft HWIL simulation credibility and increasing the risk of the use of HWIL simulation of weapons systems performance evaluation and decision-making.

Uncertainty analysis of aircraft HWILS is mainly implemented through the holistic, comprehensive research on aircraft HWILS various uncertain factors in different stages. The analysis includes the exploration of the aircraft HWILS uncertainty quantification method, a comprehensive analysis of the simulation system input, the external environment as well as the simulation system inherently uncertainty, the quantification of the uncertainty distribution of the simulation system output, the reasonable assessment of the degree of uncertainty factors on simulation credibility. The analysis may guide simulation modeling, model validation and HWILS system credibility evaluation to improve the HWILS credibility and abilities of simulation validation, evaluation and decision supporting accurately.

L. Zhang et al. (Eds.): AsiaSim 2016/SCS AutumnSim 2016, Part IV, CCIS 646, pp. 524–532, 2016.
DOI: 10.1007/978-981-10-2672-0_54

2   Research on Uncertainty Analysis Method of Aircraft HWIL

From the view of the HWIL simulation process, the simulation modeling uncertainties contains simulation modeling uncertainty, simulation running uncertainty and simulation evaluation uncertainty, as shown in Fig. 1. Simulation modeling uncertainty is the main factor causing uncertainty in the simulation running. Simulation running uncertainty is an important factor causing uncertainty in simulation evaluation.

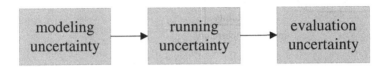

Fig. 1. HWIL simulation uncertainty

The process of uncertainty analysis is as follows: Firstly, analyzing all kinds of uncertainty elements which is the basis of uncertainty impact analysis; Secondly, for all types of uncertainty factors, obtaining efficient data; Thirdly, extracting main uncertainties; Finally, building the uncertainty mathematics model and obtaining result uncertainty distribution using uncertainty analysis method to support the uncertainty impact analysis (Fig. 2).

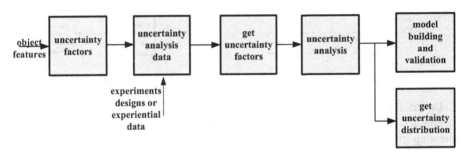

Fig. 2. Simulation uncertainty analysis process

This section focuses on aircraft HWILS uncertainty factor analysis, uncertainty factors extraction and research on uncertainty analysis method, laying the foundation for subsequent application research.

2.1   Uncertainty Factors Analysis

Uncertainty in aircraft simulation modeling mainly exists in the process of physical modeling, mathematical modeling and simulation model implemented, seen in Fig. 3. Uncertainty in aircraft HWILS running exists in these parts of the test environment, experimental design, and a combination of factors, detailed in Fig. 4. Uncertainty in simulation evaluation exists in these parts of data acquisition, data itself, data analysis methods, data analysis model, simulation results, assessment methods and etc., seen in Fig. 5.

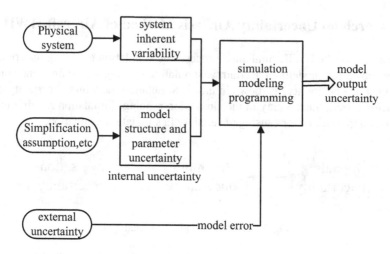

Fig. 3. Simulation modeling uncertainty

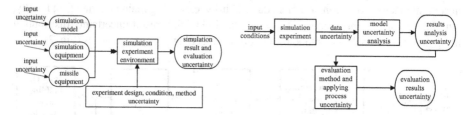

Fig. 4. Simulation running uncertainty   **Fig. 5.** Simulation evaluation uncertainty

Uncertainty mainly includes two categories: random uncertainty and cognitive uncertainty. The former describes the inherent randomness and volatility of model and operating environment, and also an inevitable uncertainty (such as: discrete error/ rounding truncation error, etc.); cognitive uncertainty describes the uncertainty caused by lack of data, cognitive biases, incomplete information. Uncertainty is mainly in the form of "random", "fuzzy", "gray" and so on.

HWILS uncertainty is not a single type of uncertainty, is a comprehensive uncertainty As for the same uncertainty, it's not absolute to judge whether the uncertainty is randomness or cognitive Usually this is up to the object under study, environment, problems concerned, available information and personnel experience. Random uncertainty is usually described by probabilistic methods, modeled by random variables or random processes; and cognitive uncertainty described by fuzzy mathematical theory, interval analysis theory, evidence theory, the uncertainty theory.

2.2 Extraction of the Uncertainty Factors

For cognitive uncertainty, validation methods can be used to extract structure uncertainty and parameter uncertainty by comparing simulation data to actual data.

Random uncertainty can be assessed by verification method. Such as rounding errors may be measured by being compared with the simulation results computed by more advanced computer equipment; human programming error can be acknowledged by redundancy check, discretization error can be evaluated by the method of changing the particle size.

2.3   Research on the Uncertainty Analysis Method of HWIL

2.3.1   Research on Uncertainty Analysis Method in Simulation Modeling

Uncertainty in aircraft simulation modeling process mainly includes two categories: random uncertainty and cognitive uncertainty, which can be described by random, fuzzy, incomplete information and data inconsistency. The research on uncertainty can be carried out based on a random, gray, fuzzy, rough and other uncertainty analysis methods (such as exploratory analysis, evidence theory, probability theory, information entropy theory and data mining, etc.). At the same time, M&S mixed uncertainty analysis problems can be properly solved by Bayesian network analysis method, evidence network analysis method, and gray system theory analysis method

- Bayesian network is a kind of graphical description based on network structure with conditional probabilities describing the association and influence among each information element. Joint distribution can be decomposed to several probability distributions less complex using independence relationships between variables to reduce the complexity of expression. Meanwhile, priori knowledge and data can be combined to avoid data over-fitted effectively.
- Evidence network model is a combination of qualitative and quantitative methods. The expression of network structure is the qualitative knowledge which means the causal link between events. The expression of the network parameters is the quantitative knowledge which describes the impact from the reason to the result.
- Grey system theory makes use of a small amount of known data to find the system output characteristics by the cumulative generation, accumulation and other mathematical methods. This method is an important way to solve uncertainty analysis of the system with the internal mechanism unknown.

2.3.2   Research on Uncertainty Analysis Method in Simulation Running

This section focuses on the study of uncertainty analysis method about simulation environment, experimental design, and combined effects.

- Research on uncertainty analysis method in simulation environment

Uncertainty in simulation environment is the comprehensive effect result of simulation model, simulation devices and aircraft devices. Uncertainty analysis of all various types of equipment/models includes three parts: input uncertainty, internal uncertainty, and output uncertainty (Fig. 6).

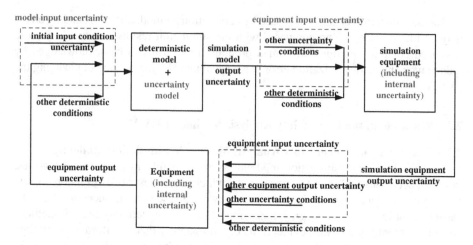

Fig. 6. Simulation environment uncertainty

– Research on uncertainty analysis methods in simulation model

On the one hand, input uncertainty analysis is made to obtain initial conditions distribution by using statistical analysis methods, On the other hand, initial input conditions uncertainty model can be made by using approximate modeling methods (such as polynomial regression models/Kriging model, etc.). Internal uncertainty analysis is mainly made to uncertainty modeling and model checking by using statistical analysis, data mining, and other consistency comparison methods, Based on the simulation model system in which all of the uncertainty models are introduced, uncertainty transfer effect is analyzed by using the random and cognitive analysis methods. Output uncertainty analysis is made on the basis of obtaining valid data from mathematical simulation and HWIL simulation, then the output distribution model can be determined using random expansion method, Monte Carlo method, interval analysis, evidence theory.

– Research on uncertainty analysis methods in simulation equipment

Input uncertainty mainly comes from the simulation model output uncertainty and uncertainty in other environments. Other environmental uncertainty can be obtained using statistical analysis methods and theoretical deduction. Internal uncertainty analysis can be made to uncertainty modeling by using conventional simulation modeling methods such as mechanism modeling method, black box modeling method and combining methods, or to make statistical error model by using statistical analysis methods, or to improve the model credibility by using consistency comparison methods. Output uncertainty is mainly reflected in the simulation device error. The error range, the mean, the main distribution, distribution type, etc., may be obtained using statistical analysis methods. Meanwhile, these serve as the main source of input uncertainty of aircraft test equipment. Comprehensive uncertainty analysis of simulation equipment can be made through the use of data mining, uncertainty analysis methods combined with random and intervals, random and fuzzy, fuzzy and interval, etc. to establish simulation device uncertainty model.

- Research on uncertainty analysis methods in simulation experiment design

Experimental Design uncertainties mainly include the uncertainty caused by the test conditions, test design, test methods. Uncertainty analysis process and methods of the test conditions are similar to model input uncertainty analysis. Because of different choice of test design method, test design cannot cover all test conditions. So uncertainty analysis of test design is made by using statistical analysis methods. Uncertainty analysis of test method is made according to the difference of the simulation results under different test methods. Based on the difference of the result consistent degree, the impact of different test method to simulation output is analyzed.

- Research on uncertainty analysis method in simulation running

Combined effects among simulation experiment design and simulation environments lead to uncertainties in simulation running, which influence uncertainty in simulation results. Uncertainty in simulation running is mixed uncertainty, not a kind of uncertainty, so uncertainty analysis hybrid methods are used to analyze the comprehensive uncertainty influence. Among them, mixing uncertainty analysis methods include stochastic-interval analysis methods, fuzzy-random and random-fuzzy methods having two main approaches (information entropy and scaling transformation) of realization, methods based on fuzzy-interval analysis, methods based on stochastic theory and evidence/Bayesian network.

2.3.3 Research on Uncertainty Analysis Method of Simulation Result

The simulation results include two kinds of data: one kind is static data, such as miss distance; the other is dynamic time-series data, such as posture information. The simulation result is not a single type of uncertainty, may be based on a class or a combination of uncertainty.

Based on data characteristics, there are two ways to implement uncertainty analysis of simulation results. One is the uncertainty analysis methods based on the static and dynamic data type; the other is the analysis method based on the uncertainty type. To determine the importance of each uncertainty factor affecting the simulation results, we choose sensitivity analysis methods, such as regression analysis, principal component analysis and correlation analysis, to eliminate the less-affected factors.

- Research on uncertainty analysis method based on static and dynamic data type

For dynamic time series data, analysis methods mainly include three types: time-domain method, frequency-domain method and time-frequency domain method. In each domain, it can be divided into linear model, nonlinear model and the stochastic model. Typical linear time-domain models are like regression analysis. Stochastic linear models are like auto-regression model, moving average model, ARMA model, ARIMA model, in which front three models are for stationary time series, the latter model is mainly for non-stationary time series. Non-linear models mainly include the neural network model and etc. Frequency-domain analysis methods have all kinds of spectral estimation and etc. Time - frequency domain analysis methods are like window Fourier transformation, wavelet transform. Among them, the linear model is mainly used to extract the global regularity of the time series, not to show the impact of short-term and unexpected events. Nonlinear methods such as neural networks pay more attention to describing the impact of partial and short-term factors. In practical applications, these methods are usually combined to use for objective description of objects.

For static data such as miss distance, we pay more attention to range and distribution of the data making use of the combined methods of statistical analysis and interval analysis. Statistical analysis is used to describe the spatial distribution of the uncertainty of the data; interval analysis is used to describe the cognitive uncertainty in data. Also, based on the characteristics of the concerned data, common uncertainty analysis methods, such as statistical methods, evidence theory, Bayesian networks, fuzzy theory interval analysis and other methods can be selected to make analysis.

- Research on data analysis method based on uncertainty types
  - Probability theory and stochastic process theory can be used to make analysis random data. We select different mining methods of random data according to simulation data quantity. These methods such as Bayesian Analysis, least squares method, neural networks, decision trees are selected when the amount of data is large. These methods such as SVM, least squares method, regression analysis methods are selected when the amount of data is small.
  - These methods, such as gray association and gray clustering classification are suitable to make analysis gray data which is small or incomplete.
  - Analysis methods like fuzzy set theory are used to study the uncertainty of fuzzy data which can not be clearly defined; analysis methods such as interval number classification/regression/cluster are used to analyze interval uncertainty.
  - These methods, such as stochastic-interval analysis methods, fuzzy-random and random-fuzzy methods, fuzzy- interval methods can be used to make analysis mixed type data.

3   Application Research on the Typical Uncertainty Analysis

Taking the aircraft HWILS as example, we select a typical part of the test environment to make application research on uncertainty analysis.

- Application research on simulation model uncertainty

In order to obtain the output uncertainty of simulation model, 27 test conditions were designed to obtain test data using orthogonal design. Based on these conditions, simulation tests are made to obtain simulation output. Statistical analysis method is used to analyze data to obtain the distribution of the simulation equipment input.

Statistical result of 27 simulation test data: the inner shaft angular velocity $(-10, 10)$ accounts for 99.76 %, the central axis angular velocity $(-10, 10)$ accounts for 99.69 %, the outer shaft angular velocity $(-10,10)$ accounts for 99.73 %. Three axis angular velocity data out of $(-10, 10)$ is less than 1 %.

- Application research on simulation equipment uncertainty.

Taking simulate turntable for example, application research on simulation equipment uncertainty is made.

In order to analyze the uncertainty of the turntable itself: First, uncertainty data of turntable itself are obtained by repeating 32 tests under typical test condition. Then, the uncertainty error models of turntable are made using statistical analysis, regression analysis, least squares methods, etc. Finally, the correctness of the uncertainty analysis results is validated by 27 different simulation data of orthogonal design.

Statistical result of 32 data: 95 % of the angular velocity errors of inner shaft falls in (−0.0275, 0.0246), the average error is −1.6623e-004, variance is 1.7190e-004. 95.0 % of the angular velocity errors of outer shaft falls in [− 0.05 0.03], mean is −0.009, variance is 0.0012.

From the histogram, error distribution does not meet the normal distribution. When the KS test and rank sum test are adopted, the error distribution does not meet the normal distribution at the 95 % confidence interval. Finally, the t distribution test is adopted, and the error distribution belongs to t distribution.

Compared with the two-order polynomial, the fitting results of the first order polynomial (formula: Y = − 0.00011 −0.01042 * X.) are more ideal. The estimated standard deviation is 0.00848, fitting degree is 0.4126, and the probability that the fitting is zero is less than 0.0001.

In order to verify the rationality of the envelope curve model, 27 test conditions of orthogonal design were made, and the coverage rate of the fitting result is calculated based on 27 simulation data. In 27 conditions, the percentage of data fitting interval is over 98 %, and the minimum is 98.04 %, and the maximum is 98.64 % and the average is 98.29 %.

- Application research with uncertainty error model introduced into system simulation model

Taking ins for example, uncertainty error is introduced into the system simulation model to analyze the impact of inertial navigation error on system output. The Monte Carlo method is used to obtain adequate data and to support analysis. All of the drop point dispersion are included in the drop point accuracy specifications. The full impact analysis of the uncertainty to the system would be implemented through experimental design in the following work.

4 Conclusions

Based on the analysis of uncertainty factors in aircraft HWILS modeling, running and evaluation, uncertainty analysis methods in aircraft HWILS are proposed. The application research on simulation model and equipment of typical aircraft HWILS was carried out using statistics method, interval analysis method and envelopment analysis method. The existed uncertainty analysis results were introduced to the system model to analyze the impact of the uncertainty on the system. The adaptability of the uncertainty methods is verified to improve the credibility of HWILS system.

References

1. Ke, H.-F., Chen, Y.-G., et al.: Electric test equipment uncertainty information processing technology. National Defense Industry Press, Beijing (2013)
2. Chen, X.-Q., Yao, W., Qi, O.-Y.: Aircraft Uncertainty Multidisciplinary Design Optimization Theory and Application. Science Press (2013)
3. Oberkampf, W.L., Helton, J.C., et al.: Challenge problems: uncertainty in system response given uncertain parameters. Reliab. Eng. Syst. Saf. **85**(1–3), 11–19 (2004)
4. Tan, P.-N., Steinbach, M., Kumar, V.: Introduction to Data Mining. People Post Press, Beijing (2012)

Design and Implementation of Fault Patterns Online Evaluation Simulation System for Aircraft

Wen-hua Kong[✉]

Beijing Electro-Mechanical Engineering Institute, Beijing, 100074, China
kongwenhua@263.net

Abstract. Fault patterns online evaluation simulations are extremely useful tools for aircraft to carry out fault's localization at rapidly and repairing in short order, as well as to improve reliability, applicability, security and effectiveness of aircraft in an operational environment. This article proposes a universal framework of fault patterns online simulation evaluation for aircraft using fault patterns injection and fault data reappearance in online. By introducing reasonable and appropriate abstraction of entity and input or output interface, the conceptual model of aircraft system are achieved. The software of fault injection and a prototype of simulation system are obtained, and verified in subsystem of aircraft oriented control computer. Simulation results are provided and they show that this work perform better.

Keywords: Aircraft · Fault pattern · Fault injection · Fault reappearance · Online evaluation simulation

1 Introduction

With increasing of informationization and integration of the aircraft, the technical bottlenecks were increasingly emerged with serious influence on safeguarding collectivity power of the aircraft, such as precision accommodation of the spare parts, concomitant maintain at ahead, monitor of quality, evaluation of operational effectiveness, technical upgrade to prolong the life-span, etc. It has played important role in decreasing time of fault diagnoses and boosting up the ability of maintaining to develop technologies of fault patterns online evaluation simulation for aircraft.

2 Related Works

In recent years, there are numerous research results on fault patterns modeling and fault patterns simulation.

- For Fault pattern modeling: Aim at the low validity and precision of fault model make the phenomena of fault latency occur frequently in testability simulation, the method of fault modeling is provided based on Bayesian networks and object-oriented technology, a seven-members fault model is founded, and the fault behavior condition

© Springer Science+Business Media Singapore 2016
L. Zhang et al. (Eds.): AsiaSim 2016/SCS AutumnSim 2016, Part IV, CCIS 646, pp. 533–542, 2016.
DOI: 10.1007/978-981-10-2672-0_55

vector or the relative fault vector could be received by Bayesian positive or negative consequence, to avoid assembled explode phenomena in fault injection test [1]. For the problem of the faults which take place when the large-scale complex armament equipment is used are difficult to analyze and deal with, a method of fault modeling and simulation was proposed by analyzing fault's basic properties characteristics, the fault attribute description model and state parameter database were set up, and the fault propagation with simulation technology and neural network arithmetic was reasoned to simulate the fault phenomenon and its development process [2]. According to the need of circuit fault simulation of actuator system, the circuit simulation model is created using the professional circuit simulation software such as Proteus, the time domain response and frequency domain response of the model are analyzed, the analysis result shows that the circuit model is capable of well imitating the response of actuator system [3]. Aim at the problem of integrated modeling of equipment integrated logistics support (ILS) system, the methods of making general description to and building ILS simulation models with XML, integrated and general presentation to all meta-models of ILS simulation is realized [4]. In addition, introducing the traditional method of fault tree analysis, fault tree was built which did not work as top-affair, fault tree models of simulation were established by using Monte-Carlo random sampling method [5]. It lays a good foundation for fault pattern modeling.

- For Fault patterns simulation: Flight failure data in database is important basis for effectively solving all kinds of potential safety hazard in plane flying, but there are not able to directly recognize the entity correlation between the failure data, traditional dada miming method need repetitious correlating and inefficient, a fault data mining method for flight safety database based on artificial immune algorithm is presented to obtain the fault data correlation [6]. By using HLA fault injection tool to realize the fault injection based on simulation, and doing many experiments on key equipment, the safety of target simulation system was fully tested, the reliability of train control system can be evaluated effectively [7]. The structural framework of Launch Vehicle simulation system is designed, taking faults in dynamic system as an example, a fault simulation based on MATLAB/Simulink is performed for supporting its fault diagnosis and isolation, as well as increasing the reliability [8]. For the situation lacking of testability validation platform for current airborne equipment developing, an airborne equipment test verification system is put forward, and the basic functions of the aircraft fuel measurement system and operation mode by Hardware-in-the-loop simulation(HILS) are achieved, avoiding simulation tolerance caused by inaccurate modeling and improving the degree of confidence of the simulation. Using several ways such as probe fault injection, simulation fault injection, software fault injection to achieve a variety of typical fault simulation of the system under test, thus to verify the airborne equipment fault detection and isolation performance [9].

The disadvantage of all simulation methods in above is not able to diagnose the fault in real time and evaluate the fault in online. Along with increasing the complexity of mission, developing aircraft system with high reliability has become urgent. For increasing the reliability of aircraft system, one of the key techniques is developing real-time fault diagnosis for localizing fault at rapidly and maintenance without accident.

3   A Comprehensive Approach

After the Fault Mode Effect and Compromise Analysis (FMECA) has been done for all potential faults in aircraft system by using theories and tools of the reliability, the fault patterns of aircraft system can be obtained, then the fault model-base were established. The real-time concurrent dynamic simulation platform was found by utilizing the modern technologies such as concurrent engineering, dynamic simulation and real-time network communication. Developing tools of fault rejection and fault data mining, the goal of fault localization and reappearance at rapidly, as well as fault evaluation in online can be reached.

Figure 1 illustrates the common framework of fault patterns online evaluation simulation system that allows connecting the different subsystems as fault data collection, fault pattern generation & correct, fault diagnose, main control simulation computer, and real-time dynamic concurrent simulation, etc.

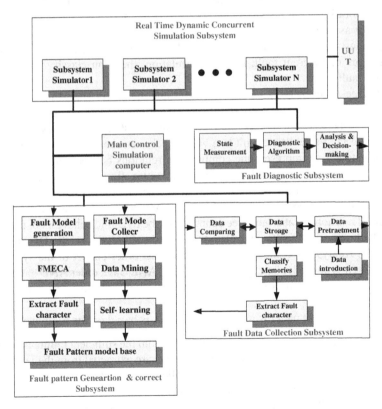

Fig. 1. Common framework of fault patterns online evaluation simulation system

The fault data collection subsystem executes completely the mission of fault data treatment that offers a set of services: collection of fault data, classification of fault data, pretreatment of fault data, and extraction of fault character. It also provides the database of fault characters for the fault patterns generation & correct subsystem to constitute the model of fault patterns.

The fault data generation & correct subsystem executes the mission of modeling for fault patterns and model correcting that offers some services such as self-learning of fault character from existing fault information included phenomena, causes, mechanism, solving methods, and extraction of fault rules. This subsystem can make the best of real time simulation and data mining to improve model of fault pattern, so that supports high fidelity online evaluation simulation of the fault patterns for aircraft.

4 Theory and Scheme

4.1 Modeling of Fault Patterns

Faults usually show as some phenomena that equipment unexpected, such as lose of functions, retrogression of performance, etc. For the degree of existence, they can classify as temporarily or chronically fault. For the process of happen and developing, they can classify as paroxysmal or gradual faults. For the severity of aftermath, they can classify as destructive or nondestructive fault. For the cause of happen, they can classify as exogenous or inherent fault. For the correlation, they can classify as primary or secondary fault.

Fault Tree Analysis (FTA) is a useful ways and means for analyzing fault patterns of system. Fault tree can distinctly show internal correlations of the system to represent logistic nexus between fault of assembly and fault of system. There are static fault tree and dynamic fault tree. Static fault tree was built in various logic gates such as AND gate, OR gate etc., to represent the combination relations between fault agents of the bottom layer in graphics mode. The cut set is the combination of basic agents that incurs failure of the system. The least cut set is the combination of minimum basic agents that incurs top failure of the system, and fault patterns represent as the least cut set of failure of system. Traditional static fault tree cannot describe dynamic behaviors of the system such as fault restoring, faults interrelated time, and cold repertory etc. Dynamic Fault Tree (DFT) Analysis is commonly to solve the least order cut set of the system with importing new types of logistic gates such as prior AND gate, order AND gate, and hot backup gate etc. In contrast to static fault tree, the DFT appends constraints of schedule [10].

The proposed fault patterns modeling with FTA is based on the following steps:

1. All the least cut set are obtained by using FTA from the sufficient failure phenomena of the aircraft system, and the basic fault agents are extracted from the least cut set.
2. The basic fault models are built by collecting, concluding, classifying, and abstracting the corresponding basic fault agents from assembly of bottom and outer of the system. The simulation cases corresponding to basic fault agents are provided with setting as different parameters in basis fault models.

3. Fault pattern simulation models are built by combination of simulation cases with some special restrictions and setting as correlative attributes such as START or STOP of simulation with special activities.

Indeed, a whole simulation model of fault pattern summarizes the 3-layers framework, illustrated in Fig. 2.

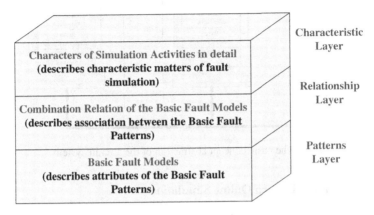

Fig. 2. The 3-layers framework of fault pattern simulation model

4.2 Abstraction of Simulation Objects

The aircraft system are usually developed as a comprehensive and robust system to ingrate with multi-subsystems such as flight control subsystem, electrical subsystem, inertia subsystem, dynamical subsystem, altimeter subsystem and rudder subsystem, etc. Each subsystem has various real-time requirements as hard or soft real time, so the aircraft system must operates in a real-time environment of linkage.

Commonly, a fault to happen is always depending on some subsystems, so we can divide the aircraft system into two aspects: the Units under Test (UUT) and the Linkage of Environments (LE). Figure 3 illustrates basic concept abstraction of the aircraft system, and proposes abstractions of all subsystems as follows:

1. Software of Subsystem (SS): application programs operating in all subsystems, represented as SS.
2. Services of Subsystem (SC): service platform to execute software of all subsystems, included operating system, memories interface, hardware I/O and drivers, represented as SC.
3. Hardware Interface (HI): the hardware interface to support one subsystem communicating with other ones, represented as HI.
4. Linkage of Environment (LE): the set of all subsystems communicating with UUT, represented as LE.

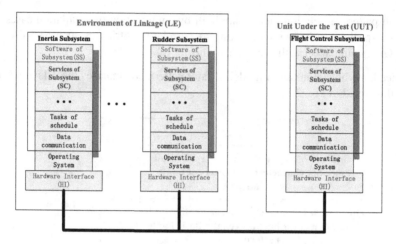

Fig. 3. The basic concept abstraction of the aircraft system

4.3   Scheme of Fault Pattern Online Simulation

The purpose of this work is to add tools of fault injection into the real time simulation environment of the outer UUT. This research proposes a non-inclusive scheme to test the reliability, security and usability of UUT. Specifically, when one fault from a defined fault space was emerged in special context of invalidation, it may be easier to validate whether the UUT can deal with correctly and its response can meet requirements of design.

Figure 4 illustrates theory of simulation test based on fault injection. Considering factors as cost, expense and efficiency etc., the LE of UUT is usually established by simulation instead of physical LE, the input signal of load driver included fault information are rejected, and output are generated from UUT. In the LE of simulation, the extended objects as fault injector are always added.

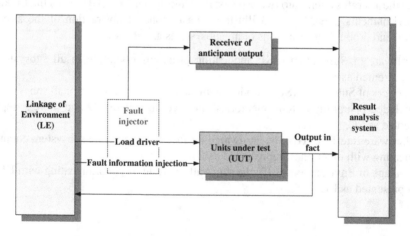

Fig. 4. Theory of simulation test based on fault injection

The UUT can generate the behaviors as follows:

1. If UUT is not to access the interface that fault information were injected, the behaviors of UUT are same as the original behaviors not to inject fault information.
2. Worked at the load driver, the invalidation of UUT may be appeared. The fault will be active, if the control streams of UUT access through the interface of communication that fault information were injected in.

Figure 5 illustrates theory of fault simulation test based on data reappearance. The environment of executing simulation that is composed of UUT and LE of simulation can be established by modeling and simulation. The data of flight test gained in outer range included fault information will be delayed boosting at frame time in nature to produce data streams corresponding with real time simulation. Setting up the initial conditions similar to ones of flight test, the delayed data streams executes reappearance in real time simulation environment to localize the fault by comparing value of output from simulation system with value of the original fault data streams at the same moment.

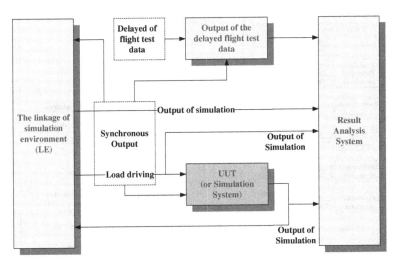

Fig. 5. Theory of simulation test based on data reappearance

5   Description of Simulation System Design

5.1   Functions

In order to complete fault pattern online evaluation simulation, the Real Time Concurrent Simulation System (RTCSS) will be established to develop the functions as follows:

1. To accomplish simulation of the Linkage Environment of UUT outer.
2. To accomplish communication of information between UUT and LE in real time.
3. To setup initial conditions such as fault pattern, fault status, and initial condition of flight etc.
4. To accomplish injection of faults in special time or regulative number.

5. To accomplish reappearance of the flight test data streams included fault information boosting at frame time in reality.
6. To accomplish analysis and memory of simulation results.

5.2 System Framework and Design

Figure 6 depicts framework of the RTCSS. A RTCSS system like the one in Fig. 7 would generally consist of a LE, a subsystem of fault injection and fault data reappearance, and a subsystem of graphical display. The subsystem of fault injection and fault data reappearance would generally consist of fault patterns base, fault injection block, fault

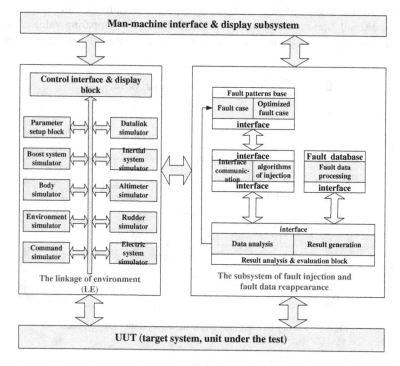

Fig. 6. The framework of real time concurrent simulation system

Fig. 7. The hardware of fault patterns online evaluation simulation system prototype

data reappearance process block, and result evaluation block. Fault patterns base includes fault case base, the base of optimized fault case, and interface.

5.3   Implement of Prototype and Validation

Based on the control computer of aircraft as UUT, we developed a prototype of the fault patterns online evaluation simulation system as shown in Fig. 7. It provided a software toolkit mainly consisted of fault modeling block and fault real time simulation block. Fault modeling block provides a help for user to model the basic fault pattern, generate automatically codes of simulation model and configure document executing in real time simulation environment.

To simulation for combination of multi-fault patterns, it provides three types of routines as combination in absolutely, orderly, and repeatedly. According to special simulation conditions, the more complicated faults like as reality are generated in freely combination scheme. Figure 8 shows a simulation case of combination fault in absolutely that inertial system outputs a abnormal height value of −500 m at 40 ms. Figure 9. Shows simulation result of a combination fault in repeatedly that inertial system output abnormal height value happened total three times in the whole of simulation course, and the duration of time that fault happened is 20 ms.

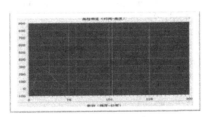

Fig. 8. The case of combination fault in absolutely that inertial system outputs a abnormal height value of −500 m at 40 ms

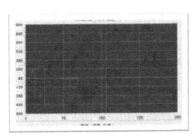

Fig. 9. The case of combination fault in repeatedly that inertial system output abnormal height value happened total three times in the whole of simulation course, and the duration of time that fault happened is 20 ms

6 Future Works

This research proposes a universal framework for fault patterns online simulation evaluation for aircraft using fault patterns injection and fault data reappearance in online. By introducing reasonable and appropriate abstraction of entity and input or output interface, the conceptual model of aircraft system are achieved. The software of fault injection and a prototype of simulation system are obtained, and verified in subsystem of aircraft oriented control computer. Simulation results are provided and they show that this work perform better.

In future, we will consummate the model base of fault patterns in progressively, spread application for aircraft system to achieve fault localization and fault reappearance in system-level.

References

1. Li, T., Qiu, J., Liu, G.: Research on fault model technology in testability simulation based fault injection experiment. Chin. J. Mech. Eng. **20**(16), 1923–1927 (2009)
2. Liang, F., Zhang, Z., Gao, Q., et al.: Research on fault modeling and simulation technology of large-scale armament equipment. Chin. J. Syst. Simul. **23**(Supp. 1), 42–46 (2011)
3. Zhang, K., Zeng, Q.: Research on circuit simulation method for actuator system. Chin. J. Aeronaut. Comput. Tech. **45**(3), 95–98 (2011)
4. Gao, J., Sun, T., Shi, S., et al.: Research on the integrated modeling of Equipment Integrated Logistics Support ILS) simulation. Chin. J. Acad. Armored Force Eng. **23**(4), 6–9 (2009)
5. Bian, X., Mou, C.: Simulation model and fault tree analysis for AUV. In: IEEE Proceedings Mechatronics and Automation, pp. 4453–4457 (2009)
6. Luo, X., Liu, K., Luo, Z.: Simulation of optimization mining for fault data in flight database. Chin. J. Comput. Simul. **31**(5), 89–92 (2014)
7. Yi, Q., Cai, B., Shang, G., et al.: Application of the fault injection method on train control simulation system. Chin. J. Railway Signal. Commun. **49**(1), 66–70 (2013)
8. Cheng, L., Cai, Y., Mu, L., et al.: Fault simulation of launch vehicle flight based on MATLAB/Simulink. Chin. J. Armament Autom. **27**(9), 8–11 (2008)
9. Wu, Z., Jing, B., Yu, S., et al.: Design and implement of testability verification system based on HILS. Chin. J. Comput. Measur. Control **21**(9), 2349–2351 (2013)
10. Kong, W., Su, Y., Yang, L.: Research on methods of modeling of fault patterns for aircraft. In: China Simulation Technology Intercommunication Conference (2012)

Data Fusion of Small Sample Flying Test Data and Big Sample Simulation Test Data Based on Equivalent Sample for Equipment Efficiency Evaluation

Xiaolei Ning[1(✉)], Yingxia Wu[1], Hailin Zhang[1], and Xin Zhao[1,2]

[1] Key Laboratory of Guided Weapons Test and Evaluation
Simulation Technology, China HuaYin Ordnance Test Center, Huayin, China
ningxiaolei21@163.com
[2] Shang Hai Jiao Tong University, Shanghai, China

Abstract. How to fuse the small flying test data and the big simulation test data is such a difficult research hot in small sample data solution field. Bayesian formula is usually adopted to solve this problem, but when it is used directly, the simulation test data always drowns the flying test data. To solve the above problem, an improved Bayesian formula for static data fusion is put forward based on simulation equivalent flying sample, which introduces the crediblity degree in forms of equivalent flying sample to Bayesian formula. And at the same time, we give out an analysis of theory and applications counter measures. The numerical computations show the feasibility of the improved method.

Keywords: Data fusion · Equivalent sample · Simulation · Bayesian formula

1 Introduction

As the rapid development of the simulation technology, it has already been equivalent to the flying test for equipment performance evaluation. Although the flying test data size is small, the simulation test data size is big. How to solve the two kinds of data comprehensively is still a difficult work to range test engineer, but is most important and significant for weapon capability estimation. Bayesian method is usually used to solve such hard problem. It takes simulation test data as prior distribution and modifies it making use of flying data, so we can finally get the posterior distribution. Bayesian formula supports a structure for different test data to fuse, and in most of the cases it can get a good result. But when used to fuse the small flying data and the big simulation data, it will still faces the below deficiency.

(1) The big simulation data drowns the small flying data that is the flying data won't work to the final fusion result at all;
(2) Posterior distribution is insensitive to the credibility of simulation system.

In order to overcome the above two shortcomings of Bayesian formula, we put forward a new Bayesian formula based on simulation equivalent to flying sample (equivalent sample, ES) to fuse the small flying test data and the big simulation data,

L. Zhang et al. (Eds.): AsiaSim 2016/SCS AutumnSim 2016, Part IV, CCIS 646, pp. 543–552, 2016.
DOI: 10.1007/978-981-10-2672-0_56

which takes the simulation data as flying test sample based on the simulation test precision so that the result can be improved greatly.

2 Mathematical Description of Test Data Fusion

Suppose the flying test data be $X = (X_1, X_2, \ldots, X_n)$ and the simulation test data be $Y = (Y_1, Y_2, \ldots Y_m)$. X has a good credibility degree but the sample number is small while the credibility degree of Y is comparatively low but the sample number is big. How to fuse the two different kinds of test data is needed badly to done. This problem can be mathematically described as follows.

$$(\theta, \vartheta) = f(X, Y) \tag{1}$$

Where θ, ϑ are the estimated parameters; $f(\cdot)$ is the estimation function. The implementing procedure is described in Fig. 1.

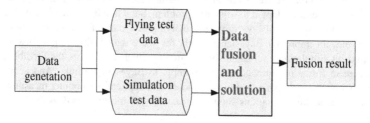

Fig. 1. The implementing procedure of data fusion

3 Bayesian Formula and Its Defect for Test Data Fusion

Bayesian formula is different from traditional statistical method, which combines the prior distribution and the site data to infer the posterior distribution. The Bayesian formula is described as follows.

$$h(\theta/x) = f(\theta/x)\pi(\theta) / \int_{\theta} f(\theta/x)\pi(\theta)d\theta \tag{2}$$

Where $h(\theta/x)$ is posterior distribution; $\pi(\theta)$ is prior distribution; $f(\theta/x)$ is sampling distribution or likely distribution. From formula (2) we can infer that Bayesian method relates to the value of $\pi(\theta)$ and $h(\theta/x)$, where how to choose $\pi(\theta)$ is most contentious. Conjugate prior distribution is a popular choose. The point estimation formula of the typical conjugate normal distribution is

$$\hat{\mu} = \left(\frac{n\hat{X}}{\tau_0^2} + \frac{\mu_0}{\tau_1^2}\right) \bigg/ \left(\frac{n}{\tau_0^2} + \frac{1}{\tau_1^2}\right) = \left(\frac{\hat{X}}{\tau_0^2/n} + \frac{\mu_0}{\tau_1^2}\right) \bigg/ \left(\frac{1}{\tau_0^2/n} + \frac{1}{\tau_1^2}\right) \tag{3}$$

Where $\hat{X} = \mu$, and $\hat{\mu}$ can be seen as the weighted average of the means of samples and priory mean, and it has business with the sample number, population variance and simulation variance. Concrete mathematical relationship can be described as follows: (1) the variance is bigger, and the weighted coefficient is smaller; (2) the sample number is smaller, and the weighted coefficient is smaller. The relationship above is obviously reasonable, because when the test sample number is bigger, the information $\hat{\mu}$ carried is more, so we should give a bigger weighted coefficient to it; on the other hand when variance bigger, it means that the test sample or prior distribution has less information of population distribution, and so we should give a smaller weighted coefficient. However, Bayesian formula used to fuse the flying test data and the simulation test data still faces the defect: the weighted coefficient of the flying test sample is $\frac{n}{\tau_0^2}\Big/\left(\frac{n}{\tau_0^2} + \frac{1}{\tau_1^2}\right)$, the weighted coefficient of simulation test is $\frac{1}{\tau_1^2}\Big/\left(\frac{n}{\tau_0^2} + \frac{1}{\tau_1^2}\right)$. The weighted coefficients both ignore the simulation size m, but obviously it should work same to the flying sample n, so that when the simulation test system has a high test precision, but the fusion data cannot be sensitive to it.

4 Bayesian Statistical Inference Based on Equivalent Sample

4.1 Equivalent Sample and How to Calculate

Bayesian formula ignores the simulation sample size, so obviously we can add simulation sample to Bayesian formula to improve its property. But how to add simulation sample m to the ordinary Bayesian formula is of difficulty. We add it to formula (3) directly.

$$\hat{\mu} = \left(\frac{n\hat{X}}{\tau_0^2} + \frac{m\mu_0}{\tau_1^2}\right)\Big/\left(\frac{n}{\tau_0^2} + \frac{m}{\tau_1^2}\right) = \left(\frac{\hat{X}}{\tau_0^2/n} + \frac{\mu_0}{\tau_1^2/m}\right)\Big/\left(\frac{1}{\tau_0^2/n} + \frac{m}{\tau_1^2/m}\right) \quad (4)$$

So the flying data weighted coefficient is $\frac{n}{\tau_0^2}\Big/\left(\frac{n}{\tau_0^2} + \frac{m}{\tau_1^2}\right)$ and the simulation weighted coefficient is $\frac{m}{\tau_1^2}\Big/\left(\frac{n}{\tau_0^2} + \frac{m}{\tau_1^2}\right)$. The simulation test sample size m is usually big, so $\frac{m}{\tau_1^2}\Big/\left(\frac{n}{\tau_0^2} + \frac{m}{\tau_1^2}\right)$ is nearly to 1. Figure 2 plots out the relationship between the weighted coefficient and the test sample size. In Fig. 2, 1 stands for the flying coefficient, and 2 stands for the simulation coefficient.

From Fig. 2, we can conclude as the simulation sample size rises, the simulation weighted coefficient also goes up largely and the flying weighted coefficient goes down conversely. So the test estimation result is totally decided by the simulation test data, so that the flying test data nearly no contributions to estimation result because of its small comparative weighted coefficient. So it is unfit to add simulation test number to formula (3) directly. To solve this problem, we define the simulation equivalent to fly test sample number, namely equivalent sample (ES).

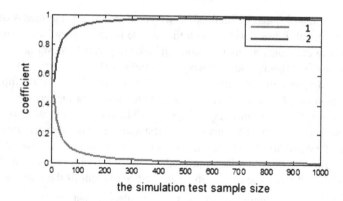

Fig. 2. The relationship between the weighted coefficient and the simulation test sample size

Concept 1. Simulation equivalent to fly test number (equivalent sample, ES). The simulation test number which has the equal estimation precision to the flying test.

For example, let simulation test sample size be m, and the precision be 0.2. At the same condition, we gain the flying test estimation precision which is also 0.2 and calculated by the test sample M. So we call the ES of simulation test sample size m is M. That is m times simulation test precision is the same to the M flying test precise. The concrete calculation procedure of ES is described in Fig. 3.

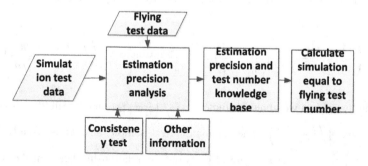

Fig. 3. The procedure of calculating ES

Step1. Calculate the simulation estimation precision: Simulation precision ΔE is decided by the credibility C, it is obvious that when C is big, the simulation precision is high. So far, there exist so many research results about calculating the credibility of simulation test system, such as statistical method, spectral analysis, and dynamics relational analysis and difference analysis. In this paper, we don't focus on the credibility research, so we can use the existing calculation result $C(0 \leq C \leq 1)$ directly. Obviously, when simulation error is equal to 0, then $C = 1$; Simulation error tends to infinity, then $C = 0$.

Set C as x-axes and the simulation precision as y-axes, that is x = 0, ΔE, or y tends to infinity; $C = 1$, or x = 1, ΔE, or y = 0. From the above analysis, we can infer that simulation error goes down as the credibility degree decreases. The equation is

$$\Delta E = f(C) \tag{5}$$

Figure 4 plots out the error changes as the credibility degree C rigidly.

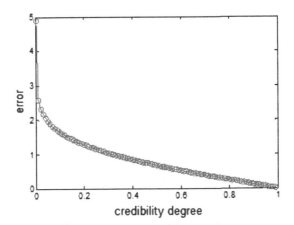

Fig. 4. The curve of credibility degree and error

The area of missile test target is 2.3 m × 2.3 m. And a simple function between the credibility degree and error is to normalize the target area by divide 1.15.

Step2. Calculate the equivalent sample based on simulation estimation error: We calculate the equivalent sample size by simulation estimation precision based on the Crammer-Rao lower limit of the mean

$$\Delta E = \frac{\sigma^2}{M} \Rightarrow M = \frac{\sigma^2}{\Delta E} \tag{6}$$

In fact, estimation error is decided by the credibility degree C and simulation test sample number mutually, and their estimated error lower limit is σ^2/M add σ^2/m separately. The calculation formula of equivalent sample is converted to

$$\Delta E = \frac{\sigma^2}{M} + \frac{\sigma^2}{m} \Rightarrow M = \frac{\sigma^2}{\Delta E - \frac{\sigma^2}{m}} \tag{7}$$

According to formula (7), we can see that m is very big, so σ^2/m is very small. The error is almost decided by the credibility of the simulation system. Figure 5 plots out the curve of estimation and equivalent sample number.

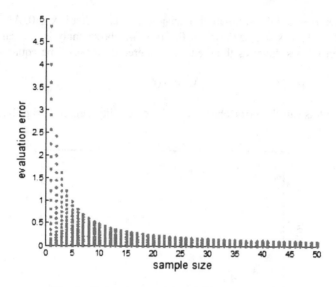

Fig. 5. Estimation precision and test sample size

4.2 Bayesian Statistical Inference Based on ES

Put ES into formula (3) and we can derive the improve Bayesian statistical inference formula is

$$\hat{\mu} = \left(\frac{n\hat{X}}{\tau_0^2} + \frac{M\mu_0}{\tau_1^2} \right) \Big/ \left(\frac{n}{\tau_0^2} + \frac{M}{\tau_1^2} \right) \tag{8a}$$

The weighted coefficient is decided by the flying test number n, variance τ_0, ES M, and variance τ_1. Formula (8a) is the point estimation and Formula (8b) gives out the interval estimation.

$$\left[\mu - \sigma_1 u_{1-\alpha/2}, \ \mu + \sigma_1 u_{1-\alpha/2} \right] \tag{8b}$$

Where μ is calculated by formula (8a); $\sigma_1^2 = \left(\sigma_0^{-2} + \tau^{-2} \right)^{-1}$, $\sigma_0^{-2} = \sigma^{-2}/n$, $\tau^{-2} = \tau^{-2}/M$.

4.3 Prior Distribution Robustness Analysis

Let μ_0 be the mean of prior distribution and τ_1^2 be variance. When τ_1^2 definite, formula (9) and formula (10) gives out the sensitive equation for different precision mean μ_0 of prior distribution.

$$\hat{\mu} = \left(\frac{n\hat{X}}{\tau_0^2} + \frac{\mu_0 + \Delta\mu}{\tau_1^2}\right) \Big/ \left(\frac{n}{\tau_0^2} + \frac{1}{\tau_1^2}\right) = \left(\frac{n\hat{X}}{\tau_0^2} + \frac{\mu_0}{\tau_1^2} + \frac{\Delta\mu}{\tau_1^2}\right) \Big/ \left(\frac{n}{\tau_0^2} + \frac{1}{\tau_1^2}\right)$$

$$\Delta\hat{\mu} = \left(\frac{\Delta\mu}{\tau_1^2}\right) \Big/ \left(\frac{n}{\tau_0^2} + \frac{1}{\tau_1^2}\right) \tag{9}$$

$$\hat{\mu} = \left(\frac{n\hat{X}}{\tau_0^2} + \frac{M(\mu_0 + \Delta\mu)}{\tau_1^2}\right) \Big/ \left(\frac{n}{\tau_0^2} + \frac{M}{\tau_1^2}\right) = \left(\frac{n\hat{X}}{\tau_0^2} + \frac{M\mu_0}{\tau_1^2} + \frac{M\Delta\mu}{\tau_1^2}\right) \Big/ \left(\frac{n}{\tau_0^2} + \frac{M}{\tau_1^2}\right)$$

$$\Delta\hat{\mu} = \left(\frac{M\Delta\mu}{\tau_1^2}\right) \Big/ \left(\frac{n}{\tau_0^2} + \frac{M}{\tau_1^2}\right) \tag{10}$$

4.4   ES Robustness Analysis

Let ΔM be the error of ES, then put it into formula (8)

$$\hat{\mu}_0 = \left(\frac{n\hat{X}}{\tau_0^2} + \frac{(M + \Delta M)\mu_0}{\tau_1^2}\right) \Big/ \left(\frac{n}{\tau_0^2} + \frac{(M + \Delta M)}{\tau_1^2}\right)$$

$$= \left(\frac{n\hat{X}}{\tau_0^2} + \frac{(M\mu_0)}{\tau_1^2} + \frac{(\Delta M\mu_0)}{\tau_1^2}\right) \Big/ \left(\frac{n}{\tau_0^2} + \frac{(M)}{\tau_1^2} + \frac{(\Delta M)}{\tau_1^2}\right) \tag{11}$$

$$= \left(\frac{n\hat{X}}{\tau_0^2} + \frac{(M\mu_0)}{\tau_1^2}\right) \Big/ \left(\frac{n}{\tau_0^2} + \frac{(M)}{\tau_1^2} + \frac{(\Delta M)}{\tau_1^2}\right) + \left(\frac{(\Delta M\mu_0)}{\tau_1^2}\right) \Big/ \left(\frac{n}{\tau_0^2} + \frac{(M)}{\tau_1^2} + \frac{(\Delta M)}{\tau_1^2}\right)$$

$$\Delta\hat{\mu} = \hat{\mu}_0 - \hat{\mu}$$
$$= \left(\frac{n\hat{X}}{\tau_0^2} + \frac{(M\mu_0)}{\tau_1^2}\right) \Big/ \left(\frac{n}{\tau_0^2} + \frac{(M)}{\tau_1^2} + \frac{(\Delta M)}{\tau_1^2}\right) + \left(\frac{(\Delta M\mu_0)}{\tau_1^2}\right) \Big/ \left(\frac{n}{\tau_0^2} + \frac{(M)}{\tau_1^2} + \frac{(\Delta M)}{\tau_1^2}\right)$$
$$- \left(\frac{n\hat{X}}{\tau_0^2} + \frac{m\mu_0}{\tau_1^2}\right) \Big/ \left(\frac{n}{\tau_0^2} + \frac{m}{\tau_1^2}\right) \tag{12}$$

When $\Delta M > 0$

$$\Delta\hat{\mu} = \hat{\mu}_0 - \hat{\mu} < \left(\frac{1}{\frac{n}{\tau_0^2} + \frac{(M)}{\tau_1^2}} - \hat{\mu}\right) \times \left(\frac{(\Delta M)}{\tau_1^2}\right) \tag{13}$$

When $\Delta M < 0$

$$\Delta\hat{\mu} = \hat{\mu}_0 - \hat{\mu} > \left(\frac{1}{\frac{n}{\tau_0^2} + \frac{(M)}{\tau_1^2}} - \hat{\mu}\right) \times \left(\frac{(\Delta M)}{\tau_1^2}\right) \tag{14}$$

Take below numerical calculation for example.

True distribution: $N(0.85, 0.6)$; Prior distribution: $N(0.82, 0.4)$.

Sample 50 times from the true distribution; Sample 200 times from the prior distribution. Table 1 gives the estimation results.

Table 1. The estimation results of different methods

Order	True value	50 test number estimation	Simulation estimation	Bayesian estimation	Proposed estimation	Equivalent sample
1	0.36	0.3474	0.1488	**0.1900**	**0.3614**	0.1
2	0.36	0.3611	0.1645	**0.2055**	**0.3396**	10
3	0.36	0.3599	0.1532	**0.1961**	**0.2251**	100
4	0.36	0.4053	0.1311	**0.1874**	**0.1874**	200

Figure 6 plots out the curve of ES and estimation result. Where 1 stands for true value, 2 stands for flying evaluation, 3 stands for simulation evaluation, 4 stands for Bayesian evaluation, and 5 stands for improved Bayesian evaluation. From Fig. 6, we can conclude that as ES arises, its estimation error is bigger. That is because the nearer to the true distribution, the bigger its weighted coefficient.

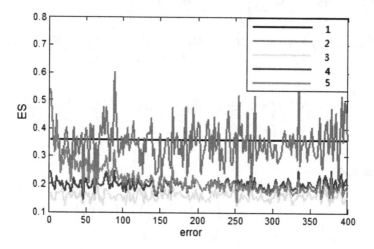

Fig. 6. The curve of estimation error and ES

5 Mathematical Calculation and Discussion

Population distribution: $N(\theta, 100)$; Prior distribution: $N(100, 225)$.

Then $\sigma_0^{-2} = \sigma^{-2}/n = 10^{-2}$, $\sigma_1^2 = \left(\sigma_0^{-2} + \tau^{-2}\right)^{-1} = 8.32^2$, $\mu_1 = \left(\frac{n\bar{x}}{\tau_0^2} + \frac{\mu_0}{\tau_1^2}\right) / \left(\frac{n}{\tau_0^2} + \frac{1}{\tau_1^2}\right) = \left(\frac{x}{100} + \frac{100}{225}\right) / \left(\frac{1}{100} + \frac{1}{225}\right)$.

Table 2. Numerical calculation

Order	Method	Point estimation	Interval estimation	Interval estimation length	Note
1	Typical statistical	115	[94.07, 126.69]	39.2	No prior information
2	Bayesian	110.3846	[94.07, 126.69]	36.62	M = 0
3	Bayesian	106.4286	[93.5975, 119.2597]	25.6622	M = 3
4	based	114.3617	[95.1833, 33.5401]	38.3568	M = 0.1
5	on ES	102.7551	[94.3551, 11.1551]	16.7999	M = 10

We can infer for Table 2 as equivalent sample raises and $\sigma_1^2 = \left(\sigma_0^{-2} + \tau^{-2}\right)^{-1}$ gradually decreases. Interval length is shorter, while equivalent sample is related to the credibility of the simulation system so we cannot raise the precision of interval estimation only by raising the simulation test sample size.

6 Engineering Application

Suppose two kinds of missile simulation test system have the same credibility C. and according to this, we calculate ES is 12. Take ES into formula (8a) to calculate hit probability seen in formula (15). Table 3 gives out the results with 28 flying test sample as the parameter basis. From Table 3 we can see that the improved method has a better estimation precision and stability.

$$p = \int_{-1.15}^{1.15} \frac{1}{\sqrt{2\pi}\sigma_x} \exp\left(\frac{x-\mu_x}{2\sigma_x}\right) dx \int_{-1.15}^{1.15} \frac{1}{\sqrt{2\pi}\sigma_y} \exp\left(\frac{x-\mu_y}{2\sigma_y}\right) dy \qquad (15)$$

Table 3. Calculation results of hit probability

Order	Flying test number	Point estimation	Bayesian estimation	Bayesian method based on ES
1	7	0.691326549697723	0.856154328960746	0.873498290428811
2	8	0.725268648482275	0.875059962697252	0.878241151910924
3	9	0.811898315813202	0.835466546590073	0.871988745895479
4	10	0.835900895629994	0.838654574864252	0.873861204434915
5	11	0.843465894406031	0.842191221855891	0.871377785997356
6	12	0.795439801487625	0.874870928491419	0.877052628304263
7	15	0.850590225424434	0.863021382077539	0.874478934878240
8	20	0.868974907814598	0.865907231989436	0.872414616550522
9	25	0.936028463538721	0.881144518672818	0.879070275284815
10	28	0.875369397379790	0.875369545534435	0.875370686214146

7 Conclusions

We put forward an improved Bayesian statistical inference formula to fuse the small flying test data with high credibility and the big simulation test data with low credibility relative to flying test data. And we can conclude

- Define the simulation equivalent flying sample concept. We take simulation test system as equivalent flying test system to calculate comprehensively to avoid that the big simulation test data draws the small flying test data.
- Have a higher precision, because it follows the advantage of fusing the prior information and site information and also makes use of the credibility.
- Be suitable to binomial and exponential distribution. Therefor it can estimate the success or index, hit accuracy index, reliability index and so on.

References

1. Hao, Q.-Y., Hu, M.-B., Cheng, X.-Q., Song, W.-G., Jiang, R., Wu, Q.-S.: Pedestrian flow in a lattice gas model with parallel update. Phys. Rev. E **82**(2), 2365–2376 (2010)
2. Castellano, C., Fortunato, S., Loreto, V.: Statistical physics of social dynamics. Rev. Mod. Phys. **81**(2), 591–646 (2009)

Research on VV&A Strategy of Modeling and Simulation for Rocket Motor

Yun-teng Ma$^{(\boxtimes)}$, Xue-ren Wang, Bai-lin Zha, Jin-jin Wang,
Yi-ang Shi, and Hui-peng Yan

Institute of High Technology, Xi'an 710025, China
lukem@qq.com

Abstract. In the process of modelling and simulation (M&S) for rocket motor, verification, validation and accreditation (VV&A) is of great importance to shorten the research period and save research cost. By analyzing the problems that frequently occur in the process of M&S for rocket motors, Specific verification and validation strategy was proposed in this paper; Three working stages of zero-dimension internal ballistic for certain solid rocket motor were modeled and simulated, whose effectiveness was later analyzed by using methods of goodness-of-fit as well as gray correlation analysis. The result shows: Compared with average evaluation system, such a strategy is able to provide the effectiveness in every stage of M&S for rocket motors with quantitative indicators, in addition to making more use of test data, which provides basis for analyzing, evaluating and improving M&S system for rocket motors.

Keywords: Modeling and simulation (M&S) · Verification, validation and accreditation (VV&A) · Rocket motor

1 Introduction

As an analytical method, modeling and simulation has been more and more widely used in many areas to improve product development efficiency and save development costs. However, whether the simulation results can truly reflect the actual or envisaged product performance is an important problem to be carefully considered for large complex systems such as rocket engines. Therefore, the verification, verification and validation (VV&A) is playing a more and more important role in many fields, especially in the development of weapons systems.

About the research of VV&A, the United States started earlier. American scholars Biggs and Cawthore comprehensively evaluated of the missile AGM-28 simulation system in 1962 [1]. In 1996 the United States issued the Department of defense directive (DoD Instructive 5000.61) [2], established VV&A working group of the military M&S, and the formed practice VV & a standard for the Department of defense in 2008 (MIL-STD-3022), which also marked the development of VV&A M&S to a systematic and comprehensive stage [3].

However, VV&A has not been widely used in all fields of M&S [3]. Many complex simulation systems have been developed and have not been systematically checked.

© Springer Science+Business Media Singapore 2016
L. Zhang et al. (Eds.): AsiaSim 2016/SCS AutumnSim 2016, Part IV, CCIS 646, pp. 553–560, 2016.
DOI: 10.1007/978-981-10-2672-0_57

Therefore, the establishment of VV&A framework for the rocket engine M&S is of great significance to solve the above problem.

2 Framework of VV&A for Rocket Engine M&S System

The ideal state of modeling and simulation system is to be able to replace or very close to the actual situation. And the factors influencing the accuracy of rocket engine modeling and simulation are mainly expressed in the following aspects: Simplification of mathematical model, selection of computational grid, selection of the calculating methods and influence of random factors. In the process of VV&A should be analyzed aiming at the above problems.

2.1   Verification of M&S for Rocket Motor

There are many M&S verification methods, such as standard test method, multi person review and simulation software reliability theory check, etc. According to the understanding of the concept of verification, the rocket engine M&S verification can be considered from the aspects like mathematical model, simulation algorithm and simulation result (Fig. 1(a)).

With the maturity of M&S technology, many researches are able to meet the above requirements, but it is not sure whether the M&S and the actual system are completely consistent. This is because the actual test results are not a fixed value, but a probability distribution. Now, the usual practice is to take the average number of test results. But this does not reflect all the information of the test, and is also a waste of resources. In order to improve the credibility of the results of M&S, the modeling and simulation system has to be verified.

2.2   Validation of VV&A for Rocket Motor

Verification process is a very important part of VV&A, it mainly inspects if the model output is sufficiently close to the actual system behavior process, that is, the study of M&S in the induction of the credibility. This part should be completed with lots of simulation data and a small amount of test data [4].

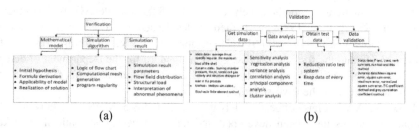

(a)   (b)

Fig. 1. Content of Verification and Validation

The simulation data of the verification process is a large number of random initial values generated by multiple simulations based on the distribution of initial parameters of the engine or the boundary conditions. Engine simulation data is usually divided into two types: static data and dynamic data. Static data such as average thrust, specific impulse, the maximum load of the shell can be regarded as random variables, while dynamic data, such as burning chamber pressure, thrust, nozzle exit gas velocity and structure changes of load in the process can be regarded as a stochastic process.

Force and load response of the integral structure of the rocket engine are usually analyzed by the method of finite element analysis. It is also needed to use the method of stochastic finite element to simulate the performance parameters of structural material, the geometrical size of structure and the load distribution in the process of verification. Stochastic finite element method is applied to the governing Eq. (1), and the distribution law of the variation of the load response and the structure performance can be obtained.

$$KU = F \tag{1}$$

And according to the size of the coefficient of variation, we can choose the random finite element Taylor expansion stochastic finite element (TSFEM), perturbation stochastic finite element method (PSFEM), Neumann expanded Monte-Carlo stochastic finite element (NSFEM) and other methods [5].

Before the stochastic finite element calculation, it is necessary to carry out the discretization of the random field. For the finite element mesh has nothing to do with the random field, in order to simplify the calculation, usually choose is a more sparse random field mesh rather than the finite element mesh would be adapted, the mesh density of whom is determined by correlation distance proposed by Vanmorcke [6–9].

The detail methods and strategies in validation process are listed in Fig. 1(b).

2.3 Accreditation of M&S for Rocket Engine

Validation process is of great significance for modeling and simulation system reliability research. It is mainly achieved by the authority of the combination of V&V results and acceptance criteria for the comprehensive evaluation. At present, the development trend is to extract and integrate the facts and data of expert knowledge and experience into clauses, which constitute the knowledge base. Combined with the method of reasoning machine and the analytic hierarchy process, the comprehensive evaluation of the system is carried out [10, 11].

3 Example Analysis

This paper takes a full surface combustion tubular mounted solid propellant rocket motor as an example. Through a zero dimensional interior ballistic model, ascending, balance and descending period, are simulated and calculated. Through the preparation of the simulation and verification integration process, the entire modeling and simulation system is comprehensively V&V analyzed.

3.1   Interior Ballistic Simulation Model of Solid Rocket Motor

The main parameters of a solid rocket engine are shown in Table 1.

According to the initial parameters, the differential equation of combustion chamber pressure with time is established by mass conservation, gas state equation and burning rate relation [12]:

$$\frac{V_c}{\Gamma^2 c^{*2}} \cdot \frac{d(p_c)}{dt} = \rho_p A_b a p_c^n - \frac{p_c A_t}{c^*} \tag{2}$$

During the rising phase, because the time is very short, the combustion chamber initial air volume V_C and burning surface area A_b as constant, separation of variables can be obtained.

Table 1. Parameters of solid motor

Parameters	Value
Tubular charge	14
External charge diameter/mm	140
Internal charge diameter/mm	36
Length of charge/mm	1740
Combustion temperature/K	2360
Throat diameter/mm	216
Nozzle expansion ratio	2.5
Buring rate coefficient	0.97
Pressure exponent	0.51

$$dt = \frac{V_c}{\Gamma^2 c^{*2}} + \frac{dp_c}{\rho_p A_b a p_c^n - \frac{p_c A_t}{c^*}} = \frac{V_c}{\Gamma^2 c^* A_t} \cdot \frac{dp_c}{\rho_p A_b c^* a K p_c^n - p_c}$$

The combustion chamber pressure in the working section can be obtained from the integral of the instantaneous equilibrium pressure formula.

According to the relationship between mass conservation and adiabatic expansion, we can understand the relationship between the pressure and the time of the combustion chamber after shutdown:

$$p_c = p_{ceq} \left[\frac{2V_c}{2V_c + \Gamma \sqrt{RT_f A_t}(k-1)t} \right]^{\frac{2k}{k-1}}$$

The above equations are discredited and the appropriate time step is set to simulate the three stages of the engine operation. Simulation results and engine test results are shown in Fig. 2.

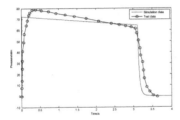

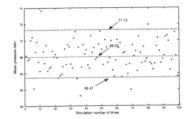

Fig. 2. Pressure graph of simulation and test   **Fig. 3.** Variable trend of pressure in chamber with times of simulating

3.2   VV&A Analyses for Interior Ballistic Simulation

Verification for M&S. In the modeling process, in order to simplify the calculation, some of the smaller items are ignored. For instance, in the derivation of formula (2), ρ_c/ρ_p is regarded as a trace and ignored. Normally under engine operating conditions,

$$p_c = 9.81MPa; \qquad T_f = 3000K; \qquad \rho_p = 1600kg/m^3$$

So

$$\rho_c = \frac{p_c}{RT_f} = 8.175kg/m^3, \frac{\rho_c}{\rho_p} = 0.0051$$

So it can be ignored for it is to the trace compared with 1. In practical applications, the choice should be appropriately made based on the required accuracy.

In the process of simulation, the method of discretization was used to calculate the differential equations, and the calculation efficiency and error are directly related to the time step, and the appropriate time step should be determined according to the stability of the algorithm.

Validation for M&S. According to previous ground test data, the solid rocket motor internal ballistic calculation parameters of the distribution can be obtained (Table 2). The random process is added in the simulation model, and after multiple simulation, combustion chamber pressure results as shown in Fig. 3.

Obviously, combustion chamber pressure fluctuates around a value. In order to further analyze the distribution, the simulation results are distributed in the form of distribution to identify and estimate the distribution parameters, so as to analyze the system sensitivity and model robustness. For small sample test data, the method

Table 2. Normal distribution of initial parameters

Random variable	Mean value	Standard deviation
Charge density/kg/cm^3	1612.965	1.015
Buring rate coefficient	0.097	0.00132
Characteristic velocity/(m/s)	1378.153	4.074

goodness of fit can be used to test the consistency of the static simulation data and test data. The results of distribution identification and parameter estimation are shown in Fig. 4.

When the charge density, burning rate coefficient and the pressure exponent changes in the same degree, the distribution of the thrust of the engine is identified, which turned out to be subject to normal distribution and γ distribution, and its distribution parameters are shown in Table 3.

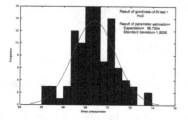

Fig. 4. Distribution distinguishing and parameter

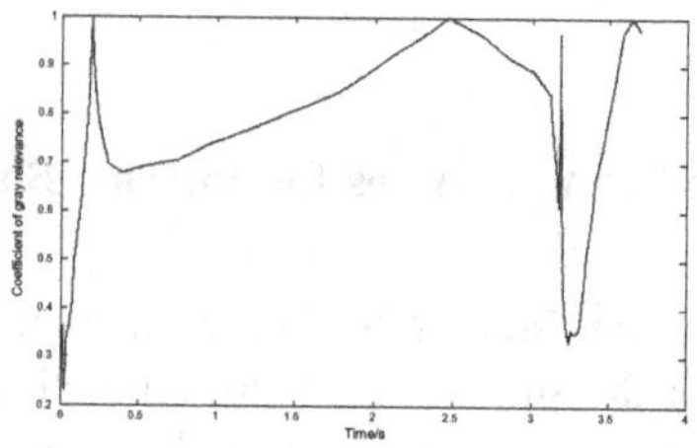

Fig. 5. Variable trend of coefficient of gray relevance with coming time

Dynamic data (shown in Fig. 2) should be preprocessed before validation, the simulation data and test data should be adjusted at the same time by intercepting the effective data segment, interpolation, fitting and smoothing method.

Taking into account the scale of test sample data is small, using TIC analysis and gray correlation coefficient method for dynamic data validation.

Table 3. Distribution of thrust when initial parameters changed

Distribution Variable parameters	Normal distribution Expectation/kg	γ distribution		
		Standard deviation	shape parameter	scale parameter
Charge density	54736.530	1265.345	1900.746	28.797
Buring rate coefficient	54541.256	1123.446	2384.939	22.869
Pressure exponoent	54483.027	2342.011	555.643	98.054

The result of TIC analysis is listed in Table 4, where TIC coefficient ρ meets $0 \leq \rho \leq 1$. The better the simulation results, the smaller the TIC coefficient, and the closer the deviation ratio and the variance ratio to 0, while covariance ratio to 1. It can be seen from the results that the simulation data can reflect the change trend of the actual system.

TIC coefficient can only give a comprehensive judgment on the simulation results. The grey correlation coefficient method can be used to validate the simulation data and test data at different time points. If the condition of the resolution is 0.3, the grey correlation degree is 0.80387, which means overall correlation degree is high. The time variation curve of the grey correlation coefficient is shown in Fig. 5. It can be seen that the correlation coefficient of balance section is more than 0.7, while is smaller in ascending and descending period, which means zero dimensional internal ballistic model has larger simulation error in ascending and descending period.

Table 4. Result of TIC analyzing

Parameters of TIC analyzing	Value
TIC coefficient	0.0666
Deviation ratio	0.11079
Variance ratio	0.028214
Covariance ratio	0.861

4 Conclusion and Future Work

- Combined with rocket engine modeling and simulation process, according to the characteristics of simulation data, the paper analyzed the emphasis and main work in VV&A process, which provides the basis of analyzing the credibility of M&S for rocket engine.
- The paper set a certain type of solid rocket motor as an example, presented the VV&A strategy of M&S for solid rocket motor combined with distribution recognition, hypothesis test, TIC coefficient method and grey correlation, which contrasted and gave the quantitative index of the simulation data and the test data modeling and simulation process of analysis, identification of the integrated use of distribution, hypothesis testing, tic coefficient method and gray correlation method contrast and give the quantitative index of the simulation data and the test data. The results show that the zero dimensional interior ballistic model can reflect the actual change trend for the steady-state simulation results, while dynamic process simulation accuracy is not high, which means more factors should be considered.
- VV&A for rocket engine is of great significance, working in the whole process of M&S, which is somehow complex. To conduct a comprehensive and accurate calibration, cooperation level of different departments should be increased, a more accurate evaluation standard should be made, so that VV&A strategy would enrich and develop continuously.

References

1. Tang, J., Zha, Y., Li, G.: An overview of the research on VV&A in simulation. Comput. Simul. **11**(23), 82–85 (2006)
2. DMSO: Instruction 5000.61. DoD Modeling and Simulation (M&S) Verification, Validation, and Accreditation [EB/OL] (1996). http://www.dmso.mil
3. Sun, Y.: Research of Verification Validation and Accreditation Technology in Modeling and Simulation. Nanjing University of Science & Technology, Nanjing (2005)
4. Jiao, P.: Research on VV&A Theory and Method of Missile Guidance Simulation System. National University of Defense Technology (2010)
5. Der Kiureghian, A.: Finite element methods in structural safety studies. In: James, Y.T.P. (ed.) Streetural Safety Studies, pp. 40–52 (1986)
6. Phcon, K.K., Quek, S.T., Chow, Y.K.: Reliability analysis of pile settlement. J. Geotech. Engrg, ASCE **116**(11), 1717–1735 (1990)
7. Vanmarcke, E.: Random Fields: Analysis and Synthesis. MIT Press, Cambridge (1983)
8. Vanmarcke, E., Shinozuka, M.: Random fields and stochastic finite element method. Struct. Safety **3**, 143–146 (1986)
9. Vanmarcke, E.: Stochastic finite element analysis. In: Masanmobu (ed.) Probabilistic Methods in Structural Engineering, New York, pp. 278–294 (1981)
10. Zhou, Z., Zhang, S.: Modeling method and model accreditation of virtual prototype missile system. Comput. Simul. **21**(10), 18–20 (2004)
11. Sargent, R.G.: Verification and validation of simulation models. In: Proceedings of 1994 WSC, pp. 77–87 (1994)
12. Dan, L., Hu, B., Li, J., Zhang, Z.: Research of digital simulation of internal ballistic performance of a solid rocket motor. J. Solid Rocket Technol. (1), 27–38 (2003)

Author Index

Printed in the United States
By Bookmasters